An Anthology

INTERNATIONAL WAR

An Anthology

Second Edition

Edited by
Melvin Small
Wayne State University
and
J. David Singer
University of Michigan

The Dorsey Press
Chicago, Illinois 60604

Cover credit: UPI/Bettmann Newsphotos   © 1985 by Media Resources

© RICHARD D. IRWIN, INC., 1989

Sponsoring editor: Leo A. W. Wiegman
Project editor: Lynne Basler
Production manager: Bette Ittersagen
Cover Design: Hunter Graphics
Compositor: Graphic World Inc.
Typeface: 10/12 Times Roman
Printer: Malloy Lithographing, Inc.

LIBRARY OF CONGRESS
Library of Congress Cataloging-in-Publication Data

International war : an anthology / edited by Melvin Small and J. David Singer.—2nd ed.
    p.   cm.
  Bibliography: p.
ISBN 0-256-07115-2 (pbk.)
    1. War. I. Small, Melvin, 1939– II. Singer, J. David (Joel David), 1925–
U21.2.I58 1988
    355'.02—dc19

88–16176

CIP

Printed in the United States of America

1 2 3 4 5 6 7 8 9 0 ML 5 4 3 2 1 0 9 8

Preface to the First Edition

Because war today threatens the people of so many nations—if not humanity as a whole—and because it has been so ubiquitous an activity for so long and in so many parts of the world, we tend to think of it as inherent in the human condition. Indeed, many accept the view that is an inexorable and inevitable consequence of "human nature," either in the biological or sociological sense. But the picture is not quite that grim. First of all, despite the frequency of international disputes and crises, war itself remains a relatively rare event, even in the nineteenth or twentieth centuries. If we calculate the number of nations that have existed since the end of the Napoleonic Wars in 1815 to 1985, and the number of years that each has been a sovereign state, we find that the world *could* have experienced about 16,000 nation-years in which international war was underway. Yet there have been, in those 170 years, only 120 major international wars, averaging about one year in duration and four participants, for a total of "merely" 600 nation-years, or less than 4 percent of the *possible* total. We do not for a moment want to make light of the 31 million soldiers who were killed in actual combat and the many millions of civilians who died in connection with these wars. Nor do we minimize the incredible waste of physical and human treasure that has gone into the preparation for war since 1815. Similarly, the psychological and political mobilization for wars, fought or not fought, has exacted an inestimable toll in human misery. Despite all of this, international war remains a relatively rare catastrophe.

In addition to the fact that many nations and people *have* been spared the horrors of war in modern times, in many regions of the world in centuries gone by war was virtually unknown. Moreover, there are regions and cultures that exist today (and others in the past) in which *any* form of collective armed violence is unheard of. Such mass violence has been condemned not only by philosophers and theologians, but by a remarkable array of leaders and politicians throughout the centuries.

In other words, it may not be an act of childlike naïveté to believe that the global village may yet return to a long, and perhaps even permanent, period of peace. It is this faith that prompts us to prepare the volume at hand. Despite all of the ominous signs and the apparent inability of citizens and leaders to learn from their past errors, we are far from persuaded that the next and perhaps last war is foreordained. The odds are not good, but neither are they appalling, and our purpose here is to change them, however slightly, in the hopeful direction. That hope rests, admittedly, on the questionable premise that we *can* learn from our errors (as well as our successes) and can then apply the lessons in time.

On the other hand, this is not one of those books that rests on the "education is our only hope" assumption. More and more people are "educated" each year, and the number of university graduates worldwide has shown as spectacular an increase since World War II as the percentage increases in literacy. So far, education in general has exercised a negligible effect on human acceptance of war as a legitimate if unattractive enterprise, and that activity known as "peace education" has achieved little more. We have, then, a rather different notion of education and learning in mind as we bring this book to completion. For example, as Americans, we refuse to accept the folklore and fairy-tales that pass for knowledge of world affairs in our own culture. Although we are believers in liberal democracy, we nevertheless reject the smug assumption that this form of political regime is any less war prone than others; historical evidence shows that regime type has little to do with the frequency with which nations initiate or are drawn into war. In addition, as professionals in history and political science, we have no illusions that either or both of our disciplines have most or all of the answers.

Our approach here, then, is skeptical and eclectic. Where reproducible evidence exists, we will present some of it; where systematic analysis is available, regardless of discipline, we will sample that literature; and where creative and ingenious insights are found, regardless of culture or epoch, we will select with care and pleasure. Our aim is not merely to arouse concern, despite the importance of that. Nor is our aim simply to remind you of the diversity—and longevity—of viewpoints on the causes of war or alternative prescriptions for its elimination. While these are legitimate aims for an anthology such as this, we have a more ambitious and pragmatic aim as well: to help each of our readers become more insightful, knowledgeable, curious, and skeptical, on the one hand, and more socially and politically active on the other. If and when those citizens of the world who are "educated" decide to really try to understand the dynamics of the war cycle and to then do something about it, we will be well on our way to obliterating the scourge of war and to creating conditions under which we might be able to live, not in blissful harmony, but in a humane, competent, and dignified world that is safe for conflict.

As we prepared this anthology, we were confronted with an immediate thorny problem. The fields of diplomatic and military history, international relations, and peace and conflict studies, from which we planned to select the bulk of our readings, are so rich and diverse that we would have needed a library of anthologies to do justice to our subject. One can imagine putting together a valuable anthology on international war from one source alone, perhaps the *Journal of Peace Research* or the *Journal of Conflict Resolution,* two of the many new journals for peace and conflict studies that have developed since World War II. Given our embarrassment of intellectual riches, we have opted for a strategy that emphasizes breadth over depth. We have spread our net widely as we searched for material that reflected broad approaches to the subject. We were interested in presenting both substantive findings and diverse methodologies. This means, for example, that when we offer a Marxist analysis or a pacifist program, we do not offer an anti-Marxist or an antipacifist rejoinder. To do so would severely limit our domain. We compensate in our introductions, where we point out each article's controversial or debatable aspects. More important, our suggested reading list that follows each article generally includes views antagonistic to the main presentation.

Thus, we offer a smorgasbord of approaches, disciplines, and findings, all of which we feel have something important to say about international war. As with any smorgasbord, not all of the items will appeal to all readers. Each, nevertheless, is worth sampling since it represents a view of international war that has influential adherents in the scholarly and diplomatic worlds. Given the distance we need to go to understand how to create a more peaceful international environment, we cannot afford to reject any plausible approach to our problem.

In most cases, we have eliminated the original footnotes from our selections. In addition, few are reprinted in entirety. We trust our editing has preserved the main thrust of each article without jeopardizing its scholarly integrity.

The authors are indebted to Virginia Corbin, Sarajane Miller Small and Mark Small for their invaluable assistance during the final stages of preparation. They also thank many of the individual copyright holders for their graciousness in permitting their work to be reprinted.

Melvin Small
J. David Singer

Preface to the Second Edition

Since our anthology was first published in 1985, it has been adopted at colleges throughout the United States most often for use in courses on international war, international relations, the history and sociology of war, and peace and conflict studies. It was designed originally as an integral part of the "War" telecourse that was presented on PBS in 1985 and 1986. We soon discovered that many of our adoptions came from courses totally unrelated to the television series. We had hoped that this would be the case since few such anthologies are available to scholars who teach courses on international war and conflict.

After hearing from many of those scholars, as well as others who used the anthology in conjunction with the telecourse, we decided to make some changes in the second edition. Many of the critical suggestions that were made had to do with the several articles that reflected a quantitative approach. In reshaping this edition, we have nevertheless retained most of them. We believe that quantitative international politics is an important and valid approach to the study of the causes of war. Students in history and the humanities, as well as those in the social sciences, should know something about the strengths and weaknesses of this approach.

We have, however, added articles of a more traditional nature. For example, to Chapter 1, The History of War, heretofore a rigidly empirical section, we have added two pieces by traditional historians. Moreover, we have dropped two of the narrower sociological articles on officers and authority from Chapter 2, The Military Experience, and replaced them with three additional combat narratives. Many of our readers requested more of those classic literary accounts of men and women in battle.

Overall then, we have dropped three articles from the original anthology and added eleven new articles—Dyer and Kennedy in Chapter 1; Crane, Moorehead, and Pelfrey in Chapter 2; Roosevelt and the Methodist Bishops in Chapter 3; Fabbro in Chapter 4, Blainey and Choucri and North in Chapter 5, and Prioreschi in Chapter 7.

We trust that our additions have made this anthology a better one. For the many helpful comments that we have received offering suggestions for improvement, we are most grateful.

M. S.
J. D. S.

Suggested Readings

Beer, Francis A. *Peace against War*. San Francisco: Freeman, 1981.

Beitz, Charles A. and Theodore Herman, eds., *Peace and War*. San Francisco: Freeman, 1973.

Bouthoul, Gaston. *Le Défi de la Guerre (1740–1974)*. Paris: Presses Universitaires de France, 1976.

Brown, Seyom. *The Causes and Prevention of War*. New York: St. Martin's, 1987.

Dedring, Jurgen. *Recent Advances in Peace and Conflict Research: A Critical Survey*. Beverly Hills: Sage, 1976.

Falk, Richard A, and Samuel S. Kim, eds. *The War System: An Interdisciplinary Approach*. Boulder, Colo: Westview, 1980.

Farrar, L.L. Jr., ed. *War: A Historical, Political, and Social Study*. Santa Barbara: ABC-Clio, 1978.

McNeil, Elton, ed. *The Nature of Human Conflict*. Englewood Cliffs, N.J.: Prentice-Hall, 1965.

Nelson, Keith L., and Spencer C. Olin, Jr. *Why War? Ideology, Theory, and History*. Berkeley: University of California, 1979.

Peace and World Order Studies: A Curriculum Guide. New York: World Policy Institute, 1988.

Stoessinger, John. *Why Nations Go to War*. New York: St. Martin's, 1982.

Contents

INTERNATIONAL WAR

An Anthology

CHAPTER 1

The History of War

We live in a violent age. Newspapers and electronic media are full of reports from battlefields in almost all of the regions of the world. Each week, thousands perish in civil wars, wars of national liberation, and traditional interstate conflicts.

At the same time, millions of people throughout the world have never experienced war in their lifetimes. Moreover, nations that have fought one another for hundreds of years are now members of political and military alliance systems; their mutual borders are undefended.

How violent then is our age? We know that as long as humans have organized themselves into communities, warfare has been an integral part of their lives. The scenarios of international conflict described by classical historians more than 2,000 years ago seem all too familiar today. Athens and Sparta or Rome and Carthage could be England and Germany or the United States and the Soviet Union in our own century.

Even as those classical historians began to document *their* now ancient wars, they were dealing with an institution that was as old as human civilization. Gwynne Dyer surveys some of "The Origins of War" in the first selection in this chapter. Employing anthropological and archeological evidence, he evaluates the function of war in primitive society as well as the development of the warrior caste.

For many readers, Dyer's journey through the millennia almost back to the caves may seem too remote to help us understand contemporary war. This should not be the case with the next selection that examines war since the beginning of the modern state system.

Paul Kennedy is interested in the reasons for "The Rise and Fall of the Great Powers" since 1500. In a provocative and magisterial study, he describes the interaction between economic growth and military power that helps us understand both the causes and the outcomes of the world wars that have periodically shaken up the international system.

Dyer's and Kennedy's contributions reflect the traditional approach to the study of history and international war. Over the past forty years, scholars in the social sciences have worked over the same data employing more empirical techniques. Attempting to emulate the hard sciences, they use methods in their research quite different from those used by the more humanistic scholars. While their narratives may not be as compelling or entertaining, their analyses often are convincing.

To return to our original question then, How violent is our age? Another way to

1

place today's wars in perspective is to compare them statistically to the wars of the recent past.

More important in a scientific sense, the compilation of such an historical record is essential to our primary concern, the variety of explanations for why nations go to war. In order to explain war, it must be first described. To be sure, war has been described by bards, chroniclers, and historians for centuries. In most cases, however, while their accounts are insightful and moving, they do not approach the problem in a systematic fashion with the sort of methodological rigor displayed in our own selection, "Patterns in International Warfare, 1816–1980."

In order to produce our catalogue of international wars since 1816, we used explicit criteria and reproducible procedures to sort through the bewildering array of facts, nonfacts, and impressions from many national, ethnic, and ideological perspectives. Our resulting data set, produced with an eye towards historical validity and statistical reliability, describes all wars since 1816 that involved independent states and that resulted in at least 1,000 battle deaths.

For some, the period from 1816 to 1980 may be too brief to allow one to generalize about historical patterns in war. Employing many of the same techniques, Jack Levy in "Historical Trends in Great Power War," moves back in time to 1495. Although Levy describes only major-power war, most of the significant military and political interaction in history has involved, in one way or another, the actions of the major powers. Thus, his list and findings offer another perspective on a broad sweep of the military history of the world.

Not all interstate conflicts lead to war. Indeed, only a small percentage of those in which military threats or even the modest use of force are employed ever result in full-scale war. One approach to the "why war?" question compares aspects of those conflicts that terminated in war with those that saw the contending parties withdraw from the brink. Charles S. Gochman and Zeev Maoz present such an approach in "Militarized Interstate Disputes, 1816–1976."

The last three articles in this chapter describe war and military conflict throughout history. They tell us how much war has been fought by which nations during which time periods. They offer benchmarks to enable us to evaluate our own era and even to make cautious predictions about the future. Finally, they delimit an empirical domain in which we can attack the question of the correlates and causes of war.

Reading 1

THE ORIGINS OF WAR

Gwynne Dyer

Notes from the Editors

War is as old as civilization. In this selection from his larger work, War, *Gwynne Dyer discusses some of the earliest examples of war between groups. A military historian and journalist interested primarily in contemporary conflict, Dyer sees the causes of war, as well as the combat experience, remaining relatively constant through the millennia.*

Although the evidence is fragmentary, anthropologists and archeologists have been able to describe the earliest societies and their interactions with one another. Dyer suggests that the state and the army developed together—human progress was in good measure dependent upon military power. For Dyer, there is a certain irony contained in the history of modern society with increases in what we call "civilization" accompanied by increases in the savagery and barbarism of warfare. Indeed, precivilized societies were apparently less savage and barbaric in their martial conflicts than their successors.

Dyer also sees continuity in the role and values of the soldier: whether defending a pharaoh 4,000 years ago or a czar seventy-five years ago, the warrior has expressed himself in deed and literature in approximately the same fashion.

The point of his book, War, *as well as his acclaimed PBS television series of the same name, is that war as an institution is now dysfunctional. Dyer is concerned that we will be unable to rid our system of this pervasive institution before civilization itself is destroyed in the final war.*

The soldier was one of the first inventions of civilization, and he has changed remarkably little over the ten thousand years or so that armies have existed. The teenage Iranian volunteers stumbling across minefields east of Basra in 1984 or the doomed British battalions going over the top in the July Drive on the Somme in 1916 were taking part in the same act of sacrifice and slaughter that destroyed the young men of Rome at Cannae in 216 B.C.; the emotions, the odds, and the outcome were fundamentally the same. Battle, the central act of warfare, is a unique event in which ordinary men willingly kill and die as though those extraordinary actions were normal and acceptable, and changing weapons and tactics have not altered those essential elements of its character.

However, the *consequences* of war can and do change. In our time, the likely consequences of war have grown drastically and irreversibly, so that they potentially include the destruction of the entire human habitat: war and civilization, which were born as Siamese twins, may also end together. But the drastic change in the scale of

Reprinted from Gwynne Dyer, *War* (Chicago: The Dorsey Press, 1985), pp. 4–19. Reprinted by permission of BMR.

war in our time has been caused by the application of modern science, industry, and organizational skills to an ancient institution that still obeys its ancient rules.

Moreover, war has always had an innate tendency to expand to the absolute limit of the resources available to the societies waging it, and sometimes far beyond their capacity to accept punishment. Force is the ultimate argument, and once it has been invoked, the only effective reply is superior force; the internal logic of war has frequently caused it to grow far bigger in scale than the importance of the issue originally in dispute would justify. World War I is a striking example; the third world war will be even more convincing, if there is anyone left to convince.

Yet modern soldiers do not behave any more ruthlessly than their ancestors. The residents of Dresden and Hiroshima in 1945 suffered no worse fate than the citizens of Babylon in 680 B.C., when the city fell to Sennacherib of Assyria, who boasted: "I levelled the city and its houses from the foundations to the top, I destroyed them and consumed them with fire, I tore down and removed the outer and inner walls, the temples and the ziggurats built of brick, and dumped the rubble in the Arahtu canal. And after I had destroyed Babylon, smashed its gods and massacred its population, I tore up its soil and threw it into the Euphrates so that it was carried by the river down to the sea." It was a more labor-intensive method of destruction than nuclear weapons, but the effect (at least for an individual city) was about the same.

Most of the major cities of antiquity sooner or later met a fate similar to Babylon's—some of them many times, over the centuries—when the fortunes of war eventually left them exposed to their enemies. The difference between the destruction ancient military commanders wrought in war and what the commanders of today's strategic nuclear forces could do in war is determined mainly by their respective technologies and resources, not by a different mentality. And that "military mentality," despite the idealism and sentimentality in which it has traditionally indulged to soften the realities of the trade, has always had a cold and steady awareness at the professional level that the key to military success is efficient killing. Today it's better cluster bombs or heat-seeking missiles, but the search for efficiency was the same when the only means of introducing lethal bits of metal into an enemy's body was by muscle-power. The following, for example, are instructions on the use of the sword in a Roman army training manual:

> A slash cut rarely kills, however powerfully delivered, because the vitals are protected by the enemy's weapons, and also by his bones. A thrust going in two inches, however, can be mortal. You must penetrate the vitals to kill a man. Moreover, when a man is slashing, the right arm and side are left exposed. When thrusting, however, the body is covered, and the enemy is wounded before he realises what has happened. So this method of fighting is especially favoured by the Romans.

But if the willingness of soldiers to kill and the tendency of war to become as destructive as the existing technology and resources will permit have both been relatively constant throughout human history, then we must consider an unwelcome possibility: that war is the inevitable accompaniment of *any* human civilization, and that a technologically advanced culture like our own will sooner or later become involved in a war in which all the available technology and resources are committed to the task of destruction. There is a daunting amount of evidence to support this belief, but there is also a fundamentally important fact that offers some kind of hope. War is part of our history, but it is not in at all the same sense part of our prehistory. It is one of the innovations that occurred between nine and eleven thousand years ago when the first civilized societies were coming into being. What has been invented can be changed; war is not in our genes.

> Walbiri society did not emphasise militarism—there was no class of permanent or professional warriors; there was no hierarchy of military command; and groups rarely engaged in wars of conquest. . . . There was in any case little reason for all-out warfare between communities. Slavery was unknown; portable goods were few; and the territory seized in a battle was virtually an embarrassment to the victors, whose spiritual ties were with other localities.

Only a generation ago the Walbiri aborigines of Australia still lived in small bands in a hunting-and-gathering economy, as the entire human race did for at least 98 percent of its history, and although every male Walbiri was a warrior, their way of fighting did not resemble what we call "war." Very few people got killed; there were no leaders, no strategy, and no tactics; and only the kinship group affected by the issue at stake— most often revenge for a killing or a ritual offense committed by another group, and hardly ever territory—would take part in the fighting.

We cannot directly examine the primitive societies from which the first civilizations arose (for they disappeared in the process), but hundreds of Old Stone Age societies have survived into the recent past or present in the Western Hemisphere and Oceania, in most parts of which "civilization" arrived with the Europeans over the past few hundred years. There is no reason to believe that these modern examples of hunting-and-gathering cultures are significantly different from those that inhabited the Middle East ten or fifteen thousand years ago, and almost all of them have the same attitude toward "war": it is an important ritual, an exciting and dangerous game, and perhaps even an opportunity for self-expression, but it is not about power in any recognizable modern sense of the word, and it most certainly is not about slaughter.

It is no surprise that a race that lived largely by hunting and that knew effective techniques for killing animals would have the same techniques available for killing its own members. Since conflict is inevitable, it is also not surprising that people sometimes kill people. Some moralists suggest that this is the human race's original sin, pointing out that few other higher species deliberately kill their own members, but the reason for our relative distinction in this area seems to be simply that man is an evolutionary latecomer to killing, sprung from a long line of nonpredators. That means the weapons our ancestors learned to use in hunting over the past few million years were not accompanied by the inhibitions against using them on our own species that hereditary predators generally have. No doubt this lack could prove to be the fatal flaw in human nature, but the important point about precivilized societies is that people did not kill people *much*.

The dominant trend in the history (and prehistory) of human culture has been the creation of larger and larger groups within which each member is defined as "one of us": a kinsman, a fellow tribesman, a fellow citizen. Ten thousand years ago the average human being's social horizon was the fifty to two hundred members of his own band of hunter-gatherers, all of whom knew each other personally; there are ten states in the world today in which over one hundred million people are considered "one of us." The advantages of living in societies where large numbers of people can cooperate with each other in innumerable ways and contribute all their individual and collective achievements to an ever-growing pool of wealth and knowledge are beyond dispute; we owe almost everything we have of value to this accumulated heritage. But there is also a dark side to living in large groups.

Within each group, it has meant the creation of impersonal and often harsh controls to enforce cooperation and to keep the social peace. Most of the large-scale societies of history (and of the present) are to a greater or lesser extent tyrannies. And as the societies we live in have grown larger, so have the conflicts between them; indeed they have changed radically and have become the modern phenomenon of war. The logical end point of living in ever larger groups is the evolution of a politically united world society in which every human being is regarded as "one of us," but the penultimate stage in which we live, with the world divided into about three dozen powerful states and over a hundred weak ones, is probably the most violent, and certainly the most dangerous, phase of human history.

At the outset, there was little violence against individuals and no danger to humanity. All of humankind lived in small groups that made their living by hunting and gathering, each moving around within a relatively vast territory and having little contact with any other band. The Bushman population of South Africa before the arrival of the blacks and the whites, for example, is estimated to have been ten or twenty thousand people living in one or two hundred bands, occupying a territory of some 350,000 square miles—around two or three thousand square miles per band.

Within each Bushman band, which was made up of a dozen or so related families, there was no center of authority and little specialization of role beyond the fact that the men hunted and the women gathered plant food and cared for the children. There was some cooperation between hunters in larger projects, like building fences to trap game, but each family was mainly dependent on its own efforts for food. The extreme isolation of each band is shown by the great diversity in the Bushman languages; in some cases even neighboring bands were unable to understand each other.

Since every family was essentially autonomous, there was little cause for violent conflict between members of the same band. Each band had a strong sense of its own territory and reacted strongly to infringements of its boundaries, but the fact that the Bushman's principal weapon was the poisoned arrow, slow-acting but inevitably fatal, imposed great restraint even on clashes between different bands.

> Within Bushman bands to this day, everything possible is done to defuse situations that could lead to clashes between individuals in which poisoned arrows might eventually be exchanged. If it reaches this stage, both belligerents are likely to die in lingering agony. . . . In their relations with other bands . . . the poisoned arrow was the Stone Age equivalent of a nuclear deterrent. . . . The slow action of the poison left a stricken adversary ample time in which to avenge the suffering that lay ahead of him.

There was some violence, but no such thing as war in the Bushman's world before more complex cultures arrived in South Africa, and the same was true of other hunter-gatherers living in societies essentially confined to a single band. They were rarely capable of imagining a degree of coordination that would make it possible to conquer another band and hold its territory, nor indeed would there have been much point. Other bands had few material possessions worth seizing, slaves were practically valueless in that sort of subsistence economy (where they could do little more than feed themselves), and additional territory was generally of only marginal use to migratory hunters. But there must have been enough population pressure on food resources, here and there in the distant past, to drive some bands of hunter-gatherers into serious conflict, for even the first increase in the scale of human groups was almost certainly driven by military considerations.

There is no way we can ever know when the first bands linked together into tribes incorporating some thousands of individuals, for it involved no change in the economic basis of society that would have left physical evidence behind. It must have been at least ten thousand years ago, for the tribe is a necessary intermediate step between the tiny hunting band and the first civilized states, but it could have been fifty thousand years ago or more in some areas. The essence of the change was that various hunting bands created a broader common identity, mainly by establishing complex ties of kinship among themselves (there was not necessarily any chief or central authority), in order to increase their fighting strength. And the consequence was that the hunters redefined themselves as warriors, whose main source of pride and self-respect came from their prowess in killing not animals, but other men.

Many modern tribal societies own herds of animals or practice primitive agriculture, which gives them some material incentive to raid each other, but all the early tribes were still hunter-gatherers, so the only possible source of serious conflict between them was over scarce hunting grounds. This was probably not a frequent occurrence, but once the new form of social organization had been created, it tended to persist. Its most striking features were the dominance of a warrior class—and the depoliticization of women.

Within the traditional small hunting band, where men and women both provided food and the center of power was the individual family, the effective political power of women was probably not much less than that of men. But in the new tribal societies, where military considerations were paramount and warriors made the important decisions collectively, women were automatically excluded from power, for men could be warriors, and women—at least at that time—could not.

> Because the men fought the wars, it was they who reaffirmed the right to decide between war and peace. Such decisions required high political authority. In a sense, men became politically preeminent because they were militarily preeminent. And they became militarily preeminent because . . . primordial kinship culture . . . gave the club or the spear to the spouse with greater muscular throwing power. . . . Men are above women in politics because men are warriors and not because men were in some societies the breadwinners.
>
> —Ali A. Mazrui

It all seems perfectly logical, and there certainly must have been occasions in the past when small bands were genuinely driven to amalgamate into larger tribal societies dominated by the warrior ethic through stark military and economic necessity. (Otherwise, why would they have bothered?) And yet one is left with the sneaking suspicion that this was mainly a vast prehistorical con game, for the fact is that there was still not much to fight about most of the time for the overwhelming majority of tribal societies living in a hunting-and-gathering ecomony.

Of all the hundreds of societies of this type encountered during the great phase of European maritime expansion into the Stone Age world of the Western Hemisphere, Oceania, and parts of Africa, there is scarcely one recorded example of a tribe being locked into a death struggle with its neighbors because of population pressure and economic scarcity. They were almost all continuously involved in low-level warfare against their neighbors in their spare time, but nobody thought "winning" was sufficiently important to put much thought into organizing warfare efficiently; rather, it provided justification for the fact that the warriors ran everything, and gave meaning to their lives.

This sort of tribal warfare is almost always very limited and bound by ritual. "Battles" are often prearranged, but once they begin, they are not much more than the sum of the individual actions of many warriors acting on their own without direction or coordination. The fighting often stops for the day after one side has exacted a death, with the losers mourning their loss and the other side celebrating its victory within sight of each other. There are often deliberate steps taken to ensure that the killing does not get too efficient. There is a New Guinea tribe, for instance, that is well aware that arrows with flights are more accurate and always fits feathers to its hunting arrows—but leaves them off its war arrows.

Similarly, the Piegan and Shoshoni Indians, who engaged in large-scale battles on foot before the use of horses spread to the American plains, used to form lines facing each other that were just barely within arrow range and shoot at their opponents while taking cover behind shields three feet in diameter. Though they also had more lethal weapons—lances and battle-axes—they never closed in to use them unless they had overwhelming numerical superiority.

There are no figures for the number of people this kind of warfare has killed, although down the trackless millennia of our prehistory it must amount to tens of millions. Among the Eskimos, whose prehistory ended in this century, it killed practically nobody, but among more warlike cultures it may have been the eventual cause of death for quite a large proportion of the adult men. But there is still a vital distinction: primitive warfare is not lethal, nor even very destructive, to the societies that indulge in it. Individuals get killed, a few at a time—mostly young males, who are both biologically and economically the most dispensable members of the tribe—but the society survives intact.

Even the most warlike of Old Stone Age people, like the Indians of North America, regarded warfare much more as a ritual activity—part art form, part healthy outdoor exercise—than as a practical instrument for achieving economic and political aims, and therefore it never became the object of human ingenuity seeking to make it more efficient. "The idea of conquest never arose in aboriginal North America, and this made it possible for almost all these Indian tribes to do a very extreme thing: to separate war from the state," wrote anthropologist Ruth Benedict in 1959. But it was not an extreme thing; it was normal and natural in primitive peoples.

> The state was personified in the Peace Chief . . . but he had nothing to do with war. . . . Any man who could attract a following led a war party when and where he could, and in some tribes he was in complete control for the duration of the expedition. But this lasted only until the return of the war party. The state . . . had no conceivable interest in these ventures, which were only highly desirable demonstrations of rugged individualism.

In fact, the highest honor a warrior could gain among the Indians of the Great Plains was not to kill the enemy, but to "count coup"—to approach the enemy without weapons and touch him with a stick or his hand. The point of intertribal warfare was to give the warriors an opportunity to demonstrate their courage. The most famous and respected Comanche warrior of his time was a man who acquired a blanket made by the Utes, his tribal enemies, and used it to walk in among them unarmed.

> After dark, he drew his blanket over his head and sauntered into the Ute encampment. From within one of the lodges he heard the songs of a hand game in progress. Protected by his disguise, he walked right through the door to join the spectators. Nobody paid any attention to him. Casually and slowly moving about he touched one after another all the Utes in the lodge. When he had touched them all, he strolled out and rejoined his friend. He had counted coup on twenty enemies at once. It was a great deed.

Though precivilized warfare served various ritual and magical purposes and may have had broader social functions, it was predominantly a rough male sport for underemployed hunters, with the kinds of damage-limiting rules that all competitive sports have. This is borne out by the fact that war tends to bulk larger and get more destructive among the more sophisticated aboriginal peoples, who have moved on to primitive agriculture or herding; the warriors have even more free time, and they are beginning to acquire material interests to defend. Quincy Wright, who studied data from 633 primitive cultures, concluded that "the collectors, lower hunters and lower agriculturalists, are the least warlike. The higher hunters and higher agriculturalists are more warlike, while the highest agriculturalists and the [pastoral peoples] are the most warlike of all."

It seems almost as if we were gradually working up to the kind of war that civilization would bring with it, and perhaps we were. But the gulf between primitive and civilized societies is as vast in warfare as it is in other respects. The essence of the Neolithic revolution was not the discovery, between 9000 and 7000 B.C. in various parts of the Fertile Crescent, that food could be obtained more reliably and in far greater abundance by planting and harvesting crops and taming and breeding animals, nor even the huge increase in population density that these discoveries made possible. It was the insight that human will and organization could exercise control over the natural world—and over large numbers of human beings.

"To exert power in every form was the essence of civilisation; the city found a score of ways of expressing struggle, aggression, domination, conquest—and servitude," wrote Lewis Mumford about the first civilizations of mankind. The roots of human civilization lie in states so absolutist and so awesomely cruel that even the death camps of Nazi Germany would have been regarded as a moral commonplace. Civilization, first and foremost, was the discovery of how to achieve power over both nature and people, and it cannot be denied that it went to our heads: on the one hand, pyramids and irrigation canals; on the other hand, wars of extermination.

That is not to say that civilization is therefore a Bad Thing or that it is necessarily doomed to destroy itself. It is civilization that gives the human experiment its meaning, and it is possible to overcome an unfortunate early upbringing. There was probably never any choice in the matter anyway; it is difficult to imagine any basis for the first civilizations other than the brutal exercise of absolute power. But we do carry our history within us, and ten thousand years later our civilization faces the prospect of an abrupt end because of the enduring institution that was the key invention of the first civilized men: military power.

> I am afeard there are few die well that die in battle.

> —Shakespeare, *Henry V*.

> To avoid death he shrank back into the host of his companions; but as he went back Meriones, dogging him, threw the spear and struck between navel and genitals where beyond all places death in battle comes painfully to pitiful mortals. There the spear struck fast driven and he, writhing about it . . . gasped for a little while, but not long, until fighting Meriones came close and wrenched the spear out from his body.

> —Homer, *Iliad*

It can never be proved, but it is a safe assumption that the first time five thousand male human beings were ever gathered together in one place, they belonged to an army. That event probably occurred around 7000 B.C.—give or take a thousand years—and it is an equally safe bet that the first truly large-scale slaughter of people in human history happened very soon afterward.

The first army almost certainly carried weapons no different from those that hunters had been using on animals and on each other for thousands of years previously—spears, knives, axes, perhaps bows and arrows. Its strength did not lie in mere numbers; what made it an army was discipline and organization. This multitude of men obeyed a single commander and killed his enemies to achieve his goals. It was the most awesome concentration of power the human world had ever seen, and nothing except another army could hope to resist it.

The battle that occurred when two such armies fought has little in common with the clashes of primitive warfare. Thousands of men were crowded together in tight formations that moved on command and marched in step. Drill, practiced over many days and months until it became automatic, is what transformed these men from a mob of individual fighters into an army. (The basic forms of military drill are among the most pervasive and unchanging elements of human civilization. The Twelfth Dynasty Egyptian armies of 1900 B.C. stepped off "by the left," and so has every army down to the present day.)

And when the packed formations of well-drilled men collided on the forgotten battlefields of the earliest kingdoms, what happened was quite impersonal, though every man died his own death. It was not the traditional combat between individual warriors. The soldiers were pressed forward by the ranks behind them against the anonymous strangers in that part of the enemy line facing them, and though in the end it was pairs of individuals who thrust at each other with spears for a few moments before one went down, there was nothing personal in the exchange. "Their shields locked, they pushed, fought, killed and died. There was no shouting, and yet not silence either, but rather such a noise as might be made by the angry clash of armed men."

The result of such a merciless struggle in a confined space is killing on an unprecedented scale. Hundreds or thousands of men would die in half an hour, in an area no bigger than a couple of football fields. "The battle over, one could see on the site of the struggle the ground covered with blood, friend and foe lying dead on one another, shields broken, spears shattered and unsheathed swords, some on the ground, some fixed in corpses, some still held in the hands of the dead. It was now getting late, so they dragged the enemy corpses inside their lines, had a meal and went to rest."

And the question we rarely ask, because our history is replete with such scenes, is, How could men do this? After all, in the tribal cultures from which we all come originally, they could not have done it. Being a warrior and taking part in a ritual "battle" with a small but invigorating element of risk is one thing; the mechanistic and anonymous mass slaughter of civilized warfare is quite another, and any traditional warrior would do the sensible thing and leave instantly. Yet civilized men, from 5000 B.C. or from today, will stay at such scenes of horror even in the knowledge that they will probably die within the next few minutes. The invention of armies required more than just working out ways of drilling large numbers of people to act together, although that was certainly part of the formula. A formation of drilled men has a different psychology—a controlled form of mob psychology—that tends to overpower the personal identity and fears of the individuals who make it up.

> You're dealing here with complicated psychological states. No man in battle is really sane. The mind set of the soldier on the battlefield is a highly disturbed mind, and this is an epidemic of insanity which affects everybody there, and those not afflicted by it die very quickly.
>
> William Manchester, World War II veteran

> People say, well, I could never kill a man. That's bullshit. They can. Anybody can kill. It takes more to make one man kill than it does the next. The training helps a lot; it gets you there. But combat—you know, once they start shooting at you, if you don't shoot back, you're a damned fool.
>
> U.S. veteran, Vietnam

By the time it has become clear to the individual soldier seeing civilized war for the first time that a battle is no place for a sane man to be, there is often physically no way to leave—and in all armies the penalty for trying to leave is death at the hands of your own side. But even experienced soldiers who know what to expect submit themselves to the ordeal of battle again and again, more or less willingly, because to do otherwise is to disgrace themselves in front of the people whose respect is the foundation of their own self-respect: their fellow soldiers. Men will kill and die rather than lose face, but the face that is being saved, the image that is being preserved, is that of the tribal warrior of the precivilized past, who fought for personal glory and stood a very good chance of surviving the fight.

Aggression is certainly part of our genetic makeup, and necessarily so, but the normal human being's quota of aggression will not even cause him to kill acquaintances, let alone wage war against strangers from a different country. We live among millions of people who have killed fellow human beings with pitiless efficiency—machine-gunning them, using flame throwers on them, dropping explosive bombs on them from twenty thousand feet up—yet we do not fear these people. The overwhelming majority of those who have killed, now or at any time in the past, have done so as soldiers in war, and we recognize that that has practically nothing to do with the kind of personal aggression that would endanger us as their fellow citizens.

We assume that people will kill if they find themselves in a situation where their own survival is threatened, and nobody needs lessons to learn how to die. What is less obvious is that practically anybody can be persuaded and manipulated in such a way that he will more or less voluntarily enter a situation wherein he must kill and perhaps die. Yet if that were not true, battles would be impossible, and civilization would have taken a very different course (if indeed it arose at all).

> Man, supposing you and I, escaping this battle, would be able to live on forever, ageless, immortal, so neither would I myself go on fighting in the foremost nor would I urge you into the fighting where men win glory. But now, seeing that the spirits of death stand close around us in their thousands, no man can turn aside or escape them, let us go on and win glory for ourselves, or yield it to others.
>
> —Sarpedon of the Lykians

> Come on, you sons of bitches! Do you want to live forever?
>
> Gunnery Sgt. Dan Daly, USMC, Belleau Wood, 6 June 1918

Patriotism, religion, the belief that you are defending your home and family, are powerful reasons for men to fight, but mercenary troops with none of those motives to sustain them have often fought to the death too. The most important single factor that makes it possible for civilized men to fight the wars of civilization is that all armies everywhere have always exploited and manipulated the ingrained warrior ethic that is the heritage of every young human male.

It is not that soldiers delude themselves about the possibility of dying in battle or about the terrible things that weapons do to living flesh; on the contrary, they are all too aware of it. Even the earliest surviving accounts of battle dwell in almost obsessive anatomical detail on how death comes to soldiers: "Ideomeneus stabbed Erymas in the mouth with the pitiless bronze, so that the brazen spear smashed its way clean through below the brain in an upward stroke, and the white bones splintered, and the teeth were shaken out with the stroke and both eyes filled up with blood, and gaping he blew a spray of blood through the nostrils and through his mouth, and death in a dark mist closed over him."

Soldiers know about violent death in all its forms, and though they have their preferences among the forms—there was, for example, an irrational but understandable preference in the trenches of World War I for death by bullets rather than by artillery fire, because a close shell explosion would distort and rend the victim's body into scarcely human fragments—nevertheless they accept the chance of death. But what they require in return is the assurance (or the illusion) that their death will not be wasted or unnoticed or meaningless. Yet most soldiers' deaths in civilized warfare are all of those things. The tribe will not mourn the fallen warrior's death or sing songs about his prowess, and the purposes of the war have little to do with his personal life, even in the unlikely event that his death affects its outcome. So to make the bleak realities of civilized war more acceptable to the regimented soldiers of civilization there is a universal conspiracy to pretend that they still dwell in a moral and psychological landscape of a more bearably human scale: that of the distant tribal past.

From the earliest recorded history, the language that civilized armies consistently used to describe their slaughterhouse battles employs the old vocabulary of the primitive warrior. Soldiers are heroes doing deeds of valor, not number fifty-four in the second rank of the fifth cohort. Battles are decided by such deeds of valor, not by numbers or better weapons or sheer chance; every man counts. And of course the victims of these falsehoods generally collaborate in the deceit, even if they are veterans who have seen battle before, because to question them would be to undermine the value of their own courage and professionalism.

It is doubtful that some single cynical genius of the distant past invented this doublethink, whereby the soldier's trade is always described in warrior's terms. More likely it evolved over many generations out of necessity, but it is nevertheless sure of the great majority of descriptions of battle from the time of Sargon of Akkad to John Wayne's war movies. Even now the old vocabulary and the old perspective predominate, especially in the military. They have to, or soldiers would not do their jobs. But the reality is different, and always has been.

> Aramu the Urartian, being struck with fear by the terror of my mighty army . . . withdrew from his city and went up into the mountains of Adduri. Then I went up after him and fought a mighty battle in the mountains. With my army I overthrew 3,400 warriors; like Adad I brought a great raincloud down upon them; with the blood of the enemy I dyed the mountain as if it had been wool, and I captured their camp. Then Aramu, to save his life, fled to an inaccessible mountain. In my mighty strength I trampled on his land like a wild bull, and his cities I reduced to ruins and consumed with fire.
>
> —Shalmaneser III of Assyria, on the campaign against Urartu

When Shalmaneser took Arzashku, the royal capital of Urartu (near Lake Van in eastern Turkey), he impaled the defenders on sharpened stakes and then piled their severed heads against the city's walls. We know this because he boasted of his deed on bronze gates he had erected in the city of Imgur-Enlil, near his capital of Nineveh. The Assyrians had the reputation of being particularly ruthless even in the ancient world, but Shalmaneser's behavior was by no means unusual.

One of the very earliest records of Egypt, dating from around 3200 B.C., shows the Pharaoh Narmer (who may have been the man who united the entire kingdom for the first time) with the headless bodies of slain enemies. The oldest inscription that has survived from Mesopotamia is the Stele of the Vultures, which shows carrion birds fighting over the entrails of soldiers killed in the battle in which Eannatum of Lagash defeated the rival city-state of Umma. War has been the constant companion of civilization, and most of the time it has been waged with savage cruelty toward the defeated—far more remorseless and efficient cruelty than most of the world's "savages" have ever displayed. And the reason for this is contained in the way that civilization was born.

There is practically no direct evidence regarding the political and military structure of the earliest civilizations, when various tribes in the Middle East were first learning how to grow crops and domesticate animals, and when the first villages began to grow into towns. But war must already have been changing into a disciplined business with political and economic purposes that we would understand, for as early as 7000 B.C. there was at least one fortified town: Jericho. The population was probably no more than two thousand, crammed into a space of about ten acres, but Jericho was surrounded by a massive wall twelve feet high and six and a half feet thick, flanked by a circular stone tower and encircled by a deep ditch. The citizens of Jericho felt they had wealth worth defending, and they lived in a world where others would try to take it from them by force and could not be stopped by lesser defenses.

It was in this earliest period, and over the next four thousand years—half of the history of civilization—that armies and states must have evolved into more or less the forms in which we know them today, but we know nothing about the details of the process, for writing had not been invented. By the time written records started about five thousand years ago, the state and the army were already fully formed institutions of great antiquity. Nevertheless, it is possible to deduce how these twin institutions emerged and grew steadily in scale and power until they towered above the mortal men who supported them.

The basis of civilization is agriculture, which transforms the land into a valuable possession requiring protection. In many parts of the ancient Middle East this protection was probably provided at first simply by transforming the tribal warriors into a loosely organized militia. This is already a momentous change. Warfare had become a purposeful activity with serious consequences for the whole community in the case of defeat, and so there was every incentive to apply human ingenuity to improving the organization and tactics of the tribal militia. But in the most fertile lands of all, in the great river valleys of the Nile and Euphrates, organization was needed on a far wider scale.

Both these regions are flood plains where the rivers, left to their own devices, will inundate the land for a few months of the year and leave it relatively parched for the rest. To farm these areas effectively, men must raise levees to keep the river within bounds and then build elaborate networks of irrigation canals and dikes to lead the water into the fields and retain it. Given the unreliability of the flood (seven years out of ten the Nile delivered either too much water or too little), the farmers must also lay up reserves of grain in the good years to share out in the bad. All this requires a central authority able to plan and coordinate the work of large numbers of people over wide areas—and the human race has never been short of people willing to volunteer for the job of running things.

> Ashurbanipal, the Great King, the Mighty King, King of the Universe . . . who from beyond the Tigris even to Mount Lebanon and the Great Sea has brought into submission at his feet the whole of the land of Lake, the land of Suhi as far as the city of Rapiku. . . .

Inscription on boundary stone, Assyrian Empire

Doubtless self-interest provided some degree of voluntary cooperation among the small peasant communities living side by side in the river valleys (in many cases they would have been of the same or related tribes), but it is equally certain that a significant degree of compulsion was necessary to unite their efforts. We know that the compulsion was supplied by military force, because that was the dominant means of enforcing obedience at the time the historical record begins. It also makes logical sense. The successful users of military force would gain control over a large area, which would prosper from better coordination of its efforts in farming the flood plain. The rulers of the area would then gain further power from having control over these increased resources, and so the system becomes self-sustaining and self-perpetuating. The state and the army were indeed Siamese twins.

Precisely who invented the first real armies, and how, we can never know. It may even have come about in different ways in different places. In one case a village militia may have discovered the rudiments of discipline and gained experience in a series of intervillage squabbles, and then been taken in hand by a prehistoric Napoleon who saw the possibilities in a systematic program of conquest. (He may have been more interested in loot, slaves, and rape than in creating the basis for a complex and productive farming economy, but his conquests would nevertheless produce the latter effect.)

In another case, an agricultural area may have been conquered by warriors from a tribe of hungry nonfarmers who then turned themselves into a military ruling caste. It is even conceivable that in some cases the initial work of political and economic unification over quite large areas proceeded without violence, but in a world where armies have come into being, even such a pacific society will survive only if it rapidly develops an army of its own.

> Shalmaneser, the Mighty King, King of the Universe, a King without rival, the Autocrat, the Powerful One of the Four Regions who shatters the princes of the whole world, who has smashed all his foes like pots. . . . Conqueror from the Upper Sea to the Lower Sea—the lands of Hatti, Luhute, Adri, Labnana, Kue, Tabali, Melidi. Discoverer of the sources of the Tigris and the Euphrates.

Another case of false modesty

There was more to these earliest states than just an army, of course. They had to have an administration that organized the work of irrigation and collected the tithes of grain (the universal form of taxation) that fed the ruler's courts, the soldiers, and the bureaucrats themselves. The centers of administration became the first cities, where a nonfarming population pursued not just the tasks of government but a rapidly diversifying variety of trades and services. And since the exercise of authority is both cheaper and easier if it rests on something beyond the mere threat of naked force (though that remains the final sanction), the old tribal religions were modified into state religions in which the gods underwrite the rulers' authority. Frequently the rulers themselves were declared minor gods, and more often than not the priesthood and the state bureaucracy were the same thing.

There was also, in the ancient kingdoms, a persistent phenomenon that is all too familiar to the citizens of modern states: the intoxication of power. Though no man can have absolute power, the illusion of it is engendered at all levels in a state administration that is backed by the right and ability to punish or even kill those who disobey. The practical basis for ordinary moral behavior is the recognition of shared humanity and mutual vulnerability, which is precisely what is destroyed by the illusion of absolute power. Thus those who controlled the first civilized states—which were all, without exception, totalitarian tyrannies—felt entitled to torture and kill their own subjects for any act of defiance and to massacre entire populations of foreigners who threatened their power. The former assumption is still very common, and the latter universal, in the states of today.

> Tell me one operation of war which is moral. . . . Sticking a bayonet into a man's belly, is that moral? Then they say, well, of course strategic bombing involved civilians. Civilians are always involved in major wars.
>
> After all, previous wars ended up in the besieging of major cities, and in besieging a city what was the idea? To cut off all supplies, and the city held out if it could until they'd eaten the last dog, cat, and sewer rat and were all starving, and meanwhile the besieging forces lobbed every missile they could lay their hands on into the city, more or less regardless of where those missiles landed, as an added incentive to surrender. . . .
>
> Sir Arthur Harris, head of RAF Bomber Command, 1942–45

There is no significant difference between what Shalmaneser III did to Arzashku in 858 B.C. and what British Bomber Command and the United States Eighth Air Force did to Dresden in 1945. Shalmaneser, being Assyrian, unquestionably took more pleasure in it, and the means of execution seem rather more exotic to us, but the ultimate consequences for the victims were identical. So was the moral basis for both acts. According to the conventional morality of every civilized society, it is justifiable and indeed praiseworthy to inflict death and suffering on the enemy when states are at war with each other. From time to time there have been quibbles about including noncombatants in the category of "enemy," but they are not to be taken seriously in a world of nuclear weapons.

No human beings can escape the category of potential enemy, for the rules of the international system decree that all states are always potentially at war with each other. Within the past two hundred years Britain and France, France and the United States, the United States and Britain, have all been both enemies and allies; Italy has gone from alliance to enmity with Germany and back again five times since 1914. Some things have changed since ancient times: the rules for the behavior of the rulers toward the ruled have been modified considerably within some states, particularly in the past few centuries. But other things have not changed at all: the international environment of armed and perilous anarchy in which all states live had already taken on its present form five thousand years ago.

Each state is solely responsible for its own survival and can only ensure it by having sufficient military force, either on its own or in alliance with others, to resist the armies of those who are in a position to threaten it. The threat is real: over 90 percent of all the states that have ever existed have been destroyed—and often their people with them—because they failed to have enough military power available at the critical moment. It is a lesson that is indelibly engraved in the consciousness of every government from Pharaoh Narmer's to Premier Gorbachev's.

Nobody now alive, nor anybody on this side of the historical horizon, has "chosen" war instead of peace; that would be like saying that someone has chosen to breathe air instead of water. Individual leaders and even whole nations may decide from time to time that they want a particular war (though far more wars begin as a result of miscalculation), and other leaders and countries may strive desperately to stay at peace, but it all takes place in a political context wherein war is always an option. That context has been the same since the beginning of recorded history. Indeed, it is almost certainly a good deal older than history. . . .

Suggested Readings

Cottrell, Leonard. *The Warrior Pharaohs*. London: Evans: 1968.

Davie, M.R. *The Evolution of War: A Study of its Role in Early Societies*. Port Washington: Kennikat, 1968.

Homer. *Iliad*. Chicago: University of Chicago, 1951.

Luckenbill, Daniel David. *Ancient Records of Assyria and Babylon*. Chicago: University of Chicago, 1926.

Mead, Margaret. *Cooperation and Conflict among Primitive Peoples*. Boston: Beacon, 1961.

Vagts, Alfred. *A History of Militarism*. New York: Norton, 1937.

Reading 2

THE RISE AND FALL OF THE GREAT POWERS

Paul Kennedy

Notes from the Editors
Since 1500, the international system has experienced at least nine world wars. All of them resulted in dramatic shifts in the relative power and status of the major states and a new rank ordering of the key players in the games of international politics. Historian Paul Kennedy studied the rises and declines in the fortunes of the major powers since the beginning of the modern state system.

In this introduction to his long and sophisticated book, he sketches the results of his examination of economic developments and military capabilities. Kennedy discovered a pattern that holds true for the entire 500-year period. Differential changes in the rates of economic growth led to changes in the military balances that ultimately produced victory or defeat in world war. Such was the case with Spain, the Netherlands, Austria, France, England, and even the contemporary United States. All of those "superpowers" experienced declines in their relative power that could be traced to their being overtaken by others in various aspects of economic and industrial development.

Moreover, all of the top dogs became top dogs by extending their political and economic holdings and alliances. The defense of those holdings, however, led to too much spending on military ventures and not enough on domestic economic health and growth.

Kennedy demonstrates how the study of history's wars can help us understand today's international system. Moreover, he contends that just because the United States has begun to slip relative to its position in 1945 is no reason to expect the total eclipse of its power. By understanding the apparent laws or patterns of history, one can adjust to and prepare for the inevitable, but not necessarily disastrous, alterations in the great power system that are taking place at the present time.

. . . The relative strengths of the leading nations in world affairs never remain constant, principally because of the uneven rate of growth among different societies and of the technological and organizational breakthroughs which bring a greater advantage to one society than to another. For example, the coming of the long-range gunned sailing ship and the rise of the Atlantic trades after 1500 was not *uniformly* beneficial to all the states of Europe—it boosted some much more than others. In the same way, the later development of steam power and of the coal and metal resources upon which it relied massively increased the relative power of certain nations, and thereby decreased the relative power of others. Once their productive capacity was enhanced, countries would normally find it easier to sustain the burdens of paying for large-scale armaments in peacetime and of maintaining and supplying large armies and fleets in wartime. It sounds crudely mercantilistic to express it this way, but wealth is usually needed to underpin military power, and military power is usually needed to acquire and protect wealth. If, however, too large a proportion of the state's resources is diverted from wealth creation and allocated instead to military purposes, then that is likely to lead to a weakening of national power over the longer term. In the same way, if a state overextends itself strategically—by, say, the conquest of extensive territories or the waging of costly wars—it runs the risk that the potential benefits from external expansion may be outweighed by the great expense of it all—a dilemma which becomes acute if the nation concerned has entered a period of relative economic decline. The history of the rise and later fall of the leading countries in the Great Power system since the advance of western Europe in the sixteenth century—that is, of nations such as Spain, the Netherlands, France, the British Empire, and currently the United States—shows a very significant correlation *over the longer term* between productive and revenue-raising capacities on the one hand and military strength on the other. . . .

. . . At the beginning of the sixteenth century it was by no means apparent that the last-named region [Europe] was destined to rise above all the rest. But however imposing and organized some of those oriental empires appeared by comparison with Europe, they all suffered from the consequences of having a centralized authority which insisted upon a uniformity of belief and practice, not only in official state religion but also in such areas as commercial activities and weapons development. The lack of any such supreme authority in Europe and the warlike rivalries among its various kingdoms and city-states stimulated a constant search for military improvements, which interacted fruitfully with the newer technological and commercial advances that were also being thrown up in this competitive, entrepreneurial environment. Possessing fewer obstacles to change, European societies entered into a constantly upward spiral of economic growth and enhanced military effectiveness which, over time, was to carry them ahead of all other regions of the globe.

While this dynamic of technological change and military competitiveness drove Europe forward in its usual jostling, pluralistic way, there still remained the possibility that one of the contending states might acquire sufficient resources to surpass the others, and then to dominate the continent. For about 150 years after 1500, a dynastic-religious bloc under the Spanish and Austrian Habsburgs seemed to threaten to do just that, and the efforts of the other major European states to check this "Habsburg bid for mastery" occupy the whole of Chapter 2. . . . The chief theme of this chapter is that despite the great resources possessed by the Habsburg monarchs, they steadily overextended themselves in the course of repeated conflicts and became militarily top-heavy for their weakening economic base. If the other European Great Powers also suffered immensely in these prolonged wars, they managed—though narrowly—to maintain the balance between their material resources and their military power better than their Habsburg enemies.

The Great Power struggles which took place between 1660 and 1815 cannot be so easily summarized as a contest between one large bloc and its many rivals. It was in this complicated period that while certain former Great Powers like Spain and the Netherlands were falling into the second rank, there steadily emerged five major states (France, Britain, Russia, Austria, and Prussia) which came to dominate the diplomacy and warfare of eighteenth-century Europe, and to engage in a series of lengthy coalition wars punctuated by swiftly changing alliances. This was an age in which France, first under Louis XIV and then later under Napoleon, came closer to controlling Europe than at any time before or since; but its endeavors were always held in check, in the last resort at least, by a combination of the other Great Powers. Since the cost of standing armies and national fleets had become horrendously great by the early eighteenth century, a country which could create an advanced system of banking and credit (as Britain did) enjoyed many advantages over financially backward rivals. But the factor of geographical position was also of great importance in deciding the fate of the Powers in their many, and frequently changing, contests—which helps to explain why the two "flank" nations of Russia and Britain had become much more important by 1815. Both retained the capacity to intervene in the struggles of west-central Europe while being geographically sheltered from them; and both expanded into the *extra-European* world as the eighteenth century unfolded, even as they were ensuring that the continental balance of power was upheld. Finally, by the later decades of the century, the Industrial Revolution was under way in Britain, which was to give that state an enhanced capacity both to colonize overseas and to frustrate the Napoleonic bid for European mastery.

For an entire century after 1815, by contrast, there was a remarkable absence of lengthy coalition wars. A strategic equilibrium existed, supported by all of the leading Powers in the Concert of Europe, so that no single nation was either able or willing to make a bid for dominance. The prime concerns of government in these post-1815 decades were with domestic instability and (in the case of Russia and the United States) with further expansion across their continental landmasses. This relatively stable international scene allowed the British Empire to rise to its zenith as a global power, in naval and colonial and commercial terms, and also interacted favorably with its virtual monopoly of steam-driven industrial production. By the second half of the nineteenth century, however, industrialization was spreading to certain other regions, and was beginning to tilt the international power balances away from the older leading nations and toward those countries with both the resources and organization to exploit the newer means of production and technology. Already, the few major conflicts of this era—the Crimean War to some degree but more especially the American Civil War and the Franco-Prussian War—were bringing defeat upon those societies which failed to modernize their military systems, and which lacked the broad-based industrial infrastructure to support the vast armies and much more expensive and complicated weaponry now transforming the nature of war.

As the twentieth century approached, therefore, the pace of technological change and uneven growth rates made the international system much more unstable and complex than it had been fifty years earlier. This was manifested in the frantic post-1880 jostling by the Great Powers for additional colonial territories in Africa, Asia, and the Pacific, partly for gain, partly out of a fear of being eclipsed. It also manifested itself in the increasing number of arms races, both on land and at sea, and in the creation of fixed military alliances, even in peacetime, as the various governments sought out partners for a possible future war. Behind the frequent colonial quarrels and international crises of the pre-1914 period, however, the decade-by-decade indices of economic power were pointing to even more fundamental shifts in the global balances— indeed, to the eclipse of what had been, for over three centuries, essentially a *Eurocentric* world system. Despite their best efforts, traditional European Great Powers like France and Austria-Hungary, and a recently united one like Italy, were falling out of the race. By contrast, the enormous, continent-wide states of the United States and Russia were moving to the forefront, and this despite the inefficiencies of the czarist state. Among the western European nations only Germany, possibly, had the muscle to force its way into the select league of the future world Powers. Japan, on the other hand, was intent upon being dominant in East Asia, but not farther afield. Inevitably, then, all these changes posed considerable, and ultimately insuperable, problems for a British Empire which now found it much more difficult to defend its global interests than it had a half-century earlier.

Although the major development of the fifty years after 1900 can thus be seen as the coming of a bipolar world, with its consequent crisis for the "middle" Powers . . . this metamorphosis of the entire system was by no means a smooth one. On the contrary, the grinding, bloody mass battles of the First World War, by placing a premium upon industrial organization and national efficiency, gave imperial Germany certain advantages over the swiftly modernizing but still backward czarist Russia. Within a few months of Germany's victory on the eastern front, however, it found itself facing defeat in the west, while its allies were similarly collapsing in the Italian, Balkan, and Near Eastern theaters of the war. Because of the late addition of American military and especially economic aid, the western alliance finally had the resources to prevail over its rival coalition. But it had been an exhausting struggle for all the original belligerents. Austria-Hungary was gone, Russia in revolution, Germany defeated; yet France, Italy, and even Britain itself had also suffered heavily in their victory. The only exceptions were Japan, which further augmented its position in the Pacific; and, of course, the United States, which by 1918 was indisputably the strongest Power in the world.

The swift post-1919 American withdrawal from foreign engagements, and the parallel Russian isolationism under the Bolshevik regime, left an international system which was more out of joint with the fundamental economic realities than perhaps at any time in the five centuries covered in this book. Britain and France, although weakened, were still at the center of the diplomatic stage, but by the 1930s their position was being challenged by the militarized, revisionist states of Italy, Japan, and Germany—the last intent upon a much more deliberate bid for European hegemony than even in 1914. In the background, however, the United States remained by far the mightiest manufacturing nation in the world, and Stalin's Russia was quickly transforming itself into an industrial superpower. Consequently, the dilemma for the *revisionist* "middle" Powers was that they had to expand soon if they were not to be overshadowed by the two continental giants. The dilemma for the status quo middle Powers was that in fighting off the German and Japanese challenges, they would most likely weaken themselves as well. The Second World War, for all its ups and downs, essentially confirmed those apprehensions of decline. Despite spectacular early victories, the Axis nations could not in the end succeed against an imbalance of productive resources which was far greater than that of the 1914–1918 war. What they did achieve was the eclipse of France and the irretrievable weakening of Britain—before they themselves were overwhelmed by superior force. By 1943, the bipolar world forecast decades earlier had finally arrived, and the military balance had once again caught up with the global distribution of economic resources.

The last two chapters of this book examine the years in which a bipolar world did indeed seem to exist, economically, militarily, and ideologically—and was reflected at the political level by the many crises of the Cold War. The position of the United States and the USSR as Powers in a class of their own also appeared to be reinforced by the arrival of nuclear weapons and long-distance delivery systems, which suggested that the strategic as well as the diplomatic landscape was now entirely different from that of 1900, let alone 1800.

And yet the process of rise and fall among the Great Powers—of differentials in growth rates and technological change, leading to shifts in the global economic balances, which in turn gradually impinge upon the political and military balances—had not ceased. Militarily, the United States and the USSR stayed in the forefront as the 1960s gave way to the 1970s and 1980s. Indeed, because they both interpreted international problems in bipolar, and often Manichean, terms, their rivalry has driven them into an ever-escalating arms race which no other Powers feel capable of matching. Over the same few decades, however, the global productive balances have been altering faster than ever before. The Third World's share of total manufacturing output and GNP, depressed to an all-time low in the decade after 1945, has steadily expanded since that time. Europe has recovered from its wartime batterings and, in the form of the European Economic Community, has become the world's largest trading unit. The People's Republic of China is leaping forward at an impressive rate. Japan's postwar economic growth has been so phenomenal that, according to some measures, it recently overtook Russia in total GNP. By contrast, both the American and Russian growth rates have become more sluggish, and their shares of global production and wealth have shrunk dramatically since the 1960s. Leaving aside all the smaller nations, therefore, it is plain that there already exists a *multi*polar world once more, if one measures the economic indices alone. Given this book's concern with the interaction between strategy and economics, it seemed appropriate to offer a final (if necessarily speculative) chapter to explore the present disjuncture between the military balances and the productive balances among the Great Powers; and to point to the problems and opportunities facing today's five large politico-economic "power centers"—China, Japan, the EEC, the Soviet Union, and the United States itself—as they grapple with the age-old task of relating national means to national ends. This history of the rise and fall of the Great Powers has in no way come to a full stop. . . .

. . . [T]he problem which historians—as opposed to political scientists—have in grappling with general theories is that the evidence of the past is almost always too varied to allow for "hard" scientific conclusions. Thus, while it is true that some wars (e.g., 1939) can be linked to decision-makers' fears about shifts taking place in the overall power balances, that would not be so useful in explaining the struggles which began in 1776 (American Revolutionary War) or 1792 (French Revolutionary) or 1854 (Crimean War). In the same way, while one could point to Austria-Hungary in 1914 as a good example of a "falling" Great Power helping to trigger off a major war, that still leaves the theorist to deal with the equally critical roles played then by those "rising" Great Powers, Germany and Russia. Similarly, any general theory about whether empires pay, or whether imperial control is affected by a measurable "power-distance" ratio, is likely—from the conflicting evidence available—to produce the banal answer sometimes yes, sometimes no.

Nevertheless, if one sets aside *a priori* theories and simply looks at the historical record of "the rise and fall of the Great Powers" over the past five hundred years, it is clear that some generally valid conclusions can be drawn—while admitting all the time that there may be individual exceptions. For example, there is detectable a causal relationship between the shifts which have occurred over time in the general economic and productive balances and the position occupied by individual Powers in the international system. The move in trade flows from the Mediterranean to the Atlantic and northwestern Europe from the sixteenth century onward, or the redistribution in the shares of world manufacturing output away from western Europe in the decades after 1890, are good examples here. In both cases, the economic shifts heralded the rise of new Great Powers which would one day have a decisive impact upon the military/territorial order. This is why the move in the global productive balances toward the "Pacific rim" which has taken place over the past few decades cannot be of interest merely to economists alone.

Similarly, the historical record suggests that there is a very clear connection *in the long run* between an individual Great Power's economic rise and fall and its growth and decline as an important military power (or world empire). This, too, is hardly surprising, since it flows from two related facts. The first is that economic resources are necessary to support a large-scale military establishment. The second is that, so far as the international system is concerned, both wealth and power are always *relative* and should be seen as such. Three hundred years ago, the German mercantilist writer von Hornigk observed that

> whether a nation be today mighty and rich or not depends not on the abundance or security of its power and riches, but principally on whether its neighbors possess more or less of it.

In the chapters which follow, this observation will be borne out time and again. The Netherlands in the mid-eighteenth century was richer in *absolute* terms than a hundred years earlier, but by that stage was much less of a Great Power because neighbors like France and Britain had "more . . . of it" (that is, more power and riches). The France of 1914 was, absolutely, more powerful than that of 1850—but this was little consolation when France was being eclipsed by a much stronger Germany. Britain today has far greater wealth, and its armed forces possess far more powerful weapons, than in its mid-Victorian prime; that avails it little when its share of world product has shrunk from about 25 percent to about 3 percent. If a nation has "more . . . of it," things are fine; if "less of it," there are problems.

This does not mean, however, that a nation's relative economic and military power will rise and fall *in parallel*. Most of the historical examples covered here suggest that there is a noticeable "lag time" between the trajectory of a state's relative economic strength and the trajectory of its military/territorial influence. Once again, the reason for this is not difficult to grasp. An economically expanding Power—Britain in the 1860s, the United States in the 1890s, Japan today—may well prefer to become rich rather than to spend heavily on armaments. A half-century later, priorities may well have altered. The earlier economic expansion has brought with it overseas obligations (dependence upon foreign markets and raw materials, military alliances, perhaps bases and colonies). Other, rival Powers are now economically expanding at a faster rate, and wish in their turn to extend their influence abroad. The world has become a more competitive place, and market shares are being eroded. Pessimistic observers talk of decline; patriotic statesmen call for "renewal."

In these more troubled circumstances, the Great Power is likely to find itself spending much *more* on defense than it did two generations earlier, and yet still discover that the world is a less secure environment—simply because other Powers have grown faster, and are becoming stronger. Imperial Spain spent much more on its army in the troubled 1630s and 1640s than it did in the 1580s, when the Castilian economy was healthier. Edwardian Britain's defense expenditures were far greater in 1910 than they were at, say, the time of Palmerston's death in 1865, when the British economy was relatively at its peak; but which Britons by the later date felt more secure? The same problem, it will be argued below, appears to be facing both the United States and the USSR today. Great Powers in relative decline instinctively respond by spending more on "security," and thereby divert potential resources from "investment" and compound their long-term dilemma.

Another general conclusion which can be drawn from the five-hundred-year record presented here is that there is a very strong correlation between the eventual outcome of the *major coalition wars* for European or global mastery, and the amount of productive resources mobilized by each side. This was true of the struggles waged against the Spanish-Austrian Habsburgs; of the great eighteenth-century contests like the War of Spanish Succession, the Seven Years War, and the Napoleonic War; and of the two world wars of this century. A lengthy, grinding war eventually turns into a test of the relative capacities of each coalition. Whether one side has "more . . . of it" or "less of it" becomes increasingly significant as the struggle lengthens.

One can make these generalizations, however, without falling into the trap of crude economic determinism. Despite this book's abiding interest in tracing the "larger tendencies" in world affairs over the past five centuries, it is *not* arguing that economics determines every event, or is the sole reason for the success and failure of each nation. There simply is too much evidence pointing to other things: geography, military organization, national morale, the alliance system, and many other factors can all affect the relative power of the members of the states system. In the eighteenth century, for example, the United Provinces were the richest parts of Europe, and Russia the poorest—yet the Dutch fell, and the Russians rose. Individual folly (like Hitler's) and extremely high battlefield competence (whether of the Spanish regiments in the sixteenth century or of the German infantry in this century) also go a long way to explain individual victories and defeats. What does seem incontestable, however, is that in a long-drawn-out Great Power (and usually coalition) war, victory has repeatedly gone to the side with the more flourishing productive base—or, as the Spanish captains used to say, to him who has the last escudo. Much of what follows will confirm that cynical but essentially correct judgment. And it is precisely because the power position of the leading nations has closely paralleled their relative economic position over the past five centuries that it seems worthwhile asking what the implications of today's economic and technological trends might be for the current balance of power. This does not deny that men make their own history, but they do make it within a historical circumstance which can restrict (as well as open up) possibilities. . . .

Suggested Readings

Gilpin, Robert. *War and Change in World Politics*. Cambridge: Harvard University, 1961.

Modelski, George. "The Long Cycle of Global Politics and the Nation-State." *Comparative Studies in Society and History* 20 (April 1978), pp. 214–35.

Ranke, Leopold von. "The Great Powers." In *Leopold von Ranke, The Theory and Practice of History,* eds. George G. Iggers and Konrad von Moltke. Indianapolis: Bobbs-Merrill, 1973, pp. 65–101.

Rosecrance, Richard. *The Rise of the Trading State*. New York: Basic Books, 1985.

Wallerstein, Immanuel. *The Modern World System*. 2 vols. New York: Academic Press, 1974, 1980.

Reading 3

PATTERNS IN INTERNATIONAL WARFARE, 1816–1980

Melvin Small and J. David Singer

Notes from the Editors

Historian Melvin Small and political scientist J. David Singer have been studying the correlates and causes of war together for twenty-five years. Before they could begin their analyses, they had to define international war, the main variable in their study. Employing a systematic, empirical approach in the Correlates of War Project, they were dissatisfied with previous anecdotal compendia of wars and battles. Thus, they chose to describe all international wars of a certain level of violence (at least one thousand battle-related deaths) fought by independent members of the international system since 1815.

In the article that summarizes findings from The Wages of War *(1972) and* Resort to Arms *(1982), Singer and Small are not concerned with civil wars, although they examine them in other contexts, nor are they concerned with wars fought by political entities that are not in the international system. Their resulting listing is smaller than many previous catalogues but more rigorous in terms of battle death and duration data.*

Their article reveals that not all nations fight in international wars and that not all time periods share equally in the number of wars begun and the number of deaths suffered. A careful examination of their data offers insights into the "why war?" question, and may even offer hope to those who fear that war is endemic to the human condition.

In 1980, Small and Singer listed eight wars as ongoing. As of this writing (1988), those eight wars have not ended.

Since Thucydides, scholars and statesmen have speculated about the causes and consequences of conflict between nation states. Despite the earnest efforts of countless generations of investigators, it is only within the past several decades that any promising attack on the problem of the causes of war has been mounted. In our judgment, the important turning point in man's long quest to understand this recurrent phenomenon occurred in the 1930's, when Quincy Wright and Lewis F. Richardson began to employ operational, quantitative techniques in the description and analysis of the most pernicious product of international relations.[1]

Inspired by the work of these pioneers, and borrowing many of their methodological and theoretical innovations, we have initiated a project whose major objective is to identify the variables that are most frequently associated with the onset of war, from the Congress of Vienna to the present.[2] Our first requirement was to describe and measure the dependent variable, and ascertain the trends and fluctuations in the

Portions of this article first appeared in "Patterns in International Warfare, 1816–1965," *Annals of American Academy of Political and Social Science* 391 (September 1970), pp. 145—55. Those portions are reprinted by permission of Sage Publications, Inc., the publisher of the journal.

frequency, magnitude, severity, and intensity of war during that period. This task has now been completed and the data base we have developed allows us to generalize with some degree of confidence about patterns in international violence over the last century and a half.[3] Before we turn to such generalizations, however, we should explain briefly the data acquisition and coding procedures employed in our study.

Identifying the Wars

Most major studies of war suffered from an absence of methodological precision and an invisibility of coding rules.[4] These practices often resulted in the impressionistic analysis by anecdote of the few famous and large wars by political theorists, or the hyper-empirical analysis of every conceivable sort of violence by scholars with a mathematical orientation. Aware of the pitfalls inherent in both approaches, we have adopted criteria and rules which we feel allow maximum practicality and efficiency but which do not violate intellectual standards of reliability and validity.

Thus, we began by delimiting the system in which we were interested. Although it would be useful to know something about violence in all polities for all recorded time periods, such an approach would find us laboring far into the foreseeable future in the often barren vineyards of the historians. The period since 1815, which is manageable in terms of the availability of historical sources, satisfies our need both for systemic continuity and for a time span long enough to allow for any permutations in the level of violence to evidence themselves. Within these temporal bounds, we were concerned primarily with wars fought by members of the international system against fellow members (interstate wars) and against independent or colonial entities which did not qualify for membership in the system (extra-systemic wars). To qualify for membership in the international system, a state needed to have a population of at least 500,000 and diplomatic recognition from legitimizers within the international community.[5] In the period after 1920, membership in the League of Nations or the United Nations was used as an alternate criterion in some cases. The adoption of such a scheme results in a system with 23 members in 1816, 34 in 1870, 61 in 1920, 124 in 1965, and 155 in 1980.

As for the wars themselves, we gathered data on those conflicts in which the battle-connected deaths for all systemic combatants taken together surpassed 1,000. A slightly more complicated procedure was used to determine the inclusion or exclusion of some extra-systemic wars.[6] All the qualifying wars were codified in terms of severity (or battle deaths of system-member participants) and magnitude (or total number of nation-months that system-member participants spent in combat). The 118 wars which met our criteria are listed in chronological order in Table 1, with the 67 interstate wars shown in italics. Alongside each war is its rank position in terms of battle deaths, nation months, and a simple intensity measure—number of battle deaths divided by number of nation months.[7]

Trends and Cycles

After the basic data were reordered according to the amount of war begun, under way, and terminated each year, we were able to search for secular trends and periodicity

TABLE 1   International War, 1816–1980

Name of War	Battle Deaths	Nation Months	Battle Deaths per Nation Months
British-Maharattan (1817–1818)I*	81.5	77.0	81.0
Greek (1821–1828)C	42.5	14.0	92.0
Franco-Spanish (1823)	104.5	57.0	108.0
First Anglo-Burmese (1823–1826)I	42.5	33.0	64.0
Javanese (1825–1830)C	42.5	19.0	84.0
Russo-Persian (1826–1828)I	67.0	49.5	82.0
Russo-Turkish (1828–1829)	11.0	30.0	18.0
First Polish (1831)C	42.5	73.0	28.0
First Syrian (1831–1832)C	53.5	60.0	54.0
Texan (1835–1836)C	104.5	78.0	100.0
First British-Afghan (1838–1842)I	33.0	20.0	73.0
Second Syrian (1839–1840)C	50.0	85.0	29.0
Franco-Algerian (1839–1847)I	42.5	12.0	99.0
Peruvian-Bolivian (1841)I	104.5	102.5	45.5
First British-Sikh (1845–1846)I	93.5	94.0	62.0
Mexican-American (1846–1848)	38.0	21.0	74.0
Austro-Sardinian (1848–1849)	57.0	47.0	63.0
First Schleswig–Holstein (1848–1849)	63.0	53.5	76.0
Hungarian (1848–1849)C	20.0	65.0	16.0
Second British-Sikh (1848–1849)I	93.5	87.0	80.0
Roman Republic (1849)	88.5	81.0	79.0
La Plata (1851–1852)	98.0	62.0	103.0
First Turco-Montenegran (1852–1853)I	67.0	89.0	37.0
Crimean (1853–1856)	8.0	7.0	25.0
Anglo-Persian (1856–1857)	81.5	72.0	86.0
Sepoy (1857–1859)C	75.0	38.0	98.0
Second Turco-Montenegran (1858–1859)I	80.5	63.0	85.0
Italian Unification (1859)	28.0	74.0	21.0
Spanish-Moroccan (1859–1860)	53.5	70.0	48.0
Italo-Roman (1860)	104.5	102.5	45.5
Italo-Sicilian (1860–1861)	104.5	80.0	96.0
Franco-Mexican (1862–1867)	33.0	8.0	94.0
Ecuadorian-Colombian (1863)	104.5	102.5	45.5
Second Polish (1863–1864)C	67.0	56.0	77.0
Spanish-Santo Dominican (1863–1865)I	60.0	55.0	68.0
Second Schleswig-Holstein (1864)	70.0	68.0	71.0
Lopez (1864–1870)	6.0	5.0	36.0
Spanish-Chilean (1865–1866)	104.5	51.0	110.0

TABLE 1   *(continued)*

Name of War	Battle Deaths	Nation Months	Battle Deaths per Nation Months
Seven Weeks (1866)	25.0	61.0	22.0
Ten Years (1868–1878)C	13.5	9.0	51.0
Franco-Prussian (1870–1871)	9.0	34.0	13.0
Dutch-Achinese (1873–1878)I	63.0	18.0	104.0
Balkan (1875–1877)C	53.5	41.0	67.0
Russo-Turkish (1877–1878)	7.0	48.0	3.0
Bosnian (1878)C	75.0	35.5	33.0
Second British-Afghan (1878– 1880)I	72.5	46.0	87.0
Pacific (1879–1883)	46.0	6.0	107.0
British-Zulu (1879)I	75.0	84.0	58.5
Franco-Indochinese (1882–1884)I	70.0	35.0	93.0
Mahdist (1882–1885)C	33.0	24.0	65.0
Sino-French (1884–1885)	47.0	45.0	57.0
Central American (1885)	104.5	102.5	45.5
Serbo-Bulgarian (1885)I	84.5	99.0	30.0
Sino-Japanese (1894–1895)	42.5	53.5	49.0
Franco-Madagascan (1894–1895)I	63.0	71.0	58.5
Cuban (1895–1898)C	22.0	27.0	40.0
Italo-Ethiopian (1895–1896)I	58.0	68.0	52.0
First Philippine (1896–1898)C	84.5	37.0	106.0
Greco-Turkish (1897)	84.5	82.5	78.0
Spanish-American (1898)	53.5	75.0	39.0
Second Philippine (1899–1902)C	70.0	22.0	101.0
Boer (1899–1902)C	29.0	32.0	55.0
Boxer Rebellion (1900)	79.0	66.0	83.0
Ilinden (1903)C	84.5	92.0	56.0
Russo-Japanese (1904–1905)	11.0	26.0	20.0
Central American (1906)	104.5	86.0	89.0
Central American (1907)	104.5	82.5	95.0
Spanish-Moroccan (1909–1910)	53.5	49.5	61.0
Italo-Turkish (1911–1912)	33.0	36.0	53.0
First Balkan (1912–1913)	17.0	43.0	17.0
Second Balkan (1913)	18.0	88.0	4.0
World War I (1914–1918)	2.0	3.0	5.0
Russian Nationalities (1917– 1921)C	22.0	25.0	41.0
Russo-Polish (1919–1920)	13.5	23.0	24.0
Hungarian-Allies (1919)	48.5	68.0	43.0
Greco-Turkish (1919–1922)	22.0	15.0	60.0
Riffian (1921–1926)C	26.0	16.0	75.0
Druze (1925–1927)C	72.5	39.0	91.0

TABLE 1   *(concluded)*

Name of War	Battle Deaths	Nation Months	Battle Deaths per Nation Months
Sino-Soviet (1929)	78.0	76.0	69.0
Manchurian (1931–1933)	19.0	31.0	31.0
Chaco (1932–1935)	11.0	17.0	32.0
Italo-Ethiopian (1935–1936)	33.0	59.0	38.0
Sino-Japanese (1937–1941)	5.0	10.0	11.0
Changkufeng (1938)	91.0	102.5	34.0
Nomohan (1939)	27.0	64.0	26.0
World War II (1939–1945)	1.0	1.0	2.0
Russo-Finnish (1939–1940)	16.0	79.0	6.0
Franco-Thai (1940–1941)	96.5	90.0	42.0
Indonesian (1945–1946)C	96.5	40.0	109.0
Indochinese (1945–1954)C	15.0	11.0	50.0
Madagascan (1947–1948)C	90.0	42.0	105.0
First Kashmir (1947–1949)I	93.5	58.0	102.0
Palestine (1948–1949)	59.0	44.0	72.0
Hyderabad (1948)I	104.5	110.0	9.0
Korean (1950–1953)	3.0	4.0	19.0
Algerian (1954–1962)C	37.0	13.0	88.0
Russo-Hungarian (1956)	53.5	98.0	12.0
Sinai (1956)	77.0	106.5	15.0
Tibetan (1956–1959)C	24.0	28.0	42.0
Sino-Indian (1962)	104.5	95.5	66.0
Vietnamese (1965–1975)	4.0	2.0	35.0
Second Kashmir (1965)	61.0	92.0	27.0
Six Day (1967)	36.0	108.0	1.0
Israeli-Egyptian (1969–1970)	65.0	29.0	97.0
Football (1969)	88.5	109.0	10.0
Bangladesh (1971)	48.5	102.5	8.0
Philippine-MNLF† (1972–)C			
Yom Kippur (1973)	39.0	92.0	14.0
Turco-Cypriot (1974)	93.5	106.5	23.0
Ethiopian-Eritrean (1974–)C			
Vietnamese-Cambodian (1975–)			
Timor (1975–)C			
Saharan (1975–)C			
Ogaden (1976–)C			
Ugandan-Tanzanian (1978–1979)	80.5	52.0	90.0
Sino-Vietnamese (1979)	30.0	97.0	7.0
Russo-Afghan (1979–1988)			
Irani-Iraqi (1980–)			

*Extrasystemic wars are shown with I (imperial) or C (colonial) following the listing.
†Continuing wars are shown without rankings

over the past century and a half. Looking first at secular trends, contrary to what might have been expected, no trend, either upward or downward, is evident. That is, whether we concentrate upon frequencies, magnitudes, severities, or intensities, we do not find appreciably more or less war in any of the sub-epochs covered. Of course, there were more battle deaths in the twentieth century than in the nineteenth (thanks to the impact of the two World Wars and the Korean conflict), but when the figures are normalized for the number of nations in the system, this trend disappears. International war, therefore, appears to be neither on the rise or the decline. It is true, however, that extra-systemic wars have been decreasing in frequency; but this is entirely a product of the liquidation of formal colonial empires and the expansion of the international system to include all independent entities.

While such findings might cheer those who intuitively feared that we have been experiencing an ever-increasing amount of war as we approach the apocalypse, they must be balanced with the more dismal finding that there appears to be a strong tendency toward periodicity in the system's war experiences. Although cycles are not apparent when we examine the amount of war beginning in each year or time period, a vague periodicity emerges when we focus on measures of the amount of war under way. That is, discrete wars do not necessarily come and go with regularity; but with some level of interstate violence almost always present there are distinct and periodic fluctuations in the amount of that violence. The 15- to 20-year cycle in the amount of nation months of war is suggested in the data.

Others have discerned similar cycles which could be related, among other things, to the time needed for a generation to "forget" the last bloody conflict.[8] It must be remembered that such analyses assume an interdependence between the martial activities of all system members, and that, for example, the incidence of war in the Balkans presumably affects the incidence of war on the Iberian Peninsula or even in Southeast Asia. Interestingly, no cyclical patterns are apparent when we examine the military experiences of the individual nations that participated in several wars. Thus, we must be rather tentative in affirming the existence of periodicity in the incidence of war, for our one strong pattern shows up only when we isolate one set of variables among many. Much more work needs to be done before we can accept completely the notion of a 15–20 year cycle, although these preliminary findings suggest the direction in which this work should go.

Seasons and Wars

Another way to approach the temporal variable is to examine the relationship between season and month and the incidence of war. According to the folklore, the onset and termination of war should be determined, in part, by climatological conditions which might affect military mobility and efficiency, and the growing and harvesting seasons which might, in turn, affect provisioning and recruiting an army. Some contemporary analysts would expect most wars to begin between March 22 and April 20 under the sign of bellicose Aries, and the fewest to begin between September 24 and October 23 when the gentle Libra is dominant.

To some degree, our data support the common folklore although the verdict is mixed for the astrologists. Of the 118 wars, 74 began in either spring or autumn and only 44 in summer and winter. This pattern does change somewhat over time; for example, "only" 23 of the 42 wars fought since 1920 began in autumn or spring. No one season or month stands out when it comes to the termination of war. This latter finding, when compared to the onset patterns, lends credence to the thesis that policy makers are influenced by the season when they consider a war/no-war decision, but that once the war is under way, more nonrational factors militate against weather or supplies playing such a crucial role. Of course, much of this is conjecture. Before we can attest with certainty to the proposition that weather and climate weigh heavily with the decisionmaker, we must compare similar sets of crises, which did and did not terminate in war, with specific seasonal variables.

The War Proneness of Nations

Whereas systemic patterns of international violence are most interesting to the political theorist, the record of individual nations' martial activities has long fascinated historians. Many have argued that some nations (perhaps during certain periods) are more aggressive than others, or that some ethnic groups are naturally warlike whereas others are naturally pacific. At the same time, repeated involvement in war may not necessarily relate to any innate characteristic but merely to the misfortune of being geographically proximate to predatory powers. By computing the number and severity of wars experienced by each nation during its tenure in the system, we can obtain a more accurate indication of the distribution of wars among the nations, and whether, indeed, certain nations, or certain classes thereof, are more prone to war involvement than others.

In terms of the sheer number of international wars, France leads the field with 22, England fought in 19, Turkey and Russia 18, and Italy (including its predecessor, Sardinia) 12. All of these nations were members of the system for the full 165 years. Spain, which fought in 10 wars, and the United States, which fought in 8, are two other charter members of the system with significant war experience. Those with a shorter tenure are led by China with participation in 11 wars, Greece and Japan with 9, Austria-Hungary with 8, and Germany (including its predecessor, Prussia) with 6. As might be expected, these nations also sustained the most battle deaths, with Russia, Germany, China, France, Japan, England, Austria-Hungary, Italy, and Turkey, in that order, all suffering 750,000 or more. Moreover, 39 percent of all the system's nation months of war were accounted for by 5 nations—France, England, Turkey, Spain, and Russia—and 40 of the 51 extra-systemic wars were fought by 6 states—England 12, France 8, Turkey 7, Russia 5, Spain 5, and Holland 3.

Obviously, major powers were the most war-prone, with Turkey, Spain, and Greece the only non-majors to appear in this firmament.[9] No major powers were able to escape this scourge, which may, in fact, turn out to be a prerequisite for achievement of that exalted status. On the other hand, most of the smaller states, and especially those in extra-European regions, enjoyed a fairly pacific record in terms of international war. Many of these, of course, experienced long and bloody civil conflicts. Still, the fact that more than half the nations which were at one time or another members of the system were able to escape international war entirely suggests that military conflict between nations is not so common a systemic activity as some have posited.

National Military Achievement

Although some nations have fought in more wars than others, they have done so with varying degrees of success. Indeed, success in warfare might predict to frequency of involvement. A nation which loses several wars might behave with great circumspection in order to avoid the necessity of having to go to war again. Alternately, a military loss might foster a revanchist spirit, or worse yet, it could tempt a third power which felt it could easily defeat the nation whose military record was less than impressive. The data upon which one might base such generalizations are offered in Table 2, which shows each nation's record of victories and defeats in all international wars, followed by its record for interstate wars only.[10]

Thanks to their choice of enemies and allies, as well as their military capabilities and skills, most of the major powers have done rather well. The nine nations which were at one time or another major powers hold six of the first seven positions and eight of the first thirteen in terms of won-lost records. The one major power absent from this galaxy, China, achieved its poor record while it was a minor power—since 1950 China has won two wars and tied in another. Turkey, as was expected, has a dismal history in this realm, but the Italians, often maligned for their legendary military ineptitude, nevertheless emerged victorious in nine of their twelve engagements.

The Initiation of Interstate War

A history of involvement in international war is a necessary but not sufficient indication of a nation's bellicosity. The determination of the initiator of military conflict, however, may tell us a bit more about a nation's aggressive proclivities. When we speak of initiation here, we are merely identifying the nation(s) which made the first attack on an opponents' armies or territories. Clearly, initiator and aggressor are not always identical, as a participant might provoke its adversary into military action by mobilization or other aggressive diplomatic or economic actions. But the designation of the initiator of military aggression should nevertheless provide some tentative clues as to the relative belligerency of system members.

In examining the interstate wars in which we were able to make this designation, we find that Italy was the actual initiator (or on the side of the initiator) on 9 occasions, France and Russia played that role on 7 occasions, Germany and Japan on 6 and Austria-Hungary and Bulgaria on 4. But when we turn from sheer number of initiations to the frequency of initiation compared to the total number of war experiences, some of the nations on this infamous list look a little less bellicose. Whereas Italy initiated or fought on the side of the initiator in 9 of her 11 interstate wars, Germany in 5 of her 6, Japan in 6 of her 9, Austria-Hungary in 4 of her 6, and Bulgaria in all of her 5, France initiated only 7 of her 14 interstate wars and Russia 7 her 13. Among

TABLE 2   National Performance in International War

Nation Name	All Wars	Interstate Wars
United Kingdom	16 - 2 - 1	6 - 0 - 1
France	15 - 6 - 1	9 - 4 - 1
USSR (Russia)	13 - 5 - 0	9 - 4 - 0
Italy/Sardinia	9 - 3 - 0	9 - 2 - 0
Japan	7 - 2 - 0	7 - 2 - 0
United States of America	6 - 1 - 1	5 - 1 - 1
Israel	4 - 0 - 1	4 - 0 - 1
Yugoslavia/Serbia	4 - 1 - 0	4 - 0 - 0
Rumania	4 - 1 - 0	4 - 1 - 0
Brazil	3 - 0 - 0	3 - 0 - 0
Austria-Hungary	5 - 3 - 0	3 - 3 - 0
Greece	4 - 2 - 1	4 - 2 - 1
Germany/Prussia	4 - 2 - 0	4 - 2 - 0
Netherlands	3 - 1 - 1	1 - 0 - 1
Belgium	2 - 0 - 1	2 - 0 - 1
Chile	2 - 0 - 0	2 - 0 - 0
Poland	2 - 0 - 0	2 - 0 - 0
Mongolia	2 - 0 - 0	2 - 0 - 0
India	3 - 2 - 0	1 - 2 - 0
Canada	1 - 0 - 1	1 - 0 - 1
Colombia	1 - 0 - 1	1 - 0 - 1
Nicaragua	1 - 0 - 0	1 - 0 - 0
Portugal	1 - 0 - 0	1 - 0 - 0
Mecklenburg Schwerin	1 - 0 - 0	1 - 0 - 0
Czechoslovakia	1 - 0 - 0	1 - 0 - 0
Norway	1 - 0 - 0	1 - 0 - 0
Tanzania/Tanganyika	1 - 0 - 0	1 - 0 - 0
South Africa	1 - 0 - 0	1 - 0 - 0
New Zealand	1 - 0 - 0	1 - 0 - 0
Spain	5 - 5 - 0	2 - 3 - 0
El Salvador	2 - 2 - 0	2 - 2 - 0
Ethiopia	1 - 1 - 1	1 - 1 - 1
Thailand	1 - 1 - 1	1 - 1 - 1
Australia	1 - 1 - 1	1 - 1 - 1
Guatemala	1 - 1 - 0	1 - 1 - 0
Paraguay	1 - 1 - 0	1 - 1 - 0
Argentina	1 - 1 - 0	1 - 1 - 0
Bavaria	1 - 1 - 0	1 - 1 - 0
Baden	1 - 1 - 0	1 - 1 - 0
Wuerttemburg	1 - 1 - 0	1 - 1 - 0
Two Sicilies	1 - 1 - 0	1 - 1 - 0
Pakistan	1 - 1 - 0	1 - 1 - 0

TABLE 2   *(concluded)*

Nation Name	All Wars	Interstate Wars
Vietnam Democratic Rep.	1 - 1 - 0	1 - 1 - 0
Korea Dem. People's Rep.	0 - 0 - 1	0 - 0 - 1
Bulgaria	2 - 3 - 0	2 - 3 - 0
Mexico	1 - 2 - 0	1 - 1 - 0
Peru	1 - 2 - 0	1 - 1 - 0
Korea Republic of	0 - 1 - 1	0 - 1 - 1
Philippines	0 - 1 - 1	0 - 1 - 1
Ecuador	0 - 1 - 0	0 - 1 - 0
Hanover	0 - 1 - 0	0 - 1 - 0
Saxony	0 - 1 - 0	0 - 1 - 0
Hesse Electoral	0 - 1 - 0	0 - 1 - 0
Hesse Grand Ducal	0 - 1 - 0	0 - 1 - 0
Modena	0 - 1 - 0	0 - 1 - 0
Tuscany	0 - 1 - 0	0 - 1 - 0
Cyprus	0 - 1 - 0	0 - 1 - 0
Uganda	0 - 1 - 0	0 - 1 - 0
Libya	0 - 1 - 0	0 - 1 - 0
Iran (Persia)	0 - 1 - 0	0 - 1 - 0
Lebanon	0 - 1 - 0	0 - 1 - 0
Saudi Arabia	0 - 1 - 0	0 - 1 - 0
Kampuchea (Cambodia)	0 - 1 - 0	0 - 1 - 0
Vietnam Republic of	0 - 1 - 0	0 - 1 - 0
China	4 - 6 - 1	3 - 6 - 1
Bolivia	0 - 2 - 0	0 - 2 - 0
Papal States	0 - 2 - 0	0 - 2 - 0
Finland	0 - 2 - 0	0 - 2 - 0
Denmark	0 - 2 - 0	0 - 2 - 0
Morocco	0 - 2 - 0	0 - 2 - 0
Iraq	0 - 2 - 0	0 - 2 - 0
Turkey/Ottoman Empire	7 -10 - 1	5 - 5 - 1
Honduras	0 - 3 - 0	0 - 3 - 0
Hungary	0 - 3 - 0	0 - 3 - 0
Syria	0 - 3 - 0	0 - 3 - 0
Jordan	0 - 3 - 0	0 - 3 - 0
Egypt/UAR	0 - 4 - 1	0 - 4 - 1

those nations with significant war experience which are absent from this list and therefore, perhaps more pacific, are: the two "sick men" of Asia, Turkey and China and three Balkan states, Greece, Rumania, and Yugoslavia. As for the two Anglo-Saxon major powers, England initiated one war and the United States two.

The decision to initiate hostilities is related, in part, to the expectation of victory. Few governments would move first militarily unless they expected that such preemption had a high probability of victory or, at least, of national survival. Not surprisingly, then, we find that initiators emerged victorious in 46 of the 62 interstate wars. As for battle fatalities, in almost three quarters of the cases, the initiators lost fewer men than their opponents. This is an impressive record when one considers that an attacking force is generally assumed to lose more personnel than a defending force in a given engagement.

Of course, in 35 percent of the cases, the initiator turned out to be a major power attacking a minor power. Of the 22 wars which saw such a one-sided confrontation, the major power won 20 of those contests. When minors fought minors, the initiator won 17 times and lost 11, but when majors fought majors, the initiators won 3 times and lost 6. Thus, initiation of hostilities appears to have been a major advantage to the combatants, but an advantage which decreased in importance when the two sides were more nearly equal in power.

Conclusion

The above figures provide a brief, and necessarily superficial, overview of the incidence of war in the modern international system. While they are of some intrinsic interest, their major value is more instrumental in nature. That is, with such data as summarized here (and reported more fully in our *Wages of War* and *Resort to Arms*) an accelerated assault on the problem of the causes of war becomes feasible. A variety of researchers, reflecting diverse disciplines and numerous theoretical orientations, have undertaken systematic searches for the factors that account for this organized tribal slaughter. Whether the focus be on economic or strategic, psychological or technological phenomena, the dependent variable data are now at hand and have been used with good results. Our major purpose was to make such research possible, and as we continue to explore the problem from our particular point of view, we hope others will do likewise. Although the odds do not seem particularly favorable, we might just unravel the mystery of war's regularity before we stumble into its final occurrence.

NOTES

1. Quincy Wright, *A Study of War,* 2 vols. (Chicago: University of Chicago Press, 1942); Lewis F. Richardson, *Statistics of Deadly Quarrels* (Chicago: Quadrangle, 1960). In the third volume of his *Social and Cultural Dynamics* (New York: American Book, 1937), Pitirim A. Sorokin also applied empirical techniques to a longitudinal study of warfare.

2. For a description of the project and a sampling of its wares, see J. David Singer (ed.), *The Correlates of War I* (New York: Free Press, 1979) and Singer (ed.), *The Correlates of War II* (New York: Free Press, 1980).

3. Most of the material in this article is reported in other forms in J. David Singer and Melvin Small, *The Wages of War, 1816–1965: A Statistical Handbook* (New York: John Wiley, 1972) and Small and Singer, *Resort to Arms: International and Civil Wars, 1815–1980* (Beverly Hills, Sage, 1982).

4. Even Wright and Richardson's pathbreaking works suffer from these shortcomings to some degree. Except for the most recent period, Wright did not order his study of wars in terms of magnitude or severity, nor did he present operational criteria for defining his universe. For his part, Richardson did not distinguish between the status of political entities engaged in conflict, nor was he interested in the casualties suffered by the separate participants in the wars he studied.

5. A complete explanation of membership criteria is found in J. David Singer and Melvin Small, "The Composition and Status Ordering of the International System, 1815–1940," *World Politics* 18, no. 2 (January, 1966), 236–282, and Small and Singer, "The Diplomatic Importance of States," *ibid.*, XXV (July, 1973), 577–99.

6. Because many nineteenth century imperial conflicts achieved a casualty level of 1,000 battle deaths only after five or ten years, we decided that such a conflict had to average 1,000 battle deaths a year for the system member in order to qualify for inclusion in our list.

7. Battle-death and nation-month scores for extra-systemic wars reflect only the war experiences of system members. Many of these wars would have ranked considerably higher on all indices had we included non-member battle deaths and nation months.

8. See, for example, Frank H. Denton, "Some Regularities in International Conflict, 1820–1949," *Background*, 9, no. 4 (February, 1966), 283–296; Frank H. Denton and Warren Phillips, "Some Patterns in the History of Violence," *Journal of Conflict Resolution*, 12, no. 2 (June, 1968), 182–195; Edward R. Dewey, *The 177 Year Cycle in War, 600 B.C.–A.D. 1957* (Pittsburgh: Foundation for the Study of Cycles, 1964); J.S. Lee, "The Periodic Recurrence of Internecine Wars in China," *The China Journal* 14, no. 3 (March, 1931), 111–115, 159–162.

9. Our major powers (reflecting the historians' consensus) were England 1815–1980, France 1815–1940, 1945–1980, Germany 1815–1918, 1925–1945, Russia 1815–1917, 1921–1980, Austria-Hungary 1915–1918, Italy 1860–1943, United States 1899–1980, Japan 1895–1945, and China 1950–1980.

10. In some cases, the distinction between victor and vanquished was difficult to make, but in the end we "declared" a victor in all but one of the wars. For our purposes, nations like Poland and Belgium in World War II, while defeated in the initial stages of the war, were considered victors since they emerged at war's end on the side of the winning coalition. Italy, Rumania, and Bulgaria, which joined the Allies after being defeated as members of the Axis, were considered as having been both winners and losers.

Suggested Readings

Dewey, Edward R. "The 177 Year Cycle in War, 600 B.C.–A.D. 1957." Pittsburgh: Foundation for the Study of Cycles, 1964.

Moyal, J. S. "The Distribution of Wars in Time." *Journal of the Royal Statistical Society* 112 (1949), pp. 446–58.

Richardson, Lewis F. *Statistics of Deadly Quarrels*. Chicago: Quadrangle, 1960.

Urlanis, Boris T. *Wars and the Population of Europe*. Moscow: Government Publishing House, 1960.

Wood, David. *Conflict in the Twentieth Century*. Adelphi Papers 48. London Institute for Strategic Studies, 1968.

Wright, Quincy. *A Study of War*. Chicago: University of Chicago, 1965.

Reading 4

HISTORICAL TRENDS IN GREAT POWER WAR, 1495–1975

Jack Levy

Notes from the Editors

Working in the same genre as Small and Singer, political scientist Jack Levy examines a much longer time period (1495–1975) and a more limited set of nations, the great powers. Like Small and Singer, he is interested in the quantification of patterns and trends in warfare through history and what these suggest about war in our time and the immediate future.

Obtaining good data for wars in the fifteenth through twentieth centuries is a formidable task. However, since Levy examines only great power wars, about which much has been written, and because many of them involved relatively small numbers of battle deaths, his figures are reliable.

He finds that great power wars have become less frequent over the long time span he studied. On the other hand, those that have been fought in recent periods have been, in general, more serious in terms of severity, intensity, magnitude, and concentration than earlier great power wars.

As with all studies of the history of international conflict, the extent to which our great power system can be compared to previous great power systems is unclear. In addition, the impact of nuclear weapons on great power war poses another theoretical problem. Some observers maintain that the presence of nuclear arsenals are responsible for the United States and Soviet Union not having gone to war in crisis situations that, in earlier times, would have produced world war.

However his data are interpreted, Levy's carefully researched catalogue of great power war is most useful for those interested in studying the causes and consequences of international war.

. . . The preceding data analysis leaves little doubt regarding historical changes in wars between the Great Powers over the last five hundred years. Great Power wars have been rapidly diminishing in frequency but increasing in extent, severity, intensity, concentration, and (to a certain degree) magnitude. That is, Great Power wars have involved an increasing number of belligerent Powers, and nation-years of war, and have become increasingly violent in terms of absolute and per capita battle deaths and their relative number per nation-year of war. Of the important dimensions of Great Power war defined here, only its frequency has diminished and only its duration has been relatively constant over time. The hypothesis that Great Power wars have become less frequent but more serious or destructive is confirmed beyond any reasonable doubt.

Reprinted with permission from Jack Levy, "Historical Trends in Great Power War, 1495–1975," *International Studies Quarterly* 26 (June 1982), pp. 278–300. © International Studies Association.

TABLE 1   Great Power Wars

War	Dates[a]
War of the League of Venice	1495-1497
Neapolitan War	1502-1504
War of the Holy League	1511-1514
Austro-Turkish War	1512-1519
Second Milanese War	1515-1515
First War of Charles V	1521-1526
Ottoman War	1521-1531
Second War of Charles V	1526-1529
Ottoman War	1532-1535
Third War of Charles V	1536-1538
Ottoman War	1537-1547
Fourth War of Charles V	1542-1544
Siege of Boulogne	1544-1546
Arundel's Rebellion	1549-1550
Ottoman War	1551-1556
Fifth War of Charles V	1552-1556
Austro-Turkish War	1556-1562
Franco-Spanish War	1556-1559
Scottish War	1559-1560 (1560)
Spanish-Turkish War	1559-1564
First Huguenot War	1562-1564
Austro-Turkish War	1565-1568
Spanish-Turkish War	1569-1580
Austro-Turkish War	1576-1583
War of the Armada	1585-1604
War of the Three Henries	1589-1598
Austro-Turkish War	1593-1606
Spanish-Turkish War	1610-1614
Spanish-Turkish War	1618-1619
Thirty Years War–Bohemian Period	1618-1625 (1621)
Thirty Years War–Danish Period	1625-1630
Thirty Years War–Swedish Period	1630-1635
Thirty Years War–Swedish-French Period	1635-1648
Franco-Spanish War	1648-1659
Anglo-Dutch Naval War	1652-1654
Great Northern War	1654-1660
English-Spanish War	1656-1659
Ottoman War	1657-1664 (1661)
Anglo-Dutch Naval War	1665-1667
Revolutionary War	1667-1668
Dutch War of Louis XIV	1672-1678
Ottoman War	1682-1699
Franco-Spanish War	1683-1684
War of the League of Augsburg	1688-1697

TABLE 1   *(concluded)*

War	Dates[a]
Second Northern War	1700-1721 (1715)
War of the Spanish Succession	1701-1713
War of the Quadruple Alliance	1718-1720
British-Spanish War	1726-1729
War of the Polish Succession	1733-1738
War of the Austrian Succession	1739-1748
Seven Years War	1755-1763
War of the Bavarian Succession	1778-1779
War of the American Revolution	1778-1784
French Revolutionary Wars	1792-1802
Napoleonic Wars	1803-1815
Crimean War	1854-1856
War of Italian Unification	1859-1859
Austro-Prussian War	1866-1866
Franco-Prussian War	1870-1871
World War I	1914-1918
Russian Civil War	1918-1921
Russo-Japanese War	1939-1939
World War II	1939-1945
Korean War	1950-1953

a. For wars which do not begin as Great Power wars, the date of intervention
   of the second Power is given in parentheses.

The description of historical trends is easier than their explanation, however. Before it could be fully accepted, such an explanation would itself have to be tested against the historical evidence. This would require the operationalization and measurement of the explanatory variables (and plausible control variables as well) in as systematic a manner as we have dealt with the dependent variable. This is an enormous task lying far beyond the scope of this study. Having rigorously and systematically described longitudinal trends in Great Power wars, we can here only hypothesize about their theoretical explanations, by identifying the important variables and suggesting plausible theoretical linkages.

Of all the trends, perhaps most puzzling is the relatively unchanging duration of Great Power war. We might have expected that improvements in communications and logistics would have increased the speed of military operations on the battlefield and that innovations in military technology and the increasing destructiveness of military conflict would have increased the costs of war; both would presumably force an earlier termination of the hostilities. Obviously, there are other variables which counteract this tendency. While the costs of war have become much greater, the gradual industrialization of basically agricultural societies has increased their economic capacity to sustain a war and accept the costs. We might also hypothesize that, in spite of the enormous changes in military technology, the defense has managed to keep up with the offense, so that it takes equally long to obtain a decisive advantage on the battlefield. Finally, the increasing organizational momentum and incrementalism generated by a larger and more firmly entrenched bureaucracy, and the increasing political insecurity of elites (deriving from the decline of dynastic legitimacy) in conjunction with increasing nationalist pressures, both make it ever more difficult to withdraw from a costly but inconclusive war.

Equally interesting is the fact that an ever-increasing number (and proportion) of Great Powers have been participating in these wars. We might hypothesize that this derives in part from the increasing interdependence of the modern Great Power security system. As the Great Powers evolved from dynastic to nation-states, their "national interests," as well as their capabilities to project power in defense of their interests, tended to expand and their commercial relationships also became closer. The Great Powers came increasingly to perceive their own strategic and economic interests as dependent on power relationships in the system as a whole, and were increasingly likely to intervene in external wars to maintain a "balance of power" or their own influence and prestige. Hence the extent (and also the magnitude) of Great Power war has increased over time.

Let us now consider the increasing destructiveness of war in terms of severity, intensity, and concentration. The most obvious explanation, of course, is *technological:* the major changes not only in the destructive power of weapons, but also in their range, accuracy, volume of fire, mobility, and penetrability, and the speed and efficiency of military transport and communications systems. In addition, there has been an increasing economic capacity to produce a larger quantity of weapons and support systems. Much of the increased capacity for violence over the past centuries can be traced to the changes in production and transport generated by the industrial revolution; the mechanization of war at the beginning of the twentieth century; the development of airpower a few decades later; and (in terms of potential destruction for the future) the development of nuclear weapons and global delivery systems by the second half of this century.

Technological innovation alone, however, cannot fully explain the increasing destructiveness of Great Power wars in the last five centuries. There are several interrelated political, socioeconomic, and cultural factors contributing to the gradual emergence of total war. Let us briefly consider these in approximate chronological sequence. First was the increasing *rationalization* of military power under the state, beginning in the late fifteenth century and intensifying after the legal codification of the existing sovereign state system at Westphalia. The wars for the personal honor, vengeance, and enrichment of kings and nobles in Middle Ages (which may have contributed to their frequent but limited nature) were increasingly replaced by the "rational" use of force as an efficient instrument of policy for the achievement of political objectives, first by dynastic/territorial political systems and ultimately by nation-states. The seriousness of the wars grew proportionally with the expansion of these political objectives, from personal gain, to the territorial aggrandizement of the state, to the national ambitions of an entire people.

Reinforcing this was the increasing *centralization* of political power within the state. This began with the gradual subordination of feudal interests to centralized state authority in the early sixteenth century, and intensified in the late seventeenth century with the development of an administrative and financial system capable of supporting a military establishment and providing the logistical basis for an expanded military effort.

Contributing further to the power of states and their ability to make war was the *commercialization* of war beginning in the early seventeenth century. There was an increasingly symbiotic relationship between the state and the commercial classes. Commerce generated the wealth necessary to sustain war, and war in turn became a means of expanding commerce. In the mercantilist conception, commerce was a continuation of war (with an admixture of other means) and war was a continuation of commerce. The merchants' enthusiasm for war diminished somewhat as this mercantilist system was replaced by free trade in the late eighteenth century, but the link was hardly broken and subsequent economic progress contributed further to the state's capacity for war.

This period also marked the emerging *popularization* of war: the rise of nationalism and popular ideology, the institution of conscripted manpower, and the creation of the "nation in arms." Each of these phenomena contributed to the enhancement of the military power of the state.

The state's ability to utilize these expanding resources was furthered by the *professionalization* of military power in the late nineteenth century. This refers to the development of a peacetime military establishment directed by a new professional military elite that was independent of the aristocracy, headed by a general staff system, run according to new principles of scientific management, and supported by a system of military academies. These developments not only increased the efficiency of the conduct of war; they also enhanced the legitimacy of the military profession and contributed to the trends toward militarism, the acceptance of the values of the military subculture as the dominant values of society. At the same time, the earlier moral and cultural restraints on war associated with the Christian and Humanist traditions were gradually eroded by the materialism and individualism of industrial society.

These trends culminated in World War II with what Millis calls the *scientific revolution* in war: the harnessing, for the first time, of the entire scientific, engineering, and technological capacities of the nation directly for the conduct of the war. This mobilization of the intellectual as well as material and social resources of the nation for the purposes of enhancing military power continues now in peacetime. These political, social and cultural developments, in conjunction with technological innovation, have been largely responsible for the increasing destructiveness of war.

Let us consider some plausible explanations for the declining frequency of Great Power war. It can generally be argued that the potential benefits of Great Power war have not kept up with their rising human and economic costs. Warfare has involved enormous increases in casualties and human suffering, the physical destruction of industrial infrastructure, and opportunity costs for society deriving from increasing costs of weapons systems, manpower, and logistics. The greater tendency toward external intervention in Great Power war further raises the costs or reduces the potential benefits from war, whether by adding the military burden of an additional enemy or by necessitating the sharing of the gains with an ally.

The declining legitimacy of Great Power war has increased its diplomatic and domestic political costs. Finally, the changing bases of national power and the declining value of territorial conquest have reduced the potential benefits of Great Power war, as has the increasing congruence between state and ethnic boundaries (at least for the Great Powers). These increasing costs of Great Power war relative to its perceived benefits have reduced its utility as a rational instrument of state policy and largely account for its declining frequency. . . .

Suggested Readings

Beer, Francis A. "How Much War in History: Definition, Estimates, Extrapolations, Trends." *Sage Professional Papers in International Studies*, vol. 3, 02–030. Beverly Hills, Calif.: Sage, 1974.

Carter, Charles. *The Western European Powers, 1500–1700.* Ithaca, N.Y.: Cornell University, 1971.

Howard, Michael. *War in European History.* Oxford: Oxford University, 1976.

Levy, Jack. *War in the Modern Great Power System, 1945–1975.* Lexington: University of Kentucky, 1983.

Montross, Lynn. *War Through the Ages.* New York: Harper & Row, 1960.

Reading 5

MILITARIZED INTERSTATE DISPUTES, 1816–1976

Charles S. Gochman and Zeev Maoz

Notes from the Editors

Political scientists Charles S. Gochman and Zeev Maoz move back one step from the beginning of war to examine conflicts between nations that involved at least minor military engagements or threats to use force to settle the dispute. Working within the framework of the Correlates of War project and developing and employing data from that project, they look at regions, nations, and pairs of nations that have become involved in what they call militarized disputes from 1816 to 1976.

In many ways, their coding problems were even more difficult than those faced by Small and Singer who looked only at wars. Gochman and Maoz, along with a team of research assistants, had to scour the diplomatic history textbooks and document collections for detailed and valid accounts of the diplomatic and military interactions in the disputes they were studying.

Their analyses offer yet another indicator of patterns of conflict in the international system and suggest the validity of looking at conflict behavior over long time periods and over several geographic regions. The patterns they discovered persisted through most of their temporal and spatial domains.

As with the incidence of war since 1816, and even earlier, the major powers are again the prime participants either as initiators or targets of disputatious behavior. The advent of nuclear weapons and of other technological changes seems to have little impact on the overall Gochman-Maoz findings. The fact that nations in these disputes retreated from the brink of war in more than nine out of ten cases may be an optimistic finding for some.

. . . Fourteen types of military acts, clustered into three broad categories, are included in the Correlates of War militarized interstate dispute data set. These acts and associated categories are as follows:

Threat of Force

- *threat to use force:* threat by one state to use its regular armed forces to fire upon the armed forces or territory of another state
- *threat to blockade:* threat by one state to use ships or troops to seal off the territory of another state so as to prevent either entry or exit

Charles S. Gochman and Zeev Maoz, "Militarized Interstate Disputes 1816–1976: Procedures, Patterns and Insights," *Journal of Conflict Resolution* 18 (December 1984), 588–89, 606–15. Copyright © by Sage Publications, Inc. Reprinted by Permission of Sage Publications, Inc.

- *threat to occupy territory:* threat by one state to use military force to occupy the whole or part of another state's territory
- *threat to declare war:* threat by one state to issue an official declaration of war against another state

Display of Force

- *alert:* a reported increase in the military readiness of a state's regular armed forces, directed at another state
- *mobilization:* the activation by a state of previously inactive armed forces
- *show of force:* a public demonstration by a state of its military capabilities, not involving combat operations, directed at another state

Use of Force

- *blockade:* use of ships or troops by one state to seal off the territory of another state so as to prevent entry or exit
- *occupation of territory:* use of military force by one state to occupy the whole or part of another state's territory for a period of at least 24 hours
- *other use of military force:* use of regular armed forces of a state to fire upon the armed forces, population, or territory of another state or to enter the territory of another state for a period of less than 24 hours
- *seizure:* the seizure by one state of material or personnel from another state for a period of at least 24 hours
- *clash:* military hostilities between the regular armed forces of two or more states that last for less than 24 hours and in which the initiator of the hostilities cannot be identified clearly
- *declaration of war:* an official statement by one state that it is in a state of war with another state
- *war:* sustained military hostilities between the regular armed forces of two or more states, resulting in 1000 or more battle fatalities; a minimum of 100 battle fatalities or 1000 troops in active combat is required before a state is considered to be a participant in a war

For the purpose of grouping individual acts (incidents) into temporally bounded disputes, three rules were employed. First, the incidents had to involve the same or an overlapping set of state actors. Second, the incidents had to involve the same issue or set of issues. Third, the elapsed time between consecutive incidents could not exceed six months. The highest level of hostility and violence that a dispute could reach is what Small and Singer classify as a "war." A dispute was considered to have ended either when there were no codable incidents for a period of six months or when a war terminated.

National Dispute Proneness and Enduring Rivalries

. . . [I]t is time to identify and rank individual states according to the frequency of their dispute involvements and to identify enduring rivalries among pairs of states.

Throughout the article we have noted conflict-related differences between major and minor powers—in particular, the disproportionate frequency with which major powers participated in and initiated interstate disputes. Our findings concerning the frequency of such behavior are consistent with a variety of studies focusing on interstate wars that have determined that the most powerful states have tended to be the most war prone. To illustrate the applicability of the "powerful and war prone" hypothesis to the dispute behavior of individual states, we have constructed Table 8.

Table 8 lists the 30 most dispute-prone states in the interstate system, ranked in terms of the number of their dispute involvements during the 161 years of our temporal domain. The most striking findings in this table are that these 30 states have initiated over 70% (N = 681) and were primary targets in over 60% (N = 587) of all militarized interstate disputes. Equally important is that 9 of the 10 most dispute-prone states are, or have been, major powers.

In addition, Table 8 shows that a high rank on total number of dispute involvements generally has implied that a state was active both as an initiator and as a primary target in interstate disputes. The correlation between the number of times a state initiated and the number of times it was a primary target in a dispute is high (r = .80). In this sense, the data in Table 8 appear to challenge some conventional notions about revisionist and status quo states, a point to which we will return below.

Finally, Table 8 reveals that the states that have been most often the initiators or primary targets in disputes also have been the most frequent joiners in ongoing disputes (r = .83). Consistent with our previous observations regarding patterns of dispute expansion, we find a high correlation between the number of times a given state has joined on the initiator's side and the number of times it has entered on the target's side (r = .82), suggesting that third-party entrants have not systematically favored the initiators or the targets in disputes.

There are, however, several features that seem to distinguish between the dispute profiles of major powers and those of minor powers. First, both the total number of dispute involvements and, particularly, the frequency of joining ongoing disputes have been considerably higher for major powers than for minor powers. Related to this is the fact that, with the exception of Japan, major powers have been more likely to initiate disputes than to have been targets, whereas minor powers have been, on average, equally likely to be initiators or targets.

While the major powers have not differed from the minor powers in terms of patterns of support for initiators and targets in ongoing disputes, the former have tended to enter such disputes with a considerably higher frequency than the latter. This suggests that the perception of their global responsibilities for determining the nature of systemic or regional order may entice major powers to participate actively in disputes among

TABLE 8 National Dispute Proneness: Initiation, Target, and Involvement Figures for the Most Dispute-Prone Nations, 1816–1976[a]

Nation	Initiation				Target				Total		
	No. Init.	Freq. Init.	Join Init.	Freq. Join	No. Tar.	Freq. Tar.	Join Tar.	Freq. Join	No. Inv.	Freq. Inv.	Rank Inv.
U.K.	78	.484	24	.149	42	.261	37	.230	181	1.124	1
U.S.A.	67	.416	18	.112	51	.317	24	.149	160	0.994	2
USSR	59	.369	22	.138	35	.219	15	.094	131	0.819	3
France	42	.267	36	.229	28	.178	21	.134	127	0.802	4
Germany	45	.346	16	.123	37	.285	9	.069	107	0.823	5
Italy	35	.217	19	.118	17	.106	10	.062	81	0.503	6
Turkey	14	.087	8	.050	41	.255	14	.087	77	0.478	7
China	36	.308	5	.043	26	.222	3	.026	70	0.598	8
Japan	20	.180	2	.018	25	.225	8	.072	55	0.495	9
Austria-Hungary[b]	18	.124	13	.090	11	.076	10	.069	52	0.359	10
Peru	25	.180	4	.029	14	.101	4	.029	47	0.338	11
Israel	25	.862	0	.000	19	.655	1	.034	45	1.552	12
Greece	19	.130	3	.021	15	.103	6	.041	43	0.295	13
Chile	25	.181	0	.000	14	.101	3	.022	42	0.304	14.5
Argentina	17	.125	1	.007	21	.154	3	.022	42	0.309	14.5
Spain	13	.081	4	.025	17	.106	3	.019	37	0.230	16
Portugal	18	.112	1	.006	12	.075	1	.006	32	0.199	17.5
India	17	.567	0	.000	15	.500	0	.000	32	1.067	17.5
Ecuador	11	.089	2	.016	14	.114	1	.008	28	0.228	19
Brazil	11	.073	2	.013	14	.093	0	.000	27	0.179	21.5
Mexico	8	.055	2	.014	16	.110	1	.007	27	0.185	21.5
Holland	5	.032	5	.032	15	.096	2	.013	27	0.172	21.5
Pakistan	7	.233	1	.033	18	.600	1	.033	27	0.900	21.5
Yugoslavia	10	.103	2	.021	11	.113	3	.031	26	0.268	24.5
Thailand	12	.133	2	.022	8	.089	4	.044	26	0.289	24.5
Bolivia	11	.085	0	.000	12	.093	1	.008	24	0.186	26
Paraguay	9	.111	2	.025	12	.148	0	.000	23	0.284	28.5
Egypt	10	.152	0	.000	7	.106	6	.091	23	0.348	28.5
Bulgaria	7	.101	4	.058	6	.087	6	.087	23	0.333	28.5
Colombia	7	.048	1	.007	14	.096	1	.007	23	0.158	28.5

a. Frequency figures were obtained by dividing the number of dispute involvements in the appropriate column by the number of years the given state has qualified as a system member.

b. The figures for Austria-Hungary include the dispute involvement history of post-World War I Austria.

third parties. Minor powers, on the other hand, may be less directly concerned by disputes among third parties or less able to intervene, hence the lower frequency of joining ongoing disputes.

One of the most illuminating insights from Table 8 is the comparison between the raw numbers of dispute involvements for states and the frequency of their dispute involvements. Although major powers have ranked very high in terms of total numbers of dispute involvements, some of the states with the highest annual frequency of dispute involvements have been newly independent minor powers such as Israel, India, Pakistan, and several other African and Asian states. While the correlation between the raw number of involvements and the annual frequency of involvements is statistically significant ($r = .60$, $p < .001$), it is not as high as one might expect given the "powerful and war prone" hypothesis. The importance of this finding lies in what it may portend for the future. The challenges to world peace in the contemporary era and in the near-term future do not derive solely from confrontations emanating from major power struggles, but also from conflicts among minor powers. These latter conflicts are equally pernicious, given the propensity of major powers to join ongoing disputes. If the frequency of national dispute proneness is any indicator, the trouble spots in the contemporary era and near-term future lie in the Middle East, Africa, and Asia, and, consequently, increased major power involvement in these regions is as potentially explosive as are the more salient, but infrequent, confrontations in Europe.

These impressions become increasingly pronounced when we examine the figures on enduring rivalries presented in Table 9. Table 9 presents, for each region of the world and for extraregional relationships, the pairs (dyads) of states that most often have engaged in disputes with one another. There are no surprises in terms of the identity of these enduring rivalries. However, several points are worth noting. First, almost all of the states on our list of dispute-prone nations (Table 8) have been involved in enduring rivalries (Table 9). This is particularly noticeable for major powers, which have engaged persistently and frequently in conflicts with one another. In regions containing two or more major powers (i.e., Europe and Asia, as well as the extraregional category), the majority of enduring rivalries have been between major powers. Moreover, with the exception of the Turko-Greek rivalry in Europe and the Indo-Pakistani and Thai-Cambodian rivalries in Asia, all other rivalries in these two regions involved at least one major power. Note in this context that Turkey appears to have been a favorite target of hostilities in Europe and that it participated in many of the traditional European rivalries. The "sick man of Europe" does not appear to be an unfounded moniker.

The predominance of major power participation in enduring rivalries, however, should not overshadow the bitterness of enduring minor-minor rivalries. As was the case with the frequency of dispute proneness of newly independent states, the newly formed rivalries among minor powers in the Middle East, Africa, and Asia are the most frequently manifested and, hence, appear to be an important source of threat to world order. Neither our examination of national dispute proneness nor our survey of enduring rivalries provides unambiguous support for the conventional division of states into revisionist (offensive) and status quo (defensive). While a few, mainly powerful, states have engaged in the overwhelming proportion of interstate disputes, there appears

TABLE 9 Enduring Rivalries, 1816–1976: The Most Dispute-Prone Dyads, by Regions

Region	No. of Disputes	Frequency of Disputes[a]
Americans		
U.S.A.-Mexico	20	0.137
Chile-Argentina	17	0.125
Peru-Ecuador	15	0.122
Bolivia-Paraguay	11	0.136
Chile-Peru	10	0.072
Europe		
U.K.-USSR/Russia	24	0.149
Turkey-Greece	23	0.158
USSR/Russia-Turkey	21	0.130
Italy-Turkey	17	0.106
France-Germany	16	0.123
U.K.-Turkey	16	0.099
France-Turkey	14	0.088
Austria-Hungary/Austria-Italy	12	0.083
France-USSR/Russia	12	0.075
France-Italy	11	0.069
U.K.-Germany	10	0.077
U.K.-France	9	0.056
Africa		
Zambia-Rhodesia	8	0.667
Somalia-Ethiopia	7	0.412
Middle-East		
Israel-Syria	17	0.586
Israel-Egypt	12	0.414
Israel-Jordan	8	0.276
Asia		
India-Pakistan	18	0.600
Russia/USSR-Japan	18	0.162
China-Japan	13	0.117
Russia/USSR-China	13	0.111
Thailand-Cambodia	11	0.458
China-India	10	0.333
Extra-Regional		
U.S.A.-China	17	0.145
U.S.A.-USSR	16	0.099
U.S.A.-Spain	15	0.093
U.S.A.-U.K.	12	0.075
U.K.-Japan	11	0.099
France-China	9	0.077
U.K.-China	9	0.077
USSR-Iran	9	0.074

[a]Frequency figures were obtained by dividing the total number of disputes for any given dyad by the number of years that the "youngest" nation of the dyad qualified for system membership.

to be no clear-cut distinction between those states that are to be found on the initiator's side and those that are to be found on the target's. Without delving into the details of individual disputes, it is not possible to make definitive statements about national dispositions toward restructuring or defending the extant order. But the simple, *prima facie* assumption that the initiators of disputes should by and large be revisionist states and the targets in disputes should largely be status quo states finds little sustenance in our data.

Finally, contrary to some previous investigations of interstate conflict, our findings seem to display marked consistency over time and across levels of analysis. This consistency may be more a result of our descriptive emphasis than any methodological weaknesses in earlier conflict studies, and a closer analytic inquiry into the determinants of various dispute attributes undoubtedly would shed more light on this issue. The Correlates of War data and our findings also open the door to new avenues of investigation. For example, the identification of enduring rivalries provides at least a preliminary response to complaints concerning lack of knowledge about "international enemies" and suggests the centrality of this phenomenon in world politics, particularly among, but not exclusively limited to, the major powers.

Conclusions and Implications

Three themes have run throughout this article. First, patterns of dispute behavior have been more persistent over time than we often assume. Second, when these patterns have changed, the changes have been evolutionary in nature and have paralleled changes in the size and composition of the interstate system. Third, despite the diversity of the political units that make up the interstate system, patterns of dispute behavior are generalizable across geographic boundaries. What do these themes suggest for the years ahead?

We have seen that historical periods traditionally have been marked by initial declines and subsequent increases in the numbers of interstate disputes, and the nuclear era has been no exception. As our data show, following an ititial decline after World War II, there was a dramatic upswing in the frequency of militarized disputes through 1976. While our evidence is incomplete, the years since 1976 appear to have been highly disputatious. There have been seven interstate wars and a large number of very volatile subwar conflicts. One contributing factor to dispute activity—the number of sovereign states in the system—appears to have leveled off, thereby relieving some upward pressure on absolute dispute frequency. Another important factor—the degree of dissensus on the "rules" of the international order—does not seem to have diminished. Thus we suspect that high absolute levels of dispute activity will prevail in the near-term future. If past trends are any indicator, the real danger lies in the possibility that the current dissensus may be manifested in global conflagration, a phenomenon that marked the end of the two preceding periods—the age of imperialism and the interwar era. The historical alternative has been a great power concert or condominium; a more cooperative restructuring that affords significant participation by other—governmental and nongovernmental—actors is largely without historical precedent.

Major powers traditionally have been both the primary challengers and the primary defenders of the international order; their technological capacity and demographic and military attributes provide them with both the incentives and the means to define the nature of that order. During the nuclear era, major power participation in militarized disputes has actually increased, relative to the proportion of the interstate system membership that they constitute. And, if anything, the large number of minor powers that have achieved their independence since 1946 has increased the arena for major power competition. Consequently, we can expect to see a continuance of active major power involvement in interstate disputes, especially as joiners in the numerous minor power conflicts.

We also can expect that the median duration of interstate disputes will not be significantly different in the future from what it has been in the past, despite changes in weapons technology and the increasing need for governments to maintain public support for foreign adventures. The fact that interstate disputes traditionally have been brief reduces the likelihood that public attentiveness to foreign affairs or opposition to foreign adventures will have a significant impact on the duration of most disputes. Similarly, because the great majority of interstate disputes never escalate to the large-scale use of military force, the impact of weapons technology on the duration of the average dispute seems to be minimal. Even with respect to war, a perusal of the seven cases of large-scale hostilities since 1976 reveals both very brief and relatively lengthy encounters. Thus, at this point, there seems to be little hard evidence to suggest that changes in military technology have had a significant and predictable impact on the duration of military engagements.

The data that we have point to a long-term trend of increased use of force in interstate disputes, associated with the growth in the number of sovereign minor powers. This trend has probably peaked, but it does not appear likely that it will decline any time soon. However, with the large number of predicted minor-minor disputes in the years ahead, the proportion of disputes escalating to war should remain low, so long as major powers do not intervene on opposing sides. In the past, such interventions have been uncommon, but when they did occur, they dramatically increased the probability of war. The current propensity of the Chinese, Soviets, and Americans to back opposing protagonists in volatile Third World disputes does not bode well in a world of nuclear weapons, where the uncontrolled escalation of an initially limited dispute could prove calamitous.

The fact that the number of disputes among minor powers has increased significantly during the nuclear era has meant that the locus of interstate dispute activity has shifted from Europe to Asia, Africa, and the Middle East. States in these regions have managed to develop a number of enduring rivalries with remarkably high frequencies of dispute involvement. Six of seven wars since 1976 have erupted among states from these three regions, and many of the most volatile subwar disputes in the past few years have occurred there. Neither economic nor cultural ties have been effective in inhibiting the outbreak or escalation of these disputes. Given past trends and current turmoil, these more newly formed regions appear destined in the years immediately ahead to host large numbers of interstate disputes.

Our empirical findings suggest that it is not appropriate to view the nuclear era as somehow unique with regard to conflictive interactions among states. Undoubtedly, nuclear weapons have made a difference. National leaders have appeared more cautious when the utilization of such weapons has seemed possible. But most aspects of dispute behavior that we have examined show considerable continuity across historical eras. This is not to deny that changes have occurred, such as the shift in the locus of dispute activity. Rather, it is to suggest that, in many aspects, states behave today pretty much as they did in the past; the differences are in the composition and size of the interstate system. In recent years, we have witnessed American forces fighting in Vietnam, Russian troops in combat in Afghanistan, Chinese soldiers undertaking punitive strikes against Vietnam, and British troops enforcing their claims in the South Atlantic. Smaller and more newly independent states also have sought to impose their claims by means of military force. The image of a British armada off the coast of Argentina and the struggle for those desolate islands that the British call the Falklands may strike one as remarkably "nineteenth centuryish." Yet these events bring home, as perhaps no scholarly discourse can, the constancy and timelessness of basic interstate relations. Technology has changed; the objectives, motives, and methods of states remain the same.

Suggested Readings

Blechman, Barry M. and Stephen S. Kaplan. *Force Without War*. Washington, D.C.: Brookings Institution, 1978.

Eckhart, William and Edward Azar. "Major World Conflicts and Interventions, 1945–1975." *International Interactions* 5 (January 1978), pp. 75–110.

James, Patrick. *Crisis and War*. Kingston: McGill-Queens Unversity, 1987.

Maoz, Zeev. *Paths to Conflict*. Boulder, Colo.: Westview, 1982.

Siverson, Randolph M. and M. Tennefoss. "Interstate Conflicts: 1815–1965." *International Interactions* 9 (July 1982), pp. 147–48.

Wilkenfeld, Jonathan et al., eds. *Foreign Policy Behavior*. Beverly Hills, Calif.: Sage, 1980.

CHAPTER 2

The Military Experience

For as long as there has been civilization, there have been soldiers and officers who have trained, fought, and sometimes died for their countries.

How and why they go about their duties is the general subject of this chapter.

Most societies have relied upon a military caste to handle the various aspects of national defense. In some cases, the fighting has been left to professional soldiers. In others, especially in modern times, mass armies composed of conscripts, led by professionals, have been the major military combatants. Whether professional or citizen soldier, Greek hoplite or German uhlan, all soldiers share common experiences. There is the universal experience of basic training, in which recruits learn the skills of their trade, their role in the hierarchy, and military codes and values. For some, there is also the combat experience. There, on the battlefield, discipline, courage, bravery, martial skills, and self-sacrifice combine to produce the military effect desired. Soldiers, especially those who have experienced combat, are a special breed. It is not surprising that those who have fought in wars often feel a closeness to their enemies that they do not feel for the civilians of their respective countries.

The study of the military experience does not lead one directly to the causes of war. It is true, however, that the military in many polities throughout history has played a central role in decision making on the eve of war. In fact, many nations now, and in earlier periods, have been directed exclusively by generals, admirals, and their cadres. Irrespective of the power of the military in society, the state of military preparedness often figures prominently in war/no war decisions. Moving back from the immediate crisis, the growth and development of armies, navies, and weapons systems have also been important to decision makers as they evaluated the perceived threats posed by their adversaries. Finally, the success or failure of arms, which always has diplomatic repercussions, is linked to the relative quality of the military institutions confronting one another on the battlefield.

From earliest recorded history to the era of air power, military combat did not change dramatically. As late as the nineteenth and early twentieth centuries, the strategies and tactics of the great generals of antiquity were often studied in the world's military academies. The first article in this section, Polybius' description of "The Battle of Cannae" between Rome and Carthage in 216 B.C., offers one example of the contemporary relevance of ancient military history. Although much has changed over the past 2,000 years, one finds much that is familiar in the general's exhortation to his troops, the carefully laid battle plans gone awry, the element of surprise, and the attendant tales of glory and gore.

The long (1861–1865) and bloody American Civil War has attracted considerable attention from military historians and novelists. Stephen Crane's *The Red Badge of Courage* is one of the most famous fictionalized accounts of combat in that war that pitted brother against brother. Crane examined one Civil War battle through the eyes of a young soldier. The fear, confusion, and occasional exhilaration of the combat experience are depicted in a magnificantly direct and authentic manner by the celebrated novelist.

Over a half-century later, World War I (1914–1918), an even bloodier conflict, brought the entire European continent into our first "total war." Yet, Polybius and Stephen Crane would have understood and empathized with the soldiers who fought at "Gallipoli" in 1915. Despite the advent of terrifying new weapons, the campaign along the Turkish Straits described by Alan Moorehead in our third selection ultimately brought soldiers face to face with their enemy, often in hand-to-hand combat.

The Vietnam War (1958–1975), although fought by Americans with the latest high-tech weaponry, also revealed aspects of the most elemental and universal of military experiences. On the ground, much of the combat involved small units that engaged one another sometimes only yards apart. In William Pelfrey's novel *The Big V,* the hero experiences emotions not unlike those experienced by Crane's protagonist. The salty language, the antagonism towards officers, the frightful tensions, and the ultimate acceptance of death suggest that little has changed in the nature of the military experience over the centuries.

Soldiers are called upon to make the supreme sacrifice to defend their nations. The combat soldier, especially, is confronted daily by the prospect of death or maiming. Few ever become accustomed to this occupational hazard. J. Glenn Gray explores "The Soldier's Relation to Death" in the fifth selection in this chapter. It is a complex relation met by different soldiers in different fashions.

Well-disciplined and well-trained soldiers are prepared to face death in war. This preparation most likely increases their odds of survival and contributes to the effectiveness of their units. Millitary training is a tricky business. Throughout history, the drill instructor or the sergeant major has been one of the central figures in the building of a soldier. To the outsider, they appear to be stern taskmasters at best and ruthless tyrants at worst. As John H. Faris reveals in the last selection in this chapter, "The Impact of Basic Combat Training," professional drill instructors not only instill military discipline and values in their charges; they also come to earn their respect and admiration.

Reading 6

THE BATTLE OF CANNAE

Polybius

Notes from the Editors

In 216 B.C., in a major battle in the Second Punic War, two Roman consuls, Aemilius and Terentius, led over 80,000 soldiers into battle at Cannae in Italy against the legions of the great general Hannibal of Carthage. The Greek historian Polybius (203–120 B.C.) wrote about the preparations for this battle and the ensuing combat in his Histories.

The excerpt is interesting for several reasons. In the first place, we read a Roman general's exhortation to his troops, an inspirational talk meant to uplift soldiers on the eve of battle. With a few changes, Aemilius' speech could have been delivered by latter-day generals such as Napoleon, Hindenburg, or Patton.

More interesting is the account of the massive, bloody clash between the Roman and Carthaginian legions. Polybius describes the strategies of both sides, how the various units were employed, and how the best-laid plans break down in the chaos of the fray. Even over two thousand years ago, commanders who took swift and decisive action as the battle ebbed and flowed were usually successful. Hannibal and Aemilius were literally in the thick of the fight, in part to inspire their troops by their example. It was only in this century that generals began to spend much of their time behind the lines, far from the combat.

The Carthaginians were clear victors in the battle of Cannae. For awhile, their victory enabled them to become a powerful rival to Rome itself. Yet, ultimately they were defeated, perhaps a sign of the transitory nature of victory and how difficult it is to maintain "Number One" status in the international system.

Having arrived at the camp and united their forces, they made known the will of the Senate to the soldiers, and Aemilius exhorted them to do their duty in terms which evidently came from his heart. He addressed himself especially to explain and excuse the reverses which they had lately experienced; for it was on this point particularly that the soldiers were depressed and stood in need of encouragement. "The causes," he argued, "of their defeats in former battles were many, and could not be reduced to one or two." But those causes were at an end; and no excuse existed now, if they only showed themselves to be men of courage, for not conquering their enemies. Up to that time both Consuls had never been engaged together, or employed thoroughly trained soldiers: the combatants on the contrary had been raw levies, entirely unexperienced in danger; and what was most important of all, they had been so entirely ignorant of their opponents, that they had been brought into the field, and engaged in

---

From *The Histories of Polybius* (translation by Evelyn S. Schuckburgh), Vol. I (London, Macmillan, 1889), pp. 264–275.

a pitched battle with an enemy that they had never once set eyes on. Those who had been defeated on the Trebia were drawn up on the field at daybreak, on the very next morning after their arrival from Sicily; while those who had fought in Etruria, not only had never seen the enemy before, but did not do so even during the very battle itself, owing to the unfortunate state of the atmosphere.

But now the conditions were quite different. For in the first place both Consuls were with the army: and were not only prepared to share the danger themselves, but had also induced the Consuls of the previous year to remain and take part in the struggle. While the men had not only seen the arms, order, and numbers of the enemy, but had been engaged in almost daily fights with them for the last two years. The conditions therefore under which the two former battles were fought being quite different, it was but natural that the result of the coming struggle should be different too. For it would be strange or rather impossible that those who in various skirmishes, where the numbers of either side were equal, had for the most part come off victorious, should, when drawn up all together, and nearly double of the enemy in number, be defeated.

"Wherefore, men of the army," he continued, "seeing that we have every advantage on our side for securing a victory, there is only one thing necessary,—your determination, your zeal! And I do not think I need say more to you on that point. To men serving others for pay, or to those who fight as allies on behalf of others, who have no greater danger to expect than meets them on the field, and for whom the issues at stake are of little importance,—such men may need words of exhortation. But men who, like you, are fighting not for others, but themselves,—for country, wives, and children; and for whom the issue is of far more momentous consequence than the mere danger of the hour, need only to be reminded: require no exhortation. For who is there among you who would not wish if possible to be victorious; and next, if that may not be, to die with arms in his hands, rather than to live and see the outrage and death of these dear objects which I have named? Wherefore, men of the army, apart from any words of mine, place before your eyes the momentous difference to you between victory and defeat, and all their consequences. Enter upon this battle with the full conviction, that in it your country is not risking a certain number of legions, but her bare existence. For she has nothing to add to such an army as this, to give her victory, if the day now goes against us. All she has of confidence and strength rests on you; all her hopes of safety are in your hands. Do not frustrate those hopes: but pay back to your country the gratitude you owe her; and make it clear to all the world that the former reverses occurred, not because the Romans are worse men than the Carthaginians, but from the lack of experience on the part of those who were then fighting, and through a combination of adverse circumstances." With such words Aemilius dismissed the troops.

Next morning the two Consuls broke up their camp, and advanced to where they heard that the enemy were entrenched. On the second day they arrived within sight of them, and pitched their camp at about fifty stades' distance. But when Aemilius observed that the ground was flat and bare for some distance round, he said that they must not engage there with an enemy superior to them in cavalry; but that they must rather try to draw him off, and lead him to ground on which the battle would be more in the hands of the infantry. But Gaius Terentius being, from inexperience, of a contrary opinion, there was a dispute and misunderstanding between the leaders, which of all things is the most dangerous. It is the custom, when the two Consuls are present, that they should take the chief command on alternate days; and the next day happening to be the turn of Terentius, he ordered an advance with a view of approaching the enemy, in spite of the protests and active opposition of his colleague. Hannibal set his light-armed troops and cavalry in motion to meet him, and charging the Romans while they were still marching, took them by surprise and caused a great confusion in their ranks. The Romans repulsed the first charge by putting some of their heavy-armed in front; and then sending forward their light-armed and cavalry, began to get the best of the fight all along the line: the Carthaginians having no reserves of any importance, while certain companies of the legionaries were mixed with the Roman light-armed, and helped to sustain the battle. Nightfall for the present put an end to a struggle which had not at all answered to the hopes of the Carthaginians. But next day Aemilius, not thinking it right to engage, and yet being unable any longer to lead off his army, encamped with two-thirds of it on the banks of the Aufidus, the only river which flows right through the Apennines,—that chain of mountains which forms the watershed of all the Italian rivers, which flow either west to the Tuscan Sea, or east to the Hadriatic. This chain is, I say, pierced by the Aufidus, which rises on the side of Italy nearest the Tuscan Sea, and is discharged into the Hadriatic. For the other third of his army he caused a camp to be made across the river, to the east of the ford, about ten stades from his own lines, and a little more from those of the enemy; that these men, being on the other side of the river, might protect his own foraging parties, and threaten those of the enemy.

Then Hannibal, seeing that his circumstances called for a battle with the enemy, being anxious lest his troops should be depressed by their previous reverse, and believing that it was an occasion which required some encouraging words, summoned a general meeting of his soldiers. When they were assembled, he bid them all look round upon the country, and asked them, "What better fortune they could have asked from the gods, if they had had the choice, than to fight in such ground as they saw there, with the vast superiority of cavalry on their side?" And when all signified their acquiescence in such an evident truth, he added: "First, then, give thanks to the gods: for they have brought the enemy into this country, because they designed the victory for us. And, next to me, for having compelled the enemy to fight,—for they cannot avoid it any longer,—and to fight in a place so full of advantages for us. But I do not think it becoming in me now to use many words in exhorting you to be brave and forward in this battle. When you had had no experience of fighting the Romans this was necessary, and I did then suggest many arguments and examples to you. But now seeing that you have undeniably beaten the Romans in three successive battles of such magnitude, what arguments could have greater influence with you in confirming your courage than the actual facts? Now, by your previous battles you have both possession of the country and all its wealth, in accordance with my promises: for I have been absolutely true in everything I have ever said to you. But the present contest is for the cities and the wealth in them: and if you win it, all Italy will at once be in your power; and freed from your present hard toils, and masters of the wealth of Rome, you will by this battle become the leaders and lords of the world. This, then, is a time for deeds, not words: for by God's blessing I am persuaded that I shall carry out my promises to you forthwith." His words were received with approving shouts, which he acknowledged with gratitude for their zeal; and having dismissed the assembly, he at once formed a camp on the same bank of the river as that on which was the larger camp of the Romans.

Next day he gave orders that all should employ themselves in making preparations and getting themselves into a fit state of body. On the day after that he drew out his men along the bank of the river, and showed that he was eager to give the enemy battle. But Aemilius, dissatisfied with his position, and seeing that the Carthaginians would soon be obliged to shift their quarters for the sake of supplies, kept quiet in his camps, strengthening both with extra guards. After waiting a considerable time, when no one came out to attack him, Hannibal put the rest of the army into camp again, but sent out his Numidian horse to attack the enemy's water parties from the lesser camp. These horsemen riding right up to the lines and preventing the watering, Gaius Terentius became more than ever inflamed with the desire of fighting, and the soldiers were eager for a battle, and chafed at the delay. For there is nothing more intolerable to mankind than suspense; when a thing is once decided, men can but endure whatever out of the catalogue of evils it is their misfortune to undergo.

But when the news arrived at Rome that the two armies were face to face, and that skirmishes between advanced parties of both sides were daily taking place, the city was in a state of high excitement and uneasiness; the people dreading the result, owning to the disasters which had now befallen them on more than one occasion; and foreseeing and anticipating in their imaginations what would happen if they were utterly defeated. All the oracles preserved at Rome were in everybody's mouth; and every temple and house was full of prodigies and miracles: in consequence of which the city was one scene of vows, sacrifices, supplicatory processions, and prayers. For the Romans in times of danger take extraordinary pains to appease gods and men, and look upon no ceremony of that kind in such times as unbecoming or beneath their dignity.

When he took over the command on the following day, as soon as the sun was above the horizon, Gaius Terentius got the army in motion from both the camps. Those from the larger camp he drew up in order of battle, as soon as he had got them across the river, and bringing up those of the smaller camp he placed them all in the same line, selecting the south as the aspect of the whole. The Roman horse he stationed on the right wing along the river, and their foot next them in the same line, placing the maniples, however, closer together than usual, and making the depth of each maniple several times greater than its front. The cavalry of the allies he stationed on the left wing, and the light-armed troops he placed slightly in advance of the whole army, which amounted with its allies to eighty thousand infantry and a little more than six thousand horse. At the same time Hannibal brought his Balearic slingers and spearmen across the river, and stationed them in advance of his main body; which he led out of their camp, and getting them across the river at two spots, drew them up opposite the enemy. On his left wing, close to the river, he stationed the Iberian and Celtic horse opposite the Roman cavalry; and next to them half the Libyan heavy-armed foot; and next to them the Iberian and Celtic foot; next, the other half of the Libyans, and, on the right wing, the Numidian horse. Having now got them all into line he advanced with the central companies of the Iberians and Celts; and so arranged the other companies next these in regular gradations, that the whole line became crescent-shaped, diminishing in depth towards its extremities: his object being to have his Libyans as a reserve in the battle, and to commence the action with his Iberians and Celts.

The armour of the Libyans was Roman, for Hannibal had armed them with a selection of the spoils taken in previous battles. The shield of the Iberians and Celts was about the same size, but their swords were quite different. For that of the Roman can thrust with as deadly effects as it can cut, while the Gallic sword can only cut, and that requires some room. And the companies coming alternatively,—the naked Celts, and the Iberians with their short linen tunics bordered with purple stripes, the whole appearance of the line was strange and terrifying. The whole strength of the Carthaginian cavalry was ten thousand, but that of their foot was not more than forty thousand, including the Celts. Aemilius commanded on the Roman right, Gaius Terentius on the left, Marcus Atilius and Gnaeus Servilius, the Consuls of the previous year, on the centre. The left of the Carthaginians was commanded by Hasdrubal, the right by Hanno, the centre by Hannibal in person, attended by his brother Mago. And as the Roman line faced the south, as I said before, and the Carthaginian the north, the rays of the rising sun did not inconvenience either of them.

The battle was begun by an engagement between the advanced guard of the two armies; and at first the affair between these light-armed troops was indecisive. But as soon as the Iberian and Celtic cavalry got at the Romans, the battle began in earnest, and in the true barbaric fashion: for there was none of the usual formal advance and retreat; but when they once got to close quarters, they grappled man to man, and, dismounting from their horses, fought on foot. But when the Carthaginians had got the upper hand in this encounter and killed most of their opponents on the ground,—because the Romans all maintained the fight with spirit and determination,—and began chasing the remainder along the river, slaying as they went and giving no quarter; then the legionaries took the place of the light-armed and closed with the enemy. For a short time the Iberian and Celtic lines stood their ground and fought gallantly; but, presently overpowered by the weight of the heavy-armed lines, they gave way and retired to the rear, thus breaking up the crescent. The Roman maniples followed with spirit, and easily cut their way through the enemy's line; since the Celts had been drawn up in a thin line, while the Romans had closed up from the wings towards the centre and the point of danger. For the two wings did not come into action at the same time as the centre: but the centre was first engaged, because the Gauls, having been stationed on the arc of the crescent, had come into contact with the enemy long before the wings, the convex of the crescent being towards the enemy. The Romans, however, going in pursuit of these troops, and hastily closing in towards the centre and the part of the enemy which was giving ground, advanced so far, that the Libyan heavy-armed troops on either wing got on their flanks. Those on the right, facing to the left, charged from the right upon the Roman flank; while those who were on the left wing raced to the right, and dressing by the left, charged their right flank, the exigency of the moment suggesting to them what they ought to do. Thus it came about, as Hannibal had planned, that the Romans were caught between two hostile lines of Libyans—thanks to their impetuous pursuit of the Celts. Still they fought, though no longer in line, yet singly, or in maniples, which faced about to meet those who charged them on the flanks.

Though he had been from the first on the right wing, and had taken part in the cavalry engagement, Lucius Aemilius still survived. Determined to act up to his own exhortatory speech, and seeing that the decision of the battle rested mainly on the legionaries, riding up to the centre of the line he led the charge himself, and personally grappled with the enemy, at the same time cheering on and exhorting his soldiers to the charge. Hannibal, on the other side, did the same, for he too had taken his place on the centre from the commencement. The Numidian horse on the Carthaginian right were meanwhile charging the cavalry on the Roman left; and though, from the peculiar nature of their mode of fighting, they neither inflicted nor received much harm, they yet rendered the enemy's horse useless by keeping them occupied, and charging them first on one side and then on another. But when Hasdrubal, after all but annihilating the cavalry by the river, came from the left to the support of the Numidians, the Roman allied cavalry, seeing his charge approaching, broke and fled. At that point Hasdrubal appears to have acted with great skill and discretion. Seeing the Numidians to be strong in numbers, and more effective and formidable to troops that had once been forced from their ground, he left the pursuit to them; while he himself hastened to the part of the field where the infantry were engaged, and brought his men up to support the Libyans. Then, by charging the Roman legions on the rear, and harassing them by hurling squadron after squadron upon them at many points at once, he raised the spirits of the Libyans, and dismayed and depressed those of the Romans.

It was at this point that Lucius Aemilius fell, in the thick of the fight, covered with wounds: a man who did his duty to his country at that last hour of his life, as he had throughout its previous years, if any man ever did. As long as the Romans could keep an unbroken front, to turn first in one direction and then in another to meet the assaults of the enemy, they held out; but the outer files of the circle continually falling, and the circle becoming more and more contracted, they at last were all killed on the field; and among them Marcus Atilius and Gnaeus Servilius, the Consuls of the previous year, who had shown themselves brave men and worthy of Rome in the battle. While this struggle and carnage were going on, the Numidian horse were pursuing the fugitives, most of whom they cut down or hurled from their horses; but some few escaped into Venusia, among whom was Gaius Terentius, the Consul, who thus sought a flight, as disgraceful to himself, as his conduct in office had been disastrous to his country.

Such was the end of the battle of Cannae, in which both sides fought with the most conspicuous gallantry, the conquered no less than the conquerors. This is proved by the fact that out of six thousand horse, only seventy escaped with Gaius Terentius to Venusia, and about three hundred of the allied cavalry to various towns in the neighborhood. Of the infantry ten thousand were taken prisoners in fair fight, but were not actually engaged in the battle: of those who were actually engaged only about three thousand perhaps escaped to the towns of the surrounding district; all the rest died nobly, to the number of seventy thousand, the Carthaginians being on this occasion, as on previous ones, mainly indebted for their victory to their superiority in cavalry: a lesson to posterity that in actual war it is better to have half the number of infantry, and the superiority in cavalry, than to engage your enemy with an equality in both. On the side of Hannibal there fell four thousand Celts, fifteen hundred Iberians and Libyans, and about two hundred horse.

The ten thousand Romans who were captured had not, as I said, been engaged in the actual battle; and the reason was this. Lucius Aemilius left ten thousand infantry in his camp that, in case Hannibal should disregard the safety of his own camp, and take his whole army on to the field, they might seize the opportunity, while the battle was going on, of forcing their way in and capturing the enemy's baggage; or if, on the other hand, Hannibal should, in view of this contingency, leave a guard in his camp, the number of the enemy in the field might thereby be diminished. These men were captured in the following circumstances. Hannibal, as a matter of fact, did leave a sufficient guard in his camp; and as soon as the battle began, the Romans, according to their instructions, assaulted and tried to take those thus left by Hannibal. At first they held their own; but just as they were beginning to waver, Hannibal, who was by this time gaining a victory all along the line, came to their relief, and routing the Romans, shut them up in their own camp, killed two thousand of them; and took all the rest prisoners. In like manner the Numidian horse brought in all those who had taken refuge in the various strongholds about the district, amounting to two thousand of the routed cavalry.

The result of this battle, such as I have described it, had the consequences which both sides expected. For the Carthaginians by their victory were thenceforth masters of nearly the whole of the Italian coast which is called *Magna Graecia*. Thus the Tarentines immediately submitted; and the Arpani and some of the Campanian states invited Hannibal to come to them; and the rest were with one consent turning their eyes to the Carthaginians: who, accordingly, began now to have high hopes of being able to carry even Rome itself by assault.

On their side the Romans, after this disaster, despaired of retaining their supremacy over the Italians, and were in the greatest alarm, believing their own lives and the existence of their city to be in danger, and every moment expecting that Hannibal would be upon them. For, as though Fortune were in league with the disasters that had already befallen them to fill up the measure of their ruin, it happened that only a few days afterwards, while the city was still in this panic, the Praetor who had been sent to Gaul fell unexpectedly into an ambush and perished, and his army was utterly annihilated by the Celts. In spite of all, however, the Senate left no means untried to save the State. It exhorted the people to fresh exertions, strengthened the city with guards, and deliberated on the crisis in a brave and manly spirit. And subsequent events made this manifest. For though the Romans were on that occasion indisputably beaten in the field, and had lost reputation for military prowess; by the peculiar excellence of their political constitution, and the prudence of their counsels, they not only recovered their supremacy over Italy, by eventually conquering the Carthaginians, but before very long became masters of the whole world.

Suggested Readings

Delbruck, Hans. *History of the Art of War,* I. Westport: Greenwood, 1975.

Keppie, Lawrence. *The Making of the Roman Army: From Republic to Empire.* London: Batsford, 1984.

Lazenby, John F. *Hannibal's War: A Military History of the Second Punic War.* Warminster, England: Aris and Phillips, 1974.

Livius, Titiu. *Hannibal the Scourge of Rome.* Cambridge: Cambridge University, 1934.

Reading 7

THE RED BADGE OF COURAGE

Stephen Crane

Notes from the Editors

Stephen Crane's short novel about the experiences of young Henry Fleming at the Battle of Chancellorsville on May 1 and 2, 1863, is considered an American classic. His account of the military experience in the United States Civil War, one of the bloodiest civil wars in history, shocked readers in 1895 who had grown up with a romantic image of the heroic War Between the States. Indeed, veterans of the war, professional military people, and nationalists attacked Crane for depicting bumbling officers, cowardly soldiers, and the mindless chaos and bloodshed of warfare.

Crane was born six years after the close of the Civil War. Relying on memoir and newspaper accounts, he produced the first novel that was devoted exclusively to soldiers at war. So vivid and authentic was his account, particularly the thoughts that raced through the mind of his hero, that many still find it impossible to believe that Crane was neither a veteran nor an eyewitness to the carnage about which he wrote. Walt Whitman wrote that "the real war will never get in the books." Crane may have come close with his graphic account.

Soldiers in later wars, as well as historians, have found in the Red Badge of Courage *a universality that transcends the Civil War experience. For many, the novel is one of the most effective antiwar pieces ever written.*

The brigade was halted in the fringe of a grove. The men crouched among the trees and pointed their restless guns out at the fields. They tried to look beyond the smoke.

Out of this haze they could see running men. Some shouted information and gestured as they hurried.

The men of the new regiment watched and listened eagerly, while their tongues ran on in gossip of the battle. They mouthed rumors that had flown like birds out of the unknown.

"They say Perry has been driven in with big loss."

"Yes, Carrott went t' th' hospital. He said he was sick. That smart lieutenant is commanding 'G' Company. Th' boys say they won't be under Carrott no more if they all have t' desert. They allus knew he was a ——"

"Hannises' batt'ry is took."

"It ain't either. I saw Hannises' batt'ry off on th' left not more'n fifteen minutes ago."

From *The Red Badge of Courage* (New York: D. Appleton, 1895), pp. 54–73.

"Well ———"

"Th' general, he ses he is goin' t' take th' hull command of th' 304th when we go inteh action, an' then he ses we'll do sech fightin' as never another one reg'ment done."

"They say we're catchin' it over on th' left. They say th' enemy driv' our line inteh a devil of a swamp an' took Hannises' batt'ry."

"No sech thing. Hannises' batt'ry was 'long here 'bout a minute ago."

"That young Hasbrouck, he makes a good off'cer. He ain't afraid 'a nothin'."

"I met one of th' 148th Maine boys an' he ses his brigade fit th' hull rebel army fer four hours over on th' turnpike road an' killed about five thousand of 'em. He ses one more sech fight as that an' th' war 'll be over."

"Bill wasn't scared either. No, sir! It wasn't that. Bill ain't a-gittin' scared easy. He was jest mad, that's what he was. When that feller trod on his hand, he up an' sed that he was willin' t' give his hand t' his country, but he be dumbed if he was goin' t' have every dumb bushwacker in th' kentry walkin' 'round on it. So he went t' th' hospital disregardless of th' fight. Three fingers was crunched. Th' dern doctor wanted t' amputate 'm, an' Bill, he raised a heluva row, I hear. He's a funny feller."

The din in front swelled to a tremendous chorus. The youth and his fellows were frozen to silence. They could see a flag that tossed in the smoke angrily. Near it were the blurred and agitated forms of troops. There came a turbulent stream of men across the fields. A battery changing position at a frantic gallop scattered the stragglers right and left.

A shell screaming like a storm banshee went over the huddled heads of the reserves. It landed in the grove, and exploding redly flung the brown earth. There was a little shower of pine needles.

Bullets began to whistle among the branches and nip at the trees. Twigs and leaves came sailing down. It was as if a thousand axes, wee and invisible, were being wielded. Many of the men were constantly dodging and ducking their heads.

The lieutenant of the youth's company was shot in the hand. He began to swear so wondrously that a nervous laugh went along the regimental line. The officer's profanity sounded conventional. It relieved the tightened senses of the new men. It was as if he had hit his fingers with a tack hammer at home.

He held the wounded member carefully away from his side so that the blood would not drip upon his trousers.

The captain of the company, tucking his sword under his arm, produced a handkerchief and began to bind with it the lieutenant's wound. And they disputed as to how the binding should be done.

The battle flag in the distance jerked about madly. It seemed to be struggling to free itself from an agony. The billowing smoke was filled with horizontal flashes.

Men running swiftly emerged from it. They grew in numbers until it was seen that the whole command was fleeing. The flag suddenly sank down as if dying. Its motion as it fell was a gesture of despair.

Wild yells came from behind the walls of smoke. A sketch in gray and red dissolved into a moblike body of men who galloped like wild horses.

The veteran regiments on the right and left of the 304th immediately began to jeer. With the passionate song of the bullets and the banshee shrieks of shells were mingled loud catcalls and bits of facetious advice concerning places of safety.

But the new regiment was breathless with horror. "Gawd! Saunders's got crushed!" whispered the man at the youth's elbow. They shrank back and crouched as if compelled to await a flood.

The youth shot a swift glance along the blue ranks of the regiment. The profiles were motionless, carven; and afterward he remembered that the color sergeant was standing with his legs apart, as if he expected to be pushed to the ground.

The following throng went whirling around the flank. Here and there were officers carried along on the stream like exasperated chips. They were striking about them with their swords and with their left fists, punching every head they could reach. They cursed like highwaymen.

A mounted officer displayed the furious anger of a spoiled child. He raged with his head, his arms, and his legs.

Another, the commander of the brigade, was galloping about bawling. His hat was gone and his clothes were awry. He resembled a man who had come from bed to go to a fire. The hoofs of his horse often threatened the heads of the running men, but they scampered with singular fortune. In this rush they were apparently all deaf and blind. They heeded not the largest and longest of the oaths that were thrown at them from all directions.

Frequently over this tumult could be heard the grim jokes of the critical veterans; but the retreating men apparently were not even conscious of the presence of an audience.

The battle reflection that shone for an instant in the faces on the mad current made the youth feel that forceful hands from heaven would not have been able to have held him in place if he could have got intelligent control of his legs.

There was an appalling imprint upon these faces. The struggle in the smoke had pictured an exaggeration of itself on the bleached cheeks and in the eyes wild with one desire.

The sight of this stampede exerted a floodlike force that seemed able to drag sticks and stones and men from the ground. They of the reserves had to hold on. They grew pale and firm, and red and quaking.

The youth achieved one little thought in the midst of this chaos. The composite monster which had caused the other troops to flee had not then appeared. He resolved to get a view of it, and then, he thought he might very likely run better than the best of them.

There were moments of waiting. The youth thought of the village street at home before the arrival of the circus parade on a day in the spring. He remembered how he had stood, a small, thrillful boy, prepared to follow the dingy lady upon the white horse, or the band in its faded chariot. He saw the yellow road, the lines of expectant people, and the sober houses. He particularly remembered an old fellow who used to sit upon a cracker box in front of the store and feign to despise such exhibitions. A thousand details of color and form surged in his mind. The old fellow upon the cracker box appeared in middle prominence.

Some one cried, "Here they come!"

There was rustling and muttering among the men. They displayed a feverish desire to have every possible cartridge ready to their hands. The boxes were pulled around into various positions, and adjusted with great care. It was as if seven hundred new bonnets were being tried on.

The tall soldier, having prepared his rifle, produced a red handkerchief of some kind. He was engaged in knitting it about his throat with exquisite attention to its position, when the cry was repeated up and down the line in a muffled roar of sound.

"Here they come! Here they come!" Gun locks clicked.

Across the smoke-infested fields came a brown swarm of running men who were giving shrill yells. They came on, stooping and swinging their rifles at all angles. A flag, tilted forward, sped near the front.

As he caught sight of them the youth was momentarily startled by a thought that perhaps his gun was not loaded. He stood trying to rally his faltering intellect so that he might recollect the moment when he had loaded, but he could not.

A hatless general pulled his dripping horse to a stand near the colonel of the 304th. He shook his fist in the other's face. "You've got to hold 'em back!" he shouted, savagely; "you've got to hold 'em back!"

In his agitation the colonel began to stammer. "A-all r-right, General, all right, by Gawd! We-we'll do our—we-we'll d-d do—do our best, General." The general made a passionate gesture and galloped away. The colonel, perchance to relieve his feelings, began to scold like a wet parrot. The youth, turning swiftly to make sure that the rear was unmolested, saw the commander regarding his men in a highly resentful manner, as if he regretted above everything his association with them.

The man at the youth's elbow was mumbling, as if to himself: "Oh, we're in for it now! oh, we're in for it now!"

The captain of the company had been pacing excitedly to and fro in the rear. He coaxed in schoolmistress fashion, as to a congregation of boys with primers. His talk was an endless repetition. "Reserve your fire, boys—don't shoot till I tell you—save your fire—wait till they get close up—don't be damned fools ——"

Perspiration streamed down the youth's face, which was soiled like that of a weeping urchin. He frequently, with a nervous movement, wiped his eyes with his coat sleeve. His mouth was still a little way open.

He got the one glance at the foe-swarming field in front of him, and instantly ceased to debate the question of his piece being loaded. Before he was ready to begin— before he had announced to himself that he was about to fight—he threw the obedient, well-balanced rifle into position and fired a first wild shot. Directly he was working at his weapon like an automatic affair.

He suddenly lost concern for himself, and forgot to look at a menacing fate. He became not a man but a member. He felt that something of which he was a part—a regiment, an army, a cause, or a country—was in a crisis. He was welded into a common personality which was dominated by a single desire. For some moments he could not flee, no more than a little finger can commit a revolution from a hand.

If he had thought the regiment was about to be annihilated perhaps he could have amputated himself from it. But its noise gave him assurance. The regiment was like a firework that, once ignited, proceeds superior to circumstances until its blazing vitality fades. It wheezed and banged with a mighty power. He pictured the ground before it as strewn with the discomfited.

There was a consciousness always of the presence of his comrades about him. He felt the subtle battle brotherhood more potent even than the cause for which they were fighting. It was a mysterious fraternity born of the smoke and danger of death.

He was at a task. He was like a carpenter who has made many boxes, making still another box, only there was furious haste in his movements. He, in his thought, was careering off in other places, even as the carpenter who as he works whistles and thinks of his friend or his enemy, his home or a saloon. And these jolted dreams were never perfect to him afterward, but remained a mass of blurred shapes.

Presently he began to feel the effects of the war atmosphere—a blistering sweat, a sensation that his eyeballs were about to crack like hot stones. A burning roar filled his ears.

Following this came a red rage. He developed the acute exasperation of a pestered animal, a well-meaning cow worried by dogs. He had a mad feeling against his rifle, which could only be used against one life at a time. He wished to rush forward and strangle with his fingers. He craved a power that would enable him to make a world-sweeping gesture and brush all back. His impotency appeared to him, and made his rage into that of a driven beast.

Buried in the smoke of many rifles his anger was directed not so much against the men whom he knew were rushing toward him as against the swirling battle phantoms which were choking him, stuffing their smoke robes down his parched throat. He fought frantically for respite for his senses, for air, as a babe being smothered attacks the deadly blankets.

There was a blare of heated rage mingled with a certain expression of intentness on all faces. Many of the men were making low-toned noises with their mouths, and these subdued cheers, snarls, imprecations, prayers, made a wild, barbaric song that went as an undercurrent of sound, strange and chantlike with the resounding chords of the war march. The man at the youth's elbow was babbling. In it there was something soft and tender like the monologue of a babe. The tall soldier was swearing in a loud voice. From his lips came a black procession of curious oaths. Of a sudden another broke out in a querulous way like a man who had mislaid his hat. "Well, why don't they support us? Why don't they send supports? Do they think ——"

The youth in his battle sleep heard this as one who dozes hears.

There was a singular absence of heroic poses. The men bending and surging in their haste and rage were in every impossible attitude. The steel ramrods clanked and clanged with incessant din as the men pounded them furiously into the hot rifle barrels. The flaps of the cartridge boxes were all unfastened, and bobbed idiotically with each movement. The rifles, once loaded, were jerked to the shoulder and fired without apparent aim into the smoke or at one of the blurred and shifting forms which, upon the field before the regiment, had been growing larger and larger like puppets under a magician's hand.

The officers, at their intervals, rearward, neglected to stand in picturesque attitudes. They were bobbing to and fro roaring directions and encouragements. The dimensions of their howls were extraordinary. They expended their lungs with prodigal wills. And often they nearly stood upon their heads in their anxiety to observe the enemy on the other side of the tumbling smoke.

The lieutenant of the youth's company had encountered a soldier who had fled screaming at the first volley of his comrades. Behind the lines these two were acting a little isolated scene. The man was blubbering and staring with sheeplike eyes at the lieutenant, who had seized him by the collar and was pommeling him. He drove him back into the ranks with many blows. The soldier went mechanically, dully, with his animal-like eyes upon the officer. Perhaps there was to him a divinity expressed in the voice of the other—stern, hard, with no reflection of fear in it. He tried to reload his gun, but his shaking hands prevented. The lieutenant was obliged to assist him.

The men dropped here and there like bundles. The captain of the youth's company had been killed in an early part of the action. His body lay stretched out in the position of a tired man resting, but upon his face there was an astonished and sorrowful look, as if he thought some friend had done him an ill turn. The babbling man was grazed by a shot that made the blood stream widely down his face. He clapped both hands to his head. "Oh!" he said, and ran. Another grunted suddenly as if he had been struck by a club in the stomach. He sat down and gazed ruefully. In his eyes there was mute, indefinite reproach. Farther up the line a man, standing behind a tree, had had his knee joint splintered by a ball. Immediately he had dropped his rifle and gripped the tree with both arms. And there he remained, clinging desperately and crying for assistance that he might withdraw his hold upon the tree.

At last an exultant yell went along the quivering line. The firing dwindled from an uproar to a last vindictive popping. As the smoke slowly eddied away, the youth saw that the charge had been repulsed. The enemy were scattered into reluctant groups. He saw a man climb to the top of the fence, straddle the rail, and fire a parting shot. The waves had receded, leaving bits of dark *débris* upon the ground.

Some in the regiment began to whoop frenziedly. Many were silent. Apparently they were trying to contemplate themselves.

After the fever had left his veins, the youth thought that at last he was going to suffocate. He became aware of the foul atmosphere in which he had been struggling. He was grimy and dripping like a laborer in a foundry. He grasped his canteen and took a long swallow of the warmed water.

A sentence with variations went up and down the line. "Well, we've helt 'em back. We've helt 'em back; derned if we haven't." The men said it blissfully, leering at each other with dirty smiles.

The youth turned to look behind him and off to the right and off to the left. He experienced the joy of a man who at last finds leisure in which to look about him.

Under foot there were a few ghastly forms motionless. They lay twisted in fantastic contortions. Arms were bent and heads were turned in incredible ways. It seemed that the dead men must have fallen from some great height to get into such positions. They looked to be dumped out upon the ground from the sky.

From a position in the rear of the grove a battery was throwing shells over it. The flash of the guns startled the youth at first. He thought they were aimed directly at him. Through the trees he watched the black figures of the gunners as they worked swiftly and intently. Their labor seemed a complicated thing. He wondered how they could remember its formula in the midst of confusion.

The guns squatted in a row like savage chiefs. They argued with abrupt violence. It was a grim pow-wow. Their busy servants ran hither and thither.

A small procession of wounded men were going drearily toward the rear. It was a flow of blood from the torn body of the brigade.

To the right and to the left were the dark lines of other troops. Far in front he thought he could see lighter masses protruding in points from the forest. They were suggestive of unnumbered thousands.

Once he saw a tiny battery go dashing along the line of the horizon. The tiny riders were beating the tiny horses.

From a sloping hill came the sound of cheerings and clashes. Smoke welled slowly through the leaves.

Batteries were speaking with thunderous oratorical effort. Here and there were flags, the red in the stripes dominating. They splashed bits of warm color upon the dark lines of troops.

The youth felt the old thrill at the sight of the emblem. They were like beautiful birds strangely undaunted in a storm.

As he listened to the din from the hillside, to a deep pulsating thunder that came from afar to the left, and to the lesser clamors which came from many directions, it occurred to him that they were fighting, too, over there, and over there, and over there. Heretofore he had supposed that all the battle was directly under his nose.

As he gazed around him the youth felt a flash of astonishment at the blue, pure sky and the sun gleaming on the trees and fields. It was surprising that Nature had gone tranquilly on with her golden process in the midst of so much devilment.

Suggested Readings

Catton, Bruce. *America Goes to War*. New York: Hill and Wang, 1958.

Colvert, James B. *Stephen Crane*. New York: Harcourt, Brace, Jovanovich, 1984.

McWhiney, Grady and Perry Jamieson. *Attack and Die: Civil War Military Tactics and the Southern Heritage*. Tuscaloosa, Ala.: University of Alabama, 1982.

Mitchell, Lee Clark, ed. *New Essays on the Red Badge of Courage*. Cambridge: Cambridge University, 1986.

Shaara, Michael. *The Killer Angels*. New York: Ballantine, 1974.

Wiley, Bell I. *The Life of Billy Yank*. Indianapolis: Bobbs-Merrill, 1952.

———. *The Life of Johnny Reb*. Indianapolis: Bobbs-Merrill, 1946.

Reading 8

GALLIPOLI

Alan Moorehead

Notes from the Editors

World War I (1914–1918), the most lethal war of modern times until World War II (1939–1945), resulted in the death of more than nine million soldiers from fifteen countries. The Gallipoli campaign of April 1915–January 1916 was one of the bloodiest engagements of the war.

Allied with the Russians, the British decided to try to open the Dardanelles as part of a plan to defeat Turkey, a German ally that was tying down much needed Russian troops. The controversial expedition, involving a landing on the strait and then an advance to dislodge the Turkish forces commanding the high ground, was marked by poor planning and battlefield blunders, particularly on the part of the British officers.

Both sides suffered heavily. Of the one million soldiers committed to the campaign, more than half suffered casualties. And the Allies had to withdraw without anything, save Turkish deaths, to show for their efforts.

Like Stephen Crane, Alan Moorehead did not witness the carnage first hand. A foreign correspondent during World War II and a popular author and novelist, he employed the rich memoir material and official records to compile his now classic Gallipoli. *An Australian, he had a special interest in the campaign since much of the Allied fighting involved Anzacs, soldiers from Australia and New Zealand.*

Moorehead's battle scenes capture the terror of combat at close range with machine guns, artillery, and even off-shore cannons creating a virtual hell for the mostly inexperienced, but incredibly brave, young men involved in the fatal expedition. This was the war in which the defensive weapons were superior to the offensive weapons. On this front, as well as the Western Front, time and again each side's offensives failed to produce the breakthrough that could lead to a decisive victory. Moorehead shows that despite the general hatred for the enemy, a certain respect, even camaraderie, prevailed during the lulls between the battles.

There is some dispute as to who ordered the attack on the Anzac bridgehead on the night of May 18. Liman von Sanders says that he himself made the plan and he takes the responsibility for it; others believe that it was conceived by Enver when he first visited the peninsula on May 10, and the circumstances of the enterprise do, in fact, bear the impress of Enver's headlong cast of mind. There was no subtlety or caution about the matter: some 42,000 men under the command of Essad Pasha were assembled, and their orders were nothing less than to demolish the whole Anzac bridgehead at a single blow. By nightfall it was hoped that the last Dominion soldier would have been killed, captured or driven into the sea, and that the entire Turkish army would have then been free to turn south to deal with the remainder of Hamilton's forces at Cape Helles.

At this time the Australian and New Zealand Corps had dwindled to some 10,000 effective men, and it was only by luck that a brigade which had been sent round to Cape Helles earlier in the month was returned to Birdwood on the eve of the battle. This brought his numbers to a total of about 17,000, of which 12,500 were available for fighting in the front line. They were thus outnumbered by more than three to one.

The Anzac position had by now become very clearly defined: it was a shallow triangle, covering about 400 acres, its base, a mile and a half long, resting on the sea, its apex reaching to the slopes of Sari Bair about a thousand yards from the shore. In order to avoid the fire of the British Fleet the Turks had dug their trenches almost on top of the Anzac lines, and at some places the two sides were divided by not more than ten yards. The situation at Quinn's and Courtnay's Posts in the centre of the line was fantastic; directly behind the Australian trench (which was kept packed with men by day and night), a steep cliff fell away to the gully below, and the Turks had only to make an advance of five yards in order to drive a wedge through the bridgehead to the sea. But this they never could succeed in doing, though they attacked repeatedly during the first half of May. No-man's-land at these and other points was no larger than a small room, and it was the easiest thing in the world for the Turks to toss a hand grenade into the Anzac trenches. The only real defence against this was to throw the grenade smartly back again before it exploded; except for a few jam tins which were filled with explosive at a makeshift workshop on the beach, the Australians had no such weapons of their own. No man could expose the smallest fraction of his body for an instant without being shot, and even a periscope hoisted for a moment above the parapet was immediately shattered. An extreme tension prevailed in the bridgehead; there was no hour when some new raid was not expected or delivered, no minute when shells were not crashing among them or bullets screaming overhead. The soldiers managed to sleep through this racket at odd hours of the day and night, but it was never a sufficient rest. No one was ever safe. On May 14 General Bridges, the commander of the Australian Division, was mortally wounded, and the following day Birdwood had his hair parted by a bullet while he was looking through a periscope. The wound turned septic and was very painful but he continued in command.

There was an intense hatred of the Turks among the Dominion soldiers. Most of them had grown up in a world of clear and obvious values; a fight was a fight, you knew who your enemy was and you stood up to him and had it out, fairly and squarely, in the open. It was in this spirit that they had volunteered for service in the Army. The charge was the thing, the quick and palpable blow in the face that knocked the man down. War, in fact, was an extension of the pub brawl, and it had in it the elements of rioting, of street fighting, of instant physical revenge.

But nothing of the kind had happened at Gallipoli. From the day they had landed the soldiers had scarcely ever seen the enemy; he lurked unseen in the heights above, he sniped down on them and caught them unawares, he stood back at a safe distance with his guns and burst his shrapnel above their heads, and there seemed to be no effective way of retaliating. After more than three weeks of this the soldiers were beginning to feel an increasing sense of frustration and of impotent anger in their narrow bridgehead. A claustrophobia had developed; they felt that they had been caught in a trap, and there seemed to be something unfair in this kind of fighting in which they were never given a chance of showing their real courage and their strength.

Beyond this there was at this early stage another and perhaps deeper feeling that there was a monstrosity and inhumanity about the Turks: they were cruel and sinister fanatics, capable of any sort of vice and bestiality—in brief, it was the popular picture that had been drawn of them by Byron and the emotions of Gladstonian liberal England. The Turks were 'natives'—but natives of a peculiarly dangerous and subtle kind. And so the Australian and New Zealand soldiers fought, not an ordinary man, but a monster prefigured by imagination and by propaganda; and they hated him.

Despite these things, perhaps even because of them, an extraordinary cheerfulness and exaltation possessed the men in the front line. Living with the instant prospect of death, all pettiness, all the normal anxieties and jealousies of life, deserted them, and they developed an almost mystical feeling towards the extreme danger that surrounded them. The fighting became an elaborate and exciting game in which they were all immensely engrossed, and it was only when they were retired to rest for a while in some half-haven under the cliffs that they became aware again of the miseries of their situation, the monotonous food, the endless physical discomfort, the impossible limits of a life in which even a canteen of fresh water or a bathe in the sea were the utmost luxuries.

By now death had become a familiar, and they often talked about it in a half-derisive deprecating slang. In the same way as the Chinese will laugh at other people's pain it became a huge joke when the men bathing off the beach were caught in a burst of shrapnel, or when some poor devil had his head blown off while he was in the latrine. There had to be some sort of expression which would help to rationalize the unbearable circumstances of their lives, some way of obtaining relief from the shock of it all, and since tears were impossible this callous hard-boiled laughter became the thing. They were not fatalists. They believed that a mistake had been made in the landing at Gaba Tepe and that they might easily have to pay for it with their lives; but they very much wanted to go on living, they were all for the battle and they hoped and believed obscurely that in the end they would win.

These high spirits, this fineness and integrity created by the powerful drug of risk, might not perhaps have continued indefinitely under such a strain, but there had certainly been no weakening in morale when, on May 18, the soldiers became aware that something unusual was happening in the enemy lines.

An unaccountable silence spread through the hills before them. For the first time since they had landed the fearful racket of the Turkish howitzers died away, and for several minutes at a stretch no rifle or machine-gun was fired. In this strange quiet most of the day went by. Then at five o'clock in the evening a tremendous artillery barrage broke out, and it continued for about half an hour. It chanced that on this day a naval aircraft had been sent out to fix the position of an enemy warship in the straits, and on his return the pilot reported that he had seen large numbers of men massing behind the Turkish lines. Later in the day this information was confirmed by a second pilot who had also seen enemy soldiers coming across the straits in boats from the Asiatic side; and from the battleship *Triumph* there was a further report that Turkish reinforcements were marching north from Cape Helles to the Anzac front. On hearing this, Birdwood sent a message to his two divisional commanders warning them to expect an attack that night; the men were to stand to arms at 3 a.m., which was half an hour before the usual time.

The night turned cold and misty, and when the moon went down at 11:35 p.m. there was hardly a sound along the front except for the breaking of the waves on the shore. Suddenly at fifteen minutes to midnight, a fusillade of rifle fire which was heavier than anything that had been heard before burst out from the Turkish trenches, and as it spread along the line the Anzac commanders kept telephoning to their outposts to ask if they were being attacked. But nothing followed, and presently the uproar dwindled into silence again. At 3 a.m. the men were roused, and they took their places on the firing steps with their bayonets fixed to their rifles. It was still cold and most of them were wearing their overcoats.

Hardly five minutes had gone by when a shout of warning went up from one of the outposts, and a company of Turks was seen advancing down a ravine known as Wire Gully in the centre of the line. There had been no preliminary bugle call, none of the usual shouts of Allah, Allah: merely these shadowy forms in the half-darkness and the long line of bayonets. The Australians opened fire from either side of the gully, and immediately the enemy bugles sounded and the charge began. Everywhere along the line the Turks jumped up from their hiding places and in a dark cloud swept forward over the broken ground.

At most places the oncoming enemy had to cross two or three hundred yards before they reached the Anzac entrenchments, and so there was half a minute or more when they were exposed in the open and quite defenceless. Very few of them survived even that amount of time. There was a kind of cascading movement in the battle; directly one line of soldiers had come over the parapet and been destroyed another line formed up, emerged into view and was cut down. For the first hour it was simply a matter of indiscriminate killing, but presently the Australians and New Zealanders began to adopt more systematic methods: when a Turkish officer appeared they deliberately withheld their fire until he had assembled the full company of his men in the open. Then all were destroyed together. At some points it became a kind of game to pick off the survivors as they ran back and forth across the battlefield like terrified rabbits in search of cover. Here and there some few of the Turks did manage to get into the Anzac trenches, but they survived only for a few minutes; there was a quick and awful bayoneting and then the tide receded again.

As daylight broke the battle assumed the character of a hunt, with the Turkish officers serving in the role of beaters driving the game on to the guns. A wild, almost berserk excitement filled the Australian and New Zealand ranks. In order to get a better view many of the soldiers jumped up and sat astride the parapets and from there they blazed away at the screaming mass of Turks before them. The Anzac soldiers who had been held in reserve could not bear to be left out of the fight; they came pressing forward offering to pay for a place on the firing line. In one trench two soldiers actually fought one another with their fists for a vacant position on the parapet, and there was a kind of mad surrealism in the shouts and cries along the line as each new Turkish rush came on. 'Backsheesh,' 'Imshi Yallah,' 'Eggs is cooked.'[1] Once an Australian was heard shouting to the Turks as they fell back from his trench, *'Saida* (good-bye). Play you again next Saturday.'

By 5 a.m., when a hot sun was beginning to stream down on to the battlefield, the attack was broken. But the orders to the Turks were that they should continue the fight until they got through to the sea, and so they went on with the struggle for another six hours, each new charge getting a little feebler than the last. Mustafa Kemal had been reduced to the command of a single division, the 19th, for the period of the offensive, and he alone, of the four divisional commanders engaged, had succeeded in making any headway. When at midday Essad Pasha decided to break off the action 10,000 of his men had fallen, and of these some 5,000, dead, dying and wounded, were lying out in the open between the trenches.

Other heavier battles than this were fought at Gallipoli, but none with such a terrible concentration of killing, none so one-sided, and none with so strange an aftermath. Through the long afternoon the wounded lay with the dead on the battlefield, and although the trenches on either side were only a yard or two away no one could go out and bring them in without taking the risk of being instantly shot.

'No sound came from that dreadful space,' the Australian history of the campaign relates, 'but here and there some wounded or dying man, silently lying without help or any hope of it under the sun which glared from a cloudless sky, turned painfully from one side to the other, or slowly raised an arm towards heaven. . . .'

By three in the afternoon the work was practically done. There were two crises: it was discovered at the last minute that the Turks' watches were eight minutes ahead of the British, and a hurried adjustment had to be made. Then, as the hour for the ending of the truce was approaching, a shot rang out. Standing there in the open with tens of thousands of rifles pointed towards them the burial parties stood in a sudden hush, but nothing followed and they returned to their work again.

At four o'clock the Turks near Quinn's Post came to Herbert for their final orders, since none of their own officers were about. He first sent back the grave-diggers to their own trenches, and at seven minutes past four retired the men who were carrying the white flags. He then walked over to the Turkish trenches to say good-bye. When he remarked to the enemy soldiers there that they would probably shoot him on the following day, they answered in a horrified chorus, 'God forbid.' Seeing Herbert standing there, groups of Australians came up to the Turks to shake hands and say good-bye. 'Good-bye, old chap; good luck.' The Turks answered with one of their proverbs: 'Smiling may you go and smiling may you come again.'

All the remaining men in the open were now sent back to their lines, and Herbert made a last minute inspection along the front, reminding the Turks that firing was not to begin again for a further twenty-five minutes. He was answered with salaams, and

---

[1] Or 'Eggs-a-cook,' an expression used by the Egyptian vendors when they sold eggs to the Anzac troops during their stay in Egypt.

he too finally dropped out of sight. At 4:45 p.m. a Turkish sniper fired from somewhere in the hills. Immediately the Australians answered and the roar of high explosive closed over the battlefield again.

There had been some irregularities. On both sides a good deal of surreptitious digging had been done, and both Turkish and British staff officers had strolled about no-man's-land, covertly studying the lie of each other's trenches. It was even said— and the story has never been denied in Turkey—that Kemal had disguised himself as a sergeant and had spent the whole nine hours with various burial parties close to the Anzac trenches.

Much the most important result of the battle and the truce, however, was that from this time onwards all real rancour against the Turks died out in the Anzac ranks. They now knew the enemy from their own experience, and he had ceased to be a propaganda figure. He was no longer a coward, a fanatic or a monster. He was a normal man and they thought him very brave.

This camaraderie with the enemy—the mutual respect of men who are committed to killing one another—was not peculiar to Gallipoli for it existed also in France; but on this isolated battlefield it had a special intensity. The Australian and New Zealand troops refused to use the gas-masks that were now issued to them. When they were questioned about this they made some such reply as, 'The Turks won't use gas. They're clean fighters.'[1]

Had the soldiers known Enver a little better they might not have been so certain of this; yet perhaps they did know Enver, for politicians generally were held in contempt at Gallipoli and by both sides, and in a way that seldom occurred in the second world war. Soon many of the British began to feel as Herbert felt: that the campaign need never have been fought at all had only the politicians acted more responsibly in the beginning.

The extreme ferocity with which the battles were fought at Gallipoli gives no inkling of the compassion that the opposing soldiers in the front line felt for one another. In the periods of comparative calm which followed May 19 at Anzac, the most bizarre incidents occurred. Once a staff officer visiting the front saw with astonishment that a number of Turks were walking about behind their lines in full view of the Australians. He asked, 'Why don't you shoot?' and was answered, 'Well, they're not doing any harm are they? Might as well leave the poor beggars alone.' Later in the campaign there was an old Turk who apparently had been given the job of doing the washing for his platoon. Regularly each day he emerged from his trench and hung out the wet shirts and socks in a line along the parapet, and no Allied soldier would have dreamed of shooting him. The Turks on their side usually withheld their fire from the survivors of wrecked ships, and in the front line at least their prisoners were treated with kindness.

There was a constant traffic of gifts in the trenches, the Turks throwing over grapes and sweets, the Allied soldiers responding with tinned food and cigarettes. The

---

[1]Gas was never used at Gallipoli.

Turks had no great love for British beef. A note came over one day: 'Bully beef—non. Envoyez milk.' It became an accepted practice to wave a 'wash-out' to a sniper who missed: there would be the sudden crack of a rifle, the bullet screaming past the Turk's head, then the laugh from the enemy trench, the waving of a spade or a bayonet and the words in English softly shouted, 'Better luck next time, Tommy.'

Once or twice private duels were fought. While the rest of the soldiers on both sides held their fire an Australian and a Turk would stand up on the parapets and blaze away at one another until one or the other was wounded or killed, and something seemed to be proved—their skill, their wish 'to dare', perhaps most of all their pride. Then in a moment all would dissolve into the horror and frenzy of a raid or a setpiece battle, the inhuman berserk killing.

Between the two extremes, between the battles and the truce, between fighting and death, the men had to come to terms with their precarious existence. They soon developed habits that fitted their mad surroundings, and they did this very rapidly and very well. The rabbit warren of trenches and dugouts at Anzac became more familiar to them than their own villages and homes. By night ten thousand shaded fires were lit in niches in the cliffs, ten thousand crude meals were cooked; they slept, they waited for their precious mail, their one reminder of the lost sane world, they put the individual extra touch to their dug-outs—another shelf in the rock, a blanket across the opening, a biscuit tin to hold a tattered book. They knew every twist in the paths where a sniper's bullet would come thudding in, they accepted wounding as they might have accepted an accident on the football field, they argued about the war and the confined beehive politics of their battalions, they took the risk of bathing in the sea under the bursting shrapnel and nothing would stop them doing it. They cursed and complained and dreamed and this in fact was home.

No stranger visiting the Anzac bridgehead ever failed to be moved and stimulated by it. It was a thing so wildly out of life, so dangerous, so high-spirited, such a grotesque and theatrical setting and yet reduced to such a calm and almost matter-of-fact routine. The heart missed a beat when one approached the ramshackle jetty on the beach, for the Turkish shells were constantly falling there, and it hardly seemed that anyone could survive. Yet once ashore a curious sense of heightened living supervened. No matter how hideous the noise, the men moved about apparently oblivious of it all, and with a trained and steady air as though they had lived there all their lives; and this in itself was a reassurance to everyone who came ashore. The general aspect was of a vast mining camp in some savage desert valley. Close to the shore were the dug-outs of the generals, the wireless station, the telephone exchange, the searchlights, a factory for making bombs, a corral for Turkish prisoners, a smithy. Scores of placid mules sheltered in the gully until at nightfall they began their work of taking ammunition and supplies to the men in the trenches in the hills above—the water ration was a pannikin a day. There was a smoking incinerator near the jetty, and it erupted loudly whenever an unexploded bullet fell into the flames. An empty shellcase served as a gong for the headquarters officers' mess. They ate bully beef, biscuits, plum and apple jam, and just occasionally frozen meat; never vegetables, eggs, milk or fruit.

Above the beach a maze of goat tracks spread upward through the furze and the last surviving patches of prickly oak, and at every step of the way some soldier had made his shelter in the side of the ravine: a hole dug into the ground, the branches of trees or perhaps a piece of canvas for a roof, a blanket, a few tins and boxes, and that was all. As one progressed upward there were many crude notices of warning against the enemy snipers: Keep Well to Your Left. Keep Your Head Down. Double Across One at a Time. Then finally the trenches themselves, where all day long the men stood to their arms, watching and watching through their periscopes for the slightest movement in the enemy lines. Cigarettes dangled from their mouths. They talked quietly.

Hamilton came over to the bridgehead on May 30 and saw, 'Men staggering under huge sides of frozen beef: men struggling up cliffs with kerosene tins full of water; men digging; men cooking; men cardplaying in small dens scooped out from the banks of yellow clay—everyone wore a Bank Holiday air; evidently the ranklings and worries of mankind—miseries and concerns of the spirit—had fled the precincts of this valley. The Boss—the bill—the girl—envy, malice, hunger, hatred—had scooted away to the Antipodes. All the time, overhead, the shell and rifle bullets groaned and whined, touching just the same note of violent energy as was in evidence everywhere else. To understand that awful din, raise the eyes twenty-five degrees to the top of the cliff which closes in the tail end of the valley and you can see the Turkish hand-grenades bursting along the crest, just where an occasional bayonet flashes and figures hardly distinguishable from Mother Earth crouch in an irregular line. Or else they rise to fire and are silhouetted against the sky and then you recognize the naked athletes from the Antipodes and your heart goes into your mouth as a whole bunch of them dart forward suddenly, and as suddenly disappear. And the bomb shower stops dead—for the moment; but, all the time, from that fiery crest line which is Quinn's, there comes a slow constant trickle of wounded—some dragging themselves painfully along; others being carried along on stretchers. Bomb wounds all; a ceaseless silent stream of bandages and blood. Yet three out of four of "the boys" have grit left for a gay smile or a cheery little nod to their comrades, waiting for their turn as they pass, pass, pass, down on their way to the sea.

'There are poets and writers who see naught in war but carrion, filth, savagery and horror. The heroism of the rank and file makes no appeal. They refuse war the credit of being the only exercise in devotion on the large scale existing in this world. The superb moral victory over death leaves them cold. Each one to his taste. To me this is no valley of death—it is a valley brim full of life at its highest power. Men live through more in five minutes on that crest than they do in five years of Bendigo or Ballarat. Ask the brothers of these very fighters—Calgoorlie or Coolgardie miners— to do one quarter of the work and to run one hundredth the risk on a wages basis— instanter there would be a riot. But here—not a murmur, not a question; only a radiant force of camaraderie in action.'

From May onwards many of the men discarded their uniforms, and except for a pair of shorts, boots and perhaps a cap, went naked in the sun. Even in the frontlines they fought stripped to the waist, a girl, a ship or a dragon tattooed on their arms. . . .

Suggested Readings

Falls, Cyril B. *The Great War, 1914–1918*. New York: Capricorn, 1959.

Hart, Basil H. Liddell. *The Real War, 1914–1918*. London: Faber and Faber, 1930.

Hamilton, Ian. *Gallipoli Diary*. New York: Doran, 1920.

Mackenzie, Compton. *Gallipoli Memories*. Garden City, N.Y.: Doubleday, 1930.

Sanders, Otto Liman von. *Five Years in Turkey*. Annapolis: U.S. Naval Institute, 1927.

Reading 9

THE BIG V

William Pelfrey

Notes from the Editors

William Pelfrey was a history major at Wayne State University who, after graduation in 1967, enlisted in the United States Army and was ultimately sent to Vietnam. Pelfrey kept diaries of his experiences and, when he returned, wrote The Big V, *one of the best Vietnam War novels. Like Stephen Crane, he concentrated on one young man, Henry Winsted, and his reactions to combat and death.*

At first glance the Vietnam War appeared to be unlike the Punic War, the Civil War, and World War I. It was a guerrilla war fought by troops against an often unseen enemy. Civilian populations caught up in the conflict posed problems for soldiers who were supposed to concentrate their fire on military *personnel and structures. In addition, it was a highly mechanized war for the Americans and their South Vietnamese allies, with helicopters, tactical air support, and high-tech means of communication changing dramatically the nature of battle.*

On the other hand, particularly in the small-scale action described by Pelfrey in this segment from his novel, the combat experience in Vietnam War was very much like that in the three previous wars. Young Winsted sees his first battlefield deaths and learns to deal with them. He expresses the resentment of many citizen soldiers to the "lifers," or career officers. He begins to adjust to the dramatic highs of battle that come few and far between the relatively normal, and sometimes tedious, down time of an American grunt in Vietnam.

Many who write about the Vietnam War stress the importance of the image of Hollywood, John Wayne, and World War II motion pictures. Soldiers constantly compared their experiences to those depicted on film and television, which they had grown up with. And many who write about Vietnam pepper their novels with the salty language of the military. Soldiers have always cursed. Literary conventions have kept their colorful language from the civilian population until the 1960s. As recently as the post World War II era, Norman Mailer's classic The Naked and the Dead *was withheld from publication until the author replaced one especially offensive profanity with the words* fug *and* fugging. *Pelfrey's language, which may still offend some readers, is authentic and, if anything, understated. Why soldiers use language that is rejected by polite society is an interesting question that again points up the differences between soldiers and civilians.*

. . . "Raider eight-five this is Raider three-four, over," using the standard Hollywood call sign procedure.

"This is Raider eight-five."

Reprinted from *The Big V* by William Pelfrey (New York: Avon, 1984), pp. 67–73, by permission of Liveright Publishing Corporation. Copyright © 1972 by William Pelfrey.

"Roger, this is Raider three-four, have completed hamlet inspection, negative sit-rep. Am proceeding back to your location at this time, over."

"This is Raider eight-five, understand, negative sit-rep, you'll sierra papa at this time. How's my copy, over?"

"This is Raider three-four, good copy. Negative further, out."

Fleming hooked the handset back to his chest.

"Okay, let's move out."

Mastion clamped his shotgun closed and moved to the point, shotgun tucked under his arm and combing the red moustache with his other hand.

The chief giggled and waved.

Lieutenant Chivington waved back. "Numah one, Papa-san."

Everyone else in the village stared quietly. The bastard with my Milky Way was still at the chief's side.

Plei Jan. Pacified village.

We had gone five hundred meters down the trail when the tubes popped. Three thups, three tubes. We all froze. Not more than five seconds and we heard the hollow rushing and rumbling. Looking back it was so much like a movie. It always was; as I reminisce, that's the most striking and revolting thing about it.

They came in as we were diving to the bush. Falling hollow rumbling, split-second suction noise just before the explosion goes, a solid reverberating explosion, unlike C-4. Fleming was hit with that first volley and screamed, one short hoarse piercing scream, cut off.

Phil had thrown himself behind Fi Bait and me and ran to the other side of the trail to help Fleming just as the tubes popped again. This time six rounds, two per tube.

Fi Bait hit my shoulder, grabbed the handset and started yelling.

"Break break break, this is seven-three-seven, fire mission! All stations break."

"Send your grid seven-three-seven."

The rounds came in. I about shit, pressing both hands on the steel pot. One hit on the trail between us and Phil. I heard the shrapnel cut and whiz through the leaves around me. I was scared shitless. In a fire fight you're too busy shooting back to get scared. But you're helpless against mortars; all you can do is lie there and listen to the thups of the tubes and wait for the explosions and shrapnel. Helpless. That hollow tumbling rushing as they come in, suction as the explosion goes.

"Come up on grid 864-036. ASAP, we've got in-coming and WIAs."

"Roger, 864-036."

Fleming was quiet.

"Anybody else hit?" Phil screamed.

No answers. I looked over at him through the smoke. He was folding the poncho, standard field expediency for a sucking chest wound.

It was too quiet. Just like in the goddamned movies. Too quiet, staring across at Phil. Where was the next one going to hit? Sweating and panting, I wanted to run, do *something*.

"Seven-three-seven, that grid is a friendly village, over."

"They're fuckin mortarin us, you shit-bird!"

They popped again, muffled thups stopping the blood in my face. I gulped and tucked my chin deeper into my chest. Just lying there, knowing it was coming.

"God damn it, level the place!"

"That's a registered village, you idiot."

"They're bringin the max on us for Christ's sake!"

This time the dispersion was greater. All hit ahead of us and right on the trail. Maybe they figured we'd be running. Someone screamed from near the point.

"How bad?" yelled Phil.

"My fucking shoulder." It was Taylor, from Pennsylvania.

Phil ran up the trail clutching his medical bag. I saw him leap, running like a football back breaking through the line. He had jettisoned his ruck and rifle.

The acrid smoke floated through the bush and Fi Bait screamed again above the silence.

"God damn it they're killin us! Give me a battery six HE. Give me a goddamned arc light."

"This is red leg four-seven. That's a big negative. You know I can't fire on a friendly village without higher authorization, over."

"Kiss my ass motherfucker!"

"Seven-three-seven you use that kind of talk on this radio and you'll have an Article Fifteen waitin for you, boy."

"What the fuck's wrong with you?"

Fai Bait no longer screamed but was plaintive, face flushed, skin drawn tight around the eyes.

No more rounds came in. They probably figured we would be retaliating with artillery and had moved back out of the village. The whole thing couldn't have lasted over three minutes.

"This is red leg . . ."

Fi Bait keyed the handset so the voice couldn't come through.

"This is seven-three-seven, kiss my ass, lifer. Negative further, out."

At the time I was too stunned by the situation to think about it, but looking back that stands out as one of the most beautiful scenes of my life. "Kiss my ass, lifer." I wish I had said that to somebody at some time in my military career.

The silence was maddening, just like the fire fight, approaching panic. All you could do was lie there, waiting for something to happen. I watched a centipede crawl down a bamboo shoot. Finally Phil came running back down the trail to Fleming.

Fi Bait dropped the handset on the damp ground and pushed my head back down so he could turn the radio off. We got up and clustered around the medic with everyone else. I was still unable to swallow my Adam's apple, eyes dry and blinking.

Two grunts picked Fleming up and lay him on the trail. The poncho lay loose on his chest, over the dressing. Blood still trickled out in two streams on the left side, puddling on the yellow dirt just like in the movies. He had probably died before Phil had finished so he didn't bother completing the job. Fleming's mouth and eyes were closed. Just like in the goddamned movies—I guess in the movies it's close to half and half, half with the eyes open, the other half shut.

Another grunt carried Fleming's pack out. I had thought Fleming was the only guy hit, but Phil nodded to the bush and two other guys went in for Lieutenant Chivington. One piece of shrapnel had cut across his face and taken his right eyebrow completely off, blood glistening down the cheek to the throat. It was like Henry Cooper's eye when Cassius Clay got to him, only the cut was much deeper, probably all the way into the skull. The front of his shirt was completely red. We later learned from base camp that he had taken a total of nineteen pieces of shrapnel in the chest and head.

I don't know, fucked up world.

Lieutenant Chivington and Fleming were both KIAs. Phil left the poncho lying on Fleming's chest. He took off each man's boots and Kell called for a dust-off. Taylor was the only WIA, and it was only a scratch. One of the first volley's three rounds had gotten both the lieutenant and Fleming. They were evidently diving for the bush when it hit, because both had their chests chewed up.

Phil gave Kell the dog tags and tied a KIA tag to each man's left big toe. We lay their gear beside the bodies and sat waiting for the medevac. A few guys opened C-ration accessory envelopes and smoked the cigarettes.

Kell popped yellow smoke when the bird came in. It hovered so high that we didn't get any backwash, the rotors slapping almost like a sixty instead of the grinding and numbing roar. The crew chief swung the Penetrator's steel arm out and lowered the cable, big white square and red cross shining down at us.

Phil and Kell secured Fleming in the sling and the crew chief hauled him up, then sent it back down for Lieutenant Chivington; then again with a basket, for their rifles, boots, and packs. Swinging the arm back in he looked down at us and flashed the peace sign. Peace sign. I remember wanting to shoot him as I stared up at the curved plastic helmet visor over his face.

The bird hovered higher above the triple canopy before arching off. Nothing was said until the rotors' noise had faded.

"Okay, let's saddle up," said Kell.

He had taken the radio out of Fleming's pack and put it in his own while waiting for the bird. We slung the packs and huddled around him, above the pool of Fleming's blood.

"Raider eight-five this is Raider three-four, over."

"Send your traffic, three-four."

"Roger, this is three-four, Kilo-India-Alphas dusted off, am proceeding to your location at this time, over."

"Roger, three-four. Come on in, boy."

Kell hooked the handset to the metal ring on his ruck strap, Mastion took the point with his shotgun and we walked back toward Jude. Kell was now in charge of the first platoon.

We stopped at four o'clock and set up our november lima in a plain of elephant grass. I don't know why we didn't keep going until finding a bamboo grove as usual; we had to send five guys out to cut enough poles and stakes for everybody's hootches. It started raining before they got back and by the time we had the hootches up we were all soaked.

I had beef and shrapnel for supper; Fi Bait had spaghetti. We hadn't spoken to each other since leaving the village. The radio was still turned off.

"You gonna send in a november lima?"

"Fuck it," he said.

I didn't want to force conversation, but I also knew if he kept the radio off and didn't turn in a november lima his shit would be flapping with the lifers.

"Want me to call it in?"

"Fuck," shaking his head, "Yeah, go ahead."

I coded our location and three on-call targets and sent them in. They didn't give any hassle about Fi Bait's tone that morning.

He lay on his back with the damp poncho liner tucked under his chin. "Tell me it ain't a fucked up world, Henry."

"I can't believe it."

"Fucking army. Fucking gooks . . . friendly village."

It rained until eight o'clock. Kell came over as soon as it stopped and told us our shifts for radio watch. Fi Bait was already asleep, at least had his eyes closed. Kell gave us the last shift and told me to wake him.

I had trouble sleeping that night. I thought back to the first fire fight, how it now seemed like an obscene game of cowboys and Indians. Kill a dink, no sweat; the blood today had been human, *real*. I thought about it and sulked nearly all night.

But I was in the Nam, I told myself that I was having trouble going to sleep only because that was the first time. As they say, "If you've seen one you've seen 'em all." I told myself that that principle applied to Americans as well as dinks. Next time it would be natural—though still sad, of course. It's just a fucked up world. After that night you would lose no sleep over KIAs, just like after actually killing one you would lose no sleep over killing dinks—so you told yourself.

I woke up Fi Bait and then Kell. It was still dark as we ate breakfast. We moved out with the sun pink behind glistening gray clouds and made it back to Jude by four o'clock, in time for a hot supper.

Captain Ferris called us over to the CP before the chow bird came in and talked about how they never would have sent us in there if they had expected anything like that. Phil was being put in for a bronze star with V, and Kell was to be promoted to staff sergeant. In the morning the chaplain would fly out for a funeral service, and the colonel would come with him to talk to us. We were to shave before getting into the chow line.

Big Sam and the medic ate at the table with Fi Bait and me.

"Bronze star, shit," said Phil.

"No use being bitter," said Sam. "At least you're gettin somethin from the army for a change."

"Gettin shit. Why don't they give me a three-day R&R?"

"You'd get the clap," said Fi Bait.

"Your mother'll be proud of a bronze star," said Sam.

The chow was hot dogs and sauerkraut with the usual quart of milk for every two men. That night it didn't rain and the four of us sat at the table talking until dark.

Gazing away from each other to the Hollywood Cambodian sunset as the talk got to Lieutenant Chivington and Fleming. Chivington had volunteered for the Nam, Fleming was US and had come in-country with Phil. I never did really know him.

After dark Sam brought a new candle over, we went into our bunker and played spades.

Suggested Readings

Caputo, Philip. *A Rumor of War*. New York: Ballantine, 1977.

Herr, Michael. *Dispatches*. New York: Knopf, 1978.

Lewy, Gunther. *America in Vietnam*. New York: Oxford, 1978.

O'Brien, Tim. *Going After Cacciato*. New York: Delacorte, 1978.

Santoli, Al, ed. *Everything We Had. An Oral History of the Vietnam War by Thirty-Three American Soldiers Who Fought It*. New York: Random House, 1981.

Summers, Harry G., Jr. *On Strategy: A Critical Analysis of the Vietnam War*. Novato, Calif.: Presidio, 1982.

Reading 10

THE SOLDIER'S RELATION TO DEATH

J. Glenn Gray

Notes from the Editors

J. Glenn Gray had just finished his graduate training in philosophy when he was drafted into the American Army in the spring of 1941. He began his military life as a private and was discharged in 1945 as a second lieutenant. While in the army, he served in combat in France and Italy and was also an intelligence officer. The Warriors (1959), from which the selection was excerpted, began as notes in the diary he kept as an observer and participant in World War II.

Gray is interested in how soldiers face death. He muses about his own experiences as well as those of military people through the ages. It is clear to him that death in combat can be dealt with in a variety of ways, depending upon the beliefs and personality of the individual soldier. He suggests that fatigue and routine tend to create a situation in which soldiers have little time or inclination to think about their own mortality. Others who do think about it are able to give meaning to their potential death in several ways. Employing philosophical, religious, and psychological insights, Gray is able to make sense out of how the presence of imminent death affects soldiers in combat.

. . . One might argue that death in war is merely a matter of increased probability, not different in principle from death in time of peace. But this would be a superficial view, for not the frequency of death but the manner of dying makes a qualitative difference. Death in war is commonly caused by members of my own species actively seeking my end, despite the fact that they may never have seen me and have no personal reason for mortal enmity. It is death brought about by hostile intent rather than by accident or natural causes that separates war from peace so completely. And the fact that death's chief victims in war are young men or youths who are just becoming men contributes greatly to the general mood. For the most part, these youths must take leave of their lives under conditions of exposure, away from home, without the possibility of the dignity and ceremony that help to moderate death's shocking character. The difference is not only between dying and getting killed. It is much more the difference between dying by disease or accident among people who know and cherish you and having your life cut off without preparation by someone who cares not at all for the anguish he causes. This creates the terrible hatred of war, particularly among civilian populations.

The majority of soldiers in modern wars, I am convinced, are able to gain only

---

Reprinted by permission of the Gray family from J. Glenn Gray, *The Warriors: Reflections on Men in Battle* (New York: Harper & Row, 1967), pp. 100–113, 116–121.

a negative relation to death. For them, death is a state and a condition so foreign and unreal as to be incomprehensible. They reject it with aversion without bringing its reality to the level of consciousness. Thus, in the summer of 1944, when I was waiting for the invasion of southern France to begin, an invasion I was to join, I wrote:

What do I think of this new adventure looming before me? Today I have thought about it for the first time. It will be dangerous, that is certain. It will also be difficult. But somehow I am unable to anticipate. I simply await—and dream of the end of the war. I daydream more than I used to.

In peacetime, young people are likely to dismiss the fact of death as something that happens to somebody else; seldom do they take seriously the certainty that they themselves will have to cope with it. In war soldiers cannot ignore death, for it is all too prevalent. But imagining what it is like to be dead is endlessly difficult. Imagination and intellect must be operative if we are to bridge the gap between life and death, and many soldiers understandably try to avoid exercising either. Battlefield dead are so passive, and life is, to our Western youth at least, bound up totally with activity and action. Soldiers fall and die in such contorted and unnatural positions, as a rule, that even their comrades find it hard to believe that, shortly before, they were alive. This is part of the mystery of death: those who enter its realm are quickly far removed from the living. In battle, where the demands of action are insistent, the process is, if possible, even more speeded up.

This morning we got word early that we had been selected as the group to enter Rome. . . . Everywhere was the picture of an Army pursuing another, ruined tanks and vehicles of all sorts, houses burned, everything hastily done. The sight of the dead soldiers did not trouble me as much as I had expected. They seemed almost part of the general wreckage, and one found it hard to believe that they had ever been alive, much less a few hours ago.

In mortal danger, numerous soldiers enter into a dazed condition in which all sharpness of consciousness is lost. When in this state, they can be caught up into the fire of communal ecstasy and forget about death by losing their individuality, or they can function like cells in a military organism, doing what is expected of them because it has become automatic. It is astonishing how much of the business of warfare can still be carried on by men who act as automatons, behaving almost as mechanically as the machines they operate.

Most of us remember with a shudder those endless pictures of Hitler's troops, before World War II, riding into one conquered country after another. They were frightening because they not only looked identical in clothing and equipment, but the set expression on their faces appeared to be vacant and purposeless. All humanity had eroded from those faces, so it seemed, and we were confronted by deadly efficient robots who were controlled by a powerful, inhuman will. So it often is in combat itself. Death comes to thousands who are only minimally conscious and snatches them away from life without their awareness of the moment or its significance.

There are two things that promote this drugged state so common in combat: training and fatigue. The routine of military life, the repetition, drill, and uniformity of response, works to dampen and dull any individual intensity of awareness. Even the civilian soldier who finds the military way quite alien and strange can learn to hold fast to the few simple rules, to be a proper cog in the vast machine, and to suspend thoughts that might unfit him for his appointed mission. He learns to expect orders from above and to pass them along to those under his control. Thinking tends to become not only painful but more and more unnecessary.

To be sure, battle often presents the soldier with novelty, demanding initiative, for which he has been unprepared. But this, too, distracts him from thought of death. He is much too busy trying to fit the novel situation into the well-worn patterns of response he has been practicing for many months or years. What does his commander expect of him in this unprecedented situation? Should he advance, stay where he is, or retreat? His mind becomes so preoccupied with the mechanics of action that larger issues never enter, and self-awareness is dimmed to the vanishing point. This is as true of the general as it is of the private soldier, perhaps more true of the general, to whom the battle must conform to some pattern of his long training in strategy and tactics. A psychologist would probably insist that this absorption with routine and details was the mind's escape from its fear of extinction. If so, the escape is usually effective.

The second hindrance to realization of death's imminence is the physical weariness that is usually precedent to any engagement in battle. Loss of sleep, long marches, cold food, and the nervous tension that the destruction common to forward areas evokes combine to exhaust the combat soldier. This weariness can go beyond borders that most of us ever know at other periods in our lives. It alone can so stupefy the senses that soldiers behave like sleepwalkers. Continued over a period of time, such exhaustion can induce men to welcome death as a rest and a change from what they have been doing. I wrote in my journal of my own feeling after hard, bitter months:

The days pass and I become duller of mind and tireder of the war. The way is long and sometimes I question the wisdom of it all, of continuing to live. There may be a real purpose in it all, which is perceived only at the end of the journey. Somehow I feel that is true.

This is part of the unromantic answer to the question how young men can face nearly certain death in war. It comes as a relief from what they are doing. Death appears to be rest; it is quiet, sleep, and even the most stupefied can gain some appreciation of what that means.

I have seen exhausted soldiers sleeping while exposed to the greatest danger of death. It might be said that these soldiers had won some positive relationship to death in conceiving it as sleep and rest. But in most cases, I think, this would be going too far. Men overcome by weariness are not really relating death to rest or sleep; they have simply an overwhelming feeling that change is a necessity and death is a change. Their aversion to the incomprehensible state of death has not been altered, as a few hours' rest makes clear. It has only been superseded by physical need of the most insistent kind.

Yet these explanations do not account completely for the large percentage of soldiers who die in war without being able to face death or gain any relationship to it save one of horror and aversion. The dazed consciousness must have other sources as well. In part it is also due, I believe, to the fear of pain and mutilation which bullets and shrapnel can bring. Pain is something very real in the memories of everyone, as death is not, and most combat soldiers have witnessed enough gaping wounds and listened to the agonized cries of the wounded often enough so that they cannot consciously endure the thought of the same thing happening to them. Though the dread of death may be at the bottom of conscious processes at such moments, the fear of being painfully injured is much in the foreground. This fear dulls self-awareness as effectively as fatigue and routine can and has a more lasting influence. Fear can prey on the mind to the point where it makes a soldier unfit for combat. Usually it rises just high enough to prevent reason, and with it the detachment of self-consciousness, from governing.

Above all, this stupefaction of consciousness is doubtless a function of the total environment of war. To some extent it afflicts everyone much of the time. After a few months in the combat zone, I, at least, found it hard indeed to believe in any other reality than war or to contrast it with any other state.

Sometimes I am overcome with the desire to go off by myself and live in a hermitage. I cannot face the prospect of going back to any of my old haunts after the war. I shall not want to speak of these war years, and I cannot be as I was. What is left? One does not want to die and cannot live as he would.

The past had grown so distant and unreal that another way of life was hard to imagine. The realization of oneself and the objective conditions of one's life can come in wartime with piercing intensity and unforgettable clarity. But the environment of violence and hatred commonly insulates us against revelations of ourselves by making any break-through to consciousness doubly difficult.

If the majority of soldiers gain no positive relationship to death, there are others who do, and the relationships are of numerous kinds, from the more abstract and conventional to the concrete and personal. There is a type of soldier who considers death very real for others but without power over him. These soldiers cherish the conviction that they are mysteriously impervious to spattering bullets and exploding shells. The little spot of ground on which they stand is rendered secure by their standing on it. Death is an impersonal force that can rob other men of their motion and their powers, but for them it has no body or substance at all. Some soldiers even manage to get through a long war with this conviction unimpaired. It is a conviction that is responsible for much rashness in battle, misnamed courage. Since such soldiers are freed from anxiety, they are frequently able to see the ridiculous and amusing aspects of combat life and provide much priceless cheer and humor for their comrades.

Fortunate is the unit that can count one or more of these soldiers in its ranks; and in fact most units do appear to contain them. They are a perennial phenomenon in war, a cause of wonder and admiration, as though their like had never been. Sometimes they become the subject of war tales, which quickly take on mythlike proportions. If such soldiers command men, as frequently happens, they have the capacity to inspire their troops to deeds of recklessness and self-sacrifice.

In most of these soldiers, the source of their relationship toward death—as a reality for others only—is not too difficult to discover. They have simply preserved their childish illusion that they are the center of the world and are therefore immortal. Their ego is incredibly naive and their self-confidence absurd to anyone who is capable of regarding them coldly. Civilian life contains many such naive egoists, I am convinced, but the presence of danger and the seemingly arbitrary fortunes of war weaken the illusion of indestructibility in most delayed adolescents. In others, stronger shocks are required. Until a drastic occurrence touches them closely, they preserve their fantastic faith. Perhaps their own wounding is necessary. The look of shock and outrage on such a soldier's face when that happens is likely to be unforgettable. At one cruel stroke he loses forever the faith in his physical immortality. His psychological adjustment to the new world he has to inhabit is certain to be harder than the physical recovery from his wounds. Most of us learn when we are younger, at home and gradually, to accept the sad truth that the world does not revolve around us. Even then the discovery is not easy or simple. At the front or in a field hospital, this truth is disillusioning in the extreme. The soldier who learns it there will never be the same again.

Sometimes he becomes a cynic, his former humor and lightheartedness utterly corroded by a lost trust in the world he inhabits. He may also become a coward, with blanching fear of all danger, a man henceforth useless to his military unit. . . .

. . . But in some few men the illusion of indestructibility is occasioned by deeper causes than deficient imagination or delayed adolescence. It is a function of an indomitable will to power which refuses to recognize ordinary mortality. Such men have a fanatic faith in their destiny which is only strengthened by narrow escapes and the sight of death in manifold forms. They are commonly leaders and win recognition as fearless warriors whose iron nerves and will to victory are out of all proportion to those of other men. We know these exceptional persons from the pages of military history, and perhaps many of us have seen their smaller counterparts in our own ranks. Nothing but their own death will rob them of their illusion, and it is one of the mysteries of combat that they so rarely get killed. Little do they have to recommend them as friends or comrades. As a rule, they are vain and empty, contemptuous of all who are not like themselves. Battle appears to be their very element, and in that element men will not hesitate to pay them homage. Nevertheless, it is not courage they display, not the human will triumphing over fate. If their vitality and their will are admirable in themselves, there is little that is specifically human about their whole mentality. They hardly recognize other men as such and are capable of walking over bodies, living or dead, without a qualm. In their secret hearts they despise friend and foe equally, these supreme egoists. If nature brought many such forth, the world would be more of a shambles after warfare than it customarily is. . . .

An opposite relation to death is possibly more prevalent among soldiers in modern wars and more understandable to Americans in general, even if scorned. Here death is an intimate and repugnant enemy before whose threat and presence one can only flee in terror. There are soldiers in nearly every unit who can endure every hardship and humiliation of military life without flinching, yet cannot face personal danger with any composure at all. Such soldiers feel that all bullets are intended for them and every shell likely to land on the particular spot they have selected as temporary shelter. Insatiable death lurks everywhere ready to pounce upon them, and every one of his victims they see makes them the more certain they will be the next one. These soldiers are quickly found out in combat and become the butt of their comrades' ridicule and contempt. There is a peculiar derogation in the epithet "coward" in wartime, for war of course glorifies courage above all other virtues. Hence the men who are unable to face the prospect of death without terror are so branded and must endure, at least in military service, insults and contumely of every sort. Few people ask why the coward fears death excessively or seek to understand the complex motives underlying his relation to the world or to death. In inquiring into his relation toward death as one of unreasoning terror on the part of the soldier-coward, I want to emphasize that the term "coward" is used in a more restrictive sense than is commonly done.

It is necessary to distinguish the person who is an occasional coward in the face of death from the constitutional coward. In almost everyone at times, there is a coward lurking. The literature of war is replete with instances of elite troops seized with panic fear, of the bravest soldiers fleeing in terror at some time in their career. Cowardice in this sense is, like rashness, a group phenomenon and greatly contagious. When the individual is caught unprepared, he becomes a victim of the mass will, which overflows him and sweeps him away. Students of mass psychology believe they know when and under what conditions the individual is likely to respond to these mass emotions. Commanders of troops can never be sure how their units will respond to the effect of surprise or close-contact fighting. But the constitutional coward hardly surprises anyone; he simply cannot endure combat when personal danger becomes acute.

Under peaceful conditions, this excessive fear of death might remain unknown, even to the coward himself, and after a war the coward is quite capable of concealing or forgetting it for the further duration of his life. Cowardice, like courage, is a complex quality, and it does not follow that an excessive fear of death always colors all other relations a coward sustains to life. In fact, the coward may be a good citizen, a considerate husband and father, a successful legionnaire. In most respects he is likely to be a more pleasing peacetime companion than the man who believes himself indestructible.

As moral courage is distinguishable from physical courage, a man being capable of possessing the one without the other, so physical cowardice is different from moral cowardice. Civilian life seldom gives men opportunity to test their capacity to face death. Doubtless there are thousands who have no idea whether they are cowards in the military sense. Only when they come to their deathbed will their fortitude or lack of it be revealed to themselves, and even there it may be hidden because we have learned well how to avoid the issue through the art and science of medicine.

The coward in battle, however, dies a thousand deaths, as the proverb has it, and each one is mentally painful beyond measure. Actually, of course, his physical death is more likely than is that of the courageous soldier, for he cannot remain still. Continually he suffers the illusion that another piece of earth is more secure than the one he presently inhabits. Even his sleep is troubled, since he follows in his unconscious mind the sound of incoming or outgoing shells. The slightest change in direction or distance of firing is sufficient to wake him and cause him to seek a presumably safer spot elsewhere. . . .

If the majority of American soldiers find it impossible to attain any other relation to death than that of rejection or negation, we should not hastily conclude that a positive and acceptive relation is evidence of an unnatural or deviant mentality. There are soldiers in the Anglo-Saxon world and perhaps more in Teutonic and Slavic lands, to say nothing of the Orient, for whom death is a fulfillment. Unless we try to understand the motivation of this kind of soldier, we can make no claim to grasping the full nature of *Homo furens*.

Here again, however, it is impossible to treat the genus and disregard the numerous species. Not all soldiers who find fulfillment in death seek the same kind of fulfillment, and their motivations are frequently very diverse. For some, death is only a *means* to fulfillment. Thus it is, for example, with the soldier who sacrifices his life willingly out of love for his country or for a glorified leader or for an ideal like fascism or communism. Such a soldier can enter into death in self-forgetfulness and treat it merely as an incident in comparison with the reality that fills his being. He uses death as a means by which to prove his love and devotion to something beyond himself. Death is welcomed not for itself, but as a sign of his utter faithfulness. Some leaders can call forth in their men this unbounded eagerness to die for them. The simple soldier who obeys such an impulse to self-sacrifice feels in an irrational way that his leader will be mightily satisfied with him for so doing. Any wrath his leader may nurse at a perverse turn of events will be appeased by this act of selflessness. A soldier like this steps into death, as it were, with his eyes fixed elsewhere. He has not thought much or at all about what it is like to be dead or what dying signifies, because he is overcome by enthusiasm for some living ideal or person sufficient to render his own independent existence of lesser value.

For the deeply religious soldier, on the other hand, death can be a fulfillment in a very different sense from self-sacrifice. If he chances to be a follower of those religions that teach eternal life, then physical death is a portal for him to a greater and immeasurably happier life beyond. Though the numbers of such soldiers have decreased markedly in our century, we should not forget that thousands of them still take part in every major war. I was, in fact, astonished to find how many of the farewell letters written by those condemned for the unsuccessful attempt on Hitler's life in 1944 were pervaded by faith in a life to come. Sometimes this is a minimal faith, a forlorn hope, but there can be little doubt that many soldiers cherish it still. The genuinely other-worldly consciousness, so much scorned as an escape in recent times, is increasingly misunderstood by people who take little time for reflection. Their customary charge that the hope of life after death is camouflaged egotism and vanity applies only to those who attempt to use religious faith rather than be used by it.

For the soldier who is not a foxhole convert to faith, death is something other than a barrier placed between him and the painless life on the other side. On the contrary, genuine otherworldliness regards death as an enemy only so long as the individual has not discovered his purpose in being alive, for reaching the goal is no simple process of stepping over a dark threshold. Death is, instead, a power on earth to be overcome; it is a last great obstacle and a necessary trial for the pilgrim on life's way. In the end it will prove, of course, to be a veil of illusion to the faithful one, but he must overcome the world to learn this secret. His proper posture will be to meet death face-to-face and gain the assurance that the closer he comes the more peaceful and indeed joyous his journey. If anyone doubts that such people can confront death with serenity and cheer, let him read the communications of true believers condemned to die and awaiting execution. Their one concern is commonly those who are left behind without the calm and peace that they, the condemned, have won.

Perhaps I can state this otherworldly relation to death in more concrete form. Death is a fulfillment, not in the sense of a consummation, but as the final triumph of the spirit over the forces that would hinder it from life everlasting. There are, to be sure, some kinds of otherworldliness that conceive of trials continuing after death, when the soul is in purgatory, but there any aid it receives must be external to it and not something that the soul can itself accomplish. Rather than being a barrier between me and true bliss, death is the path that brings me there when I have learned to tread it. Christian and non-Christian otherworldliness are at one in teaching that life is a process of overcoming the natural and instinctive. A rebirth is required, a change in direction which is radical, to the point where life will not be considered any longer as self-sustaining or self-explanatory, but, rather, as a gift that is redeemable by the giver at any moment under any condition. Those who are born again to the spirit, as the Christian puts it, regard death as that part of life which does not belong to one's essence. . . .

. . . Occasionally on the battlefield one is haunted by the face of a dead soldier on which there is stamped a kind of unearthly serenity. I remember a handsome young German soldier, near the end of World War II, who had been hanged by the SS troops, possibly because he wanted to surrender a few hours earlier than they. His body was swaying in the breeze beneath a tree along the road on which my jeep was traveling. I stopped and cut the rope that held him. As his body fell to the earth, face upward, my gaze was caught and held for some minutes by the expression on his regular features. Seldom have I seen a look of greater inner happiness on a human face, dead or alive. It was hard to understand how he could have maintained such an expression, for his executioners had hardly granted him the mercy of a broken neck. He had no other wound, and everything about his person and uniform was in perfect order.

I could not rid myself of the conviction that, despite his youth and the approaching end of hostilities, he had suffered gladly this death by execution at the hands of his own people. If in this particular case it is a supposition that cannot be confirmed, we do have evidence of other German soldiers who voluntarily escaped torments of conscience in Hitler's war through death brought about by his hired killers. The perceptive among them knew well enough that dying does not erase guilt, but they also knew that it is the most that conscience and religious faith can demand in situations where more appropriate atonement is not available. We need be under no illusions that only enemy nationals sought similar means of atonement, though the number in any army is not great. . . .

Suggested Readings

Hart, Adrian Liddell, ed. *The Sword and the Pen: Selections from the World's Greatest Military Writings*. New York: Crowell, 1976.

Keegan, John. *The Face of Battle*. New York: Viking, 1976.

Marshall, S.L.A. *Men Against Fire*. New York: Morrow, 1947.

Moran, Lord. *The Anatomy of Courage*. London: Constable, 1945.

Selwyn, Victor. *Poems of the Second World War*. London: Dent, 1985.

Reading 11

THE IMPACT OF BASIC COMBAT TRAINING

By John H. Faris

Notes from the Editors

In 1969, sociologist John H. Faris went through basic and advanced infantry training and came into contact with that legendary tyrannical figure, the drill instructor. Looking back at his own experiences, as well as research interviews in the following years, Faris examines the role of the drill sergeant, perhaps the most important cog in the military socialization process for young recruits.

His most surprising finding is that the drill sergeant, who appears as a shouting, dictatorial, tough leader, is often admired, liked, and even loved by the people he seems to abuse. Faris explains this apparent paradox by examining how basic training procedures socialize the recruit and then, in more detail, how the sergeant fits into that socialization process.

For most soldiers, the drill sergeant serves as a role model and as a dedicated and caring father figure. That role is carefully choreographed, albeit implicitly and subconsciously. The drill sergeant changes his behavior and attitudes as the recruits move through the basic training process. In most armies, most recruits ultimately "graduate" from basic training. The drill sergeant helps to create the illusion that it is harder to get through the process than it actually is.

Faris' article helps us understand how civilians are turned into soldiers and especially how basic training, a process common to all armies, socializes young people into the military system.

In January 1974 a high-ranking officer at an Army basic training center recounted the following incident in an interview: A graduation ceremony, normally held on the parade field, was shifted to an auditorium. When a noncommissioned officer was presented with the "Drill Sergeant of the Training Cycle" award, the graduating company cheered and applauded with great enthusiasm. The officer expressed much surprise at this apparently genuine and spontaneous display of positive affect. (It is supposed that the indoor setting, being more anonymous and less formal than the parade ground, was less inhibiting.) The fact that the officer was surprised is interesting in itself. Strong feelings of affection for their drill sergeants are very common in trainees, particularly toward the end of training. In a sample of 107 trainees interviewed over a 1-1/2-year period, 91% responded to the question, "What do you think of your drill sergeant?" in a positive way. (None were unqualifiedly negative; the rest were mixed.)

Reprinted by permission of the author from *The Social Psychology of Military Service*, edited by Nancy L. Goldman and David R. Segal (Beverly Hills, Calif.: Sage Publishing Co., 1976), pp. 13–22.

Comments such as "He's nice," "He's a great man," and "I love him, oh boy, do I love my drill sergeant" were frequent.

The officer's surprise is understandable. Drill sergeants are thought to be, and are, the source of much unpleasantness for recruits. What is comparably surprising is that not only do most trainees come to like their drill sergeant, but most trainees also have similar feelings about the Army at a time when hardships of Army life are at their peak and privileges are fewest. When asked, in the final week of training, "What do you think of the Army?" 72% responded positively and 11% negatively (remainder mixed). Comments such as "It's really together" and "I love it" were frequent. The findings that most trainees like their drill sergeant and the Army are important in light of the nature of basic training and the criticality of manpower considerations in the all-volunteer situation. This paper suggests that the explanation of the second finding (trainees' orientation to the Army) can be found in the explanation of the first (their feelings toward the drill sergeant) and that an examination of these findings can shed light on the nature of socialization into the all-volunteer ground forces.

Socialization in Basic Training

Although basic combat training is an extraordinary experience, it has been an integral part of our culture. Most men of military age have a father or brother or uncle who has experienced basic training, and dramatic depictions occur with some frequency in movies and television, along with some news documentaries. Most trainees, whether conscripts or volunteers, approach the rite of passage with trepidation. There are several features of basic training which make it extraordinary and which have persisted through the years and appear in much the same form from one post to another.

First, there is at least initially a disparagement of civilian status, which takes the form of degradation and humiliation on both the group and individual levels. Soldiers who have been to college are ridiculed as stupid for not knowing how to fasten an Army belt buckle; an entire platoon is made to feel clumsy for not being able to march as a unit. Unflattering haircuts and glaringly new, ill-fitting uniforms reduce personal dignity. The trainee's fear of authority and his ignorance of what is and what is not a legitimate order (one trainee with a high, thin voice was ordered to chew tobacco) are imposed upon to make the novice look and feel silly.

Second, basic training is characterized by extreme isolation from civilian society on the one hand and an almost complete lack of privacy from other trainees on the other. Contact with friends and relatives is much reduced, while at the same time it is almost impossible to be alone. In many basic-training barracks there are no partitions between the toilets. This is a feature of the experience with which many trainees have difficulty.

Third, much of the evaluation of performance in basic training is done at the group level rather than on the individual level. This collective evaluation (or "group punishment"—which neglects positive reinforcement on a unit basis) violates the trainee's sense of justice. For example, an entire platoon may have passes withheld because the floor under one bunk—the responsibility of one individual—was inadequately swept. This system is the source of many of the strongest complaints (though a minority of trainees perceive the function of such an approach—to develop teamwork and solidarity).

Fourth, basic combat training includes an emphasis on masculinity and aggressiveness. Expressed attitudes toward women are utilitarian and unromantic and tend to reinforce a sense of male superiority. Closely related is a high value on aggressiveness (within the appropriate context—fighting, for example, is rarely tolerated). Trainees are required to growl and scream in a savage manner, to roar "kill" (the "spirit of the bayonet") at bayonet training, and to shout rather than speak in reply to a drill sergeant. The emphasis on masculine toughness combined with the threat of being labeled feminine (in a very derogatory fashion) is traumatic for insecure trainees.

Finally, basic training is designed to place the trainee under various forms of stress, both physical and psychological. While some trainees are in better physical condition than others, mechanisms exist so that almost all experience stress. The stronger trainees may be required to carry an extra 25 pounds of machine gun or radio on a speed march. Trainees doing calisthenics are not allowed to look at one another so they can locate a group norm; therefore, each trainee may be required to do his own personal maximum of pushups. There are other forms of physical stress— hunger, thirst (in field training), and sleep deprivation. (Sex deprivation is not a particularly frequent complaint. It is plausible that other forms of stress reduce the sex drive, which may account for the persistent rumor that the mess hall food contains saltpeter.)

Psychological stress has a number of sources. Fear of failure and the companion fear of being recycled (repeating part of basic training in another company) are among the most severe types of psychological stress, especially for marginal soldiers. Psychological stress is also generated intentionally by arbitrary and sometimes conflicting demands. One drill sergeant said in an interview that he would see to it that his platoon, which had been doing very well, "won't be able to do anything right tomorrow."

The above characteristics would seem to make basic combat training a highly negative experience, and certainly they are often perceived as negative by the trainees. How, then, can we account for the finding that most trainees respond positively both to the institution which has provided them with this experience and to the drill sergeants who in most cases are the direct perpetrators of these negative experiences? The remainder of this paper will deal with how the drill sergeant manages this transformation.

Characteristics of the Drill Sergeant's Role

The career drill sergeant is a highly skilled manager of small groups. . . . A drill sergeant said in one interview:

Say I have a man with a bad attitude, doesn't care about soldiering. I put him on barracks detail for a few days, just keep him apart, and soon he's begging me to let him return to training. It's like this. Do you like parades? No, of course not. Nobody likes to go on parade. But how would you feel if someone told you that you're the only one who can't *go on parade, how'd you feel? See?*

Some drill sergeants are better able to articulate their knowledge than others, but almost all possess a variety of important skills and attributes which either are acquired through long experience and the inherited tradition or are possessed as a criterion for selection to this duty. These are as follows:

1. *The drill sergeant as role model.* In a situation where military values are preeminent and the status and achievement of the new trainee are minimal, the drill sergeant presents the image of the ideal soldier. In dramatic contrast to the trainee, the drill sergeant is competent (he has mastered all the skills required of the trainee), assured, tough, ascetic, and attractive—his uniform is usually immaculate, from well-brushed campaign hat to glistening black boots. He is obviously a military leader and is likely to wear the badge of the combat veteran. If the trainee accepts the values of the military (and most do, at least temporarily and provisionally), there is no more appropriate or accessible standard for the enlisted man to aspire to than the drill sergeant. Not surprisingly then, quite a few trainees (36 out of 144, or 25%, in a sample drawn in 1968) form the ambition of someday becoming a drill sergeant. (Almost certainly a major factor in the disenchantment with the Army that frequently occurs after basic training is the disparity between the quality of leadership provided by drill sergeants and that supplied by NCOs and officers in the rest of the Army. But it would be an error to attribute this disenchantment solely to leadership.)

2. *The drill sergeant as a father figure.* Many of the senior drill sergeants are in fact old enough to be the trainees' father. Drill sergeants often take a very paternalistic orientation toward trainees, particularly when dealing with them on an individual basis—helping with learning a skill or counseling a soldier with problems. Not infrequently the drill sergeant uses "son" instead of "you," "trainee," "shithead," and other appellations common in other situations. Trainees often come to view their drill sergeant as a substitute father and almost invariably prefer the older, experienced drill sergeant to his younger assistant (who is often virtually the same age as the trainees).

3. *The drill sergeant as dedicated and caring.* Drill sergeants put in long hours, often as long as the trainees—from 5 A.M. or so to 9 P.M. or, when there is night training, midnight or later. (As a consequence, drill sergeants tend to have unstable marriages.) While, obviously, drill sergeants are not deprived as trainees are, they often do share hardships—they participate in the speed marches, sleep in the woods on bivouacs, etc. Drill sergeants frequently go out of their way to help a trainee with a problem. A captain told of one of his drill sergeants who for more than 3 hours on his day off worked on the family car of a trainee who was being visited.

4. *The drill sergeant's situational role shifts.* The drill sergeant's orientation in the formal situation of the parade field or company-level training is markedly different from what it is in relatively less formal platoon training, meetings inside the barracks, and individual counseling. As a result, most trainees think that their platoon's drill sergeant is the best in the company, since they have never seen

the other drill sergeants in the less formal situations. Similarly, drill sergeants are much more formal and autocratic in "garrison life" and in routine training than they are in field training, particularly in overnight bivouacs and tactical maneuvers. Their manner in the latter situations suggests that this is what the Army is really about, and this impression and the accompanying sense of comradeship are reinforced by the drill sergeant's leaving behind his campaign hat (his peculiarly distinctive symbol) and wearing a steel helmet and pack like the trainees. One otherwise very unapproachable drill sergeant allowed himself to be called "Sarge" in the field. When the company returned to barracks he reverted to a despot.

5. *The drill sergeant's role-shifts over time.* As trainees begin to leave behind their civilian attachments, develop their own solidarity, master the soldier's skills, and adopt the values of the military, the drill sergeant comes to treat them, not as equals, but as worthy of eventual acceptance into the status of soldiers. There is increased relaxation and approval. One of the elements of this process, the use of humor, is important enough to be examined in depth.

Most drill sergeants use humor with great effectiveness. The first form in which this appears is ridicule, part of the degradation process. At this stage, when the trainees as a collectivity (not yet a group) are the target, it is not intended or perceived as humorous, though the form is humor. When an individual trainee is the target, the other trainees are often not permitted to engage in laughter or join in the ridicule. They are not allowed to imply that they are in a different category from the unfortunate victim.

The first time our drill sergeant met the platoon was the morning after our haircuts. We stood rigidly in what we thought was the position of attention. He stalked silently through the ranks, examining us for a few minutes. Finally, "Where's my two hippies?" Silence. "All right now, Goddammit, where's my hippies? They told me I had two longhairs." After a long and uncomfortable silence Private W. said, "I had long hair, sir." "Sir? Sir! Don't call me sir, Goddammit, I work for a living. What are you, a sissy? What d' you wanta wear that bebop hair for?" And so on, inches away from W.'s face, amidst our silent gratitude and pity.

The effectiveness of ridicule is in part dependent on the nature of the platoon at this stage. Trainees are almost complete strangers to one another, although within hours most begin to develop friendships with a bunkmate or two. The group is atomized and offers little defense to the assault of initial socialization.

Before many days, though, a wider and deeper solidarity emerges. There is a development of trainee humor both as a defense against the drill sergeants and basic training and as a means of reinforcing solidarity. A jocular griping, often coarse in form, is widespread in basic training. Some standard gripes become institutionalized— creamed beef on toast is known universally as "shit on a shingle."

Another example of the cohesion-producing function of humor is provided by Obrdlik (1943). His discussion of the gallows humor of Nazi-occupied Czechoslovakia emphasizes the importance of this humor for social control and morale.

These people have to persuade themselves as well as others that their present suffering is only temporary, that it will soon be all over, that once again they will live as they used to live before they were crushed.

Obrdlik also points out that gallows humor can be aggressive and can undermine the morale of oppressors. In basic training this can threaten the position of the drill sergeant. An inexperienced and insecure officer is particularly vulnerable, as this account of a young officer with his first command shows. The officer had sympathetically rescinded the formal reprimand of a soldier whose rifle was dirty and then had overheard that same man laughing in the barracks.

I moved on a few steps. All right, he had made a quick recovery. But was relieved. There was nothing in that. but he had seemed really upset in the armoury, shaken, as Cormack said. Now he was roaring his head off—the quality of laughter somehow caught the edge of my nerves. I stood undecided, and then wheeled around and shouted:

"Sergeant Telfer!"

He came out of his room. "Yessir?"

"Sergeant Telfer," I said, "stop that man laughing."

He gaped at me. "Laughing, sir?"

"Yes, laughing. Tell him to stop it—now."

"But . . ." he looked bewildered. "But . . . he's just laughin' sir . . ."

"I know he's just laughing. He's braying his bloody head off. Tell him to stop it."

"Right, sir." He obviously thought the sun had got me, but he strode into the barrackroom. Abruptly, Leishman's laughter stopped, then there was what might have been a smothered chuckle, then silence.

Feeling suicidal, I went back to my billet. Obviously, Leishman had thought I was a mug; I should have let the charge stick. Let someone get away with it, even a good soldier, and you have taken some of his virtue away. On the other hand, maybe he had been laughing about something else entirely; in that case, I had been an idiot to give Sergeant Telfer that ridiculous order. Either way, I looked a fool. And my Service dress didn't fit. To hell with it. I would see the adjutant tomorrow and ask for a posting.

But even the experienced trainer is not immune to an extraordinary assault, as indicated by this account by T.E. Lawrence of his basic training experience in the RAF under the assumed name of Ross. A fellow recruit, Sailor, comments to Lawrence:

"But, mate, you let the flight down, when he takes the mike out of you every time. Give the ignorant shit-bag a—— great gob of your toffology."

Next day, in the first stand-at-ease of his first period:— "Short-arse you there, Ross, what's your bleedin' monaker:—what d' you know?" Such nonplussing questions are Poulton's favorite gambit for a hazing. Spring to attention. "Sergeant," I dutifully intone. He wouldn't stop. "I asked you a question, you little——." But I am not tired at this time of day: by Sailor's advice of priggery I made to drawl out "Well, Sergeant, specifically of course we can know nothing—unqualified—but like the rest of us, I've fenced my life with a scaffolding of more or less speculative hypotheses."

The rear rank deflated appreciatively. The tired sounding, like the wind in wet trees. The Sergeant stared; then whispered to himself "Jesus——Christ." At that Sailor let out a high, sudden, singing laugh. "Flight. Attention" Poulton yelled, and the drill went forward, gingerly. "My Christ" exulted James, thumping my back later, in the hut's safety, "The silly——didn't know whether his——was bored, punched, drilled or countersunk."

Drill sergeants anticipate, preempt, and transform this process by gradually shifting from ridicule to a joking relationship. There emerges, too, the use of banter. Thus the drill sergeant manages two statuses—the superordinate noncommissioned officer socializing agent and the prospective fellow soldier and comrade-at-arms.

Banter may be verbal or may exist in the ludicrous character of a situation.

One of the men in my squad was caught with a candy bar in his laundry bag, strictly forbidden. The drill sergeant inquired, "Who's your squad leader?" He then took the candy bar, mashed it with his heel in the dirt, and directed me to put it in my pants pocket and keep it there for the rest of the day. It was a hot summer day.

One day, returning on a bus from successful training, M., a black trainee, asked the drill sergeant when he could come over to his house for dinner. The drill sergeant said that he was from Tennessee and that M. didn't have enough money to get through his front door. M. said, "C'mon Drill Sergeant, I got enough money to burn a wet elephant." All of this was in high good humor, much appreciated by the rest of the platoon.

The essential element of this joking relationship is that it requires the cooperation of the trainees. Daniels and Daniels (1964) have indicated the importance of the role of the good-natured fool in providing the focal point for the joking relationship between the drill sergeant and the trainee group.

The function of the fool as a social type makes a dramatic contrast to the sick role in basic training as described by Schneider (1953:396).

The sick role develops first as a group-sanctioned behavior, focusing the resentment of the group against the army, providing a cause celebre *for aggression against the army. But the group sanction lasts only until the group has begun to make its adjustment to aborted affectional needs, heightened masculinity demands, and brotherlike relationships. When the group begins to make its adjustment, its need for rationalization of its aggression against the army diminishes, so that it no longer supports the sick in their role. At this time the divorce between the sick and the group takes place, and the sick find themselves isolated from the group.*

This provides the limiting case to the proposition of Dentler and Erikson (1959) that cohesion forms around deviance.

The joking relationship that develops between trainees and drill sergeant is constrained by bounds. It is appropriate in some situations (riding on a bus) and unthinkable in others (inspection in ranks). Some topics, being sacred, are not permissible for joking—e.g., the drill sergeant's dignity:

After joking about dinner at the drill sergeant's house, M. made some joking remark about the drill sergeant's Smokey-the-Bear hat. This was greeted with great laughter by the platoon and provoked a threat by the drill sergeant to put us all to cleaning the mess hall grease trap with a spoon. The rest of the bus trip was in nervous silence.

There are sacred topics for trainees as well. A drill sergeant's question about the sex life of a married trainee met such stony resistance that the subject was dropped.

The skillful use of humor as a socialization mechanism is an important factor in effecting the transformation from a cohesive group with oppositional tendencies to an accommodation with and adoption of the values of the institution, while retaining the distinctions between the status of the private recruit and the veteran NCO. It is a form of seduction.

6. *Drill sergeants as perpetrators of an illusion.* Drill sergeants perform a sort of magic act which manages a serious contradiction—that between the threat of failure and the challenge of basic training, on the one hand, and the reality that almost everyone succeeds, on the other. While many trainees fear being recycled, only a few are (1–3%) and usually as a result of serious injury or illness. Failure on the comprehensive test at the end of basic training (especially since the test was made more rigorous in 1972) is a very real possibility; often fewer than 20% pass on the first administration. But almost everyone passes the second time, and virtually all the rest are "pushed through" even if it takes one or two more tries. This situation results in role strain for the drill sergeant. The organizational demand for high success rates in a situation of scarce manpower conflicts with his professional norms—that only a well-trained soldier should be permitted to graduate. Drill sergeants complain that they have to cajole, and even bribe, examiners to let the hopeless cases through. But this is the extreme case. In any event, drill sergeants must create the perception that basic training is an extraordinary challenge, one which will set the graduates apart from others, in face of the fact that almost everyone succeeds. The fact that most trainees begin to discover this is indicated by the frequent comments toward the end of training that they wish it had been tougher. When pressed further, though, they usually admit that at the time it seemed hard enough. . . .

Suggested Readings

Booth, Richard F. and Anne Hoiberg. "Change in Marine Recruits' Attitudes Related to Recruit Characteristics and Drill Instructor's Attitudes." *Psychological Reports,* 33 (August 1973), pp. 63–71.

Coates, C.H. and R.J. Pellegrin. *Military Sociology: A Study of American Military Institutions and Military Life.* Baltimore: Social Science Press, 1965.

Hackett, Sir John. *The Profession of Arms.* London: Times Publishing Company, 1962.

Little, R.W. *A Handbook of Military Institutions.* Beverly Hills, Calif.: Sage, 1971.

Milgram, Stanley. *Obedience to Authority.* New York: Harper & Row, 1974.

Moskos, Charles C., ed. *Public Opinion and the Military Establishment.* Beverly Hills, Calif.: Sage, 1971.

CHAPTER 3

Justifying War

Having examined the extent to which international war has been a part of the human landscape and psyche over the past several centuries and how soldiers and their officers train, fight, and sometimes die, we may now shift from the "how much?" question to the "how come?" question. This latter question can, of course, be subdivided into two separate and distinct issues.

First, what factors in terms of background conditions and policy moves of nations are most regularly associated with the presence and absence of war? For example, is the international system more war prone when there are certain alliance patterns or power distributions, or when certain types of nations begin to follow new types of policies? Or, do some types of nations become more war prone at some specified times in their economic development, political cycles, or national moods?

There is an appreciable difference between trying to *explain* or account for the distribution of wars across time and space, or even to account for a single war on the one hand, and trying to *justify* a given war or group of wars. Explanation is normally an appeal to reason and intellect, whereas justification is more often an appeal to passion or ideology. Another distinction is that whereas explanation seeks to account for events in the past, justification is often used to influence the future, even when it rests on an interpretation of the past. In this case, justification begins to look like rationalization, in which the spokesperson is engaged not only in trying to delude others, but perhaps him/herself as well.

These distinctions should not be overdrawn, but are nevertheless worth keeping in mind as we examine the selections in this chapter. In them, we find a very wide range of perspectives and arguments as to why certain specific wars or classes of war are—or are not—justifiable. The criteria range, of course, from the spiritual to the pragmatic, from the parochial to the catholic, and from the immediate to the eternal. The issue has concerned, even obsessed, many humans for many centuries, and even though the new technologies of war increasingly enlarge the disparity between the potential costs and the likely benefits, it will continue to engage us well into the future. As long as large groups of people can be persuaded that their poor lot in life can be bettered—or their good fortune is in jeopardy—there will be those who are willing and able to mobilize them for armed conflict. Of course, it takes more than perceived injustice or expected depradation for war to occur. A rather complex set of conditions must also be present, and those will be addressed in Chapter 4.

Our focus here, then, is on the moral and pragmatic case for and against war, with particular attention to war between nations. As to the ethical case, we immediately come up against the familiar means-ends dilemma, and given the fervor with which people hold to a particular set of moral preferences and priorities, it tends to be a dilemma of impressive proportions.

The dilemma is especially troubling to those with strong religious beliefs. Theodore Roosevelt, president of the United States from 1901 to 1909, and prominent politician thereafter, confidently appealed to scripture to support his call to arms in 1916. For him, the Old and New Testaments offered ample support for his bellicose message in "Fear God and Take Your Own Part." Many religious thinkers today would find Roosevelt's analysis of scripture controversial. For them, the pacifist message in the Bible is hard to ignore.

Nevertheless, perplexed by the ethical, logical, and practical difficulties of classifying all war (and similar forms of armed combat) as beyond the pale, some philosophers and theologians have sought a middle position by which some types of war are outlawed, but others remain legitimate. In his 1960 article, "Ethics and War: A Catholic View," our second selection, Father Joseph McKenna interprets how his church deals with the issue of justifiable war with special reference to the Cold War. McKenna does not rule out the use of nuclear weapons to defend the "free world" although he does establish a series of conditions that have to be met before a nation would resort to that dire option.

Writing almost a quarter of a century later, in the wake of antiwar activism from that same Catholic Church, Sandra Schneiders offers "New Testament Reflections on Peace and Nuclear Arms." For her part, she finds only a pacifist message in the words of Jesus and his disciples.

Three years after the Catholic Bishops presented their pastoral letter, about which Schneiders wrote, the American Methodist Bishops offered their own statement on war in the nuclear age. "In Defense of Creation" amplifies and expands upon the Catholic position on such issues as the arms race and deterrence, appealing once again to scripture for support.

Moving away from the New Testament and theological interpretations, Michael Walzer in "The Just War," an excerpt from his *Just and Unjust Wars,* tries to define an aggressive war. For him, a resort to arms is justified in wars of self-defense. Walzer's distinction between wars fought by aggressors and wars fought by defenders is an example of the distinction between abstract principle and empirical regularity. Whereas the typical war arises out of rivalry and armed competition—resting on widespread popular support—with negligible differences between the behaviors of the protagonists, few wars are forced on a nation and its people. As a result, in most instances, it is of little moral consequence who fired the first shot.

Even more dubious than the identity of the aggressor, scientifically and ethically, is the notion of motivation. Often related to, but separable from "who hit whom first?", this distinction allegedly rests on the intentions and goals—one might even say the justifications—of the opposing side. The range of interpretations is nearly boundless as we weigh the nobility or the narrowness of each nation's war objectives.

In Thucydides' famous "Melian Debate," we are witness to a discussion between the aggressors, the Athenians, who maintain that might makes right in the real world of international relations, and the Melians, who refuse to submit, because even if the alternative is *physical* destruction and occupation, submission would lead to an alleged humiliating *spiritual* destruction of their people.

In the last selection in this chapter, Melvin Small's "National Security" looks at the war/no war decision from a realist's perspective. When is national security threatened, he asks? Under what circumstances should a citizen, weighing all the options, support a call to arms? This simple and straightforward question is much more complicated than it seems at first glance.

Most of the authorities cited in this chapter accept defensive war as legally, philosophically, or politically legitimate. The problem, of course, is that few nations have ever fought anything but defensive wars whether we are talking about Poland's "invasion" of Nazi Germany in 1939 or Finland's "invasion" of the Soviet Union in that same year. Nevertheless, the definitions of just and unjust wars, wars of aggression, and national defense could become important when and if international institutions begin to play a more significant role in maintaining collective security.

Reading 12

FEAR GOD AND TAKE YOUR OWN PART

Theodore Roosevelt

Notes from the Editors

Although he won the Nobel Prize for Peace for helping to negotiate an end to the Russo-Japanese War of 1904–1905, Theodore Roosevelt is remembered more for his bellicose nationalism. "Speak softly but carry a big stick" and "Fear God and take your own part" are the sorts of maxims one associates with "Teddy."

From August 1914 through March 1917, the United States under President Woodrow Wilson played the role of a neutral in World War I. Roosevelt, whom Wilson had defeated for the presidency in 1912, came to oppose that policy. He felt his country had to become more active in the war, supporting the allegedly righteous British and French against the evil violators of neutral rights, the Germans.

In 1914 and 1915, Roosevelt published articles in popular magazines urging his fellow citizens to reject the course of allegedly cowardly pacifism that Wilson had chosen. In the compilation of his articles, Fear God and Take Your Own Part, *he attempted to show that the Christian path was the path of vigorous self-defense against the forces of aggression and ill will in the world. He railed against the advocates of peace he felt used the Bible incorrectly to support their position. For Roosevelt, both the Old and New Testaments offered evidence that righteousness was more precious than peace. It is interesting to note that when Wilson finally took his country into war in April of 1917, he used that phrase to justify his break from neutrality and Christian pacifism.*

. . . Outside of our own borders we must treat other nations as we would wish to be treated in return, judging each in any given crisis as we ourselves ought to be judged—that is, by our conduct in that crisis. If they do ill, we show that we fear God when we sternly bear testimony against them and oppose them in any way and to whatever extent the needs require. If they do well, we must not wrong them ourselves. Finally, if we are really devoted to a lofty ideal we must in so far as our strength permits aid them if they are wronged by others. When we sit idly by while Belgium is being overwhelmed, and rolling up our eyes prattle with unctuous self-righteousness about "the duty of neutrality," we show that we do not really fear God; on the contrary, we show an odious fear of the devil, and a mean readiness to serve him.

But in addition to fearing God, it is necessary that we should be able and ready to take our own part. The man who cannot take his own part is a nuisance in the community, a source of weakness, an encouragement to wrongdoers and an added burden to the men who wish to do what is right. If he cannot take his own part, then

From *Fear God and Take Your Own Part* (New York: George H. Doran, 1916), pp. 15–29, 165–66.

somebody else has to take it for him; and this means that his weakness and cowardice and inefficiency place an added burden on some other man and make that other man's strength by just so much of less avail to the community as a whole. No man can take the part of any one else unless he is able to take his own part. This is just as true of nations as of men. A nation that cannot take its own part is at times almost as fertile a source of mischief in the world at large as is a nation which does wrong to others, for its very existence puts a premium on such wrongdoing. Therefore, a nation must fit itself to defend its honor and interest against outside aggression; and this necessarily means that in a free democracy every man fit for citizenship must be trained so that he can do his full duty to the nation in war no less than in peace.

Unless we are thorough-going Americans and unless our patriotism is part of the very fiber of our being, we can neither serve God nor take our own part. Whatever may be the case in an infinitely remote future, at present no people can render any service to humanity unless as a people they feel an intense sense of national cohesion and solidarity. The man who loves other nations as much as he does his own, stands on a par with the man who loves other women as much as he does his own wife. The United States can accomplish little for mankind, save in so far as within its borders it develops an intense spirit of Americanism. A flabby cosmopolitanism, especially if it expresses itself through a flabby pacifism, is not only silly, but degrading. It represents national emasculation. . . .

Patriotism should be an integral part of our every feeling at all times, for it is merely another name for those qualities of soul which make a man in peace or in war, by day or by night, think of his duty to his fellows, and of his duty to the nation through which their and his loftiest aspirations must find their fitting expression. After the *Lusitania* was sunk, Mr. Wilson stated in effect that such a time was not the right time to stir up patriotism. This statement is entirely incompatible with having a feeling of deep patriotism at any time. It might just as appropriately have been made by George Washington immediately after his defeat at the Brandywine, or by Abraham Lincoln immediately after the surrender of Fort Sumter; and if in either of these crises our leaders had acted on any such principle we would not now have any country at all. Patriotism is as much a duty in time of war as in time of peace, and it is most of all a duty in any and every great crisis. To commit folly or do evil, to act inconsiderately and hastily or wantonly and viciously, in the name of patriotism, represents not patriotism at all, but a use of the name to cloak an attack upon the thing. Such baseness or folly is wrong, at every time and on every occasion. But patriotism itself is not only in place on every occasion and at every time, but is peculiarly the feeling which should be stirred to its deepest depths at every serious crisis. The duty of a leader is to lead; and it is a dreadful thing that any man chosen to lead his fellow-countrymen should himself show, not merely so profound a lack of patriotism, but such misunderstanding of patriotism, as to be willing to say in a great crisis what President Wilson thus said at the time of the sinking of the *Lusitania*. This statement, coupled with his statement made about the same time as to being "too proud to fight," furnishes the clue to the Administration's policy both before and since. This policy made our great democratic commonwealth false to its duties and its ideals in a tremendous world crisis, at the very time when, if properly led, it could have rendered an inestimable service to all mankind, and could have placed itself on a higher pinnacle of worthy achievement than ever before.

Patriotism, so far from being incompatible with performance of duty to other nations, is an indispensable prerequisite to doing one's duty toward other nations. Fear God; and take your own part! If this nation had feared God it would have stood up for the Belgians and Armenians; if it had been able and willing to take its own part there would have been no murderous assault on the *Lusitania,* no outrages on our men and women in Mexico. True patriotism carries with it not hostility to other nations but a quickened sense of responsible good-will towards other nations, and good-will of acts and not merely of words. I stand for a nationalism of duty, to oneself and to others; and, therefore, for a nationalism which is a means to internationalism. World peace must rest on the willingness of nations with courage, cool foresight, and readiness for self-sacrifice to defend the fabric of international law. No nation can help in securing an organized, peaceful and justice-doing world community until it is willing to run risks and make efforts in order to secure and maintain such a community.

The nation that in actual practice fears God is the nation which does not wrong its neighbors, which does so far as possible help its neighbors, and which never promises what it cannot or will not or ought not to perform. The professional pacifists in and out of office who at peace congresses pass silly resolutions which cannot be, and ought not to be, lived up to, and enter into silly treaties which ought not to be, and cannot be, kept, are not serving God, but Baal. They are not doing anything for anybody. . . .

When Mr. Wilson and Mr. Bryan made this nation shirk its duty towards Belgium, they made us false to all our high ideals; for they acted and caused this government to act in that spirit of commercial opportunism which refuses to do duty to others unless there is in it pecuniary profit for oneself. This combination of mean timidity and mean commercial opportunism is peculiarly odious because those practising it have sought to hide it by profuse outbursts of wordy sentimentality and loud professions of attachment to impossible and undesirable ideals. One of the besetting sins of many of our public servants (and of not a few of our professional moralists, lay and clerical) is to cloak weakness or baseness of action behind insincere oratory on behalf of impractical ideals. The true servant of the people is the man who preaches realizable ideals; and who then practises what he has preached.

Moreover, even as regards the pacifists who genuinely desire that this nation should fear God, it is to be remembered that if the nation cannot take its own part, the fact that it fears God will be of no practical consequence to any one. Nobody cares whether or not the feeling of the Chinese people is against international wrongdoing; for, as China is helplessly unable to take her own part, she is in practise even more helpless to take the part of any one else and to secure justice and mercy for any one else. The pacifists who are seeking to Chinafy the United States are not only seeking to bring the United States to ruin, but are also seeking to render it absolutely impotent to help upright and well-behaved nations which are oppressed by the military power of unscrupulous neighbors of greater strength.

The professional pacifists, the leaders in the pacifist movement in the United States, do particular harm by giving well-meaning but uninformed people who do not think deeply what seems to them a convincing excuse for failure to show courage and resolution. Those who preach sloth and cowardice under the high-sounding name of "peace" give people a word with which to cloak, even to themselves, their failure to perform unpleasant duty. For a man to stand up for his own rights, or especially for the rights of somebody else, means that he must have virile qualities: courage, foresight, willingness to face risk and undergo effort. It is much easier to be timid and lazy. The average man does not like to face death and endure hardship and labor. He can be roused to do so if a leader of the right type, a Washington or Lincoln, appeals to the higher qualities, including the stern qualities, of his soul. But a leader, or at least a man who holds a leader's place, earns praise and profit unworthily if he uses his gift of words to lull well-meaning men to sleep, if he assures them that it is their duty to do the easy and selfish thing, and furnishes them high-sounding phrases with which to cover ignoble failure to perform hard and disagreeable duties.

In the 33d chapter of the great prophet Ezekiel, the first six verses run as follows:

1. Again the word of the Lord came unto me, saying:

2. Son of man, speak to the children of thy people and say unto them, When I bring the sword upon a land, if the people of the land take a man of their coasts and set him for the watchman;

3. If when he seeth the sword come upon the land, he blow the trumpet and warn the people;

4. Then whosoever heareth the sound of the trumpet and taketh not warning, if the sword come and take him away, his blood shall be upon his own head;

5. He heard the sound of the trumpet and took not warning, his blood shall be upon him. But he that taketh warning shall deliver his soul.

6. But if the watchman see the sword come and blow not the trumpet and the people be not warned; if the sword come and take any person from among them, he is taken away in his iniquity; but his blood will I require at the watchman's hand.

I very heartily commend these verses to the prayerful consideration of all those in high political office, whether Presidents, Secretaries of State, or leaders of the Senate and the House at Washington; and to all male and female college presidents, clergymen, editors and publicists of pacifist tendency; and above all to the sometimes-well-meaning souls who have fallen victims to the habit of prolonged and excessive indulgence in attending universal peace meetings and giving, and listening to, lectures on immediate universal peace and disarmament. . . .

Peace is not the end. Righteousness is the end. When the Saviour saw the money-changers in the Temple he broke the peace by driving them out. At that moment peace could have been obtained readily enough by the simple process of keeping quiet in the presence of wrong. But instead of preserving peace at the expense of righteousness, the Saviour armed himself with a scourge of cords and drove the money-changers from the Temple. Righteousness is the end, and peace a means to the end, and sometimes it is not peace, but war which is the proper means to achieve the end. Righteousness should breed valor and strength. When it does breed them, it is triumphant; and when triumphant, it necessarily brings peace. But peace does not necessarily bring righteousness. . . .

The pacifists have used all kinds of arguments in favor of peaceful submission to, or refusal to prepare against, international violence and wrongdoing, and among others the very ancient arguments based upon the supposed teaching of the New Testament against war. In the first place, as I have already pointed out, this argument is quite incompatible with accepting the lesson taught by the action of the Saviour in driving the money-changers from the Temple; not to mention, incidentally, that the duty of preparedness has rarely been put in stronger form than by St. Luke in the direction that "He that hath no sword, let him sell his garment and buy one."

In the next place, the plea is merely an instance of the adroit casuistry that can twist isolated teachings of the Gospels in any required direction. As a matter of fact, the Gospels do not deal with war at all. During the period they covered there was no war in Judea, and no question arising from the need of going to war. The precepts and teachings upon which the pacifists rely apply not to war, but to questions arising from or concerning individual and mob violence and the exercise of the internal police power. In so far as sincere and logical pacifists are concerned, they recognize this fact. There are schools of pacifists who decline to profit by the exercise of the police power, who decline to protect not merely themselves, but those dearest to them, from any form of outrage and violence. The individuals of this type are at least logical in their horror even of just war. If a man deliberately takes the view that he will not resent having his wife's face slapped, that he will not by force endeavor to save his daughter from outrage, and that he disapproves of the policeman who interferes by force to save a child kidnapped by a black-hander, or a girl run off by a white-slaver, then he is logical in objecting to war. Of course, to my mind, he occupies an unspeakably base and loathsome position, and is not fit to cumber the world—in which, as a matter of fact, he exists at all only because he is protected by the maintenance by others of the very principle which he himself repudiates and declines to share. . . .

Suggested Readings

Beale, Howard C. *Theodore Roosevelt and the Rise of America to World Power.* Baltimore: John Hopkins University, 1956.

Cooper, John Milton, Jr. *The Warrior and the Priest: Woodrow Wilson and Theodore Roosevelt.* Cambridge: Harvard University, 1983.

Devlin, Patrick. *Too Proud to Fight.* New York: Oxford University, 1975.

Marks, Frederick. *Velvet on Iron: The Diplomacy of Theodore Roosevelt.* Lincoln: University of Nebraska, 1979.

May, Ernest R. *The World War and American Isolation.* Cambridge: Harvard University, 1959.

Reading 13

ETHICS AND WAR: A CATHOLIC VIEW

Joseph C. McKenna

Notes from the Editors

Joseph C. McKenna, a Jesuit scholar, outlines the Catholic position on the just war in this article published in 1960. The church has changed its position somewhat over the past quarter century, and most recently (1983) the American Catholic Bishops' Pastoral Letter challenges some of Father McKenna's venerable theses. Moreover, the world itself has changed since 1960, and nuclear war poses different problems now than it did then. Nevertheless, Father McKenna's exposition is still an important one.

Referring to scripture and commentaries on scripture, he carefully describes the Catholic Church's traditional justifications for war. The seven points he presents can be applied to historical as well as contemporary conflicts.

Father McKenna distinguishes between his church's position and that of Protestant or humanist thought. Moreover, he demonstrates how Catholic thought on war is compatible neither with absolute pacifism nor with the Realpolitik *school. Naturally, no real-life situation is ever as clear-cut as Father McKenna's examples. Honest Catholics, as well as non-Catholics, will most likely differ on the description of a given conflict, and how they perceive their own nation's role in that conflict. Throughout the centuries, Catholic and other religious officials in contending nations have often sanctified their nation's call to arms. Few nations have ever gone to war without the support of their religious establishments.*

World War II and Cold War I have influenced the moral appraisal of diplomacy much as they have influenced all systematic analysis of international relations. Commentators are now more aware that the wide gap between what is and what ought to be cannot be nullified by exhortation or legal formula or inexorable institutional evolution. They appreciate more profoundly the structure and function of power. They have learned from Mukden, Wal-Wal and Munich that accommodation can be more costly than resoluteness, and that an ethic dissociated from the world in which men live cannot give adequate moral guidance for men's living. Nevertheless the commentators remain reluctant, on both political and moral grounds, to accept *Realpolitik's* ethical outlook on the use of force. The shortcomings of yesterday's total victory have been too sobering; and Hiroshima's destruction has left a scar upon the conscience. Moral judgments on diplomacy are accordingly less simplist, less absolute, more troubled and uneasy than in the pre-war decades.

Published with permission of the author Joseph C. McKenna, S.J., and the *American Political Science Review* from "Ethics and War: A Catholic View," *American Political Science Review* 54 (September 1960), pp. 647–58.

The moral theories that have attracted most attention among students of international politics are either Protestant Christian or secular humanist in their basic orientations. This is not to say that these orientations are clearly distinguishable in any particular statement; more or less of them can be found in Niebuhr, Wolfers, Butterfield, Lefever, and Osgood among others. Less well known is a view that can be classified as Catholic or Scholastic. In the hope that this could illuminate, if it does not modify, the problems and the answers as conceived by the better known theories, the present study will put forth such a view. The position will be stated first, with such explanation as might be needed for understanding it, and some indication of differences from the Protestant and humanist conceptions. The theory can then be applied to varying hypothetical projections of the contemporary international scene. . . .

Virtually any foreign policy problem has moral implications: travel, migration, commerce, economic aid, disaster relief, colonialism, or cooperation for social welfare. The present study will be confined to the issue of war and the threat of war.

In political terms, war or the threat of war is always an instrument of somebody's policy. It is used to persuade another people to make concessions which are less distasteful to them than the death of their soldiers, the destruction of their wealth, and the occupation of their territory. But the functional description does not convey the stark reality. The tragic finality of instant death, the lingering agony of wounded life, the mental anguish of fear and separation, and the attending train of privation, disease, dishonesty and vice—all these of massive proportions—have been left out. Nuclear war could put the death in tens of millions, deform the bodies and minds of endless generations, and leave the civilized world a charred and blackened wasteland. Normal human sensitivity shudders at this vision. Sensitivity apart, war's coercive purposes repel the humanist as an irrational invasion of man's self-determining dignity. In Christian eyes, to inflict pain on one's fellows clashes with the brotherly ideals which Christ exemplified and preached.

Horrifying though the vision be, inhumane and unchristian though war seem, some segments of mankind still find a promise of gain in the use or threat of force. As long as this is so, the other segments of mankind must deal with a temptation of their own—to cancel out coercion's promise with a menace of counter-coercion. It is this which raises the moral question: Are war and threat of war legitimate, and under what circumstances? How severe may the general be in war, or the statesman in diplomacy? An important restriction of focus in examining such questions must be noted. For all the undoubted impact of environmental interaction on social decisions, the decisions are made by men. It is consequently in the perceptions of solitary minds that the practical permissive or inhibitory influence of moral considerations on community choices must be radicated. The Scholastic moralist wishes to inform the consciences not primarily of nations, but of men.

Divine revelation does not give an unqualified answer to the question of war's legitimacy. Sacred Scripture, read piecemeal with somebody's "inner light" may sound definitive; read in context with the resources of systematic hermeneutics, it remains inconclusive. The "morality of the Sermon on the Mount" is often cited as categorically condemning all resort to force. The Sermon, however, is not all "morality." It includes counsels of perfection as well as minimal commands, ascetical as well as moral guidance. Moreover, in all literalness, it was addressed to individual persons in their individual capacities, not to social collectivities or social leaders as such. Its admonitions to turn the other cheek, to resist not evil, to give your cloak to the man who takes your tunic, and to go two miles with the fellow who makes you go one (*Mt.* 5:39-41) do not necessarily imply, therefore, that the statesman and his nation are morally obliged to sacrifice every other consideration and advantage for the sake of peace. The Sermon's advices must, in fact, be harmonized with the quite different indications which appear elsewhere in Scripture. Among these is the minatory dictum of St. Paul: "But if thou dost what is evil, fear, for not without reason does it [the public power] carry the sword. For it is God's minister, an avenger to execute wrath on him who does evil." (*Rom.* 13:4) While this is directly relevant only to internal social order, it does bestow a positive moral quality upon coercive power in official hands. The interpreter of Scripture must confront with caution, then, even the incisive prohibition in the decalogue: "Thou shalt not kill." (*Ex.* 20: 13)

Primitive Christian practices and documents can be, according to Catholic belief, an alternative expression of divine revelation. They reflect the otherwise unrecorded teaching of Christ and the apostles. But these sources are no more decisive than Sacred Scripture as to the moral warrant for war. Despite an apparent reluctance to enter the army, early Christians did serve, and some achieved distinction. The feeling among them that service was incompatible with the new religious spirit hinged not upon the martial purposes of the soldier's profession but upon the idolatrous rites often associated with military life. Origen (d. 254), St. Cyprian (d. 258), and Lactantius (d. 330) can be adduced as denouncing warfare or violence; Tertullian (d. 240) held mutually contradictory positions at different stages of his career. The witness of these men, however, is understandably fragmentary. With the Christian religion persecuted, outlawed, or ignored, formal theorizing on issues of public policy was pointless. When the Edict of Constantine and the emperor's subsequent conversion gave Christians open access to civil office, a new situation was created.

St. Augustine (d. 430) then shaped the broadest early statement on the morality of war. Briefly, this regarded force as, in some situations, justified. The Augustinian statement, despite occasional discordant comments in the Middle Ages, thenceforth remained "in possession" among Catholic thinkers. The chief landmarks in its evolution were the currency given it by Gratian (c. 1150), its distinctive clarification by St. Thomas Aquinas (d. 1274), and its detailed development by the Spanish theologians Francisco Vittoria (d. 1546) and Francisco Suarez (d. 1617). Since the statement is, however, less definitive as early Christian witness than as accepted contemporary doctrine, a complete account of its historical elaboration is not to the point here. It will be enough to set forth the position as it stands today, incorporating such modifications as have found their way into it during the past three hundred years.

In the opinion of Scholastics, both defensive and offensive war can be morally justified. Supporting argumentation differs for the two types, and the offensive variety is more severely circumscribed. Although Pauline ideas are invoked in the argument, they do not seem strictly necessary; the analysis relies more heavily on reason than on revelation.

At the core of the position is the Scholastic concept of a political society. While this concept admittedly tends to a misleading hypostasization of the state, it does convey reality in terms more meaningful than the positive law fiction of corporate personality. For it relates to the intentions of morality's divine creator rather than to the artifice of human legislators. In the Scholastic view, because a civil society is a natural entity, it is divinely instituted. God, as author of man's natural needs, aptitudes and tendencies, is also author of the social structures which are built upon them. To these social structures, of which the state is one, He has attached certain objective moral characteristics.

One moral characteristic of the state is its obligation to seek the common earthly welfare of its citizens. Linked with this is a second, its right of self-defense. If the evil could with impunity impose their will upon the innocent, social life would be reduced to chaos; for the good of its citizens, then, a state unjustly attacked by force may resist by force.

The right of self-defense is not, however, absolute. It may be exercised only if action is urgently needed and no other remedy is at hand; only so much violence is allowed as will repel the unjust aggressor; a justified attack may not be resisted at all. On these restrictions of the right, Scholastics have long agreed. But two other points have recently attracted closer attention. In an important sense, the right of self-defense is founded on the requirements of a wider, equally natural, but less articulated community—that of mankind. The right aims at preventing international anarchy by restraints placed upon men of ill-will. Conceivably, this purpose would be better served in some circumstances by forbearance than by resistance; where this was the case, the state would be obligated to refrain from action. Secondly, the right of self-defense is founded on the interests of the particular community's own citizens. It aims at protecting their wealth, their lives, and their liberty. Conceivably, this objective, too, could be better achieved by self-abnegation than by self-assertion; and the state would again be obliged to let events take their course.

Another cardinal characteristic of the state is its moral authority. This is its divine authorization to rule, to exercise—with effects in the moral order itself—the functions traditionally identified with governing: to command, judge and execute. While Augustine and his followers here look to the Pauline concept of the public power, the Scholastic can derive this characteristic in sheerly rational terms, as a natural requirement of the community and therefore as a natural endowment bestowed by the community's divine author.

Upon the state's possession of moral authority turns its right of offensive war. The rights of a state or its citizens can be violated in ways other than by invasion: territory or prerogatives owing to the nation can be withheld, or the movement and commerce of its nationals can be seriously impeded. The injustice thus inflicted would call not only for reparation but—in the interests of social order—for punishment. Within a society, the individual is not free to pursue such purposes on his own; he may only appeal to public authority. As between societies, however, there is no one to whom effective appeal can be made. The moral empowerment of the injured state therefore receives a kind of extension: to pass and execute judgment on those who are normally beyond its jurisdiction. Just as the government may right wrongs and punish wrong-doers inside its boundaries, so it may act outside. If need be, it may vindicate its community's rights even by violence. The injured state becomes with respect to another nation "an avenger to execute wrath on him who does evil."

The Scholastic does not, it should be noted, stigmatize legitimate war as the "lesser evil." International crises do not confront him, in this respect at least, with true "dilemmas." Common humanist and Protestant conceptions are quite different. Ernest Lefever, for example, writes unequivocally in a somewhat wider context that "choosing the lesser of two evils . . . is more responsible than an ethic of abstention." Reinhold Niebuhr, adapting classic Lutheran theology, finds man necessitated to sin, not only by the intrinsic corruption of human nature but also by the extrinsic dilemmas of the social milieu. For the Scholastic, by contrast, sin is never inevitable; an act of self-defense or an act of vindicative justice, although imposed by circumstances which are regrettable, is morally good. This conclusion might be censured as leading to an easy identification of selfish national interest with high moral purpose. Yet the doctrine may actually be more humanizing than the other, bleaker, views. It holds conscience to account, first for the reason, then for the measure, of violence—instead of giving over the moral agent to the uninhibited hopelessness which often follows from seeing sin as unavoidable.

The justification of war in general terms does not end the discussion. Conscience must render its account on certain qualifying factors. Unless particular conditions are fulfilled, the general justification has no application to specific cases. These qualifications can be conveniently summarized under seven headings—some of which are more, some less, relevant to the problems of contemporary diplomacy.

First, the war must be declared by legitimate public authority in the country which goes to war. This requirement pertains primarily to offensive wars, since these professedly vindicate justice and are therefore an exercise of divinely authorized judicial and executive power. Historically, the condition was invoked in order to limit the military activities of lesser feudal lords. Today, it has a somewhat analogous function even with respect to the major powers. Since, in choosing war or peace, the government of any state acts as surrogate for an unarticulated international authority, its decision must be controlled by international purposes. War must aim at a good which is universal rather than exclusive. Peace and the sacrifice even of a just claim may therefore be necessary sometimes for the welfare of the wider community.

Second, the injury which the war is intended to prevent or rectify must be real and certain. An imaginary injustice cannot legitimize vindication. Both the right which has been infringed and the alleged infringement of it must have substance. The possibly unjust taking of human life is not within the ambit of the "probabilism" utilized by many Scholastics in appraising most types of moral acts. The right which is at stake in war must therefore be certainly possessed and certainly violated. Some moralists believe, in addition, that a government going to war should know for certain the other party's *moral* culpability, that it should be able to discount with complete assurance any suggestion of inadvertence or ignorance on his part. This belief again is based on the Scholastic notion of civil authority. Because authority is divine in origin and function, only a *moral* fault, as distinguished from a purely juridical, external, offense, can validate its use. As others indicate, however, human knowledge can never be sure of other men's dispositions, on which their moral guilt depends; malicious or not, the external violation of right disturbs social order and justifies its vindication. Typical injuries envisaged by the older moralists, it may be noted, included seizure or retention of territory, breach of the communal or private, the commercial or personal liberties of a country's nationals; and similar impositions on a third state.

Third, the seriousness of the injury must be proportioned to the damages that the war will cause. No criteria are laid down for weighing either factor, except that the assessment must be made in terms of moral rather than material gains and losses. Self-defense, it is agreed, almost always justifies resistance, and the positive vindication of trivial rights is never adequate reason for hostilities. Between these two accepted judgments, however, there is room for widely divergent appraisals. Some commentators contend that no vindication of any right entitles a country to wage war. For them the theory of legitimate offensive action, although retaining its technical validity, has ceased to be applicable in the modern world. They expressed this view before World War II; they regard it as irrefutably confirmed by subsequent military developments. Pope Pius XII appears to have made it his own. The potential damage of war will be totally disproportionate to any possible achievement.

Fourth—and this is closely linked with the third condition—there must be reasonable hope of success in the waging of the war. If defeat is certain, hostilities will only aggravate the injustice which occasioned them and leave a train of futile sorrow in their path. A nation defending itself against attack, however, may more readily take its chances on fighting, as Finland did in 1939, than a nation on the offensive. In extreme cases the moral value of national martyrdom may compensate for the material destruction of unsuccessful war, as with Belgium in 1914.

Commentators prophesy that the next war will have no victor. The truth of their prediction depends upon what victory can mean. It cannot mean now, if it ever did, the categorical imposition of the winning side's will upon the loser. The erosion of the victors' comparative advantage *vis-à-vis* the vanquished in both World Wars demonstrates this; even after an atomic clash, the cooperation of the defeated country will be worth bargaining for. Success can then mean, at best, the accomplishment of limited objectives. But since such accomplishment remains possible, calculation of success can still enter into the moral choice of war or peace.

Fifth, only as a last resort may hostilities be initiated. A war is clearly pointless if its ends can be attained by less painful means. Negotiation, mediation, arbitration and judicial settlement must be utilized first. Scholastics have in fact demanded, as a necessary prerequisite for military action, an ultimatum or a formal declaration of war, since these are the last measures of persuasion short of force itself. Apart from the possibility that such devices might in fact achieve their appropriate purpose, they can aid in assessing the morality of one's own decision. For they help to establish with certainty any alleged injury as a matter both of law and of fact, by at least hinting at the culpability of a party who shuns them. Moreover, if the rights and wrongs of a situation remain doubtful—in which case war would be immoral—these alternative courses furnish opportunity for compromising the issues.

Sixth, a war may be prosecuted legitimately only insofar as the responsible agents have a right intention. Even good acts are morally perverted if they are done with immoral motives. The significance of this condition should not be discounted simply because the external observer cannot pass judgment on its fulfillment. Governmental authorities are here challenged to confront continually their purposes with the un-flinching appraisal of their consciences. A war which is otherwise just becomes immoral if it is waged out of hatred. A war of self-defense becomes immoral if, in its course, it becomes an instrument of expansion. A war to vindicate justice becomes immoral if, as it goes on, it becomes a means of aggrandizement. The facility with which nations rationalize their resort to war is a commonplace of diplomatic historians. The inhibitory influence of conscience is cited less frequently—and even then, with dis-paraging cynicism; yet it has possibly prevented more wars than this world dreams of. The requirement of right intention can, in addition, debar the rash initiation of war and can bridle the vengeful dispositions which—as Kennan and others have com-plained—make for the irrational termination of hostilities in "unconditional surrender" when something just as valuable could be achieved faster, more cheaply; and in punitive clauses which fester instead of healing the wounds of the defeated.

Seventh, the particular measures used in conducting the war must themselves be moral. Noble ends do not sanctify ignoble means; evil may not be done that good may come of it. The ramifications of this restriction are wide. It raises questions about the taking of hostages, the handling of prisoners, the employment of deceptive strategems, and the resort to espionage, and, above all else today, the utilization of nuclear weapons. It might be anticipated that no conceivable use of these armaments can be justified. But the Scholastic here makes important distinctions. Discussion of these best fits the application, below, of the seven enumerated conditions to the emerging international situation. . . .

Since Scholastic ethics are—as should by now be clear—highly circumstantial, applications must wait upon "a case," upon the factual situation of any given hour. The possibilities are therefore infinite. Upon these, however, some order and limitation can be imposed by restricting discussion to contingencies which can be regarded as both typical and likely, and by seeking in these the moral course for the United States. These types and probabilities, moreover, can be viewed as under the dominance of the East-West struggle.

Within this framework, the contingencies likely to call for a moral choice of war or peace can conveniently be reduced to these: open military attack or subversion (1) by an "uncommitted" nation or by a Soviet ally against an American ally or a "neutral"; (2) by the Soviet Union itself against such an ally or neutral; (3) by the Soviet Union against the United States itself; or (4) "liberative" action by the United States against a Russian ally, or "preventive" action against Russia. The first three of these contin-gencies are occasions for defense, the fourth for initiative. Examination of the four serially, as related to the major criteria for a just war, would be tedious. It will be simpler to deal with them together, noting similarities and differences, and to answer the easier questions first. For all cases, the rightness of American intentions will be assumed.

One factor which pervades all these situations and differentiates them sharply from those contemplated by the earlier moralists is the peculiarity of the central dispute between the polar powers in this scheme. The controversy between the United States and Russia is not primarily territorial. The physical distance between the two countries is considerable, and their boundaries are not the subject of debate. At issue is security for ways of life which have been incorporated into social, economic, and political institutions. Territory is important only as it is touched by this issue of ideals. Russian military power is close to nations in Europe and elsewhere which are similar to the United States in outlook or in aspiration. Americans are reluctant to permit any expansion—at least, without the consent of the people immediately affected—of a governmental system that suppresses human liberties as the West conceives them. This reluctance rests in part on the intrinsic Christian and humanist value of freedom, and in part on the fear that similar encroachment will progressively reach out to the United States itself.

Russians expressly wish to extend the area in which their social system holds sway. This wish springs in part from the determination to maximize values which they prefer to the Western concept of freedom, and in part from the hope that the system's extension to other countries will assure its continuance at home. While Communists professedly seek their objectives only by a convincing demonstration of the superiority of communism as a way of life, the evidence seems to belie this profession; Soviet leadership will apparently use any means it can get away with, including threats, subversion, and military action. Yet American power lies close to the Soviet sphere. And because some Americans want to press back the area which has been deprived of liberty, the Russians are also concerned for security.

On both sides, security is a state of mind. The concept certainly provides no clear standard for vindicatory justice, and even where mere accommodation is concerned, it does not lend itself to diplomatic compromise or third party judgment—the less so because international executive action in support of a judgment cannot realistically be expected.

With this overshadowing controversy defined, the enumerated contingencies may be examined. The first two of them envisage a hostile movement by, for example, the UAR against Israel, Communist China against India or Pakistan, or the USSR against Sweden, Turkey, Brazil, or Ghana. Would a military response by the United States be permissible in terms of the issue alone? In none of these situations could the United States invoke self-defense in its classic conception, since American territory would remain untouched. Self-defense in its modernized version, would, however, be available as a matter of both law and morality. With several of the potential victims, the United States is linked by mutual security pacts carrying an obligation of virtually automatic collective resistance. Article 51 of the United Nations Charter sanctions spontaneous support of countries with which no formal treaty exists. Defensive action could be required for the world's common good. In the third contingency—a Soviet attack on the United States—the classic right of self-defense would clearly become operative. As for liberative action by the United States in the Russian satellites, at the level of positive international law alone this would be difficult to justify—possible, perhaps, only by stretching the human rights clauses of some peace treaties into a guarantee susceptible of intervention in their support. Preventive war could be validated if immediate hostile intentions were certain; but this had better be treated later in connection with the problem of certitude itself.

A question more haunting then the *casus belli* is the likelihood of success. American power on the side of the defender would assure the military defeat of any aggressor or combination of aggressors, save one. Possibly the United States would not even have to draw upon its nuclear arsenal—although the cost, in casualties, of a conventional war against Communist China would come very high. *Vis-à-vis* the Soviet Union, military victory would be less sure. Russia is physically and psychologically capable of long-range, large-scale, nuclear warfare. The possibility of failure against the USSR makes uncertain the expectations of victory over lesser powers which the Soviets choose to back. American favor would not, therefore, automatically assure the triumph of every American protégé.

If military success is thus questionable, diplomatic victory—at least total diplomatic victory—is even more so. The problem of proportion is implicit in that of success. Some victories would make the winner master of a seared and wasted world, not worth the trouble. Some would, at best, preserve the *status quo,* as the police action in Korea. Some would exchange new and more powerful enemies for old, as World War II did in Poland and China. Some would tie the victor down to prolonged, expensive and perhaps futile "pacification" of the vanquished, as a prospective American conquest of Russia. It can only be said, as a counter-consideration, that some situations narrow a nation's options, that diplomatic success is relative to the alternatives presented, and that diminished victory may be preferable to defeat. As game-theory might put it, it is inadvisable to play when no one can win, but once play has begun (and this is not always a free choice), the player must seek at least to minimize his losses.

Concretely, judged from the viewpoint of probable success and proportionate cause, virtually no imaginable hostilities among "neutrals" would justify partisan military intervention by the United States. War between the Arabs and Israel would not directly impinge on American security. Participation of this kind would divert energies from the principal diplomatic adversary, and—in the Middle East, at least—would provide that adversary with a tempting opportunity to increase its political influence. Contrariwise, mediatory action of some type by the American government would contribute more to peace than would involvement.

Aggression by a neutral against an ally would present a somewhat different picture. Suppose that India were to mount an attack on Pakistan, Yugoslavia on Italy, or Sweden on Norway. Treaty obligations would not bind the United States to act in all such instances. Yet moderate conventional military support of its ally would seem legitimate and hopeful. Such support would embarrass the United States because it would transform a neutral into an enemy, and would agitate waters in which the Soviet Union would then fish. But it would at the same time deter the aggressor, and it could moderate the reactions of the defender—thus making for settlement. Russian counteraction, one suspects, would be calculated not to precipitate a general war.

A direct Soviet attack upon the United States or its allies in Europe would involve stakes to which very strong, sharp reactions would be proportionate. The challenge to Western survival would be undeniable and strategic opportunities would be more favorable than in many another conceivable circumstance. More troublesome would be a Soviet move against less pivotal and more vulnerable American allies: Korea, Thailand, Pakistan, Turkey, Nationalist China, or even Japan. True, failure to respond would mean great loss of face in a world where face is an element of power. The threat to American security, however, would be less direct and immediate. Militarily, some of these places would be booby-traps which would absorb huge expenditures of men and resources in a wasteful peripheral action, or could provoke United States initiative in using nuclear weapons—and this would change the whole measure of proportion and success. On balance it would seem legitimate for the United States to give such defensive support as is needed in such areas, though remaining modest in objective and prepared for accommodation. American initiative toward liberative or preventive war is faced with all the uncertainties of outcome and of proportion mentioned earlier, which make it morally indefensible.

Two further requirements of a just war fuse into a single problem centering on the element of time. Here again the moralist is faced with a circumstantial factor which sharply differentiates contemporary diplomatic situations from those of a bygone day. Time has been one-sidedly compressed by modern technology—the time of action, but not of decision. Manned aircraft dispatched for a concerted attack on the United States can be detected, it is supposed, four hours before they strike. An enemy's use, instead, of ballistic missiles could cut this warning time to fifteen minutes. The time available for confirming or recalling American counter-measures is similarly restricted. Yet the injury which provokes a war must be real, not imaginary—and therefore known for certain; and war as a means of correcting the injury must be the last resort, utilized only when all less drastic steps have failed. Both the investigation needed to ascertain an injury and the negotiation needed to exhaust other resorts consume time. Because time is an important resource for warring powers, the fulfillment of the ethical requirements may sacrifice decisive military advantage. Besides, four hours leaves few enough moments for a moral determination and appraisal of facts; a quarter hour leaves virtually none. How does this consideration affect moral appraisal in the four contingencies previously enumerated?

As long as possession of missiles with nuclear war-heads is restricted as at present, few of these contingencies will get beyond control or correction in the time required for investigation. Neither neutrals nor Soviet satellites will take decisive military steps against other neutrals or the Western alliance; Russia itself seems unlikely to act in this fashion against neutrals. Open military measures in these contingencies would probably be conventional. The most critical of the possibilities, however, is a massive Soviet attack on major American allies or on the United States. From the military standpoint the most appropriate counterstep would be the immediate launching of a similar attack on the Soviet Union. In a period of a few hours, then, the United States would have to determine whether a suspicious Russian move was really an attack— in fact whether it was really Russian—and was unprovoked by far-flung American troops or far-flung allied governments. Doubt on any point would call for frantic and hazardous (given mutual mistrust) negotiations to call off the attack in mid-flight.

Brief though the time be, one must insist that the requirement of moral certitude be met. This does not, however, require judicial inquiry. Because it burdens the conscience of the responsible statesman, the key question is whether *he* is satisfied as to his knowledge. The outsider has the impression that, with the resources at hand, he *can* be. The very mass of any likely aggression with strategic nuclear weapons would make it identifiable with assurance. A degree of tolerance of some kinds of isolated attack or isolated provocation would be reasonable, and would probably be conceded by both sides—with counter-measures going no further than the *lex talionis*. While delivery remains the task of manned bombers, the "failsafe" procedure appears to guarantee the policy-makers's control over his retaliatory force for a period sufficient to gather his information. The long count-down, and the frequent misfires of ICBMs used in outer space research indicate that, for the moment, this control will cover unmanned vehicles, too. If an attack on an ally or the United States were established as a fact, however, further diplomatic effort at accommodation would not be required. The last peaceful resort would have been passed.

Apart from a direct attack, subversive activity inspired by the Soviet Union could effect a successful *coup* at some places within the Western defensive system, but this does not present quite the same moral problem. Governmental overthrow seems less likely to occur without warning among the United States' central allies than among the peripheral ones. Moreover, instant nuclear retaliation would not be an apt instrument for undoing such a mishap. If military counter-action were feasible, it would also be moral; but time would press less urgently than in the case of open aggression.

If an American initiative rather than reaction to a Russian attack were in question, the problems of certitude and last resort would again be different. The only substantive grounds on which such an initiative could be justified would be interpretive self-defense—the anticipation of an assured Soviet action against the United States or its friends. This limitation of substantive grounds helpfully limits the procedural consid-erations. Without certitude of imminent Russian aggression, the United States could not licitly act. Technically, this certitude is possible. Practically, it may not be. Widely scattered underground agents could report simultaneously that at H-hour ICBMs would be launched *en masse* against the United States, or that the Long-Range Air Force would rendezvous over the principal American cities. The definiteness of such infor-mation would leave only the question of whether one more diplomatic try—an ulti-matum, for example, would be necessary. Even though this would sacrifice the military advantage of a surprise defensive initiative, such an effort would, I think, be required.

The final moral criterion which must be applied to the major contingencies deals with the measures or means to be used in warfare. The use of immoral means renders immoral the very pursuit of the war by the user. In question are the means sanctioned by the responsible policy-maker, not the activities in which individuals or subordinate officials may engage on their own authority; although war does produce a flood of these activities, their moral relevance is to the balance of good and evil consequences, already discussed. As far as the policy-maker's choice is concerned, the possible resort to nuclear weapons presents the chief difficulty. A rather extensive digression back to pertinent principles of Scholastic ethics will be necessary in approaching it.

The central issue in the use of nuclear weapons is the treatment of non-combatants. In a just war enemy soldiers, and civilians engaged in close logistical supporting action like the manufacture and transport of munitions, may legitimately be killed. Because these are intimately cooperating in the materially unjust activities of the opposing state, they are "guilty"—at least in the juridical sense—of serious injustice; the troops engaged against them are agents of the public authority which is trying to restrain them. Even in "total war," however, non-combatants remain very numerous; these are "innocent," and not subject to the drastic treatment accorded to their countrymen who are closer to the battle. The moral problem arises because nuclear weapons, in some of their contemplated uses, would inflict civilian casualties numbering tens of millions.

The Scholastic seeks moral judgment for this and other methods of warfare through the "principle of double effect." In essence, this principle asserts that an evil effect may be *tolerated* as an incident to a good effect *willed*. As elaborated, the principle requires the fulfilment of four conditions. First, the two effects must issue from a human act which is in the abstract morally good, or at least indifferent; it may not be intrinsically evil. Second, causally the good effect must flow as immediately from this act as the evil effect; it may certainly not be caused by the evil effect. Third, the moral agent must, in his own mind, positively intend only the good effect, merely permitting the evil. And fourth, the good achieved must be proportionate to the evil which is incidental to it. In these terms, an act which damages the innocent can be moral if the damage is adventitious to the restraint and punishment of the guilty. Scholastics have usually regarded as legitimate the bombardment of, for example, a strategic fortress in which non-combatants have taken refuge, or a munitions plant in a populated area. The firing of projectiles is indifferent; significant military damage and unfortunate civilian casualties result simultaneously from the explosions; the agent, by hypothesis, intends only the military destruction; and the objective, again by hypothesis, is sufficiently important to outweigh the non-combatant deaths and injuries. Scholastics seem not, however, to lay down criteria for determining allowable proportions of evil and good; they appear rather to what they assume is the common human appraisal.

Although the principle of double effect leaves room, then, for some actions which harm the innocent, moralists during World War II condemned at least one common practice connected with aerial bombardment—as falling outside the limits of the principle and therefore as an immoral military measure. This was the so-called "saturation bombing" of mixed industrial and residential neighborhoods. Military men thought of the technique partly as a way to compensate for the inaccuracy of their bombers, and partly as a device for undermining the enemy's civilian morale. If one could not lay bombs with pin-point precision on a warplant, one could pour bombs lavishly on the general area in which the plant was situated. This would increase the mathematical probability of a "hit." And if the other nation's general populace brooded under the constant threat of sleepless nights, devastated homes, and death itself, their determination to struggle on could not endure. The moral critics objected that the military gain in crippling a factory bore no proportion to the damage inflicted on non-combatants; that demoralization was caused by direct attacks upon the innocent rather than being incidental to attacks on the guilty; and that it was psychologically impossible to discriminate in one's moral intention while one was spraying lethal missiles with deliberate indiscrimination over a diversified area.

For the atomic bombing of Hiroshima, these strictures were more clearly valid. Even if the bomb had been aimed at a sharply defined military target, success in destroying such an installation or complex could not outweigh the resultant deaths of 80,000 or more civilians. The American argument was that this act shortened the war and saved lives on both sides. In moral terms, the argument was irrelevant. For if it was true, the good was still the consequence of the evil, the end still did not justify the means.

The censure of American action at Hiroshima does not, however, debar all licit use of nuclear weapons. Since 1945, atomic technology and politics have changed in at least two ways significant for the moralist. The fantastic upward development of explosive potency (and of fall-out range and intensity) in the hydrogen bomb, and the unexpected harnessing of this same potency in tactical war-heads have diversified the uses upon which he must pass judgment. And the growth of the "nuclear club" to include the most likely adversaries in any major war has added a new evil consequence which he must calculate into the double-effect. This is the possibility that any single atomic explosion will provoke a widening—whether gradually or rapidly—resort to nuclear weapons. The consensus which Scholastics have reached in observing these changes could probably be summarized in these propositions. If the likelihood of expanding a nuclear conflict be set aside, even a high-yield hydrogen bomb could legitimately be dropped upon an isolated military target such as a fleet at sea. Tactical weapons could be hurled at airbases or at armies in the field. As for nuclear raids— restricted in scope—on industrial or communications centers, opinion is divided: some believe that if such an operation would be much less costly to the raider than a conventional precision attack, it would be permissible, while others insist that in the nature of the case it precludes the necessary discrimination in the raider's moral intentions.

Against this background of principle, one can turn again to likely contingencies in international affairs. By contrast with the other six criteria, the criterion of means touches the conduct of a war rather than its inception. Its relevance to entering upon a war is reflex, as an aspect of gauging proportionate good and evil consequences.

A war between neutrals, or a war initiated by Soviet satellites against a neutral or an American ally could, in an outsider's judgment, be repressed by an intervention which did not employ nuclear explosives. The generally superior arsenal of conventional American arms is capable of achieving this end. Action by Communist China may, as indicated earlier, represent an exception. True, from a military point of view, nuclear devices could be advantageous in these contingencies and, in the abstract, some of them are certainly licit. But the surest way to obviate all use of atomic weapons—and an upward spiral in their potency—is to refrain from first use.

If the Soviet Union were to initiate a war, however, the United States would almost certainly have to run the risk of "first use." The employment of atomic warheads in tactical operations against military installations or troops in the field would be permissible. This would be true, too, in the single conceivable instance of an American initiative. But in no contingency does it seem possible to justify the dispatch of high yield nuclear weapons against cities or essentially civilian areas—not even in retaliation.

This last is a hard saying. It might severely handicap the entire diplomacy of the nation which accepts it. Yet the annihilation of cities makes no political sense, and for this reason the question of such retaliation seems purely academic. There are indications that the balance of terror pivots upon fear rather of the error than of the rational intent of either side. And as long as this is so, the merit of the balance need not be sacrificed by the dismantling of its military substructure. For within the arena marked off by the balance—and nowhere else—can diplomacy maneuver and experiment with other instrumentalities of policy.

Because the present study has ranged so widely, a brief summary may be useful. Catholic thinkers believe that war can be morally justified, in the light both of reason and revelation. Given the contemporary international setting, this judgment is to all intents and purposes valid only for defensive action. The specific conditions required to legitimize specific hostilities are these: The war must be initiated by competent authority. It must be waged to meet a verified, serious injury. The good at which it aims must be proportionate to the evil which flows from it. It must be begun in the reasonable hope that its objective will be achieved. It must be undertaken only after all peaceful remedies have been exhausted. The agents responsible for the war must have a right-intention. The means employed must themselves be morally good or indifferent.

If these principles be applied to various likely projections of the present world situation, the eventuality which would most clearly justify a full-scale military response by the United States would be an attack on this country or its allies, initiated by the Soviet Union. Less clear would be an engagement among neutrals, between neutrals and American allies, or between the Soviet satellites and an American ally or a neutral. An American initiative would be permitted only in a constellation of circumstances so unique as to be virtually impossible. The use of some nuclear weapons, while legitimate in the abstract, is almost unthinkable in any but a direct American-Soviet conflict; and even in this case, their employment on civilian centers would be illicit.

With Catholic thought as here presented, it is impossible to reconcile either absolute pacificism or the *Realpolitik* which terminates ethical considerations at the water's edge. The difference between this Catholic view and Protestant or humanist thought of the "realist" tendency is primarily one of emphasis. For the Catholic thinker war is not the lesser of two evils, but the lesser of two goods (one of which appears, at the moment of choice, unattainable). Ethical factors which must be weighed into the political decision for war or peace are more carefully systematized. Even in the conduct of hostilities, moral restraints are regarded as operative. And the moderating factor of "right intention" can contribute to a settlement which is more stable because it is less vindictive. To cite these emphases as "superiorities," however, is less to the purpose than to suggest them as "differences" stimulative of reflection by the many for whom international ethics have, since 1945, acquired new urgency.

Suggested Readings

Gray, J. Glenn. *On Justifying Violence Philosophically*. New York: Harper & Row, 1970.

Horsburgh, H.J.N. *Non-Violence and Aggression*. Oxford: Oxford University, 1968.

Lackey, Douglas P. *Moral Principles and Nuclear War*. London: Rowman and Allenheld, 1984.

Neibuhr, Reinhold. *Christian Realism and Political Problems*. New York: Scribners, 1953.

Potter, Ralph B. *War and Moral Discourse*. Richmond, Va.: John Knox, 1969.

Reading 14

NEW TESTAMENT REFLECTIONS ON PEACE AND NUCLEAR ARMS

Sandra M. Schneiders

Notes from the Editors

In 1983, the American Catholic Bishops issued an important pastoral letter, The Challenge of Peace, *that challenged their nation's foreign policy, and indeed, the foreign policies of all major powers. To the bishops, nuclear war was clearly immoral and deterrence was moral only in the most narrow of contexts. Sandra M. Schneiders, a professor of religious studies, finds in the* New Testament *much to support the bishops' philosophy.*

Obviously, biblical texts have been used to support all sorts of political and moral causes. Schneiders' interpretations would not be acceptable to the religious right, the fundamentalists, and others who see nothing inconsistent between a strong national defense and Christian principles.

Schneiders, nevertheless, emphasizes Christ as a peaceful symbol, devoted to the poor and downtrodden. Those who use money for weapons that could be used to feed the hungry and shelter the homeless are in violation of His teachings. For her, the New Testament *supports the notion that national security should not be the ultimate value for a nation and its citizens. Furthermore, the* New Testament *preaches friendship, love, and reconciliation between peoples, values that current deterrence policies undermine.*

Schneiders goes beyond the bishops in her use of the New Testament *to condemn deterrence theory. Many of her arguments, however, do parallel those in the controversial pastoral letter.*

With so many others, Catholics and non-Catholics alike, I rejoiced at the prophectic witness the bishops gave to the possibility of peace and the moral leadership they provided for those who are working to bring it about. The pastoral is a major contribution to reflection and incentive to action on the most pressing issue of our time. Nevertheless, I have to conclude that the weakest element of the letter is the section on scripture. The biblical section in the final document is a major improvement over the corresponding sections in the first and second drafts. It evokes the biblical message with greater fullness and shows better the relationship between the Old and New Testaments. However, the major weakness, namely, the failure to integrate the biblical material into the central reasoning of the document, remains. . . .

Reprinted from *Catholics and Nuclear War,* edited by Philip J. Murnion, pp. 91, 96–104. Copyright © 1983 by The National Pastoral Life Center. Reprinted by permission of the Crossroad Publishing Company.

The New Testament Contribution to the Question of Peace and Nuclear Arms

There are numerous possible approaches to the New Testament data which bear upon the questions with which we are concerned. I will explore five aspects of the New Testament message which seem to me particularly important for reflection on peace and nuclear arms. In line with the observations in the preceding section I will try to show not what could conceivably be justified as a consonant with New Testament demands, but what the Christian vocation as presented in the Gospels seems to call us to in the face of the incessant build-up of nuclear arms in our country and abroad. In other words, I will attempt to bring the inner dynamics of Christian discipleship into dialogue with the inner dynamics of the current situation in order to expose the challenge that the former addresses to the latter. In what follows I shall, first, look briefly at the Christian mandate to make peace; second, and in somewhat greater detail, explore the radicality of the Christian love commandment; third, examine the ministry of reconciliation as the concrete locus of peacemaking and Christian love; fourth, look at Jesus' preferential option for the poor in relation to military spending. Finally, I shall make some suggestions about the bearing of the Gospel's "reversal dynamic" on the practical question of political realism in the present situation.

Christian Vocation to Peace. The Sermon on the Mount (Mt. 5–7; cf. Lk. 6:17–49), and especially the Beatitudes, is recognized by most scholars as a kind of Christian *Magna Carta,* an aphoristic description of the Christian vocation. Only one of the beatitudes has as its reward the ultimate gift of becoming a child of God. "Blessed are the peacemakers, for they shall be called children of God" (Mt. 5:9).

The New Testament notion of peace is rooted in that marvelously comprehensive Old Testament conception of *shalom.* Peace, in the biblical perspective, is not simply the absence of conflict but is that plentitude of life which involves length of days in fullness of strength, covenantal unity within the community and with God, freedom from fear of enemies or calamity, and the immortality achieved through one's descendants when one is finally gathered to one's ancestors.

In John's Gospel the essential gift flowing from the resurrection of Jesus is that peace which the world cannot give (Jn. 14:27 and 20:19). And as John Donahue shows in great detail, it is particularly Luke's Gospel and the Acts of the Apostles which present both the vocation of Jesus and that of the New Testament community as a vocation to preach the "good news of peace" (Acts 10:36). The letters of Paul contain frequent exhortations to the new Christian communities to build, foster, protect, and cherish peace among themselves and with their neighbors (e.g., 2 Cor. 12:11–12 and elsewhere).

We are called by the Gospel not merely to avoid aggression or conflict but to actively announce and bring about peace. If this peace is fullness of life as God's Community living together in freedom from fear, and if the condition of both the possibility and realization of justice is such peace (cf. Jas. 3:18), it seems that we must raise serious questions about preparation for war even when such preparation is undertaken as a way of preventing war. The philosophy which regards preparedness for and willingness to engage in war as the best safeguard of peace is radically opposed to the Gospel of Christ. This opposition must create a dilemma for the Christian in regard to deterrence policies based on a balance of terror.

Probably, the most difficult question with which the bishops wrestled in the writing of the pastoral was the question of deterrence, the possession of massive arsenals of nuclear weapons as an incentive to the enemy not to declare war. It seems to me that there are two aspects of the gospel vocation to be peacemakers which challenge the possession of nuclear weapons, even for purposes of deterrence. The first has to do with fear and the second with intention.

Biblical *shalom* involves, in an integral way, freedom from fear. Fear, widespread and constant, is one of the most devastating direct results of the stockpiling of nuclear weapons. We are holding ourselves and all of our sisters and brothers in a web of terror. It is difficult not to raise the question of whether the manufacture and stockpiling of this lethal potential is not so contrary to our Christian vocation to make peace, to establish the conditions of fullness of life in freedom from fear, as to be intolerable as a Christian option for any reason whatsoever.

The second perspective from which deterrence seems questionable in the light of the gospel vocation to make peace has to do with intention. Since the atomic explosion at Hiroshima in 1945 the popes and the episcopal magisterium have insisted repeatedly that the use of nuclear weapons and even the threat or intention to use them are strictly immoral. The pastoral takes the same position. But it is extremely difficult to see what real deterrent force the mere possession of nuclear weapons, if one is publicly committed not to use them under any circumstances, really has. The possession of nuclear weapons as a deterrent seems to imply the willingness to use them if provoked. The United States government has made it perfectly clear that it rules out neither retaliation nor first strike. There is a terrible logic in this position if one intends to be realistic about deterrence. But this only raises again the question of whether the moral acceptability of possession of nuclear weapons is not more academic than morally realistic.

The Christian Love Commandment. All four Gospels, but particularly the Gospel of John, present the command to love one's fellow human beings as the very heart of the lifestyle Jesus sought to establish among his disciples. This commandment is rooted in the second great commandment of the Mosaic law (cf. Dt. 6:5 and Lv. 19:18): to love one's neighbor as oneself. But Jesus' presentation of it goes well beyond the Old Testament injunction in two important ways.

First, Jesus *universalized* the command which bound the Israelites to love the members of their own people with whom they were united by ethnic and religious bonds and who had not forfeited their right to that love by infidelity to the covenant obligations. Jesus commands his disciples to love even those who are not members of their own community: "If you love those who love you, what reward have you? . . . And if you salute only your brothers and sisters, what more are you doing than others?" (Mt. 5:46–47; cf. also Lk. 6:32–34) He even commands them to love their enemies, not just the anonymous collective enemy such as the Samaritans (cf. Lk. 10:29–37) but the personal enemy who was actually persecuting them (Mt. 5:44, cf. Lk. 6:27). The specific motive of this astounding love, like that of making peace, is "so that you may be children of your Father who is in heaven" (Mt. 5:45; cf. Lk. 6:35). Our vocation to become children of God is intimately bound up with our capacity and obligation to seek unity among ourselves.

Second, Jesus *intensified* the love command. Not only are his disciples to love universally; they are actually to refrain even from resisting evil done against them and positively to return good for evil, praying for their persecutors, and willingly accepting further harm rather than do harm to protect or avenge themselves (cf. Mt. 5:38–42; Lk. 6:27–31). In John's Gospel this love of the enemy is given its final development as the command of universal love in imitation of Jesus' love for us. Furthermore, the Christian's love of others implies the willingness to lay down one's life for those one loves, even as Jesus laid down his life for us (Jn. 15:12–13). No one may remain "enemy" for those who have accepted the love of God in Jesus.

It is in the Gospel of John, in the last discourses, especially chapters 13 and 15, that we have the fullest and most original presentation of the Christian love command. According to the Fourth Gospel the relations among Christians are rooted in the fact that they are all God's children. Jesus came to give power to become children of God to those who believed in him (Jn. 1:12). By sharing in Jesus' own filiation through the gift of the Spirit his disciples become his brothers and sisters (Jn. 20:17) and brothers and sisters of one another. But Jesus, at the Last Supper, both by word and gesture, indicated that the full development of this sibling relationship is friendship. He no longer calls his disciples servants but friends because he has chosen them and because he has, in a certain real way, abolished their natural inferiority to him, made them his equals, by sharing with them everything he had received from his Father (cf. Jn. 15:12–17).

The relationship of friendship, a relationship of equality, mutuality, complete sharing of material and spiritual goods, which Jesus establishes between himself and his disciples must, he says, be the model of their relationships among themselves. They are to love one another as he has loved them (Jn. 15:12). Indeed, this is, in the Fourth Gospel, the single identifying mark of the Christian (Jn. 13:34–35) and the means by which they will draw all other people to participate in the saving revelation of Jesus: "That they may be one even as we [Jesus and the Father] are one, I in them and thou in me, that they may become perfectly one, so that the world may know that thou hast sent me" (Jn. 17:22–23).

The ultimate expression of this love of friendship is the willingness to lay down one's life for one's friends. To love as Jesus has loved us is not only not to injure the other but actually to choose the other's life over our own if the choice comes to that. Jesus chose to die rather than to kill (cf. Jn. 18:36), and he made his death not an unwilling submission to violence but the free preference to suffer violence rather than to inflict it (cf. Jn. 19:11) in order to validate beyond any possibility of doubt his offer of divine friendship.

Of all the conclusions we might draw from these reflections on the nature of the Christian love command I would suggest only two at this point. First, if the distinctive character of Christian love is friendship and the very essence of friendship is equality and mutual total self-gift, then all relations of superiority/inferiority are out of place among Christians. How can we, as Christians, cooperate in building a national defense policy whose intention is to establish and maintain not only superiority over our adversaries but dominance carried to the point of absolute world supremacy?

My second conclusion has to do with the universality of the love comand in the Gospel. As Christians we cannot regard others as our enemies because we must love our enemies, thus making them our friends. We are actually called to prefer the life of our friend to our own. How, then, can we support a defense policy which generates and aggravates mistrust between nations and relies on felt hostility toward the "enemy" to keep the "national will" strong? It is precisely the conflict in the Christian conscience between the call to take up arms against enemy regimes and the obligation that such action implies of killing real people whom one must, as a Christian, love as Jesus has loved us that has made Christian conscientious objection an increasingly frequent phenomenon among people whose devotion to the values of democracy cannot be doubted.

The Ministry of Reconciliation.   We are called to make peace in a world enmeshed in animosity, to love universally in a world structured by mutual fear and hatred. It is this conflicting reality which, it seems to me, establishes the ministry of reconciliation as the primary practical expression of a Christian stance in a violent world.

Paul presents Jesus as the expression of God's reconciling action among us. "God was in Christ reconciling the world to himself" (2 Cor. 5:19) and the one "who through Christ reconciled us to himself . . . gave us the ministry of reconciliation" (2 Cor. 5:18).

In the Gospels Jesus is presented as giving numerous concrete injunctions concerning the task of overcoming division between ourselves and others. We are to bless those who curse us, pray for those who abuse us, offer the other cheek to the one who strikes us, give our coat to the one who steals our cloak, and refrain from reclaiming the goods that have been taken from us (Lk. 6:27–30). Virtually all reputable scripture scholars recognize that these injunctions cannot be made a literal code for the handling of interpersonal conflicts. They represent, in the form of concrete examples, the real ideal of Christian reconciliation. Yet, the Christian's attitude and desire is not to "even the score" but to dissolve enmity, to soften hatred with love, and to make it possible for the one who is doing the evil to stop doing it without fear of being destroyed. The cycle of violence cannot be broken by retaliation but only by forgiveness.

Jesus' demand that his disciples renounce retaliation as a means of achieving justice has historically been one of the most unrealizable of ideals, whether at the individual or at the societal level. He consistently struggled against injustice toward himself and others. He did not stand idly by wishing for the conversion of those who constituted themselves his enemies. He defended himself against those who sought to entrap him, escaped physically when he could, and protected his outcast friends against the cleverness of the self-righteous defenders of morality. Nevertheless, what we see very clearly in Jesus' own behavior is his refusal, even under the most unjust attack and extreme provocation, to resort to retaliation or the threat of retaliation. Because Jesus would not use violence he could not threaten violence.

One of the most encouraging and original sections of the pastoral is Part III, "The Promotion of Peace: Proposals and Policies." It clearly points out the numerous possibilities open to us for the pursuit of peace without recourse to war or the threat of war. At the heart of these proposals is a constant concern with reconciliation. Peoples must come to know each other so that they can trust one another. Nations must commit themselves to the building and honoring of international institutions and procedures for the resolution of conflicts. The art of peacemaking must be studied and taught. Retaliation and the threat of retaliation can never achieve peace and must finally be renounced in favor of the constant effort at reconciliation to which the Gospel calls us.

Preferential Option for the Poor.   Throughout the Gospel we are confronted with Jesus' self-definition as the physician sent to the sick (cf. Mt. 9:12), the savior sent to sinners (Mt. 9:12–13), the divine shepherd of God sent to the lost sheep (cf. Lk. 15:3–7), the long-awaited messiah anointed to preach good news to the poor (Lk. 4:18). Jesus is born of poverty to a mother who celebrates Yahweh's historical choice of the lowly, the hungry, and the downtrodden (cf. Lk. 1:47–55). He chooses to associate with the poor and the sinners (Mt. 9:11; Lk. 7:34 and elsewhere), and finally dies, stripped even of his clothes (Jn. 19:23–24), in utter destitution. Jesus' choice of solidarity with the poor is perhaps the most unmistakable characteristic of his life among us.

As the Statement of the Holy See to the United Nations in 1976 so graphically stated, the overproduction of military devices is an act of aggression against the poor "for even when they are not used, by their cost alone, armaments kill the poor by causing them to starve." If, as bearers of the name of Christ, we must embody Jesus' own preferential option for the poor, it is hard to see how we can tolerate, much less endorse, our government's clear preferential option for military spending at the cost of daily increasing unemployment, hunger, disease, and social unrest here and abroad.

Although the pastoral devotes less space to this issue than one might wish, stressing the need for a more equitable world order if peace is to be established rather than the gospel imperative of solidarity with the poor, it is nonetheless strong and insistent on our obligation to order our economic priorities according to the Gospel.

The "Reversal Dynamic" of the Gospel.   Surely anyone reading the above arguments, and especially the questioning of the possession of nuclear weapons for purposes of deterrence, will raise the issue of political realism, the issue raised repeatedly by the Reagan administration as the process surrounding the pastoral developed.

The question comes down to the rather simple dilemma: as long as the Soviet Union is armed with nuclear weapons do we have any choice but to maintain a superior arsenal for defense and deterrence? On the basis of the Gospel I would answer: yes, we do have a choice. The mystery of Jesus' resurrection is the grounds for the Christian defiance of death. For us, death is not the ultimate tragedy (cf. Mt. 10:28) and thus not something which must be avoided at any cost. Security, much less invulnerability, is therefore not the ultimate value for us who are challenged to be willing to lose our life in order to find it (Mt. 10:39), to fall to the ground and die in order to bear fruit (Jn. 12:24–25). Our Judeo-Christian heritage says nothing if not that power is made perfect in infirmity (2 Cor 12:5–10), that God can and does use the weak to confound the strong (1 Cor. 1:26–31). Like the Israelites who had to learn not to trust in horses and chariots (cf. Ps. 20:7–8) and Jesus who refused to summon the legions of heaven (Mt. 26:53) or the forces of earth (Lk. 22:51) to his defense, can we not, in faith, lay down our arms?

To some this is undoubtedly a counsel of madness if not despair. But even from a human point of view it might be possible to argue the Christian position. Even the current administration has admitted that a nuclear war would mean disaster for victors and vanquished alike. The medical and scientific communities are in agreement that there will be no victors in a nuclear exchange. Our weapons, as defense, are useless, and their stockpiling daily increases the chance of their accidental or deliberate use.

But, as the pastoral points out so well, to say that we have no military defense is not to say that we have no defense at all. It does say that we must rechannel our efforts from military build-up into the building of international agencies of conflict resolution, engagement in mutually respectful and honest negotiations, and the solution of the problem of unjust distribution of resources which underlies so much of the world's tension. To lay down our arms is not to abandon defense, but to abandon useless and, quite possibly, immoral posturing. And it would place all the burden of world opinion on any nation which remained armed or threatened to use arms. I would want to argue that no use of nuclear weapons, either by firing or by threat, and thus probably also by possession, is moral or effective. We have nothing to gain by keeping them and everything, literally, to lose.

Yet, the basic issue is not whether this is a reasonable strategy. The Gospel's peacemaking mandate, its love command, the ministry of reconciliation which it entrusts to the Christian community, the preferential option for the poor to which it calls us, and the reversal dynamic inaugurated by the resurrection of Jesus which it proclaims are not just the requirements of human nature or the conclusion of enlightened rationality. They are a new wine which must burst the wineskins of the ancient dynamics of competition and conflict, aggression and hatred, retaliation, the oppression of the poor and the weak by the rich and powerful, and the search for unlimited human security and national supremacy upon which our current defense policy is based. In other words, the Gospel's contribution to our reflection on war and peace is neither accidental nor purely exhortatory. It is substantive and structural. The question is whether the dynamics of Christian discipleship are reconcilable with the dynamic of national policy in the area of defence. If the answer is no, then those who call themselves Christians have hard choices to make. One of the most encouraging signs of the maturity and commitment of Christians in our time is that increasing numbers of Christians are making those choices and making it clear that the source of their convictions and their actions is the Gospel they profess.

Suggested Readings

Bainton, Roland H. *Christian Attitudes Toward War and Peace: A Historical Survey and Critical Reevaluation*. Nashville: Abingdon, 1978.

Gremillion, J. *The Gospel of Peace and Justice*. New York: Orbis, 1979.

Krauthammer, Charles. "On Nuclear Morality." In *Nuclear Arms: Ethics, Strategy, Politics*, ed. R. James Woolsey. San Francisco: ICS, 1984, pp. 11–21.

McSorley, Richard. *New Testament Basis of Peacemaking*. Washington D.C.: Georgetown University Center for Peace Studies, 1979.

National Conference of Catholic Bishops on War and Peace. *The Challenge of Peace: God's Promise and Our Response*. Washington, D.C.: U.S. Catholic Conference, 1983.

O'Brien, D.J. and T.A. Shannon. *Renewing the Earth: Catholic Documents on Peace, Justice and Liberation*. Garden City, N.Y.: Image, 1977.

Reading 15

IN DEFENSE OF CREATION: THE NUCLEAR CRISIS AND A JUST PEACE

The United Methodists Council of Bishops

Notes from the Editors

John Wesley, the founder of the Methodist Church, considered war to be the ultimate evidence of humankind's sinful condition. In 1986, elders of that church produced In Defense of Creation: The Nuclear Crisis and a Just Peace.

In many ways, this document resembles the celebrated Catholic Bishops' pastoral letter of 1983, but it takes a less ambiguous stand on the concept of nuclear deterrence. Whereas the Catholic Bishops suggested that deterrence might be morally acceptable if it was viewed as a transitory stage on the way to disarmament, the Methodist Bishops reject the concept completely.

Echoing the argument in Schneiders' amplification of the Catholic position, the Methodist Bishops stress the wasteful as well as the dangerous nature of the arms race. They call attention to the resources that might otherwise be employed to feed the hungry, shelter the homeless, and provide opportunity to the underprivileged.

They issue a call for their clergy and congregations, as well as all citizens of the world, to educate themselves about the issues and to urge their leaders to heed the call for disarmament. Needless to say, like the Catholic Bishops and other clerical peacemakers, the Methodist Bishops offer little in a practical way to explain how Russian, American, and other leaders will beat their swords into plowshares. Moreover, in the United States, a significant and politically powerful segment of the Protestant faith, the fundamentalists, supports the nuclear arming of America and warns its congregations about the dangers inherent in attempting to make a deal with the atheists and anti-Christs in the Kremlin.

We write in defense of creation. We do so because the creation itself is under attack. Air and water, trees and fruits and flowers, birds and fish and cattle, all children and youth, women and men live under the darkening shadows of a threatening nuclear winter. We call The United Methodist Church to more faithful witness and action in the face of this worsening nuclear crisis. It is a crisis that threatens to assault not only the whole human family but planet earth itself, even while the arms race itself cruelly destroys millions of lives in conventional wars, repressive violence, and massive poverty.

We seek the fullest and fairest possible discussion not only of the convictions that we have tried to state clearly but also of alternative and critical views. We pray that our churches may become redemptive models of peaceable diversity even as they struggle for reconciliation and unity in Christ.

The Heritage of Faith and the Call to Peace

The transcendent dimensions of the nuclear crisis make biblical dramas of the human predicament more vivid and more appropriate than most previous generations could know. Too much Christian discussion of war and peace over the intervening centuries has lost the breadth and depth of scriptural understanding of creation, God's action in history, the world of nations, and human destiny. Nuclear issues raise questions of freedom and responsibility, the end of history, the meaning of power and security, and spiritual despair. The Bible gives us a faith view and a world view spacious enough to comprehend the enormity of just such issues.

At the heart of Old Testament Scripture is the Hebrew understanding of *shalom*. *Shalom* means positive peace, joyful peace, just peace. *Shalom* is harmony between humanity and all of God's creation. In *shalom* there is no contradiction between justice and peace or between peace and security or between love and justice (Isaiah 32:16–18; Jeremiah 29:7). In the *shalom* of God's good creation, every person of every race in every nation is a sacred being, made in God's image and entitled to life and peace, health and freedom.

But the *shalom* of God's good creation has been broken by the fallenness and violence of sinful human creatures. The powers of government are not only legitimate expressions of the creation's natural order of political community; they are necessary constraints upon human sinfulness. When governments themselves become destroyers of community and threats to the creation, when they presume to usurp the sovereignty that belongs to God alone, they are rightly subject to challenge and correction, protest and resistance. *Shalom* discloses an alternative community—alternative to the idolatries, oppressions, and violence that mark the ways of many nations.

Jesus Christ, the Incarnation of God, comes to us as the presence and promise of *shalom*. He comes heralded by angels who sing: "Glory to God and peace on earth!" He invokes the most special blessings upon peacemakers (Matthew 5:9). He commands us to love our enemies; for he knows, even if we do not, that if we hate our enemies, we blind and destroy ourselves (Matthew 5:43–46; Luke 6:27–38). He weeps when he foresees the city reduced to rubble and dust because the people do not know "the things that make for peace" (Luke 19:41–44).

Paul's letters announce that Jesus Christ is our peace. It is Christ who has "broken down the dividing wall of hostility," creating one new humanity (Ephesians 2:14–19). It is Christ who calls us to become ambassadors of a new creation, a new Kingdom, a new order of love and justice (2 Corinthians 5:17–20). It is Christ who has "disarmed the principalities and powers" (Colossians 2:15). Beyond all brutality and suffering and death, God's costly gift of peace awaits us. Peace is the ultimate victory—peace that the world itself cannot give.

We believe the nuclear crisis poses fundamental questions of faith that neither the pacifist nor just-war traditions have adequately addressed. We invite pacifists and nonpacifists among our people not only to recapture their common ground, such as their moral presumption against all war and violence, but to undertake together a fresh inquiry into those transcendent issues that stretch far beyond private conscience and rational calculation.

The just-war tradition, originating with Saint Ambrose and Saint Augustine in the fourth and fifth centuries, set forth seven principles concerning the morality of going to war and the conduct of warfare. Three of those principles are especially tested by nuclear warfare and have helped us form our own judgments.

First, we are convinced that no actual use of nuclear weapons offers any *reasonable hope of success* in achieving a just peace.

Second, we believe that the principle of *discrimination* (requiring the immunity of noncombatants from direct attack) is bound to be horribly violated in any likely use of nuclear weapons not only because of the widespread effects of blast, fire, radioactive fallout, and environmental damage but also because of the unlikelihood that any resort to nuclear weapons by major powers can result in a strictly controlled or "limited" nuclear war.

Third, we cannot imagine that the norm of *proportionality* can be meaningfully honored in a nuclear war, since such a war could not be waged with any realistic expectation of doing more good than harm.

These considerations impel us to say *No,* a clear and unconditioned *No,* to nuclear war and to any use of nuclear weapons.

But our *No* is more than a matter of ethical calculation; it is a rejection of that nuclear idolatry that presumes to usurp the sovereignty of the God of *shalom* over all nations and peoples. Vengeful judgment and mass destruction are clearly contrary to the will of God and to the moral order of creation.

In the roundedness of *shalom,* a just-war ethic is never enough. Our churches must nurture a *new theology for a just peace.* Our searching of the Scriptures and historical traditions, along with our discernment of the most salient religious issues in the nuclear crisis, has led us to formulate a provisional list of guiding principles for a theology for a just peace. . . .

The Nuclear Challenge to Faith

Theological understandings of justice and peace in the nuclear crisis must be informed by a distinction between two sets of nuclear issues. There are the *primal issues* of blast, fire, and fallout and their more- or less-direct physical impact. There are also the *consequent issues,* the second- and third-generation issues, which have to do with the many long-term ramifications of all nuclear technologies not only for the physical environment but for all human institutions and behavior: political, economic, scientific, educational, cultural, and psychological. Our churches must give more urgent response to these consequent issues. These are the issues that stretch farthest beyond the classical war-peace debate. They cut most sharply into the fabric of our cultural and institutional life. They make most clear that the nuclear crisis is a matter of *social justice as well as world peace.*

Nuclear deterrence has too long been reverenced as the idol of national security. In its most idolatrous forms it has blinded its proponents to the many-sided requirements of genuine security. There can be no unilateral security in the nuclear age. Security requires economic strength and stability, environmental and public health, educational quality, social well-being, public confidence, and global cooperation.

Whatever claims may be made for deterrence policies since 1945, the future is shadowed by the increasingly perilous trends of recent years. The moral case for deterrence, even as an interim ethic, has been undermined by unrelenting arms escalation. It has been discredited by the invidious discrimination between nuclear-weapon states and those that have renounced nuclear rights under the 1970 Non-Proliferation Treaty. Nuclear deterrence has become a dogmatic license for perpetual hostility between the superpowers and for their rigid resistance to significant measures of disarmament. A still more fundamental flaw is at the very core of nuclear deterrence: a contradiction between inordinate confidence in the rationality of decision makers and the absolute terror of annihilation.

The ideology of deterrence must not receive the churches' blessing, even as a temporary warrant for holding on to nuclear weapons. The lingering possession of such weapons for a strictly limited time requires a different justification: *an ethic of reciprocity* as nuclear-weapon states act together in agreed stages to eliminate their nuclear weapons. Such an ethic is shaped by a realistic vision of *common security* and the escalation of mutual trust rather than mutual terror.

We do not believe that *strategic defenses* offer either an alternative to deterrence or an enhancement of deterrence. We cannot as bishops claim the expertise to assess all the technologies involved. However, moral and political dimensions of this quest for nuclear defenses can and must be made understandable to our church members. Space defenses may well have provocative and dangerous offensive implications. They threaten to become obstacles to new arms-control agreements. They violate the clear intent and spirit of the ABM Treaty of 1972 and risk the demise of that treaty. At estimated costs of up to one trillion dollars, the US Strategic Defense Initiative (SDI) would surely be the most expensive project ever undertaken by any government or any other institution—with enormous economic and social consequences.

We repeat our conviction that the churches must act on the understanding that the nuclear arms race is not simply an antiwar issue. *The nuclear arms race is an issue of social justice.* Justice is offended in the double standard under which some nations presume nuclear weapons for themselves while denying them to others. Justice is outraged in the unending vertical proliferation of nuclear weapons by the superpowers in violation of Article VI of the Non-Proliferation Treaty. Justice is abused in the overwhelming power of nuclear-weapon states to threaten the self-determination, security, and very life of nonaligned and nonbelligerent nations. Justice is forsaken in the squandering of wealth in the arms race while a holocaust of hunger, malnutrition, disease, and violent death is destroying the world's poorest peoples. Justice is defiled by the superpowers' implication in conventional arms races and proxy wars in the Third World, causing much present suffering and threatening escalation into a nuclear war. The possibilities of nuclear terrorism by revolutionary movements are seriously aggravated by such injustices.

The Arms Race and American Society

Christian concern for social justice has both domestic and international dimensions. Every social institution of militarized states has been profoundly affected by the *consequent* issues: the systemic "fallout" of military technologies and policies. In the United States, democratic decision making has been sharply limited by the speed of missiles, the bureaucratic momentum of technology, and the pervasive web of military-industrial-political-scientific interests. Domestic politics has witnessed the demagogic and deceitful exploitation of nuclear fears to silence the voices of reason.

The US military buildup between 1980 and 1985 has cost $1.2 trillion, or more than $20,000 for an average family of four. In fiscal year 1986, military and related spending will amount to more than half of all discretionary spending by Congress. US arms are now being purchased with food stamps, welfare checks, rent subsidies, Medicaid payments, school lunches, and nutrition supplements for poor mothers and their children. Half of the nation's Black children and two fifths of all Hispanic children now live in poverty. The productivity of the American economy has been severely retarded by the disproportionate allocation of scientific and technical personnel and research funds to military purposes. A decline in industrial efficiency has incurred enormous foreign trade deficits and caused the loss of millions of industrial jobs.

The racial dimensions of this struggle over national priorities are increasingly acute. Black teenage unemployment in May 1985 was 40.4 percent and was concentrated in the deteriorating inner core of older cities, where housing, health services, and education are most deficient. Without a sharp new governmental focus on inner city peoples, racial polarization is bound to intensify. Clearly, the demilitarization of America must be accompanied by a powerful new national commitment to equal opportunity for racially disadvantaged peoples.

The "nuclearism" that permeates a whole culture is reflected psychologically in a simultaneous denial of the problem and a sense of helplessness to cope with it. There is a growing fear of "futurelessness" among young people. For young people and for all citizens, the legitimate need for self-respect as a nation must be lifted above the relentless barrage of aggressive, competitive, and chauvinistic sentiments that assault them not only in political rhetoric but also in commercial, recreational, and even educational institutions. Peacemaking must be celebrated as a patriotic commitment.

These domestic burdens of the arms race weigh heavily on other nations as well. The prospects for political liberalization, economic progress, and social well-being for the peoples of the Soviet Union are tragically diminished by the enormous investment of their government in the military sector. The economic and social development of some of the world's poorest countries are distorted and constrained by inordinate arms expenditures and repressive military establishments.

The Arms Race and World Community

Our consciousness of the biblical truth that all the peoples of earth are one whole human family has been vivified for our generation as never before by the emergence of both global threats and global bonds. The nuclear crisis is not primarily a matter of missiles; it is a crisis of human community. The US-Soviet conflict is the most serious stumbling block to a peaceable and survivable world community. The Soviet Union remains an authoritarian state, obsessed with secrecy, repressive of most forms of public protest, overbearing and sometimes brutal in its attempts to dominate states along its borders. The invasion of Afghanistan is the most recent example. But millions of Soviet citizens are united in their national pride, in their passion for peace and security, in their determination not to be militarily inferior, and in the sacrifices they have made for economic and technological progress.

We have come to recognize that anti-Soviet fears, which are manipulated for political and ideological purposes, are perhaps the main hindrance on the US side to constructive arms negotiations. Each government has given the other abundant cause for grievance since 1917. But the American and Soviet peoples share a common humanity, a common aversion to war, a common horror of nuclear weapons, and a common hope for their economic and social well-being. More than ninety-five percent of the world's fifty thousand nuclear weapons are in the arsenals of the United States and Soviet Union, clearly indicating their mutual responsibility for reversing the arms race. While each superpower has some statistical advantages, each can totally destroy the other nation and the whole human family—not once, but many times.

As Christians our capacity to address these moral questions is greatly enhanced by our ecumenical bonds with tens of millions of Christian sisters and brothers in the Soviet Union. This endurance of religious faith and practice seven decades after the Bolshevik Revolution is one of the most remarkable spiritual triumphs of modern history.

The new cold war between the United States and Soviet Union extends to every continent. It tends to turn every North-South issue of economic and social justice into an East-West issue of military confrontation. It is a major source of injustice to the world's poorest peoples, whether through squandering of resources, neglect, repression, exploitation, proxy wars, nuclear arrogance, or failure to construct the institutions of multilateral cooperation required for humane development. We implore all United Methodists to testify to their governments that the national aspirations and human rights of Black South Africans, Central Americans, and Filipinos must not be forsaken for "national security" or anti-Soviet policies.

Policies for a Just Peace

The necessity of reconstructing USA-USSR relations is the crux of the nuclear crisis and an imperative of justice and freedom to all earth's peoples. That reconstruction involves developing a regular and systematic pattern of consultation, including an annual summit conference, between the highest political and military leaders of both countries.

We support the following transitional measures *toward a nuclear-free world:*

1. A comprehensive test ban as the first step toward a mutual and verifiable freeze on the testing, production, and deployment of nuclear weapons—and also as an urgent measure to strengthen the Non-Proliferation Treaty.
2. Consolidation of existing bilateral treaties (ABM Treaty of 1972 and SALT II Treaty) and phased but rapid reduction of nuclear arsenals, while calling upon all other nuclear-weapon states to agree to parallel arms reductions, to the eventual goal of a mutual and verifiable dismantling of all nuclear armaments.
3. Bans on all offensive and defensive space weapons.
4. A no-first-use (of nuclear weapons) agreement, accompanied by withdrawal of all battlefield nuclear weapons from forward defense areas and also by assurances that no conventional force buildups are preconditions of such a policy.

We oppose all major counterforce weapons on both sides (including US MX, Trident, and Pershing II missiles and Soviet SS-18 and SS-19 land-based missiles, Typhoon submarines and missiles, and SS-20 intermediate-range missiles).

We oppose all efforts to achieve nuclear superiority or to promote confidence in "limited nuclear war," and all weapons systems that hold out false hopes of effective defenses against nuclear weapons.

We believe a political climate more conducive to negotiations might well be fostered by independent US or Soviet initiatives, such as a moratorium on nuclear tests, on flight tests of strategic weapons, or on production of fissionable materials for weapons purposes. Such initiatives would be an invitation to reciprocity. They would demonstrate a willingness to risk a small beginning of trust when nations must choose between growing trust and mutual destruction. Reciprocity also means a readiness to respond to the peaceful initiatives of the other side.

We urge renewed commitment to building the institutional foundations of common security, including UN peace-keeping forces, new instruments of mediation and verification, agencies to facilitate economic conversion, and global systems of governance in matters of economic justice, human rights, and environmental conservation.

We propose that the inseparability of peace and justice be made manifest in truly substantial *disarmament funds for development*. Such funds would be devoted to those economic development activities of the United Nations most effectively aimed at the basic human needs of the world's poorest peoples.

We believe the prime alternative to hostility and violence is nurtured in the ways of peacemaking itself. We therefore urge a much stronger commitment to peace research, studies, and training at all levels of education. We encourage special study of nonviolent civilian defense and peacemaking forces.

We recognize that both the imperatives of peacemaking and impulses to violence are to be found in all world religions. We therefore urge educational and religious institutions to develop substantial programs of study, dialogue, and action between Christians and other faith communities in the common quest for peace. . . .

Suggested Readings

Bennett, J.C. *Nuclear Weapons and the Christian Conscience*. New York: Scribners, 1962.

Brandt, Richard B. *War and Moral Responsibility*. Princeton: Princeton University, 1973.

Nye, Joseph S., Jr. *Nuclear Ethics*. New York: Free Press, 1986.

Paul, Ellen Frankel et al., eds. *Nuclear Rights/Nuclear Wrongs*. Oxford: Basil Blackwell, 1986.

Sheils, W.J., ed. *The Church and War*. Oxford: Basil Blackwell, 1983.

Reading 16

THE JUST WAR

Michael Walzer

Notes from the Editors

When, if ever, can a war be justified? Under what circumstances do our legal, ethical, and moral principles permit nations and individuals to take up arms against one another? Political philosopher Michael Walzer, one of the leading experts on just war theory, has attempted to answer these and related difficult questions.

In this selection from his celebrated book, Just and Unjust Wars *(1977), Walzer presents elements of a theory of aggression. For him, a war is justified to combat an aggressor not only for the nation attacked but for the rest of the members of the international system. Aggressive states should be resisted with force and, if necessary, punished after their defeat. Although most observers would probably agree with a justification of war having to do with resisting aggression, the definition of aggression has posed insurmountable problems. Both the League of Nations and the United Nations have labored unsuccessfully for over sixty years trying to find a universally acceptable and practical definition of aggression.*

Finding an acceptable definition of aggression is complicated by the concept of structural violence. According to some observers, a war to overthrow an unjust social and economic order is also justified. That is, aggression need not be limited to a direct military attack but can also be defined in terms of a regime's suppression of its own citizens. Today's wars of national liberation are often justified by their supporters by resort to variants of the concept of structural violence.

The Legalist Paradigm

If states actually do possess rights more or less as individuals do, then it is possible to imagine a society among them more or less like the society of individuals. The comparison of international to civil order is crucial to the theory of aggression. I have already been making it regularly. Every reference to aggression as the international equivalent of armed robbery or murder, and every comparison of home and country or of personal liberty and political independence, relies upon what is called the *domestic analogy*. Our primary perceptions and judgments of aggression are the products of analogical reasoning. When the analogy is made explicit, as it often is among the lawyers, the world of states takes on the shape of a political society the character of

Reprinted from *Just and Unjust Wars* by Michael Walzer. Copyright © 1977 by Basic Books. Reprinted by permission of Basic Books, pp. 58–63.

which is entirely accessible through such notions as crime and punishment, self-defense, law enforcement, and so on.

These notions, I should stress, are not incompatible with the fact that international society as it exists today is a radically imperfect structure. As we experience it, that society might be likened to a defective building, founded on rights; its superstructure raised, like that of the state itself, through political conflict, cooperative activity, and commercial exchange; the whole thing shaky and unstable because it lacks the rivets of authority. It is like domestic society in that men and women live at peace within it (sometimes), determining the conditions of their own existence, negotiating and bargaining with their neighbors. It is unlike domestic society in that every conflict threatens the structure as a whole with collapse. Aggression challenges it directly and is much more dangerous than domestic crime, because there are no policemen. But that only means that the "citizens" of international society must rely on themselves and on one another. Police powers are distributed among all the members. And these members have not done enough in the exercise of their powers if they merely contain the aggression or bring it to a speedy end—as if the police should stop a murderer after he has killed only one or two people and send him on his way. The rights of the member states must be vindicated, for it is only by virtue of those rights that there is a society at all. If they cannot be upheld (at least sometimes), international society collapses into a state of war or is transformed into a universal tyranny.

From this picture, two presumptions follow. The first, which I have already pointed out, is the presumption in favor of military resistance once aggression has begun. Resistance is important so that rights can be maintained and future aggressors deterred. The theory of aggression restates the old doctrine of the just war: it explains when fighting is a crime and when it is permissible, perhaps even morally desirable. The victim of aggression fights in self-defense, but he isn't only defending himself, for aggression is a crime against society as a whole. He fights in its name and not only in his own. Other states can rightfully join the victim's resistance; their war has the same character as his own, which is to say, they are entitled not only to repel the attack but also to punish it. All resistance is also law enforcement. Hence the second presumption: when fighting breaks out, there must always be some state against which the law can and should be enforced. Someone must be responsible, for someone decided to break the peace of the society of states. No war, as medieval theologians explained, can be just on both sides.

There are, however, wars that are just on neither side, because the idea of justice doesn't pertain to them or because the antagonists are both aggressors, fighting for territory or power where they have no right. The first case I have already alluded to in discussing the voluntary combat of aristocratic warriors. It is sufficiently rare in human history that nothing more need be said about it here. The second case is illustrated by those wars that Marxists call "imperialist," which are not fought between conquerors and victims but between conquerors and conquerors, each side seeking dominion over the other or the two of them competing to dominate some third party. Thus Lenin's description of the struggles between "have" and "have-not" nations in early twentieth-century Europe: ". . . picture to yourselves a slave-owner who owned 100 slaves warring against a slave-owner who owned 200 slaves for a more 'just' distribution of slaves. Clearly, the application of the term 'defensive' war in such a case . . . would be sheer deception . . ." But it is important to stress that we can penetrate the deception only insofar as we can ourselves distinguish justice and injustice: the theory of imperialist war presupposes the theory of aggression. If one insists that all wars on all sides are acts of conquest or attempted conquest, or that all states at all times would conquer if they could, then the argument for justice is defeated before it begins and the moral judgments we actually make are derided as fantasies. Consider the following passage from Edmund Wilson's book on the American Civil War:

> *I think that it is a serious deficiency on the part of historians . . . that they so rarely interest themselves in biological and zoological phenomena. In a recent . . . film showing life at the bottom of the sea, a primitive organism called a sea slug is seen gobbling up small organisms through a large orifice at one end of its body; confronted with another sea slug of an only slightly lesser size, it ingurgitates that, too. Now the wars fought by human beings are stimulated as a rule . . . by the same instincts as the voracity of the sea slug.*

There are no doubt wars to which that image might be fit, though it is not a terribly useful image with which to approach the Civil War. Nor does it account for our ordinary experience of international society. Not all states are sea-slug states, gobbling up their neighbors. There are always groups of men and women who would live if they could in peaceful enjoyment of their rights and who have chosen political leaders who represent that desire. The deepest purpose of the state is not ingestion but defense, and the least that can be said is that many actual states serve that purpose. When their territory is attacked or their sovereignty challenged, it makes sense to look for an aggressor and not merely for a natural predator. Hence we need a theory of aggression rather than a zoological account.

The theory of aggression first takes shape under the aegis of the domestic analogy. I am going to call that primary form of the theory the *legalist paradigm,* since it consistently reflects the conventions of law and order. It does not necessarily reflect the arguments of the lawyers, though legal as well as moral debate has its starting point here. Later on, I will suggest that our judgments about the justice and injustice of particular wars are not entirely determined by the paradigm. The complex realities of international society drive us toward a revisionist perspective, and the revisions will be significant ones. But the paradigm must first be viewed in its unrevised form; it is our baseline, our model, the fundamental structure for the moral comprehension of war. We begin with the familiar world of individuals and rights, of crimes and punishments. The theory of aggression can then be summed up in six propositions.

1. *There exists an international society of independent states.* States are the members of this society, not private men and women. In the absence of a universal state, men and women are protected and their interests represented only by their own governments. Though states are founded for the sake of life and liberty, they cannot be challenged in the name of life and liberty by any other states. Hence the principle of non-intervention, which I will analyze later on. The rights of private persons can be recognized in international society, as in the UN Charter

of Human Rights, but they cannot be enforced without calling into question the dominant values of that society: the survival and independence of the separate political communities.

2. *This international society has a law that establishes the rights of its members—above all, the rights of territorial integrity and political sovereignty.* Once again, these two rest ultimately on the right of men and women to build a common life and to risk their individual lives only when they freely choose to do so. But the relevant law refers only to states, and its details are fixed by the intercourse of states, through complex processes of conflict and consent. Since these processes are continuous, international society has no natural shape; nor are rights within it ever finally or exactly determined. At any given moment, however, one can distinguish the territory of one people from that of another and say something about the scope and limits of sovereignty.

3. *Any use of force or imminent threat of force by one state against the political sovereignty or territorial integrity of another constitutes aggression and is a criminal act.* As with domestic crime, the argument here focuses narrowly on actual or imminent boundary crossings: invasions and physical assaults. Otherwise, it is feared, the notion of resistance to aggression would have no determinate meaning. A state cannot be said to be forced to fight unless the necessity is both obvious and urgent.

4. *Aggression justifies two kinds of violent response: a war of self-defense by the victim and a war of law enforcement by the victim and any other member of international society.* Anyone can come to the aid of a victim, use necessary force against an aggressor, and even make whatever is the international equivalent of a "citizen's arrest." As in domestic society, the obligations of bystanders are not easy to make out, but it is the tendency of the theory to undermine the right of neutrality and to require widespread participation in the business of law enforcement. In the Korean War, this participation was authorized by the United Nations, but even in such cases the actual decision to join the fighting remains a unilateral one, best understood by analogy to the decision of a private citizen who rushes to help a man or woman attacked on the street.

5. *Nothing but aggression can justify war.* The central purpose of the theory is to limit the occasions for war. "There is a single and only just cause for commencing a war," wrote Vitoria, "namely, a wrong received." There must actually have been a wrong, and it must actually have been received (or its receipt must be, as it were, only minutes away). Nothing else warrants the use of force in international society—above all, not any difference of religion or politics. Domestic heresy and injustice are never actionable in the world of states: hence, again, the principle of non-intervention.

6. *Once the aggressor state has been militarily repulsed, it can also be punished.* The conception of just war as an act of punishment is very old, though neither the procedures nor the forms of punishment have ever been firmly established in customary or positive international law. Nor are its purposes entirely

clear: to exact retribution, to deter other states, to restrain or reform this one? All three figure largely in the literature, though it is probably fair to say that deterrence and restraint are most commonly accepted. When people talk of fighting a war against war, this is usually what they have in mind. The domestic maxim is, punish crime to prevent violence; its international analogue is, punish aggression to prevent war. Whether the state as a whole or only particular persons are the proper objects of punishment is a harder question, for reasons I will consider later on. But the implication of the paradigm is clear: if states are members of international society, the subjects of rights, they must also be (somehow) the objects of punishment.

Suggested Readings

Gallie, W.B. *Philosophers of Peace and War.* Cambridge: Cambridge University, 1978.

Johnson, James Turner. *Can Nuclear War Be Just?* New Haven: Yale, 1984.

Klassen, W. "The Just War: A Summary." *Peace Research Reviews* 7 (September 1978), pp. 1–70.

Melzer, Jehuda. *Concepts of a Just War.* Leyden: A.W. Sijthoff, 1975.

Phillips, Robert L. *War and Justice.* Norman: University of Oklahoma, 1984.

Ramsay, Paul. *The Just War: Force and Political Responsibility.* New York: Scribners, 1968.

Tooke, J.D. *The Just War in Aquinas and Grotius.* Naperville, Ill.: Allenson, 1965.

Reading 17

THE MELIAN DEBATE

Thucydides

Notes from the Editors
Thucydides (455–400 B.C.), the chronicler of the Peloponnesian Wars, is considered
one of the founders of the study of political theory. In his history of the great wars between
Athens and Sparta (431–404 B.C.), Thucydides not only presents an account of the
battles and politics of the era, but offers a wealth of commentary on international relations
and human behavior.

He himself fought for his beloved Athens in the war, an Athens which became less
admirable as it moved, under wartime conditions, from a democracy to a more autocratic,
imperialistic state. In 416 B.C., aspects of this new Athens can be seen in the famous
Melian debate. Melos was a Spartan colony that had remained neutral in the Peloponne-
sian Wars. Nevertheless, the Athenians wanted to bring the island formally under their
own control. Before commencing hostilities, spokespersons for both sides argued their
respective cases—the Athenians for Melian capitulation, the Melians for their own in-
dependence and for justice and morality in international relations.

The Athenians argued, among other things, that might makes right and that a nation
concerned with defending its national interest should not take into account moral issues.
The Melians explained their unwillingness to surrender in terms of the need for a people
to defend their integrity, irrespective of the consequences.

Many of the ideas expressed in the Melian debate are similar to current debates
about the relations between nations.

. . . the Athenians next made an expedition against the island of Melos with thirty ships of their own, six Chian, and two Lesbian, twelve hundred hoplites and three hundred archers besides twenty mounted archers of their own, and about fifteen hundred hoplites furnished by their allies in the islands. The Melians are colonists of the Lacedaemonians who would not submit to Athens like the other islanders. At first they were neutral and took no part. But when the Athenians tried to coerce them by ravaging their lands, they were driven into open hostilities. The generals, Cleomedes the son of Lycomedes and Tisias the son of Tisimachus, encamped with the Athenian forces on the island. But before they did the country any harm they sent envoys to negotiate with the Melians. Instead of bringing these envoys before the people, the Melians desired them to explain their errand to the magistrates and to the dominant class. They spoke as follows: "Since we are not allowed to speak to the people, lest, forsooth, a multitude should be deceived by seductive and unanswerable arguments which they

Reprinted from Benjamin Jowett, *Thucydides*, Book V (London: Oxford University Press, 1900), pp. 167–77.

would hear set forth in a single uninterrupted oration (for we are perfectly aware that this is what you mean in bringing us before a select few), you who are sitting here may as well make assurance yet surer. Let us have no set speeches at all, but do you reply to each of several statements of which you disapprove, and criticise it at once. Say first of all how you like this mode of proceeding."

The Melian representatives answered: "The quiet interchange of explanations is a reasonable thing, and we do not object to that. But your warlike movements, which are present not only to our fears but to our eyes, seem to belie your words. We see that, although you may reason with us, you mean to be our judges; and that at the end of the discussion, if the justice of our cause prevail and we therefore refuse to yield, we may expect war; if we are convinced by you, slavery."

Ath.

"Nay, but if you are only going to argue from fancies about the future, or if you meet us with any other purpose than that of looking your circumstances in the face and saving your city, we have done; but if this is your intention we will proceed."

Mel.

"It is an excusable and natural thing that men in our position should neglect no argument and no view which may avail. But we admit that this conference has met to consider the question of our preservation; and therefore let this argument proceed in the manner you propose."

Ath.

"Well, then, we Athenians will use no fine words; we will not go out of our way to prove at length that we have a right to rule, because we overthrew the Persians; or that we attack you now because we are suffering any injury at your hands. We should not convince you if we did; nor must you expect to convince us by arguing that, although a colony of the Lacedaemonians, you have taken no part in their expeditions, or that you have never done us any wrong. But you and we should say what we really think, and aim only at what is possible, for we both alike know that into the discussion of human affairs the question of justice only enters where there is equal power to enforce it, and that the powerful exact what they can, and the weak grant what they must."

Mel.

"Well, then, since you set aside justice and invite us to speak of expediency, in our judgment it is certainly expedient that you should respect a principle which is for the common good; that to every man when in peril a reasonable claim should be accounted a claim of right, and that any plea which he is disposed to urge, even if failing of the point a little, should help his cause. Your interest in this principle is quite as great as ours, inasmuch as you, if you fall, will incur the heaviest vengeance, and will be the most terrible example to mankind."

Ath.

"The fall of our empire, if it should fall, is not an event to which we look forward with dismay; for ruling states such as Lacedaemon are not cruel to their vanquished enemies. With the Lacedaemonians, however, we are not now contending; the real danger is from our many subject states, who may of their own motion rise up and overcome their masters. But this is a danger which you may leave to us. And we will now endeavour to show that we have come in the interests of our empire, and that in what we are about to say we are only seeking the preservation of your city. For we want to make you ours with the least trouble to ourselves, and it is for the interests of us both that you should not be destroyed."

Mel.

"It may be your interest to be our masters, but how can it be ours to be your slaves?"

Ath.

"To you the gain will be that by submission you will avert the worst; and we shall be all the richer for your preservation."

Mel.

"But must we be your enemies? Will you not receive us as friends if we are neutral and remain at peace with you?"

Ath.

"No, your enmity is not half so mischievous to us as your friendship; for the one is in the eyes of our subjects an argument of our power, the other of our weakness."

Mel.

"But are your subjects really unable to distinguish between states in which you have no concern, and those which are chiefly your own colonies, and in some cases have revolted and been subdued by you?"

Ath.

"Why, they do not doubt that both of them have a good deal to say for themselves on the score of justice, but they think that states like yours are left free because they are able to defend themselves, and that we do not attack them because we dare not. So that your subjection will give us an increase of security, as well as an extension of empire. For we are masters of the sea, and you who are islanders, and insignificant islanders too, must not be allowed to escape us."

Mel.

"But do you not recognise another danger? For, once more, since you drive us from the plea of justice and press upon us your doctrine of expediency, we must show you what is for our interest, and, if it to be for yours also, may hope to convince you: Will you not be making enemies of all who are now neutrals? When they see how you are treating us they will expect you some day to turn against them; and if so, are you not strengthening the enemies whom you already have, and bringing upon you others who, if they could help, would never dream of being your enemies at all?"

Ath.

"We do not consider our really dangerous enemies to be any of the peoples inhabiting the mainland who, secure in their freedom, may defer indefinitely any measures of precaution which they take against us, but islanders who, like you, happen to be under no control, and all who may be already irritated by the necessity of submission to our empire—these are our real enemies, for they are the most reckless and most likely to bring themselves as well as us into a danger which they cannot but foresee."

Mel.

"Surely then, if you and your subjects will brave all this risk, you to preserve your empire and they to be quit of it, how base and cowardly would it be in us, who retain our freedom, not to do and suffer anything rather than be your slaves."

Ath.

"Not so, if you calmly reflect: for you are not fighting against equals to whom you cannot yield without disgrace, but you are taking counsel whether or not you shall resist an overwhelming force. The question is not one of honour but of prudence."

Mel.

"But we know that the fortune of war is sometimes impartial, and not always on the side of numbers. If we yield now, all is over; but if we fight, there is yet a hope that we may stand upright."

Ath.

"Hope is a good comforter in the hour of danger, and when men have something else to depend upon, although hurtful, she is not ruinous. But when her spendthrift nature has induced them to stake their all, they see her as she is in the moment of their fall, and not till then. While the knowledge of her might enable them to beware of her, she never fails. You are weak and a single turn of the scale might be your ruin. Do not you be thus deluded; avoid the error of which so many are guilty, who, although they might still be saved if they would take the natural means, when visible grounds of confidence forsake them, have recourse to the invisible, to prophecies and oracles and the like, which ruin men by the hopes which they inspire in them."

Mel.

"We know only too well how hard the struggle must be against your power, and against fortune, if she does not mean to be impartial. Nevertheless we do not despair of fortune; for we hope to stand as high as you in the favour of heaven, because we are righteous and you against whom we contend are unrighteous; and we are satisfied that our deficiency in power will be compensated by the aid of our allies the Lacedaemonians; they cannot refuse to help us, if only because we are their kinsmen, and for the sake of their own honour. And therefore our confidence is not so utterly blind as you suppose."

Ath.

"As for the Gods, we expect to have quite as much of their favour as you: for we are not doing or claiming anything which goes beyond common opinion about divine or men's desires about human things. For of the Gods we believe, and of men we know, that by a law of their nature wherever they can rule they will. This law was not made by us, and we are not the first who have acted upon it; we did but inherit it and shall bequeath it to all time, and we know that you and all mankind, if you were as strong as we are, would do as we do. So much for the Gods; we have told you why we expect to stand as high in their good opinion as you. And then as to the Lacedaemonians—when you imagine that out of very shame they will assist you, we admire the innocence of your idea, but we do not envy you the folly of it. The Lacedaemonians are exceedingly virtuous among themselves, and according to their national standard of morality. But, in respect of their dealings with others, although many things might be said, they can be described in few words—of all men whom we know they are the most notorious for identifying what is pleasant with what is honourable, and what is expedient with what is just. But how inconsistent is such a character with your present blind hope of deliverance!"

Mel.

"That is the very reason why we trust them; they will look to their interest, and therefore will not be willing to betray the Melians, who are their own colonists, lest they should be distrusted by their friends in Hellas and play into the hands of their enemies."

Ath.

"But do you not see that the path of expediency is safe, whereas justice and honour involve danger in practice, and such dangers the Lacedaemonians seldom care to face?"

Mel.

"On the other hand, we think that whatever perils there may be, they will be ready to face them for our sakes, and will consider danger less dangerous where we are concerned. For if they need our aid we are close at hand, and they can better trust our loyal feeling because we are their kinsmen."

Ath.

"Yes, but what encourages men who are invited to join in a conflict is clearly not the good-will of those who summon them to their side, but a decided superiority in real power. To this no men look more keenly than the Lacedaemonians; so little confidence have they in their own resources, that they only attack their neighbours when they have numerous allies, and therefore they are not likely to find their way by themselves to an island, when we are masters of the sea."

Mel.

"But they may send their allies: the Cretan sea is a large place; and the masters of the sea will have more difficulty in overtaking vessels which want to escape than the pursued in escaping. If the attempt should fail they may invade Attica itself, and find their way to allies of yours whom Brasidas did not reach: and then you will have to fight, not for the conquest of a land in which you have no concern, but nearer home, for the preservation of your confederacy and of your own territory."

Ath.

"Help may come from Lacedaemon to you as it has come to others, and should you ever have actual experience of it, then you will know that never once have the Athenians retired from a siege through fear of a foe elsewhere. You told us that the safety of your city would be your first care, but we remark that, in this long discussion, not a word has been uttered by you which would give a reasonable man expectation of deliverance. Your strongest grounds are hopes deferred, and what power you have is not to be compared with that which is already arrayed against you. Unless after we have withdrawn you mean to come, as even now you may, to a wiser conclusion, you are showing a great want of sense. For surely you cannot dream of flying to that false sense of honour which has been the ruin of so many when danger and dishonour were staring them in the face. Many men with their eyes still open to the consequences have found the word 'honour' too much for them, and have suffered a mere name to lure them on, until it has drawn down upon them real and irretrievable calamities; through their own folly they have incurred a worse dishonour than fortune would have inflicted upon them. If you are wise you will not run this risk; you ought to see that there can be no disgrace in yielding to a great city which invites you to become her ally on reasonable terms, keeping your own land, and merely paying tribute; and that you will certainly gain no honour if, having to choose between two alternatives, safety and war, you obstinately prefer the worse. To maintain our rights against equals, to be politic with superiors, and to be moderate towards inferiors is the path of safety. Reflect once more when we have withdrawn, and say to yourselves over and over again that you are deliberating about your one and only country, which may be saved or may be destroyed by a single decision."

The Athenians left the conference: the Melians, after consulting among themselves, resolved to persevere in their refusal, and made answer as follows: "Men of Athens, our resolution is unchanged; and we will not in a moment surrender that liberty which our city, founded seven hundred years ago, still enjoys; we will trust to the good fortune which, by the favour of the Gods, has hitherto preserved us, and for human help to the Lacedaemonians, and endeavour to save ourselves. We are ready however to be your friends, and the enemies neither of you nor of the Lacedaemonians, and we ask you to leave our country when you have made such a peace as may appear to be in the interest of both parties."

Such was the answer of the Melians; the Athenians, as they quitted the conference, spoke as follows: "Well, we must say, judging from the decision at which you have arrived, that you are the only men who deem the future to be more certain than the present, and regard things unseen as already realised in your fond anticipation, and that the more you cast yourselves upon the Lacedaemonians and fortune and hope, and trust them, the more complete will be your ruin."

The Athenian envoys returned to the army; and the generals, when they found that the Melians would not yield, immediately commenced hostilities. They surrounded the town of Melos with a wall, dividing the work among the several contingents. They then left troops of their own and of their allies to keep guard both by land and by sea, and retired with the greater part of their army; the remainder carried on the blockade.

About the same time the Argives made an inroad into Phliasia, and lost nearly eighty men, who were caught in an ambuscade by the Phliasians and the Argive exiles. The Athenian garrison in Pylos took much spoil from the Lacedaemonians; nevertheless the latter did not renounce the peace and go to war, but only notified by a proclamation that if any one of their own people had a mind to make reprisals on the Athenians he might. The Corinthians next declared war upon the Athenians on some private grounds, but the rest of the Peloponnesians did not join them. The Melians took that part of the Athenian wall which looked towards the agora by a night assault, killed a few men, and brought in as much corn and other necessaries as they could; they then retreated and remained inactive. After this the Athenians set a better watch. So the summer ended.

In the following winter the Lacedaemonians had intended to make an expedition into the Argive territory, but finding that the sacrifices which they offered at the frontier were unfavourable they returned home. The Argives, suspecting that the threatened invasion was instigated by citizens of their own, apprehended some of them; others however escaped.

About the same time the Melians took another part of the Athenian wall; for the fortifications were insufficiently guarded. Whereupon the Athenians sent fresh troops, under the command of Philocrats the son of Demeas. The place was now closely invested, and there was treachery among the citizens themselves. So the Melians were induced to surrender at discretion. The Athenians thereupon put to death all who were of military age, and made slaves of the women and children. They then colonised the island, sending thither five hundred settlers of their own.

Suggested Readings

De Ste Croix, G.E.M. *The Origins of the Peloponnesian War*. Ithaca: Cornell University, 1972.

Fleiss, Peter J. *Thucydides and the Politics of Bipolarity*. Baton Rouge: Louisiana State University, 1966.

Grundy, George. *Thucydides and the History of His Age*. Oxford: Blackwell, 1948.

Hornblower, Simon. *Thucydides*. Baltimore: Johns Hopkins University, 1987.

Kagan, Donald. *The Archidamian War*. Ithaca: Cornell University, 1974.

Woodhead, Arthur Geoffrey. *Thucydides on the Nature of Power*. Cambridge: Harvard University, 1970.

Reading 18

NATIONAL SECURITY

Melvin Small

Notes from the Editors
National security *is one of those common terms, used by diplomats and citizens alike,
that has rarely been defined. Most people readily agree that national security, whether
Russian, American, Chinese, or Jordanian, must be defended. And many would agree
with Richard Nixon who suggested that national security is threatened whenever a nation's
chosen leader determines that it is.*

*In the selection that follows, historian Melvin Small tries to define and assess the
issue for the U.S. In* Was War Necessary? *(1980) from which the selection was taken,
he asked if it was necessary for the United States to enter the wars in which it fought.*

*His approach is a controversial one, especially since he prefers a narrow military
definition of national security. On the other hand, he does explore the possible economic,
political, and moral components of the concept. Throughout the excerpt, Small emphasizes
the difficulty of constructing a definition of national security that would be acceptable to
most observers. Also, he raises the complex issue of the justification for preventive war.*

*The selection poses a fundamental question to the reader: Under what circumstances
would he or she individually approve a call to arms?*

. . . In the system in which we have been operating since our earliest days, a
system without an international police force, a nation must take up arms when it is
attacked or is in imminent danger of being attacked. War may also be justified when
a nation's bases, vessels, or formal allies are attacked. From my perspective, all other
wars should be avoided whether they are fought to defend the balance of power, to
secure markets, or to uphold international morality.

Is this, as some contend, a naive neoisolationist position? Cannot all threats to
the balance of power, markets in Asia, and international morality ultimately become
imminent threats to national security? Obviously, the definition of "imminent" needs
clarification. Would not an attack have been imminent had Hitler defeated Russia and
England in 1941, or Germany won World War I and established economic supremacy
throughout the developing world, or the British been able to continue to trample on
our flag with impunity during the Napoleonic Wars?

Of course, if we accept these arguments, then we should seriously consider taking
out Libyan nuclear installations before those alleged fanatics develop the capability to
bury us. Or perhaps we should contrive a way to destroy the Organization of Petroleum

Reprinted with permission of the author Melvin Small from *Was War Necessary: National Security and
U.S. Entry into War, 1812–1950* (Beverly Hills, Calif.: Sage, 1980), pp. 17–24.

Exporting Countries before our economic system falls apart, or declare war on South Africa for her affronts to human dignity.

Few would seriously consider such policy recommendations today although they are the logical corollaries of perceiving threats to our national security as more than just direct military threats. All of which brings us back to that sticky problem of national security. If we are going to argue that the only wars that are justified are those fought to protect national security, then we must define that elusive concept. When is national security threatened? What is national security?

It might help if we considered threats to national security to be of three general kinds—direct military threats, economic threats, and threats to national honor. All, except pacifists, would take up arms when an enemy invaded our shores, and even pacifists might resist nonviolently. Almost everybody would take up arms when the enemy was aboard vessels on the way to the attack. But in the latter case, how do we know that they are not on a training mission? To take the most extreme example, suppose that on December 6, 1941, we had intercepted the Japanese fleet 500 miles from Pearl Harbor. A good number of Americans would have opposed an aggressive move on our part until we knew for sure that those aircraft carriers were not on a goodwill visit to Mexico or Chile. How could we have established for certain what their intentions were? Did we have to wait until the bombs started to fall?

Still on the military threat, most of us agree that we should go to war when someone makes a military incursion across our frontier. Where is our frontier? On the Rhine? The 38th Parallel? Havana? Had Hitler beaten England and then decided to take over Canada, could we have allowed him time to gain a foothold along our vast northern border? Or to change the perspective somewhat, could the Russians have afforded to sit idly by in 1956 while their fraternal neighbor, Hungary, was invaded by agents of the CIA? Did not Russia's strategic frontier begin at the Hungarian border? Although the definition of frontier is ambiguous, I define national security in terms limited to a direct military attack on our own soil or on the soil of a near neighbor whose conquest would leave us in a dangerously weakened position. Such a definition would exclude the domino theory that said we must stop "them" in Vietnam because Vietnam is only four jumps away from the United States, as in Vietnam-Malaya-Philippines-Hawaii.

Many argue that national security can be threatened by enemy activities that fall well short of military attack. If a nation threatens to upset the balance of power—as did Napoleon, Hitler, and perhaps Stalin or Truman—it may capture so much of the world's wealth and resources that other nations will suffer a serious decline in their living standards. With that decline could come mass unemployment, depression, and domestic political instability. Therefore, as in the case of America's relationship to Germany in World War I, even though the Kaiser posed no immediate military threat, had he won the war, his economic leverage would have been so great and his intentions so hostile that our economic and political stability would have been placed in jeopardy. Ultimately, Germany would have been able to convert economic dominance into military or political dominance.

To make the economic threat even more direct and relevant, one might argue that if forces opposed to our survival gained control of all of the oil-producing areas of the world, our national security would be threatened and we would have to go to war. For myself, I do not think economic arguments justify the loss of one citizen in war. I would prefer to do without oil and lower my standard of living than go to war for markets and raw materials. Of course, as the quality (or is it quantity?) of life declines, many lives might be lost in civil war—but I would take my chances on that happening.

Naturally, an American can more easily hold to such principles than citizens of countries such as Japan, who are dependent on free international trade. At various times in history, sustained economic blockades and boycotts directed against them could have led to mass starvation.

Attacks on a nation's honor or prestige represent a third sort of national security threat, and perhaps the most complicated one of all. If another nation invades disputed border areas, attacks our citizens and their property, makes illegal seizures of our vessels, or otherwise assaults our sovereignty, national security is said to be threatened. For one thing, if we accept such offenses without a fight, third parties may consider us a weakling nation, easily bullied and dominated. The international system is full of countries looking for easy prey. That nation which does not stand up for its honor will ultimately face a direct military threat to its security. In addition, a nation that allows its honor to be sullied will suffer a loss of general respect among its own people that could lead to political dislocation and civil turbulence.

In 1898, Spain faced a difficult choice. Either give the Cubans their freedom and lose the last vestige of imperial glory or fight a war against the United States she knew she could not win. To give in to U.S. demands for Cuban independence would have been humiliating and so, with only the slightest chance of finding European allies, Spain chose the path of war. As expected, she lost not only the war but also Cuba, the Philippines, Puerto Rico, and Guam. At the cost of all this real estate, in addition to 5,000 battle deaths, Spanish honor was maintained.

In 1939, Finland refused to give the Russians a huge chunk of territory near Leningrad in exchange for barren arctic wastes. Russia proceeded to invade its tiny neighbor, a nation whose friends were already involved in their own war. After a bloody struggle, Finland surrendered. She suffered 50,000 battle deaths, thousands more were injured, made homeless, and orphaned, and much of the country lay in ruins. She also was compelled to relinquish more territory than the Russians had originally demanded. Undoubtedly, Finnish honor was preserved. Observers thrilled to the courageous struggle waged by the little Davids in the infamous Winter War. Today, Finns walk proudly in the world; their national integrity and self-respect have been enhanced because of their celebrated resistance to aggression. They may also have escaped satellization in 1948 because of the toughness displayed in 1939–1940. But were other options available in 1939 and was not the price they paid for protecting national honor too high?

In a comparable situation, Czechoslovakia, a strong and progressive small power, did not take up arms against Germany when the Sudetenland was wrenched from her in 1938 and she did not fight the following year when the entire country was absorbed into the Third Reich. Most likely, though the Czechs could have mounted stiffer resistance than did the Poles later in the same year, in the end the Germans would have crushed them. Deciding that in this case discretion may have been the better part of valor, the realistic Czechs chose to sully their reputation and accept aggression without a fight. In exchange, the country emerged from World War II relatively unscathed. Although forced to live as Nazi vassals, and although some citizens and minorities were shipped off to the camps or suffered Lidices, many Czechs were able to protect their lives and property.

Denmark's experience with the question of national honor in World War II may be the most interesting of all. To this day, many Danes profess to be disturbed by their countrymen's attitudes in the spring of 1940. Unlike the Norwegians, Dutch, Belgians, and Poles, the Danes did not resist a German takeover. More important, they even accepted, albeit without enthusiasm, membership in the Anti-Comintern Pact which made them tacit allies of the Nazis. From 1940 to 1943, Denmark enjoyed self-government, there was little underground activity, and scant personal and physical damage to the country. An effective undergound did develop after 1943, especially after the Nazis took away what was left of Danish political freedom. In the fall of that same year, the Danes were able to foil Hitler's secret plans to round up Danish Jews. Almost the entire nation worked together to smuggle 7,500 Jews to Sweden before the Gestapo could ship them off to the crematoria. Despite this well-publicized gesture, Denmark's position during the war is still an important issue in the country. Why, they ask themselves, did they not fight like other small European states? Of course, what did the Poles, Belgians, Dutch, and Norwegians gain from their futile struggles— a clearer conscience, greater national peace of mind? In exchange for those unmeasurable rewards, they were visited with devastation, death, quislings, and concentration camps. Was Denmark's honor soiled in 1940? If so, what has been the effect on her national character and her respect among her own citizens and the rest of the nations of the world?

Given logistic considerations, the Danes made the wisest choice in 1940. Had they resisted for a while, the Nazi effort elsewhere (especially in Norway) conceivably might have faltered, but this was unlikely. Above all, the Danes can always talk about their assistance to the Jews, unique assistance that salvaged national honor with a realistic and effective gesture. The Danish people were too sensible to waste their lives by throwing themselves at Nazi tanks. What would have happened to their national conscience had they not the glorious Jewish incident to recall? Very little, I think, for a history of resistance and heroism would have been written anyway.

Some cynical Danes even claim that their resistance was not effective. To those who have grown up on Hollywood portrayals of European resistance movements, this comes as a shock. We expect that every Frenchman, Dane, Belgian, and Norwegian helped the Allies by blowing up rail lines, protecting downed fliers, and sending secret coded messages from short-wave transmitters hidden in the basements of local cafes. As the powerful documentary film *The Sorrow and the Pity* demonstrates, most Frenchmen, like most citizens in similar plights, sat out World War II, neither overtly nor covertly resisting. In a few years, after memories of the war faded, national honor was assuaged by inflating scattered acts of resistance into a widespread national patriotic movement. Is this merely self-delusion? If it is, can a nation survive it? I think so, and consequently am suspicious of arguments claiming that a failure to stand up to a stronger bully must lead to a decline in self-esteem that can be translated into a threat to national security.

If a nation sees that war is the only outcome of a diplomatic duel unless it accepts less than half a loaf, and if it does not stand much of a chance of winning that war, then it is best to take less than half the loaf. It is said that aggressors can never be sated—give them the Sudetenland and they will eventually come back for more. Perhaps, but not every diplomatic rival is Hitler. One should put off the day of final reckoning until national survival is at stake. Then "better dead than Red," and maybe not even then. This is not a pacifist's approach to international conflict. It represents a course of rationality and prudence.

Undoubtedly, justifications for war based upon unemotional analyses of the military, economic, and prestige components of national security are not entirely satisfactory. What is missing from these calculations is the righteous war, the war to save suffering peoples. To some degree, this moral criterion dovetails with the prestige criterion. Our national security is said to be dependent upon the maintenance of our prestige and our prestige is, in turn, partially dependent upon the fulfillment of our implicit national commitment to rescue nations from oppressors. Those who justify war according to some form of moral imperative do not like to talk about anything as base as national security. To them, any war fought to defend the freedom of others is a rational war.

Such an approach, though noble, makes little sense. In the first place, people who run nations do not make war for those exalted purposes, even though they may convince themselves and their citizens that they are entering the battle to save humanity. No doubt in many wars, one side's strategic interests coincided with what appeared to be the interests of humanity. Nevertheless, I cannot identify a single war in modern history that was launched primarily for reasons of morality. This is not to say that we cannot or should not support the morally preferable side in a war. Such a determination is easiest in wars in which one group is fighting for liberation from oppression. Nevertheless, the selection of the morally superior side should not be confused with the notion that governments go to war because of moral considerations.

All statesmen in recent times have claimed that they were fighting their wars for only the most moral purposes. The Nazis fought to save the world from Jewish domination, the United States to defend the democrats of Seoul against the butchers of Pyongyang, the Russions to liberate Hungary from counterrevolutionaries, the Chinese to destroy Tibetan feudalism, and the Indians to assist their persecuted brothers in Bangladesh. All of these cases, and countless more, represent ex post facto justifications for decisions based upon considerations of Realpolitik. Even the war the United States fought against the Axis had little to do with morality at the start. If we did enter for higher spiritual purposes, then why were we not in the ranks in 1939 and 1940 when Hitler was overrunning country after country? Once in the war, Americans were told they were fighting to rid the world of the fascist scourge. In the 1950s and 1960s, if our interventions were based upon a desire to free peoples from oppression in Korea, Vietnam, Cuba, and the Dominican Republic, where were we in Spain or Greece?

Our morality, as well as the morality of other nations, is highly selective and inconsistent. One leader's morality is another's immorality, one leader's freedom is another's oppression. Even philosophers and theologians are unable to agree on universally acceptable definitions of moral and immoral international behavior. In any event, moral justifications have never been directly related to the decision makers' definitions of national security. To oppose war on humanistic grounds and then to eliminate moral arguments from our analyses may seem paradoxical. Yet given the impossibility of defining morality, it would be futile to devote much attention to the issue of just wars. If anything, the case against war becomes all the stronger when we use the realpoliticians' own cost-benefit analysis against them.

Suggested Readings

Beard, Charles A. *The Idea of National Interest*. New York: Macmillan, 1934.

Morgenthau, Hans. *In Defense of the National Interest*. New York: Knopf, 1951.

Pusey, Merlo J. *The Way We Go to War*. Boston: Houghton Mifflin, 1969.

Wheeler, Gerald E. "National Security." *Encyclopedia of American Foreign Policy,* II ed. Alexander DeConde. New York: Scribner's, 1981, pp. 523–34.

Wolfers, Arnold. "National Security as an Ambiguous Symbol." *Political Science Quarterly* 67 (December 1952), pp. 481–502.

CHAPTER 4

The Causes of War, Part 1

Almost all disciplines that deal with human behavior have made contributions to our understanding of aggression, conflict, and war. This chapter is devoted to five general disciplinary frameworks, each of which has been employed profitably by students of international war.

Some biologists and psychologists seek the roots of war in humankind's aggressive tendencies. These tendencies allegedly show up from time to time in our individual and collective interactions in families, communities, nations, and even in the international system. Sometimes our aggression is channeled into peaceful, even creative activities. Other times it leads to violence and war. According to this view, since nations are collections of individuals who can all be pugnacious, it is only natural for them to find themselves in mortal combat on occasion. At the level of the decision maker with authority for a war/no war decision, one can imagine how his or her personally aggressive traits might help determine the outcome of that decision. Decision makers are, after all, humans capable of irrational behavior, captive to their emotions that, in turn, may be affected by psychological and physiological factors.

Much of the theorizing in this realm is based upon animal experimentation. Scientists observe gulls or monkeys, run rats through mazes, and stimulate fish with electric shocks. They then draw analogies between those animals' levels of aggressive behavior, under certain conditions, and that of humans. Needless to say, scientists, as well as philosophers, raise a host of objections to this facile analogizing, none the least of which has to do with the apparent emotional, intellectual, and even spiritual differences between humans and the so-called lower animals.

In the first selection in this chapter, "The Biology of Human Aggression," James A. Schellenberg surveys major developments in this area from Darwin's voyage to the Galapagos in the mid-nineteenth century to the rise of the new field of sociobiology in the mid-twentieth century. The passage of time has not stilled the debate over the value of the contributions that the biological sciences make to our understanding of human, and not just animal, conflict.

Many psychologists tend to sidestep the debate over instinctual versus learned aggression. They are most interested in what triggers aggression in humans and how that aggression might be contained or controlled. In their studies of frustration, misperception, and attitude change, for example, we learn about stimuli that lead to aggressive behavior and how individuals displace or project their aggression. As in the biological studies, psychological studies often involve controlled laboratory experiments from which are extrapolated theories about how people relate to one another in their communities and how nations and their leaders relate to one another in the international system. Carried to an extreme, the findings from psychological experiments with freshmen in their introductory college classes sometimes end up as theories about why the United States invaded Grenada in 1983.

Not speaking for all psychologists, Sigmund Freud, the founder of psychoanalysis, tried to answer the question "Why War?", the second article in this chapter. Writing over fifty years ago, Freud applied some of the concepts of his subdiscipline to the history of human conflict. Members of his guild today might disagree with his emphasis upon a biologically-determined theory of aggression.

David Fabbro in "Peaceful Societies" employs research from anthropology in a novel way to discover why some humans do not behave aggressively towards one another. Instead of asking Freud's question, "Why war?" Fabbro asks, "Why peace?" By examining seven societies that do not engage in violence, in particular their child-rearing, governance, and problem-solving methods, Fabbro searches for patterns that might lead the rest of humankind toward less aggressive activities.

Much of the debate about the causes of conflict revolves around those who stress individual factors, such as the biologists and the psychologists, and those who stress structural factors, such as the economists. For many, economic interpretations provide the most powerful tools for understanding the causes of societal conflict. In their simplest sense, these interpretations claim that nations go to war to obtain resources, markets, and territory to enhance or protect national wealth. In earlier times, much of the wealth of a nation literally flowed into the coffers of the kings and their cronies. In our own era, national economic health is a prime determinant of domestic political stability and national power, both central to the survival of a regime.

In addition, foreign adventures have often been linked to domestic instability as leaders try to rally their disgruntled populace around the flag through the refocussing of attention to a real or imagined external threat to national security. Economic approaches may also be linked to psychological approaches when one considers national mood as a factor that contributes to an environment supportive of an aggressive foreign policy. Some historians, for example, talk of a "psychic crisis" in the United States in the 1890s, produced in part by the depression of 1893, that led to American imperialism.

Millions of people around the world today believe that Marxist analysis best explains why nations war with one another. The Soviet authors of the fourth article in this section, "The Economic Foundations of Wars: A Soviet View," apply the theories of Karl Marx and V. I. Lenin to contemporary conflict. Not all Marxists agree with this official interpretation, nor do many scholars who consider themselves to be non-Marxist economic determinists.

Many political scientists also concentrate on the system in their studies of international relations. Some borrow from the psychological and biological sciences, others from economics, while still others emphasize an approach unique to their discipline. Even before there was such a thing as political science, political philosophers like Machiavelli began to describe and prescribe rules of rational international behavior. Over the centuries, the realist paradigm emerged from such contributions, a paradigm that often lies behind modern studies of diplomatic and martial interaction.

In their analysis of Hans Morgenthau's contributions to that paradigm, James E. Dougherty and Richard L. Pfaltzgraff, Jr., present one view of "The Realist Approach to International Conflict." According to the realists, political relationships are governed by objective rules which, when followed, produce the most stable and peaceful system possible. Conflict of interest is assumed in every domestic and international relationship. However, violence or war is not the necessary outcome of that conflict as long as every state follows its own limited national interest.

As with previous approaches, many political scientists and other students of war do not accept all of the assumptions of realism. For some, it serves better as a critique of morally or ideologically based diplomacy than as a key to understanding conflict in the international system.

The use of any of the five approaches presented here does not preclude the use of the other four. One can imagine employing contributions from biology, psychology, anthropology, economics, and political science in concert to explain why nations come into conflict or why they go to war. Some approaches may be more useful in illuminating the underlying causes of a conflict; others may be helpful in explaining crisis behavior. The application of some of these general disciplinary approaches to specific case studies is the subject of Chapter 5.

Reading 19

THE BIOLOGY OF HUMAN AGGRESSION

James A. Schellenberg

Notes from the Editors

In The Science of Conflict *(1982), sociologist James A. Schellenberg explores the major explanations for human conflict and evaluates conflict resolution techniques. In his chapter on the biological approach to conflict, reprinted here, he examines the development of theories from Charles Darwin to Konrad Lorenz and on to Edward O. Wilson.*

Is aggression learned or innate? That is the issue which has produced heated scholarly debate for many years. If aggression is innate or instinctive, then we may have a long way to go to eliminate violent conflict from human society. If aggression is mostly learned, then through our schools and other socialization processes we should be able to "create" individuals who are more gentle and less prone to violence.

One major question posed in much of the research and theorizing in the field is whether one can draw an analogy between an individual and a collectivity such as a nation. Another, even more serious problem, has to do with the relationship between humans and animals. Most of the work in the field has involved the study of animals, sometimes as complex and advanced as monkeys, often as simple and unhumanlike as rats or small fish. Does the behavior of a rat in a maze have anything to do with the way humans behave?

Even if one accepts a biological approach and supports the notion that aggression is primarily instinctive, all is not lost. There are those who argue that humans, the highest form of animals, sublimate their aggressive instincts through nonlethal outlets, such as the participating in or watching of sports. In any event, the relationship of biology to international conflict is an ambiguous one about which no consensus has emerged.

Is a propensity for social conflict somehow rooted in our nature as members of the human species?

This question cannot adequately be answered with a simple yes or no. In pursuing an answer, we will first examine the revolution in thinking about human origins and human nature which is associated with the work of Charles Darwin (1809-82). We will then discuss some of the social implications of Darwinism as seen by other theorists in the second half of the nineteenth century. Finally, we will consider some of the Darwinian currents of thought today, and then draw our conclusions (tentative though they may be) about the biological basis of human conflict and aggression.

The Origin of Darwinism

The theory of evolution was no sudden hypothesis in Charles Darwin's mind. The idea had long existed in one form or another (Darwin's own grandfather had written a book on the subject), and Darwin early questioned the assumption of permanently fixed species. It was during the five years that the young Darwin served as a naturalist aboard the *Beagle* (1831–36) that his thoughts on evolution began to take shape. However, he still lacked an explanation for why or how evolutionary change occurred.

The main purpose of the expedition of the *Beagle* was to survey the coast of South America. Darwin contributed to this purpose with important geological observations. These observations clearly supported the notion that present landforms were produced by slow evolutionary changes from previous forms, as was indeed claimed in the recently published *Principles of Geology* (first edition 1830–33) by Charles Lyell. But Darwin's curiosity roamed widely to other matters for observation—the various types of plants found in different places, the strange variations in forms of animals, and the strange customs of primitive Indians and only marginally civilized gauchos. He collected a fascinating variety of biological specimens, and his written observations in the form of his *Journal* (1839) were soon published.

But even more important than Darwin's discoveries on this expedition were the unanswered questions which arose. Different geological strata encased different forms of life; does this not indicate an evolution of life forms as well as the earth forms in which they are found? And how are we to understand the important similarities between extinct varieties and present plants and animals in the same area? Or the present differences between similar forms in different locations? Some form of biological evolution seemed a necessary part of the answer for each of these questions.

But Darwin still had no explanation of what could account for the major changes necessary to transform a species. For months after his return to England, Darwin pondered the subject of how evolution might take place. Changes in domesticated breeds of plants and animals offered some clues, and they demonstrated the importance of a careful selection of preferred types. But how could selection be produced in nature? The answer came to Darwin quite suddenly, as he recounts in his *Autobiography*:

In October 1838, that is, fifteen months after I had begun my systematic enquiry, I happened to read for amusement Malthus on Population, *and being well prepared to appreciate the struggle for existence which everywhere goes on from long-continued observation of the habits of animals and plants, it at once struck me that under these circumstances favourable variations would tend to be preserved, and unfavourable ones to be destroyed. The results of this would be the formation of a new species.*

Natural environments, in other words, select a new species by the gradual effect of differential death rates of the previous population. Those more apt to survive are "naturally selected" to become the emerging form.

Darwin was extremely cautious about his new idea, for he realized its sharp departure from the generally accepted opinions of fellow scientists. Then too there were other kinds of opinions—such as those of his devout new wife, to whom he had resolved to say nothing about his radical new ideas. It was not until four years later that Darwin set forth in a brief manuscript his idea of natural selection, but he made no move to publish this. What he did publish instead were such books as *Coral Reefs* (1842) and *Geological Observations on South America* (1846). In 1858, twenty years after he had first conceived the idea of natural selection, he at last worked on a book to present this theory. Then, however, in the mail came a letter from the East Indies, where Alfred R. Wallace was engaged in research as a naturalist. With this letter was an essay which, Darwin was horrified to discover, was almost an exact summary of his own theory. This moved Darwin into action. He sought the advice of scientific friends, who arranged for Wallace's essay and an abstract of Darwin's ideas to be presented together to the scientific world. Darwin then hurried to bring out a fuller statement the next year, which took the form of his celebrated *Origin of Species* (1859).

The full title of his book, *The Origin of Species by Means of Natural Selection or the Preservation of Favored Races in the Struggle for Life,* makes clear the central importance of natural selection in Darwin's theory of evolution. In his introduction he summarized this idea as follows:

As many more individuals of each species are born than can possibly survive; and as, consequently, there is a frequently recurring struggle for existence, it follows that any being, if it vary however slightly in any manner profitable to itself, under the complex and sometimes varying conditions of life, will have a better chance of surviving, and thus be naturally *selected.*

In the hundreds of fact-filled pages that follow, the theory of biological evolution is systematically developed. Although natural selection is not presented as a total explanation, it is seen as the most important factor in the origin and change of species. "Thus," he says in his final paragraph, "from the war of nature, from famine and death, the most exalted object which we are capable of conceiving, namely, the production of the higher animals, directly follows."

In the *Origin* Darwin says nothing about the evolution of man. He does suggest that "much light will be thrown" in the future by similar analyses concerning "the origin of man and his history." But that is the extent of Darwin's discussion of human origins in that book. Twelve years later, in *The Descent of Man,* he attempted to follow up on this direction of analysis. While still the central theme, natural selection is here joined by a number of other ideas which were only briefly presented or hinted at in the *Origin of Species.*

The Descent of Man includes attention to, as factors in evolution, the inheritance of acquired characteristics, special accidents of heredity, what Darwin calls "correlated variation" (features which are not themselves adaptive but happen to be developed along with those which are), and differential fertility. Especially emphasized is "sexual selection" or preferential mating, which directly results in differential fertility. In fact, the full title of the book is *The Descent of Man and Selection in Relation to Sex,* and a discussion of sexual selection actually constitutes most of the book. It is among higher animals that sexual selection becomes important in evolution; among lower animals "perceptive and intellectual faculties are not sufficiently advanced to allow of the feelings of love and jealousy, or of the exertion of choice." Sexual selection takes place in two kinds of "sexual struggle" between rivals: one is typically between males who seek "to drive away or kill their rivals," while the other is a more subtle competition for the attentions and favors of the opposite sex (male or female). In both cases, we have the basis of a rivalry between individuals within a species in seeking to mate which is a more direct confrontation than is the impersonal competition of natural selection.

Social Darwinism

Other than in his extended discussion of sexual selection, Darwin had little to say about social or group factors in human evolution. He did briefly refer to the importance of "social instincts" which higher animals have acquired gradually "for the good of the community." Man, however, has "few or no special instincts"; social motives in humans, said Darwin, are much more influenced by learning than is the case with other animals. Other than making such general points, Darwin himself contributed little to what has come to be called "social Darwinism."

Other writers were far less reticent in tracing the implications of Darwinism for society. One whom Darwin cited with general approval ("our great philosopher," he called him at one point) was his fellow Englishman, Herbert Spencer. Spencer was an even more thoroughgoing evolutionist than Darwin, extending this idea to the far reaches of human society and, indeed, the entire universe. Spencer also talked about the importance of "survival of the fittest" (a phrase which Darwin borrowed from him) before the *Origin of Species* appeared.

In his *First Principles,* published in 1862, Spencer sets forth a universal law of evolution. It is this:

Evolution is an integration of matter and concomitant dissipation of motion, during which the matter passes from an indefinite, incoherent homogeneity to a definite, coherent heterogeneity, and during which the retained motion undergoes a parallel transformation.

Such evolution was viewed as a cosmic law of nature—applicable alike to what Spencer distinguished as the *inorganic* (physical), *organic* (biological), and *superorganic* (or sociocultural) realms.

On the superorganic level, societies may be seen as significant integrations which continually increase in coherence and heterogeneity. This view of human society is parallel to the conception of biological organisms as emergent wholes. Societies, like individual organisms, develop their integrities or unities through a struggle for survival, a struggle which in large part pits society against society. Competition for survival is therefore characteristic of both individual organisms and societies, and in this struggle are forged the characteristic forms taken by animal species and/or human societies.

Fear is endemic in the uncertainties of early forms of human society, which leads to religious and political forms of social control. Especially prominent is a military form of social organization. Militarism makes possible the combination of smaller groups into larger units, thus extending the scope of social organization. With the expanding scope of social organization, however, more emphasis can be given to peaceful pursuits. Gradually, then, as the scope of human society expands, the plasticity of society increases and individual spontaneity and initiative assume more importance.

Coercion becomes less and less necessary as a basis of social integration as more effective institutions of human cooperation prove their survival value. Spencer's view of the general evolution of society may thus be described as a transition from "military" (or coercively controlled) to "industrial" (or functionally cooperative) forms of social organization.

As we move more and more toward an industrial society—that is, one of peaceful interdependence—obvious conflict becomes more muted. But, according to Spencer, competition is still going on indirectly, pitting individual against individual and institutional form against institutional form. This is nature's way of discriminating between the more fit and less fit forms. And the less we consciously interfere with the process the better, for the most adaptive (and therefore best) forms are those which emerge gradually out of this long-term competition for survival. This, of course, led Spencer directly to the political position of *laissez-faire,* arguing for a bare minimum of governmental regulation. This should allow, he believed, maximum room for the competitive process, which produces the gradual improvement of human society.

In the United States, William Graham Sumner was soon arguing somewhat similar views. Conflict over the means of subsistence is the underlying fact which shapes the nature of human society, according to Sumner. But Sumner emphasized group factors (including the binding power of folkways and mores, which are arbitrarily evolved by groups) more strongly than did Spencer, and Sumner had less optimism about the direction of evolutionary change.

Spencer and Sumner were among the founding fathers of the discipline of sociology in England and the United States, respectively. Both were thoroughgoing evolutionists, and both saw a central role for the application of natural selection to institutions of human society. Meanwhile, on the European continent an even more extreme form of social Darwinism was being propounded in the name of sociology by Ludwig Gumplowicz. In 1883 Gumplowicz published his most famous work, *Der Rassenkampf (Race Conflict),* followed two years later by his *Outlines of Sociology.* He too tried to base his sociology upon natural science foundations; and for Gumplowicz, as for Spencer and Sumner, conflict between societies is a basic theme in social evolution. But especially unlike Spencer, Gumplowitz did not perceive these conflicts as becoming reduced and more individualized with the development of civilization. War between groups, in his view, has always been the main proving ground for the evolution of human social forms—and so it remains today.

At the heart of social conflict for Gumplowicz is conflict between races and nationality groups. To begin with, he assumes (in contrast to Darwin, incidentally) a polygenetic origin (that is, for different races at different times) of mankind. He further assumes the existence of an inherent animosity between persons of different races. Once the means of warfare became developed, it was only natural that war would be a constant feature of humanity. With war comes the possibility of the conquest of one group by another and the development of a strong state to ensure a means for domination. With the consolidation of larger political units (through war and conquest), a greater differentiation develops within the society. From then on, the range of conflict increases within societies to add to that between societies as, in the words of Gumplowicz, "the life and death struggle between hordes anthropologically different becomes a contest between social groups, classes, estates and political parties." Class conflict is an especially prominent feature in developed states. In origin the dominant class usually represents a conquering group, but over time new classes develop to complicate the power relationships. Primary elements in the formation of the class system are opposing economic interests as well as the formation of alignments necessary to allow effective domination by a ruling group. The desire for greater material welfare for one's group and a drive toward domination over other groups provide the constant stimuli for further conflicts of class against class and nation against nation.

Throughout the writings of Gumplowicz runs a strong naturalistic emphasis. "The alpha and omega of sociology," as he summarized it, "its highest perception and final word is: human history is a natural process." In this natural process, however, it is human groups, not individuals, which constitute the fundamental units. Indeed, according to Gumplowicz,

It is not man himself who thinks, but his social community; the source of his thoughts is in the social medium in which he lives, the social atmosphere which he breathes, and he cannot think naught else that what the influences of his social environment concentrating upon his brain necessitate. . . . Man is not self-made mentally any more than he is physically. His mind and thoughts are the product of his social medium, of the social element whence he arose, in which he lives.

Given this social determinism, Gumplowicz can give no basis for considering social reality as anything other than it is. Conflict is endemic in the nature of human society, and there is nothing which we can do about it. Sociology can contribute nothing to help man resolve these conflicts, for they will continue to be resolved primarily through physical force. What social science can best contribute is understanding—and resignation. By adding to our knowledge of the basic laws of human society, according to Gumplowicz, "sociology lays the foundations for the morals of reasonable resignation, morals higher than those resting on the imaginary freedom and self-determination of the individual."

Today no sociologists apply the Darwinian ideas of evolution and natural selection to human society quite so thoroughly as did their late-nineteenth-century counterparts. No one generalizes so freely and with such optimism as Spencer, or so broadly and with such pessimism as Gumplowicz. Human society can be said to evolve, but in such an infinitely more complex manner than do biological organisms that sociologists generally hold that natural selection as a biological idea has little relevance. But does it not still have *some* value for understanding the nature of society?

Most sociologists today would admit some room for the principle of natural selection in the evolution of cultural traits—as *cultural* evolution, though, quite distinct from biological evolution. We are able to fly, for example, not because we have a pair of appendages which we have been gradually adapted for millions of years to serve as wings, but because of tools produced by the human brain and hand. These tools themselves undergo a kind of evolution, as new forms of airplanes prove themselves better adapted to our needs than previous forms. So, a kind of natural selection goes on in determining the products of human culture which are most likely to survive. But note: we are not now talking of the survival of human individuals or groups. We are talking about the survival of cultural forms, forms which are generally shared by humans and which fairly easily pass from group to group. We are not talking of anything which is the special property of biologically identifiable groups, such as families, clans, tribes, or races.

Some social scientists have argued that cultural evolution has completely displaced biological evolution as a factor of significant change for humans. Weston LaBarre, for example, makes this claim:

The human hand is the adaptation to end all adaptations: the emancipated hand has emancipated man from any other organic evolution whatsoever. *With man, genetic evolution and organic experiments have come to an end. Without involving the animal body and its slow, blind genetic mechanisms, man's hands make the tools and the machines which render his own further physical evolution unnecessary; they replace the slow, cumbrous, expensive, uncertain, and painful mechanism of organic evolution with the swift, conscious, biologically free, and painless making of machines.*

Not all social scientists would agree that humans are now free from further biological evolution. Most would argue that such organic change is overshadowed by cultural evolution, but that biological evolution is still going on. Whether or not such organic change may be an important factor in our cultural adaptability and social behavior (other than by giving us our brains and hands in the first place) is one of the most hotly disputed questions among today's social scientists. Even those who most confidently ridicule the excesses of nineteenth-century social Darwinism find some of the same arguments coming from their colleagues in biology in the final decades of the twentieth century. Darwinism is once again becoming a center of controversy among scholars. In the next section we will examine how new currents of science— especially those bearing the names of "ethology" and "sociobiology"—are addressing themselves to the subject of the biology of human aggression.

The New Biology of Conflict

How much has happened in the hundred years since Darwinism became a major force in social science! Yet, strangely, how similar are some of the controversies engaging social scientists today to those of a century ago. The place of biological evolution in the understanding of human society is an issue which is still not at rest. This issue serves as the focus of renewed scientific and ideological debate, centering especially on the role of genetics in structuring human behavior.

As social science developed in the final decades of the nineteenth century and the opening years of the twentieth century, an evolutionary perspective provided a dominant framework for analysis. Early American sociology, for example, such as that represented by Lester F. Ward or William Graham Sumner, was cast solidly in the perspective of evolution—both biological and cultural. Early social psychology also followed an evolutionary perspective. Then, beginning in the second decade of the twentieth century and increasing in the 1920s and 1930s, came a disenchantment with such an approach. Evolutionary theory was viewed as too broad and all-encompassing for a scientific analysis of behavior. What seemed needed was a more limited framework, and anthropology, psychology, and sociology alike turned to the more patient accumulation of facts. Evolutionary theory was considered too speculative to have much to say for scientific studies of human behavior.

Then came the rapid advancement of genetic research in the third quarter of the twentieth century and, at the same time, marked progress in systematic behavior studies of lower animals. A new science called "ethology" was developed to study comparative animal behavior patterns, with a special emphasis upon the instinctive roots of such behavior. Popularizations of this work by Robert Ardrey, Konrad Lorenz, and Desmond Morris soon brought home to the literate public the implications of ethology for understanding human social behavior. Finally, in 1975, a still newer science, "socio-biology," was announced by E. O. Wilson and projected to take over eventually a broad area of science ranging from ethology to sociology. Immediate controversy soared about the pretensions of this newest science and especially about its claims regarding the genetic bases of behavior.

Since central issues for the interpretation of human conflict and aggression are at stake, it is relevant that we at least review briefly this recent literature. Let us give special attention to Lorenz's *On Aggression* (a leading example of ethology). Later we will briefly examine Wilson's *Sociobiology*.

Much of *On Aggression* consists of a mature scientist's review and reflection on data with which he has first-hand experience—such as fighting behavior among cichlid species of fish or, his personal favorite, the greylag goose. Combining these with the research of others, he builds generalizations about aggression as a spontaneous response which is instinctively elicited by certain triggering occasions, with the occasions differing from species to species. Within each species there is a patterned regularity of the way aggression against fellow members of the species is expressed as well as the occasions for this aggression. Aggression is frequently highly ritualized, typically allowing for attack and submission to be expressed with little actual danger to life. Displacement of aggression upon substitute objects also frequently occurs, especially in highly social species.

In Lorenz's view, the natural mechanisms of aggression and its control are closely related to different forms of animal social organization. He points to four different types of social organization observed among various animal species. The simplest form is the anonymous crowd, a simple aggregation of members who band together for convenience or protection. Aggression is not characteristic within such simple "flocks" of birds or "schools" of fish. A second system of organization is the territorial group—members of a species which share a similar area, such as a nesting colony, which they defend against intruders. A third system is a tribal group, such as an extended family of rats which will attack any rat with the wrong kind of smell. All three of these systems of social organization are based on some vague consciousness of kind, but without requiring individual personal identities. The fourth system of social organization, the bond, is formed on the basis of individual identities. Here both love and hate become important features, with elaborate forms of courtship and intergenerational concern within the family group, along with highly expressive aggression against outsiders.

The particular forms of aggressive behavior, Lorenz holds, have been developed in each species through natural selection. They therefore always have some general evolutionary purpose, or perhaps a combination of particular purposes. The most general and common evolutionary function of animal aggression is the spacing out of the species. Such territorial dispersion facilitates population control (those more dispersed having lower life chances) and provides a reasonably effective environment for those remaining (enough food and mates, for example). More particular forms of aggressive behavior may function to facilitate sexual selection (such as access for a male to a particular female), brood defense, and the establishment of stable social relations (for example, through hierarchical "pecking orders"). Each species has its distinctive place in nature, and thus its distinctive combination of evolutionary functions fulfilled by aggression. And man? Says Lorenz:

 . . . *it is more than probable that the destructive intensity of the aggression drive, still a hereditary evil of mankind, is the consequence of a process of intra-specific selection which worked on our forefathers for roughly forty thousand years, that is, throughout the Early Stone Age. When man had reached the stage of having weapons, clothing, and social organization, so overcoming the dangers of starving, freezing, and being eaten by wild animals, and these dangers ceased to be the essential factors influencing selection, an evil intra-specific selection must have set in. The factor influencing selection was now the wars waged between hostile neighboring tribes.*

At any rate, man is seen as having his aggression as strongly rooted in his biological heritage as is true for other species. Indeed, he seems unusually murderous, for his development of weapons came so fast that he has not yet evolved the biological mechanisms of restraint—so common in the ritualized aggression of other species.

Humanity today, in the view of Lorenz, is left with a considerable burden in the control of its aggression. How are we to do this? In his final chapter, Lorenz considers a number of approaches toward controlling aggression. He dismisses simple moralistic condemnation and the elimination of aggressive cues as ineffective approaches, and the possibility of eliminating the aggressive drive through eugenic planning is also seen as a false lead (mainly because we do not know which desirable human traits might at the same time be lost). With what then are we left? Redirection seems to be Lorenz's main formula. He sees competitive sports as an especially promising area. He also talks about developing collective enthusiasm for causes of human betterment which can inspire us to heights of achievement and glory, as did the wars of old. Other forms of cultural control of aggression also should be furthered, he suggests. Finally, we are given the prescription of insight—to see our own behavior within a proper perspective. Two forms of this insight, either of which should aid our collective survival, are a sense of humor and a sense of our place in the natural order. Either assists us in developing the perspective necessary to help restrain that murderous impulse which lurks within.

The most problematic issue raised by Lorenz's work for us is that of the inherited nature of an aggressive drive, especially when we consider human behavior. Despite all the recent achievements in genetics, we are still a long way from identifying the precise genetic code for human inheritance. Even when we are able to derive a statistic called a "heritability index" (to measure the extent to which a given characteristic varies in response to known differences in heredity), its interpretation remains fraught with difficulties. For one thing, attempts to measure the heritability of aggression have not given either very high or very consistent results. This suggests that, at least for humans, aggression has a far greater learned component than Lorenz appears to allow.

However, we should recognize that in the higher vertebrates, including humans, there are rather clearly patterned neurological correlates of aggressive behavior. Centers of the brain associated with different kinds of aggressive responses have been identified and their functions described. Experimentally, it has been possible to manipulate aggression by hormone treatments and brain stimulation. But we should not neglect consideration of the sequence of events by which these physiological mechanisms normally operate. The brain centers most involved in aggression typically respond to signals given after some external stimulus is interpreted, and endocrine levels are typically affected in response as well. Aggression is not simply created from within; the physiological ingredients are themselves normally the result of perceptions about external events. As a leading student of animal behavior, John Paul Scott, concludes a discussion of the physiology of aggression:

The important fact is that the chain of causation in every case eventually traces back to the outside. There is no physiological evidence of any spontaneous stimulation for fighting arising within the body.

The points that we have just considered appear to be at variance with Lorenz's conception of aggression as a spontaneous response which is instinctively elicited by certain triggering occasions. At least for the higher vertebrates, the spontaneity appears in highly qualified fashion. Certain triggering occasions (for example, there is a fair amount of research to implicate aversive and frustrating stimuli with aggression) may indeed be associated with aggression, but this association depends significantly on past learning—especially in the case of humans.

Enter Sociobiology

Where *On Aggression* gives a leading naturalist's interpretations of aggression in humans and other animals, *Sociobiology* presumes to lay out a completely new science for the analysis of social behavior of animals of all types. Although conflict and aggression are not the central themes in this work, they are featured with enough prominence to make a few comments about this book relevant here.

Edward O. Wilson is an expert on insect societies, but his interests also cover broad questions of population biology and social organization in all species. These interests he proposes to bring together in the new science of sociobiology. His enormous book, *Sociobiology: The New Synthesis,* reviews exhaustively the literature of the social life of animals, especially as interpreted within the framework of population biology. Within this framework, social evolution is viewed essentially as biological evolution. Genetic change is assumed to be the basis for changes in both the physical structure and the behavioral functioning of a species. Broadly speaking, then, features of social behavior are seen as genetically selected for, even if precise genes may not be identified. Wilson, however, is somewhat more cautious than Lorenz in talking about aggression as an instinct. Aggression is seen as genetic in the sense that, according to Wilson, "its components have proved to have a high degree of heritability," but he sees no general instinct of aggression. Rather, there are particular patterns of aggressive behavior which different species have found to be adaptive for their particular survival purposes. For example, displays of territorial defense are apt to be developed when the food supply is relatively limited and the costs of such defense are not too large. However, should defense prove too costly, a less territorial pattern is apt to be evolved. In evolving their particular patterns, says Wilson:

Species are entirely opportunistic. Their behavior patterns do not conform to any innate restrictions but are guided, like all other biological traits, solely by what happens to be advantageous over a period of time sufficient for evolution to occur.

Wilson identifies eight different categories of aggressive behavior: (1) territorial aggression, (2) dominance aggression, (3) sexual aggression, (4) parental disciplinary aggression, (5) weaning aggression, (6) moralistic aggression, (7) predatory aggression, and (8) antipredatory aggression. He emphasizes that aggression "is a mixture of very different behavior patterns serving very different functions" in different species. Even within the same species a wide variation in aggressive response is possible. He cites the example of how differently the rattlesnake will respond when wrestling with another rattlesnake, when stalking small prey, when dealing with a large animal, or when countering a rattlesnake-eating king snake. Four very different ways of fighting are all here shown by the same species of snake, each adapted to its special circumstances.

Wilson has little to say about human aggression, other than to assume that a characteristic "so widespread and easily invoked" can hardly be neutral or negative in affecting species or group survival. True, there is great variability in the aggressive behavior of humans. "But," continues Wilson,

in order to be adaptive it is enough that aggressive patterns be evoked only under certain conditions of stress such as those that might arise during food shortages and periodic high population densities. It also does not matter whether the aggression is wholly innate or is acquired part or wholly by learning. We are now sophisticated enough to know that the capacity to learn certain behaviors is itself a genetically controlled and therefore evolved trait.

Here Wilson seems to be trying to avoid a heredity-versus-learning issue by viewing both as broadly within the adaptive processes of evolutionary change. He also suggests that the adaptive value of a particular behavior pattern for a species will not always be easily apparent to an observer.

In this final chapter, Wilson gives some attention to the distinctive plasticity and cultural nature of the human species, but his analysis of human social evolution is still essentially in terms of genetic evolution. Human institutions appear to have been selected for by the genetic advantages they gave to early human groups. Little room is provided for viewing cultural evolution as itself a primary determining force. It is this omission which most dismays sociologists and anthropologists about sociobiology.

An example of Wilson's tendency to emphasize biological evolution to the neglect of cultural influences may be seen in his treatment of warfare. He suggests that war has played a significant role in the genetic evolution of humans, helping to spur general mental and cultural advance as well as selecting for military traits. Although possibly not universal (". . . some isolated cultures will escape the process for generations at a time, in effect reverting temporarily to what ethnographers classify as a pacific state"), warfare is viewed by Wilson as a significant general factor in human evolution. Anthropologists, however, have not shown any consensus in support of such an interpretation. Ashley Montagu counters with the view that "up to some twelve thousand years ago war played an insignificant role" in evolution, and that in the last 12,000 years war has become either biologically irrelevant or dysgenic.

In pointing out various functions of war for primitive man, some anthropologists point to important contrasts between war fought within the tribe (often highly ritualized and associated with a male-supremacist cultural complex) and war between tribes (less common in the simplest societies than war within the tribe). It has been shown that these forms of warfare tend to be pursued in quite different fashions by rather different societies. Only in the case of intertribal war is the conflict relatively unrestrained and true victory or defeat a generally realistic outcome.

Marvin Harris gives us an example of a largely cultural interpretation of early warfare. He views warfare within the tribe primarily in terms of cultural ecology. His analysis of warfare among the Maring of New Guinea, for example, suggests that it functioned primarily to prevent too great a pressure on the carrying capacity of the environment. It did this indirectly, by (1) placing a premium upon producing young men for fighting, thus leading to (2) infanticide or neglect of young females, thus (3) providing effective population control, and thus (4) reducing the pressure on available natural resources. War also more directly assisted the conservation of natural resources by keeping certain battle-related or recently abandoned areas out of cultivation for important periods of time. While such factors may have had some secondary significance for genetic selection (selecting males for fighting qualities), their main importance lies in the cultural order. Harris concludes that "war has been part of an adaptive strategy associated with particular technological, demographic, and ecological conditions" but that this does not require us to "invoke imaginary killer instincts or inscrutable or capricious motives to understand why armed combat has been so common in human history."

We do not mean to present Harris' views as the final word on the meaning of primitive warfare; we use them mainly in contrast to the implications put forward by the sociobiologists. The general significance of such a contrast will be considered further in the final section of this chapter.

Beyond Nature?

Humans have often prided themselves on being more apart from than a part of nature. Recognizing our distinctive mode of adaptation—with conceptual thought, language, and a proliferation of tools—we are tempted to put ourselves in a very special place in relation to other forms of life. This leads to a desire to see our past as sharply different from that of other forms of life, to see our present as not bound by the constraints of our specific biological nature, and to see our future in terms of an infinite extension of our ability to control the forces of nature.

The Darwinian revolution—including its contemporary expressions in ethology and sociobiology—has forced us to reconsider this view of man. We now have another view of human origins, and our awareness of the biological limitations of our species has also grown. Even our vision of the future is more and more shaped by the recognition that we can continue to exist on our planet only as a part of an intricate web of life.

No doubt this renewed humility concerning our species is fundamentally good for us. But it is possible that we may be so caught up in the spirit of the Darwinian revolution that we might lose our sense of the peculiar distinctiveness of humans as cultural beings. We are a culture-creating species, whose linguistic patterns and systems of technology are as much a part of our world as are its flora and fauna. This is no doubt a result of our own distinctive prehistory selection and evolution. But it also imposes limitations on the way we should see natural selection and evolution as applied to ourselves.

One of the mistakes we may make in uncritically accepting Darwinism is to overgeneralize the idea of natural selection. Natural selection does not necessarily imply some underlying primacy of conflict over cooperation. If nature is sometimes, as a Victorian poet put it, "red in tooth and claw," so too is it also often a symphony of marvelous coordination. Survival is in part competitive, and the particular natures of species are shaped by this competitive legacy. But they are also shaped by the legacy of ways they have come to cooperate within the species and with other forms of life. When we come to humans, the role of cooperation within the species is greatly enhanced. To create and pass on a culture requires an unusual degree of common identity and group coordination. It is unlikely that such a culture-bearing species would have a greater endowment of aggressive genes than would most other mammals.

Another possible error which may be encouraged by an uncritical Darwinism is the assumption that biological evolution is the key to the future progress of our species. With this assumption usually goes the corollary that since biological evolution is not subject to any fundamental purposive control, there is little we can do to plan for our own long-term progress. We are, in this view, products of a blind progression, a progression which will continue to unfold blindly in the future according to the chance happenings of genetics and natural selection. But this view ignores the extent to which we are products of our culture as well as our genes, and it neglects the extent to which we can control and modify our culture. Human cultures do not suddenly transform themselves in response to human wishes, but there is at least some room for consciously guided change. To ignore this is to ignore what is probably most distinctively human.

Charles Darwin himself offers a beautiful example of what we are cautioning against. In one of his few pronouncements directly relevant to public policy, he said:

Man, like every other animal, has no doubt advanced to his present high condition through a struggle for existence consequent on his rapid multiplication; and if he is to advance still higher, it is to be feared that he must remain subject to a severe struggle. Otherwise he would sink into indolence, and the more gifted men would not be more successful in the battle of life than the less gifted. Hence our natural rate of increase, though leading to many and obvious evils, must not be greatly diminished by any means. There should be open competition for all men; and the most able should not be prevented by laws or customs from succeeding best and rearing the largest number of offspring.

The full logic of this position is difficult for us to accept in these days of contraception and planned parenthood. Darwin is actually suggesting a contrasting policy of encouraging "the largest number of offspring" to join in the struggle for life itself. Such a clear expression of social Darwinism can make sense only if we systematically turn our backs on our capacity as humans to exert control over the conditions of our life. This control does not always come easily. Much of it occurs through the collective accumulation of culture, of which we are not often very self-conscious. But there is room for at least a partly planned cultural supplement to the blind process of evolution through natural selection. This cultural supplement does not always incline us toward peace, but at least it raises the possibility of a more conscious creation of broader avenues of human cooperation than the age-old "survival of the fittest."

Suggested Readings

Ardrey, Robert. *The Territorial Imperative*. New York: Atheneum, 1966.

Eibl-Eibesfeldt, I. *The Biology of Peace and War*. New York: Viking, 1979.

Lorenz, Konrad. *On Aggression*. New York: Harcourt Brace Jovanovich, 1966.

Montagu, M.F. Ashley. *The Nature of Human Aggression*. New York: Oxford University, 1976.

Scott, John Paul. *Aggression*. Chicago: University of Chicago, 1975.

Weigele, Thomas. "Decision-Making in an International Crisis: Some Biological Factors." *International Studies Quarterly* 17 September 1973, pp. 295–336.

Wilson, E.O. *Sociobiology: The New Synthesis*. Cambridge: Harvard University, 1975.

Reading 20

WHY WAR?

Sigmund Freud

Notes from the Editors

In 1931, the International Institute of International Cooperation was asked by the League of Nations to arrange for intellectual exchanges between prominent world figures concerning the issues of global importance. Albert Einstein, the great nuclear physicist, wrote on behalf of the Institute to Sigmund Freud, the founder of psychoanalysis, about his views on aggression, war, and conflict. Freud responded in his native German in an article that was published in 1933. Ominously, perhaps, the article was banned in Germany.

Freud, who had written earlier on war, had touched on some of the same themes in The Future of Illusion *(1927) and* Civilization and its Discontents *(1930). In this article he stresses his belief in the human instinct for violence or destruction, an instinct balanced by one for love or life. Although the instinct for destruction had produced untold wars and murders through the centuries, Freud was ultimately optimistic. He felt that humankind was capable of "displacing" the destructive instinct and, moreover, he saw a general sublimation of violence as the collective intellect of civilization developed.*

In many ways, Freud, a psychoanalyst, seems to be in agreement with those who emphasize biological predetermination. However, his interest in how citizens can be led into destructive activities by their leaders reflects more of a social scientific approach to the problem. It is interesting to note that Freud, who ends his essay optimistically, had to flee for his life in 1939 after the Nazis took over his native Austria.

. . . It is a general principle, then, that conflicts of interest between men are settled by the use of violence. This is true of the whole animal kingdom, from which men have no business to exclude themselves. In the case of men, no doubt, conflicts of *opinion* occur as well which may reach the highest pitch of abstraction and which seem to demand some other technique for their settlement. That, however, is a later complication. To begin with, in a small human horde, it was superior muscular strength which decided who owned things or whose will should prevail. Muscular strength was soon supplemented and replaced by the use of tools: the winner was the one who had the better weapons or who used them more skillfully. From the moment at which weapons were introduced, intellectual superiority already began to replace brute muscular strength; but the final purpose of the fight remained the same—one side or the other was to be compelled to abandon his claim or his objection by the damage inflicted

From *Collected Papers,* Vol. 22, pp. 204–207, 209–211, 214, by Sigmund Freud, edited by James Strachey. Published by Basic Books, by arrangement with the Hogarth Press and The Institute of Psycho-Analysis, London. Reprinted with permission.

on him and by the crippling of his strength. That purpose was most completely achieved if the victor's violence eliminated his opponent permanently—that is to say, killed him. This had two advantages: he could not renew his opposition and his fate deterred others from following his example. In addition to this, killing an enemy satisfied an instinctual inclination which I shall have to mention later. The intention to kill might be countered by a reflection that the enemy could be employed in performing useful services if he were left alive in an intimidated condition. In that case the victor's violence was content with subjugating him instead of killing him. This was a first beginning of the idea of sparing an enemy's life, but thereafter the victor had to reckon with his defeated opponent's lurking thirst for revenge and sacrificed some of his own security.

Such, then, was the original state of things: domination by whoever had the greater might—domination by brute violence or by violence supported by intellect. As we know, this regime was altered in the course of evolution. There was a path that led from violence to right or law. What was that path? It is my belief that there was only one: the path which led by way of the fact that the superior strength of a single individual could be rivalled by the union of several weak ones. *L' union fait la force*. Violence could be broken by union, and the power of those who were united now represented law in contrast to the violence of the single individual. Thus we see that right is the might of a community. It is still violence, ready to be directed against any individual who resists it; it works by the same methods and follows the same purposes. The only real difference lies in the fact that what prevails is no longer the violence of an individual but that of a community. But in order that the transition from violence to this new right or justice may be effected, one psychological condition must be fulfilled. The union of the majority must be a stable and lasting one. If it were only brought about for the purpose of combating a single dominant individual and were dissolved after his defeat, nothing would have been accomplished. The next person who thought himself superior in strength would once more seek to set up a dominion by violence and the game would be repeated *ad infinitum*. The community must be maintained permanently, must be organized, must draw up regulations to anticipate the risk of rebellion and must institute authorities to see that those regulations—the laws—are respected and to superintend the execution of legal acts of violence. The recognition of a community of interests such as these leads to the growth of emotional ties between the members of a united group of people—communal feelings which are the true source of its strength.

Here, I believe, we already have all the essentials: violence overcome by the transference of power of a larger unity, which is held together by emotional ties between its members. What remains to be said is no more than an expansion and a repetition of this.

This situation is simple so long as the community consists only of a number of equally strong individuals. The laws of such an association will determine the extent to which, if the security of communal life is to be guaranteed, each individual must surrender his personal liberty to turn his strength to violent uses. But a state of rest of that kind is only theoretically conceivable. In actuality the position is complicated by the fact that from its very beginning the community comprises elements of unequal strength—men and women, parents and children—and soon, as a result of war and conquest, it also comes to include victors and vanquished, who turn into masters and slaves. The justice of the community then becomes an expression of the unequal degrees of power obtaining within it; the laws are made by and for the ruling members and find little room for the rights of those in subjection. From that time forward there are two factors at work in the community which are sources of unrest over matters of law but tend at the same time to a further growth of law. First, attempts are made by certain of the rulers to set themselves above the prohibitions which apply to everyone— they seek, that is, to go back from a dominion of law to a dominion of violence. Secondly, the oppressed members of the group make constant efforts to obtain more power and to have any changes that are brought about in that direction recognized in the laws—they press forward, that is, from unequal justice to equal justice for all. This second tendency becomes especially important if a real shift of power occurs within a community, as may happen as a result of a number of historical factors. In that case right may gradually adapt itself to the new distribution of power; or, as is more frequent, the ruling class is unwilling to recognize the change, and rebellion and civil war follow, with a temporary suspension of law and new attempts at a solution by violence, ending in the establishment of a fresh rule of law. There is yet another source from which modifications of law may arise, and one of which the expression is invariably peaceful: it lies in the cultural transformation of the members of the community. . . .

Thus we see that the violent solution of conflicts of interest is not avoided even inside a community. But the everyday necessities and common concerns that are inevitable where people live together in one place tend to bring such struggles to a swift conclusion and under such conditions there is an increasing probability that a peaceful solution will be found. Yet a glance at the history of the human race reveals an endless series of conflicts between one community and another or several others, between larger and smaller units—between cities, provinces, races, nations, empires— which have almost always been settled by force of arms. Wars of this kind end either in the spoliation or in the complete overthrow and conquest of one of the parties. It is impossible to make any sweeping judgement upon wars of conquest. Some, such as those waged by the Mongols and Turks, have brought nothing by evil. Others, on the contrary, have contributed to the transformation of violence into law by establishing larger units within which the use of violence was made impossible and in which a fresh system of law led to the solution of conflicts. In this way the conquests of the Romans gave the countries round the Mediterranean the priceless *pax Romana*, and the greed of the French kings to extend their dominions created a peacefully united and flourishing France. Paradoxical as it may sound, it must be admitted that war might be a far from inappropriate means of establishing the eagerly desired reign of 'everlasting' peace, since it is in a position to create the large units within which a powerful central government makes further wars impossible. Nevertheless it fails in this purpose, for the results of conquest are as a rule short-lived: the newly created units fall apart once again, usually owing to a lack of cohesion between the portions that have been united by violence. Hitherto, moreover, the unifications created by conquest, though of considerable extent, have only been *partial*, and the conflicts between these have called out more than ever for violent solution. Thus the result of all these warlike efforts has only been that the human race has exchanged numerous, and indeed unending, minor wars for wars on a grand scale that are rare but all the more destructive. . . .

I can now proceed to add a gloss to another of your remarks. You express astonishment at the fact that it is so easy to make men enthusiastic about a war and add your suspicions that there is something at work in them—an instinct for hatred and destruction—which goes halfway to meet the efforts of the warmongers. Once again, I can only express my entire agreement. We believe in the existence of an instinct of that kind and have in fact been occupied during the last few years in studying its manifestations. Will you allow me to take this opportunity of putting before you a portion of the theory of the instincts which, after much tentative groping and many fluctuations of opinion, has been reached by workers in the field of psychoanalysis?

According to our hypothesis human instincts are of only two kinds: those which seek to preserve and unite—which we call 'erotic', exactly in the sense in which Plato uses the word 'Eros' in his *Symposium,* or 'sexual', with a deliberate extension of the popular conception of 'sexuality'—and those which seek to destroy and kill and which we group together as the aggressive or destructive instinct. As you see, this is in fact no more than a theoretical clarification of the universally familiar opposition between Love and Hate which may perhaps have some fundamental relation to the polarity of attraction of repulsion that plays a part in your own field of knowledge. But we must not be too hasty in introducing ethical judgements of good and evil. Neither of these instincts is any less essential than the other; the phenomena of life arise from the concurrent or mutually opposing action of both. Now it seems as though an instinct of the one sort can scarcely ever operate in isolation; it is always accompanied—or, as we say, alloyed—with a certain quota from the other side, which modifies its aim or is, in some cases, what enables it to achieve that aim. Thus, for instance, the instinct of self-preservation is certainly of an erotic kind, but it must nevertheless have aggressiveness at its disposal if it is to fulfil its purpose. So, too, the instinct of love, when it is directed towards an object, stands in need of some contribution from the instinct for mastery if it is in any way to obtain possession of that object. The difficulty of isolating the two classes of instinct in their actual manifestations is indeed what has so long prevented us from recognizing them.

If you will follow me a little further, you will see that human actions are subject to another complication of a different kind. It is very rarely that an action is the work of a *single* instinctual impulse (which must in itself be compounded of Eros and destructiveness). In order to make an action possible there must be as a rule a combination of such compounded motives. This was perceived long ago by a specialist in your own subject, a Professor G. C. Lichtenberg who taught physics at Gottingen during our classical age—though perhaps he was even more remarkable as a psychologist than as a physicist. He invented a Compass of Motives, for he wrote: "The motives that lead us to do anything might be arranged like the thirty-two winds and might be given names in a similar way: for instance, 'bread-bread-fame' or 'fame-fame-bread'." So that when human beings are incited to war they may have a whole number of motives for assenting—some noble and some base, some which are openly declared and others which are never mentioned. There is no need to enumerate them all. A lust for aggression and destruction is certainly among them: the countless cruelties in history and in our everyday lives vouch for its existence and its strength. The satisfaction of these destructive impulses is of course facilitated by their admixture with others of an erotic and idealistic kind. When we read of the atrocities of the past, it sometimes seems as though the idealistic motives served only as an excuse for the destructive appetites; and sometimes—in the case, for instance, of the cruelties of the Inquisition—it seems as though the idealistic motives had pushed themselves forward in consciousness, while the destructive ones lent them an unconscious reinforcement. Both may be true.

I fear I may be abusing your interest, which is after all concerned with the prevention of war and not with our theories. Nevertheless I should like to linger for a moment over our destructive instinct, whose popularity is by no means equal to its importance. As a result of a little speculation, we have come to suppose that this instinct is at work in every living creature and is striving to bring it to ruin and to reduce life to its original condition of inanimate matter. Thus it quite seriously deserves to be called a death instinct, while the erotic instincts represent the effort to live. The death instinct turns into the destructive instinct when, with the help of special organs, it is directed outwards, on to objects. The organism preserves its own life, so to say, by destroying an extraneous one. Some portion of the death instinct, however, remains operative *within* the organism, and we have sought to trace quite a number of normal and pathological phenomena to this internalization of the destructive instinct. We have even been guilty of the heresy of attributing the origin of conscience to this diversion inwards of aggressiveness. You will notice that it is by no means a trivial matter if this process is carried too far: it is positively unhealthy. On the other hand if these forces are turned to destruction in the external world, the organism will be relieved and the effect must be beneficial. This would serve as a biological justification for all the ugly and dangerous impulses against which we are struggling. It must be admitted that they stand nearer to Nature than does our resistance to them for which an explanation also needs to be found. It may perhaps seem to you as though our theories are a kind of mythology and, in the present case, not even an agreeable one. But does not every science come in the end to a kind of mythology like this? Cannot the same be said today of your own Physics?

For our immediate purpose then, this much follows from what has been said: there is no use in trying to get rid of men's aggressive inclinations. We are told that in certain happy regions of the earth, where nature provides in abundance everything that man requires, there are races whose life is passed in tranquility and who know neither coercion nor aggression. I can scarcely believe it and I should be glad to hear more of these fortunate beings. . . .

My belief is this. For incalculable ages mankind has been passing through a process of evolution of culture. (Some people, I know, prefer to use the term "civilization".) We owe to that process the best of what we have become, as well as a good part of what we suffer from. Though its causes and beginnings are obscure and its outcome uncertain, some of its characteristics are easy to perceive. It may perhaps be leading to the extinction of the human race, for in more than one way it impairs the sexual function; uncultivated races and backward strata of the population are already multiplying more rapidly than highly cultivated ones. The process is perhaps comparable to the domestication of certain species of animals and it is undoubtedly accompanied by physical alterations; but we are still unfamiliar with the notion that the evolution of civilization is an organic process of this kind. The *psychical* modifications that go along with the process of civilization are striking and unambiguous. They consist in a progressive displacement of instinctual aims and a restriction of instinctual impulses. Sensations which were pleasurable to our ancestors have become indifferent or even intolerable to ourselves; there are organic grounds for the changes in our ethical and aesthetic ideas. Of the psychological characteristics of civilization two appear to be the most important: a strengthening of the intellect, which is beginning to govern instinctual life, and an internalization of the aggressive impulses, with all its consequent advantages and perils. Now war is in the crassest opposition to the psychical attitude imposed on us by the process of civilization, and for that reason we are bound to rebel against it; we simply cannot any longer put up with it.

Suggested Readings

Berkowitz, Leonard. *Aggression: A Social Analysis*. New York: McGraw-Hill, 1962.

Bramson, C. and G. Goethals, eds. *War: Contributions from Psychology, Sociology and Anthropology*. New York, Basic Books, 1968.

Cantril, Hadley, ed. *Tensions That Cause War*. Urbana: University of Illinois, 1950.

DeRivera, Joseph. *The Psychological Dimensions of Foreign Policy*. Columbus, Ohio: Merrill, 1968.

Feierabend, Ivo K., Rosalind K. Feierabend, and Ted Gurr, eds. *Anger, Violence, and Politics: Theories and Research*. Englewood Cliffs, N.J.: Prentice Hall, 1972.

Fornari, Franco. *The Psychoanalysis of War*. New York: Anchor, 1974.

Frank, Jerome. *Sanity and Survival: Psychological Aspects of War and Peace*. New York: Vintage, 1967.

Stagner, Ross. *Psychological Aspects of International Conflict*. Belmont, Calif.: Brooks-Cole, 1967.

White, Ralph K., ed. *Psychology and the Prevention of Nuclear War*. New York: New York University, 1986.

Reading 21

PEACEFUL SOCIETIES

David Fabbro

Notes from the Editors

Most students of peace and conflict or peace science concentrate their attention on incidents of violence and war in domestic and international systems. In this selection, David Fabbro, who was a graduate student in the University of Lancaster's Peace and Conflict Research Program, studies conflict by examining seven societies that apparently live without resort to violence in their daily interactions.

His sample, which includes groups from every continent except Europe, is described in terms of a variety of socioeconomic and ideological variables in a quest to discern commonalities or patterns. There are enough differences among them, particularly in terms of the all-important question of the production of a surplus, to confound the analysis. On the other hand, Fabbro discovers that irrespective of the geographical locus or material conditions, it appears that social justice and equality can be compatible with the absence of physical violence.

No doubt the relative isolation of most of his seven groups contributes to the low levels of violence present in their societies. Nevertheless, an examination of their socialization practices and conflict resolution techniques does suggest other explanations for their relatively peaceful condition. Whether or not these practices and techniques have application for other groups, countries, or systems remains to be seen. Fabbro hopes that studies of more violent-prone groups with similar profiles in similar regions will enhance our understanding of the causes of human conflict and aggression.

However one interprets his findings they are ultimately optimistic. If some people in today's world are able to live pacific lives, then violence may not be as integral a part of human society as many of us believe.

Introduction

The majority of work in peace research has been directed toward gaining an understanding of the sources and dynamics of direct and structural violence. Elaboration of the social preconditions of peace has all too often been neglected, viewed as an abstraction and/or utopia, or been of a purely theoretical nature. This paper is an attempt to arrest this underdevelopment by directing attention toward a number of concrete examples of peaceful societies.

From David Fabbro, "Peaceful Societies: An Introduction," *Journal of Peace Research* 15 (1, 1978), pp. 67–83. Reprinted by permission of Norwegian University Press, Oslo.

Criteria of Peace

There are a number of levels or intensities of peace which members of a society may experience. In ascending order of comprehensiveness these would include:

1. The society has no wars fought on its territory;
2. The society is not involved in any external wars;
3. There are no civil wars or internal collective violence;
4. There is no standing military-police organization;
5. There is little or no interpersonal physical violence;
6. There is little or no structural violence;
7. The society has the capacity to undergo change peacefully; and
8. There is opportunity for idiosyncratic development. . . .

Internal Factors

A number of questions have been developed in order to demonstrate various aspects of these societies, and, where sources allow, to extract the same type of information for each society.

General

1. In what type of natural habitat does the society reside?
2. How is subsistence gained?
3. What is the prevailing ideology-cosmology-world view of the society? What are the core or paramount norms which act as the basis of regulation in social inter-course?
4. On what basis is the society integrated?

Direct Violence

5. What are the major characteristics of the child socialisation process?
6. Does physical violence exist? If so, what forms does it take?
7. What conflict resolution processes exist? Are they institutionalised or informal?

Structural Violence

8. Is there any division of labour and if so does it lead to specialisation?
9. Are there any forms of socially coercive organizations which are capable of gaining compliance on the basis of power?
10. Are there any forms of hierarchy? If so are they exclusive or restrictive?
11. Who participates in decisionmaking concerning the society as a whole? Is such participation direct or mediated?
12. Who exercises social control?

13. What forms does social control take?

14. Are there any forms of discrimination which militate against an equal distribution of self-respect between individuals?

The Societies

The Semai of Malaya

1. The Semai Senoi live in western Malaya and are subdivided into eastern and western groups. Their habitat is a mixture of lowland tropical rain forest and mountain ridges.

2. The Semai gain their subsistence by hunting, trapping, fishing, and some swidden—slash and burn—agriculture. Some gathering of wild food consisting mainly of fruit is also carried out. They also have domesticated animals such as hens, ducks, and goats.

3. The religious system of the Semai is complex but does not give rise to any religious leaders or elite. Central to social organisation and the regulation of interpersonal relations is the concept of *punan*. Implicit in *punan* is the idea that making someone unhappy, especially by frustrating desires, increases the probability of that person suffering physical injury. The notion of *punan* pervades their whole lifestyle and influences matters such as child rearing and sexual relations.

4. The band is the largest form of social organisation; each one being composed of a number of nuclear families. In the west the predominant settlement pattern is a cluster of small houses which together form a homestead. The houses of the western Semai generally have between five and twenty-four inhabitants while the eastern Semai live communally in long houses which may have as many as fifty residents.

5. Semai children enjoy a considerable amount of freedom in their behaviour. If a child does not wish to engage in some activity parents do not force it to do so; such action would be *punan*. Generally children learn through voluntary imitative play. When children misbehave, adults invoke the threat of evil spirits or the occurrence of certain evil happenings to gain compliance with their wishes. Where physical punishment is used it consists of a pinch on the cheek or a tap on the hand. All child rearing practices are geared toward the personal internalisation of norms of conduct. This is especially so with children who display aggressive behaviour. In such cases the Semai deliberately do not punish such behaviour physically and so personal experience of violence is very limited. Moreover it is very difficult for children to rebel against their parents because adults do not object if a child does not wish to do something.

6. Physical violence is more or less unknown in Semai society. Apparently between 1956 and 1967 a number of cases of murder and attempted murder occurred but this appears to have arisen because of the political turbulence in Malaya in general at this time. Also the Semai apparently abandoned the very

old or sick during times of scarcity but this was done reluctantly. According to Dentan (1968:59) violence appears to terrify the Semai who meet force with passivity or flight.

7. Conflict resolution processes do exist in Semai society but they are not particularly formalised. In a dispute one party usually suffers (that is, is taken to suffer) *punan*. The victim has two courses of action available. The *punan* may be endured or the offender may be asked for compensation. Generally the offender pays it. In a dispute where both parties feel in the right they may appeal to a respected elder; but, should one of the parties think the judgement unjust it can be ignored. Disputants who become angry manifest such feelings by avoiding the other party. Generally, most quarrels are conceived of by the participants as being a personal matter.

8. There is some division of labour in Semai society but mainly in relation to hunting which is a male activity. Men, women, and children help to clear the forest for agriculture. Men and women too old to hunt supplement the diet by fishing. Domestic activities such as basket weaving or carrying water are performed by women. Both men and women plant crops but only women harvest the rice. Both sexes cook and winnow grain. There does not appear to be any specialisation of labour in Semai society; even the headman must gain his own subsistence.

9 and 10. There is no specifically political organisation within Semai bands. All elders are accorded respect on two grounds. Firstly, they have the largest amount of experience and as such are valuable sources of information. Secondly, most young people and young married couples move frequently between homesteads. Thus it is the elders who provide continuity and stability within each homestead. The foremost male elder is regarded as the headman of the group. As with all other elders, however, young people may ignore his advice. The headman keeps the peace—when disputes cannot be solved by the parties directly involved—by conciliation rather than coercion. If the headman is to function efficiently he must be respected; one who is not respected will find people turning to another elder for advice. People only recognise the headman's authority in specific situations: in the mediation of a dispute, as a group representative in external matters, and in the west, in deciding upon the selection and apportionment of land. The position of headman appears to be held by males only.

11 and 12. Theoretically all adults participate in decisionmaking and social control. Women are not formally prevented from being influential within the group but in general they apparently feel embarrassed about participating in discussions about matters of general concern. In practice a few women are influential in discussions but the majority appear to abstain. Both social control and decisionmaking are implemented through the medium of public opinion. Usually it is the older men who have the greatest influence on public opinion but paradoxically such elders are often regarded with suspicion by the rest of the group and so their authority is probably less than would appear at first sight. Another person who has a major influence on public opinion is the one who enjoys popularity. Such

popularity accrues to an individual who shares what can be afforded without appearing to calculate the cost of such generosity.

13. The main sanction is embarrassment; when public opinion goes against an individual that individual is "embarrassed" (Dentan 1968:69). Sanctions other than public opinion do not appear to exist. Strong internalised norms of behaviour combined with the influence of public opinion appear to make deviance very uncommon.

14. Self-respect appears to be fairly evenly distributed among the Semai. Children have great freedom of action and can if they wish ignore adult instructions. Men and women seem to enjoy equal sexual license with divorce and separation as frequent occurrences. It should be noted, however, that there appear to be informal barriers which prevent women from fully participating in group decisionmaking and neither do women hold the position of headman.

The Siriono of Eastern Bolivia

1. The Siriono live in the tropical rain forest centred on eastern Bolivia.

2. They are seminomadic aborigines who practice some swidden agriculture but are primarily hunter-gatherers.

3. The kinship system is based on the matrilineal extended family. A band— the highest level of social integration—is composed of a number of nuclear families who all occupy a communal hut. Each family has an area in the hut where the parents' hammocks are hung.

4. Sorcery is more or less unknown to the Siriono. Reciprocity does exist between families but it is generally forced; and, there is a general reluctance to share food which has not been produced cooperatively.

5. It is usually females who look after children although both parents spend a lot of time playing with their children. Holmberg characterises child rearing practices as: "informal, random and haphazard" (1966:203). Reward and punishment techniques are used but there is little or no physical punishment. Apparently Siriono mothers almost always cry after they have been angry with their children. Both sexes are taught early to contribute to the family economy. From about eight years of age boys accompany their fathers when hunting, while girls help with household tasks.

6. Physical violence does occur among the Siriono but fighting with weapons and clubs is rare. Males seldom express direct aggression against other males. Neither do males beat their wives but there are apparently quarrels among women, frequently culminating in fighting with digging sticks. At one stage the Siriono engaged in violence against white colonisers although it did not continue for long and did not become an institutionalised feature of Siriono society.

7. Various conflict resolution processes exist but usually disputes are settled by those who start them. An exception to this general rule arises at drinking feasts—a regular feature of social life—when quarrels are settled by wrestling matches. Any other type of fighting is frowned upon and is usually stopped by

nonparticipant men and women. There are no formal agencies of social control and the chief does not interfere in disputes. The final form of conflict resolution is fission. In this instance one of the parties to the conflict will leave the band temporarily or permanently and join another group or alternatively a number of families may leave a band and establish a new one.

8. The Siriono do practice division of labour to a small extent. Hunting is a male occupation whereas food gathering and horticulture are joint pursuits. There is no occupational specialisation, and there are no nonproductive sectors in the society. Even the chief must provide for himself.

9 and 10. Leadership which exists among the Siriono is based solely on the personal qualities of the incumbent. It appears, however, to be held by males only.

11. Participation in decisionmaking does not appear to arise because there are very few collective enterprises requiring decisions. Husband and wife or wives appear, in the given situation, equal in prestige even if this is only indicated by the fact that women start quarrels as frequently as do men.

12. Social control appears to be based on individual action toward the offender; calling for satisfaction by reference to group norms rather than group action against the offender. "Justice is an informal and private matter. . . . Generally speaking it would seem that the maintenance of law and order rests largely on the principle of reciprocity (however forced), the fear of the supernatural, sanctions and retaliation, and the desire for public approval" (Holmberg 1966:153).

13. Norms of behavior appear to be flexible as evidenced by the lack of recognition in the culture of sexual offences or theft.

14. Self-respect appears to be fairly evenly distributed. Individuals may ignore the advice of a chief if they wish. Sexism does exist as shown by the informal exclusion of women from the leadership position. Females do, however, have sexual license and hold their own drinking feasts and dances. Holmberg does not offer any evidence that women are subservient to their husbands or men in general.

The Mbuti Pygmies of the Ituri Forest

1. The pygmies live in the equatorial forest belt of central Africa.

2. The Mbuti are hunter-gatherers with the emphasis on hunting. Some bands use nets for trapping game while others rely on individual hunting with bows and arrows.

3. Their myth system is in one sense very pragmatic. According to Barrington Moore, "they have made for themselves no oppressive taboos and have about as light hearted an attitude toward their own social regulation as it is possible to have and still maintain the degree of social cohesion necessary for their particular form of society" (1972:18). They have a great feeling of identification with the forest. It is viewed as the benevolent provider of life, all good things,

and the protector from the malevolence of nonforest peoples. Rituals associated with birth, puberty, sickness, and death all symbolically express the identification between forest and pygmy which is also expressed in interpersonal relations through cooperation and mutual aid.

4. Mbuti bands are composed of several nuclear families. Their kinship system is relatively undeveloped. The extended family is the largest blood-tie group, but the Mbuti use kinship terms to relate to both blood relatives and friends.

5. Babies are breast-fed for between eighteen months and three years. Once a child has been weaned he or she may demand and expect to be disciplined by any adult. From an early age children are encouraged to imitate adult activities. By the age of six both girls and boys contribute to the general economy by helping with camp chores. From nine years of age onwards children participate in hunting in bands which use nets. At this age the form of punishment changes; ridicule replacing physical punishment. "The whole process of child training is characterised by informality and by emphasis on the child's responsibilities to the band as a whole" (Turnbull 1965:306).

6. Mbuti bands do not appear to experience much interpersonal violence. Fighting does take place between husbands and wives. The violence which does occur has a peculiar property which mitigates lethality.

> The human body is in a sense, *boru*. . . . It is a term seldom used, but the concept affords a firm basis for a code of respect for the body, abuse or mutilation of which may drive away the *pepo* causing death. Thus physical violence as a means of settling a dispute is abhorred as sacrilege. A sound thrashing is perfectly in order, but any violence that produces blood causes an opening through which *pepo* may escape (Turnbull 1966:250).

7. Various conflict resolution processes exist. The most common form is third-party intervention. Young married couples, older married couples, or elders may intervene depending on the nature of the dispute. If any one of these mediators fails then the band as a whole may take part in mediation. Individuals may also mediate in a dispute. One major form of this is intervention by the "clown." The clown is often unmarried but entitled to respect because of prowess in a skill and also because he possesses a certain amount of impartiality. Generally he mediates through the voice of ridicule or he may be singled out by the parties to the dispute as the source of their difference which he accepts without letting it get him down. Should reconciliation at the band level fail it may split into two sections or a family may join another band.

8. Some division of labour exists in Mbuti society but it is not well defined and does not lead to specialisation. Men, women, and children all participate in the hunt in bands using nets. In archer bands, men hunt without the aid of women and children. All individuals help with the gathering of vegetable foods. There are no unproductive people in Mbuti bands.

9. Political organisation is not differentiated from general social life. The

only distinction which the Mbuti make is in respect to their dealings with the Negro cultivators who live in villages on the edges of the forest.

10 and 11. It is only in relation to the village that leadership exists. One particular individual who is a past master at trickery but who is willing to appear subservient to the villagers acts as leader in the exchange relationship. In the village the other pygmies refer to him as the leader but on returning to the forest his leadership ceases. Life in the forest does not produce leadership although older people and those who are considered foremost—by virtue of their prowess— in a particular activity have influence in the band in general. Almost every adult has the right to express himself in almost any activity. It is interesting to note that even in the Negro villages during a crisis all members of the band present participate in decisionmaking even where villagers have poisoned a pygmy to bring about the desired results of sorcery. In this situation the leader does not make the decision to return to the forest, neither does the victim or the immediate family; the whole band does. The reaction of the pygmies to this threat provides an insight into their general outlook: "The pygmy attitude is ambivalent: they do not believe in supernatural powers of this order . . . their reaction is not one of fear, even when their fellows die, nor is it coloured by the desire for revenge, nor even of anger or hatred" (Turnbull 1965:304).

12. All members of a band ultimately exercise social control through the medium of public opinion.

13. The major form of sanction related to norm breaking is ridicule and the appeal to the need for mutual cooperation.

14. It would seem that self-respect is fairly evenly distributed between members of Mbuti bands. Women have an equal voice with men in all major decisions. The early encouragement of children to contribute to the general economy probably militates against the effect of feeling inadequate in an adult world. There is, however, one major drawback: marriages are arranged by parents. To offset this constraint the Mbuti practice divorce which does not appear to cause much dislocation in the lives of the individual or of the band.

The Kung Bushmen of the Kalahari Desert

1. The Kung live in the Kalahari desert of southern Africa. The desert has a mean average height of 3,000 feet above sea level. It is covered in wind-blown sand to a depth of three to four hundred feet. There are some water holes and a variety of drought-resistant plants, plus numbers of small and large game.

2. The Kung are hunter-gatherers. They have few material artifacts, the main ones being bows and arrows and digging sticks.

3. The kinship system is of a patrilineal extended family type. When the old father dies, however, that particular extended family ceases to exist; dependents who are left are usually supported by close blood relatives. A band is composed of a number of nuclear families who usually have some blood tie.

4. The Kung myth system is comparatively well developed. There are two gods, a greater and a lesser one. Neither god is inherently good or evil. The greater god created the world, animals, plants, women, and then men. The Kung pray spontaneously and, in part, it reflects the major preoccupations of life: hunger, sickness, and death. The great god, however, gave healing powers to medicine men who exist solely to cure people and do not engage in witchcraft or sorcery. Social norms that are emphasised are the institutionalised patterns of sharing and their determined striving for cooperation and harmony.

5. Kung parents are protective, gentle, and permissive in their child training. Parents do not make demands on children to help with work, Marshall maintains, because there are few household tasks to perform because of their low level of technology (1965:264). Lee, on the other hand, maintains that few demands are made on children to contribute to the general economy because a modest work effort by adults produces enough food to support all the members of a band (1968a:39). Children are always kept within sight of adults because of the dangers arising from predators and becoming lost in a featureless landscape. Children are, however, encouraged to imitate adult activities. Marshall sums up child development: "They usually fall in with group life and do what is expected of them *without* uncertainty, frustration, or fear; and expression of resistance or hostility toward their parents, the group, or each other are very much the exception" (1965:264).

6. Physical violence appears to be rare in Kung society. According to Thomas, the Bushmen deplore bravery and in their legends the heroes are the animals which survive through trickery and deception rather than force (1969:32). The Kung do practice infanticide occasionally and it generally occurs when a woman is already nursing one child.

7. Conflict or wrong-doing is usually judged and controlled through public opinion which is usually expressed through conversation. Occasionally an individual may try to obtain revenge personally and this method is ostracised by them. The headman is not a formalised judge of the people in a band. Neither can he punish a wrongdoer.

8. Division of labour exists mainly along age and sex lines and does not, with the exception of medicine men, give rise to specialisation. The major division occurs over hunting, which is a male activity. Although women gather four-fifths of the food requirement it is the men who are accorded esteem for the production of the remaining fifth in the form of meat. This situation has arisen, according to Lee, because hunting is a less predictable activity than gathering (1968a:40).

9. There does not appear to be any dividing line between political, social, or religious life.

10. Leadership does exist in Kung bands. Usually it is an inherited position which passes from father to son. But in certain circumstances people may turn away from a headman because another may be more suited. The areas of leadership are, however, circumscribed. The headman personifies the rights of a band over

a given geographical area but does not own the land in a private individual capacity. Every family has an inalienable right to the resources on the land.

11. The headman's authority extends only to the coordination of the band's movements in relation to the use of resources. Apart from the decision to move the camp it is individuals who decide on various questions. There is strong informal pressure on men to go and hunt, but it is the individual who decides with whom and where to hunt. Within hunting groups there is no leadership.

12. All the adult members of a band exercise social control, which is usually done through the medium of public opinion.

13. Norms appear to be fairly rigid in Kung society. The very ethos of mutual dependency appears to forestall much norm breaking.

14. Self-respect seems to be fairly evenly distributed. Divorce is a characteristic feature of marital life although adultery is severely condemned. Sexism does exist in several forms: whereas a man may have more than one wife, women only take one husband at a time. Neither do females appear to hold leadership positions or receive acknowledgement commensurate to the amount of food which they provide.

The Copper Eskimo of Northern Canada

1. The area which the Copper Eskimo inhabit is part of the arctic tundra. The subsoil is permanently frozen, being covered with snow during the winter months. Temperatures range from $-47°$ F to $+70°$ F in August.

2. Seals and caribou were the most abundant game animals which provided not only meat but also skins for clothing and equipment. Migratory game birds, musk oxen, squirrels, foxes, some brown bears, and salmon, lake trout, and tom cod also supplemented the diet.

3. The Copper Eskimo conceive of the world as a flat, unbroken expanse of land and sea. Above this real world, supported at its four corners by wooden pillars is another flat level abounding in animals. Above this is another level for the sun, moon, and stars, which are semispiritual beings—the sun being a woman, the moon a man, and the stars either animal or human spirits before they ascended into the sky (Jeness 1922:179). The world of human existence is partly composed of spirits which may be benign or malevolent. All people have a soul—*nappan*—which is conceived of as the vital life force. The Copper Eskimo practice propitiation of these spirits by offering food and drink. Many phenomena and unusual events are attributed to the intervention of spirits. Such an outlook means the Copper Eskimo is "a true Epicurean, holding that life is a short and uncertain thing at best, and that the wise man will grasp at what pleasures he can in his course without stopping to ponder over those things that do not directly affect his immediate welfare" (Jeness 1922:229). Relationships between individuals are based on the idea that in theory all the members of a group—a composition of a number of nuclear families—are free and equal. The Copper Eskimo are intolerant of restraint upon individual behaviour. Such values mean that their society

is a tolerant one. Only individual acts which have a direct effect upon the community as a whole are evaluated in terms of being morally good or bad. The foremost virtues of Copper Eskimo society are: peacefulness, good name, courage, energy, patience and endurance, charity toward both the young and the old, and loyal cooperation. Fair dealing and truthfulness are of secondary importance only while sexual relations are hardly considered as coming within the scope of group consideration.

4. Bands are composed of a number of nuclear families which usually have some blood ties. The composition of a band changes over time.

5. Children are suckled for three to four years and sometimes for as long as five. Rarely is the child away from its parents during this stage and the mother usually carries it with her wherever she goes. Copper Eskimo children display a certain amount of deference to adults but such behaviour does not imply passivity. Children usually address adults as their equals and will join in any conversation that is taking place and do not hesitate to interrupt and correct their parents (Jeness 1922:169). In general parents do not use corporal punishment in child rearing although "a child may receive a thump with a fist or a blow from the snow duster in the passion of the moment when it will often try to retaliate" (Jeness 1922:169). Usually, however, the shame of public disapproval is sufficient to control a child's behaviour. From the age when children start to move about on their own until puberty they are left without adult interference to a great extent.

6. Various forms of physical violence have been documented among the Copper Eskimo. They practice infanticide for material and social reasons—both the parents of a newborn child must wish to bring it up, otherwise the child is abandoned. Some physical punishment is used in child rearing but it is not consistently used as part of an established practice. Homicide does occur and Rasmussen (1932:17) intimates that it is quite frequent, a point reinforced by Palmer (1965:322). Physical violence also occurs among marriage partners although men appear to use it more frequently. Much of the violence appears to be spontaneous rather than premeditated.

7. Conflict resolution processes in Copper Eskimo bands are generally informal and take place at the interpersonal level. Only in rare instances will the band as a whole engage in joint action against an individual, leading to that person's exclusion from the group. The only remedy for minor offences such as theft or the abduction of a wife is for the individual to extract personally compensation or vengeance. It is fairly common for murderers to go unpunished but where they are punished it is always a close relative of the deceased who is responsible for retribution. This situation does not, however, lead to a hereditary vendetta system.

8. Division of labour occurs mainly along age and sex lines. Heavier work and hunting tend to devolve on males while women are responsible for all the domestic tasks. Some younger women do, however, hunt. In the caribou drives all the band participates either in the killing or the beating. Specialisation appears

to extend only to shamanism and even here individual shamans have to provide the bulk of their own material needs.

9 and 10.   There appear to be no socially coercive organisations basing their compliance on power in Copper Eskimo bands. Similarly there is no hierarchy. Certain individuals may have influence but it is restricted in application and declines with old age.

11.   All adults appear to participate directly in general group discussions; women apparently being as vociferous as men in the dance house and on caribou drives.

12 and 13.   Only in extreme cases where an individual's behaviour becomes a threat to the group as a whole will collective action ensue; in all other situations people mind their own business even to the extent of quietly standing by and witnessing a robbery or a murder (Jeness 1922:235).

14.   It appears that all men have a relatively equal amount of self-respect as do women between themselves. While, according to Jeness, "marriage involves no subjection on the part of the woman" (1922:162), he mentions cases where wives are beaten by their husbands for failing to perform, in the husbands' opinion, their tasks sufficiently quickly. But in general women participate as freely as do men in various aspects of social life. Shamanism, for example, is open to women as well as men.

The Hutterites of North America

1.   The Hutterites live in North America in both the United States and Canada in temperate grassland areas.

2.   They maintain themselves by mixed agricultural production. The surplus which they produce is sold and used to buy in various types of equipment and clothing and to establish new colonies.

3 and 4.   Hutterites are extremely religious in a Western sense. Their religious belief system is the basis of their whole material culture. Absolute authority resides in a supernatural being—God—who created everything. It is thought that human nature has a natural carnal tendency which can only be overcome by continued submission to God's will through communal living. "Self-surrender, not self-development is the divine order" (Hostetler and Huntington 1967:15). Natural carnality is overcome by teaching children the divine discipline, and until they are capable of self-control, obedience to elders. Male dominance in the culture is reflected in the creation of the universe. The male is thus the righteous example and women are required to be submissive and obedient to men.

5.   The socialisation of children cannot be characterized in terms other than authoritarian. The premise of child development is that they are expected to behave badly because they have not yet learned to cope with their carnal desires. Part of the punishment for misdemeanour is the instilling of the need to try harder in the future. This does not mean that there is no physical punishment, the reverse is in fact prevalent. "Punishment is usually physical, arbitrary, and inconsistent,

and, from the child's point of view, often unpredictable" (Hostetler and Huntington 1967:61). Much of the child's life is spent in hands other than those of its parents: with babysitters, adults in general, the kindergarten, the German school, and the English school. Children do not take their meals with adults—who eat communally—but are fed at home.

6. The only physical violence in Hutterite communities occurs—apart from the disciplining of children by adults—between the children. This plays an important role in the socialisation of the children as Hostetler and Huntington point out.

> Much of the children's play is physically rigorous and often rough. . . . They fight hard, quickly and quietly. They vie with one another, showing no physical fear of jumping off high places or pushing one another in front of the tractor. Adults generally ignore the children's dangerous games. . . . The free play of school children reinforces community values: the children learn to ignore physical discomfort and fear of injury and to minimise the importance of the body; the changing play groups teach the unpleasantness of being excluded (1967:72-73).

7. Given that a Hutterite colony is structured hierarchically, conflict resolution processes tend to be a set of decisions handed down from above. The preacher often has the task of smoothing over differences. The executive council also adjudicates in interpersonal disputes. Some potential conflict situations are structured in a random fashion as for example when a colony divides to create a new one. Who stays and who goes is done by selection from a hat.

8. There is a definite division of labour on age and sex lines. Women work predominantly in the communal kitchen and look after the hens and geese. During the busy harvesting period they also help in the fields. Men work solely with the larger animals and the land. In the kitchen and in the fields there is a hierarchy; and with the men there is also specialisation of labour.

9. It appears that Hutterites do not differentiate political and social activities and forms. Their distinction is between worldly (material) existence and spiritual life.

10. Only baptised males are eligible for departmental positions such as cattleman, pigman, or shoemaker. Between five and seven of the baptised men are elected to form an executive council. These men hold the key colony positions including first and second preacher, householder, and field manager. The executive makes decisions concerning colony life. The preacher holds the highest leadership position but his actions are subject to review by the council. The preacher has no formal training and is elected by lot from nominations of his own colony. He does not gain full power until after several years of proven leadership; he can be removed should his conduct meet with general disapproval.

11. All baptised males of a colony exercise social control, although it is often delegated to the preacher or executive for more minor breaches of norms.

12. Similarly all baptised males participate in decisionmaking on major policies and determine who will hold the leadership positions.

13. Norms of behaviour are very rigid. This is offset to an extent by the propensity of the Hutterites to forgive individuals for misdemeanours, even where the individual has left the colony to live in the world outside. The deciding factor in forgiveness appears to be repentance on the part of the individual concerned.

14. The distribution of self-respect appears to be highly skewed. The Hutterite ideology creates its own feudal structure. God is at the top, then men who preside over women, who together control children, all of whom dominate nature. As was seen above, child training is authoritarian and punishment can be arbitrary. Women do not participate in deciding colony affairs either by voting or by holding leadership positions. Sexism exists in a blatant form where women are believed to be intellectually and physically inferior to men and, whereas men reflect some of God's glory, women have weakness (Hostetler and Huntington 1967:30). This has given rise to male and female subcultures. While men attempt to avoid confrontation with the colony's power structure, women often complain because they have little to lose. The net result is a conditon where a woman "often projects her annoyance and mildly dislikes men as a group" (Hostetler and Huntington 1967:30).

The Islanders of Tristan da Cunha

1. They inhabit the island of Tristan da Cunha which is located in the South Atlantic Ocean. It includes two smaller islands within reach of rowing boat. It has a mild wet windy climate.

2. The economy of Tristan has taken three distinct forms since its initial colonisation in the early nineteenth century. During the nineteenth century it was based primarily on barter with passing ships, fresh vegetables and meat being traded for items which the islanders could not produce themselves. From about 1915 to 1940, with the end of sailing ships, Tristan was almost totally isolated from the outside world. In this period a subsistence economy was developed based on fishing, farming, gathering, and earlier hunting. Gradually after 1945 a money economy was introduced via a South African fishing company and later by various public works instituted by the British government. The islanders have always been dependent on the outside for items such as rope, canvas, wood, flour, sugar, salt, tea, and coffee. While at one stage the introduction of a money economy appeared to threaten the core values of the community, the islanders have managed to adopt it to their own ends. "The islanders refused to become 'chained to the labour market.' They refused to give up their subsistence economy with its network of reciprocal relations and its independence. These were values that they would not sacrifice for all the affluence and prosperity" (Munch 1971:306-307).

3. The islanders have many bilateral kinship ties with neither the male or female line taking precedence. This gives rise to many self-selective labour exchange relationships. The founding ethos of the community was based on the principles of equality, communal ownership, cooperation, and freedom from government control. These founding values are still the predominant ones on the island although communal ownership no longer exists.

4. Most of the inhabitants are Christians but this does not appear to have a great effect on social organisation (Munch 1964:371; Munch 1971:136—for two different examples).

5. Child-rearing practices on the island have a peculiar nature.

The importance attached to the avoidance of open violent display of aggressive feeling among Tristan people is well seen in the ways in which children are taught. . . . Paradoxically it is through threats or acts of physical punishment that children are inculcated with the importance of non-violent behaviour (Loudon 1970:307).

Parents go to great lengths to remove what they characterise as willful behaviour in children. One of the basic aims in child rearing is to instill patience so that immediate gratification of desires is not expected. To gain this end parents will tease and provoke children into displays of willful behaviour and then physically punish it. There is a graded use of physical punishment which tends to increase in severity with increasing age of the child.

6. Apart from the physical punishment of children the only other physical violence on Tristan occurs between husband and wife. Furthermore there is no theft, misdemeanour, or disturbances.

7. When some conflicts have arisen on the island individuals have intervened. On only one occasion did an outsider act in this capacity: in 1908 when an Anglican clergyman intervened in a dispute which was not purely internal to the island (Munch 1971:80-81). In fact many of the disputes which arose during the nineteenth century occurred between existing inhabitants and newcomers—generally from shipwrecks. Among the islanders themselves there is little need for third-party intervention and there are even norms militating against it because esteem is accorded to the person who minds his own business and leaves others to do as they please (Munch 1970:1302). Public opinion takes a distinct form on Tristan which Loudon has termed "public teasing," which basically is making jokes at another's expense. Although Loudon identifies this as one of the legitimated forms of hostility, it is interesting to note the issues over which it arises. "Characteristics and tendencies particularly liable to expose people to public ridicule are what may be termed cowardice, laziness, stupidity, and credulity, but above all boastfulness and self importance and over-readiness to push oneself forward" (Loudon 1970:315)[1]—that is, basically all those aspects of personal behaviour which the ethos of the community would define as normatively bad. It is interesting to note the sexism in this situation; women are neither the butt of such teasing nor do they participate in it.

8. In principle every household is economically self-sufficient. The islanders do, however, cooperate on various tasks. There are those tasks such as crewing a boat which demand cooperation and others such as berry picking to reduce the tedium. All cooperation is reciprocal. Division of labour exists on age and sex lines but does not appear to lead to occupational specialisation.

9. Political organisation only exists on Tristan insofar as it has relations with the outside world. Internally there is no leadership or organisation based on power.

A person may influence others by example rather than dictum (Munch 1970:1303). There is evidence that political organisations have been formed on two occasions. The first occurred in Britain after evacuation because of volcanic activity. Initially it was a spontaneous outburst against a bureaucrat from Whitehall who maintained that they might not be able to return to Tristan. A petition was then sent to the government and when no reply was forthcoming the islanders held a public meeting. Even in this case they had received encouragement and moral support from outsiders (Munch 1964:374). The second time was after the return to Tristan when all those men working on the new dock spontaneously walked out—under threat of dismissal—in order to travel to Nightingale Island to collect guano.

10. As was mentioned previously there is no universally recognised hierarchy on Tristan. Church authorities often tried to establish some form of authority but it was usually short-lived and always ignored where possible (Munch 1964:371).

11. Munch also mentions two cases when individuals from within the community attempted to establish themselves as leaders. The islanders spontaneously thwarted these two attempts by simply ignoring the self-styled leaders: "They had received the most severe denunciation this atomistic and pacific community would hand out to anybody: they were ignored, isolated, denied a status in the community, not by communal decree but simply as a consequence of the withdrawal of individual reciprocal relationships" (Munch 1974:256).

12 and 13. Social control exists only insofar as all the inhabitants of Tristan abide by the norms of the founding charter. The main sanction of social control rests with the withdrawal of individual reciprocal relations.

14. Only tentative comments can be made on the distribution of self-respect. One would expect there to be equality between men as all have similar tasks to perform with similar resources. Munch does mention one of the more "prominent" families in relation to the meeting in England. Women and children may suffer in this respect. They do not participate in fishing expeditions and women cook for men even during cooperative ventures such as the thatching of a house.

Discussion

The attributes selected for examination in these societies are presented in summary form in Table 8.1. Although there are differences between these groups a number of patterns emerge from this preliminary sample. It is, however, necessary to consider some other aspects of these societies in order to gain some insight into their internal dynamics.

All of these groups are essentially small, local, face-to-face communities, although some of them exist within a larger cultural milieu—there are, for example, some 40,000 Mbuti Pygmies. The small size of all these societies is a major contributory factor in their open and basically egalitarian decisionmaking and social control processes.

The five traditional groups all experience a changing composition in their membership in the short term. This "flux" derives in part from seasonal-ecological variables

TABLE 8.1 Common Factors of Peaceful Societies

Groups / Items	Semai	Siriono	Mbuti	Kung	Copper Eskimo	Hutterites	Tristan
1 Habitat	Tropical Rain Forest	Tropical Rain Forest	Tropical Rain Forest	Hot Desert	Arctic Tundra	Temperate Grassland	Temperate Grassland
2 Subsistence	Hunting-Gathering, Swiddening	Hunting-Gathering, Swiddening	Hunting-Gathering	Hunting-Gathering	Hunting, some Gathering	Mixed Agriculture	Mixed-Subsistence Agriculture
3 Cosmology	Ideational*	Ideational	Ideational	Ideational	Ideational	Ideational	Idealistic
4 Integration	Kinship & Interest	Kinship & Interest	Kinship & Interest	Kinship & Interest	Kinship & Interest	Interest & Kinship	Interest & Kinship
5 Socialisation	Permissive	Permissive	Permissive	Permissive	Permissive	Authoritarian	Authoritarian
6 Physical Violence	Little, Lethal	Little, non-lethal	Little, non-lethal	Little, Lethal	Some, Lethal	Some, non-lethal	Some, non-lethal
7 Conflict Resolution	Individual & Group	Individual, some Group	Individual & Group	Individual & Group	Individual, some Group	Group	Individual
8 Division of Labour	Yes	Yes	Yes	Yes	Yes	Yes† Specialisation	Yes
9 Coercive Organisation	No	No	No	No	No	Perhaps	No
10 Hierarchy	Yes, nonrestrictive for males	No	No	Yes, nonrestrictive for males	No	Yes, nonrestrictive for males	No
11 Decision	All adults	All adults	All adults	All adults	All adults	All male adults	All adults
12 Social Control	All	All	All	All	All	All male adults	All adults
13 Forms of Social Control	Usually psychic	Usually psychic	Usually psychic	Usually psychic	Psychic & Physical	Psychic	Psychic
14 Discrimination	Yes	Yes	Yes	Yes	Yes	Yes	Yes

*Used in Sorokin's (1962: 55-102, Vol. I) sense.

and in certain cases from need for collective activity to maintain boundary distinctions (Turnbull 1968a:135).[2] But conflicts within these groups are also partly responsible for personnel changes, fission being used as a dissociative conflict resolution form. The changing composition of these traditional societies is partly responsible for the lack of lineal leadership. To maintain such a system of control would not only be difficult given the large geographical area which these groups cover but in certain circumstances it would stand in the way of "economic" necessity in terms of the production and distribution of food (Fried 1967:106).

The traditional groups produce little or no surplus. As such, material inequality between individuals on a long-term basis is impossible. As a corollary, leadership remains on the level of personal authority rather than coercive power because there is no surplus to appropriate and utilise. According to Fried (1967:117), however, the first step in the establishment of power-based leadership is the creation of a centre for the redistribution of material surplus for the benefit of the society as a whole (as per the Mountain Arapesh, Mead 1961:34) rather than an appropriation centre for personal-sectional advancement. What these groups do produce, however, is distributed equitably. In this context the cases of Tristan da Cunha and the Hutterites are of importance. Although the domestic mode of production on Tristan undoubtedly keeps the surplus small, the more specialised techniques employed by the Hutterites create a larger one and yet no great material inequality exists within them. The Hutterites in fact hold their surplus collectively and use it for the benefit of the group as a whole. It is interesting to note that both of these groups were "created"; they were established in the historical past with specific social structures designed to achieve definite goals.

The differences in child-rearing practices between the traditional and created societies are open to a number of possible—and contradictory—explanations. Firstly, it could be argued that the latent "violence" of the created societies—the existence of surplus which does not produce material inequality—manifests itself in their authoritarian child-rearing methods. Alternatively, their violent socialisation ways are a product of their historical background. Their respective conceptions of human nature—natural carnality or willful behavior—are only a reflection of their Western European Christian origin which emphasises control rather than development and as such directly influences the way their mode of subsistence. Both Tristan da Cunha and the Hutterites have sedentary farming lifestyles which are incompatible with independent adventurous personalities which permissive child socialisation processes tend to create.

Fortunately this sample of peaceful societies is not solely composed of hunting-gathering groups. If it were so composed then the absence of large structural inequalities might be attributed to this particular level of sociocultural development. The cases of Tristan da Cunha and the Hutterites demonstrate that it is possible for a society to produce a surplus and still retain a fairly egalitarian social structure which is not maintained by the use or threat of physical violence.

Conclusion

Any points derived from this small sample of peaceful societies must necessarily be tentative. The attributes of the groups considered, however, do not point toward a basic incompatibility between social justice or equality on the one hand and an absence of physical violence on the other. The very idea that the presence of one is the "price" paid for the absence of the other may simply be a manifestation of Western—although now becoming global—culture and its concomitant hierarchical world view.

Much more work is needed on the study of peaceful patterns of social organisation in terms of increasing the sample and perhaps more importantly of locating groups where there is sufficient information for longitudinal studies. Also, comparisons with societies which are physically violent but have basically similar social structures would possibly aid in identifying factors critical in the production of peace. This area of study has links with various other approaches, in particular the study of futures (e.g., Targ 1971, Weiss 1975). This type of information would not only provide insights into how various groups have "achieved" a relatively peaceful lifestyle but also, and perhaps more importantly, would demonstrate that peace is not a utopian and by implication unobtainable goal.

Notes

The groundwork for this chapter was carried out while I was an undergraduate in the School for Independent Studies, University of Lancaster 1974-1975. Many thanks go to my supervisor of that time, David Osterberg. My thanks also go to my current supervisor Paul Smoker whose comments encouraged me to rework parts of the original. Also for various personal friends whose support has encouraged me to stay with the original idea.

1. A number of authors of works used here (Dentan 1968; Loudon 1970; Chance 1966; Hostetler and Huntington 1967) display a common tendency to use some form of neo-Freudian drive reduction model of human aggression. Thus, even these peaceful societies, according to this approach, have violence ready to break out. Such a theory of course does little to explain the variance in the distribution of violence between egalitarian band societies and nation-states for example. When dealing with such macro categories of social organisation, hierarchy and compulsive organisation appear to account for a more significant amount of the variance.

2. Contrary to the argument maintaining some form of instinctual disposition to possess land as a part of human inheritance these least complex of societies are not generally territorial in the sense of maintaining an exclusive monopoly over an area of land. Other groups may come and go, and in times of shortage an incumbent band may share the food and water resources with another less fortunate group (Fried 1967:94-98; Lee and Devore 1968a:12).

References

Balicki, A. 1968. "The Netsilik Eskimos: Adaptive Processes." Pp. 78-82, in Lee and Devore (eds.), *Man the Hunter*. Chicago: Aldine.

Benedict, R. 1935. *Patterns of Culture*. London: Routledge & Kegan Paul.

Broch, T., and J. Galtung. 1966. "Belligerence among the Primitives." *Jnl. Peace Research* 3:33-45.

Chance, N. A. 1966. *The Eskimo of North Alaska*. New York: Holt, Rinehart & Winston.

Coon, C. S. 1972. *The Hunting Peoples*. London: Cape.

Davie, M. R. 1929. *The Evolution of War: A Study of Its Role in Early Societies*. Port Washington, New York: Kennikat Press, 1968.

Dentan, R. K. 1968. *The Semai: A Non-Violent People of Malaya*. Holt, Rinehart & Winston.

Dole, G. E., and R. L. Carneiro (eds.). 1960. *Essays in the Science of Culture: In Honour of Leslie A. White*. New York: T. Y. Crowell.

Forde, D. C. 1963. *Habitat, Economy and Society: A Geographical Introduction to Ethnology*. New York: Dutton & Co.

Fourie, L. 1960. "The Bushmen of South-West Africa." Pp. 87-95 in S. and P. Ottenberg (eds.), *Cultures and Societies of Africa*. New York: Random House.

Fried, M. H. 1967. *The Evolution of Political Society: An Essay in Political Anthropology*. New York: Random House.

Friedl, E. 1975. *Women and Men: An Anthropologist's View*. New York: Holt, Rinehart & Winston.

Fromm, E. 1973. *The Anatomy of Human Destructiveness*. New York: Holt, Rinehart & Winston.

Galtung, J. 1969. "Violence, Peace and Peace Research." *Jnl. Peace Research* 6:167-191.

Gardener, P. M. 1968. "Discussion: Primate Behaviour and the Evolution of Aggression." Pp. 338-344 in Lee and Devore (eds.), *Man the Hunter*.

Gjessing, G. 1967. "Ecology and Peace Research." *Jnl. Peace Research* 4:125-139.

Godlier, M. 1975. "Modes of Production, Kinship, and Demographic Structures." Pp. 3-27, in M. Bloch (ed.), *Marxist Analyses and Social Anthropology*. London: Malaby Press.

Holmberg, A. R. 1966. *Nomads of the Longbow: The Siriono of Eastern Bolivia*. Natural History Press.

Honigman, J. J. 1968. "Interpersonal Relations in Atomistic Communities." *Human Organisation* 27:220-229.

Hostetler, J. A. 1974. *Hutterite Society*. Baltimore and London: The Johns Hopkins University Press.

————, and G. E. Huntington. 1967. *The Hutterites of North America*. New York: Holt, Rinehart & Winston.

Jeness, D. 1922. *The Life of the Copper Eskimo*. Report of the Canadian Arctic Expedition 1913-1918, Vol. XIIa. Ottawa: F. A. Acland.

————, 1946. *Material Culture of the Copper Eskimo*. Report of the Canadian Arctic Expedition 1913-1918, Vol. 16. Ottawa: E. Clouter.

Lee, R. B. 1968a. "What Hunters Do for a Living: Or How to Make Out on Scarce Resources." Pp. 30-48, in Lee and Devore (eds.), *Man the Hunter*.

————, 1968b. "Discussion: Predation and Warfare." Pp. 157-158, in Lee and Devore (eds.), *Man the Hunter*.

————, and I. Devore (eds.), 1968. *Man the Hunter*. Chicago: Aldine.

————, and I. Devore. 1968a. "Problems in the Study of Hunter-Gatherers." Pp. 3-12, in Lee and Devore (eds.), *Man the Hunter*.

Lenski, G. 1966. *Power and Privilege: An Essay in the Theory of Social Stratification*. New York: McGraw-Hill.

Loudon, J. B. 1970. "Teasing and Socialization on Tristan da Cunha." Pp. 293-331, in P. Mayer (ed.), *Socialization: The Approach from Anthropology*. London: Tavistock.

Marshall, L. 1965. "The Kung Bushmen of the Kalahari Desert." Pp. 241-278, in J.L. Gibbs (ed.), *Peoples of Africa*. New York: Holt, Rinehart & Winston.

Mead, M. 1961. *Cooperation and Conflict Among Primitive Peoples*. Boston: Beacon Press.

———. 1972. *Culture and Commitment: A Study of the Generation Gap*. London: Panther Books Ltd.

———. 1973. "Warfare is Only an Invention Not a Biological Necessity." Pp. 112-118, in C. R. Beitz and T. Herman (eds.), *Peace & War*, San Francisco: Freeman & Co., Institute Press.

Moore, B., Jr. 1972. *Reflections on the Causes of Human Misery and upon Certain Proposals to Eliminate Them*. London: Allen Lane, The Penguin Press.

Munch, P.A. 1964. "Culture and Superculture in a Displaced Community: Tristan da Cunha." *Ethnology* 3:369-376.

———. 1970. "Economic Development and Conflicting Values: A Social Experiment in Tristan da Cunha." *American Anthropologist* 72:1300-1318

———. 1971. *Crisis in Utopia: The Ordeal of Tristan da Cunha* New York: T. Y. Crowell.

———, 1974. "Anarchy and Anomie in an Anarchistic Community." *Man* 9:243-261.

Otterbein, K.F. 1970. *The Evolution of War: A Cross-Cultural Study*. Human Relations Area Files Press.

Palmer, S. 1965. "Murder and Suicide in Forty Non-Literate Societies." *Jnl. Criminal Law, Criminology, and Police Science* 56:320-324

Rasmussen, K. 1932. *Intellectual Culture of the Copper Eskimo*. Report of the Fifth Thule Expedition to Arctic North America, Vol. IX. Copenhagen: Glydendalske Boghandel, Nordisk Forlag.

Sahlins, M. 1974. *Stone-Age Economics*. London: Tavistock.

Schapera, I. 1930. *The Khoisan Peoples of South Africa: Bushmen and Hottentots*. London: Routledge & Kegan Paul, 1965.

Service, E. R. 1966. *The Hunters*. Englewood Cliffs, N.J.: Prentice-Hall.

Sipes, R. G. 1973. "War, Sports and Agression: An Empirical Test of Two Rival Theories." *American Anthropologist* 75:64-86.

Sorokin, P. 1962. *Social and Cultural Dynamics*. 4 vols. New York: Bedminster Press.

Sweet, L. E. 1973. "Culture and Agressive Action." Pp. 325-344, in C.M. Otten (ed.), *Agression & Evolution*. Lexington, Mass.: Xerox College Publishing.

Targ, H. R. 1971. "Social Science and a New Social Order." *Jnl. Peace Research* 8:207-220.

Thomas, E. 1969. *The Harmless People*. Penguin.

Turnbull, C.M. 1965. "The Mbuti pygmies of the Congo." Pp. 279-318, in J.L. Gibbs (ed.), *Peoples of Africa*. New York: Holt, Rinehart & Winston.

———. 1966. *Wayward Servants: The Two Worlds of the African Pygmy*. London: Eyre & Spottiswoode.

———. 1968a. "The Importance of Flux in Two Hunting Societies." Pp. 132-137, in Lee and Devore (eds.), *Man the Hunter*.

———. 1968b. "Discussion: Resolving Conflicts by Fission." P. 156, in Lee and Devore (eds.), *Man the Hunter*.

————, 1968c. "Discussion: Primate Behaviour and Human Aggression." Pp. 338-343, in Lee and Devore (eds.), *Man the Hunter.*

Watanabe, H. 1968. "Subsistence and Ecology among Northern Food Gatherers." Pp. 69-77 in Lee and Devore (eds.), *Man the Hunter.*

Weiss, T.G. 1975. "The Tradition of Philosophical Anarchism and Future Directions in World Policy." *Jnl. Peace Research* 12:1-17.

Wright, Q. 1964. *A Study of War.* Chicago: University of Chicago Press (abridged ed.).

Suggested Readings

Lloyd, W.B., Jr. *Waging Peace: The Swiss Experience.* Washington, D.C.: Public Affairs Press, 1958.

Melko, Matthew. *52 Peaceful Societies.* Oakville, Ontario: Canadian Peace Research Institute, 1973.

Mitchell, J.J. *Human Nature: Theories, Conjectures, and Descriptions.* Metuchen, N.J.: Scarecrow, 1972.

Mead, Margaret. *Cooperation and Competition Among Primitive Peoples.* Boston: Beacon, 1961.

Reading 22

THE ECONOMIC FOUNDATIONS OF WARS: A SOVIET VIEW

Notes from the Editors

This selection from an official Russian publication lays out a Marxist perspective on the causes of war. Marx himself devoted most of his writing to the development of capitalism and its eventual destruction by the forces of socialism. In 1916, Lenin extended Marx' analysis when he wrote Imperialism, the Highest Stage of Capitalism. *Writing from exile about a Europe at war, Lenin explained international conflict in terms of imperialist rivalries brought about by the decline of capitalism in domestic economies.*

Current Soviet ideologists have extended Lenin's analysis to our own times. They see the rise of socialism in this century hastening the decline of capitalism and producing increased aggressiveness on the part of the fast-failing western nations. In addition, the contradictions between the western states and the colonies have become exaggerated, as have the contradictions within capitalist systems themselves. For Moscow, the current world conflict and the arms race are the result of capitalism's aggressive attempts to maintain by force their pernicious system.

Marxist-Leninists maintain that when socialism completely supplants capitalism, international war will disappear from the system. As for the apparent anomaly of socialist states fighting socialist states (as was the case of China and Russia in 1969 and China and Vietnam in 1979) defenders of the ideology argue, depending upon their nationality, that one of the two self-proclaimed socialist states in those conflicts was not a "true" socialist state.

As the Soviet Union reinterprets Lenin's message in light of the Perestroika *and* Glasnost *of the Gorbachev era, the views in this piece may be softened. Undoubtedly, contemporary Kremlin leaders will seek to find more grounds for peaceful coexistence between the systems in the years to come.*

While engendering wars and determining their aims, politics is neither primary nor self-contained. It is determined by the vital interests of different classes evolved by the socioeconomic system of the exploiter state. This system, which has given rise to wars, is characterised by the domination of private ownership, the concentration of the bulk of the means of production in the hands of the exploiter classes, who exist by appropriating the surplus product created by the working people. This is what all class antagonistic formations have in common, what forms the common source of wars of the most varied type.

All wars in the past and present, those between exploiter states in pursuit of the selfish interests of slave owners, feudal lords, and the bourgeousie, as also the uprisings and wars of the working people against whom they rose when their position had

Reprinted from *Marxism-Leninism on War and Army (A Soviet View)* (Moscow: Progress Publishers, 1972), by the United States Air Force (Washington, D.C.: Government Printing Office, 1974), pp. 31–39.

become unbearable and their patience had worn out, all these wars were caused by private ownership relations and the resultant social and class antagonism in exploiter formations. However, this does not mean that the specific differences in the causes of wars have been abolished. Wars in each of the above formations and in definite historical epochs had their own, specific causes. Capitalism ushered in a new epoch in the history of wars. The basic law of capitalism is the production of surplus value. The aim of capitalist production is the constant, unlimited accumulation of profit. Capitalists cannot rest content with the mass of the surplus value being created by the proletariat of their own country. Their appetites were insatiable. They scour the world in search of high profits. Wars are a means of rapid enrichment for the capitalists and, hence, a constant travelling companion of capitalism. The system of the exploitation of man by man and the system of the destruction of man by man are two sides of the capitalist order. War is a means by which the bourgeoisie obtains new raw material sources and markets, robs foreign countries, and makes easy profits.

Capitalism created a world market for the first time in history and enlarged the number of objects over which wars were waged. Chief among them were colonies— sources of cheap raw materials and labour power, spheres for the export of goods and capital, and strongholds on international trade routes. For several centuries bourgeois Holland, Britain, France, Portugal, and other European states waged wars of conquest against weakly developed countries in order to make colonies of them. There were also wars between the capitalist countries themselves for division of the world.

Naturally, some wars under capitalism were due also to other causes. The development of the productive forces of capitalism was obstructed in many countries by national oppression and political decentralisation. The epoch from the French bourgeois revolution of 1789–1794 to the Paris Commune of 1871 saw bourgeoisie-progressive, national liberation wars among other types of war. The main content and historical purpose of these wars were to overthrow absolutism and to destroy foreign oppression.

With the transition of capitalism to the imperialist stage, the bourgeoisie states became more aggressive. This is explained by the economic features of imperialism, which is a decaying and moribund capitalism. At the turn of the century, leap-like development replaced the more or less regular spread of capitalism over the globe. This led to an unprecedented growth and intensification of all the contradictions of that system—economic, political, class and national. The struggle of the imperialist powers for markets and spheres of capital investment, for raw materials and labour power, and for world domination took on extremely sharp forms. While imperialism ruled undividedly this struggle inevitably led to destructive wars. *The basic economic sources of these wars were rooted in the deepening conflict between the modern productive forces and the economic, and also political, system of imperialism.* This was the main cause of the armed clashes between imperialist powers.

The confines of old national states, without the formation of which capitalism could not have overthrown feudalism, became too narrow for it. The productive forces of world capitalism outgrew the limited framework of bourgeois states. The whole world merged into a single economic organism and was at the same time divided up among a handful of big imperialist powers. This contradiction found expression in the striving of the bourgeoisie to export capital and to win markets for commodities they cannot sell at home, to seize raw material sources and new colonies, to destroy competitors on world markets, and to conquer world domination and, hence, to unleash wars.

The conflict between the productive forces (with the national-imperialist limits imposed on their development) and the capitalist relations of production is strikingly expressed in the uneven, leap-like economic and political development of capitalist countries under imperialism. Thus, at the beginning of the century bourgeois countries which had launched out on industrial development only recently found themselves in a favourable situation and succeeded, by a sudden forward dash, to outstrip the old industrial capitalist states in a comparatively short time. After the Second World War the share and role of the individual capitalist states changed again and the unevenness of their economic development intensified.

Uneven development inevitably leads to abrupt changes in the alignment of forces in the world capitalist system. From time to time a sharp disturbance of the equilibrium occurs within that system. The old distribution of spheres of influence among the monopolies clashes with the new alignment of forces in the world. To bring the distribution of colonies in accord with the new balance of forces, there inevitably have to be periodic redivisions of the already divided world. Under capitalism armed violence is the only way of dividing up colonies and spheres of influence.

"Capitalism," Lenin said, "has concentrated the earth's wealth in the hands of few states and divided the world up to the last bit. . . . Any further enrichment could take place only at the expense of others, as the enrichment of one state at the expense of another. The issue could only be settled by force—and, accordingly, war between the world marauders became inevitable." *As a result of the social antagonisms inherent in capitalism and the operation of the law of the uneven, leap-like economic and political development of the capitalist countries under imperialism, the contradictions between the bourgeois states aggravate to the utmost, and this leads to a division of the capitalist world into hostile coalitions, and to wars between them.*

The First and the Second World Wars burst forth on this economic basis. The imperialists of all countries, the entire world system of capitalism were guilty of them. These wars had catastrophical results for the international bourgeoisie, promoted the formation of the world socialist community and the collapse of the colonial system of imperialism. However, the ruling circles of the imperialist states did not draw the necessary conclusions from them.

Reasons for the Greater Aggressiveness of the Imperialist States Today

Formerly the aggravation of the contradictions between these states or their coalitions was the main reason responsible for the striving of imperialist states to unleash wars. These contradictions continue to aggravate. However, the main contradiction now is that between the two opposing social systems—capitalism and socialism.

The contradictions between the two world systems are class contradictions. The socialist system greatly diminishes the sphere of imperialist exploitation and domination, creating conditions in which capitalism will lose the privileges it still enjoys.

Socialism has a revolutionising influence on the working people in the capitalist countries, the colonies, and dependent countries.

Another reason for the growing aggressiveness of modern imperialism is that the contradictions between the imperialist states, on the one hand, and the colonies and recent colonies, on the other, have greatly aggravated. Under the influence of the example set by the Soviet Union—once a backward agrarian country and now a mighty industrial power—and that of the successes achieved by other socialist countries, the popular masses in Asia, Africa, and Latin America have launched a national liberation revolution. Deep antagonisms divide the imperialist states and the countries that have won national independence or are still fighting for liberation.

The imperialist predators are willing to resort to any means, fair or foul, to preserve and strengthen their colonial possessions. They attempt to suppress the national liberation struggle of the African peoples by force of arms, they unleash wars in the Southeast Asian countries, and organise reactionary coups in the Latin American states. Colonialism and neocolonialism are the direct and indirect cause of many conflicts threatening to plunge mankind into a new war.

The third cause is the exacerbation of the internal contradictions of capitalism after the Second World War. This is linked, first and foremost, with the continuing aggravation and deepening of the general crisis of capitalism, with the fact that the main contradiction of capitalist society, that between labour and capital, continues to grow. The transition from monopoly capitalism to state-monopoly capitalism, under which the monopolies merge with the state, intensifies the exploitation of the working people, makes science and technology and the growing productive forces serve the aim of enriching a handful of monopolists. Exploitation has never been as hideous as it is today. Even when business conditions are favourable, millions of people, workers, and intellectuals are unemployed, and peasants are ruined and evicted from their land. At the same time a small number of powerful monopolies are profiting from the exploitation of the working people, from the arms race and aggressive wars.

State monopoly capitalism is responsible for the unprecedented intensification of militarism, including the economic and ideological fields. Militarisation permeates the entire life of bourgeois society. The production of mass-destruction weapons eats up an enormous part of the national income of the bourgeois states. During the past twenty years U.S. military spending has increased more than forty-eight-fold over that in the two prewar decades. More than 75 percent of the total expenditure in the U.S. federal budget is directly or indirectly channeled to military needs. The growth in weapons production in the main imperialist states makes other countries spend large funds on strengthening their defence too.

The imperialist state is becoming a militaristic police state. The economic superstructure rising on the basis of finance capital and the politics and ideology of the finance oligarchy strengthen the state's aggressiveness. Under state-monopoly capitalism "big business," the political leaders and the top brass controlling the state, make it pursue a policy aimed at preparing a war against the Soviet Union and other socialist states.

The sharp diminution of the sphere of action of the imperialist forces and the extreme aggravation of the contradictions under state-monopoly capitalism make the economic and political development of the bourgeois countries ever more uneven. This is the fourth reason responsible for the greater aggressiveness of the imperialist states.

In recent years serious changes have taken place in the relation of forces within the capitalist world. This process is continuing. Intense exploitation of the working people through the system of state-monopoly capitalism, relatively small military spending over a long period of time, the high level of capital investments, and the comparatively rapid growth of labour productivity, the application of the fruits of scientific and technological progress, and the considerable material assistance given to them by the United States and some other countries have led to rapid economic advance in West Germany and Japan. For several years the West European countries and Japan outstripped the United States in economic growth rates. Lately, however, their roles have changed again.

This deepened the contradictions between the United States and the European capitalist countries and Japan. The competitive struggle in Western Europe has also taken on sharper forms, including the Common Market and other state-monopoly associations. New forms of international economic associations and new ways of dividing markets have emerged, as have also new centres of attraction and new hotbeds of contradictions. All this must be taken into account when the economic reasons for military clashes are investigated.

The triumph of socialist revolutions and the transition of a growing number of countries to the socialist road have greatly weakened imperialism. But, imperialism does not want to give up its positions without struggle. The class-social antagonisms between the two social systems are growing ever more distinct and at times assume very sharp forms.

The contradiction between capitalism and socialism is stronger than the inter-imperialist contradictions. It reflects all the contradictions of the epoch and leaves a deep mark on all major international events. It should be remembered that the growth of the forces of socialism and the upsurge of the class and national liberation struggle are attended by the growing aggressiveness of the monopoly bourgeoisie, which fights social progress by all and every means and attempts to preserve its class privileges and riches at all costs.

The advance of the world socialist system and other factors do much to exacerbate interimperialist contradictions. They exert a dual influence. On the one hand, they strengthen the will of the imperialist powers to unite, to create military, political, and other alliances; on the other, they deepen the contradictions between them. This corroborates Lenin's statement that "two trends exist; one, which makes the alliance of all the imperialists inevitable; the other, which places the imperialists in opposition to each other—two trends, neither of which has any firm foundation."

After the Second World War the first tendency naturally grew stronger in the course of the struggle waged by the imperialist powers against the socialist system. Imperialist states energetically strengthened their aggressive military blocs, signed bilateral pacts, etc. For the first time in history the main imperialist powers, the United States, Britain, West Germany, and others joined a single military alliance directed against the socialist system.

Naturally, the fact that there are two opposite tendencies in the development of the imperialist system makes every alliance of the capitalist countries contradictory and unstable. Such alliances (organisations) directed against the socialist countries and the national liberation movement do not resolve the economic and political contradictions between the individual capitalist countries in those alliances and within every one of them but, on the contrary, further deepen and aggravate them. Besides, the setting up of organisations involving a number of capitalist countries inevitably leads to a growth of the contradictions within these organisations and struggle against outsiders. At present, however, these interimperialist contradictions are dampened by the even sharper class antagonisms. That is why a war between the big imperialist states, though still possible, is far less likely now than it was before.

Thus, the world imperialist system is torn by deep and sharp antagonisms. These are contradictions between labour and capital and between the people and the monopolies, growing militarisation, the disintegration of the colonial system, the antagonisms between the young national states and the old colonial powers, and, most important, the rapid growth of world socialism that undermines and erodes imperialism, weakens it, and spells its doom.

In view of the above the imperialists tend to save capitalism through war, the danger of which is great at present and is threatening all the people of our planet. *It is precisely because capitalism at its highest stage has entered the period of its decline and ruin and is going through a new, third state of its general crisis that its aggressive strivings are not decreasing but are incessantly growing.*

Imperialist aggression is spearheaded against the socialist community and only the strength of the countries in the community, notably that of the Soviet Union, prevents international reaction from unleashing a world military conflict. At the same time the antagonisms between the handful of highly developed imperialist powers and the young developing countries are growing sharper. The imperialists attempt with all the means at their disposal to hamper the peoples from carrying out radical changes in their social systems. With this aim in view they unleash local wars, instigate military coups, and organise plots and interventions.

Socioeconomic Conditions for the Establishment of Peace

War, as Marxism-Leninism has shown scientifically, is not a permanent feature in history. The historical inevitability of transition of all or at least of the main countries to socialism creates the economic basis for banning wars from the life of society and for establishing eternal peace. Mankind has already attained a stage of development in which there are material prerequisites determining not only the possibility but also the objective need for the victory of the new, socialist system, under which the causes breeding wars and military conflicts will disappear. Lenin wrote: "Our aim is to achieve a socialist system of society, which, by eliminating the division of mankind into classes, by eliminating all exploitation of man by man and nation by nation, will inevitably eliminate the very possibility of war."

The modern productive forces have created the material prerequisites and the objective need for the transition of mankind to socialism. Because of their high level of development and social character an extensive division of labour has been established between different countries, and close economic ties have been formed. The development of sea, land, and air transport has made it possible to cover distances between countries in no time.

Modern scientific and technological progress opens up broad prospects for the rapid development of the productive forces and for the radical improvement of the material conditions in all countries. The introduction of its enormous achievements on a mass scale, the extensive use of nuclear energy for peaceful purposes, and the comprehensive automation of production will give mankind unheard-of wealth, which we must not risk losing just to please a handful of warmongers.

However, the long-since-obsolete capitalist relations of production prevent the use of the enormous achievements made by production, science, and technology in the interests of all members of society, and also equal economic cooperation between the peoples.

Under capitalism already there is a clearly expressed tendency toward the setting up of a single world economy managed according to a common plan, a tendency that will undoubtedly develop further and will fully assert itself once socialism is established on a global scale. Socialism will remove the barriers between countries and nations imperialism has set up, and will unite mankind into a single workers' collective. The triumph of socialism in all countries will bring a social system "whose international rule will be *Peace,* because its national rules will be everywhere the same—*Labour!*"

These prophetic words which were spoken by Marx as early as 1870, have been fully borne out by the peace-loving policy of the Soviet Union and other socialist countries, by the new relations between them. These are relations of fraternal cooperation and mutual assistance between countries, in which the leading role is played by the working class, and in which the working people themselves are the masters of their destiny and are building a new life without the bourgeoisie. The socialist community embodies the objective invincibility of mankind's movement toward eternal peace.

Now the world socialist system determines the main trend of human society's historical progress. The further transformation of the world socialist system into the decisive factor in mankind's social development will express not only the chief content, trend, and main distinctive features of history, but also the entire process of that development, all its paths and specific features.

But, as long as the economic basis of wars and their only source—imperialism—continue to exist, as long as imperialist policy and ideology are aimed at preparing and unleashing military conflicts, the economic and military might of the Soviet Union and the entire socialist community and the policy and ideology of the building and defence of socialism and communism will have to play an important part in preventing wars and reining in the aggressive imperialist forces.

Suggested Readings

Curtin, Philip, ed. *Imperialism*. New York: Harper & Row, 1971.

Hobson, John A. *Imperialism*. Ann Arbor: University of Michigan, 1965.

Kara, Karel. "On the Marxist Theory of War and Peace." *Journal of Peace Research* VI, 1 (1968), pp. 1–27.

Lenin, V.I. *On War and Peace*. San Francisco: China Books and Periodicals, 1966.

Magdoff, Harry. *The Age of Imperialism: The Economics of United States Foreign Policy*. New York: Monthly Review Press, 1969.

Milovidov, A.S. and V.G. Koslov, eds. *The Philosophical Heritage of V.I. Lenin and Problems of Contemporary War*. Moscow: Military Publishing House, 1972.

Schumpeter, J.A. *Imperialism and Social Classes*. New York: Kelley, 1951.

Vigor, P.H. *The Soviet View of War, Peace and Neutrality*. London: Routledge and Kegan Paul, 1975.

Reading 23

THE REALIST APPROACH TO INTERNATIONAL CONFLICT

James E. Dougherty and Richard L. Pfaltzgraff Jr.

Notes from the Editors

James E. Dougherty and Richard L. Pfaltzgraff Jr. are the authors of an influential text in international relations, Contending Theories of International Relations *(1981). In the excerpt reprinted here, they analyze the thoughts of Hans Morgenthau, one of the leading figures in the so-called realist school.*

Morgenthau, who himself wrote several influential textbooks during the first two decades after World War II, was concerned about the moralism, idealism, and indeed, naivete, in America's foreign relations. For him, as well as diplomat-historian George Kennan with whom he has often been linked, leaders should concentrate solely on the pursuit of their nation's interest in international relations. If all nations pursued their national interest, the system would be relatively stable, with the "balance of power" mechanism keeping potential troublemakers in check.

This does not mean, of course, that realistic practitioners are in agreement over the definition of national interest and the means one should use to protect it. For example, Morgenthau became one of the more outspoken critics of the Vietnam War. Yet that war was supported and extended by a very realistic president, Richard Nixon, and his national security advisor, Henry Kissinger, who also promulgated the "realist" line. Although they disagreed over tactics, Morgenthau's conception of diplomacy was closer to Nixon's than it was to Jimmy Carter's and Ronald Reagan's, both of whom were too ideological for Morgenthau.

Hans J. Morgenthau (1904–1980), sets forth six principles of realist theory. First, he suggests that political relationships are governed by objective rules deeply rooted in human nature. Since these rules are "impervious to our preferences, men will challenge them only at the risk of failure." If these rules themselves cannot be changed, Morgenthau's determinism holds that society can be improved by first understanding the laws that govern society and then by basing public policy on that knowledge.

In theorizing about international politics it is necessary to employ historical data for examining political acts and their consequences. In systematizing these vast amounts of historical data, the students of politics should place themselves "in the position of a statesman who must meet a certain problem of foreign policy under certain circumstances," and ask themselves, "what the rational alternatives are from which a statesman may choose who must meet this problem under these circumstances (presuming always that he acts in a rational manner), and which of these rational alternatives this particular statesman, acting under these circumstances, is likely to choose. It is the testing of this rational hypothesis against the actual facts and their consequences that gives meaning to the facts of international politics."

Second, Morgenthau contends that statesmen "think and act in terms of interest defined as power" and that historical evidence proves this assumption. This concept, central to Morgenthau's realism, gives continuity and unity to the seemingly diverse foreign policies of the widely separated nation-states. Moreover, the concept "interest defined as power" makes possible the evaluation of actions of political leaders at different points in history. To describe Morgenthau's framework in more contemporary language, it is a model of interaction within an international system. Using historical data, Morgenthau compares the real world with the interaction patterns within his model.

In his view, international politics is a process in which national interests are adjusted:

The concept of the national interest presupposes neither a naturally harmonious, peaceful world nor the inevitability of war as a consequence of the pursuit by all nations of their national interest. Quite to the contrary, it assumes continuous conflict and threat of war to be minimized through the continuous adjustment of conflicting interest by diplomatic action.

Third, Morgenthau acknowledges that the meaning of "interest defined as power" is an unstable one. However, in a world in which sovereign nations vie for power, the foreign policies of all nations must consider survival as their minimum requirement. All nations are compelled to "protect their physical, political, and cultural identity against encroachments by other nations." Thus national interest is identified with national survival. "Taken in isolation, the determination of its content in a concrete situation is relatively simple, for it encompasses the integrity of the nation's territory, of its political institutions, and of its culture." As long as the world is divided into nations, Morgenthau asserts, the "national interest is indeed the last word in world politics." Interest, then, is the essence of politics.

Once its survival is assured, the nation-state may pursue lesser interests. Morgenthau assumes that nations ignore the national interest only at the risk of destruction. Yet in twentieth-century foreign policy formulation, lesser interests have sometimes preceded the national interest. Had Great Britain in 1939-1940 based her policy toward Finland upon legalistic-moralistic considerations, backed with large-scale military aid against Soviet aggression, then Britain's position might have been weakened so as to assure her destruction by Nazi Germany. Britain would have neither restored Finland's independence nor safeguarded her most vital national interest, that of physical survival. Only when the national interest most closely related to national survival has been safeguarded can nations pursue lesser interests.

Fourth, Morgenthau states that "universal moral principles cannot be applied to the actions of states in their abstract, universal formulation, but that they must be filtered through the concrete circumstances of time and place." In pursuit of the national interest, nation-states are governed by a morality which differs from the morality of individuals in their personal relationships. In the actions of statesmen *qua* statesmen, the political consequences of a particular policy become the criteria for judging it. To confuse an individual's morality with a state's morality is to court national disaster. Because the primary official responsibility of statesmen is the survival of the nation-state, their obligations to their citizenry require a different mode of moral judgment from that of the individual.

Fifth, Morgenthau asserts that political realism does not identify the "moral aspirations of a particular nation with the moral laws that govern the universe." In fact, if international politics is placed within a framework of defining interests in terms of power, "we are able to judge other nations as we judge our own." This aspect of Morgenthau's realism bears resemblance to Niebuhr's thought and in turn to Augustinian theology.

Sixth, and finally, Morgenthau stresses the autonomy of the political sphere. Political actions must be judged by political criteria. "The economist asks: 'How does this policy affect the welfare of society, or a segment of it?' The lawyer asks: 'Is this policy in accord with the rules of law?' The moralist asks: 'Is this policy in accord with moral principles?' And the political realist asks: 'How does this policy affect the power of the nation?'"

In power struggles, nations follow policies designed to preserve the status quo, to achieve imperialistic expansion, or to gain prestige. In Morgenthau's view, domestic and international politics can be reduced to one of three basic types: "A political policy seeks either to keep power, to increase power, or to demonstrate power."

Although the purpose of a status quo policy is to preserve the existing distribution of power, the nation adopting such a policy does not necessarily act to prevent all international change. Instead, status quo nations seek to thwart change that may produce fundamental shifts in the international distribution of power. Morgenthau cites the Monroe Doctrine as an example of a status quo policy that fulfills his two criteria. First, it was designed to maintain the prevailing power balance in the Western Hemisphere. Second, it expressed the unwillingness of the United States to prevent all change. Instead, the United States would act only against change that threatened the existing distribution of power. Likewise, treaties concluded at the end of wars invariably codify the then prevailing status quo.

Imperialism is the second major alternative available to nations. This is a policy designed to achieve a "reversal of existing power relations between nations." The goals of imperialist powers include local preponderance, continental empire, or world domain. Nations may adopt imperialistic policies as a result of victory, defeat, or the weakness of other states. A state whose leaders expect victory may alter its objectives from the restoration of the status quo to a permanent change in the distribution of power. Moreover, a defeated nation may adopt an imperialistic policy to "turn the scales on the victor, to overthrow the status quo created by his victory, and to change places with him in the hierarchy of power." Finally, the existence of weak states may prove irresistible to a strong state.

To attain imperialistic objectives, states may resort to military force or to cultural and economic means. Military conquest is the oldest and most obvious form of imperialism. Economic imperialism is not as effective a technique as military conquest. If one imperialistic state cannot gain control over another by military means, it may attempt to do so by economic capabilities. Cultural imperialism represents an attempt to influence the human mind "as an instrument for changing the power relations between two nations."

According to Morgenthau, states may pursue a policy of prestige. This may be "one of the instrumentalities through which the policies of status quo and of imperialism try to achieve their ends." Its objective is to "impress other nations with the power one's own nation actually possesses, or with the power it believes, or wants the other nations to believe, it possesses." Morgenthau suggests two specific techniques of this policy: diplomacy and the display of force. A policy of prestige succeeds when a nation gains such a reputation for power that the actual use of power becomes unnecessary—the political shadow allegedly cast by military power. . . .

Morgenthau is concerned not only about the quest for power, but also with the conditions for international peace. His concept of international order is closely related to his concept of national interest. The pursuit of national interests that are not essential to national survival contributes to international conflict. In the twentieth century, especially, nations have substituted global objectives for more limited goals that, in Morgenthau's view, constitute the essence of national interest. Modern nationalism, combined with the messianic ideologies of the twentieth century, has obscured the national interest. In the guise of extending communism or "making the world safe for democracy," nations intervene in the affairs of regions not vital to their security. For example, Morgenthau, like Kennan, opposed American military intervention in South Vietnam because Southeast Asia allegedly lay beyond the most vital interests of the United States, and because the United States would find it impossible, except perhaps with a vast expenditure of resources, to maintain a balance of power in Southeast Asia. In contrast, he expressed great concern about Soviet influence in Cuba because of its geographic location in close proximity to the United States.

Even in an international system without ideologically motivated foreign policies, competition between opposing nation-states is likely. Like many other realists, Morgenthau views the balance of power as the most effective technique for the management of power in an international system based on competitive relationships among states. He defines balance of power as (1) a policy aimed at a certain state of affairs; (2) an actual state of affairs; (3) an approximately equal distribution of power; and (4) any distribution of power. However, it is not the balance of power itself, but the international consensus upon which it is built that preserves international peace. "Before the balance of power could impose its restraints upon the power aspirations of nations through the mechanical interplay of opposing forces, the competing nations had first to restrain themselves by accepting the system of the balance of power as the common framework of their endeavors." Such a consensus "kept in check the limitless desire for power, potentially inherent, as we know, in all imperialisms, and prevented it from becoming a political actuality."

The international consensus which sustained the balance of power before the twentieth century no longer exists. Structural changes in the international system have drastically limited, if not rendered ineffective, the classical balance of power. In Morgenthau's view, the balance of world power through the early 1960s rested with two nations, the United States and the Soviet Union, rather than with several great powers. He contended that allies of one superpower could shift their alignment to the other superpower, but they could not alter significantly the distribution of power because of their weakness relative to either the United States or the Soviet Union. Nor was any third power of sufficient strength as to be capable of intervening on either side and greatly changing the power distribution.

Like the balance of power, diplomacy plays a crucial role in the preservation of peace. In fact, a precondition for the creation of a peaceful world is the development of a new international consensus, in the formation of which diplomacy can contribute to "peace through accommodation." Morgenthau decries the "deprecation of diplomacy" in the twentieth century. The diplomat's role has been diminished by the development of advanced communications, by public disparagement of diplomacy and diplomats, and by the tendency of heads of government to conduct their own negotiations in summit conferences. The rise in importance of international assemblies, the substitution of open diplomacy for secrecy, and the inexperience on the part of the superpowers contributed to the decline of diplomacy during much of the twentieth century. Morgenthau clearly prefers a diplomacy similar to that of the international system before the twentieth century. His views on traditional diplomacy as a means for adjusting national interests resemble those of Sir Harold Nicolson, a leading twentieth-century British diplomatist and theoretician of diplomatic practice.

If it is to be revived as an effective technique for managing power, diplomacy must meet four conditions. (1) Diplomacy must be divested of its crusading spirit. (2) Foreign policy objectives must be defined in terms of national interest and must be supported with adequate power. (3) Nations must view foreign policy from the point of view of other nations. (4) Nations must be willing to compromise on issues that are not vital to them. If diplomacy can be restored to a position of importance, Morgenthau believes, it may not only contribute to "peace through accommodation," but also to the creation of an international consensus upon which more adequate world political institutions can be built. . . .

Suggested Readings

Clausewitz, Carl von. *On War*. London: Penguin, 1968.

Hinsley, F.H. *Power and the Pursuit of Peace*. Cambridge: Cambridge University, 1963.

Kissinger, Henry A. *A World Restored*. New York: Grosset and Dunlap, 1964.

Machiavelli, Niccolo. *The Prince*. New York: Appleton, 1947.

McNeil, William H. *The Pursuit of Power*. Chicago: University of Chicago Press, 1982.

Thompson, Kenneth W. *Political Realism and the Crisis of World Politics*. Princeton: Princeton University, 1960.

CHAPTER 5

The Causes of War, Part 2

Of all the chapters in this anthology, this was the most difficult to design. We present here seven pieces of original research written during the past three decades that represent several methodological approaches to the study of war. By no means do they represent all of the exciting new approaches in the discipline. Further, they suggest only a small fraction of the insight and knowledge being produced by innovative social scientists and humanists working in international relations and peace and conflict studies today.

In our first selection, the summary chapter from *The Causes of War*, Geoffrey Blainey presents what he learned from his analysis of war from the eighteenth century to the present. Blainey's propositions, derived from a traditional humanistic approach to historical data, deal with many of the theories and variables that are employed in the more empirically based studies that follow.

One important concern of peace scientists has been coalition theory, and especially, how various alliance and alignment configurations affect international stability. Diplomatic history abounds with examples of shifting alliances apparently stabilizing or destabilizing the so-called balance of power. Until recently, most of those who wrote about this issue used selected historical anecdotes to prove or disprove theories about the relationship between alliances and war.

In "Multipolar Systems and International Stability," Karl W. Deutsch and J. David Singer tackle the problem in a different fashion. They examine one major corollary of the balance of power model that predicts more international stability as the system moves from bipolarity to multipolarity. Unlike many of the earlier contributions in this area, theirs uses mathematical models to test hypotheses. Although their models are abstract, real historical data have been used to test them in recent years. The article is an example of how scholars apply scientific techniques to immediately relevant problems of war and peace. Deutsch and Singer wrote at a time when the world was indeed shifting from bipolarity to multipolarity. They hoped that their conclusions would interest the policy makers.

Arms races are another central concern of policy makers and scholars alike. Some, like George Washington, among others, counsel *Si vis pacem, para bellum*—If you desire peace, you must prepare for war. Others contend that the erection of a military establishment to defend a nation against a putative enemy both increases tensions and compels that enemy to build a comparable military establishment. In the end, the arms race, spurred by mutually perceived political conflict, may come to produce more tension and instability than the original conflict itself.

In "Arms Races and Escalation," our third selection, Michael D. Wallace, with the aid of a computer, determines the frequency with which the outbreak of war has been preceded by an arms race. Beginning with a rich set of data on war and military expenditures, Wallace constructs an inventive arms-race-index formula that allows him to test empirically the classic hypothesis.

Alliance configurations and arms races are background variables that generally relate to the underlying causes of conflict in the international system. Nazli Choucri and Robert C. North looked at those variables, as well as others, in their attempt to understand the underlying causes of World War I. By examining the structure of the system from 1870 to 1914 and the interactions of the major powers, they hoped to determine what led to the outbreak of war in the summer of 1914.

The last three articles in this chapter involve the immediate origins of World War I. Although each views those origins from a different perspective, they are primarily interested in how one may apply the lessons of that tragedy to conflict resolution today.

Most wars are not welcomed by those who seem to stumble into them. Time and again, crises are exacerbated by the way decision makers miscalculate and misperceive each others' intentions and capabilities. In Ralph K. White's discussion of "Misperception in Vienna on the Eve of World War I," insights from social psychology and psychology are used to examine the pictures in the heads of Austrian decision makers. White delves into the historical documentation from the period to elicit from Austrian statements several dramatic types of misperception and self deception. Without such misperception and self deception, and perhaps with more perfect knowledge of others' perceptions and intentions, wars such as World War I might be avoided.

Diplomatic historians tend to eschew computers and models and bury themselves in the archives, armed only with their intellect and investigative skills. They often emerge with a convincing account of their subject, although their methodology is vague and their assumptions unstated. Nevertheless, for the single case study, it is difficult to imagine a better way to attack a problem than through the traditional immersion in the documents, primary documents that resist rigorous coding or categorization. And, of course, the historian's narrative approach can make for good reading.

Using a historian's approach, L.L. Farrar, Jr. evaluates the options available to the decision makers in "The Limits of Choice: July 1914 Reconsidered." Farrar moves beyond Vienna to all of the major capitals as he examines the decision points that, it seems now, led inexorably to the blazing of the guns of August. At first glance, Farrar's conclusion, that in most cases the diplomats made the most rational decisions for their nations, seems at variance with White's. Yet it is possible for people to behave rationally on the bases of their views of reality, inaccurate though those views may be.

However rationally the leaders may have behaved during July and August of 1914, they did plunge the world into The Great War. The Cuban Missile Crisis of 1962 was one frightening global crisis that was resolved peacefully. Ole R. Holsti, Richard A. Brody, and Robert C. North are interested in "The Management of International Crisis," and how the 1962 case differed from the 1914 case. They employed a content analysis of many of the same documents that Farrar examined, as well as those available for the Cuban crisis, to identify behaviors and bargaining strategies that may lead nations away from the abyss.

Much of this social-scientific empirical research on the correlates and causes of war has been supported by government agencies. In part, governments are interested in contributing to our existential knowledge base. They have also expressed interest in applying some of the findings in a practical way to their day-to-day analyses of diplomatic interactions. In the main, however, little has been produced in this realm that has been of immediate utility to foreign policy practitioners. They find most of the studies to be too rarified intellectually or too general to be *directly* relevant to their endeavors. On the other hand, much of the new behavioral approach to international relations has found its way into the literature used in the universities. Thus, in a slow, almost osmotic process, today's students, who will be tomorrow's diplomats, should be using these approaches and insights in the decades to come.

Reading 24

SOME CAUSES OF WAR

Geoffrey Blainey

Notes from the Editors

In 1973, Geoffrey Blainey, a professor of economic history, published the widely acclaimed The Causes of War. *Blainey examined all major international wars since 1700 and most of the prominent theories about their causes. In one sense, his book is a paean to the importance of history to understanding contemporary international conflict. Blainey contends that even with nuclear weapons, nations today tend to behave the way nations have behaved over the past three centuries.*

He began his analysis in an unorthodox manner by studying periods of peace, and he was forced to admit that some of the more celebrated periods of peace defy simple explanation. He then looked at such causes of war as military overoptimism, the role of third parties, domestic turbulence, economics, the influence of climatological factors, ideology, accident, arms races, and historic enmities.

Blainey's approach depends upon the narrative techniques of the traditional historian. Thus, even though his examples are aptly chosen, his interpretations perceptive, and conclusions sound, some students of war may find fault with this intuitive, nonreplicable, and ultimately unscientific, method.

The selection reproduced here is his straightforward conclusion—the thirty-three general propositions about war, peace, and neutrality he developed through the body of the analysis. Although much of what he has turned up seems not surprising or controversial, several of his propositions are new and indeed thought provoking.

The Causes of War

1. There can be no war unless at least two nations prefer war to peace.

2. Just as peace comes only through the agreement of the fighting nations, so war comes only through the agreement of nations which had previously been at peace.

3. The idea that one nation can be mainly blamed for causing a war is as erroneous as the idea that one nation can be mainly praised for causing the end of a war. Most current explanations of war, however, rest on these errors.

4. If it is true that the breakdown of diplomacy leads to war, it is also true that the breakdown of war leads to diplomacy.

5. While the breakdown of diplomacy reflects the belief of each nation that

Geoffrey Blainey, *The Causes of War* (London: Macmillan, 1973), pp. 245–49. Reprinted with permission of The Face Press, A Division of Macmillian, Inc. © Geoffrey Blainey, 1973.

it will gain more by fighting than by negotiating, the breakdown of war reflects the belief of each nation that it will gain more by negotiating than by fighting.

6. Neutrality, like war and peace, depends on agreement. Sweden and Switzerland, for instance, have remained neutral for more than a century and a half not only because they chose neutrality but because warring nations permitted them to remain neutral.

7. War and peace are more than opposites. They have so much in common that neither can be understood without the other.

A Framework of Causes

8. War and peace appear to share the same framework of causes. The same set of factors should appear in explanations of the

outbreak of war;
widening of war by the entry of new nations;
outbreak of peace;
surmounting crises during a period of peace; and,
of course, the ending of peace.

9. When leaders of rival nations have to decide whether to begin, continue or end a war, they are, consciously or unconsciously, asking variations of the same question: they are assessing their ability or inability to impose their will on the rival nation.

10. In deciding for war or peace national leaders appear to be strongly influenced by at least seven factors:
  i. military strength and the ability to apply that strength efficiently in the likely theatre of war;
  ii. predictions of how outside nations will behave if war should occur;
  iii. perceptions of whether there is internal unity or discord in their land and in the land of the enemy;
  iv. knowledge or forgetfulness of the realities and sufferings of war;
  v. nationalism and ideology;
  vi. the state of economy and also its ability to sustain the kind of war envisaged;
  vii. the personality and experience of those who shared in the decision.

11. Wars usually begin when two nations disagree on their relative strength, and wars usually cease when the fighting nations agree on their relative strength. Agreement or disagreement emerges from the shuffling of the same set of factors. Thus each factor is capable of promoting war or peace.

12. A change in one factor—the defection of an ally or the eruption of strife in the land of the enemy—may dramatically alter a nation's assessment of its bargaining position. In the short term that factor could wield an influence which seems irrationally large.

13. When nations prepare to fight one another, they have contradictory

expectations of the likely duration and outcome of the war. When those predictions, however, cease to be contradictory, the war is almost certain to end.

14. Any factor which increases the likelihood that nations will agree on their relative power is a potential cause of peace. One powerful cause of peace is a decisive war, for war provides the most widely-accepted measure of power.

15. Even a decisive war cannot have permanent influence, for victory is invariably a wasting asset.

16. A formula for measuring international power is essential: ironically the most useful formula is warfare. Until the function of warfare is appreciated, the search for a more humane and more efficient way of measuring power is likely to be haphazard.

Varieties of War

17. To precede war with a formal 'declaration of war' is usually regarded as normal behaviour, but the evidence since 1700 suggests that it was abnormal. The Japanese surprise attack on Pearl Harbour in 1941 belonged to a strong international tradition.

18. Wars confined to two nations were fought usually on the geographical fringes rather than near the core of world power.

19. A general war or a world war began usually as a war between two nations and then became a series of wars which were interlocked and were fought simultaneously. An explanation of a general or many-sided war should therefore be structurally similar to the explanation of several two-sided wars.

20. A civil war was most likely to develop into an international war when one side in the civil war had ideological, racial or other links with an outside nation.

21. A general war was usually, by the standards of the age, a long war. Even in the era of nuclear weapons a general war—if it occurs—will probably be a long war.

22. It is doubtful whether any war since 1700 was begun with the belief, by *both* sides, that it would be a long war.

23. The idea that great advances in the technology of warfare inevitably led to shorter wars was held by many generations but falsified by many wars.

Flaws in Current Theories of War and Peace

24. Most of the popular theories of war—and the explanations by many historians of individuals wars—blame capitalists, dictators, monarchs or other individuals or pressure groups. These theories, however, explain rivalry and tension rather than war: rivalry and tension between countries can exist for generations without producing war.

25. Governments' aims and ambitions are vital in explaining each war, but

to emphasise ambitions and to ignore the *means* of implementing ambitions is to ignore the main question which has to be explained. For the outbreak of war and the outbreak of peace are essentially decisions to implement aims by new *means*. To attempt to explain war is to attempt to explain why forceful *means* were selected.

26. The evidence of past wars does not support the respectable theory that an uneven 'balance' of power tends to promote war. If the theory is turned upside down, however, it has some validity.

27. The evidence of past wars does not support the scapegoat theory and its assumption that rulers facing internal troubles often started a foreign war in the hope that a victory would promote peace at home.

28. The evidence of past wars does not support the 'one pair of hands' theory of war: the belief that a nation busily making money will have no spare energy or time for the making of war.

29. The idea that the human race has an innate love of fighting cannot be carried far as an explanation of war. On the statistical evidence of the last three or thirteen centuries it could be argued with no less validity that man has an innate love of peace. Since war and peace mark fluctuations in the relations between nations, they are more likely to be explained by factors which themselves fluctuate than by factors which are 'innate'.

30. War-weariness in a nation often promotes peace and war-fever promotes war, but there have been notable instances where war-weariness promoted war.

31. The Manchester theory argues that increasing contact between nations— through common languages, foreign travel and the exchange of commodities and ideas—dispels prejudice and strongly promotes peace. The evidence for this theory, however, is not convincing.

32. No wars are unintended or 'accidental'. What is often unintended is the length and bloodiness of the war. Defeat too is unintended.

33. Changes in society, technology and warfare in the last three centuries spurred some observers to suggest that international relations were thereby so revolutionised that past experience was largely irrelevant. There is much evidence, however, to suggest that there is considerable continuity between the era of cavalry and the era of intercontinental missiles.

Suggested Readings

Fuller, J.F.C. *The Conduct of War 1789–1961: A Study of the Impact of the French, Industrial and Russian Revolutions on War and its Conduct.* London: Eyre and Spottiswoode, 1961.

Howard, Michael. *War in European History.* Oxford: Oxford University, 1976.

Nef, John Ulric. *War and Human Progress: An Essay on the Rise of Industrial Civilization.* New York: Norton, 1950.

Neustadt, Richard and Ernest R. May. *Thinking in Time: The Uses of History For Decision Makers.* New York: Free Press, 1987.

Singer, J. David, ed. *The Correlates of War II: Testing Some Realpolitic Models.* New York: Free Press, 1980.

Taylor, A.J.P. *The Struggle for Mastery in Europe, 1848–1918.* Oxford: Oxford University, 1954.

Reading 25

MULTIPOLAR SYSTEMS AND INTERNATIONAL STABILITY

Karl W. Deutsch and J. David Singer

Notes from the Editors

In 1964, political scientists Karl Deutsch and J. David Singer examined some of the balance of power literature with special attention to the differences between bipolarity and multipolarity. Was the system more stable when two major powers dominated it, as was the case since World War II, or when power was shared among more than two majors, as was becoming the case when the article was written?

During much of the eighteenth and nineteenth centuries, Europe was said to be governed by a balance of power system in which as few as four and as many as seven nations were relatively equal. Supposedly, through the near-automatic operation of the balance of power—in which each nation acted in a way to keep any one nation or alliance from dominating—the system was preserved in relative peace.

Not satisfied with the folklore, Deutsch and Singer suggest ways to test the hypothesis/ proposition that a multipolar system is inherently more stable than a bipolar system. Emphasizing the interaction-opportunity enhancement as well as the decline in attention that one state may give to another as the number of states increase, Deutsch and Singer opt for the multipolar system. They warn, however, that balance of power systems ultimately break apart and that perhaps the shift from a bipolar to a multipolar world has only gained the international system a few more years of breathing space before the predictable next—and perhaps last—major war.

In the classical literature of diplomatic history, the balance-of-power concept occupies a central position. Regardless of one's interpretation of the term or one's preference for or antipathy to it, the international relations scholar cannot escape dealing with it. The model is, of course, a multifaceted one, and it produces a fascinating array of corollaries; among these, the relationship between the number of actors and the stability of the system is one of the most widely accepted and persuasive. That is, as the system moves away from bipolarity toward multipolarity, the frequency and intensity of war should be expected to diminish.

To date, however, that direct correlation has not been subjected to rigorous scrutiny by either abstract or empirical test. For the most part, it has seemed so intuitively reasonable that a few historical illustrations have been accepted as sufficient. This is, on balance, not enough to support a lawful generalization; it must eventually be put to the historical test. This will be done eventually, but in the interim this hypothesis should at least be examined on formal, abstract grounds. The purpose of this article, therefore, is to present two distinct—but related—lines of formal, semi-quantitative,

Reprinted with permission from *World Politics*, Vol. 16, No. 3 (April 1964), pp. 390–406. Copyright © 1964 by Princeton University Press. Reprinted with permission of Princeton University Press.

argument as to why the diffusion-stability relationship should turn out as the theoretician has generally assumed and as the historian has often found to be the case.

A Probabilistic Concept of International Political Stability

Stability may, of course, be considered from the vantage point of both the total system and the individual states comprising it. From the broader, or systemic, point of view, we shall define stability as the probability that the system retains all of its essential characteristics; that no single nation becomes dominant; that most of its members continue to survive; and that large-scale war does not occur. And from the more limited perspective of the individual nations, stability would refer to the probability of their continued political independence and territorial integrity without any significant probability of becoming engaged in a "war for security" with the time scale introduced as a limiting factor.

The Accelerated Rise of Interaction Opportunities

The most obvious effect of an increase in the number of independent actors is an increase in the number of possible pairs of dyads in the total system. This assumes, of course, that the number of independent actors is responsive to the general impact of coalition membership, and that as a nation enters into the standard coalition it is much less of a free agent than it was while non-aligned. That is, its alliance partners now exercise an inhibiting effect—or perhaps even a veto—upon its freedom to interact with non-alliance nations.

This reduction in the number of possible dyadic relations produces, both for any individual nation and for the totality of those in the system, a corresponding diminution in the number of opportunities for interaction with other actors. Although it must be recognized at the outset that, in the international system of the nineteenth and twentieth centuries, such opportunities are as likely to be competitive as they are to be cooperative, the overall effect is nevertheless destabilizing. The argument is nothing more than a special case of the widely employed pluralism model.

In that model, our focus is on the degree to which the system exhibits negative feedback as well as cross-pressuring. By negative—as distinguished from positive or amplifying—feedback, we refer to the phenomenon of self-correction: as stimuli in one particular direction increase, the system exhibits a decreasing response to those stimuli, and increasingly exhibits tendencies that counteract them. This is the self-restraining system, manifested in the automatic pilot, the steam-engine governor, and most integrated social systems, and it stands in contrast to the self-aggravating as seen in forest fires, compound interest, nuclear fission, runaway inflation or deflation, and drug addiction.

The pluralistic model asserts that the amplifying feedback tendency is strengthened, and the negative feedback tendency is weakened, to the extent that conflict positions are superimposed or reinforcing. Thus, if all clashes and incompatibilities in the system produce the same divisions and coalitions—if all members in class Blue line up *with* one another and *against* all or most of those in class Red—the line of cleavage will be wide and deep, with positive feedback operating both within and between the two classes or clusters. But if some members of class Blue have some incompatible interests with others in their class, and an overlap of interests with some of those in Red, there will be some degree of negative or self-correcting feedback both within and between the two classes.

This notion is analogous to that of cross-cutting pressure familiar to the student of politics. Here we observe that every individual plays a fairly large number of politically relevant roles and that most of these pull him in somewhat different attitudinal, behavioral, and organizational directions. For example, if an individual is (1) a loving parent, (2) a member of a militant veterans' organization, (3) owner of a factory, and (4) a Catholic, the first and third factors will tend to deflect him toward a "coexistence" foreign policy, the second will pull him toward a "holy war" orientation, and his religious affiliation will probably (in the 1960's) produce a deep ambivalence. Likewise, following Ralf Dahrendorf's formulation, if status difference is a major determinant of conflict exacerbation, and an individual is head of a family, a bank teller, and president of the lodge, he will coalesce with and against different people on different issues. In each of these cases, his relatively large number of interaction opportunities produces a set of cross-pressures such as largely to inhibit any super-imposition or reinforcement. The consequence would seem to favor social stability and to inhibit social cleavage; increasing differentiation and role specialization in industrial society has, in a sense, counteracted the Marxian expectation of class warfare.

Thus, in any given bilateral relationship, a rather limited range of possible interactions obtains, even if the relationship is highly symbiotic. But as additional actors are brought into the system, the range of possible interactions open to each—and hence to the total system—increases. In economics, this accretion produces the transformation from barter to market, and in any social setting it produces a comparable increase in the range and flexibility of possible interactions. Traditionally, social scientists have believed—and observed—that as the number of possible exchanges increases, so does the probability that the "invisible hand" of pluralistic interests will be effective. One might say that one of the greatest threats to the stability of any impersonal social system is the shortage of alternative partners.

If we assume, then, that any increase in the number of independent actors *is* conducive to stability, the question remains as to the quantitative nature of this correlation. Is there any particular level at which the system cannot be made more stable by the addition of new actors, or less stable by the loss of existing actors? Is there, furthermore, some critical level at which small changes become crucial? Our response must be based, of course, on the degree to which each single increment or decrement affects the number of possible dyads, or bilateral interaction opportunities, in the system. That effect is found by applying the standard formula for possible pairs:

$$\frac{N(N-1)}{2}$$

thus, in a purely bipolar system, only one dyad or pair is possible, while a tripolar situation produces three pairs, four actors produce six pairs, five produce ten possible pairings, and so on, as shown in Figure 1.

This figure indicates rather dramatically the degree to which the number of in-

FIGURE 1 Interaction Opportunity

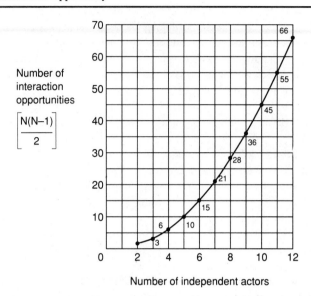

dependent actors affects the possible number of dyads, and thus interaction opportunities. Even as we move from bipolarity to a tripolar system, the interaction opportunities within the system triple, and when another single actor is added the possible dyadic relations increase by three, and so on, with each addition in the actor column producing an increment of N-1 in the interaction opportunity column. Intuitively, the student of international politics would note that until N reaches five, there is an insufficient number of possible dyads, and that beyond that level the stability-enhancing increment begins to grow very sharply.

So far, we have operated from the conservative assumption that all nations have identical interests, concerns, and goals, and though we would not want to exaggerate in the opposite direction, one cannot overlook the diversity that does exist. A landlocked nation can hardly offer fishing rights in its coastal waters, an agricultural surplus nation will seldom purchase those same foodstuffs, two underdeveloped nations are most unlikely to exchange machine tools, and a permanent member of the Security Council cannot be expected to give much for assurance of a seat in that organ. Every nation's needs and supplies differ, and the more nations there are, the greater will be the number and diversity of trade-offs available to the total system. As possible trade-offs increase, the greater the possibility for compensatory and stabilizing interactions to occur. That is, in a system characterized by conflict-generating scarcities, each and every increase in opportunities for cooperation (i.e., to engage in a mutually advantageous trade-off) will diminish the tendency to pursue a conflict up to, and over, the threshold of war.

Finally, membership in an alliance not only exercises a negative quantitative impact on a nation's interaction opportunities, but affects the quality of those that do continue to exist. On the one hand, the pattern-maintenance needs of the alliance will

FIGURE 2   Share of Attention

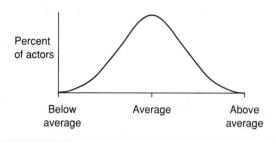

be such as to *minimize* (a) the range of issues over which it will conflict with an alliance partner, and (b) the intensity of such intra-alliance conflicts as are permitted. On the other hand, the establishment of such a clear-cut ingroup-outgroup division can only lead to an *increase* in the range and intensity of any conflicts with non-alliance actors.

To summarize, one logical explanation for the correlation between number of independent actors and the probability of armed conflict lies in the realm of enhanced interaction opportunities, observed in terms of their quantity, diversity, and qualities.

The Accelerated Diminution in the Allocation of Attention

A second line of argument that should also support the hypothesized correlation between multipolarity and stability revolves around the notion of attention available for conflict. Here we assume that, as the number of independent actors in the system increases, the share of its attention that any nation can devote to any other must of necessity diminish. The argument need not, of course, postulate that each additional actor will attract an equal share of the attention of each of the other actors, or necessarily attract the same share as those already in the system. That share will be a function of many considerations and may vary rather widely. Let us assume, then, that any nation's total external attention—that is, its information-processing and resource-allocating capabilities—will be distributed among all others in the system according to a normal distribution, as illustrated in Figure 2.

In this figure, we suggest that a very few of the total number of actors in the system receive very little of A's attention, that most of them receive a moderate share of that attention, and that a very few receive an impressively heavy share of it. But regardless of the shape of this attention distribution curve, the fact is that every actor claims *some*.

If those receiving a minimal share of A's attention were to disappear into a coalition, this would have only a minor impact on the amount of attention now left over for A to redistribute among the remaining independent actors. But if coalition were to occur among some of those receiving a greater share of that original attention, A would then be able to deal with the members of that coalition with fewer demands on its information-processing and energy-allocating capabilities; as a consequence,

FIGURE 3   Allocation of Attention

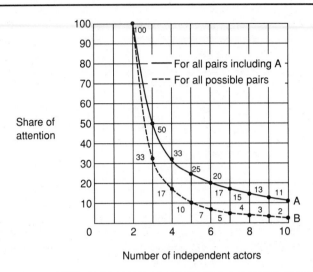

Number of independent actors

that remaining for allocation to the other actors in the system would be appreciably increased.

Now the limited attention capability of each nation in the system must be allocated between two different sets of relationships. First priority will tend to go to all of those dyadic relationships in which it is a partner, while the dyads of which it is not a member will receive a lesser, but not insignificant, degree of attention. Some recent illustrations of this latter demand might be found in the attention which the United States has expended on the Soviet-Yugoslavian, British-Egyptian, or Indian-Pakistan dyads, or which the U.S.S.R. devoted to the Arab-Israeli, Cuban-American, or Franco-Algerian pairings. Regardless of membership or non-membership, each nation must spread its attention among most of the dyads in the system.

What, then, is the effect of any trend toward or away from bipolarity upon that distribution of attention? In Figure 3, we plot that distribution according to the assumption that, with each single addition to the number of independent actors, the total number of dyads in which nation A is a member will also increase by one, following the formula N-1. With each increment in the number of dyads of which A may be a member, the amount of attention available for any one such pairing will drop, as shown in the upper (solid line) curve. Thus three actors produce two possible dyads that include A, with an average of 50 per cent of A's attention available for each; four actors produce three such pairs and 33 per cent of A's attention for each; and five actors produce four A-inclusive dyads, with only 25 percent of his attention available to each.

When we drop the condition that only those dyads of which A (any actor) is a member can constitute a drain on A's attention, and assume that *every* possible dyad will make some such demand, the attention curve responds even more rapidly to an increase in the number of independent actors. As the lower (dotted line) curve indicates, each new actor increases the total number of dyads by the:

$$\frac{N(N - 1)}{2}$$

formula, as already used earlier in Figure 1, with the percentage of share of attention available to each dyad dropping even more sharply.

Why should these rapid decreases in percentage of available attention exercise any effect upon the stability of the system? In communication theory, it is generally recognized that below a certain signal-to-noise ratio, the signal is essentially undetectable; that is, it loses prominence as its strength vis-à-vis the noise (or random disturbance) in the system diminishes. The same general principle would seem to apply to social interaction; as Rapoport and Schelling have pointed out, interaction between any two nations may be viewed as a special case of the interchange of messages between them. Each state in this case would have to treat the messages from its most prominent adversary of the moment as the signal relevant to this incipient conflict in or before its early stage of escalation; and it would tend to treat all other messages, concerning all other pairs of states, as noise of relatively little relevance to this particular conflict.

The general requirement of at least a minimal signal-to-noise ratio would then hold for this incipient conflict, as it would hold for any other communication process; and we shall assume that is approximately by the ratio of governmental attention to foreign messages from this particular rival, to all other messages concerning other states or pairs of states. Just what this signal-to-noise ratio—or, here, minimal attention ratio—would have to be is a question of empirical fact. Signal-to-noise ratios of 100:1 are not uncommon in electronic communication systems. It is perhaps not excessive to assume that the minimal attention ratio for an escalating conflict would have to be 1:9, since it does not seem likely that any country could be provoked very far into an escalating conflict with less than 10 per cent of the foreign policy attention of its government devoted to the matter.

If we require a minimal attention of 10 percent for an escalating conflict, the likelihood of such conflicts thus will decline sharply with the decline of the average attention that any one government has available for any one of the remaining actors in the international system.

The decline of this average available attention with an increasing number of actors in the system has been graphed in curves A and B in Figure 3, as discussed earlier. We can now show on the same graph the lines of minimal attention ratios required to permit average probabilities of, say, 20, 10, or 5 per cent for an escalating conflict between any two actors in the system. Several such lines, at 10, 20, 30 . . . per cent levels of an assumed minimum attention ratio, have been drawn in Figure 3. Their intersections with curves A and B show how quickly the increase of the number of actors will remove an international system from the danger zone, or how fast a diminution in the number of actors will increase the average risk of escalating conflict among the remainder.

As far as it goes, this graphic representation confirms the greater stability of multipolar systems, and it suggests some quantitative findings. It shows that the average share of available attention for any one conflict drops sharply as soon as there are more than three power centers in the system, and more gently after there are more than five such centers; and it further suggests that the stability of the system may depend critically on the *critical attention ratio*—that is, on the proneness of countries to enter into escalating conflicts even if only a small part of their government's attention is engaged in this particular quarrel.

Thus, if some minimum percentage of a nation's external attention is required for that nation to engage in behavior tending toward armed conflict, and the increase in number of independent actors diminishes the share that any nation can allocate to any other single actor, such an increase is likely to have a stabilizing effect upon the system.

Some Implications for Richardson's Model of Escalating Conflict

The task of this section will be to correlate the propositions concerning the greater stability of multipolar systems in international politics, especially as recently formalized by Morton Kaplan, with the Richardson model of conflict; and to show that the former proposition can be treated as a special case of the general Richardson model.

In the Richardson model of the arms race, or of similar competitive relations, conflict behavior of each of two parties is seen as growing at an exponential rate, similar to the growth of compound interest or to the progress of an explosion. The rate of this growth is described by a pair of differential equations in which one party's increase in armaments—or of other competitive behavior—is perceived as a threat and becomes the motivating input for the corresponding reciprocal or retaliatory response of the other. Thus, if country A had spent in the previous year $90 million on armaments, while its rival B had spent $100 million, and if A now tries to equal B and increases its armaments budgets from $90 million to $100 million, and if country B, which previously had spent $100 million, tries to maintain the previous ratio of arms budgets, then B must now spend $111 million in the following year; whereupon A, if its rulers still aim at parity with B, will now increase its budget accordingly to $111 million, forcing B to defend its old proportionate lead by raising its arms budget by $12.3 million to $123.3 million, so that not only the absolute amounts but also the *increases* in arms spending on both sides are growing in every round, and the arms race will accelerate in ever-growing steps until some limit or breakdown is attained.

This simple model would hold equally for bipolar and multipolar systems. In the latter systems, one might imagine that it could apply to every possible pair of nations in the rivalry, and thus to 10 pairs in a five-power system, to 15 pairs in a six-power world, and generally to

$$\frac{N(N-1)}{2}$$

powers in an N-power system. If country A wanted at least to keep its proportionate lead against *each* of its rivals, it would have to maintain its level in an exponentially growing arms race with the most quickly growing of these rivals, because this would automatically increase its lead over all the rest. If all powers followed this type of policy, the total pace of arms competition for all countries would be set by the fastest growing competitor.

This model, however, seems too simple. It may be more reasonable to assume that a country is most likely to respond to an increase in the arms expenditure of a rival only in regard to that part which appears likely to be deployed or directed against itself.

In the case of a bipolar world, this consideration would make very little difference. The strongest country, A, would have to fear almost the full amount of the increment in the strength of the next strongest power, B, since in this bipolar world the third and fourth ranking powers, C and D, and all the lesser powers down to N, are almost negligible in their strength in comparison to A and B. These negligible lesser powers would thus not require any significant allocation of B's resources to ensure against the risk of having to fight them, and practically all of B's strength would remain available for use against A, forcing A in turn to increase its own efforts to the full extent required to maintain its own margin of strength in relation to B's growth.

Matters are quite different, however, in a multipolar world. In a four-power system, C and D, the third and fourth ranking nations, are already nearly as strong as A and B, the top and second-rank powers. Accordingly, B may have to allocate more than one-half of its resources—and of its increment in these—to the possibility of having to fight C or D, and thus B may have left less than one-half of its increment for a credible increase in its threat against A. The effect of A's behavior, according to the Richardson model, would be correspondingly less, since A would have to raise its arms budget only to the extent needed to hold its proportionate lead in regard to one-half or less of B's increment in arms expenditure. The arms race in a completely rational world would thus tend to be slower under multipolar conditions than under bipolar ones.

A different line of reasoning suggests the same result. Richardson's original model assumed that the motivation for a state to try to maintain its proportionate lead over the arms level of another was autonomously generated within the state itself. Once the national subsystems of the international political system had this motivation, in Richardson's model, then the consequences of an escalating arms race followed under the conditions that he specified. It was the competitive motivations of the national states, in Richardson's thought, that produced the competitive character of the international system. Many writers on international politics, from Machiavelli onward, have taken the opposite view. The larger system, they have maintained, is itself competitive to start with, in that it rewards appropriate competitive behavior and penalizes the failure to compete by the pitiless elimination of the laggards and the weak. Machiavelli's princes, Adam Smith's businessmen, and Charles Darwin's animals all must compete for survival in their respective systems, on pain of being wiped out otherwise, regardless of their subjective motivation. In time, each of these systems is expected to select for survival primarily those subsystems that have responded most adequately to its competitive pressure. Which rival subsystem happened to exercise this competitive pressure at the moment is secondary in each of these theories. If this particular rival had been absent, another would have taken his place and served the same function of offering a compelling challenge to competitive behavior.

This type of thinking has remained familiar in the popular rhetoric of arms competition. The world is such, the argument used to run—or the adversary is such, it has run more recently—that "there is no choice" but arms competition or national doom through surrender or defeat. Regardless of the motivations of its own people, its own political system, and its own decision-makers, any state in such a situation must respond to the challenge of an arms race or else perish.

How strong is this externally derived pressure upon a state to increase its own armaments for the sake of survival, regardless of any other values or motivations produced by its domestic political system? Clearly, it is proportional only to that part of the increment in a rival's armament that is not likely to be balanced by a shift in alliances under a balance-of-power policy. In a bipolar world, a 10 per cent increase in the arms spending of power A must be answered by an equal increment in the arms of B, and the escalation process may then proceed at 10 per cent increments for each cycle. In a world of four approximately equal powers, a rise in the arms level of power A from 100 to 110 would give A's coalition, I—consisting, say, of A plus C—only a strength of 210 against the rival coalition II, consisting of B and D, with a strength of 200. The superiority of coalition I over coalition II would thus be not 10 but only 5 per cent; the offsetting armaments needed by coalition II would only have to be of 5 per cent; the subsequent increments of the escalation would likewise be of this lesser order of magnitude; and escalation would proceed more slowly.

In a similar six-power world, a 10 per cent increase in the armament of one power would compel an increment of only about 3 per cent in the arms spending of the three members of the rival coalition. A ten-power world in the same situation would only be forced to a 2 per cent arms rise for each of five powers. Generally, every increase in the number of powers would slow down the speed of Richardsonian escalation.

If we drop the assumption of approximately equal powers in a multipolar world, the same general result follows. So long as most powers are free to move laterally from one coalition or alignment to another, their self-interest will favor such balance-of-power policies as to produce very nearly evenly matched coalitions, each of them composed quite possibly of members of unequal power. In such a mobile multipolar world, no government needs to fear a moderate decline in national power as potentially disastrous. It can survive as a second-class power as safely or precariously as it did as a first-class one, provided only that it joins in time the appropriate new alliance or alignment. Arms increases by a rival power, which in a bipolar world might pose a fatal threat, might call in a multipolar world for little more than a quick adjustment of alliances.

Some Implications for the Diffusion of Nuclear Weapons

If an increase in the number and diplomatic mobility of actors may slow down the process of arms escalation, it would by the same reasoning also slow down any process of de-escalation. Here, too, a one-sided arms reduction in a two-power world may elicit an equal response by the other power, while in a multipolar world the effect of any such unilateral initiative would be much weaker.

If we are chiefly interested in rapid de-escalation—that is, in partial or complete disarmament—a multipolar world may prove more intractable than a bipolar one; and we may view the emergence of French, German, Japanese, or Communist Chinese national power with justified alarm. If we are mainly concerned, on the contrary, with preventing any rapid escalation of the two-power arms competition between the United States and the Soviet Union, a shift toward a multipolar world may appear preferable.

At this point, of course, the bare and abstract arguments pursued thus far become quite insufficient. In our analysis of alternative international power systems we have abstracted from all other qualities of the states, governments, and national political systems within them. At the point of policy choice, however, these hitherto neglected aspects may be the decisive ones. A bipolar system in which each of the two rival powers is likely to be moderate and cautious in its policy initiatives and responses might be a great deal safer than a multipolar world containing one or several well-armed powers whose governments or politically relevant strata were inclined to incompetence or recklessness. As elsewhere, so also in international politics a stable general system could be wrecked by the introduction of unstable components.

At the present time, the importance of this latter point may well be decisive. Each of the present major nuclear powers—the United States, Britain, and the Soviet Union—has been politically stable, in the sense that each has retained its particular type of government for over forty years. None of these three countries has been notable for initiating large and reckless military enterprises. Among the middle-level and smaller powers, most likely to press for nuclear weapons during the next decade—which include France, Germany, Japan, Mainland China, Nationalist China, and perhaps Egypt and others—there are several whose recent history lacks any comparable evidence of stability in domestic institutions and caution in international affairs. If this stage should be followed by the dissemination of nuclear weapons among a still larger number of countries, including inevitably at least some with still less stable domestic regimes and less cautious military policies, the instability of the international system would be still more dangerous. For these reasons, any successful efforts by the United States and other powers to slow down the dissemination of nuclear weapons would tend to increase the stability of the international system. In the present article, devoted to an abstract argument, these matters can only be indicated, but they must not be forgotten.

One other problem, however, should be discussed here: the time horizon under which the stability of international systems is evaluated. A multipolar world, though often more stable in the short run than a bipolar one, has its own problem of long-run political stability, and it is to this that we must now turn our attention.

The Long-Run Instability of Multipolar Systems

On the basis of these considerations, it might seem that a multipolar system could last forever, or for a very long time, by always opposing the ambitions of its currently top-ranking member; and this is indeed what some writers have claimed as a virtue of the balance-of-power system. In each of the sections above, however, we have dealt with considerations of an essentially short or middle-run nature, with a rather incomplete view as the natural consequence.

There are at least two analytic reasons why this relatively benign long-run outcome cannot be expected. For one thing, if we accept the usual zero-sum assumption of

Machiavelli and the classic theory of games—according to which any gain by one contender can occur only through an equal loss by one or more of his rivals—then we must assume that each contending power ordinarily will try to acquire all the territory and population it can at the expense of its rivals, and that it will do nothing to create new rivals for itself. The model thus provides for the possibility of the destruction of states whose rulers misjudged the precise balance of strength at the moment, or whose economies and populations no longer yielded the increasing increments in arms spending and military effort required by the competition, but this model does not provide for the creation of new states. If the probability of states perishing is small, but larger than zero, and the probability of substantial new powers arising is zero in terms of this model, then the model will predict a diminishing number of effective contenders, leading eventually to a two-power world or to the survival of a single power, as in the case of the reduction of the many governments of classic antiquity to the two-power clash of Rome and Carthage, and of Rome's final long monopoly of power in the Mediterranean world until new forces entered from outside the region.

The second line of reasoning is based on considerations of statistics. Thus far we have taken probabilities only in terms of their central tendencies, rather than in terms of the variance of possible outcomes and their distribution. If we assume these outcomes to be normally distributed around some mean, then the usual outcome of an increment in threat by power A against power B in a multipolar system will consist in both A's and B's finding enough allies, respectively, to match the power of their respective coalitions and to produce the relatively moderate outcomes predicted by the classic balance-of-power model. In rare cases, however, corresponding to one tail of the distribution, state A will find a great preponderance of allies and become able to destroy its current enemy, B, completely; and in other rare cases—corresponding to the other tail of the distribution—A must expect to find itself facing an overwhelming coalition of adversaries that will destroy it. In the short run, only the moderate central tendencies of the distribution of outcomes of the coalition-forming process will be frequent enough to be taken into account, but in the long run the balance-of-power world must be expected to produce eventually dramatic and catastrophic changes, both locally and at last at the system level. The number of years after which long-run rather than short-run phenomena are likely to prevail will depend on the frequency of international crises, and on the shape of the distribution of balanced and unbalanced coalitions, respectively, as outcomes of the coalition-forming process.

This expectation seems in good agreement with the historical data. No balance-of-power system has lasted longer than a few centuries, and most of the original powers contending in such systems have survived as independent powers only for much shorter periods.

The classic descriptive and analytical views of two-power confrontations and of the balance of power among several contenders have been formalized by several writers. The most prominent models, of the tight bipolar and multipolar world, respectively, can be interpreted in terms of the dynamic model of conflict by Lewis F. Richardson. The results suggest that the Richardson model, with very simple assumptions, can be made to include the bipolar and multipolar models as special cases. This combined model then suggests some general inferences in predictions about trends that appear to accord well with historical data. In the long run, according to this model, even multipolar systems operating under the rules of balance-of-power policies are shown to be self-destroying, but both in the short and the long run the instability of tight bipolar systems appears to be substantially greater. It seems plausible that, *if the spread of nuclear weapons could be slowed down or controlled,* a transition from the bipolar international system of the early 1950's to an increasingly multipolar system in the 1960's might buy mankind some valuable time to seek some more dependable bases for world order.

Suggested Readings

Gulick, Edward Vose. *Europe's Classical Balance of Power.* Ithaca: Cornell University, 1955.

Healey, Brian and Arthur Stein. "The Balance of Power in International History." *Journal of Conflict Resolution.* 17 (March 1973), pp. 33–62.

Modelski, George. "Kautilya." *American Political Science Review* 58 (September, 1964), pp. 549–60.

Rosecrance, Richard A. *Action and Reaction in World Politics.* Boston: Little, Brown, 1963.

Sabrosky, Alan Ned. *Polarity and War.* Boulder, Colo.: Westview, 1985.

Waltz, Kenneth N. "International Structure, National Force, and the Balance of World Power." *Journal of International Affairs* XXI, 2 (1967), pp. 215–31.

Wight, Martin. "The Balance of Power." Herbert Butterfield and Martin Wight, eds., *Diplomatic Investigations.* Cambridge: Harvard University, 1968, pp. 149–75.

Reading 26

ARMS RACES AND ESCALATION

Michael D. Wallace

Notes from the Editors
Ever since World War I, political theorists have considered arms races to be among the
most important causes of war. Naturally, nations usually begin to arm because of some
real or perceived political rivalry, but the race itself sometimes can become as important
as the original cause(s) for the arms buildup.

Although in recent years, mathematical modelers have produced articles and books
on arms races, few have employed historical data in their studies. Using the Correlates
of War project data on arms expenditures, military disputes, and wars, political scientist
Michael Wallace examines ninety-six disputes between major powers from 1816 to 1965.
He is concerned about the percentage of those disputes that were preceded by arms races
and the percentage of that subset that resulted in war. That is, Wallace asks whether
arms races are more likely to precede disputes that led to war than disputes that were
resolved peacefully.

In order to conduct his study, he developed an arms race index to calculate the
rates of change in arms expenditures between the two parties in a dispute. Needless to
say, the fashioning of the index and the obtaining of good data, especially for the nineteenth
century, was a difficult task.

Wallace discovers that disputes that led to war were preceded by arms races in
twenty-three of twenty-eight cases, while those disputes not preceded by an arms race
terminated in war only three out of seventy-one times. Although he cannot say that arms
races "cause" war, his study convinces him that they are strongly correlated with the
outbreak of war.

Introduction

More than 30 years have passed since Lewis Fry Richardson began his pioneering treatise on the dynamics of arms races (Richardson, 1960), and nearly two decades have gone by since J. David Singer (1958) and Samuel Huntington (1958) staked out their positions on opposite sides of the "armaments-tensions" debate. In the intervening years, a great deal has been written concerning the onset and dynamic evolution of arms races,[1] and on the relationship between national capabilities and likelihood of violent conflict.[2] Yet, oddly enough, virtually nothing written to date has shed much light on the central question these pioneering works address: does the existence of an arms race between two states significantly increase their probability of going to war?

It is only necessary to peruse the current debate over the parturient SALT II

Reprinted from *Journal of Conflict Resolution* 23 (March 1979), pp. 3–16. Copyright © 1979 by Sage Publications, Inc. Reprinted by permission of Sage Publications, Inc.

negotiations to realize that the outlines of the controversy have remained essentially unchanged since classical times. On the one side, Vegetius's doctrine "si vis pacem para bellum" finds its contemporary expression amongst the partisans of military expansion in both the Pentagon and the Kremlin. They argue that only a strong military posture can deter an opponent's military adventurism, which, unchecked, would lead to armed conflict. In other words, it is not arms races that lead to war, but rather a nation's failure to maintain capabilities vis-à-vis its potential rivals and adversaries.

On the other side of this debate are those who believe that military expansion per se contributes to the danger of war. It is argued, to begin with, that military expansion is self-defeating, in that it is likely to provoke a similar countervailing expansion by the other side. Moreover, the mutual threat posed by such competitive military growth intensifies other conflicts and contentions among nations, leading to additional uncertainty and insecurity, further pressures for military expansion, and so on in a vicious, escalating circle. In short, the partisans of the "arms race" school do not see the competitive acquisition of military capability as a neutral instrument of policy, still less as a means to *prevent* war, but rather as a major link in the complex chain of events leading to armed conflict.

Given the central role this debate has played in current policy discussions, and considering the magnitude of the stakes involved in the nuclear age, it is long past time that some direct scientific evidence were brought to bear on the matter. That is what I shall attempt here.

In order to address the question in a systematic manner, two preliminary conceptual matters must be dealt with. First, we must decide what is to be meant by an "arms race," and second, we must specify the *process* by which arms races may be thought of as influencing the probability of war.

The Definition of an Arms Race

Turning first to the definition of an arms race, the literature presents numerous alternatives.[3] While many of these differ in some respects, there are two elements common to all. First, arms races involve simultaneous abnormal rates of growth in the military outlays of two or more nations. Second, in an arms race these result from the competitive pressure of the military rival itself, and not from domestic forces exogenous to this rivalry.

Beginning with the second of these two components of a definition, it is clear that, at a minimum, we can only speak of an "arms race" between nations whose foreign and defense policies are heavily interdependent; the behavior and capabilities of each nation must be highly salient to the other nations. Thus, it is meaningless to speak of an "arms race" between nations with little contact with or interest in each other. But more than this is required. The capabilities of the putative military rivals must not only be mutually salient, but also roughly comparable. However great their mutual antagonism, and however rapidly their armed forces grow, it would make little sense to speak of an "arms race" between, say, the United States and Cuba, or the Soviet Union and Iran. In short, arms races can exist only amongst the great powers, or amongst local powers of comparable military standing within the same region.

The next question is, what are we to understand as the "abnormal growth" which constitutes an arms race? Clearly, not *all* competitive or simultaneous increases qualify. Throughout most of the nineteenth and twentieth centuries, a majority of nations, and virtually all of the great powers, have made continual qualitative and quantitative additions to their armed forces. More often than not, these have been undertaken in a spirit of rivalry—country X wishing to possess bigger battleships than Y or more armoured divisions than Z. Yet these competitive acquisitions are not "arms races"; the average annual rate of growth has not usually exceeded 4 or 5% in real terms, and an examination of historical accounts indicates that contemporary elites have worried very little about them.

At frequent intervals, however, this pattern of normal arms *competition* is transformed into a runaway arms *race* through some combination of domestic, diplomatic, and strategic pressures.[4] The competition now becomes a matter of great, perhaps paramount salience for both sides. The annual rate of growth in military capability occasionally climbs to a figure in excess of 10%, even as much as 20 or 25%. In short, the onset of an arms race is characterized by a sharp acceleration (significant increase in the rate of increase) in military capability. It is these "runaway accelerations" that we shall term "arms races" for the purposes of this paper.

From Arms Race to War

In specifying the impact which rapid military growth has upon the probability of war, two problems arise. First, how do we distinguish empirically between genuine competitive arms races as described above, and mere coincidental military "accelerations"? For example, between 1937 and 1939, both Britain and the United States increased the size and quality of their armed forces many times over, yet it would be absurd to speak of them as engaging in an arms race.

The second problem arises from the fact that military acquisitions by *themselves* are extremely unlikely to provoke military hostilities. Even in the era of "counterforce" and "flexible response," few responsible observers suggest that any nation would initiate violent hostilities with a power of comparable size *solely* to protect or enhance its military-strategic position. Some other factor or factors must lead nations into a dispute or confrontation of sufficient severity that the military dangers created by the arms race are transformed from chronic irritants into acute threats to national survival.

Both of these problems are easily solved by turning the central question on its head. Instead of asking whether or not bilateral or multilateral runaway arms growth enhances the likelihood of war, we can pose the problem this way: "Do serious disputes between nations engaged in an arms race have a significantly greater probability of resulting in all-out war than those between nations exhibiting more normal patterns of military competition?" Presumably, if two nations are on opposite sides of a serious dispute, any military acquisition they might make will be directed towards each other at least in part. At the same time, such a dispute provides the theoretical preconditions for the transition from war preparation to war initiation.

The Domain

As is customary with studies using Correlates of War Project data, the test period for our hypotheses will extend from 1816 to 1965. In this paper we shall consider only *great power* disputes and wars occurring during this period, that is, those in which there was at least one great power on each side. There are two reasons for this. First, we noted that rough equivalence of capability was a crucial prerequisite for an arms race, ruling out consideration of "major vs. minor" wars and disputes. Although rough equivalence of capability often obtains among hostile lesser powers, these are often dependent upon great powers for weapons and political support to the extent that their decisional autonomy is open to question. A second difficulty is that data concerning the military capability of, and disputes concerning, lesser powers is far less reliable than the corresponding information for the majors.

In sum, it was felt that any major extension of the test population at this stage would muddy the waters, and possibly confuse the results. There is one important exception, however. In those cases where there occurs a dispute between a great power and a minor power bound in a military alliance to another great power, we consider this to be a great power dispute.

The population of "great powers" is that used by Singer and Small (1966), and comprises Britain from 1815 to 1965; France from 1816 to 1940, and 1945 to 1965; the United States from 1898 to 1965; Italy from 1860 to 1943; Germany from 1816 to 1918, and 1923 to 1945; Austria-Hungary from 1816 to 1917; Russia from 1816 to 1917, and from 1920 to 1965; Japan from 1904 to 1945; and China from 1950 to 1965.

Serious Disputes

As the data collected by the Correlates of War Project on serious international disputes have not yet appeared in print, a brief summary of the coding rules is in order here. Briefly, for our purposes a *dispute* is a military confrontation between two or more nations not deadly enough to qualify as a war defined by Singer and Small. However, it must be "serious enough for one of the parties involved to threaten to commit, or actually commit, significant military resources to resolve the dispute" (Levy, 1977). We consider this a commitment to have a specific series of acts initiated by the official representatives of a power and clearly a commitment directed towards another great power. This series of acts comprises the following: the act of blockade, declaration of war, seizure or occupation of territory, the use of military forces, the mobilization of armed forces, and the seizure of foreign personnel or materiel. In all, a total of 96 disputes between major powers met our criteria; a complete list will be found in Table 1.

The Wars

Of these 96 serious dispute dyads, only 23 resulted in the outbreak of full-scale war as defined by Singer and Small (1972). Included are all military clashes in which at least one great power participated on each side, and which resulted in at least 1,000 battle-related fatalities. Only one departure is made from the Singer-Small codifica-

TABLE 1   Serious Disputes Between Major Powers 1816–1965

Year	Nations Involved		Escalation to War	Arms Race Index
1833	UK	Russia	No	2.73
1833	France	Russia	No	0.17
1836	Russia	UK	No	1.00
1840	France	Russia	No	12.90
1840	France	Germany	No	0.66
1849	UK	Russia	No	1.02
1849	France	Russia	No	36.27
1850	Germany	Austria	No	9.54
1853	UK	Russia	Yes	0.06
1853	France	Russia	Yes	31.74
1854	Austria	Russia	No	53.80
1859	France	Austria	Yes	120.91
1861	UK	Russia	No	0.16
1866	Germany	Austria	Yes	148.61
1866	Italy	Austria	Yes	575.14
1867	France	Italy	No	55.00
1870	France	Germany	Yes	8.91
1875	France	Germany	No	1.19
1877	UK	Russia	No	3.22
1878	UK	Russia	No	0.88
1878	Austria	Italy	No	0.48
1885	UK	Russia	No	4.93
1887	Germany	France	No	1.07
1888	Italy	France	No	7.17
1888	Austria	France	No	8.35
1888	England	France	No	1.63
1893	Austria	Russia	No	0.23
1895	Russia	Japan	No	61.53
1897	UK	Russia	No	0.17
1898	UK	France	No	0.35
1899	UK	Germany	No	0.39
1900	Japan	Russia	No	53.17
1902	US	Germany	No	0.15
1902	US	UK	No	0.01
1903	US	UK	No	0.07
1904	UK	Russia	No	0.07
1904	Russia	Japan	Yes	221.00
1905	Germany	France	No	0.04
1911	Germany	France	No	2.48
1911	Germany	UK	No	28.07

TABLE 1 *(continued)*

Year	Nations Involved		Escalation to War	Arms Race Index
1912	Russia	Austria	No	0.02
1912	Austria	Italy	No	0.37
1913	Italy	France	No	43.39
1914	Germany	UK	Yes	133.20
1914	Germany	France	Yes	231.25
1914	Germany	Russia	Yes	205.35
1914	Austria	UK	Yes	90.00
1914	Austria	France	Yes	156.25
1914	Austria	Russia	Yes	138.75
1915	Italy	Germany	Yes	811.30
1915	Italy	Austria	Yes	912.38
1917	US	Germany	Yes	349.68
1923	UK	Russia	No	0.04
1931	US	Japan	No	0.53
1932	UK	Japan	No	0.85
1932	US	Japan	No	1.05
1934	Italy	Germany	No	14.58
1934	Russia	Japan	No	0.13
1935	Japan	Russia	No	106.13
1935	UK	Italy	No	38.21
1936	UK	Germany	No	112. 68
1936	France	Germany	No	5.56
1937	Russia	Japan	No	51.47
1937	Japan	US	No	28.28
1938	Russia	Japan	No	14.96
1938	UK	Germany	No	90.06
1938	France	Germany	No	25.97
1939	Japan	France	No	11.49
1939	UK	Japan	Yes	261.23
1939	France	Germany	Yes	495.51
1940	Italy	UK	Yes	559.65
1940	Italy	France	Yes	643.70
1940	Japan	UK	No	39.98
1940	Japan	France	No	11.49
1941	Germany	Russia	Yes	221.61
1941	US	Japan	Yes	314.58
1945	Japan	Russia	Yes	102.93
1946	US	Russia	No	0.03
1948	Russia	US	No	0.32
1948	Russia	UK	No	0.25

TABLE 1   *(concluded)*

Year	Nations Involved		Escalation to War	Arms Race Index
1948	Russia	France	No	10.01
1953	Russia	US	No	68.72
1953	Russia	UK	No	41.80
1954	China	UK	No	22.89
1956	China	US	No	25.03
1956	Russia	France	No	61.89
1956	Russia	UK	No	53.05
1958	China	US	No	65.02
1958	UK	Russia	No	0.19
1960	US	Russia	No	6.34
1961	US	Russia	No	14.14
1962	US	China	No	103.73
1962	US	Russia	No	122.10
1964	US	Russia	No	30.70
1965	China	UK	No	81.43
1965	China	US	No	47.97

tions. In the case of those wars which involved more than two powers, each dyad is coded separately. Thus, for example, World War II is coded as an initiation of Franco-German and Anglo-German hostilities in 1939, an Anglo-Italian and Franco-Italian outbreak in 1940, and a Russo-German and Japanese-American conflict initiated in 1941. This was done to avoid the practical and conceptual difficulties of aggregating military capabilities of nations entering the conflict at different times.

The Measurement of Military Capability

The next step in the operational test of our hypotheses is the development of an index of military capabilities. For present purposes, we shall use annual *aggregate military expenditures*. Included in this total are both regular and extraordinary expenditures for all regular armed forces, as well as proceeds from borrowings in aid of the military. Both metropolitan and colonial expenditures are included. However, we *exclude* unexpended appropriations, military pensions, and expenditures on police, frontier guards, and reserves.

At this point, a few words of justification are in order. Obviously, many will argue that expenditures for armed forces do not always reflect true military capabilities; to use expenditures as an index would be to assume that military "cost-effectiveness" remains constant through time and space. Obviously, this is not the case, and represents a major potential source of bias in the index. But, in mitigation two points may be made.

First, while military efficiency varies widely, it tends to change fairly slowly. As we shall see, our measurement of the severity of an arms race is made with reference to a time-span of ten years. Within this time period, changing cost-effectiveness is unlikely to be a problem.

Moreover, we shall be concerned here not with the absolute level of military expenditures, but rather with their *rates of change* (deltas) from year to year. Thus, the problem of comparing absolute levels across nations does not arise.

We have not specified operational criteria for wars, disputes, and military capabilities. It remains to distinguish operationally between those instances of military growth which are to be characterized as "arms races," and those which are not. This is not quite as easy as it might seem at first blush, and to make a valid and useful distinction, we shall have to enlist the aid of some recent developments in applied mathematics that are unlikely to be familiar to most social scientists.

An Arms Race Index

It is easier to set down the conditions which an operational definition of an arms race must satisfy than it is to meet them. First and foremost, the measure should distinguish clearly between the "normal" incrementation of arms levels and abnormal "runaway" growth. Second, it should be sensitive only to *competitive* growth, where both sides are increasing rapidly and simultaneously. Third, given the occasional problems of data accuracy which persist despite our best efforts, the measure should be founded on as solid a data base as possible. Finally, it should be relatively *less* sensitive to the rates of arms growth further away in time.

The application of these criteria rules out several initially plausible index construction procedures. Measures based upon mean rates of increase do not satisfy the first and fourth criteria, as they are likely to average together observations made before and after the onset of the arms race. Moving averages go a long way towards satisfying the fourth criterion, but are still likely to "average out" periods of fast and slow growth. Indices based upon growth immediately prior to the dispute are likely to involve only two or at most three data points, leaving themselves extremely vulnerable to error. Finally, indices based upon the direct measurement of the *acceleration* of the arms race also run into problems with criterion three, since more data points are required for an unbiased estimate of the rate of acceleration than for the simple rate of change.

In this paper, a completely different approach will be employed. Instead of detecting the existence of an arms race by measuring the rate of increase or acceleration in arms spending directly, the issue shall be determined by extrapolating from a polynomial function fitted to the arms expenditure data for ten years prior to the onset of the dispute or war. This polynomial function shall be used to estimate the time rate of change (delta) for each nation for the year prior to the dispute. The existence of an arms race prior to the dispute or war shall be determined by obtaining the *product* of the national rates of change for each side, with higher values representing "arms-race" dyads. By calculating national rates of growth on the basis of a ten-year data series, and by constructing the final index in a multiplicative fashion, we ensure that only long-term, intense, bilateral growth in arms expenditures will score high on our arms race scale. The calculated arms race index values for each dyad are displayed in Table 1.

TABLE 2

	Arms Race	No Arms Race
War	23	3
No War	5	68

The Results

Given these values, how does our hypothesis fare? Even by inspection, it is clear that the mean arms race score for nation-dyads entering into full-scale warfare is much greater than the corresponding score for "no war" dyads — 292.2 compared with only 23.0. The probability that this difference would occur by chance is less than one in 10,000.

In other words, pairs of nations which end up going to war are characterized by much more rapid military growth in the period immediately prior to the conflict than those which do not resolve their conflicts by other means. The predictive power of this relationship can be seen more clearly if we dichotomize the independent variable to produce a 2 × 2 table. In Table 2, we see that a high arms race score for a pair of nations correctly predicts the outbreak of war 23 out of 28 times, and conversely, a low score correctly predicts the *non*escalation of a dispute 68 out of 71 times, for an overall "batting average" of 91 cases out of 99. . . .

As interesting as the strength of the relationship are the identities of some of the "incorrect predictions." Included among the five conflicts preceded by an arms race which did *not* result in war are the remilitarization of the Rhineland, the Munich Crisis, and the Cuban Missile Crisis. In each of these cases, the consensus of historians has it that war was averted only by the narrowest of margins.

Interpreting the Findings

The relationship between arms races and conflict escalation uncovered in this study is unusually strong. For this reason, great caution must be exercised in interpreting its meaning. First, it is worth emphasizing that these findings do *not* imply that an arms race between the powers necessarily results in war. To prove this, it would be necessary to show not only that arms races lead to the escalation of conflicts, but also that they play an important role in the *initiation* of such conflicts. No such evidence has been adduced here.

Moreover, the findings do not provide incontrovertible proof of a *causal* link between arms races and conflict escalation; they establish only that rapid competitive military growth is strongly *associated* with the escalation of military confrontations into war. It is conceivable that this result is a spurious effect of the level of ongoing hostility and tension between powers. It is possible that, when they are very great, such tensions simultaneously stimulate military competition and induce a greater propensity to war. If such is the case (and this itself would have to be demonstrated by further research), then arms races, while remaining a valuable "early warning indicator" of war, could not be considered a causal factor in war onset.

But despite these caveats, it will not do to interpret the findings too conservatively. When two great powers engage in acts of military force or violence against one another, we cannot but assume that their relationship is characterized by a considerable degree of hostility and tension. Yet, in only 3 of 71 cases did such acts lead to war when not preceded by an arms race. Conversely, when an arms race *did* precede a significant threat or act of violence, war was avoided only 5 out of 28 times. It is difficult to argue, therefore, that arms races play *no* role in the process of leading to the onset of war.

The policy implications of this are obvious and immediate. The findings support with hard evidence the intuitive fears of those who argue that an intensification of the superpower arms competition could lead to a "hair-trigger" situation in which a major confrontation would be far more likely to result in all-out war. Thus, they underline the urgency of present efforts to curb the looming quantitative and qualitative expansion of superpower strategic arsenals.

Footnotes

1. Useful summaries and critiques of this extensive literature are to be found in Rapoport (1957), Busch (1970), Chaterjee (1974), Zinnes (1976), Gillespie et al. (1977), and Hollist (1978).

2. See, for example, Singer, Bremer, and Stuckey (1972); Wallace (1974); and Choucri and North (1974).

3. See Huntington (1958); Richardson (1960); Milstein and Mitchell (1968); and Busch (1970).

4. See Luterbacher (1975), and Wallace (1976; 1978).

References

Busch, P.C. (1970) "Mathematical models of arms races," in B.M. Russet, What Price Vigilance? New Haven, CT: Yale Univ. Press.

Chaterjee, P. (1975) Arms, Alliances, and Stability. Delhi: Macmillan.

Choucri, N. and R. North (1975) Nations in Conflict: Population, Expansion, and War. San Francisco: W.H. Freeman

Gillespie, J.V., D.A. Zinnes, P.A. Schrodt, G.S. Tahim, and R.M. Rubison (1977) "An optimal control model of arms races." Amer. Pol. Sci. Rev. 81, 1(March):226-244.

Hollist, W.L. [ed.] (1978) Exploring Competitive Arms Processes. New York: Marcel-Dekker.

Huntington, S.P. (1958) "Arms races: prerequisites and results," in C.J. Friedrich and S.E. Harries (eds.) Public Policy. Cambridge, MA: Harvard Univ. Press.

Levy, A. (1977) "Code's manual for identifying serious inter-nation disputes, 1816-1965." Correlates of War Project internal memo, Ann Arbor, Michigan.

Luterbacher, U. (1975) Dimensions historiques de modeles dynamiques de conflict. Leiden: A.W. Sythoff.

Milstein, J.S. and W.C. Mitchell (1969) "Computer simulation of international processes: the Vietnam War and the pre-World War I naval race." Peace Research Society Papers 12.

Rapoport, A. (1957) "Lewis F. Richardson's mathematical theory of war." J. of Conflict Resolution 1 (September):249-299.

Richardson, L.F. (1960) Arms and Insecurity. Pittsburgh: Boxwood.

Sard, A. and S. Weintraub (1971) A Book of Splines. New York: John Wiley.

Singer, J.D. (1958) "Threat perception and the armament-tension dilemma." J. of Conflict Resolution 2, 1(March):90-105.

_____ S. Bremer, and J. Stuckey (1972) "Capability distribution, uncertainty, and major power war, 1820-1965," in B.M. Russett (ed.) Peace, War, and Numbers. Beverly Hills: Sage Publications.

Singer J.D., and M. Small (1966) "The composition and status ordering of the international system, 1815-1940." World Politics 18(January):236-282.

_____ (1972) The Wages of War. New York: John Wiley.

Wallace, M.D. (1973) War and Rank Among Nations. Lexington, MA: D.C. Heath.

_____ (1976) "Arms races and the balance of power: a preliminary model." Applied Mathematical Modeling 1, 2(September):83-92.

_____ and J.M. Wilson (1978) "Non-linear arms race models: a test of some alternatives." J. of Peace Research 15, 2:175-192.

Zinnes, D.A. (1976) Contemporary Research in International Relations. New York: Free Press.

Suggested Readings

Art, Robert J. *The Influence of Foreign Policy on Seapower: New Weapons and Weltpolitik in Wilhelmian Germany*. Beverly Hills, Calif.: Sage, 1973.

Bueno de Mesquita, Bruce. *The War Trap*. New Haven: Yale University, 1981.

Mosley, Hugh G. *The Arms Race: Economic and Social Consequences*. New York: Heath, 1985.

Schelling, Thomas C. *Arms and Influence*. New Haven: Yale University, 1966.

Pelz, Stephen. *Race to Pearl Harbor: The Failure of the Second London Naval Conference and the Onset of World War Two*. Cambridge: Harvard University, 1974.

Smoker, Paul. "Fear in the Arms Race." *Journal of Peace Research* I (1964), pp. 55–64.

Reading 27

THE UNDERLYING CAUSES OF WORLD WAR I

by Nazli Choucri and Robert C. North

Notes from the Editors

For over a quarter of a century, social scientists at Stanford University have been studying the causes of war, using content analysis, mathematical models, and computers. Although most of their work involves the crisis in the summer of 1914 that led to World War I, political scientists Nazli Choucri and Robert C. North stepped back from that six-week period to examine international interactions from 1870 to 1914.

In Nations in Conflict *(the first half of which contains an excellent traditional narrative account of the period), they developed and tested a model of the effects of five key variables on the conflict behavior of the six major European powers. They determined that colonial expansion, colonial conflict, military capability, alliances, and international violence—which they describe quantitatively—were central to understanding international conflict in the period prior to the outbreak of the Great War.*

Choucri and North then fashioned a system of simultaneous equations, which they employed with real data, to predict international behavior. Although they failed to come up with a unified model that worked for all countries during all time periods, some of their strongest findings are important. A nation's colonial expansion was predicted by population density, alliance activity by the military expenditures of nonallies, colonial conflict, and violent behavior by the violence of other nations.

Statisticians have criticized some of the methodological assumptions that Choucri and North were compelled to make. Historians and other humanistically oriented scholars have noted, as they often do with quantitative works, "we knew it all the time." The authors themselves acknowledge their inability to predict the outbreak of World War I in 1914 from their analysis.

Nevertheless, this major work from the Stanford project is an innovative approach to understanding conflict during a celebrated period of explosive colonial expansion, tight alliance systems, and arms races that has long fascinated scholars.

The many links identified so far indicate in general that rather strong paths exist from domestic growth to expansion and military expenditures, from there to alliances, and then to violence-behavior. However, our analysis reveals that international violence can be reached from different initial conditions and along different paths. . . .

In this chapter we shall attempt to pull the pieces together by summarizing the links discussed in Chapters 11–15 and demonstrating their interdependence. We shall examine the relative importance of several factors—domestic growth, expansion, intensity-of-intersections, alliances, military expenditures, etc.—affecting the vio-

Reprinted with permission from Nazli Choucri and Robert C. North, *Nations in Conflict* (San Francisco: Freeman, 1975), pp. 245–52.

lence-behavior of the nations in our study, and note which paths to violence are statistically significant. . . .

Our statistical findings generally confirm the links hypothesized in our model. Only a few findings were difficult to interpret. Certain relationships proved much stronger than others, depending on the period and the country examined. In addition, the paths to violence-behavior are somewhat different for each of the six nations, and even the paths for a single nation vary according to which period (the full period or a subperiod) was analyzed. Despite this multiplicity of paths, *the explanatory power of the variables remains strong*. Our findings therefore sustain the usefulness of the model in the study of international systems.

The case of Britain illustrates the extent to which violence-behavior can be traced to domestic factors of growth and expansion. The population and national-income variables, in various combinations, proved to be important determinants of colonial area (expansion) and military expenditures. Expansion (colonial area) led to increased conflict with other nations over colonial matters (intersections) and thus, at least during the early years of the period studied, to increased military expenditures. These increases contributed to violence-behavior primarily through the intervening link of alliances. This brief sketch leaves out many important relationships in the case of Britain. . . . [It] clearly illustrates the extent to which other factors were operative. For example, it is important to note that Britain's violence-behavior was influenced by foreign factors such as violence-of-others and military-expenditures-of-nonallies. On balance, however, at least one distinct path to violence-behavior emerges from expansion through intensity-of-intersections, military expenditures, and alliances, a path that originates in the dynamics of domestic growth.

In the case of France only one path to violence-behavior is demonstrated, although there are many contributing factors. Expansion (colonial area) appears strongly determined by domestic factors; unlike the case of Britain, however, expansion is not significantly related to intensity-of-intersections. A clear path can be traced from domestic growth (including population growth) to expansion (colonial area), through military expenditures and alliances, to violence-behavior.

For Germany the situation is quite different. Germany's violence-behavior can be attributed only to violence-of-others. German expansion (colonial area), although generated primarily by growth factors, is not linked to intensity-of-intersections or military expenditures. This is a unique case; all the other powers show a link from expansion to the rest of the model. . . . [It] shows three processes *not* linked: (a) the process of expansion, (b) the interconnection of military expenditures, intensity-of-intersections, and alliances, and (c) the factors contributing directly to violence-behavior. Thus, the hypothesized linkage of these three processes was not substantiated in the case of Germany.

In the case of Italy the variables are highly interconnected, as shown by the four distinct paths between violence-behavior and expansion (colonial area), and thus between violence-behavior and population density. Two of these paths pass through intensity-of-intersections, and two through military expenditures. Despite this complexity, the importance of intersections and military expenditures is clear.

In the case of Russia only one distinct path to violence appears; again, however, there are many contributing factors. Domestic factors lead to expansion (colonial area), and this to intensity-of-intersections. There is a direct (but negative) path from inter-sections to violence. Probably more important are the further positive links with military expenditures, alliances, and particularly violence-of-others.

Finally, for Austria-Hungary three distinct paths to violence emerge, but with many contributing factors. The most direct can be traced from expansion (colonial area) through intensity-of-intersections to violence-behavior. A second path leads from expansion to military expenditures, then to intersections, and then to violence-behavior. A third passes through expansion, military expenditures, and alliances (negative) to violence-behavior. In short, intensity-of-intersections, military expenditures, and alliances are the most important contributors to the violence-behavior of Austria-Hungary. This is the only case in which violence-of-others is not a determinant of violence-behavior.

Despite the different paths described above, a fairly clear pattern in the causes of violence-behavior emerges. Expansion (colonial area), stimulated by population growth (density) and technological advance (national income per capita), generally leads to increased intensity-of-intersections. The relationship of expansion to military capability is more complex. In our analysis the link between colonial area and military expenditures is occasionally negative, particularly for those nations whose colonial expansion was blocked or otherwise frustrated. (Only the findings for Germany show no statistically significant relations between colonial area and the other endogenous variables of the model.) Intensity-of-intersections is also related to the nondomestic factors of violence-of-others and colonial-area-of-nonallies, although a nation's own violence-behavior occasionally had some impact. (Again, Germany is a unique case; intensity-of-intersections is generated almost entirely by domestic factors.) The variables military expenditures, intensity-of-intersections, alliances, and violence-behavior are quite highly interconnected, that is, several paths join them. Although violence-behavior is generated by both domestic factors (alliances, military expenditures, and intensity-of-intersections) and foreign factors (military-expenditures-of-nonallies, violence-of-others), the foreign factors generally predominate.

Our analysis thus substantiates our hypothesis that a nation's defense-related capabilities (the military, and sometimes alliances) are largely generated by domestic growth. But this growth may evoke violence-behavior from other powers and, in return, the violence (as well as growth) of others evokes even further violence-behavior. In short, the violence-behavior of one power appears to be related to the violence-behavior of other powers. . . .

The intersection variable is not as consistently significant as we had postulated. This is surprising in view of the powerful colonial thrusts of Britain, France, and Germany, and the numerous collisions among them. The relative weakness of the intersection variable may be due to vulnerability in our procedure for obtaining quantified data (including measurement error), a possible redundancy between intensity-of-intersections and violence-behavior, or to some other failures of analysis. Of course, it is also possible that compared with all interactions among the major powers, intersections (conflicts over colonial interests) did not in fact exert as direct and powerful an influence on either military capabilities or violence-behavior as we had postulated. As our analysis reveals, it is likely that intersections were only one element in a large network of interdependent factors.

Although reaction to the spending of nonallies appears to have had an effect on growth in military expenditures, the trends uncovered by our analysis seem to support the idea . . . that a country's behavior and its interaction with other countries is in great part influenced by bureaucratic politics. Except for periods immediately following a war, bureaucratic demands are for increases, not reductions, in allocations. Thus, the influence of the previous year's allocations is considerable. The significance of bureaucratic politics, of growth in population and technology, and other domestic considerations in accounting for military expenditures does not mean that the notion of competition (or arms race) is useless in explaining military spending levels. It does mean that domestic growth is an important determinant of these levels. In addition, competition may be a powerful *rationalization* for increasing military spending.

The approval of a country's military budget, like the acquisition of colonial territory, is likely to be the outcome of several public and private interests, some of which may have little to do directly with any specific foreign threat. During the period 1870–1914 there was a considerable convergence of colonial and military interests— in some instances they were almost inseparable. Military interests thus converged with industrial, commercial, and bureaucratic interests. It would not be surprising, therefore, to find pressure in many parts of government and society for yearly increases in defense spending. In addition, it is far easier for decision-makers to act by only tinkering with previous budgets (incrementalism) rather than constantly rethinking priorities, and there is strong evidence that they usually do act in that fashion.

The strong influence of military expenditures on intensity-of-intersections should not be surprising in view of the part played by the armies and navies of the major powers during 1870–1914 in acquiring, protecting, policing, and often administering colonial territories, and in securing sea and overland trade routes. That is, if a power deploys its troops and warships to serve its colonies, and another power behaves similarly, one would expect their interests to collide. The notable findings of our analysis of intersections is that the intensity of a nation's intersections is best explained by that nation's own military expenditures and, secondly, by violence-of-others. Once again, internal socio-economic dynamics seem to generate activities with strong external consequences.

The number of alliances, which is generally related to the degree of violence-behavior, tends to be influenced by military-expenditures and population-times-national-income (both domestic variables), as well as by intensity-of-intersections.

Violence-behavior generally is a reactive process. The level of violence is not as strongly linked to conflicts of national interests (intersections), military capability, or alliances as we had hypothesized. Nevertheless, increases in these dimensions often provoke some response by a rival power, which in turn stimulates violence-behavior— clearly an action-reaction process. Thus, our hypothesized links throughout the model still appear to be extremely important, but in an indirect and always complex form.

Although the narrow time frame and limited measures in our study make it impossible to provide anything like conclusive evidence, it is safe to conclude that hereafter, as a consequence of our findings, theories of war will have to take into account domestic socio-economic processes as well as foreign relations. It is all the more important, therefore, that much research remains to be done on the ways in which economic factors influence the expansion of national activities and conflicts of national interests. Particularly, much work needs to be done on incorporating more sensitive measures of trade in a political model, and including other economic measures, such as foreign investment and flow of resources. The linkage of population, technology, expansion, and violence uncovered in our analysis might have been stronger if the economic variables had been more refined. . . .

Suggested Readings

Domke, William K. *War and the Changing Global System*. New Haven: Yale University, 1988.

Joll, James. *The Origins of the First World War*. London: Longman, 1984.

Langer, William Leonard. *The Diplomacy of Imperialism*. New York: Knopf, 1951.

Mayer, Arno J. *The Persistence of the Old Regime: Europe to the Great War*. New York: Pantheon, 1981.

Organski, A.F.K. and Jacek Kugler. *The War Ledger*. Chicago: University of Chicago, 1980.

Williamson, Samuel R., Jr. *The Politics of Grand Strategy: Britain and France Prepare for War, 1904–1914*. Cambridge: Harvard University, 1969.

Reading 28

MISPERCEPTION IN VIENNA ON THE EVE
OF WORLD WAR I

by Ralph K. White

Notes from the Editors

World War I is a favorite case study of students of the causes of war. It owes its popularity not only to its scope but to the fact that almost all of the relevant archives from almost all of the major participants have been available to researchers since the 1920s. Governments threw open their archives to demonstrate to critics at home and abroad that they acted prudently and rationally during the six-week crisis that began at Sarajevo on June 28, 1914 when the Austrian archduke was assassinated, and ended on August 4 when most of the European powers were at war.

Social psychologist Ralph K. White wrote Nobody Wanted War *in 1968 as a response to American involvement in the Vietnam War. He is most concerned with misperceptions in international relations that have led all too often to the paradox of the unwanted war.*

In the following excerpt from his book, White describes the Austro-Serbian crisis of July 1914 and how the actions taken by both sides led to World War I. He is interested in Austria's perception of herself as a major power, the international system, and Serbian intentions. White discerns six major misperceptions shared by Austrian decision makers that led them to precipitate a war that they did not want to fight. Although he here only discusses Austria, social psychologists offer the same sort of analysis of misperceptions of other major powers on the eve of World War I, as well as on the eve of other wars.

White realizes that he is dealing only with what historians call the "immediate" causes of war. All the same, he suggests that a social-psychologist's approach has a lot to tell us about the underlying causes too, for many of those classic causes, as he sees them, were related to nationalism.

The Sequence of Events, 1914

Since the sequence of events is important in understanding how the First World War began, and since even the bare essentials may be hazy in many readers' minds, a brief summary is presented herewith:

June 28, 1914. The Austrian Archduke Francis Ferdinand was assassinated in Sarajevo by a militant Serbian nationalist protesting against the Austro-Hungarian rule over Serbians and other Yugoslavs.

At that time the Austro-Hungarian empire in Central Europe included not only what is now Austria and Hungary but also what is now Czechoslovakia, most of what

---

Excerpt from *Nobody Wanted War* (Garden City, Doubleday, 1968), pp. 7–20, by Ralph K. White. Copyright © 1968 by Ralph K. White. Reprinted by permission of Doubleday, a division of Bantam, Doubleday, Dell Publishing Group, Inc.

is now Yugoslavia, and much of what is now Poland and Rumania. All of these nationalities were restless, even though the Austro-Hungarian rule over them was relatively mild and progressive. A very dangerous element in the situation, from the Austrian point of view, was the small independent nation of Serbia, just south of Austria-Hungary, which was obviously hoping to expand by uniting with its Yugoslav brothers then under Austro-Hungarian rule. From the Austrians' point of view, therefore, the murder of the Archduke was extremely dangerous as a symptom of the disintegration their empire was faced with, since they regarded the murder as instigated by "criminal" Serbian nationalists aided and abetted by the Serbian government in Belgrade.

July 5. The German Kaiser and his Chancellor, Bethmann-Hollweg, assured their ally, Austria-Hungary, of German support if Austria decided to react "firmly" to the Serbian danger.

July 23. Austria-Hungary sent Serbia an ultimatum making a number of demands.

July 25. Serbia replied to the ultimatum accepting all of the demands but one— the one that provided for Austro-Hungarian participation in police activity within Serbia. Austria-Hungary, regarding this last demand as crucial, rejected the Serbian reply, broke off diplomatic relations, and began to prepare for war.

Feverish diplomatic activity ensued. Russia, enormously larger than Austria, regarded Serbia as her protégé and protested Austria's action. Germany however, also much stronger than Austria and with a much more modern and efficient army than Russia's, stood firmly by Austria and seemed clearly ready to fight at Austria's side if Austria were attacked by Russia. France was similarly allied with Russia. England, loosely allied with France and Russia in the Triple Entente, did her best to get the issue resolved by negotiation, but failed.

July 29. Germany tried unsuccessfully to keep Austria from attacking Serbia.

By this time, however, a new and decisive element was entering the situation: the mobilization of Russia's enormous but cumbersome military machine. The Germans, thoroughly alarmed by the prospect of a war on two fronts, with Russia on one side and France on the other, demanded that Russia stop her mobilization. Russia refused and the war began with a German strike at France through Belgium, which consolidated British feeling and ensured that Britain would enter the war on the anti-German side.

Austrian Perceptions

On the day when Austria-Hungary broke relations with Serbia, setting in motion the escalation that transformed a local dispute into a world war, the perception of the situation in Austrian minds was radically different from the perception of it in the minds of Austria's enemies—a perception that sustained those enemies (ultimately including the United States) through more than four years of one of the bloodiest wars in history. Austria's enemies saw her declaration of war on Serbia as cold-blooded, calculating aggression. In their minds, the militarists who ruled Imperial Germany and controlled Austria had decided to use the minor Serbian dispute as a pretext to launch a war that they believed would give them mastery, first of Europe and then of the world.

Historical scholarship in the 1920s established a view of these events that includes a more understandable conception of what was in Austrian minds at the time. Historians are now in fair agreement that Austria, not Germany, was the prime mover. Germany clearly tried to prevent a major European war. From the Austrian point of view Serbia was carrying on an intolerable agitation against Austria-Hungary, not even stopping at assassination, that had to be punished. Unless Serbia was punished, nationalist agitation throughout the Austro-Hungarian Empire would get worse, threatening its very existence.

To be sure, there were other thoughts in the minds of Austrians. One was the terrifying possibility of a larger war. Russia, with her enormous army, might come in. But surely (the Austrians thought) the Czar of Russia, who lived in fear of assassination himself, must realize that the Hapsburg emperor could not tolerate the sort of agitation that had prompted the assassination of the Archduke. He must see that Austria-Hungary's very existence as a bastion of civilization and order in Central Europe depended on her standing firm in this new crisis and teaching the conspirators in Belgrade an unforgettable lesson. Since the German Kaiser had seen the justice of Austria's position and was standing firmly by her, the Czar would hardly be so rash as to intervene; he must know that the consequences of a world war would be incalculable. In any case, the risk must be run; if the Serbian nationalist agitation among the Serbs and Croats still under Austrian rule were allowed to continue, it could quickly spread to the other nationalities within the Austro-Hungarian family of nations, and Austria-Hungary herself would disappear as a Great Power—which was, of course, unthinkable.

If this is a fair picture of what was happening in Austrian minds, it suggests that their reality world was distorted by six forms of misperception:

1. A diabolical enemy-image

2. A virile self-image

3. A moral self-image

4. Selective inattention

5. Absence of empathy

6. Military overconfidence

1. *The Diabolical Enemy-Image:* In the central focus of Austrian minds was the "criminal" character of the "assassins" who had violated all standards of human decency and were endangering the very survival of the beneficent Austro-Hungarian empire. In this black-and-white picture the black was more fully in focus than the white. To Austrians it seemed that such men, and the conspiracy in Belgrade that was responsible for their actions (though this point remained controversial to detached observers) were so flagrantly evil that all right-minded people, even Russians, must see the need to "punish" them.

The Germans too saw devils. Although before July 30 they only gave "loyal" support to Austria (and, on July 29, tried unsuccessfully to restrain her), on July 30 the news of Russian mobilization threw the Germans into panic. To the Kaiser it appeared that the Russians, French, and British were seizing upon the Serbian dispute as a pretext to attack both Germany and Austria. In an extraordinary instance of displacement of hostility, at precisely the moment when the British were trying desperately to stave off major war, the Kaiser saw them as the head and center of a plot against him. On the margin of a diplomatic note he wrote: "The net has been suddenly thrown over our head, and England sneeringly reaps the most brilliant success of her persistently prosecuted, purely *anti-German world policy,* against which we have proved ourselves helpless, while she twists the noose of our political and economic destruction out of our fidelity to Austria, as we squirm isolated in the net (italics in the original)." Though the Kaiser could scarcely be called psychotic, this passage has the ring of pure paranoia. To him, the British plot was real. With Germany's very existence at stake, he felt that Russia should be given no more time to get its enormous but cumbersome military machine under way. He decided on a strike-first policy, and once that decision was made, the Great War had begun.

2. *The Virile Self-Image:* In 1914, the Austrians were not alone in their preoccupation with prestige and their feeling that humiliation would be intolerable. Each of the Great Powers feared "losing our position as a Great Power" and sinking to the status of a second-class power. In each case, after a firm stand had been taken, governments were acutely conscious of the danger of backing down, or seeming to back down. They were less vividly aware of the pain and death of tens of millions of human beings that might result if there were no compromise. This was true until the general Russian mobilization, when fear took over as the ruling emotion in Germany, if not in Austria-Hungary, and led directly to a strike-first policy. Before that time, the ruling emotion had been not fear of attack but fear of humiliation. The chief dimension in which national decision-makers judge themselves, and expected to be judged by others, was not good vs. bad, or right vs. wrong, but strong vs. weak. The essential goal apparently was to be, and to seem, strong and courageous. The essential thing was to take a firm stand, a strong stand, and to do it with such firmness and such obvious lack of fear, on one's own part and on the part of one's allies, that the potential enemy would surely back down.

3. *The Moral Self-Image:* In the crisis of 1914 the Austrians had a black-and-white picture in which only evil was attributed to the Serbian enemy and only good the the Austro-Hungarian self. While their own moral nobility was perhaps less salient in the Austrians' minds than the diabolical character of the enemy or their own need to take a firm stand in the interest of self-preservation, the Austrian self that they thought worth preserving was also noble: peace-loving (they never for a moment sought a bigger war, and always feared it), civilized (they were a bastion of civilization in a Central Europe threatened by the barbarian tide of pan-Slavism), economically rational (their empire was prospering in unity and would suffer economically if broken up), orderly (the Serbian assassins were violating elementary standards of law and order), and democratic (theirs was a limited monarchy, and the subject peoples were advancing toward full autonomy as rapidly as possible).

It is not necessary to deny some truth in each of these propositions; it is necessary only to notice that the Austrians' picture was expurgated at one crucial point. It did not include even a candid consideration of the possibility that this noble nation might now be committing aggression. The Austrian ultimatum to Serbia included what the Serbs regarded as a virtual demand for submission to Austrian authority, and when this was not clearly accepted by Serbia, Austria broke relations and began to mobilize for war. In the eyes of most of the world, this was aggression. It was aggression also by almost any clear definition of the term; for example, if aggression is defined as the use of force or threat of force on another nation's territory and against the wishes of the majority of the politically conscious people of that nation, Austria's action was aggression, however much it may have been provoked. But the Austrians did not call it that, or seriously think about what to call it. To them it was not aggression at all, but a firm stand, or bringing the criminals to justice. Here again there was selective inattention. The charge of aggression was not answered in their minds; it was ignored.

There was also in their minds a curious sort of automatism—a feeling that they could not do otherwise. The initial steps on the road to war were taken with a feeling of necessity; to do otherwise would be suicide. Once the initial steps were taken, Austrian minds were gripped by what Anatol Rapoport has called "the blindness of involvement." As the Emperor Francis Joseph put it, "We cannot go back now." All moral guilt was thus shifted from the Austrians themselves to an impersonal Fate or Necessity. This was shown most strikingly at two key points: Austria's refusal to reconsider her course of action on July 25, when the conciliatory Serbian reply to the Austrian ultimatum was seen even by the German Kaiser as "doing away with every reason for war," and her refusal to draw back even when Germany, on July 29, exerted very strong pressure on her to do so. On that day the German Chancellor, Bethmann-Hollweg, wired the Austrians: "we cannot allow Vienna to draw us lightly, and without regard to our advice, into a worldwide conflagration." Berchtold, the Austrian Foreign Minister, had the bit in his teeth, and had put on blinders; with a "courageous" unwillingness to consider any alternative course of action, he stepped over the brink of the precipice.

The strong German pressure on Austria to draw back also points up how mistaken our own diabolical image of Germany was, throughout the First World War. Americans generally assumed that Austria, much weaker than Germany, must have been playing a subordinate role in the Kaiser's plans for war and world conquest. Actually Austria, encouraged by the "blank check" which Germany had heedlessly given her on July 5, went a good deal further than Germany wanted her to. The "puppet" got out of hand. Like much of history, this series of events was largely a matter of sheer thoughtlessness and failure to communicate. Germany can be blamed not so much for malice or for dreams of world conquest as for ordinary carelessness. She should have tried sooner and harder to stop Austria. But one thing is now fairly well agreed upon by scholars: Germany did not try to precipitate a European war. She tried to prevent it.

4. *Selective Inattention:* Of all the psychological mechanisms involved in the misperceptions we have been considering, perhaps most pervasive is one that

in some contexts may be called "resistance" or "repression" (though the Freudians give a more restricted meaning to each of these terms). Harry Stack Sullivan has referred to it more broadly as "selective inattention." It is involved on both sides of a black-and-white picture, when white or gray elements on the enemy side are glossed over and attention focuses only on the black, and vice versa.

In nations stumbling toward war there are usually at least three other definable types or aspects of selective inattention: narrow time-perspective, narrow space-perspective, and absence of empathy. The Austrians in 1914 were vividly aware of only one aspect of the future as they perceived it: the catastrophic disintegration that they thought likely (with much reason) if they could not cope firmly with Serbian nationalism. But the parts of this anxiety-filled image were not cognitively well defined. It did not distinguish clearly, for example, between what would happen if they merely dealt firmly with Serbian and other agitators within their own borders and what would happen if, in the process of punishing Serbia, they sent troops across their borders into a neighboring state. To the rest of the world this distinction seemed the distinction between legitimate maintenance of internal stability and illegitimate aggression that could precipitate world war. But in anxious Austrian minds it was all of a piece: a need to punish Serbia, as vigorously as possible, in order to prevent destruction and vindicate the image of Austria-Hungary as a virile nation.

In addition, the Austrians failed to pay attention to other future possibilities, including Russian intervention, and the kind of breakup of the Austrian empire that later occurred as a result of the war that Austria herself precipitated.

A restriction in the Austrians' space-perspective was represented by their failure to pay much attention to countries other than the two that were the main focus of their attention (themselves and Serbia), and the two that were somewhat in the periphery (Russia, whose intervention they feared, and Germany, whose strong stand by Austria was counted on to deter Russian intervention). Two countries that were soon to become involved, France and England, were present in Austrian minds but apparently not seriously considered. America, which was to join the Allies nearly three years later—partly because of the American impression at the outset that Germany and Austria had committed aggression—was apparently not considered at all.

5. *Absence of Empathy:* Even in the case of Serbia, the enemy that was in the bright central focus of Austrian attention, the Austrians seemed to fail almost completely to realize how the situation looked from another point of view. They did not see that to a Serbian patriot the Austrian demands appeared to be naked aggression, calling for a struggle to the last drop of patriotic Serbian blood. They did not see how Russian pride, smarting after a number of setbacks including the high-handed Austrian annexation of Bosnia six years earlier, would respond to a new arbitrary extension of German-Austrian power in an area where the Russians felt that their honor and their interest were involved. They failed to see that, while the Russian Czar himself was peacefully inclined and would try to avoid a major war, his close advisers were not necessarily so pacific, and that Russia might become entangled in a situation in which its pride and prestige were so deeply

involved that war might seem the only alternative to intolerable humiliation. Like/ the Germans, the Austrians resisted negotiations, which would have compelled them to see clearly and to cope with other viewpoints. They failed to anticipate the swing of the pendulum of the Kaiser's mood from careless overconfidence to panic once the Russian general mobilization had started and the British entry into the war seemed likely.

The Austrians failed to see how the British and French would fear a collapse of the balance of power if they left Russia to fight alone against a smaller but far more efficient German army, or how British public opinion would react if the panicky Germans, anxious to capitalize on their one great asset, the superior efficiency and speed of their forces, were to invade France through Belgium. They did not realize that America would regard their attack on Serbia as a big country bullying a small one, and would similarly regard Germany's march through Belgium—that America's sympathies would be immediately engaged on the side of the Allies, and the way would thus be prepared for America ultimately to enter the war. In short, the Austrians were so wrapped up in their own anxiety and their own righteous indignation that they had little attention left for considering what was real to anyone else.

6. *Military Overconfidence:* It is paradoxical but true that exaggerated fear can be combined with exaggerated military confidence. The Austrians, for example, had what now seems an exaggerated fear of the spreading disaffection of nationalities within their empire that would result if they failed to take a stand against Serbia. At the same time, until the Russian mobilization, they were excessively confident that they could teach Serbia a lesson and, with strong German support, keep Russia from intervening. Like the Germans, they pinned their hopes on the possibility of localizing the issue, enjoying mastery and venting righteous indignation within a small sphere while remaining safe from the mastery impulse and the righteous indignation of others in a larger sphere. They were wrong. They misperceived. Reality differed from their perception of it chiefly in that they were inattentive to the possibility that strong allies of Serbia (Russia, France, Britain, America) might scorn to be intimidated by the Kaiser's appearance at Austria's side "in shining armor." They did not see that their potential enemies, like themselves, might be living up to an indomitable self-image, fearful of showing fear, and therefore irrationally ready to fight.

Underlying Causes

The causes of any war are usually discussed under two heads: immediate, "precipitating" causes—assumed to be relatively superficial—and long-term, underlying causes. Up to this point our analysis of World War I has been only in terms of its immediate or precipitating causes. Is this superficial? Were there deeper causes that have not been touched?

Certainly there were other forces at work. Four factors often cited as underlying causes are nationalism, militarism, economic imperialism, and the system of competitive alliances into which Europe was divided in 1914. Each of these had deep historical roots, and the mere mention of them is enough to suggest how much has been omitted in the above historical sketch. But even in this brief discussion it is appropriate to ask two questions:

Were the immediate, precipitating causes perhaps less superficial than is commonly supposed?

After all, these are the causes that were most directly, demonstrably related to the fateful decision that directly produced the war. Austria's breaking of relations with Serbia and her mobilization for war, Russia's general mobilization, the panicky German response to Russian mobilization—these actions, and the motives, assumptions, and misperceptions that produced them, were direct and unequivocal causes of the war's outbreak. Abstractions such as militarism and economic imperialism are both more indirectly and more equivocally related to what occurred.

Take, for instance, militarism. This high-level abstraction, insofar as it means anything beyond our dislike of war and of the arms associated with it, has two concrete meanings: an arms race, with its concomitant of heightened fear and suspicion, and a disproportionate influence of military men in the decisions that lead to war.

An arms race certainly existed in the years before 1914, especially in the competition between the German and the French armies and between the German and the British navies. But it would be hard to show that either race contributed even indirectly to the decisions of the Austrians, the Russians, and the Germans that directly precipitated war.

As for undue influence of military men upon diplomatic decisions, it probably existed in Russia but not, to any high degree, in either Austria or Germany. In Austria the decisions were apparently made primarily by the civilian Foreign Minister, Berchtold, backed by the Emperor, Francis Joseph, and in Germany by the civilian Chancellor, Bethmann-Hollweg, backed by the Kaiser. In neither case is it clear that militarism had any essential part in what occurred.

Economic imperialism as a cause of war has been the favored explanation of Marxists and others who have pictured the First World War as the inevitable outcome of capitalist rivalry for markets, raw materials, and investment opportunities. Innumerable writers have discovered in economic imperialism a profound and "scientific" explanation for the mystery of the occurrence of war in a world in which the common people, at least, hate war. But this explanation is hard to reconcile with the stubborn, inconvenient fact that the prime movers in starting the First World War were not the advanced capitalist nations, Great Britain, France, and Germany. The prime movers were Serbia, Austria-Hungary, and Russia, which were engaged not in a scramble for overseas markets and raw materials but in an old-fashioned struggle for territory, power, prestige, national independence, and (at least in Austrian minds) national survival.

Competitive alliances also call for consideration as one of the forces behind the war. It is true that the alliance of Germany with Austria-Hungary, the alliance of France with Russia and the looser entente that included Great Britain as well as France and Russia were crucial factors in the immediate, dramatic spread of the war. Once Austria and Russia were embroiled, the war spread and became a conflagration that included Germany, France, and Great Britain. A local conflict was transformed, senselessly, into a general one. A distinction should be made, however, between factors that caused the war and factors that caused it to spread. The initial conflict was essentially between Austria and Serbia, with Russia's support of Serbia serving to bring two major countries, Austria and Russia, into collision. That presumably would have occurred whether either country had allies or not. Germany at first gave Austria a blank check, but later tried to restrain her. If that attempt had succeeded, the war probably would not have occurred, and the alliance system would have had to be credited with stopping a war instead of producing one.

Nationalism, however, was clearly a basic cause. The crisis of 1914 was shot through with nationalism from beginning to end. To take just one country: Austria's diabolical image of Serbia was an image of a national enemy, endangering Austria's national survival. Her virile and moral self-image was an image of a national self. Her selective inattention shielded her from disturbances of a national black-and-white picture and from reconsidering a course of action that she regarded, however mistakenly, as essential to national survival. (Sinking to the status of a second-class power seemed to the Austrians almost equivalent to national extinction.) The empathy that Austria's decision-makers did not have was empathy with national enemies, and Berchtold's jaunty, feckless overconfidence was overconfidence in a national self, backed by a national ally.

Every step in our analysis could be described also as a study of one or another aspect of nationalism, defined provisionally as identification (of individuals and governments alike) with a national self-image and a consequent mobilization of powerful motives—such as the desire for power and prestige—on behalf of that image. Negatively, nationalism can be described as an absence of any concept of a self larger than the nation. With the possible exception of the Catholic church, and of course their alliance with Germany, the Austrians in 1914 had virtually no supranational self-images (such as Europe, or the United Nations, or the human race), with which they could identify. The same can be said of all other actors in the drama.

Earlier national history and underlying causes—including psychological ones—may be important, then, in helping to account for the growth and shaping of the nationalism that now seems to have been of decisive importance during the war crisis itself. And that leads to a second question:

Were psychological factors, including misperception, important also in the growth of nationalism, and should they therefore be recognized among the underlying as well as the precipitating causes of the war?

For full understanding of the nationalism that pervaded Europe in 1914, the history of the preceding two or three centuries must be studied. For example, Austria's glorious victories over the Turks and Metternich's special dynastic version of nationalism help one to understand the atmosphere and rhetoric of Vienna in 1914.

The historical record alone, however, is hardly enough to explain it. It is also important to ask whether Austrian and other nationalists derived unconscious satisfactions, throughout these centuries, from picturing their own nations as virile and moral, whether (more mysteriously) they also drew unconscious satisfaction from picturing their enemies as diabolical, and if so, why. One must ask whether there is a deep psychological need to identify with symbols of *something* larger and better than the individual self, and try to analyze the social factors that link this need to some symbols (religious, ideological, or national) rather than others. . . .

Suggested Readings

Axelrod, Robert. *Structure of Decision: The Cognitive Maps of Political Elites*. Princeton: Princeton University, 1976.

Bronfenbrenner, Urie. "The Mirror-Image in Soviet American Relations: A Social Psychological Report." *Journal of Social Issues* XVII, 3 (1961), pp. 45–56.

Holsti, Ole R. "Cognitive Dynamics and the Image of the Enemy." *Journal of International Affairs* 221, 1 (1967), pp. 16–39.

Janis, Irving. *Victims of Group Think: A Psychological Study of Foreign Policy Decisions and Fiascos*. Boston: Houghton Mifflin, 1972.

Jervis, Robert. *Perception and Misperception in International Politics*. Princeton: Princeton University, 1976.

Reading 29

THE LIMITS OF CHOICE: JULY 1914 RECONSIDERED

L. L. Farrar, Jr.

Notes from the Editor

L. L. Farrar, Jr. is a historian interested in the causes of war who, like many of his colleagues, focuses on the rich documentation of World War I for his case study. After surveying the social scientist's competing approaches to decision making in a crisis, he outlines the major events of the July 1914 crisis and how each of the major powers reacted to them.

Farrar concludes that the outbreak of World War I was the logical result of rational policy considerations. By examining the diplomatic and military choices available to the decision makers, he is able to demonstrate the complexity of the situation and how one could continually choose the best of the perceived available options at each of the decision points and still end up in a war that nobody wanted.

All the actors in this tragedy were hoping for a diplomatic victory. None could accept a diplomatic defeat in political terms. In the end, war became a plausible alternative; at least it held out the hope of "victory" when diplomatic victory could not be obtained.

Farrar also maintains that his study supports an eclectic approach to crises that borrows from situational, systems, and decision-making analyses. Whichever approach one favors, Farrar's findings, solidly based in the documents, offer a rather pessimistic perspective on the causes of World War I.

The discussion of the outbreak of World War I was a classic historical debate. It raised most historical questions. Not only academics but also politicians, journalists, and the educated public became involved. A considerable number of scholars made reputations debating it. It was probably the most burning historical question for the interwar generation and produced a vast quantity of original documents and secondary literature. But the great effort produced little agreement. This paradox seemed to make nonsense of history: the more men knew, the less they agreed. The debate seemed to demonstrate that history is nothing more than national propaganda, subjective prejudice, or intellectual exercise. This conclusion was partially justified since many participants sought immediate political objectives rather than historical objectivity. Indeed it was precisely those political implications of the debate, which attracted public attention, that virtually insured against objectivity. In this sense the debate tells us more about the interwar period than the prewar period. However much the participants genuinely sought to explain the prewar period, their disagreement was due largely to questions of interpretation, since the facts could be generally agreed upon after pub-

Reprinted from *Journal of Conflict Resolution* 16 (March, 1972), pp. 1–23. © 1972 Sage Publications, Inc. Reprinted by permission of Sage Publications, Inc.

lication of the official documents. The debate is therefore understandable only if these interpretations are isolated.

Competing Interpretations of the Crisis

The July crisis can be understood in terms of four basic interpretations: responsibility, chance, limited choice, and multiple explanation. The most commonly argued interpretation and starting point for the interwar debate was responsibility. During the war each government had naturally sought to mobilize popular support with the assertion that the enemy was responsible for the war. After the war there was an understandable psychological and political compulsion to believe that someone else had been responsible. The Versailles Treaty established so firmly the concept of responsibility as the framework of debate that at first it was seldom questioned. The concept was applied in varied and frequently contradictory ways. Some argued that all governments to some degree were responsible and that this responsibility could be ranked. (Most recently this view has been put by Remak, 1971.) Others asserted that only some governments were responsible. Still others blamed specific groups within governments or societies such as the military, revengeful politicians, foreign ministries, conservatives, industrialists, or other interest groups. The concept of responsibility was also interpreted in different ways. Some interpreters perceived conscious decisions to seek war—a responsibility of commission. More found conscious decisions to risk, although not to seek, war—a lessened responsibility of commission. Probably even more saw unconscious willingness to risk war and conscious desire to avoid war—responsibility of omission, that is, statesmen were responsible because they had been irresponsible. Thus responsibility of commission depended primarily on motives, while responsibility of omission depended largely on consequences.

Increasingly the concept of chance competed with responsibility as the interwar years passed. Like responsibility this interpretation had immediate political implications. It seemed to facilitate international reconciliation by justifying the dismantlement of the Versailles Treaty. Its appeal since World War II is the implied warning against precipitating World War III by mistake. It rejected responsibility of commission; since no one had wanted war, no one was responsible. It also rejected responsibility of omission; irresponsibility precluded responsibility. Instead incompetence, weakness, stupidity, miscalculation of risks, and unforeseen events were seen as the real causes of war. Some argued a lack-of-great-man theory: if a great statesman like Bismarck had existed, the war might have been prevented. Many regarded seemingly coincidental events such as the assassination and the military timetables as critical. A few believed a crisis mentality paralyzed statesmen. Still others were even less specific and blamed "fate"—in the sense of bad luck.

The concept of limited choice was specifically advocated by few participants in the debate, but was implied by all those who asserted that the old diplomatic system had caused the war. Like responsibility and chance, limited choice had fundamental political implications. If the international system had caused war to break out in 1914, war might recur unless that system were changed. This interpretation implied rejection of responsibility and chance as explanations for the war following the July crisis. It suggested instead that the cause lay in long-term factors, such as the alliance system,

militarism, nationalism, economic competition and imperialism, anachronistic diplomacy, domestic political problems, the press and public opinion, a pervasive sense of
doom, and/or "fate"—in the sense of destiny. Some or all of these forces limited so
severely the options open to statesmen that war was a virtual certainty once the crisis
began.

The concept of multiple explanation became increasingly popular as mounting
evidence made the July crisis seem more complex and therefore less susceptible to
any single explanation. Like the other interpretations it had fundamental political
implications. If the outbreak of war could not be easily explained, it would be difficult
to adjust the system in order to avoid its recurrence. Multiple explanation rejected the
assumption basic to the other interpretations that *one* cause could be isolated and
assumed. Thus all interpretations which perceived *both* long-term (limited choice) *and*
short-term (responsibility and chance) causes fall under the general rubric of multiple
explanation.

I find limited choice the most satisfactory explanation. Once the crisis began, the
choices perceived by European statesmen proved so narrow that war was virtually
unavoidable. The fact that other hypothetical choices can be suggested in retrospect
does not in itself diminish the usefulness of this interpretation. Instead the critical
issue is whether the statesmen of 1914 can realistically be expected to have chosen
alternatives which might have avoided war. The perceptions of these statesmen were
profoundly affected by the prevailing view of the great-power system and the consequent role of great-power statesmen. All great-power statesmen assumed that it was
their primary duty to protect and expand the power of their states by diplomacy if
possible, and by war if necessary. When confronted with the choice between a peace
which seemed detrimental to their state's interests and a less disadvantageous or even
advantageous war, they regarded it as their duty to opt for war. Thus the central
problem in understanding the 1914 crisis becomes one of analysing the choices with
which the statesmen of 1914 were confronted and of deciding whether or not they
could reasonably be expected to have made fundamentally different decisions within
the existing conditions.

Literature on International Crises

There is a considerable amount of social science literature on international crises.
It can be roughly divided into the three general categories of decision-making, situation
analysis, and system analysis. Before applying the limited choice interpretation to the
1914 crisis, it may be useful to examine some of these works. Doing so should help
focus my analysis and suggest some of its implications.

Decision-making.   The concern of the present study—how choices were
made during the crisis—makes the large body of literature on decision-making relevant.
Most germane to the present study are the excellent works of Abel (1941) and Russett
(1962, 1967). Abel argues that decisions for war have been neglected because of the
tendency to see war as a response to external, impersonal occurrences (e.g., population
pressures, business cycles, mass psychoses) and to assume a cause-effect schema such
as is used in the natural sciences. He suggests instead that war is the outcome of a

process of development in which innumerable and often unique factors play differing roles. Thus one should analyze processes rather than seek causes. His purpose is therefore "to show the background from which decision emerges." He sees government as the locus of decision: "Throughout recorded human history, the initiators of war were individuals and groups who held power." A conflict situation occurs when these groups are threatened or frustrated. The crisis develops as neither side accedes and the range of possible solutions narrows. The conflict reaches a climax when negotiations fail and intimidation proves ineffective. The ultimate choice is forced upon the dominant group—the alternatives of either resigning from its position of dominance or employing violence as a radical means of solving its problem." But this is only the final, not the critical step. "The experience of a crisis does not directly or necessarily precipitate war." It is merely the final step of a process which began with "the decision by the leaders . . . to use physical force as a means of resolving an anticipated or actual critical situation." Abel contends that this decision is not reached on the spur of the moment or as a result of immediate circumstances. It is "based upon a careful weighing of chances and of anticipating consequences," and not "precipitated by emotional tensions, sentimentality, crowd behavior, or other irrational motivations." Furthermore "the rational, calculating decision is reached far in advance of the actual outbreak of hostilities," usually from one to five years before. He bases this conclusion on a study of twenty-five major wars and illustrates it with the Austrian decision of 1791–92, the Austrian decision of 1909–14, the Italian decision of 1933–36, and the German decision of 1934–39. In the second illustration he argues that "the conclusion is inescapable that the Austrian power group . . . had made up their minds to have war with Serbia several years before the outbreak of hostilities and were only awaiting a favorable opportunity. The opportunity came with the assassination of the Archduke Ferdinand." Thus wars are caused by the rational, calculated, and premeditated decisions (of small power-groups) that war is desirable. They can be prevented only by making war undesirable (through credible deterrence) and by community control over power groups.

Despite his admonition that war is "not the inevitable and invariant effect of some 'cause'," Abel's thesis comes very close to the long-term responsibility explanation which historians have traditionally applied. I would argue that this tends to narrow the focus excessively and to make policy unduly rigid. His view also implies that rulers are evil individuals and essentially different from the ruled. I would argue that rulers are not inherently evil but forced by their roles to make decisions and that they are not essentially different from their populations. However I do find Abel's view useful in two senses. It emphasizes the interdependence of crisis and precrisis events; in particular, it sees the crisis as a result of precrisis decisions. Furthermore it presents the decision-making process as essentially a calculation rather than an emotional, irrational response to the crisis situation.

Russett (1967) emphasizes the rationality of decision-making in his insightful article on Pearl Harbor. He rejects the specific argument that the Japanese decision was "inexplicable" or "irrational" because it was unwise, and doubts the general argument that it is precisely during crises that "men are least able to weigh calmly the cost of their acts and the likelihood of counteraction." Furthermore he contends that the Japanese decision was not due to specific Japanese characteristics, peculiarities of the personalities of Japanese statesmen, or the pressure of circumstances. Instead he maintains that the Japanese decision was based on a rational and prolonged calculation of the utility and probable results of various options. Japanese leaders decided that war with the United States was necessary because of assumptions about the general situation and because of Japanese requirements. Thus "American deterrent policy failed not because Japanese leaders really expected to win, but because they saw no alternative to war." As Russett recognizes, this is a different interpretation of the decision for war than argued by North (1967) and others, below. Russett suggests—and I would agree—that, although leaders may evidence signs of stress during a crisis, the crisis is due not to the stress but to decisions taken previously. I would also concur in his view that personality characteristics are not significant during a crisis.

In his article on Pearl Harbor, Russett seems to have changed his mind considerably from the view he had put previously. In an earlier article (1962), he argued that the outbreak of most wars could be best understood in terms of an automobile accident. Like a car crash, wars resulted not from previous decisions but from a situation. If the time for reaction was short, the communication poor, and the stress on decision-makers high, war would result. War could have been avoided in 1914 by a "cooling-off treatment." This view comes close both to the traditional war-by-mistake thesis and the situational approaches discussed below. In distinguishing between accidental and deliberate wars, however, Russett may have anticipated the logic of his later interpretation. He asserts that "Hitler in 1939 consciously ran at least the high risk of war for the achievement of certain aims, and the resulting conflict was not 'accidental'." This would be his subsequent view of the Japanese decision in 1941. It could also be applied in 1914. Like most of those who apply the war-by-mistake thesis, Russett equates accidental with unintentional and thus uses the automobile-accident model. I would alter the automobile analogy to stock car racing where the decision to enter implies the high likelihood of crashes, but no crash is specifically planned.

Situation Analysis.   Russett's earlier article typifies much of the work on crises which has been done by social scientists. In general these scholars argue that the decision for war is less the result of general circumstances or previous decisions than the crisis situation itself. This approach is well represented by the perspective work of Hermann (1969, 1972). As he defines it, "situational analysis . . . assumes that the action of an agent (in this case an international actor) is a function of the immediate situation he confronts" (1969). Hermann proceeds to develop a typology of six situations on the basis of the three variables: threat, time, and surprise. A crisis is at one end of this spectrum of situations and is characterized by high threat, short time for decision, and surprise. He argues elsewhere (1972) that at least four "models dealing specifically with behavior in crisis" exist: individual stress, organizational response, hostile interaction, and cost calculation. The individual stress model focuses on the decision-maker's internalization of national goals and the resultant personal stress on him when these goals are threatened in a crisis. The organizational response model is concerned primarily with the locus of and participants in decision-making which tends to occur at high levels and to involve few decision-makers during a crisis. The hostility interaction model concentrates on the variable of hostility—the perception and expression of which is regarded by decision-makers as critical. Finally the cost calculation model presents crisis behavior primarily as a result of cost-benefit calculation. Although previous experience and decisions, as well as the general international situation, are calculated into these models, the main emphasis is placed on the crisis itself.

This concentration on the crisis situation is the main characteristic of the extensive and painstaking work of North, Ole Holsti, Brody, Zinnes, Koch, and others, which constituted my own introduction to social science literature on international crises. North (1967) is quite specific on the relationship between crisis and background. He argues that "to identify background trends or events as causal agents seems to impute an element of determinism that unfolding history may not warrant. It makes the outbreak of war, when it comes, appear inescapable, that is, beyond the capacity of any leadership to prevent." He grants "the importance of historical perspective, the identification of persisting animosities, expectations, ambitions and conflicts, and the context and circumstances from which the crisis emerged." But his focus is "upon the way a crisis is handled, upon how it is managed, rather than upon its origins, . . . more particularly how various leaders perceived these phenomena [and] relationships . . . between perception and overt behavior." His conclusion is that "the world war was at least in part a consequence of miscalculations associated with the local conflict and of a kind of panic that seized certain leaders—especially the Kaiser—when, under extremely high tension, they felt themselves 'surrounded' and hopelessly threatened." The crisis caused "spiraling tension;" the tension caused misperceptions; the misperceptions caused miscalculations; the miscalculations caused hostile actions; the hostile actions caused war. As he notes, North disagrees with Abel's argument that decisions are rational calculations: "At almost every major turning point the men who made the crucial decisions were strongly affected by essentially emotional, non-rational phenomena." Perceived threat is the critical element and overrides rational calculation: "Perceptions of one's own inferior capability, if anxiety, fear, or perceptions of threat or injury are intense enough, will fail to deter a nation from going to war." In short, there is a "typical chain of events" or "conflict spiral" which seems to operate in crises (North, 1969).

It is on this crisis mechanism that North, Holsti, and others concentrate their attention. The operative problem becomes the measurement and the relationship of variables which may affect the process. Consequently data on the "conflict spiral" has been collected by North, Brody, and Holsti (1964). Perceptions of hostility have been related to capability and behavior (Zinnes, North, and Koch, 1961; Zinnes, 1968). Holsti (1963) has sought to devise measurements for international tension. The effects of a crisis on decision-makers' perceptions of time, alternatives, and communication have been examined by Holsti (1965, 1972). The ultimate objective is isolation of critical factors which will facilitate control or "crisis management." The model for a properly managed crisis—i.e., one which does not eventuate in war—is the Cuban Missile Crisis of 1962. When compared with 1914, the critical characteristics of the 1962 crisis seem to have been greater negotiating time, preservation of alternatives, and better communication (Holsti, *et al.,* 1969; Holsti, 1972). In short, war occurred in 1914 because the crisis was mismanaged by the statesmen but was avoided in 1962 because the crisis was well-managed.

The ultimate form of situation analysis is simulation and gaming. In a structured laboratory situation the variables which are assumed to be critical are tested against the actual historical results. At least two very interesting experiments of this type have been done on the 1914 crisis. Kessler and de Sola Pool (1969) sought to simulate information processing during a crisis in order to understand the process of deterrence. They explored how much of the behavior of political decision-makers in a crisis could be explained by psychological mechanisms. They concluded that the differing perceptions of statesmen (the tsar and the kaiser) were due primarily to information processing during the crisis. It is not clear from the experiment to what extent the differences are due to personalities as compared with the roles individuals play and the perspectives these roles imply (e.g., national interest).

Another fascinating example of this type of experiment is the attempt by Hermann and Hermann (1969) to simulate the outbreak of World War I. Their main variables are the personalities of the major decision-makers, background information, and communication during the crisis. Although small divergences occur, the simulation approximates historical reality quite closely in terms of general result (war) and patterns of communication (within and between alliances). The Hermanns attribute some of the divergences primarily to personality mismatching between players and actual crisis participants, and thus conclude that personality is an important consideration in a crisis. In a later statement Hermann (1971) speculates that "personality characteristics may have more effect on policy in times of crisis when compared to noncrisis. . . . In crises, . . . much of the bureaucratic apparatus falls away in the decision process and . . . the values and personality dispositions of strong leaders are much more likely to be manifest in the decisions." Nonetheless he agrees that "there were important determinants for example in the 1914 situation which constrained choice—or at least, led individuals to perceive their choices to be limited."

The importance of personality characteristics in a crisis is clearly an important and complex question which warrants a good deal more intensive work. My own view would differ from Hermann's and would conform with that of Russett (1967), who allows for the possibility that personality affects crises, but doubts that possibility, and believes that roles are a more important consideration. As for the simulation and gaming experiments, they appear to me to be a very exciting and potentially profitable effort to test propositions derived by studying history. In a very primitive and intuitive way the case study which follows is an attempt to apply a kind of simulation of the hypothetical options which are then tested against what I regard as the historical choices—i.e., those which the statesmen actually made. My basic assumption is that the decision-makers were in a sense "programmed" for the crisis and war by their conception of the state system, national goals, and their proper roles as statesmen. However this sort of assumption could be tested rigorously only in a simulation like the ones discussed above.

Situation analysis can be evaluated on the levels of accuracy, assumptions, and interpretation. Though some of the details can be questioned, the accuracy of most of the data produced by this analysis seems to me to be quite high. Likewise its assumptions about the relative importance and procedures for measurement of variables are by and large persuasive. Assumptions about correlations between variables are clearly more speculative and thus open to criticism (see, for instance, the criticism of North, Brody, and Holsti, 1964). There is of course even greater room for difference of opinion on matters of interpretation. There are commonsense correlations—as between hostility and mobilization, perceived, and expressed hostility, etc.—which may be usefully demonstrated more specifically. Yet the question remains as to whether these correlations constitute causality. Does hostility cause mobilization? Does stress cause hostile actions? Or are these features of crisis behavior the manifestation of previous attitudes and decisions? As North's critique suggests, hostility and mobilization "may—at least in some cases—be only the outer shell of the real motives and calculations entering into the actual war-making decisions." In short the problem boils down to the question: Is crisis behavior the cause or the symptom of a phenomenon whose causes lie in the precrisis period? My own view is that the crisis is best interpreted as the result of precrisis causes. This does not mean that the crisis is unimportant. On the contrary, as in pathology, it is useful to trace the course of the disease as well as to seek its causes.

System Analysis.   The general alternative to situation analysis is system analysis. The two approaches imply fundamental differences for the perception of crises. Whereas situation analysis assumes that crisis behavior is due largely to crisis conditions, system analysis assumes that crisis behavior is largely attributable to precrisis conditions. For the first, crises are the cause; for the second, they are the effect. It is impossible to do justice here to the literature on system analysis (any more than it is to situation analysis), but, as examples, two studies by one researcher may serve to suggest its thrust. Through the work of Morton Deutsch (1961, 1969) runs the theme that conflicts will recur as long as the existing system persists. He sees the central problem as the resolution of conflict in a productive rather than a destructive way. The key to productive resolution of conflict is "mutual trust, . . . mutual interests, and mutual respect." This mutuality requires agreement that each party has a stake in the other's welfare. It can be fostered by "conditions of normative order," which should be created by improving communication and establishing common rules and values. In short, productive conflict resolution assumes a cooperative rather than a competitive system. The 1914 system was, however, a competitive system. It was characterized by the conditions of destructive conflict, the tendency to expand and to escalate often independent of the specific cause. In existence were the impulses to such escalation and expansion—a competitive process, misperception and biases, and a process of commitment to the conflict. Thus the system of 1914 was predisposed to destructive conflict.

Expressed in greater detail elsewhere (Farrar, 1971), my own view is in general agreement with Deutsch. The state system of 1914 was competitive. The preservation and expansion of state power was the fundamental operating assumption of statesmen and probably of most citizens. This principle was best symbolized in the self-stylization of the various governments as "the great powers." The decision between war and peace was made on the basis of state interest; a state's interest could not be sacrificed for the general good of peace. The great powers had committed themselves by 1914 to policies which were incompatible if tested. In 1914 they were tested. Thus I would argue that war occurred less because of specific crisis behavior than because of general assumptions and operating principles at work in the great-power system.

Conceptualization of the 1914 Crisis

The interpretation which follows analyzes decisions made during the stages of the crisis. The crisis is herein separated into two general phases, designated as the Austro-Serbian Stage (June 28–July 22) and the European Stage (July 23–August 4). The crisis is divided at July 23—i.e., with the Austro-Hungarian ultimatum to Serbia—because it is seen to mark the point at which generally secret diplomatic preparations end and generally public diplomatic action begins. Clearly the crisis can be divided at other points. For example Holsti (1970) divided the crisis at July 28 because of increased tension and loss of control. The stages can also be further subdivided. For the present analysis, however, the preparation-action division seems most useful since the behavior during the action phase seems to follow from the decisions made in the preparation stage.

The behavior of statesmen during the crisis is treated in essentially decision-making terms. Within each main stage, the crucial events are identified, the issues implied for each participant are indicated, the hypothetical options suggested, and the actual choices explained. The choices are explained largely in policy terms, i.e., calculations of costs and benefits and of probabilities, rather than in terms of crisis circumstances (stress, anxiety, etc.). These decisions are summarized in Tables 1 and 2 near the beginning of each section discussing one stage of the crisis.

The Austro-Serbian Stage, June 28–July 22

The assassination of Archduke Francis Ferdinand on June 28, 1914, inaugurated what the Kaiser had presciently predicted would be "the third chapter of the Balkan war in which we shall all become involved" (Fischer, 1964, 57–58). The assassination forced Austria-Hungary and Serbia into direct confrontation for the first time. The Austro-Serbian crises of the previous eighteen months had proven false beginnings for several reasons. Vienna had not yet become entirely convinced that its existence depended on crushing Serbia. Serbian nationalism had touched the monarchy only indirectly in Albania and in the Balkans in general. The previous crises had remained under the control of the two governments. However subsequent events culminating in the assassination had altered the situation. Vienna had become increasingly desperate because of the development of the Balkan situation in general. The assassination seemed to prove that Serbian nationalism was a direct—rather than an indirect—threat to the monarchy. It also seemed to demonstrate that relations between the two countries could not be controlled by their governments. In short, the situation had become both more desperate and less containable.

The motives of the assassins and of secret Serbian national societies were probably complex. They may have feared that Austria-Hungary would preserve Albania, establish an anti-Serbian Balkan league, or even resolve the South Slav problem within the monarchy. Conversely they may have been more anxious to activate the moderates in their own government than to anticipate the militants in Vienna. It is equally possible that their thinking was vague but dominated by the anarchist conviction that violence of any kind would serve the cause of Serbian nationalism in some unforeseeable way. The very nature of such secret organizations makes it unlikely that their motives will ever be known precisely. However their motives are less important than their actions which forced Belgrade and Vienna to confront their irreconcilable objectives.

The ultimate objectives more than the conscious policies of Belgrade and Vienna made a conflict between them virtually unavoidable. Vienna sought unsuccessfully to prove official Serbian complicity. It was unlikely since the assassination faced Belgrade with the awkward choice between making amends or appearing aggressive. It was equally unlikely that the Serbian government could have prevented the assassination since the societies symbolized the national movement and were immensely difficult to control; these considerations made it hard for the Serbian government to move against the societies even after the assassination. The Serbian government therefore contributed in a negative way to the crisis by not preventing the assassination although it did not believe it could have done otherwise. The same may be said of the Austro-Hungarian government. It played a part in the assassination in the sense that Francis Ferdinand presented himself in Sarajevo as a target for assassination. However the preservation of the monarchy depended in part on its ability to demonstrate Habsburg authority in areas where it was jeopardized by Serbian nationalism. Both Vienna and Belgrade had done what seemed necessary. But what would preserve Austria-Hungary as a great power would provoke Serbian nationalism, and what would satisfy Serbian nationalism would threaten Austria-Hungary as a great power. Thus coexistence seemed virtually impossible and conflict almost inevitable.

The assassination forced Vienna to make a fundamental choice. Hypothetically it had the options of reform, renunciation, and reprisal (see Table 1, Section A). Vienna might have sought to nullify the threat of Serbian nationalism by pacifying the South Slavs inside the monarchy with domestic reform. However reform was not a practical means of preserving the monarchy since the ruling minorities—particularly the Magyars—probably would have seceded rather than renounce their privileges. Alternatively Vienna might have sought to preserve the existence of the monarchy by renouncing its great-power status and becoming a mandate of the other great powers. This decision was never seriously contemplated since Austria-Hungary—like any state—would consider becoming a mandate only when it had already ceased to be a power and the only alternative was dissolution. Consequently the only option was to remove the threat of Serbian nationalism by reprisal.

This logic seemed to confirm a program which had already been devised in Vienna before the assassination provided the pretext for its implementation. This program reiterated more strongly than ever the Viennese argument for establishing a Balkan league under Austro-Hungarian control and at Serbian expense by the conclusion of an alliance with Bulgaria and the improvement of relations with Romania and Greece. The syndrome of anxiety and arrogance which had become increasingly characteristic of Austro-Hungarian thinking was expressed in the polarization of alternatives: either the monarchy would be preserved by reconstruction and domination of the Balkans or it would collapse. Austro-Hungarian leaders argued for implementation of the program with circular logic. It would succeed if Russia renounced the Balkans. Russia would renounce the Balkans if it were not yet prepared to risk war or if Russian support for Serbia could be made to appear aggressive. The program would fail if Russia refused to renounce the Balkans, but Russian refusal would merely demonstrate that it was already determined to destroy Austria-Hungary. Since Austro-Hungarian chances

TABLE 1 Critical Events, Issues, Alternatives, and Choices in the Austro-Serbian Stage of the Crisis (June 28–July 22)

Section	Dates	Government	Event	Issue	Alternatives and Choice*
A	June 28–July 5	Austria-Hungary	Assassination of Francis Ferdinand	Austro-Hungarian policy toward Serbia and self-preservation	(a) Reform of Austria-Hungary (b) Renunciation of Austro-Hungarian great-power status and appeal to other powers (c) *Reprisal against Serbia*
B	July 5	Germany	Austro-Hungarian request for support	Austro-German alliance	(a) Refusal of support to Austria-Hungary (b) Restraint of Austria-Hungary (c) *Reassurance of unqualified support for Austria-Hungary*
C	July 5–22	Germany	Austro-Hungarian response to assassination	Preserve Austria-Hungary and diplomatic victory for Germany and Austria-Hungary	(a) Open involvement (b) *Covert involvement* (c) Noninvolvement
D	July 5–22	Austria-Hungary	Austro-Hungarian response to the assassination	Preparation for military reprisal against Serbia	(a) *Unacceptable ultimatum, then attack* (b) Attack without ultimatum

	Date	Country	Interest	Alternatives
E	June 28–July 22	Russia	Russian influence in the Balkans	(a) Refuse support to Serbia (b) Reassure Serbia of unqualified support (c) *Restrained support of Serbia*
F	June 28–July 22	France	Franco-Russian alliance	(a) Refuse support to Russia (b) *Reassure Russia of unqualified support* (c) Restrain Russia
G	June 28–July 22	France	Franco-Russian alliance	(a) Refuse support to Serbia (b) Reassure Serbia of unqualified support (c) *Restrained support to Serbia*
H	June 28–July 22	Britain	Status quo, balance of power, and thus peace	(a) Refuse support to France (b) Reassure France of unqualified support (c) Restrain other powers (d) Mediation (e) *Inaction and avoid choice*

*The alternative in italics was the actual choice made.

for survival would diminish with time, an immediate confrontation with Russia was preferable to postponement. Thus either eventuality argued for implementation of the Austro-Hungarian program.

Austro-Hungarian policy is generally criticized but this criticism is misleading. Berchtold is almost universally stigmatized for seeking to preserve a doomed empire at the risk of a European war. Although espoused by pacifists and apologists for the other powers, this criticism could have little relevance for Austro-Hungarian statesmen. It was their duty to preserve Austria-Hungary, not peace. Since they perceived that Austria-Hungary was doomed unless war was risked, it was their responsibility to risk war. This criticism, directed at Berchtold personally, implies that other Austro-Hungarian statesmen might have acted differently. Although hypothetically possible, it is unlikely; indeed it is more likely that Berchtold postponed rather than precipitated the use of force. Most leading Austro-Hungarian statesmen regarded war with Serbia as necessary even though they recognized that it would probably cause a European war. After initial opposition to the use of force, even Tisza concluded that "we could not do otherwise." Consequently, if Berchtold is criticized, his Austro-Hungarian colleagues must share the responsibility for risking war to preserve their state. However all great-power statesmen did the same and must therefore share the criticism. In fact if in contrast to Austria-Hungary the other powers were viable in peace but vulnerable in war, their statesmen must be criticized even more than the statesmen in Vienna. Thus it is inconsistent to criticize Austro-Hungarian policy because it risked war if the European system presupposed that a great power would defend its existence by risking war. In this sense Austro-Hungarian policy was determined by circumstances.

Since Austro-Hungarian domination over Serbia seemed to require Russian renunciation of Serbia which seemed to require German support for Austria-Hungary, Austro-Hungarian domination over Serbia seemed to depend on German support. The Austro-Hungarian request for support confronted German leaders with three hypothetical choices (see Table 1, Section B). They could refuse, restrain, or respond. German policy on the eve of war had shifted among these three courses and could be explained in large measure as an effort to maintain both peace and the alliance with Austria-Hungary, but the Austro-Hungarian request for support necessitated a German choice between maintaining the alliance or the peace. If Germany refused or restrained Vienna in order to preserve peace, it risked Austro-Hungarian dissolution or defection to the Entente and thus the destruction of the alliance. Conversely if it supported Vienna to preserve the alliance, it risked war. In fact the alliance was jeopardized over the long run even if Berlin supported Vienna's efforts to resolve the dispute with Serbia. The alliance assumed Austro-Hungarian dependence on Germany in the Balkans, particularly with regard to the Austro-Serbian problem. If the Austro-Serbian problem were resolved, as implied by Vienna's request for support, Austria-Hungary would need Germany less and probably pursue a more independent policy. Likewise if Germany no longer supported Austria-Hungary in the Serbian question, Berlin might seek better relations with Russia. Better Russo-German relations would affect the Franco-Russian alliance. Thus the Austro-Serbian dispute was one of the foundation stones not only of the Austro-German alliance but of the whole alliance system. The Germans were therefore faced with an awkward choice between two evils: On the one hand rapid Austro-Hungarian dissolution or defection if they refused or restrained

Vienna; on the other, subsequent Austro-Hungarian defection if they supported Vienna.

Berlin's response was determined by its evaluation of the alliance. German great-power status depended in part on Austria-Hungary as a diversion for Russia if war occurred. If war were not perceived as imminent, Germany could refuse or restrain Austria-Hungary in order to preserve peace and seek an alternative to the alliance. Indeed some German diplomats favored the latter course early in the July crisis. If war were perceived as inevitable or even imminent, Germany could not risk the alliance. In the spring of 1914 war seemed increasingly imminent to German leaders, primarily because of Franco-Russian military preparations. At the same time the likelihood of Austro-Hungarian diversion from the Russian front or even dissolution of the monarchy seemed to increase because of problems with Romania and Italy. The assassination seems to have persuaded German leaders not only that an Austro-Serbian *modus vivendi* was impractical but also that the Serbian threat to Austria-Hungary would increase. In short the prospect of Austro-Hungarian dependability decreased as the prospect of war increased. Restraining Vienna would only postpone war until a less advantageous juncture when Austria-Hungary was weaker and the Franco-Russian alliance was stronger. Thus German leaders decided that it was necessary to support Vienna.

German support for Vienna implied the eventualities of a German diplomatic victory or immediate war. German leaders hoped several considerations would make a diplomatic victory possible. Russia might not support Serbia, either because Russian military preparations were not completed or because the Tsar might refuse to condone regicide. Even if Russia wanted to support Serbia, France might restrain Russia or at least refuse to support it. Britain might restrain the Franco-Russian alliance or at least refuse to support it. Such eventualities would constitute a German diplomatic victory since they would allow Germany to preserve Austria-Hungary and thus the alliance. They might even shatter the enemy alliance. However German leaders recognized and assumed the risk of war, for they were aware from the beginning of the crisis that Austria-Hungary planned to attack Serbia, that Russia was unlikely to sacrifice Serbia, that France would probably support Russia, and that Britain might join France. Berlin anticipated this eventuality with circular logic like that used in Vienna. If war did not come in 1914, it was inevitable by 1917. War was preferable in 1914 because Austria-Hungary was stronger and Franco-Russian preparations incomplete. Furthermore British intervention seemed less certain in 1914 than in 1917 if the Anglo-Russian naval negotiations during the spring of 1914 were an accurate indication of British intentions. Thus either eventuality which could follow from supporting Vienna seemed preferable to the alternative.

German leaders made their decision to support Vienna with even less serious consultation or dissent than their counterparts in Vienna. This has usually been interpreted as proof either of German stupidity or aggressiveness, but it can also be viewed as an indication that German leaders perceived no alternative. Their alternatives had seemed to polarize. On the one hand, restraint of Austria-Hungary seemed to imply its dissolution, thus weakening the Austro-German alliance and constituting a threat to German great-power status; on the other hand, support of Austria-Hungary seemed to imply its revival, thus strengthening of the Austro-German alliance and preserving or even extending German great-power status. Like their Austro-Hungarian counterparts, German leaders were motivated both by anxiety and by arrogance. This mentality insured that they would perceive no alternative compatible with their view of German interests. Indeed granted their assumptions about German interests and the existing situation, there was none. It would therefore have been both illogical and irresponsible for them to jeopardize German power in order to preserve peace. In this sense, their decision was determined by circumstances.

Having decided to support Vienna, the Germans were next confronted with the question of how. Here again they had three hypothetical choices: open involvement, covert involvement, or noninvolvement (see Table 1, Section C). Between its assurance of support to Vienna (on July 5) and the presentation of the Austro-Hungarian ultimatum to Serbia (on July 23), the Germans sought to create conditions conducive to diplomacy or, failing that, military success by supporting Austria-Hungary and confronting Russia with a diplomatic defeat. If Russia were forced to accept diplomatic defeat, the Franco-Russian alliance might be threatened and its ability to conduct war in 1917 jeopardized. Alternatively if Russia refused to accept diplomatic defeat and opted instead for war, it might improve the chances for German military success in 1914 by alienating Britain and thus forcing the Franco-Russian alliance to fight without British assistance. Consequently far from moderating Austro-Hungarian policy toward Serbia, Berlin urged Vienna to present Europe with a *fait accompli*. By doing so Vienna would not only confront Russia with a diplomatic defeat but would also deter mediatory proposals which could preclude both Austro-Hungarian revival and an Austro-German diplomatic victory. Meanwhile Berlin pursued these objectives with its own policy of localization which was based on the assertion that the Serbian question was a strictly Austro-Hungarian (i.e., local) rather than European problem. To buttress this assertion and avoid alarming the Franco-Russian alliance into warning Austria-Hungary or Britain into proposing mediation, Berlin claimed ignorance of Austro-Hungarian intentions and assumed an air of studied calm. However Berlin also made it clear that the alternative to localization was war, in order to deter Franco-Russian resistance or to make it look like aggression, and thus alienate Britain. Thus Germany opted for covert involvement and pursued the dual policy of encouragement in Vienna but localization elsewhere.

Vienna moved slowly however. Although Austro-Hungarian leaders were agreed on the aim of a reprisal against Serbia, they were not agreed on the means. They had two basic alternatives: attack with or without diplomatic preparation (see Table 1, Section D). Since other powers—particularly Russia—were unlikely to perceive the assassination as sufficient justification for destroying Serbian independence, Tisza persuaded his colleagues to present Serbia with an ultimatum designed to justify crushing Serbia by making Serbia assume the onus of provocation. This procedure trapped Vienna in a vicious cycle however. Vienna could perhaps justify its destruction of Serbia as far as the other powers were concerned if Serbia rejected an Austro-Hungarian ultimatum, but not if it accepted the ultimatum. Vienna could insure rejection only if it posed unacceptable conditions (which it sought to do). However Austro-Hungarian reprisal would not seem justified by rejection of unacceptable conditions but only of acceptable conditions. In short, Serbia had to commit suicide to justify its murder by Austria-Hungary. Vienna's ultimatum policy was however not only unlikely to succeed but also involved risks for the monarchy. If Serbia accepted the ultimatum, Austria-Hungary would have to choose between the ultimatum and war. If Vienna abided by the ultimatum, it imposed conditions on itself as much as on Serbia. Conversely if Vienna attacked despite Serbian acceptance, it would appear even more aggressive than if it had attacked Serbia without the ultimatum. Thus although Berlin repeatedly urged haste to insure success, Vienna's delay in formulating the ultimatum probably did not affect its success. In the final analysis Austro-Hungarian policy could not escape its contradictions.

The assassination forced Russian leaders to confront fundamental issues. Like Berlin when asked for support by Vienna, St. Petersburg had the three hypothetical choices of renouncing, reassuring, or restraining Serbia (see Table 1, Section E). Theoretically it was possible that Russia would renounce Serbia, but Russian great-power status assumed the protection of its interests, including its influence in the Balkans which depended in turn on its patronage of Serbia. Thus Serbia depended on Russia which added to the Austro-Serbian tension. Because Russian great-power status depended in part on its support of Serbia, renouncing Serbia was not a viable option. Likewise it was hypothetically possible that Russia could reassure Serbia of its unqualified support, as Berlin had done for Vienna. However Russian protection of Serbia against Austria-Hungary depended in turn on deterring German support for Austria-Hungary, which was possible by winning French support, and perhaps British support. It was advantageous to avoid alienating Britain by appearing provocative because of unqualified Russian support to Serbia. Consequently unqualified Russian support for Serbia was not practical. Since only restrained support remained, Russia urged Serbia to accept all Austro-Hungarian demands compatible with its independence. This sole recourse in fact served Russian interests by perpetuating Austro-Serbian tension which was a precondition of Russian great-power status. Nonetheless Russian policy was determined by circumstances, in the sense that Russian leaders perceived no viable alternative.

French leaders had the analogous hypothetical choice among the options of refusing, reassuring, or restraining Russia (see Table 1, Section F). It was theoretically possible for them to refuse to support or restrain Russia, but French great-power status necessitated the alliance with Russia. The alliance assumed Russian dependence on France, which resulted in Russo-German tension and added to Austro-Serbian tension. Consequently a French refusal to support or to restrain Russia was not a valid option. Therefore Paris reassured St. Petersburg of its unqualified support, as Berlin had done for Vienna. Hypothetically France had the same options with Serbia (see Table 1, Section G) but consideration of Britain's reaction precluded such an option—as it did for Russia—and France instead endorsed Russian restraint of Serbia. As in the case of Russia, this sole recourse in fact served French interests by perpetuating Austro-Serbian tension which was a precondition of French great-power status. Nonetheless French policy was determined by circumstances, in the sense that no viable alternative was perceived by French leaders. Thus all the continental powers had committed themselves to policies which had been dictated by events.

Only the British remained uncommitted. Unlike the continental powers, Britain had not yet been forced to make a choice among the options of refusal, reassurance, or restraint (see Table 1, Section H). On the contrary, British interests seemed best served by avoiding this choice as long as possible. British great-power status depended on preserving both its colonial hegemony and the continental balance of power. Both

TABLE 2 Critical Events, Issues, Alternatives, and Choices in the European Stage of the Crisis (July 23–August 4)

Section	Dates	Government	Event	Issue	Alternatives and Choice*
A	July 23–25	Serbia	Austro-Hungarian ultimatum	Serbian reply to the ultimatum	(a) Rejection (b) Submission (c) *Humiliation, i.e., qualified acceptance*
B	July 25–26	Russia, France, and Britain	Serbian reply to the ultimatum	Conflict between Austria-Hungary and Serbia	(a) Reject Serbian reply (b) *Accept Serbian reply*
C	July 25	Austria-Hungary	Serbian reply to the ultimatum	Conflict with Serbia	(a) Accept Serbian reply (b) *Reject Serbian reply*
D	July 25–31	Germany	Austro-Hungarian rejection of Serbian reply	Austro-German alliance	(a) Restrain Austria-Hungary (b) *Reassure Austria-Hungary of German support*
E	July 25	Russia	Austro-Hungarian rejection of Serbian reply	Russian influence in the Balkans	(a) *Support Serbia* (b) Restrain Serbia (c) Renounce Serbia
F	July 28	Russia	Austro-Hungarian declaration of war on Serbia	Russian influence in the Balkans	(a) Submission, or renounce Serbia (b) Continued warnings (c) *Military threat*
G	July 28–31	Germany	Russian mobilization	Austro-German alliance	(a) Submission (b) *Support Austria-Hungary and military counter-threat against Russia*

H	July 31	Germany	Russian mobilization	French support for Russia	(a) *Military threat against France* (b) No military threat against France
I	July 31	France	German military threat against France	Franco-Russian alliance	(a) Submission (b) *Rejection*
J	July 31	Germany	French rejection of German threat	Austro-German alliance	(a) Revoke threats against France and Russia (b) *Implement threats*
K	July 23–August 4	Britain	Austro-Hungarian ultimatum, Serbian reply, etc.	Status quo, balance of power, and peace	(a) Inaction (b) *Mediation*
L	July 23–August 4	Germany, France, Russia, and Austria-Hungary	British mediation	Austro-German and Franco-Russian alliances	(a) Accept British mediation (b) *Reject British mediation*
M	August 4	Britain	German threat to France (and Belgium)	Franco-British alliance and balance of power	(a) Inaction (b) Renounce France, Belgium, and balance of power (c) *Military counter-threat to Germany*
N	August 4	Germany	British military threat	British entry against Germany	(a) Submission (b) *Rejection*

*The alternative in italics was the actual choice made.

purposes were suited by the existing alliance system. The Austro-German alliance served to perpetuate British colonial hegemony by tying down the Franco-Russian alliance in Europe, and the Franco-Russian alliance helped to preserve the European balance by checking Germany. It was therefore logical that Britain should endeavor to maintain the status quo by preserving peace. However it was also logical that the continental powers should seek to exploit for their own purposes this British interest in maintaining the status quo. Berlin hoped it could induce London to second the German policy of localization. The British reply, that localization could not succeed if it implied destruction of Serbian independence, was both realistic and also reflected British interests. Localization in the German sense would either resolve the Serbian problem, which was a precondition for the existing alliance system, or precipitate a European war. Meanwhile Paris and St. Petersburg hoped British interest in maintaining the status quo would induce London to restrain Berlin and Vienna. The British refused on the ground that it would thereby jeopardize the possibility of mediation. Instead the British urged a compromise which would preserve the Austro-Serbian problem and avoid the extremes of complete resolution or war, but the compromise-message failed to elicit response. In fact a compromise was impossible since resolution of the Austro-Serbian problem would threaten Russian great-power status and thus the Franco-Russian alliance, and nonresolution would threaten Austro-Hungarian great-power status and thus the Austro-German alliance. Consequently it seemed to London that peace and the status quo might best be preserved by British inaction, since the continental powers might remain cautious as long as Britain remained uncommitted. Thus rather than forcing a British commitment, circumstances forced Britain into noncommitment. However the logic worked both ways. If Britain could discourage the eruption of an Austro-Serbian crisis by not choosing sides, it could also avoid choosing sides only as long as the crisis did not erupt. A crisis was, however, implicit in the decisions already taken by the continental governments and would become explicit if all abided by these decisions.

The European Stage, July 23–August 4

The first, or Austro-Serbian, stage of the crisis reached its climax and the actual European crisis began with the delivery of the Austro-Hungarian ultimatum to Serbia on July 23. Measured in terms of published official documents per day of the crisis from June 28 to August 4, the diplomatic activity of the participant governments was between ten and fifteen times as intense after July 23 as before. The ultimatum implied that Vienna sought a diplomatic victory, under threat of military operations, which would presumably be forgone if the ultimatum were accepted. It confronted the Serbian government with three hypothetical choices: rejection, submission, or humiliation (see Table 2, Section A). Serbia could reject the ultimatum out of hand and thereby risk having to stand alone against Austria-Hungary. Or it could submit completely and thereby renounce its political independence to Austria-Hungary. Or it could win Russo-French support by accepting their advice to navigate between these extremes and to accept a diplomatic humiliation but preserve its independence. Although the Serbian government may have considered the extreme alternatives, it eventually opted for the middle road. In fact, this was the best of all possible choices for Serbia since it would either force Austria-Hungary to recognize Serbia's right to exist if Austria-Hungary accepted, or force Russia to defend Serbia if Austria-Hungary refused. The Entente powers and even the Kaiser reacted with relief to the Serbian reply since it seemed to facilitate the solution least unsatisfactory to the powers—i.e., at Serbian expense but without jeopardizing the balance of power (see Table 2, Section B). Thus as the crisis was about to explode, it seemed most likely to be defused by Serbia's action.

The Serbian answer hypothetically placed Vienna in the awkward situation of choosing between the alternatives of accepting or rejecting (see Table 2, Section C). The Serbs had refused to commit suicide by accepting the ultimatum unqualifiedly or to justify murder by rejecting the ultimatum. Vienna could now accept the Serbian reply and thus win a diplomatic victory at the price of renouncing military operations and recognizing Serbia's right to existence. Or Vienna could reject the Serbian answer and opt instead for military operations at the risk of triggering a European war. A diplomatic victory might have offered the advantages of establishing Austria-Hungary's right to limited intervention into Serbian affairs. It might even have included a European guarantee of Austro-Hungarian existence against Serbia in exchange for an equivalent Austro-Hungarian guarantee to Serbia. However such a diplomatic victory implied the disadvantage that Europe rather than Austria-Hungary would resolve the Serbian problem. Experience had taught Vienna to expect little satisfaction from the other powers. Above all a compromise solution assumed that Austro-Serbian coexistence was possible, whereas Austro-Hungarian statesmen assumed it was not. In short, the logic of early July still seemed to pertain in late July. Since they were determined to preserve the monarchy, the statesmen in Vienna perceived no choice but to reject the Serbian reply and solve the Serbian problem themselves, even at the risk of European war.

The Austro-Hungarian decision confronted the continental powers with the implications of their policies. The issue was now whether they would abide by their previous decisions at the risk of war or alter their decisions at the risk of their great-power status. Berlin was confronted with the hypothetical choice between restraining or reassuring Vienna (see Table 2, Section D). German leaders may have yielded briefly to the temptation of escaping this choice by finding a compromise solution, but a compromise solution necessitated a fundamental change of German policy which was never seriously considered. On the contrary Berlin encouraged Vienna to begin military operations quickly in order to force a Russian choice between diplomatic defeat and war (see Table 2, Section E). Berlin clarified this choice with its own localization argument that Russian intervention into the Austro-Serbian dispute would constitute aggression against Austria-Hungary. Confronted with this situation the Russians had three hypothetical options: submission, continued diplomatic warnings, or military threat (see Table 2, Section F). They did not seriously consider submission and had become convinced that further diplomatic warnings were pointless. They therefore sought to restructure the issue from the German contention of localization to Europeanization with the assertion that the Austro-Serbian problem was European, not strictly Austro-Hungarian. This formula would constitute diplomatic victory for Russia and diplomatic defeat for Austria-Hungary since it would institutionalize Serbian independence and thus Austro-Hungarian insecurity. Meanwhile Russia rejected a diplomatic defeat as implied in the Austro-Hungarian declaration of war on Serbia. Russian leaders demonstrated that they preferred war to diplomatic defeat by announcing mobilization first against Austria-Hungary and then against Germany. In short they presented Germany with the choice between diplomatic defeat and war. The Germans rejected the Russian threats and replied with their own threat of mobilization (see Table 2, Section G), but the German counter-threat was rejected in turn by the Russians. Thus threats of war had failed to make Serbia, Austria-Hungary, Russia, or Germany accept diplomatic defeat.

Diplomatic defeat might have been accepted only if a threat of war had been credible, but none could have been credible. Such a threat can be credible only if it implies immediate defeat. Immediate defeat assumes concentration of forces, but none of these powers concentrated against any of the others, because doing so would have contradicted basic strategic and diplomatic assumptions. Austria-Hungary did not concentrate its forces against Serbia because it assumed that it would be unnecessary if Russia renounced Serbia and impossible if Russia supported Serbia. Russia did not concentrate its forces against Austria-Hungary or Germany because it assumed that it would be necessary to fight both or neither. If it fought both, it preferred to divide its forces. Germany did not concentrate against Russia because it too assumed that it would have to fight both France and Russia or neither. If it fought both, it preferred to concentrate on France. Thus none of these threats succeeded because none was coordinated with basic strategic and diplomatic assumptions. They might have succeeded had these assumptions proven fallacious, but the threats were necessary only if the assumptions were valid. Thus the threats of war could have succeeded only if they had been unnecessary and failed when they were necessary. However the threats had to succeed if war were to be avoided, and so war could not be avoided by Austro-Hungarian, Russian, or German threats against one another.

War might have been avoided however, if France accepted diplomatic defeat, which it might have done had a German threat been credible—if it were threatened with immediate military defeat by Germany's concentrating forces against it. In fact German strategists did plan a concentration against France precisely because they believed it could be defeated quickly (whereas Russia could not) and because doing so corresponded with their basic strategic and diplomatic assumptions. German leaders assumed Germany would have to fight both Russia and France or neither, because Russia would opt for war only if supported by France. Thus French decisions rather than German threats would determine Russian policy. French decisions could be affected only by a German threat to France. It was therefore appropriate that this was the only threat German strategists prepared. It was also the only threat during the crisis which coordinated military strategy with diplomatic policy in the sense of confronting France with the possibility of immediate defeat (see Table 2, Section H). Like the previous threats it did not necessitate war, since it offered the French the alternative of diplomatic defeat. The French were consequently confronted with the choice between diplomatic defeat and war (see Table 2, Section I). The French rejection implied that the German threat was not credible. Perhaps no threat would have been credible if diplomatic defeat was not conceivable because a defeat required renouncing Russia and thus French great-power status. The French refusal confronted Germany with a hypothetical choice between diplomatic defeat and war (see Table 2, Section J). Berlin might have chosen diplomatic defeat if it had felt that the war could not be won or that the price of winning would be too high, i.e., if the long-run Franco-Russian threat had been credible. However, diplomatic defeat implied renunciation of Austria-Hungary and thus German great-power status. The Germans therefore opted for war instead of diplomatic defeat. The French and German decisions demonstrated that no military threat was sufficiently credible to make the continental powers accept a diplomatic defeat which implied loss of great-power status. War was avoidable only if diplomatic defeat was acceptable because the threat of war was credible. Thus war was unavoidable.

The only escape from this logic seemed to be British mediation. The Austro-Hungarian ultimatum to Serbia confronted Britain with the hypothetical alternatives of inaction or mediation (see Table 2, Section K). Since inaction implied genuine disinterest, it was not acceptable to the British. Mediation was therefore undertaken because it implied preservation of the status quo and thus Britain's pivotal position in the balance of power. Britain confronted the continental powers with the choice of accepting or rejecting mediation (see Table 2, Section L). British mediation could succeed only as long as the balance of power was accepted by all the powers. The powers would do so as long as they believed it was unnecessary to change it in order to preserve their great-power status. British mediation might therefore have succeeded before the assassination, but then it had seemed unnecessary and undesirable to the British. It seemed necessary only after the assassination, in fact only after the ultimatum. However the ultimatum indicated that the balance of power was no longer accepted by all the continental governments. Austria-Hungary and Germany had committed themselves to alter it by destroying Serbian independence in order to preserve their own great-power status. France and Russia had committed themselves to defend Serbian independence in order to preserve their great-power status. These two positions were irreconcilable and British mediation could have succeeded only if one side had been willing to accept diplomatic defeat. None would do so since each equated diplomatic defeat with loss of great-power status, and British mediation could therefore not have succeeded after the ultimatum, or even the assassination. Thus it was caught in a paradox; it could succeed when it seemed unnecessary and could not succeed when it did seem necessary. The fact that mediation was tried is frequently interpreted as proof that it was practical but that it failed because of British mistakes. This criticism is unjustifiable and misleading. British mediatory efforts were not a case of losing peace by mistake but of mistaken efforts to save peace when it was already lost.

Conclusions: The Limits of Choice

Each power did what seemed necessary to remain a power. All perceived a choice among diplomatic victory, diplomatic defeat, and war. All preferred diplomatic victory since it implied the rewards of war without the risks, but one power could win diplomatic victory only if another accepted diplomatic defeat. All rejected diplomatic defeat since it implied the price of military defeat without the possibility of victory. War at least implied the possibility of victory as well as defeat. Thus diplomatic victory was impossible because diplomatic defeat was inconceivable, whereas war was conceivable. Consequently when a choice seemed imperative, war became inevitable.

The interpretation suggested here has implications for our understanding of the

1914 crisis. Traditionally most historical studies of the crisis have presented it as the result of design, blunder, chance, or some combination. More recently social scientists have argued that it was the result of circumstantial factors (e.g., stress, hostility, etc.). Few studies have perceived the crisis as the logical result of rational policy considerations. This article has sought to fill this gap. Only by having all possible views of the crisis can we fully understand its complexity.

The present interpretation also has ramifications for the study of crises in general. No single crisis can provide a model for all crises, but it can provide a useful case study, and better understanding of individual cases can increase our knowledge of the general phenomenon. The 1914 crisis is a particularly interesting case because of its historical importance, the amount of information available, and the number of studies it has inspired. The best work done recently on the crisis by social scientists has concentrated on situation analysis. The interpretation herein focuses on decision-making, but follows from an analysis of the state system. Thus two other methodologies are applied to the problem of international crisis. All three—situation analysis, system analysis, and decision-making analysis—provide different but not necessarily unrelated ways of conceptualizing the problem. Until our understanding of the problem is far greater than it is at present, we cannot afford to neglect any approach which may provide new insights.

References

Abel, Theodore. The element of decision in the pattern of war, *American Sociological Review,* 1941, *6,* 853-59.

Deutsch, Morton. Some considerations relevant to national policy, *Journal of Social Issues,* 1961, *17,* 57-68.

———. Conflicts: productive and destructive, *Journal of Social Issues,* 1969, *25* (Jan.), 7-41.

Farrar, Lancelot L., Jr. Impotence of omnipotence: the paralysis of the European great power system, 1871-1914, *International Review of History and Political Science,* 1971, *8* (Nov.).

Fischer, Fritz. *Griff nach der Weltmacht: Die Kriegszeilpolitik des kaiserlichen Deutschland 1914/18.* Dusseldorf: Droste Verlag, 1964.

Hermann, Charles F. International crisis as a situational variable. In James N. Rosenau (ed.), *International Politics and Foreign Policy.* New York: Free Press, 1969, 409-421.

———. *Crises in Foreign Policy: A Simulation Analysis.* Indianapolis and New York: Bobbs-Merrill, 1969.

———. Letter to the author, 1971.

——— and Linda P. Brady. *International Crises: Insights from Behavioral Research.* New York: Free Press, 1972.

——— and Margaret G. Hermann. An attempt to simulate the outbreak of World War I. In James N. Rosenau (ed.), *International Politics and Foreign Policy.* New York: Free Press, 1969, 622-39.

Holsti, Ole R. The value of international tension measurement, *Journal of Conflict Resolution,* 1963, *7,* 608-17.

———. The 1914 case, *The American Political Science Review,* 1965, *60,* 365-78.

———. Individual differences in "definition of the situation," *Journal of Conflict Resolution,* 1970, *14,* (3, Sept.), 303-10.

——. *Crisis, Escalation and War*. Toronto: McGill-Queen's University Press, 1972.

——, Richard A. Brody, and Robert C. North. The management of international crisis: affect and action in American-Soviet relations, October 1962. In Richard C. Snyder and Dean Pruitt (eds.), *Theory and Research on the Causes of War*. Englewood Cliffs, N.J.: Prentice-Hall, 1969, 62-79.

Kessler, Allen, and Ithiel de Sola Pool. The kaiser, the tsar and the computer: information processing in a crisis. In James N. Rosenau (ed.), *International Politics and Foreign Policy*. New York: Free Press, 1969, 664-75.

North, Robert C. Perception and action in the 1914 crisis. *Journal of International Affairs*, 1967, *21*, 103-22.

——, Richard Brody, and Ole R. Holsti. Some empirical data on the conflict spiral, *Peace Research Society (International) Papers*, 1964, 1-56.

Remak, Joachim. *Sarajevo: The Story of a Political Murder*. London: Weidenfeld and Nicolson, 1959.

——. The healthy invalid: how doomed the Habsburg empire? *The Journal of Modern History*, 1969, *41* (June), 127-43.

——. 1914—the third Balkan war: origins reconsidered, *The Journal of Modern History*, 1971, *43* (Sept.), 353-66.

Russett, Bruce M. Cause, surprise, and no escape, *The Journal of Politics*, 1962, *24*, 3-22.

——. Pearl Harbor: deterrence theory and decision theory, *Journal of Peace Research*, 1967, *2*, 89-105.

Zinnes, Dina A. The expression and perception of hostility in prewar crisis: 1914. In J. David Singer (ed.), *Quantitative International Politics*. New York: Free Press, 1968, 85-119.

——, Robert C. North, and Howard E. Koch. Capability, threat, and the outbreak of war. In James N. Rosenau (ed.), *International Politics and Foreign Policy*. New York: Free Press, 1961, 469-82.

Suggested Readings

Hermann, Charles F., ed. *International Crises: Insights From Behavioral Research*. New York: Free Press, 1972.

Lafore, Laurence. *The Long Fuse: An Interpretation of the Origins of World War I*. Philadelphia: Lippincott, 1965.

Lockhart, Charles. *The Efficiency of Threats in International Interaction Strategies*. Beverly Hills, Calif.: Sage, 1973.

Schroeder, Paul. "World War I as Galloping Gertie." *Journal of Modern History* 44 (September, 1972), pp. 319–45.

H. Snyder, Glenn, and Paul Diesing. *Conflict Among Nations: Bargaining, Decision Making and System Structure in International Crises*. Princeton: Princeton University, 1977.

Tuchman, Barbara. *The Guns of August*. New York: Dell, 1971.

Reading 30

THE MANAGEMENT OF INTERNATIONAL CRISIS

Ole R. Holsti, Richard A. Brody and Robert C. North

Notes from the Editors

Ole R. Holsti, Richard A. Brody, and Robert C. North are three political scientists who worked together on a massive project at Stanford University on the causes of war, with emphasis on World War I. Their empirical approach involved the coding of diplomatic interaction during the 1914 crisis along a number of dimensions in order to see what sort of stimuli elicited what sort of responses from the chancellors and kaisers.

In the article reprinted here, they apply their approach to the Cuban Missile Crisis of 1962, a crisis that was resolved short of war, and compare their findings in that crisis to findings from the 1914 crisis. They wrote their article in 1965, well before much of the documentation relating to the Cuban Missile Crisis was released. Thus, they had to rely upon the published record of official statements. We now know much more about the crisis, including the fact that Kennedy did indeed promise to remove the famous missiles from Turkey in a quid pro quo, as long as the Russians never revealed his concession.

Nevertheless, enough of the American and Soviet diplomatic records were available to Holsti, Brody, and North to permit them to make some valuable generalizations about effective conflict-reducing strategies in a crisis. They highlight the apparent sensitivity shown by Kennedy for Khrushchev's political problems and domestic and international image, and contrast that to the relative insensitivity of decision makers who led their nations into war in the summer of 1914. Of course, critics argue that celebrating the "brilliant" crisis management of the Americans in 1962 in no way absolves the leaders for getting into a world-threatening nuclear crisis that they could and should have avoided in the first place.

In October, 1962, the first nuclear confrontation in history was precipitated by the establishment of Soviet missile sites in Cuba. For a period of approximately one week, the likelihood of a full-scale nuclear exchange between the United States and the Soviet Union was exceedingly high. Speaking of the events of the week of October 22, Attorney General Robert Kennedy recalled: "We all agreed in the end that if the Russians were ready to go to nuclear war over Cuba, they were ready to go to nuclear war, and that was that. So we might as well have the showdown then as six months later."

An examination of the events immediately surrounding the crisis, analyzed in

Reprinted by permission of the authors from Ole R. Holsti, Richard A. Brody, and Robert C. North, "The Management of International Crisis: Affect and Action in American-Soviet Relations," ed. Dean G. Pruitt and Richard C. Snyder, *Theory and Research on the Causes of War* (Englewood Cliffs, N.J.: Prentice Hall, 1969), pp. 62–79.

four rather distinct periods, offers a clear-cut case history of conflict that escalated to the brink of war—and then deescalated. This pattern can be contrasted with the crisis during the summer of 1914 which spiraled into a world war.

During the 1962 pre-crisis period President Kennedy had been under considerable domestic pressure to take action against Cuba. In addition to attacks on Administration policy by Senators Capehart, Bush, Goldwater, and Keating, the Republican Senatorial and Congressional campaign committees had announced that Cuba would be the "dominant issue of the 1962 campaign." Public opinion polls revealed an increasing impatience with American policy toward Communist influence in the Caribbean. When the President arrived in Chicago on a campaign tour in mid-October, one "welcoming" sign said: "Less Profile—More Courage."

There had been a number of rumors regarding the emplacement of Soviet missiles and troops in Cuba, but "hard" evidence was lacking; those most critical of Administration policy were not, in fact, willing to reveal their sources of information. Although Cuba had been under surveillance for some time, the first active phase of the crisis, from October 14 to October 21, began with the development of photographic evidence that Soviet missiles had indeed been located in Cuba. It was during this period that—according to President Kennedy—"15 people, more or less, who were directly consulted" developed "a general consensus" regarding the major decision to invoke a limited blockade. Unfortunately for the purposes of this analysis, there are no publicly available documents written by either Soviet or American decision-makers for the period.

The second and third periods—October 22–25 and October 26–31 respectively— might be described as the "period of greatest danger of escalation" and the "bargaining period." The present paper is primarily confined to this time span, and is not concerned with the final period, during which the agreement reached between President Kennedy and Premier Khrushchev were assertedly carried out and in which further questions regarding verification were raised.

The period of most acute danger of escalation began with President Kennedy's address to the nation on October 22. The President announced:

Within the past week unmistakable evidence has established the fact that a series of offensive missile sites is now in preparation on that imprisoned island. The purpose of these bases can be none other than to provide a nuclear strike capability against the Western Hemisphere.

Additional sites not yet completed appear to be designed for intermediate-range ballistic missiles capable . . . of striking most of the major cities in the Western Hemisphere.

This urgent transformation of Cuba into an important strategic base—by the presence of these large, long-range, and clearly offensive weapons of mass destruction—constitutes an explicit threat to the peace and security of all the Americas.

The United States would, according to the President: (1) impose a "strict quarantine" around Cuba to halt the offensive Soviet build-up; (2) continue and increase the close surveillance of Cuba; (3) answer any nuclear missile attack launched from Cuba against any nation in the Western Hemisphere with "a full retaliatory response upon the Soviet Union"; (4) reinforce the naval base at Guantanamo; (5) call for a meeting of the Organization of American States to invoke the Rio Treaty; and (6) call for an emergency meeting of the United Nations. At the same time he stated that additional military forces had been alerted for "any eventuality." James Reston reported "on highest authority" that,

Ships carrying additional offensive weapons to Cuba must either turn back or submit to search and seizure, or fight. If they try to run the blockade, a warning shot will be fired across their bows; if they still do not submit, they will be attacked.

In accordance with the Joint Congressional Resolution passed three weeks earlier, the President signed an executive order on October 23 mobilizing reserves.

In its initial response the Soviet government denied the offensive character of the weapons, condemned the quarantine as "piracy," and warned that Soviet ships would not honor it. It was also reported that Defense Minister Malinovsky had been instructed to postpone planned demobilization, to cancel furloughs, and to alert all troops. Although the issue was immediately brought before the United Nations and the Organization of American States, the events of October 22–25 pointed to a possibly violent showdown in the Atlantic, in Cuba, or perhaps in other areas of the world. President Kennedy apparently expected some form of retaliation in Berlin. In his October 22 address he specifically warned the Soviet Union against any such move: "Any hostile move anywhere in the world against the safety and freedom of people to whom we are committed—including in particular the brave people of West Berlin—will be met by whatever action is needed."

The quarantine went into effect at 10 A.M. Eastern Standard Time on October 24. At that time a fleet of 25 Soviet ships nearing Cuba was expected to test the American policy within hours. Statements from Moscow and Washington gave no immediate evidence that either side would retreat, although the Soviet Premier dispatched a letter to Bertrand Russell in which he called for a summit conference. The next day rumors of an American attack or invasion of Cuba were strengthened by the announcement by Representative Hale Boggs that, "if these missiles are not dismantled, the United States has the power to destroy them, and I assure you that this will be done." At the same time American intelligence sources revealed that work on the erection of missile sites was proceeding at full speed.

The first real break in the chain of events leading to an apparently imminent confrontation came on October 25 when twelve Soviet vessels turned back in mid-Atlantic. It was at this point that Secretary of State Dean Rusk remarked, "We're eyeball to eyeball, and I think the other fellow just blinked." Shortly thereafter the first Soviet ship to reach the patrol area—the tanker *Bucharest*—was allowed to proceed to Cuba without boarding and search.

By the following day the crisis appeared to be receding somewhat from its most dangerous level. The Soviet-chartered freighter, *Marucla* (ironically, a former American Liberty ship now under Lebanese registry), was searched without incident and, when no contraband was discovered, allowed to proceed to Cuba. In answer to an appeal from Secretary General U Thant, Soviet Premier Khrushchev had agreed to keep Soviet ships away from the patrol area for the time being. President Kennedy's reply to the Secretary General stated that he would try to avoid any direct confrontation at sea "in the next few days." At the same time, however, the White House issued a statement which said: "The development of ballistic missile sites in Cuba continues at a rapid pace. . . . The activity at these sites apparently is directed at achieving a full operational capability as soon as possible." The State Department added that "further action would be justified" if work on the missile sites continued. Photographic evidence revealed that such work was continuing at an increased rate and that the missile sites would be operational in five days.

The "bargaining phase" of the crisis opened later in the evening of October 26. A secret letter from Premier Khrushchev acknowledged the presence of Soviet missiles in Cuba for the first time. He is reported to have argued they were defensive in nature but that he understood the President's feeling about them. According to one source, "Never explicitly stated, but embedded in the letter was an offer to withdraw the offensive weapons under United Nations supervision in return for a guarantee that the United States would not invade Cuba." A second message from Premier Khrushchev, dispatched twelve hours later, proposed a trade of Soviet missiles in Cuba for NATO missile bases in Turkey; the United Nations Security Council was to verify fulfillment of both operations, contingent upon the approval of the Cuban and Turkish governments.

In his reply to Khrushchev's secret letter of Friday evening, the President all but ignored the later proposal to trade bases in Turkey for those in Cuba. At the Attorney General's suggestion, the President simply interpreted Premier Khrushchev's letter as a bid for an acceptable settlement—as if the message regarding bases in Turkey had never been received.

As I read your letter, the key elements of your proposal—which seems generally acceptable as I understand them—are as follows:

1) You would agree to remove these weapons systems from Cuba under appropriate United Nations observation and supervision; and undertake, with suitable safeguards, to halt the further introduction of such weapons systems into Cuba.

2) We, on our part, would agree—upon the establishment of adequate arrangement through the United Nations to ensure the carrying out and continuation of these commitments—(a) to remove promptly the quarantine measures now in effect and (b) to give assurance against an invasion of Cuba.

He added, however, that

. . . the first ingredient, let me emphasize, . . . is the cessation of work on missile sites in Cuba and measures to render such weapons inoperable, under effective international guarantees. The continuation of this threat, or a prolonging of this discussion concerning Cuba by linking these problems to the broader questions of European and world security, would surely lead to an intensification of the Cuban crisis and a grave risk to the peace of the world.

In responding to Khrushchev's proposal to trade missile bases in Turkey for those in Cuba, a White House statement rejected that offer: "Several inconsistent and conflicting proposals have been made by the U.S.S.R. within the last 24 hours, including the one just made public in Moscow . . . the first imperative must be to deal with this immediate threat, under which no sensible negotiation can proceed."

Despite the advent of negotiations the situation was still dangerous. On October 27 an American U-2 reconnaissance plane had been shot down over Cuba, and several other planes had been fired upon. The Defense Department warned that measures would be taken to "insure that such missions are effective and protected." At the same time it announced that twenty-four troop-carrier squadrons—14,000 men—were being recalled to active duty. The continued construction on the Cuban missile sites, which, it was believed, would become operational by the following Tuesday, was of even more concern than attacks on the U-2's. Theodore Sorensen, speaking of the events of October 27, said, "Obviously these developments could not be tolerated very long, and we were preparing for a meeting on Sunday [October 28] which would have been the most serious meeting ever to take place at the White House."

On the following morning [October 28], however, Radio Moscow stated that the Soviet Premier would shortly make an important announcement. The message was broadcast in the clear to shortcut the time required by normal channels of communication. Premier Khrushchev declared:

I regard with great understanding your concern and the concern of the United States people in connection with the fact that the weapons you describe as offensive are formidable indeed. . . . The Soviet Government, in addition to earlier instruction on the discontinuation of further work on weapons construction sites, has given a new order to dismantle the arms which you describe as offensive, and to crate and return them to the Soviet Union.

The statement made no reference to the withdrawal of American missiles from Turkey.

In reply, President Kennedy issued a statement welcoming Premier Khrushchev's "statesmanlike decision." He added that the Cuban blockade would be removed as soon as the United Nations had taken "necessary measures," and further, that the United States would not invade Cuba. Kennedy said that he attached great importance to a rapid settlement of the Cuban crisis, because "developments were approaching a point where events could have become unmanageable."

Although Khrushchev stated that the Soviet Union was prepared to reach an agreement on United Nations' verification of the dismantling operation in Cuba, Fidel Castro announced on the same day that Cuba would not accept the Kennedy-Khrushchev agreement unless the United States accepted further conditions, including the abandonment of the naval base at Guantanamo. But the critical phases of the Soviet-American confrontation seemed to be over. Despite the inability to carry out on-site inspection, photographic surveillance of Cuba confirmed the dismantling of the missile sites. The quarantine was lifted on November 21, at which time the Pentagon announced that the missiles had indeed left Cuba aboard Soviet ships.

What research questions does this sequence of events suggest? The crisis may be analyzed from several perspectives. From one point of view, it was a unique event, and not comparable to previous situations. In relation to either World War, the weapons systems of the adversaries were of incomparable magnitude. The nations, as well as their leaders, were different. Even the alerting and mobilizing of armed forces, which were so crucial to the escalation into war in the summer of 1914, resulted in a different outcome in October 1962. And certainly in its potential consequences, the Cuban crisis surpassed all previous cold war confrontations and, for that matter, any previous crisis in history. From this perspective the investigator may focus his attention on the unique characteristics of the situation.

The analyst of international relations may, on the other hand, examine the events of October 1962 in such a manner as to permit relevant comparisons with other crisis situations, both those resolved by war and those eventually resolved by non-violent

FIGURE 1   The Interaction Model

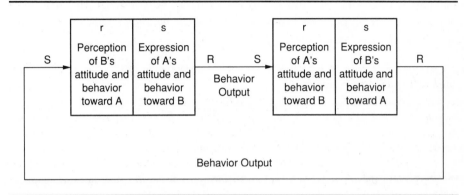

means. Are there, for example, consistent patterns of behavior that distinguish the situations which escalate into general war—as in 1914—from those in which the process of escalation is reversed?

A conceptual framework developed for such analysis is a two-step mediated stimulus-response model (S — r:s — R), in which the acts of one nation are considered as inputs to other nations. The nations are information-processing and decision-making units whose policies, in turn, can become inputs to other nations (Figure 1). The basic problem is this: given some action by nation B, what additional information is needed to account for nation A's foreign policy response?

Within the model, a stimulus (S) is an event in the environment which two or more decision-makers may perceive and evaluate differently. A stimulus may be a physical event or a verbal act, which elicits a response (R) from another nation. For example, during the early autumn of 1962, the Soviet Union began erecting launching sites for medium range ballistic missiles in Cuba (R). Regardless of the Soviet motives or intent behind this act, it served as an input or stimulus (S) to the United States, which responded by a series of steps, including the naval quarantine of Cuba (R).

In the model the perception (r) of the stimulus (S) within the national decision system corresponds to the "definition of the situation" in decision-making models. For example, the Soviet missile sites in Cuba (S) were perceived by President Kennedy as a threat to the security of the Americas (r). Finally, the "s" stage in the model represents the actor's expression of his own intentions, plans, actions or attitudes toward another actor, which becomes an action response (R) when carried out. Both "r" and "s" carry evaluative and affective loadings. Thus, irrespective of Russian intent, the Cuban missiles were perceived as a threat (r) by President Kennedy, who expressed American intent (s) to remove them from Cuba. This plan was put into effect by the quarantine (R), which then served as an input (S) to the Soviet decision-makers.

Operationally it would be much simpler, of course, to confine oneself to an analysis of actions (S and R) as do many classical formulations of international politics. In some situations the one nation's actions may be so unambiguous that there is little need to analyze perceptions in order to predict the response of the other state; consider, for example, the American response to the Japanese attack on Pearl Harbor. Unfortunately, as Kenneth Boulding and others have pointed out, it is less clear that positive actions will lead to reciprocation.

In any case, not all—or even most—foreign policy behavior is unambiguous. For political behavior, what is "real" is what men perceive to be real. Boulding has summarized this point succinctly:

We must recognize that the people whose decisions determine the policies and actions of nations do not respond to the "objective" facts of the situation, whatever that may mean, but to their "image" of the situation. It is what we think the world is like, not what it is really like, that determines our behavior.

At this point one might protest that well-trained statesmen will find little difficulty in interpreting the facts as they pertain to foreign policy. Yet one can cite example after example to the contrary. Consider, for example, the various interpretations— even among foreign policy professionals—which almost inevitably follow nearly every turn in Soviet policy. Such problems of interpretation are encountered at every point in the stream of decisions which constitute foreign policy, and *mis*perceptions may have behavioral consequences as "real" as more accurate perceptions do. Thus, since all decision-making is rooted in the perceptions of individuals, the model attempts to assess both objective and subjective factors. Other research has reinforced the belief that a model of interstate behavior must account for perceptual variables.

There have been serious doubts about the feasibility of quantifying perceptual and affective data, and the inclination, until recently, has been to emphasize "hard" variables and aggregate data.

As important as these objective data are, they may fail to take into sufficient account how human beings react. Moreover, objective data are usually compiled on an annual, quarterly, or monthly basis. While these indices may well be relied upon to reveal the trend toward an environment conducive to crisis—such as Europe in 1914 or the Cold War since 1945—they may prove less useful for the intensive study of a short time period. Thus it is particularly important for the investigator who seeks to analyze short term changes in the international system—such as the crisis situation— to incorporate subjective data into his model.

The premise that the analysis of political behavior is enriched by the incorporation of perceptual data poses special problems for the student of international relations. Clearly the standard methods of attitude measurement—the personal interview, the questionnaire, or the direct observation of decision-makers in action—can rarely be used by the social scientist who seeks to study human behavior at the international level. What he needs are instruments for measuring attitudes and actions "at a distance." This is perhaps the primary rationale for settling upon the content analysis of the messages of key decision-makers—those who have the power to commit the resources of state to the pursuit of policy goals at the international level—as an important research tool.

Source materials used for the analysis of perceptions (s and r in the model) consist of 15 United States and 10 Soviet documents, a total of nearly thirty thousand words, from the ten-day period opening on October 22—the day of President Kennedy's address on the Cuban crisis—and closing on October 31. After relevant decision-makers had been selected, *all publicly available documents,* rather than a sample, were used. For example, President Kennedy, Secretaries Rusk and McNamara, Ambassador Stevenson, and Attorney General Kennedy were selected as the key American decision-makers. *The entire verbatim text of every available document* authored by these five persons during the ten-day period was included. These documents were subjected to analysis by means of the General Inquirer system of automated content analysis via the IBM 7090 computer. This analysis provided day-by-day ratings of each party's perceptions and intentions for six variables: positive affect, negative affect, strength, weakness, activity, and passivity. In addition, the actions of each party were scaled on a dimension of degree of violence or potential violence. . . .

Looking at the action data alone, it is apparent that Soviet and American actions during the period are closely correlated; that is, the actions for both sides are most violent or potentially violent in the first three days, followed by a relatively steady decline through October 31. . . .

. . . There was a general tendency on the part of both Soviet and American decision-makers to perceive rather accurately the nature of each other's action, and then to respond in kind. . . .

. . . In each case October 25–26—previously identified as the point dividing two phases of the crisis—was the point at which mutual perceptions appeared to change. The rigidly negative-strong-active perceptions of the period of highest danger became somewhat modified at this point. Perceptions along the evaluative dimensions became more neutral and, in some cases, actually became positive. As one would expect, during the latter days of the crisis there was also an increase in perceptions of passivity. The potency dimension, on the other hand, remained predominantly on the strong side throughout the crisis period. . . . When compared with a similar analysis of the crisis which escalated into World War I, however, one interesting point emerges. In 1914, the leaders of the Dual Alliance (Germany and Austria-Hungary) consistently pursued policies with a higher level of violence or potential violence than did the members of the Triple Entente (England, France, and Russia). Over the crisis period as a whole, the actions of the Dual Alliance were significantly more violent. . . . A further analysis of the data disclosed that the only significant difference between the two alliances was in the S-r link; that is, between the actions of the other party and one's perceptions of them. German and Austro-Hungarian leaders consistently overperceived ($r > S$) the level of violence in the actions taken by members of the Triple Entente. British, French, and Russian leaders, on the other hand, underperceived ($S > r$) the level of violence of the actions of the Dual Alliance nations. The difference between the two coalitions in this respect was significantly different. . . . In terms of the $S - r : s - R$ model, this relationship between one coalition's actions (S), the other coalition's perceptions of those actions (r), and the resulting policies (R) was apparently the crucial one.

In the Cuban crisis, however, both sides tended to perceive rather accurately the nature of the adversary's actions and then proceeded to act at an "appropriate" level; that is, as the level of violence or potential violence in the adversary's actions diminished, perceptions of those actions increased in positive affect and decreased in negative affect, and the level of violence in the resulting policies also decreased. Thus, unlike the situation in 1914, efforts by either party to delay or reverse the escalation were generally perceived as such, and responded to in like manner. Whether the different patterns of action and perception found in the 1914 and Cuban cases will be found consistently to distinguish crises that escalate and de-escalate can only be determined, of course, through continuing research.

Having utilized the S − r:s − R III model to examine the pattern of Soviet and American interaction, it may be useful to attempt at least a partial explanation for the patterns with some comparisons with the 1914 crisis. Such an analysis will be concerned primarily with what might be called "styles of decision-making," and must of necessity be based on incomplete data. Although there are several accounts of the process by which American policy was formulated, such data with respect to the Soviet Union are much more fragmentary and inferential.

One major characteristic of Soviet policy during this period is clear. Unlike German leaders in 1914, Premier Khrushchev did not irrevocably tie his policy to that of a weaker—and perhaps less responsible—ally. The Cuban response to President Kennedy's address of October 22 was stronger and more unyielding than that of the Soviet Union. Premier Castro in fact ordered a general war mobilization *prior to* the delivery of the President's speech. The following day Premier Castro in effect left no room for either Cuba or the Soviet Union to maneuver: "Whoever tries to inspect Cuba must come in battle array! This is our final reply to illusions and proposals for carrying out inspections on our territory." Premier Khrushchev, on the other hand, like President Kennedy, almost immediately chose to interpret the crisis as one involving the United States and the Soviet Union alone. In his correspondence with President Kennedy during October 26–28, it is also apparent that the Soviet Premier was unwilling to let the intransigence of Dr. Castro stand in the way of a possible solution of the crisis. In his letter of October 28, in which Khrushchev offered to withdraw the missiles, there was, in fact, no acknowledgment of the necessity to obtain Cuban agreement on the terms of the settlement.

American decision-making in regard to the missiles in Cuba was characterized by a concern for action based on adequate information. The resistance of the Administration against action—despite public pressure—until photographic evidence of the missile sites was available, has already been noted. As late as Thursday, October 18, a series of alternatives was being considered pending more accurate information, and while the decision to institute a blockade was being hammered out, open discussion of the alternatives was encouraged. The President recalled that "though at the beginning there was a much sharper division . . . , this was very valuable, because the people involved had particular responsibilities of their own." Another participant in the decision-making at the highest level wrote: "President Kennedy, learning on his return from a mid-week trip in October, 1962, that the deliberation of the NSC [National Security Council] executive committee had been more spirited and frank in his absence, asked the committee to hold other preliminary sessions without him." Thus despite the very real pressure of time—the missile sites were to become operational by the end of the month—the eventual decision was reached by relatively open discussion. Group decision-making does not insure the emergence of sound policy, of course, but it does limit the probability of a decision performing a personality-oriented function.

Actually, it was not until Saturday, October 20—almost a week after the photographic evidence became available—that the general consensus developed. The President himself acknowledged that the interim period was crucial to the content of the final decision: "If we had had to act on Wednesday [October 17], in the first 24 hours, I don't think probably we would have chosen as prudently as we finally did, the quarantine against the use of offensive weapons."

Another characteristic of the decision process in October 1962 was the very conscious concern for action at the very lowest level of violence—or potential violence—necessary to achieve the goals. Senators J. William Fulbright and Richard B. Russell were among those who urged immediate invasion of Cuba, a suggestion against which the President stood firm. According to Kennedy, the decision to impose a naval quarantine was based on the reasoning that:

. . . the course we finally adopted had the advantage of permitting other steps, if this one was unsuccessful. In other words, we were starting, in a sense, at a minimum place. Then, if that were unsuccessful, we could have gradually stepped it up until we had gone into a much more massive action which might have become necessary if the first step had been unsuccessful. By this step, no irrevocable decision had been made—a number of options remained.

The concern of the President and his advisers with maintaining a number of options was based at least in part on an explicit distinction between threats and acts. The use of threats has become a more or less accepted tool of international politics in the nearly two decades of cold warring. The United States and the Soviet Union, on the other hand, had systematically abstained from direct violent action against each other. The desire to avoid killing Soviet troops was an important factor in the decision to refrain from an air strike against Cuba. Instead the quarantine shifted the immediate burden of decision concerning the use of violence to Premier Khrushchev. Even if Soviet ships refused to honor the blockade, the initial American plan was to disable the rudders of the vessels, rather than to sink them.

The flexibility provided by a number of plans requiring less than the use of unlimited violence stands in marked contrast to the situation in 1914. One factor in the rapid escalation in 1914 was the rigidity of various mobilization plans. The Russian attempt to mobilize against only Austria was anathema to the Russian generals because no such formal plan had been drawn up. According to General Dobrorolski, "The whole plan of mobilization is worked out ahead to its final conclusion and in all its detail . . . once the moment is chosen, everything is settled; there is no going back; it determines mechanically the beginning of war."

Similarly the Kaiser's last-minute attempt to reverse the Schlieffen plan—to attack only in the east—shattered Moltke, who replied:

That is impossible, Your Majesty. An army of a million cannot be improvised. It would be nothing but a rabble of undisciplined armed men, without a commissariat. . . . It is utterly impossible to advance except according to plan; strong in the west, weak in the east.

American decision-makers also displayed a considerable concern and sensitivity for the position and perspective of the adversary. This was a matter of deep concern in the development of the crisis. Unlike some of the key decision-makers in the 1914 crisis, those in October 1962 seemed to conceive a close relation between Soviet and American actions rather than two sides, each acting independently, in vacuo. Theodore Sorensen described the deliberation as follows: "We discussed what the Soviet reaction would be to any possible move by the United States, what our reaction with them would have to be to that Soviet reaction, and so on, trying to follow each of these roads to their ultimate conclusion."

This sensitivity for the position of the adversary was apparent in a number of important areas. There was a concern that Premier Khrushchev not be rushed into an irrevocable decision; it was agreed among members of the decision group that "we should slow down the escalation of the crisis to give Khrushchev time to consider his next move." An interesting example of the President's concern emerges from his management of the naval quarantine: "The President ordered the Navy screen not to intercept a Soviet ship until absolutely necessary—*and had the order transmitted in the clear*." There was, in addition, a conscious effort not to reduce the alternatives of *either* side to two—total surrender or total war. According to one participant, "President Kennedy, aware of the enormous hazards in the confrontation with the Soviets over Cuba in October, 1962, made certain that his first move did not close out either all his options or all of theirs." Sorensen added that:

The air strike or an invasion automatically meant a military attack upon a communist power and required almost certainly either a military response to the Soviet Union or an even more humiliating surrender. . . . The blockade on the other hand had the advantage of giving Mr. Khrushchev a choice, an option, so to speak, he did not have to have his ships approach the blockade and be stopped and searched. He could turn them around. So that was the first obvious advantage it had. It left a way open to Mr. Khrushchev.

Thus, unlike the 1914 situation, in which at least one ultimatum was worded so as to be incapable of execution, there was no demand which the Soviet Premier could not understand, none that he could not carry out, and none calculated to humiliate him unduly. During the summer of 1914, by way of contrast, there were numerous instances of failure on all three of these important points. The Austro-Hungarian ultimatum was deliberately worded in such a manner as to humiliate Serbia and to provoke rejection. The policy of the other powers, on the other hand, was hardly characterized by clarity. Russian decision-makers failed to communicate their initial desire to deter Vienna rather than to provoke Berlin. This was matched by England's inability to convey to German leaders their intention to intervene should the local conflict engulf the major continental powers. And, in the culminating stages of the crisis, decision-makers in the various capitals of Europe made the very types of demands upon their adversaries—notably in regard to mobilizations—which they admitted they could not reciprocate.

In seeking to account for the differences between crises that escalate beyond the control of the participants and those that eventuate in a pacific resolution, perceptual variables have a demonstrable utility. A substantial difference between the 1914 and 1962 crises was the relative clarity with which tension-reducing moves were seen by the participants in the latter period; in the 1914 crisis this clarity was eroded by the tendency to imbue the potentially tension-reducing actions of the other alliances with hostile intent.

But this is only the beginning of analyses of international politics in crisis. To strictly account for the differences in outcome a great many more cases need to be studied—cases chosen to test the role of other plausible explanatory factors (weaponry, culture, etc.). But even these two cases may have furthered our understanding of the role of affect and action in the management of international crisis.

Suggested Readings

Allison, Graham T. *Essence of Decision: Explaining the Cuban Missile Crisis.* Boston: Little, Brown, 1971.

Betts, R.K. "Analysis, War and Decisions: Why Intelligence Failures Are Inevitable." *World Politics,* 31 (October 1978), pp. 61–89.

George, Alexander L. et al., *The Limits of Coercive Diplomacy: Laos, Cuba, Vietnam.* Boston: Little, Brown, 1971.

Smoke, Richard. *War: Controlling Escalation.* Cambridge: Harvard University, 1977.

Wohlstetter, Roberta. *Pearl Harbor: Warning and Decision.* Stanford: Stanford University, 1962.

Young, Oran. *The Politics of Force: Bargaining During International Crisis.* Princeton: Princeton University, 1968.

CHAPTER 6

The Prevention of War and the Resolution of Conflict

As we have seen, the scholarly study of the correlates and causes of international war offers valuable lessons from the history of human interaction for contemporary decision makers. Unfortunately, most of the books and articles in the field do not offer immediate and practical solutions to diplomatic problems. In this chapter, we turn our attention to somewhat more applicable techniques of conflict resolution, some of which have already been used with success in prior crises.

The study of history and even prehistory reveals that not all societies during all time periods have been war prone. As we have seen, anthropologists describe scores of societies in which physical violence is all but unknown. Historians, as well, have discovered islands of relative peace amidst the turbulence of civil and international war. One such island was the thirteenth century in Europe. Roscoe Balch's, "The Resigning of Quarrels: Conflict Resolution in the Thirteenth Century," our first selection in this chapter, reveals how sophisticated mediation techniques apparently kept war to a minimum during that century. In addition, Balch identifies factors that produced an environment conducive to the peaceful settlement of disputes.

Mediation and arbitration are common techniques used in almost all cultures. Henry Paley's "The Herodotus Solution" is a more unique—and more idealistic—program for tension reduction between the Soviet Union and the United States. His peace hostage proposal calls for hundreds of thousands, perhaps millions, of mostly youthful citizen-tourists to be exchanged between the two major powers. Their presence in great numbers in each country, according to Paley, might make decision makers think twice before they bring down the missiles not only on their enemies but on their children as well.

Throughout history, brave people have confronted their enemies using tactics of civil disobedience. While they have led to success in some domestic conflicts, such tactics are more difficult to employ in international conflicts. In our third selection, Gene Sharp proposes a "Civilian-Based Defense Policy" in which the adoption of those tactics by an unarmed population might not only make an invader's lot difficult, if not impossible, but might also serve as a deterrent to an invasion in the first place.

Sharp's proposal for a nonmilitary civilian "army" is not a new one. William James was also interested in such a concept, albeit not in terms of deterrence and defense. Writing "The Moral Equivalent of War" at a time of increasing international militarism, James conceded the value of military training to a society. However, he proposed the creation of armies of young people to be disciplined and trained not to fight one another but to serve their societies in what we would today call Peace or

Job Corps. James' proposal would please those who thought that military institutions were important to their nation but would reduce the threat that such institutions posed to one's neighbors. Paley's informal citizen exchange army is a variant of the James' scheme.

Most contemporary decision makers in the major powers would probably greet the proposals offered by Paley, Sharp, and James with skepticism at best, derision at worst. Nevertheless, they have been interested in suggestions for conflict resolution that they can apply in their day-to-day negotiations. Charles E. Osgood's "Calculated De-escalation as a Strategy," our fifth selection, is a formula for a negotiating strategy that might be applied to arms control talks. His GRIT proposal is applicable in any number of other diplomatic standoffs, and, it seems, has been used, at least implicitly, by American diplomats in the past.

According to some observers interested in the prevention of war, none of the proposals offered in this chapter address the main problem in international relations, the lack of institutions to maintain peace and world order. For over a thousand years, theologians, philosophers, and political theorists have presented plans for world government or world federation. None have come close to being accepted by national leaders, all of whom jealously guard their sovereignty. It is true, of course, that since 1920, the League of Nations and then the United Nations have been in existence, serving as world parliaments and occasionally playing a salutary role resolving disputes and keeping the peace along unsettled borders.

In "An Open Letter to UN Chiefs" on the occasion of the world body's fortieth birthday, Richard Hudson, in our last selection, proposes amendments to the UN Charter that he believes will make the organization a more effective peace keeper and war preventer. Although his plan is no pie-in-the-sky program for world government, it does represent a small step in that general direction.

Interest in proposals for arms control and a general relaxation of tensions in the international system has increased in recent years. This heightened interest is related to the nuclear arms race and renewed fears of nuclear war, subjects we will examine in Chapter 7.

Reading 31

THE RESIGNING OF QUARRELS: CONFLICT RESOLUTION IN THE THIRTEENTH CENTURY

Roscoe Balch

Notes from the Editors

Historian Roscoe Balch explores the reasons why mediation techniques apparently worked well in the thirteenth century, a century that was more peaceful than those preceding and following it. Mediation employs a third party who helps the contending sides settle their differences. The process differs from arbitration, a resolution technique in which the arbitrators' independently-arrived-at judgment is often binding.

During the thirteenth century, the Church was central to many of the mediations, or the "resigning" of quarrels, as Balch describes them. As he points out, certain characteristics of the emerging international system made mediation techniques more likely to be successful in that century than in others surrounding it. Whatever the reasons for the success of peaceful conflict resolution in the thirteenth century, Balch's analysis demonstrates that the world, and different regions within the world during different time periods, has known periods of relative peace.

Although he restricts his analysis to the century in question, Balch implicitly asks why such a rational system could not work in the twentieth century. A wide variety of institutions, including the church, exist today that could easily perform mediation functions. While mediation and arbitration are used from time to time in contemporary diplomacy, few nations have been willing to surrender much of their sovereignty to even the most neutral and unbiased of third parties. Clearly, before we ever reach a point where mediation, arbitration, and even formal juridical approaches to major diplomatic problems are employed more widely, major changes will have to occur in the structure and the culture of the nation-state system.

Medieval Europe was a crazy quilt of armed political units. Allegiance patterns were complex and often confused and the weakness of all centralizing powers invited violence. It would be difficult to conceive of an era more likely to submerge itself in endemic war. To save itself, and to express an ideal, medieval society created a complex mix of peace institutions and techniques, often centering around a single idea, the resigning of quarrels to a third party.

Much of this activity can be followed in great detail. It may well constitute the largest body of experience with third party peacemaking available to modern society. It is, like most of medieval diplomatic history, a largely untold story. What follows is a preliminary sketch of the style and character of this peacemaking and an attempt to isolate a few of its salient characteristics. We may ask, also, if there is anything in

First appeared in *Peace and Change: A Journal of Peace Research* V (1) (Spring 1978), pp. 33–38. Reprinted by permission.

these characteristics which can help explain why there was so much third party activity.

The twelfth century saw the rapid development of diplomatic techniques. The growth of towns and of half independent feudal holdings outran existing legal institutions. Diplomacy often filled the gaps between firm jurisdictions, and grew beside the Law Merchant. Roman law taught the art of using agents. Diplomats began to receive *plena potestas,* full—or plenipotentiary powers. Quarrels which could not be submitted to a judicial process began to be "resigned" to a third party who might act as mediator or arbitrator. Direct relationship between these various kinds of agency cannot be demonstrated. But all grow in the same milieu.

The resigning of quarrels is also part of another context, the search for peace manifested in such developments as the Peace of the Church and the Peace of God. But whereas these can be traced to definite clerical institutions (the Peace of the Church at the end of the tenth century and the Peace of God in the late eleventh), the resigning of quarrels appears without such sponsorship as though it were, perhaps, a formalization of actions which had always existed to some extent.

Both the Peace of the Church and the Peace of God were efforts to abolish private war by expanding political authority, investing in the earlier instance a bishop and the latter a layman with the right to forcibly put down private war. They fit into the dream of Pax Romana, that is, the dream of peace through governmental centralization and control, even as the dream of a reconstituted Roman Empire did. By the end of the thirteenth century both the Peace of the Church and the Peace of God had disappeared from diplomatic documents. They did not even, like the ghost of peace through empire, echo through the words of exiled poets and alienated theologians.

In the best overview of medieval diplomacy yet written, Francois Ganshof reports that in the eleventh and twelfth centuries when all of the peace techniques were growing simultaneously, most disputes were settled by war. But in the thirteenth, fourteenth, and fifteenth centuries most disputes were settled by negotiations. When we turn and look at those settlements closely, we find an extraordinary amount of third party activity. Why, of all the peace institutions, did this one, neutral mediation and arbitration, survive to play so fruitful a role?

Some clue to this question may be provided if we note that arbitration which may be regarded as the most advanced, because the most difficult, form of third party activity, has flourished in certain other periods, although historical peace research is too undeveloped a field of scholarship for easy generalization. Two periods that have been identified are Hellenistic Greece and medieval Russia. At least 46 cases of arbitration were recorded between 300 and 100 B.C. Cities, philosophers, and even Olympic champions served as arbitrators. Ganshof believes that there was some such activity in medieval Islam. Certainly there are earlier Arabian precedents. The Kitab-al-Aghani tells us that once in Pre-Mohammedan Arabia, a bride forced her husband to make peace between two warring tribes before she would allow him conjugal relations.

One of the most eventful arbitrations of recorded history occurred in 657 in Syria, when the forces of Muawiya, being worsted in battle, placed copies of the Qur'an on their spears to signal a demand for arbitration. The pious party within the victorious army forced its leader, Ali, to accept this arbitration, which led to the founding of the Ummayad Caliphate and ultimately to the schism between Sunna and Shia.

The three areas about which most is known, Hellenistic Greece, medieval Russia, and medieval western Europe, have two things in common. One is the use of religion in supporting negotiations. The second is the diffusion of political power. Peace activities on the model of the Pax Romana attempted to overcome that diffusion, while third party activity accepted the diffusion and built upon it. The Church supported both and enjoyed success over a much longer period as a resolver of quarrels than as a centralizer of political authority.

The widespread diffusion of power was a fundamental fact of medieval life. Medieval diplomacy must and did reckon with it constantly. Any political unit or any individual capable of important political choice or initiative might deal diplomatically with the greatest of princes. Thus in 1296, we find Edward I accrediting diplomatic envoys to the barons, knights, town councilors, townsmen and good men of the country of Holland and Zeeland. The circumstances were extraordinary. But normal diplomacy could, and did, stretch to cover them. Even the relationships between kings and those who held fiefs directly of them wavered between the strictly political and judicial, and the quasi-, or even fully, diplomatic. This was true between France and Aquitaine, between France and Flanders, between England and Scotland.

Third party mediation and arbitration were spread over this entire range of thirteenth century diplomatic activity. A pope submitted to arbitration in 1244. A count of Savoy, faced with choosing his successor from among his nephews, willed the problem to arbitrators. By the end of the thirteenth century, arbitration had become the normal recourse for solving disputes which arose between mariners of different powers. What is perhaps more surprising was the frequency with which the largest powers accepted arbitration.

But if third party activity flourished in the complex and often confused dispersion of power which characterized the last three medieval centuries, that situation can hardly have been its sole cause. Eleventh century Europe was also a time of dispersed power but there was little mediation and conflicts frequently ended in war. Problems do not lead through some law of history or logic to their own solutions.

In seeking clues to the widespread success of third party activity, we might look to the forms in which it was enacted. In most instances the forms were simple. Philip the Fair conceded to Edward I power to form a truce between the king of France and the king of Aragon. In a separate document the king of Aragon granted the same permission with equal brevity. The documents of truce might well be, as in this instance they were, much more detailed. The contrast points up a significant characteristic. Third parties offering mediation or arbitration never stated, or even hinted, at possible terms in written documents. Parties resigning quarrels to third parties were equally reticent. Confidentiality was rigorously protected. The third party stepped behind the elaborate formalities of medieval statecraft. The hard bargaining was usually secret.

While the simplicity of most documents is in itself instructive, we can learn more about the tacit understandings behind them by examination of those rarer documents which are elaborate and full in their language. We observe, for example, a papal mission of reconciliation.

In 1295, Boniface VIII began his famous mediation between Philip the Fair and Edward I with letters to the two kings stressing his personal friendship for them. It is a note struck frequently though more briefly in the simpler documents of other cases.

Rudolph of Hapsburg "out of affection" concedes his quarrel with the count of Savoy to the mediation of Edward I. Alphonso of Castile "at the prayers of Edward I, husband of our sister, and for love of him" grants a truce to Philip III. The importance of the personal relationship between the third party and those he served was such that a count of Flanders declared himself no longer bound by an arbitral decision after the death of one of the arbitrators.

When Edward met with Boniface's legates, the cardinals of Albano and Palestrina, he gave two reasons for agreeing to let the pope's legates mediate. One was, " reverentie Romanae ecclesiae, quae, totius orbis caput est et magistra" ("out of reverence for the Roman church which is the head and teacher of the whole world") and because of the cardinals themselves, "because of your labors and your long journey." Such sentiments were not always sincere. We find Philip the Fair in 1297, after the *clericis laicos* dispute, submitting a quarrel to papal arbitration "because of the esteem in which he holds Boniface VII." The form, we may suspect, rather exceeded the substance.

It remains clear that third party activity frequently, if not always, was conceived as the action of a personal friend. Personal relationships were expected to transcend interest. In an age when political units were headed by hereditary rulers, personalization of peace making could flourish. Distrust must always be one of the prime obstacles to surrendering one's vital interests into the hands of another. Personal friendship like confidentiality and informality strengthened the basic factor of confidence or trust. Even when such confidence was very slender, people clung to the forms, "assuming a virtue though they felt it not."

The position of mediators was still stronger when they could call on a family tie. Thus in the last decades of the thirteenth century, Guy of Flanders was embroiled in deep and bitter quarrels with the counts of Hainault and Holland and their overlord the king of the Romans. His son-in-law, John of Brabant, served as arbitrator between his father-in-law and each of the other counts and as successful mediator between his father-in-law and the king of the Romans. Count Philip of Savoy was reconciled to Rudolf of Hapsburg by Philip's sister, Margaret of France. Instances could be multiplied endlessly.

Boniface VIII, not himself related to either Edward I or Philip the Fair, wrote for aid to St. Louis' widow who was Edward's aunt and Philip's grandmother. The pope also wrote to Amadeus of Savoy who was cousin to both kings, and to Philip's queen who was stepdaughter to Edward's brother, and to Philip's stepmother who was an aunt of Edward's son-in-law.

The peace mission which Boniface sent out stayed in the field for more than two years. On the English side of the channel, the actual negotiators became well-known personalities. One of them, the Cardinal of Albano, had received a special letter of warm welcome from the king before he reached England. A year later, the same diplomat was granted 200 marks yearly by Edward for, the Patent Roll assures us, "past services." A year later, Edward's documents speak of both cardinals as "our special friends."

Thus the form and style of third party activity was intended to foster what Sir Harold Nicholson has called "those principles of courtesy, confidence and discretion which forever remain the only principles conducive to the peaceful settlement of disputes." The frequent success of third party endeavors in the late middle ages seems to offer support to this conclusion of the distinguished practitioner and historian of diplomacy. Nicolson, himself, believed that medieval diplomatic practice was more conducive to peacemaking than that of more recent times. He offers an actual moment for the change, the coming to power of Alexander VI. Garrett Mattingly's classic, *Renaissance Diplomacy,* is based on a similar conviction. As far back as 1887, Frantz Funck-Brentano, who believed that the policy which guided diplomacy in France was the same in medieval and modern times, had made a similar observation.

To Funck-Brentano the difference lay in the all-pervading religious character of medieval diplomacy. He noted that important embassies were received in churches or chapels or at least in the palace of a bishop or in a monastery, almost never in a purely secular building. Boniface's legates began their presentation to Edward I at mass. One of them preached a sermon on the topic of peace. The next day's session began again with mass. One of Edward's bishops preached on the text of the psalmist, "I will hear what the Lord God speaks in me for he will speak peace unto his people." Funck-Brentano points to the testimony of medieval documents. Important agreements were sworn to "in the presence of the sacrament, with fingers corporally touching the gospels." Conclusion of peace required a large church, episcopal robes, often the giving of absolution. Frequently the negotiators of both sides took communion together. Although third party mediators often stepped behind the ceremonial, their efforts were surrounded by this religious diplomacy.

Like the rest of medieval diplomacy, third party activity was, in Donald Queller's words, "open to anyone who had sufficient power at his command to enter it." In medieval Russia, women of noble houses, bishops, above all the Metropolitan of Moscow, and abbots were active. The same was true in western Europe. Entering this activity was a matter of choice, ability, and character. Philip III's first queen did not take part, but his second queen, Marie of Brabant, was active. Her brother, John I of Brabant, the chivalrous knight who led three hundred picked men against an equal number under Reginald of Guelders on a dead even field at Woeringen, was often a peace maker. Among his neighbors, Guy of Flanders, John of Hainault, and Floris of Holland, though vigorous men active in diplomatic affairs, do not seem to have been mediators. The bishop of Liege in the 1280's was a skilled mediator. The name of his near neighbor, the bishop of Utrecht, does not appear.

Third party peacemaking, while it touched everything, was in some sense a movement which fired only some of the finest minds of the time and depended heavily upon them. St. Louis contributed his charisma to the cause and his personality might be thought of as a model for the mediating diplomat. His courtesy, the fine distinguishing quality of his mind, the ease and simplicity of his personal manner all cast him more naturally in the role of diplomat than of warrior. But it was above all his character, his moral authority, which enabled him to survive unpopular decisions with his prestige substantially intact.

The frequency with which the name of Edward I appears as a mediator is no accident. He once wrote to John of Brabant, "We hold above all in our desires, that before violence occurs to our friends, we might cut off the cause of dissension for all the faithful of Christ." He was a man given to large schemes. His legislation, his Welsh campaigns, his alliance system in '94–'97, all combine long range plans with careful attention to detail. His peacemaking shows the same ambition. His cousins ruled in France, his brother-in-law in Castile. He arranged marriages for his children in Aragon, in Austria, in Holland and in Brabant. In every instance the relationships involved the king of England in reconciling of quarrels. That he, himself, was involved in the war which broke the peace of the century's last decade is ironic and it illustrates the perennial difficulty of maintaining peace.

I have stressed the importance of the personal in third party activity, yet in one important class of arbitrations, those taking place according to the Law of the March, these factors hardly apply. Nor is the form religious. The Law of the March, or border, held in areas of uncertain jurisdiction between, for example, Brittany and Anjou, Gascony and Castile, Hainault and Liege, and on the Atlantic. It existed to settle grievances between private parties from different jurisdictions. Yet it was not purely private law for it allowed reprisals against the people of an offender. Conflicts were often resolved through arbitration. Each side appointed an equal number, perhaps two or three or six, arbitrators. It was common, if not universal, practice that at least one judge on each side be a trained lawyer. In cases involving mariners, one or more prominent citizens of the towns from which the ships came were often included. Hearings were held and decisions rendered. The forms and regularities of law and custom, the even number of arbiters and their competence to the task, created the confidence which was so difficult to obtain in the more purely diplomatic instances. Yet the Law of the March was dependent on the agreement of the highest authority in each political unit who must agree to participate, to appoint arbitrators, and to enforce their decisions. Thus the Law of the March was a subordinate part, a most useful tool of the larger effort at peace.

Why was the movement so strong? To what motives could the intervening third party appeal? Once again we turn from the silence of the lay mediators to the fulsome rhetoric of Boniface VIII. Basically, he presented four arguments. He "saw the horror of this ancient quarrel rising before my mind's eye." He saw much more but it was more succinctly said by Edward's man, Antony Bek, summing up the English understanding of the pope's point, every faithful Christian ought to desire peace "for the sufficient reason of the goods which it brought and of the evils which arose from the war."

The war distracted men, Boniface further argued, from the "negotium terre sancta," "the business of the Holy Land." Knowing as we do that the crusading movement had all but run its course we may be tempted to underestimate this motive, but there is no real evidence that its appeal was strong.

Thirdly, Boniface appealed to a theory of Christian kingship, calling on the kings to be mindful of the "Highest King, through whom kings reign and princes rule." War, Boniface declared, would scandalise the faithful and damage the reputation of the kings. Philip's attention was directed to the example of his grandfather, St. Louis. Clearly, there was a theory of Christian kingship to which the mediator could appeal, counterbalancing the heroic tradition of warrior kings.

The pope waited until a later letter to bring up his last argument. The war was diverting the revenues of the church away from pious purposes. His statement is limited to the economic effect of war upon the church but it would apply with equal, if not greater, force to secular revenues. Europe had come far from the simple days of the feudal host. The rising cost of war had far outstripped the revenues of even the richest states. The annual, or all but annual, campaigns of Charlemagne's time were beyond the capacities of any king of the high middle ages. When continental war finally came to Edward I, three years of it—three years in which he was never able to place in the field the army he thought necessary or fight a single great battle—still cost him in excess of 350,000 pounds. The strain caused great domestic repercussions and made the last thirteen years of his reign far more desperate, far less constructive, than the first twenty-one. While one cannot cite a single document showing a direct connection between third party activity and economic necessity, one can readily infer it.

The resigning of quarrels became a common phenomenon in a Europe where political and military power were widely diffused; where patterns of sovereignty were still uncertain; where the cost of war had become prohibitive; and where disputes were everywhere. The custom of resigning quarrels was a creative response in which the society called upon its highest ideals and married them to the actual situation. Medieval third party activity was the expression of a diplomacy which in its forms and style consciously enhanced "those principles of courtesy, confidence and discretion which forever remain the only principles conducive to the peaceful settlement of disputes."

Medieval people did not achieve perfect peace but they did peacefully resolve many disputes and thus help their society to survive most dangerous conditions and, ultimately, to prosper.

Suggested Readings

Carlston, Kenneth S. *The Process of International Arbitration*. New York: Columbia University, 1946.

Choucri, Nazli, and Robert North. "In Search of Peace Systems: Scandinavia and the North." In *Peace, War, and Numbers*, ed. Bruce Russett. Beverly Hills, Calif.: Sage, 1972, pp. 239–74.

McGuire, Brian Patrick (ed.). *War and Peace in the Middle Ages*. Copenhagen: C.A. Reitzels, 1987.

Melko, Matthew, and John Hord. *Peace in the Western World*. Jefferson, N.C.: McFarland, 1984.

Singer, J. David. "Negotiation by Proxy." *Journal of Conflict Resolution* 9 (December 1965), pp. 538–41.

Walton, Richard E. *Interpersonal Peacemaking: Confrontations and Third Party Consultations*. Reading, Mass.: Addison-Wesley, 1969.

Reading 32

THE HERODOTUS SOLUTION

Henry Paley

Notes from the Editors

Henry Paley was an educator deeply concerned about the increasing likelihood that the United States and the Soviet Union might launch a Third World War. Although his proposed Herodotus Solution would not eliminate great power rivalry, it might decrease the probability of nuclear war.

Paley recalls the Iranian Hostage Crisis (1979–80) when the United States refrained from taking forceful military action against Iran, in part because such action would have endangered the lives of the hostages. He proposes that the Russians and Americans exchange hundreds of thousands of "hostages" each year, and thus create a situation in which the decision makers on both sides would think twice before taking any action that might incinerate so many of their own children. In addition, a positive spin-off would be the exposure of a generation of young Americans and Russians to one another.

As early as the nineteen fifties, a citizen exchange organization was established in the United States with goals similar to Paley's and several remain active today. During the Vietnam War, a group of prominent Americans volunteered to go to Hanoi as hostages against U.S. bombing, but the North Vietnamese refused to allow them in. In recent years, American (and European) activists have gone to Central America to "bear witness" on the Nicaraguan-Honduran border. They hoped that by stationing themselves in the battle zone, American-backed insurgents might refrain from attacking Nicaragua for fear of killing American citizens.

Obviously, as Paley points out, his scheme faces many practical obstacles. Among the most serious is how a closed society like the Soviet Union could ever be cajoled into permitting an "army" of American young people to participate in its society, and conversely, into permitting its own youth to live in the United States for an extended period of time. Nevertheless, in a world searching for pathways away from nuclear war, Paley's somewhat fanciful scheme is, at the least, worth discussing.

The ancient Greeks gave us the key for opening the superpower stalemate. If we use it, World War III can be held hostage indefinitely.

Writing in the Fifth Century before the Christian Era, the historian Herodotus observed, "In peace, children bury their parents; war *violates the order of nature* and causes parents to bury their children."

Can there be a more painful human experience than children preceding their parents in death? It is the essence of what makes war an unnatural act. Yet international

---

Reprinted with permission from *The Metro Times,* Detroit's Weekly Publication of News and the Arts, May 30–June 5, 1984, pp. 1–5.

peace efforts ignore the natural gravitational force of society's basic building block—the family—as a checkmate to war.

We have never had a better chance to turn the Herodotus Key than now. Never have we possessed more technical capability to use it on the scale essential for its successes. And, there has never been greater incentive. The enormity of what lies beyond the brink of World War III adds urgency to the case for making this new initiative the threshold for a permanent peace.

This is not to argue for abandoning efforts underway to relieve present international tensions. It is to suggest a new strategy for the United States to introduce at the top of its peace agenda, one particularly appropriate at this point in time. Even if it failed to generate an affirmative response from our prime potential World War III adversary, it would add a dimension to America's peace effort that could not help but bolster international support for our more conventional approaches to mankind's survival challenge.

Discussions between the U.S.A. and the U.S.S.R. aimed at averting World War III continue to be obsessed with the notion that peace can be built upon a balance of military terror. The concept has never worked. It is even less likely now to produce desired outcomes than it was in the Versailles Era after World War I. We simply cannot treat present nuclear, chemical, conventional and bacteriological weaponry as if we were trading off coal-fired dreadnoughts and water-cooled machine guns.

Nor can we rely upon the illusion that the sheer scale of potential destruction contained in today's armaments is sufficient in itself to forestall World War III. We must *believe* both superpowers when they rationalize to their respective constituencies the need for shunting such an enormous proportion of national product to the technologies of destruction. Both say they have the will to use all weapons in their respective arsenals. It would be suicidal to ignore that calculated assertion.

Detente, sanctions, SALT and multinational defense treaties all orbit about the presumption that military balance is the key to averting World War III. None appear to recognize that inevitably the defensive effort of Power A is perceived as an aggressive move to Power B. And none give appropriate weight to the human foibles that can place irrational judgments behind cataclysmic trigger mechanisms.

Not At All Complex

To construct a fail-safe mechanism for holding World War III hostage requires bilateral commitment by America and Russia. To work, it requires clearly understood self-interest motivation by a broad spectrum of the inhabitants of both countries.

Without the participation of the two superpowers, World War III will not happen in our time. How long that condition will persist is speculative. But for now the U.S.A. and the U.S.S.R. are essential protagonists. On the reverse side of the same coin, if the Soviet Union and the United States were engaged in a bilateral process that exploited their respective populations' natural revulsion to war, it would inexorably sweep other powers into their peace orbit.

The Herodotus Key strategy is not at all complex. But it must be launched on a massive scale to succeed. Required is an exchange of the young between Russia and America in an order of magnitude never before seriously considered. *Every segment of each nation must feel a pervasive hostage stake, every region of both countries.*

Consider the paralysis of the most powerful nation in the world three years ago when the United States confronted the hostage crisis in Iran.

Dealing with a bush league military power, on an issue that clearly violated the most basic precept of international discourse—the sanctity of diplomatic personnel—the armed might of America was unable to force its will. We were properly concerned that military intervention would jeopardize the safety of our countrymen. The abortive rescue venture proved a near disaster. If anything, it heightened our national frustration. But it also demonstrated the utter inadequacy of armed force as a means of asserting national will when an aggrieved power's civilians are on the real estate of a hostile country *and their safety is a national priority.*

Imagine no fewer than a million young Americans and a million young Russians, drawn from a representative cross-section of each population, all volunteers, exchanged and located in every strategic area of both countries. Given the reach of these young people into virtually every community and family of both nations, it is inconceivable that the leadership of either would dare to press the World War III button. The exchangees' safety would become an irresistible national priority.

Destroying Stereotypes

Once the massive bilateral investment of youth is on the target turf of the rival superpowers, the Versailles notion of disarmament can begin to make sense. There would be growing reason to disinvest in weapons of destruction as their utility becomes increasingly moot. The shift of national resources to the infrastructure needs that would enhance the quality of life in both countries would constitute a compelling incentive for lesser world powers to seize a share of the Herodotus Key.

What are the logistical problems of a youth exchange strategy involving millions of young Americans and Russians who offer themselves to hold World War III hostage? What would be the elements of the bilateral agreement within which such an exchange is implemented?

The two nations would have to agree upon an exchange protocol covering:

- deployment of the volunteers in significant numbers within all strategic target areas
- a deployment schedule probably designed around a one-year volunteer term to assure a constant presence of exchangees
- a provision of study and work resources adequate to make the volunteer experience of value to each exchangee, assuring optimum health and safety conditions, maximum opportunity for educational enhancement of participants
- a mutually acceptable age range and a reasonable process for assuring the representative character of each nation's exchange cadre
- mutually acceptable incentives for volunteer service such as deferment from or reduced military obligations, educational support, family benefits or employment opportunities when the exchangees return to their native lands
- a means of renegotiation of the basic protocol while both volunteer cadres are

in place—a way of resolving the inevitable snafus that occur with an under-taking on this scale.

Both countries have the educational capability to implement intensive language preparation for volunteers recruited. Both have the transportation capacity to move the volume of young people called for in this massive intercontinental exchange.

What about each nation's fiscal resources to undertake the job? The only major initial add-on cost for both would be transportation. Food, shelter, recreation, education, health care—the major expenditure items of the exchange—would be approximately the same for each country if their volunteers remained home.

The additional cost of moving a million Russian youths to America and the same number of our young people to the U.S.S.R. would be infinitesimal compared to the planned additional expenditures for military armaments now anticipated by each of the superpowers.

Once implemented, the cost of supporting the exchange program would probably be a receding concern. There may even be an excess of funding as each of the competing nations strives to impress upon its volunteer visitors the virtues of its own system. It should be expected that the Russians will try to indoctrinate our exchangees and we will do the same. Both countries might compete so fervently for these young minds that there may be a tendency to be very generous with the appropriation spigots in Moscow and Washington.

There may also be some stereotypes challenged by the returning volunteers. They might not accept some of the assumptions that older Americans and Russians hold so fervently, assumptions that are now setting our course toward mutual destruction.

Bourbon, Baseball and Business

And there may be some very serious personal problems engendered by this exchange. What if some of our sons and daughters decided they wanted to remain in the U.S.S.R. and the same situation confronted Russian families? There is always the risk of being converted to borscht, ballet or bolshevism; bourbon, baseball or business. Then, too, there is Cupid, a large hazard among this age group. He has never been identified with any particular political ideology.

This is a real problem. Even so, it does seem to move us in the right direction—away from fear, hate, distrust. Perhaps the best way of handling it would be for the bilateral treaty to guarantee the return home of each volunteer. If some wish to again return abroad or to immigrate, they would have to pursue conventional procedures. Hopefully those procedures will become less onerous as we learn more about each other.

What if we offer the Herodotus Key to the Soviets and they turn us down? It is not at all unlikely, considering the reputation of Moscow for isolating visitors from abroad.

Would it be wasted motion for President Reagan to offer this exchange only to have it rejected by the Kremlin's paranoia? What would we have lost?

Might we not begin to regain the clear leadership America had at the close of World War II when not just the nations but the populations of Western Europe and what is now called the Third World perceived this country as the salient force for peace on our planet? Consider the impact of a Soviet rejection of the Herodotus Key upon the millions around the world who doubt our will to make peace and the millions more who see Uncle Sam as wearing the black sombrero in the present disarmament impasse.

We have much to gain and nothing to lose by making this offer to the Russians.

Suggested Readings

Angell, Robert C. *Peace on the March: International Participation.* New York: Van Nostrand, 1969.

Herodotus. *Histories.* London: Oxford University, 1962.

Kelman, Herbert C. "The Role of the Individual in International Relations." *Journal of International Affairs* 24 (1970), pp. 1–17.

Nye, Joseph S., and Robert O. Keohane. *Transnational Relations and World Politics.* Cambridge: Harvard University, 1972.

Reading 33

CIVILIAN-BASED DEFENSE POLICY

Gene Sharp

Notes from the Editors
Gene Sharp is one of the leading theorists of nonviolent resistance to aggression. In his books, articles, and workshops on the history and practice of civil disobedience, he has described ways in which individuals, groups, and even nations can try to defeat aggression through civil disobedience.

In his selection on civilian-based defense policy, a policy he hopes would deter or, if necessary, defeat military attack, invasion, and occupation, Sharp answers critics who consider nonviolent resisters unrealistic. Moreover, those who would join his "army" would have to be every bit as brave as regular soldiers as they confronted their traditional militarized enemy with an economic and political offensive that would temporarily destroy the infrastructure of their own nation.

Examples abound of successful applications of his general approach. In India, Gandhi (who borrowed from Thoreau) used passive resistance techniques to make the Raj ungovernable for the British. In the American South, Martin Luther King Jr. (who borrowed from Gandhi) successfully confronted the segregationists.

Sharp is aware of the magnitude of the task of organizing a population for a civilian-based defense policy. However, he may be too optimistic about the ability of any civilian population to contend with an invading society devoid of moral scruples. After all, Gandhi was dealing with the democratic British, not with the totalitarian Nazis. Nevertheless, Sharp's approach is an attractive one to those searching for ways to eliminate international, and even civil war, from human existence.

In civilian-based defense the civilian population wields diverse social, political, psychological, and economic "weapons," rather than military ones, for national defense purposes. Civilian-based defense can be defined as a defense policy utilizing prepared civilian struggle to preserve the society's freedom, sovereignty, and constitutional systems against internal coups d'etat and external invasions and occupations. The aim is to deter and to defeat such attacks. This is to be done not simply by efforts to alter the will of the attacker, but by the capacity to make effective domination and control impossible by both massive and selective noncooperation and defiance of the population and their institutions.

Civilian-based defense is a projected refinement of the general technique of non-

Reprinted with permission from *Social Power and Political Freedom*, pp. 232–49, by Gene Sharp. Hardcover edition: Boston, Porter Sargent Publisher, 1980, 440 pp., $15.95. Paperback edition: Boston, Porter Sargent Publisher, 1980, 440 pp., $8.95. Also by Gene Sharp: *The Politics of Nonviolent Action*, same publisher, and for the European application of this policy, see *Making Europe Unconquerable*, London and Philadelphia, Taylor & Francis, 1985, 311 pp.

violent action, or civilian struggle, as it has occurred widely in improvised forms in the past. This policy is an attempt deliberately to adapt and develop that technique to meet defense needs, and thereby potentially to provide, by the same capacity, deterrence to those particular forms of attack.

What Is It?

A civilian-based defense policy has three main characteristics. First, it is designed to be a defense policy capable of practical operation under existing political and international conditions, although it may also contribute to significant changes in international relations. Second, it is a civilian as contrasted to a military defense policy. Military attack would be met with the quite different nonmilitary sanctions of defiance and nonviolent noncooperation. Present military personnel would not by definition be excluded from the implementation of the policy, but military means of defense would be replaced with civilian means. Third, it is a policy to be carried out by the civilians as a whole and not conducted for them by a small group of professionals or by an organization set apart from the rest of the society (although specialists and organizations would be needed). In crises, the effectiveness of this policy would ultimately depend to a much greater degree on the active participation of the citizens themselves in the defense of their political freedom and political society than in the case of military defense.

There is almost no doubt that a civilian-based defense policy would have to be considered and adopted through the normal democratic process and governmental decision. The governmental apparatus and resources would then be available for the preparation of the new policy, which would have to be considerable, and for assistance during the changeover. It may, however, be worth exploring other possible models for adoption.

There are two important differences between civilian-based and military-based defense. Civilian-based defense is designed not only to deal with external threats to freedom by invasion, but also to defeat attempts to destroy democratic government by means of a coup d'etat, with or without external encouragement and assistance. Many parliamentary regimes have been ousted by such coups. Barring civil war, however, there has been virtually no defense capacity for such contingencies if the army leads or backs the coup as has often happened. This extension of defense capacity in the new policy would help to deter both the usual types of coups d'état and possible coups by very small political extremist groups once the military establishment has been abolished. Civilian-based defense cannot defend geographical borders or territorial integrity as such, but as a rule neither can military means. Even the superpowers cannot ensure their territories against nuclear devastation.

The purpose of civilian-based defense would be to make the establishment and maintenance of control over the country impossible and, at the same time, set in motion influences in the invader's own country that would be internationally harmful to his regime and to the military venture. The primary attempt to defend free social and political institutions, and the principles underlying them, would thus finally lead to a geographic withdrawal or collapse of the invader. The advantage of this approach is the probability that it would considerably reduce physical destruction and loss of life, while making it possible to refuse to surrender despite occupation.

Civilian-Based Defense as a Deterrent

If an aggressive regime is deciding whether or not to attempt an invasion to take possession of another country, it will usually take into consideration a number of factors. These include estimates of the relative ease or difficulty of the invasion and subsequent control of the country, and estimates of anticipated gains as compared to costs of the whole operation, including economic, political, ideological, military, and other aspects. If the prospective invasion is not based on a huge gamble or pure irrationality, the likelihood of considerably greater losses and disadvantages than gains will probably discourage or deter the invader.

It is commonly claimed that strong military defense capacity can serve as an effective deterrent by making an invasion extremely costly, reducing possibilities for success, running a very low chance of defeating it, or promising massive retaliatory destruction. There is no reason to assume, however, that military power is the only available deterrent. Invasion is not an objective in and of itself. It is seen as a way to achieve a wider purpose, which almost inevitably will involve occupation of the country. If, however, a successful invasion is to be followed by immense difficulties in occupying and controlling the society and population of the invaded territory, this may be at least as effective a deterrent as military capacity to combat the invasion. Such control on a large scale is a problem even in the absence of well-prepared capacity for resistance. George F. Kennan has argued the difficulties of achieving and maintaining control over large conquered areas.

There is no magic by which great nations are brought to obey for any length of time the will of people very far away who understand their problems poorly and with whom they feel no intimacy of origin or understanding. This has to be done by bayonets, or it is not done at all.[1]

Although he is not an advocate of civilian-based defense and has urged continuation of the nuclear deterrent, his 1957 Reith Lectures stressed the importance of the nonmilitary component of Western resistance to Communism. "The Soviet threat," he declared, "is a combined military-political threat, with the accent on the political." He propounded a "strategic doctrine addressed to this reality." This doctrine, which included military or preferably paramilitary forces, emphasized the need to strengthen the "internal health and discipline of the respective national societies, and of the manner in which they were organized to prevent the conquest and subjugation of their national life by unscrupulous and foreign-inspired minorities in their midst." Such a strategy would not be designed primarily to defend the frontiers;

but rather its defense at every village crossroads. The purpose would be to place the country in a position where it could face the Kremlin and say to it: "Look here, you may be able to overrun us, if you are unwise enough to attempt it, but you will have a small profit from it; we are in a position to assure that not a single Communist or other person likely to perform your political business will be available to you for this purpose; you will find here no adequate nucleus of a puppet regime; on the contrary, you will be faced with the united and organized hostility of an entire nation;

your stay among us will not be a happy one; we will make you pay bitterly for every day of it; and it will be without favorable long-term political prospects."

A country in a position to demonstrate its ability to do this would, he maintained, "have little need of foreign garrisons to assure its immunity from Soviet attack." Moreover, defense based largely on organized civil resistance "could be maintained at a fraction of the cost per unit of the present conventional establishments."[2]

Defense of Freedom

A reconsideration of policies and preparations for civilian-based defense would necessitate a careful examination of the principles, qualities, and institutions of the society that were deemed worthy of defense. Widespread understanding of, clarification of, and commitment to democratic principles and institutions would be an important early stage in transarmament to civilian defense. But, while defense motivations and aims ought to be under regular development and consideration, there are certain minimum principles in which general agreement should be possible. The formulation that Arne Naess has offered in regard to Norwegian defense might serve, in a modified form, as the basis for a description of the defense motivations and aims of other countries.

To defend Norway today means to defend our independence, our freedom to shape our lives within the framework of Norwegian social traditions and cultures and to change them as we wish. It is to defend a way of life against all external forces that would alter it without our consent.[3]

One of these basic principles in combatting attempted occupations and seizures of power is, as has been emphasized, that defense is the responsibility of the citizens themselves. Civilian-based defense extends the principle that the price of liberty is eternal vigilance to the strategy and specific implementation of the country's defense policy. This principle, of course, is not new. Its earlier applications are symbolized by the guns above the fireplaces in Swiss houses, the early American Minutemen, and the constitutional guarantee of the "right to bear arms." But, as Carl J. Friedrich has reiterated, technological developments, primarily in modern weaponry, have virtually destroyed this as a practical principle (except perhaps in a very indirect and abstract sense).[4] Civilian-based defense, by relying on a technique of struggle not dependent upon military technology, restores the role and importance of individuals in the defense of their freedom and political society. "Eternal vigilance" ceases to be a romantic slogan of an earlier age and becomes a fundamental principle on which the defense policy is built.

Preparations for Civilian-Based Defense

There is general agreement that although it is never easy, it is less difficult to resist a tyrannical regime while it is seeking to establish itself rather than after it has succeeded. Kennan, in reference to the seizure of power by a totalitarian regime, points to the necessity for certain states of mind and behavior among the subjects. "For the seizure of power, a certain degree of mass bewilderment and passivity are required."[5] The advance preparations and training for a civilian-based defense policy are designed precisely to prevent that condition; the usurper will encounter a population prepared to fight for its freedom. Thus, subject to the adequacy of such preparations and the effectiveness with which the struggle is conducted, the invader or internal usurper is likely to face an extraordinarily difficult task in establishing and consolidating his regime.

Adoption of a civilian-based defense policy would require both general and specific preparations. Since no country is likely to abandon military defense until it has confidence in and is prepared to apply an alternative defense policy, for a significant period these preparations would be carried out simultaneously with continued military measures. Because of their different natures, the two policies would probably require separate institutional arrangements; during the transitional period, personnel and money would be needed for both. Detailed consideration of the various aspects of preparations for civilian defense necessarily lies outside the scope of this chapter. The broad types of preparations listed here, therefore, are only suggestive of the extensive program that would have to be developed.

A major educational program to introduce the nature and purpose of the new defense policy would be needed for the country as a whole. This probably could best be implemented by central, state, and local governmental bodies, assisted by various independent institutions, such as schools, churches, trade unions, and business groups. People would be given the broad outlines of the new policy, the method of operation, and the results expected. This basic education would be designed to encourage justifiable confidence in the new policy and to instill in the general population the broad principles on which resistance in times of crisis would be based.

More specialized training would be required for particular occupational groups and for those wishing to participate in more advanced aspects of the defense policy. The specific forms of training would vary, and the levels would range from that required by local defense workers to specialist education, which could be offered by civilian-based defense counterparts of West Point. Careful consideration would be needed to determine the most desirable and effective means of such educational preparations and organizational structures for those actively involved in preparation and training programs.

Specialists in civilian-based defense could play an important role in initiating resistance, especially at the beginning of an occupation or a coup, and could in specific situations serve as special cadres for particularly dangerous tasks. They could not and should not be depended upon to carry out the resistance on behalf of the general population. Responsibility for the bulk of defense measures should be assumed by the citizenry. The specialists' role should be primarily that of assisting in training and in launching the initial resistance. It may be highly desirable to keep some specialists in reserve to guide the later stages of the resistance. In general, the leaders will be among the first imprisoned or otherwise dealt with by the usurper; thus, the population will need to have the capability to continue civilian-based defense measures on its own initiative.

None of this should be interpreted as an implication that preparations for civilian-based defense should consist only of central instructions carried out at the base of the pyramid. An effective strategy of civilian-based defense would require an analysis of the potentialities of particular factors—means of transportation, government departments, schools, and so forth—to identify the specific points at which selective non-cooperation might have a maximum impact in disrupting the operation of the whole institution or system. This is simply illustrative of the interplay that would be needed between the group largely responsible for formulating various general strategies of defense and those carrying out measures on the local level. The specific organization of a contact system or an underground would probably have to wait until after the launching of the invasion or coup; otherwise it might be much easier for the opponent to know the exact personnel and structure of the resistance system.

Civilian-based defense "war games" and defense maneuvers, as part of the preparations, have been proposed by Theodor Ebert.[6] Such war games would offer the specialists a chance to examine the viability of proposed alternative strategies and tactics for dealing with various types of threats. Maneuvers, ranging from ones to be held in local residential areas or factories to ones in cities, regions, and even the whole country, could be useful means by which the population would learn in a small way something of the practical application of the civilian-based defense principles. Such exercises might help to avoid the uncertainty and bewilderment often experienced by the population in times of invasion or coups d'état, and thereby facilitate the launching of the resistance with the maximum of resolution and unity.

Preparations for civilian-based defense should also include continued efforts to improve the society and system. In the last analysis, the more worthy the society is of defense, the better that defense will be. Alienated or unjustly treated sections of the population can be a serious threat to success. Since diffusion of power and responsibility is important in the conduct of civilian-based defense, reforms designed to give such groups a sense of participation in the community and to eradicate injustices could be a contribution by increasing both the degree of democracy and the defense potential.

Technical preparations are also necessary for civilian-based defense. It would be most desirable, for example, to provide, in advance, provisions and equipment that would lessen difficulties of communication with the population after the enemy has occupied key centers and seized established newspapers, radio stations, and other mass media. Printing and duplicating equipment for underground newspapers and resistance leaflets and broadcasting equipment could be distributed in advance. Thus, if large stocks were discovered and seized, considerable supplies would still be available to counter the enemy's propaganda and to disseminate instructions for resistance. Advance arrangements might often be possible for locating such broadcasting stations or printing plants in the territory of a friendly neighboring country as part of a civilian-based defense mutual aid agreement. Since an enemy might seek to force submission by starving the population, and since certain resistance methods (such as a general strike) would disrupt the distribution of food, emergency supplies of food should be stored locally. Alternative means of providing fuel and water during emergencies could also be explored. In particular types of crises, plans might be considered for the dispersal of major sections of the population from large cities to rural areas where control would be more difficult to exercise.

It is difficult at this point to determine what would be the best governmental arrangements for the preparation and organization of a civilian defense policy. A Department of Civilian-based Defense might be set up to provide leadership and coordination. Various types of legislation concerning the adoption and implementation of civilian-based defense, the responsibility of the citizens, and so forth, would probably be necessary.

Undermining the Opponent

The strategists and other experts in or associated with this Department of Civilian-based Defense would have prime responsibility for considering a variety of possible strategies and tactics for dealing with all conceivable forms that usurpation might take. The strategy most appropriate to a given situation would be determined in a large degree by the nature of the enemy and his objectives. All possible present and future threats and aims, therefore, would require careful advanced study, carried out together with a consideration of various strategies for dealing with each threat. In the United States this should include possible usurpations by an elected President and pseudo-constitutional seizures of power. While anticipation of and preparation for all eventualities should be made, the exact course of events is extremely difficult to predict. Provisions would also have to be made to ensure the flexibility and capacity for innovation to meet unexpected situations.

The initial stages of an attempted usurpation will be crucial in setting the mood and pattern of behavior to be developed in later periods. The attitude of the population to the invasion or coup is crucial. Traditionally, occupation following the defeat of military forces has been accompanied by feelings of dismay, confusion, and hopelessness. The defense capacity has been exhausted to no avail, and the population is left to fend for itself. This situation contributes significantly to the psychological condition that Hitler prescribed as necessary for successful occupation rule: the people of the occupied territories must admit defeat and recognize the occupation regime as their conqueror and master. Under a civilian-based defense policy, a radically different situation would exist. The country and the defense capacity would not have been defeated. The combat strength would not yet have been tested in struggle. The citizenry would have been so trained and prepared that it would not feel dismayed or confused. It would be understood that the physical distribution of soldiers and functionaries throughout the country did not constitute defeat but instead was the initial stage of a longer struggle at close range. This admittedly would be difficult, but the civilian defenders would hold advantages. Setbacks and defeats might occur; they would lead, however, not to acceptance of the usurpation but to a period of building strength and regrouping of forces under a different strategy in preparation for greater success in future campaigns. There are no white flags of surrender in civilian-based defense.

Although civilian-based defense cannot defend the geographic borders, this does not mean that nothing can be done at this initial stage. The deployment of troops can be delayed by obstructionist activities at the docks if major troop shipments come by sea, by refusing to operate the railroads, or by blocking highways with thousands of abandoned automobiles. Such acts will also make clear to the individual soldiers that any propaganda concerning the population's desire for protection against a threatening third power is not true. Other more symbolic actions with primarily a psychological intent can be undertaken to establish an attitude of resistance and defiance as early as possible. This will serve a dual purpose: *(a)* to give notice to the usurping regime, its functionaries, and its troops that the attempt to seize control and occupy the country will be firmly resisted; and *(b)* to influence the morale and behavior of the general population so that no inactive period will exist during which submission and collaboration could spread because of the absence of articulate opposition.

It will be important, as has been previously indicated, to make special efforts to communicate with the usurper's ordinary troops. They should be informed that there will be resistance. But, to minimize future suffering and increase the chances of victory, they must be helped to understand that, despite what they may have been told, the resistance will be a special type, directed against the attempt to seize control but without threatening harm to the individual soldiers. If this can be communicated, the soldiers may be more likely to help the resisting population in small ways, less likely to carry out brutalities or to conduct repression efficiently, and more likely to mutiny at a crisis point than if they expected at any moment to become targets for snipers or plastic bombs. Radio, leaflets, and personal conversations (preferably in the soldiers' own language) may be used for this purpose. Certain types of demonstrations may conceivably be held at the border or at other points where troops may enter, but their limited role will have to be recognized. Other initial actions may include the wearing of black by the whole population as a symbol of disapproval, a stay-at-home for one or more days, a general strike for a limited predetermined period, and the defiance of curfews with multitudes of the people flooding the streets and behaving in a friendly fashion to the individual soldiers, asking them to visit their homes, and urging them not to believe the propaganda they may have heard.

Strategies of Civilian Struggle

Depending on the assessment of the opponent and the situation, a well-prepared population might possibly undertake a hard campaign of comprehensive noncooperation intended to force quick defeat of the attempt to seize power. The general strike would be a key method for this kind of campaign, which has been called a "nonviolent *Blitzkrieg.*"

A program of total noncooperation with the enemy would doubtless be the most effective strategy, if the population could maintain such noncooperation with something approaching unanimity even in the face of severe repression, and if it were able to organize and continue life itself during the struggle. The difficulties of fulfilling these conditions may mean that sometimes such extensive noncooperation will not be attempted. In any case, it could be effectively practiced only for limited time periods. This strategy, therefore, might be reserved for initial attempts at quick defeat of usurpation, applied as short, extra severe resistance at particular points in the course of a long struggle, or used toward the end of a prolonged struggle to bring it to a swift, successful close.

It should already be obvious, even from this very sketchy discussion, that a variety of possible strategies may be applied in civilian-based defense. If one strategy is inappropriate in a given circumstance or after use has not proved effective, other possible strategies exist, and within each one there is considerable room for variation. Transitions from one strategy to another and from one phase of the conflict to the next are very important; flexibility without a sense of failure and realistic assessments of the state of the struggle without an abandonment of confidence and loss of initiative are crucial though difficult to achieve. If a "nonviolent *Blitzkrieg*," or total resistance, has been attempted and has not produced victory after a reasonable time, a transition to more selective resistance over a longer time schedule would be necessary.

Directly after the stage of initial symbolic resistance or after a period of general strike or total resistance, the strategy of selective resistance could be applied. Such a strategy provides for the concentration of resistance at specific points crucial to the usurper's control, or at those particularly important for the maintenance of the principles and way of life of the country.

There are several potential advantages of this strategy. First, it may involve an economic use of combat strength. For a certain period of time the main brunt of the struggle may be borne by a particular section of the population, such as an occupational group, and the rest of the population, though involved in various ways, does not constantly have to be the primary target of attack. Other sections of the population may take the lead later and assume the brunt of the struggle. Second, as tyrannical, and particularly totalitarian, regimes seek to achieve and maintain control by the stage-by-stage destruction of independent groups and institutions and the atomization of the population, selective resistance can be focused on defense of the independence of particular groups and institutions, such as trade unions, schools, and churches, that may be subject to attack at any given point. Successful resistance at these points helps both to retain and to develop the society's capacity for future resistance and its qualities of freedom. Third, selective resistance in either defensive or offensive forms may be directed at those points which symbolize important issues, for example, the freedoms of speech, religion, and assembly, in the battle of ideas between the two systems. In addition to being simply the battlegrounds over which the contest of forces takes place, they are, by the very selection and formulation of the specific issues, important factors in the ideological and psychological aspects of the struggle. "Resistance at the right point can help to communicate to an enemy, to the civilian population, and to third parties, exactly what is being fought for, and what is being opposed."[7] Last, selective resistance applied to transportation, industry, and other aspects of the economic system can be very effective in thwarting the enemy's general control and specific economic objectives. Careful selection of the issues and points of resistance may go a long way to maximize the power of the civilian defenders and to achieve successes against the usurping regime.

As selective resistance is likely to be more frequently applied than total resistance, it would be crucial to decide well ahead of time on the types of issues to which resistance must be offered and on the points at which ground must never be given even for tactical reasons, whatever the price. These would generally be points of overwhelming ideological significance or points that, if granted, would ensure the enemy control of the society. Citizens as a whole and each occupational group should be familiar with these preselected points, thereby facilitating response to particular resistance instructions or ensuring resistance at such points even if the resistance organization were destroyed. Within selective resistance, the strategy may be developed in various specific ways to counter most adequately the opponent's objectives and to accord with particular social and political conditions.

It is impossible here to suggest detailed courses of resistance in particular conflict situations or to explore all the kinds of strategic considerations and alternatives that lie within the field of strategy in civilian-based defense. No two situations are ever exactly alike. Careful investigation and planning are required to determine for a particular conflict what are the more promising strategies and tactics. The consideration of general principles of civilian-based defense strategy is a vast task, which for several reasons may be more comprehensive and difficult than military strategy. The whole population and all the institutions of the society potentially are directly involved in the struggle itself. In a nonviolent war, the battleground is not limited to geographic front lines or foreign targets. It includes the whole country, the international theater of operations in which nonmilitary support is sought against the invader, and the invader's own homeland where domestic opposition to the invader's regime and its aggression should be encouraged.

As long as the citizens remain firm and refuse to cooperate and obey, they hold the real power. The usurper can only impose that which the population is too weak to resist. A dictator is no less dependent upon the sources of power granted to him by the subjects than any other ruler. If these sources of his power can be withheld by the noncooperation and disobedience of the population, he, too, will be unable to maintain himself as a ruler.

Difficult Questions

The problem of defense, therefore, is the problem of how to act by means that undermine and finally dissolve the usurper's power to maintain his usurpation. There are admittedly a multitude of difficult questions involved in such an attempt. In addition to those already suggested, four merit special mention. (1) What is the most desirable and effective approach to the opponent's troops and functionaries in order to encourage disaffection, obtain cooperation, and perhaps finally induce a mutiny? Two diametrically opposite approaches have been suggested: social boycott, and individual fraternization combined with political noncooperation. (2) With varying degrees of individual commitment and involvement, how can the maximum level of citizenry participation be obtained? (Total participation is not necessary for success.) Since certain occupational groups may be especially vulnerable and simultaneously hold extremely important positions, their behavior requires special attention. (3) In the face of repression and brutalities, how can the defender's capacity to persist be strengthened to the utmost? Military might has been demonstrated to be incapable of imposing a regime on a population firmly determined not to accept it. It is necessary, however, to study the conditions under which this is possible and the influence on these of various types of repression, including psychological warfare, drugs, *agents provocateurs,* seizure of hostages, selective acts of terror, and vast physical destruction. (4) Can civilian-based defense be combined with military defense or at least with sabotage? Although this requires careful investigation and research, there is one important argument against the attempt to do so. The mechanisms of change in the two techniques of struggle are quite different from those in nonviolent action; the latter is seriously weakened by violence from the resisters. A combination of these may destroy the effectiveness of the civilian-based defense actions and the operation of the political *jiu-jitsu* process in which the opponent's violence, in the face of the defenders' non-violence, rebounds against his power position. This suggests that in the absence of greater knowledge it is unwise to make a hasty decision to combine them.

Possibility of Defeat

A defense of political freedom such as that proposed here would never be easy. There would be suffering, tragedies, and setbacks as well as dignity, heroism, and successes. There would be no certainty of easy or short-term victories; there would be no way of guaranteeing that such a struggle would inevitably lead to success even in the space of a few years. No technique of struggle can guarantee clear victory in every instance in which it is applied. There is a multitude of factors involved in a civilian defense struggle. If the qualities and conditions necessary for the successful operation of the mechanisms of nonviolent action are not present to a sufficient degree, victory cannot follow. Many of these factors, however, are directly and indirectly controllable by the nonviolent actionists. This is one reason why research, planning, preparations, and training are so important for civilian-based defense and significantly increase the chances of victory.

In considering the possibility of failure or of only very limited success, two factors need to be kept in mind. First, even failure after an heroic struggle by civilian-based defense is preferable to any outcome of a major nuclear war. At worst, it would mean a long, difficult, and painful existence under severe tyranny, but life would still remain, and with life the hope for eventual freedom. Emphatically, this is not a brief for the "better red than dead" type of slogan. It is not the abandonment of strength but the reverse. Nonviolent action is not a course for cowards. It requires the ability to sustain the battle whatever the price in suffering, yet would, in any case, allow a future for humanity. Second, in this type of struggle, the failure to achieve total victory does not mean total defeat. Even if the population of the occupied country should lack the capacity to drive out the invader, it could have the strength to maintain a considerable degree of autonomy for the country and a large degree of independence for the social and political institutions upon which the country's capacity for freedom largely depends. The defense struggle could also exert pressures to lessen the brutality and rigidity of sections of the invader's own government and population.

There are many reasons for believing that an adequately prepared civilian-based defense policy would make it possible to overthrow an occupation or a coup and restore political freedom. If a country makes the maximum possible effort to fulfill the requirements of a civilian-based defense policy, there are grounds for thinking that, under present international and technological conditions, civilian-based defense offers a much greater chance of success than does military defense.

The Tyrant Faces Impotence

A number of the responses that may be used to create a political ambush and to deny the invader his political and economic objectives has been indicated. It may be worthwhile, however, to briefly recapitulate these possible activities.

At the initial stage, he may find that the railways, airlines, buses and even private vehicles are not available to transport his soldiers and officials because of the refusal of transport workers and transportation experts to cooperate. He may discover the removal of key parts from the equipment or the absence of necessary fuel. He may meet a blanket refusal on the part of the existing government bureaucracy and civil servants to take any action, or they may continue to carry out the old policies, ignore his orders, and disrupt the implementation of new policies. The existing police, instead of helping to make arrests, carry over some resemblance of order, and encourage obedience to the new regime, may blatantly go on strike, disappear under new identities, or at least warn the resistance movement and population of impending arrests. Furthermore, the police may also selectively refuse to carry out orders or carry them out with such inefficiency that they are of little use.

The invader's parades of troops throughout the cities may be met with empty streets and shuttered windows, and his public receptions boycotted. Efforts may be made to undermine the loyalty of his individual soldiers and functionaries. They may be invited to dinners and parties with individuals and families and tactfully explained the aims and nonviolent means of the resistance. Attempts to utilize the economic system may be met with limited general strikes, slowdowns, refusals of assistance, or disappearance of indispensable experts, and the selective use of various types of strikes at key points in industries, transportation, and the supply of raw materials. The resistance may be publicized through prearranged channels throughout the world, including the invader's homeland.

At the intermediary stage, the enemy may gradually try to gain control of the various social institutions, either because their independence contributes significantly to the population's capacity to resist or because control is required by the tyrant's ideology or political program. By its very nature, totalitarianism must seek to bring all major social institutions under the control of the State, as a part of the atomization of the population and the regimentation of the society. If this is achieved, the future capacity for resistance will be largely destroyed for a long period. Thus, because of democratic principles and future combat capacity, civilian-based defense will firmly resist any efforts to control the society's institutions.

The attempt to use the legal court system to bolster the authority of the new regime or to enforce its orders would be met by refusals to recognize the usurping regime as legal and constitutional, and often by refusal of judges to continue to operate the courts under existing political conditions. The attempt to bring the school system under State control by dissolving independent teachers' organizations and school boards, by setting up substitute politically controlled bodies, and by introducing propaganda into the curriculum would be confronted with a refusal to recognize the dissolution of the former organizations, a refusal to include antidemocratic propaganda in the curriculum, explanations to the pupils of the issues at stake in the defense struggle, and perhaps the closing of school buildings and the holding of free private classes in the children's homes. Efforts to destroy the independence of trade unions and to establish politically controlled puppet organizations would be met by refusal to attend meetings of or pay dues to the new bodies, by persistence in recognizing only the earlier organizations, and by engaging in a series of disruptive strikes and boycotts that would cause grave difficulties for the usurping regime. Innumerable ways can be envisaged by which attempts to take over other institutions and occupational groups (the churches, management, newspapers, radio, farmers, electricians) could be opposed by similar noncooperation and defiance. There are historical precedents for all of these types of resistance. Even without advance preparations they have been highly effective in important cases. With careful advance instruction, training, and other types of preparations, there is every reason to believe that the effectiveness of such noncooperation could be greatly increased.

The failure to bring the occupied country to heel and to destroy social institutions would indicate that the society's capacity to resist had been sustained; its skill in doing so may have increased with combat experience. Moreover, the psychologic climate created would tend to produce or increase a miasma of uncertainty and dissent within the usurper's regime, in his country, and among his soldiers and functionaries. International pressures may also have been encouraged by the course of events and the defender's evident will to resist. The usurper may find that he faces not only the opposition of world public opinion but serious democratic pressures and economic embargoes on important fuels, raw materials, and manufactured products. In such a situation, repression feeds resistance—the greater the repression, the stronger the resistance. The simple numerical multiplication of noncooperating and disobedient subjects may thus defeat the would-be tyrant and bring about a restoration of liberty, enhanced with new meaning, vitality, and durability. The initial apparent success of the invasion or early stages of the coup is revealed as a mirage without lasting political reality. The real conquest is effected by the determined civilian defenders of freedom.

Footnotes

1. George F. Kennan, *Russia and the West Under Lenin and Stalin* (Boston: Little, Brown, 1961), p. 276. Copyright © 1960, 1961 by James K. Hotchkiss, Trustee, with permission of Atlantic-Little, Brown and Co.

2. George F. Kennan, *Russia, the Atom, and the West* (New York: Harper and Bros., 1958), pp. 62–65.

3. Arne Naess, "Non-Military Defense and Foreign Policy," in Adam Roberts, ed. *Civilian Resistance as a National Defense: Non-violent Action Against Aggression*, (Harrisburg, PA: Stackpole Books, 1968) p. 34.

4. Carl J. Friedrich, "The Unique Character of Totalitarian Society," in Carl J. Friedrich, ed. *Totalitarianism*, p. 56. "If men wish to defend themselves against a violent invader on the level of violence, it is the invader who dictates to the defender what methods of control he shall use." (Bart. de Ligt, *The Conquest of Violence: An Essay on War and Revolution* (New York: E.P. Dutton & Co., 1938; p. 198.)

5. George F. Kennan, "Totalitarianism in the Modern World," in Friedrich, ed., *Totalitarianism*, p. 23.

6. See Theodor Ebert, "Organization in Civilian Defense," in Roberts, ed., *Civilian Resistance as a National Defense*, pp. 271–273.

7. Roberts, "Civilian Defense Strategy," in ibid., p. 248.

Suggested Readings

Bondurant, Joan V. *Conquest of Violence*. Berkeley: University of California, 1965.

Boserup, Anders, and Andrew Mack. *War Without Weapons: Non-Violence in National Defense*. New York: Schocken, 1975.

Brock, Peter. *Pacifism in Europe*. Princeton: Princeton University, 1972.

Charney, Israel W., ed. *Strategies Against Violence: Design for Non-Violent Change*. Boulder: Westview, 1978.

Erickson, Erik. *Gandhi's Truth: On the Origins of Militant Non-Violence*. New York: Norton, 1969.

Pelton, L. *The Psychology of Non-Violence*. New York: Pergamon, 1974.

Reading 34

THE MORAL EQUIVALENT OF WAR

William James

Notes from the Editors

Published in the year of his death, William James' (1842–1910) "The Moral Equivalent of War" represents the distinguished American philosopher and psychologist's contribution to the debate between pacifists and militarists. Although World War I began only four years after publication of the article, during the previous decade peace movements around the world reacted energetically to the arms race, alliance systems, and periodic crises that threatened to send the European continent into war.

James accepts the warlike nature of humankind as well as the apparent fact that wars are endemic to the human condition. He is especially interested in the military experience and its alleged impact on society. In his best of all possible worlds, armies and martial values would not be necessary. Nevertheless, given the then widely held beliefs that not only was military service necessary but that it was a positive experience, James joins the militarists when he suggests that one could have "armies" without wars.

He proposes conscripting young people to work in armies that would do good works for society: improving the environment, raising living standards, and controlling nature. By participating in these activities, young people would develop the values of the military tradition that many in society seemed to cherish. James anticipates the American Peace and Job Corps, although those "armies" are not as martially oriented as the ones he describes.

The war against war is going to be no holiday excursion or camping party. The military feelings are too deeply grounded to abdicate their place among our ideals until better substitutes are offered than the glory and shame that come to nations as well as to individuals from the ups and downs of politics and the vicissitudes of trade. There is something highly paradoxical in the modern man's relation to war. Ask all our millions, north and south, whether they would vote now (were such a thing possible) to have our war for the Union expunged from history, and the record of a peaceful transition to the present time substituted for that of its marches and battles, and probably hardly a handful of eccentrics would say yes. Those ancestors, those efforts, those memories and legends, are the most ideal part of what we now own together, a sacred spiritual possession worth more than all the blood poured out. Yet ask those same people whether they would be willing in cold blood to start another civil war now to gain another similar possession, and not one man or woman would vote for the proposition. In modern eyes, precious though wars may be, they must not be waged solely for the sake of the ideal harvest. Only when forced upon one,

Reprinted from *McClure's Magazine*, August, 1910, pp. 463–468.

only when an enemy's injustice leaves us no alternative, is a war now thought permissible.

It was not thus in ancient times. The earlier men were hunting men, and to hunt a neighboring tribe, kill the males, loot the village and possess the females, was the most profitable, as well as the most exciting, way of living. Thus were the more martial tribes selected, and in chiefs and peoples a pure pugnacity and love of glory came to mingle with the more fundamental appetite for plunder.

Modern war is so expensive that we feel trade to be a better avenue to plunder; but modern man inherits all the innate pugnacity and all the love of glory of his ancestors. Showing war's irrationality and horror is of no effect upon him. The horrors make the fascination. War is the *strong* life; it is life *in extremis;* war-taxes are the only ones men never hesitate to pay, as the budgets of all nations show us.

History is a bath of blood. The Iliad is one long recital of how Diomedes and Ajax, Sarpedon and Hector *killed*. No detail of the wounds they made is spared us, and the Greek mind fed upon the story. Greek history is a panorama of jingoism and imperialism—war for war's sake, all the citizens being warriors. It is horrible reading, because of the irrationality of it all—save for the purpose of making "history"—and the history is that of the utter ruin of a civilization in intellectual respects perhaps the highest the earth has ever seen.

Those wars were purely piratical. Pride, gold, women, slaves, excitement, were their only motives. In the Peloponnesian war for example, the Athenians ask the inhabitants of Melos (the island where the "Venus of Milo" was found), hitherto neutral, to own their lordship. The envoys meet, and hold a debate which Thucydides gives in full, and which, for sweet reasonableness of form, would have satisfied Matthew Arnold. "The powerful exact what they can," said the Athenians, "and the weak grant what they must." When the Meleans say that sooner than be slaves they will appeal to the gods, the Athenians reply: "Of the gods we believe and of men we know that, by a law of their nature, wherever they can rule they will. This law was not made by us, and we are not the first to have acted upon it; we did but inherit it, and we know that you and all mankind, if you were as strong as we are, would do as we do. So much for the gods; we have told you why we expect to stand as high in their opinion as you." Well, the Meleans still refused, and their town was taken. "The Athenians," Thucydides quietly says "thereupon put to death all who were of military age and made slaves of the women and children. They then colonized the island, sending thither five hundred settlers of their own."

Alexander's career was piracy pure and simple, nothing but an orgy of power and plunder, made romantic by the character of the hero. There was no rational principle in it, and the moment he died his generals and governors attacked one another. The cruelty of those times is incredible. When Rome finally conquered Greece, Paulus Aemilius was told by the Roman Senate to reward his soldiers for their toil by "giving" them the old kingdom of Epirus. They sacked seventy cities and carried off a hundred and fifty thousand inhabitants as slaves. How many they killed I know not; but in Etolia they killed all the senators, five hundred and fifty in number. Brutus was "the noblest Roman of them all," but to reanimate his soldiers on the eve of Philippi he similarly promises to give them the cities of Sparta and Thessalonica to ravage, if they win the fight.

Such was the gory nurse that trained societies to cohesiveness. We inherit the warlike type; and for most of the capacities of heroism that the human race is full of we have to thank this cruel history. Dead men tell no tales, and if there were any tribes of other type than this they have left no survivors. Our ancestors have bred pugnacity into our bone and marrow, and thousands of years of peace won't breed it out of us. The popular imagination fairly fattens on the thought of wars. Let public opinion once reach a certain fighting pitch, and no ruler can withstand it. In the Boer war both governments began with bluff but couldn't stay there, the military tension was too much for them. In 1898 our people had read the word "war" in letters three inches high for three months in every newspaper. The pliant politician McKinley was swept away by their eagerness, and our squalid war with Spain became a necessity.

At the present day, civilized opinion is a curious mental mixture. The military instincts and ideals are as strong as ever, but are confronted by reflective criticisms which sorely curb their ancient freedom. Innumerable writers are showing up the bestial side of military service. Pure loot and mastery seem no longer morally avowable motives, and pretexts must be found for attributing them solely to the enemy. England and we, our army and navy authorities repeat without ceasing, arm solely for "peace," Germany and Japan it is who are bent on loot and glory. "Peace" in military mouths today is a synonym for "war expected." The word has become a pure provocative, and no government wishing peace sincerely should allow it ever to be printed in a newspaper. Every up-to-date dictionary should say that "peace" and "war" mean the same thing, now *in posse,* now *in actu.* It may even reasonably be said that the intensely sharp competitive *preparation* for war by the nations *is the real war,* permanent, unceasing; and that the battles are only a sort of public verification of the mastery gained during the "peace" interval.

It is plain that on this subject civilized man has developed a sort of double personality. If we take European nations, no legitimate interest of any one of them would seem to justify the tremendous destructions which a war to compass it would necessarily entail. It would seem as though common sense and reason ought to find a way to reach agreement in every conflict of honest interests. I myself think it our bounden duty to believe in such international rationality as possible. But, as things stand, I see how desperately hard it is to bring the peace-party and the war-party together, and I believe that the difficulty is due to certain deficiencies in the program of pacificism which set the militarist imagination strongly, and to a certain extent justifiably, against it. In the whole discussion both sides are on imaginative and sentimental ground. It is but one utopia against another, and everything one says must be abstract and hypothetical. Subject to this criticism and caution, I will try to characterize in abstract strokes the opposite imaginative forces, and point out what to my own very fallible mind seems the best utopian hypothesis, the most promising line of conciliation.

In my remarks, pacifist though I am, I will refuse to speak of the bestial side of the war-*regime* (already done justice to by many writers) and consider only the higher aspects of militaristic sentiment. Patriotism no one thinks discreditable; nor does any one deny that war is the romance of history. But inordinate ambitions are the soul of every patriotism, and the possibility of violent death the soul of all romance. The militarily patriotic and romantic-minded everywhere, and especially the professional military class, refuse to admit for a moment that war may be a transitory phenomenon in social evolution. The notion of a sheep's paradise like that revolts, they say, our higher imagination. Where then would be the steeps of life? If war had ever stopped, we should have to re-invent it, on this view, to redeem life from flat degeneration.

Reflective apologists for war at the present day all take it religiously. It is a sort of sacrament. Its profits are to the vanquished as well as to the victor; and quite apart from any question of profit, it is an absolute good, we are told, for it is human nature at its highest dynamic. Its "horrors" are a cheap price to pay for rescue from the only alternative supposed, of a world of clerks and teachers, of co-education and zo-ophily, of "consumer's leagues," and "associated charities," of industrialism unlimited, and feminism unabashed. No scorn, no hardness, no valor any more! Fie upon such a cattleyard of a planet!

So far as the central essence of this feeling goes, no healthy-minded person, it seems to me, can help to some degree partaking of it. Militarism is the great preserver of our ideals of hardihood, and human life with no use for hardihood would be contemptible. Without risks or prizes for the darer, history would be insipid indeed; and there is a type of military character which every one feels that the race should never cease to breed, for every one is sensitive to its superiority. The duty is incumbent on mankind, of keeping military characters in stock—of keeping them, if not for use, then as ends in themselves and as pure pieces of perfection—so that Roosevelt's weaklings and mollycoddles may not end by making everything else disappear from the face of nature.

This natural sort of feeling forms, I think, the innermost soul of army-writings. Without any exception known to me, militarist authors take a highly mystical view of their subject, and regard war as a biological or sociological necessity, uncontrolled by ordinary psychological checks and motives. When the time of development is ripe the war must come, reason or no reason, for the justifications pleaded are invariably fictitious. War is, in short, a permanent human *obligation*. General Homer Lea, in his recent book "The Valor of Ignorance," plants himself squarely on this ground. Readiness for war is for him the essence of nationality, and ability in it the supreme measure of the health of nations.

Nations, General Lea says, are never stationary—they must necessarily expand or shrink, according to their vitality or decrepitude. Japan now is culminating; and by the fatal law in question it is impossible that her statesmen should not long since have entered, with extraordinary foresight, upon a vast policy of conquest—the game in which the first moves were her wars with China and Russia and her treaty with England, and of which the final objective is the capture of the Philippines, the Hawaiian Islands, Alaska, and the whole of our Coast west of the Sierra Passes. This will give Japan what her ineluctable vocation as a state absolutely forces her to claim, the possession of the entire Pacific Ocean; and to oppose these deep designs we Americans have, according to our author, nothing but our conceit, our ignorance, our commercialism, our corruption, and our feminism. General Lea makes a minute technical comparison of the military strength which we at present could oppose to the strength of Japan, and concludes that the islands, Alaska, Oregon, and Southern California, would fall almost without resistance, that San Francisco must surrender in a fortnight to a Japanese investment, that in three or four months the war would be over, and our republic, unable to regain what it had heedlessly neglected to protect sufficiently, would then "disintegrate," until perhaps some Caesar should arise to weld us again into a nation.

A dismal forecast indeed! Yet not unplausible, if the mentality of Japan's statesmen be of the Caesarian type of which history shows so many examples, and which is all that General Lea seems able to imagine. But there is no reason to think that women can no longer be the mothers of Napoleonic or Alexandrian characters; and if these come in Japan and find their opportunity, just such surprises as "The Valor of Ignorance" paints may lurk in ambush for us. Ignorant as we still are of the innermost recesses of Japanese mentality, we may be foolhardy to disregard such possibilities.

Other militarists are more complex and more moral in their considerations. The "Philosophie des Krieges," by S. R. Steinmetz is a good example. War, according to this author, is an ordeal instituted by God, who weighs the nations in its balance. It is the essential form of the State, and the only function in which peoples can employ all their powers at once and convergently. No victory is possible save as the resultant of a totality of virtues, no defeat for which some vice or weakness is not responsible. Fidelity, cohesiveness, tenacity, heroism, conscience, education, inventiveness, economy, wealth, physical health and vigor—there isn't a moral or intellectual point of superiority that doesn't tell, when God holds his assizes and hurls the peoples upon one another. *Die Weltgeschichte ist das Weltgericht;* and Dr. Steinmetz does not believe that in the long run chance and luck play any part in apportioning the issues.

The virtues that prevail, it must be noted, are virtues anyhow, superiorities that count in peaceful as well as in military competition; but the strain on them, being infinitely intenser in the latter case, makes war infinitely more searching as a trial. No ordeal is comparable to its winnowings. Its dread hammer is the welder of men into cohesive states, and nowhere but in such states can human nature adequately develop its capacity. The only alternative is "degeneration."

Dr. Steinmetz is a conscientious thinker, and his book, short as it is, takes much into account. Its upshot can, it seems to me, be summed up in Simon Patten's word, that mankind was nursed in pain and fear, and that the transition to a "pleasure-economy" may be fatal to a being wielding no powers of defence against its disintegrative influences. If we speak of the *fear of emancipation from the fear-regime,* we put the whole situation into a single phrase; fear regarding ourselves now taking the place of the ancient fear of the enemy.

Turn the fear over as I will in my mind, it all seems to lead back to two unwillingnesses of the imagination, one aesthetic, and the other moral; unwillingnesses, first to envisage a future in which army-life, with its many elements of charm, shall be forever impossible, and in which the destinies of peoples shall nevermore be decided quickly, thrillingly, and tragically, by force, but only gradually and insipidly by "evolution"; and, secondly, unwillingness to see the supreme theatre of human strenuousness closed, and the splendid military aptitudes of men doomed to keep always in a state of latency and never show themselves in action. These insistent unwillingnesses, no less than other aesthetic and ethical insistencies, have, it seems to me, to be listened to and respected. One cannot meet them effectively by mere counter-insistency on war's expensiveness and horror. The horror makes the thrill; and when the question is of getting the extremest and supremest out of human nature, talk of expense sounds ignominious. The weakness of so much merely negative criticism is evident—pacificism makes no converts from the military party. The military party denies neither the bestiality nor the horror, nor the expense; it only says that these things tell but half the story. It only says that war is *worth* them; that, taking human nature as a whole, its wars are its best protection against its weaker and more cowardly self, and that mankind cannot *afford* to adopt a peace-economy.

Pacificists ought to enter more deeply into the aesthetical and ethical point of view of their opponents. Do that first in any controversy, says J. J. Chapman, *then move the point,* and your opponent will follow. So long as anti-militarists propose no substitute for war's disciplinary function, no *moral equivalent* of war, analogous, as one might say, to the mechanical equivalent of heat, so long they fail to realize the full inwardness of the situation. And as a rule they do fail. The duties, penalties, and sanctions pictured in the utopias they paint are all too weak and tame to touch the military-minded. Tolstoi's pacificism is the only exception to this rule, for it is profoundly pessimistic as regards all this world's values, and makes the fear of the Lord furnish the moral spur provided elsewhere by the fear of the enemy. But our socialistic peace-advocates all believe absolutely in this world's values; and instead of the fear of the Lord and the fear of the enemy, the only fear they reckon with is the fear of poverty if one be lazy. This weakness pervades all the socialistic literature with which I am acquainted. Even in Lowes Dickinson's exquisite dialogue, high wages and short hours are the only forces invoked for overcoming man's distaste for repulsive kinds of labor. Meanwhile men at large still live as they always have lived, under a pain-and-fear economy—for those of us who live in an ease-economy are but an island in the stormy ocean—and the whole atmosphere of present-day utopian literature tastes mawkish and dishwatery to people who still keep a sense for life's more bitter flavors. It suggests, in truth, ubiquitous inferiority.

Inferiority is always with us, and merciless scorn of it is the keynote of the military temper. "Dogs, would you live forever?" shouted Frederick the Great. "Yes," say our utopians, "let us live forever, and raise our level gradually." The best thing about our "inferiors" to-day is that they are as tough as nails, and physically and morally almost as insensitive. Utopianism would see them soft and squeamish, while militarism would keep their callousness, but transfigure it into a meritorious characteristic, needed by "the service," and redeemed by that from the suspicion of inferiority. All the qualities of a man acquire dignity when he knows that the service of the collectivity that owns him needs them. If proud of the collectivity, his own pride rises in proportion. No collectivity is like an army for nourishing such pride; but it has to be confessed that the only sentiment which the image of pacific cosmopolitan industrialism is capable of arousing in countless worthy breasts is shame at the idea of belonging to *such* a collectivity. It is obvious that the United States of America as they exist to-day impress a mind like General Lea's as so much human blubber. Where is the sharpness and precipitousness, the contempt for life, whether one's own, or another's? Where is the savage "yes" and "no," the unconditional duty? Where is the conscription? Where is the blood-tax? Where is anything that one feels honored by belonging to?

Having said thus much in preparation, I will now confess my own utopia. I devoutly believe in the reign of peace and in the gradual advent of some sort of a socialistic equilibrium. The fatalistic view of the war-function is to me nonsense, for

I know that war-making is due to definite motives and subject to prudential checks and reasonable criticisms, just like any other form of enterprise. And when whole nations are the armies, and the science of destruction vies in intellectual refinement with the sciences of production, I see that war becomes absurd and impossible from its own monstrosity. Extravagant ambitions will have to be replaced by reasonable claims, and nations must make common cause against them. I see no reason why all this should not apply to yellow as well as to white countries, and I look forward to a future when acts of war shall be formally outlawed as between civilized peoples.

All these beliefs of mine put me squarely into the anti-militarist party. But I do not believe that peace either ought to be or will be permanent on this globe, unless the states pacifically organized preserve some of the old elements of army-discipline. A permanently successful peace-economy cannot be a simple pleasure-economy. In the more or less socialistic future towards which mankind seems drifting we must still subject ourselves collectively to those severities which answer to our real position upon this only partly hospitable globe. We must make new energies and hardihoods continue the manliness to which the military mind so faithfully clings. Martial virtues must be the enduring cement; intrepidity, contempt of softness, surrender of private interest, obedience to command, must still remain the rock upon which states are built—unless, indeed, we wish for dangerous reactions against commonwealths fit only for contempt, and liable to invite attack whenever a centre of crystallization for military-minded enterprise gets formed anywhere in their neighborhood.

The war-party is assuredly right in affirming and reaffirming that the martial virtues, although originally gained by the race through war, are absolute and permanent human goods. Patriotic pride and ambition in their military form are, after all, only specifications of a more general competitive passion. They are its first form, but that is no reason for supposing them to be its last form. Men now are proud of belonging to a conquering nation, and without a murmur they lay down their persons and their wealth, if by so doing they may fend off subjection. But who can be sure that *other aspects of one's country* may not, with time and education and suggestion enough, come to be regarded with similarly effective feelings of pride and shame? Why should men not some day feel that it is worth a blood-tax to belong to a collectivity superior in *any* ideal respect? Why should they not blush with indignant shame if the community that owns them is vile in any way whatsoever? Individuals, daily more numerous, now feel this civic passion. It is only a question of blowing on the spark till the whole population gets incandescent, and on the ruins of the old morals of military honor, a stable system of morals of civic honor builds itself up. What the whole community comes to believe in grasps the individual as in a vise. The war-function has grasped us so far; but constructive interests may some day seem no less imperative, and impose on the individual a hardly lighter burden.

Let me illustrate my idea more concretely. There is nothing to make one indignant in the mere fact that life is hard, that men should toil and suffer pain. The planetary conditions once for all are such, and we can stand it. But that so many men, by mere accidents of birth and opportunity, should have a life of *nothing else* but toil and pain and hardness and inferiority imposed upon them, should have *no* vacation, while others natively no more deserving never get any taste of this campaigning life at all—*this* is capable of arousing indignation in reflective minds. It may end by seeming shameful to all of us that some of us have nothing but campaigning, and others nothing but unmanly ease. If now—and this is my idea—there were, instead of military con-scription, a conscription of the whole youthful population to form for a certain number of years a part of the army enlisted against *Nature,* the injustice would tend to be evened out, and numerous other goods to the commonwealth would follow. The military ideals of hardihood and discipline would be wrought into the growing fibre of the people; no one would remain blind as the luxurious classes now are blind, to man's relations to the globe he lives on, and to the permanently sour and hard foundations of his higher life. To coal and iron mines, to freight trains, to fishing fleets in December, to dish-washing, clothes-washing, and window-washing, to road-building and tunnel-making, to foundries and stoke-holes, and to the frames of sky-scrapers, would our gilded youths be drafted off, according to their choice, to get the childishness knocked out of them, and to come back into society with healthier sympathies and soberer ideas. They would have paid their blood-tax, done their own part in the immemorial human warfare against nature; they would tread the earth more proudly, the women would value them more highly, they would be better fathers and teachers of the following generations.

Such a conscription, with the state of public opinion that would have required it, and the many moral fruits it would bear, would preserve in the midst of a pacific civilization the manly virtues which the military party is so afraid of seeing disappear in peace. We should get toughness without callousness, authority with as little criminal cruelty as possible, and painful work done cheerily because the duty is temporary, and threatens not, as now, to degrade the whole remainder of one's life. I spoke of the "moral equivalent" of war. So far, war has been the only force that can discipline a whole community, and until an equivalent discipline is organized, I believe that war must have its way. But I have no serious doubt that the ordinary prides and shames of social man, once developed to a certain intensity, are capable of organizing such a moral equivalent as I have sketched, or some other just as effective for preserving manliness of type. It is but a question of time, of skilful propagandism, and of opinion-making men seizing historic opportunities.

The martial type of character can be bred without war. Strenuous honor and disinterestedness abound elsewhere. Priests and medical men are in a fashion educated to it, and we should all feel some degree of it imperative if we were conscious of our work as an obligatory service to the state. We should be *owned,* as soldiers are by the army, and our pride would rise accordingly. We could be poor, then, without humiliation, as army officers now are. The only thing needed henceforward is to inflame the civic temper as past history has inflamed the military temper. H. G. Wells, as usual, sees the centre of the situation. "In many ways," he says, "military orga-nization is the most peaceful of activities. When the contemporary man steps from the street, of clamorous insincere advertisement, push, adulteration, underselling and intermittent employment into the barrack-yard, he steps on to a higher social plane, into an atmosphere of service and cooperation and of infinitely more honorable em-ulations. Here at least men are not flung out of employment to degenerate because there is no immediate work for them to do. They are fed and drilled and trained for better services. Here at least a man is supposed to win promotion by self-forgetfulness and not by self-seeking. And beside the feeble and irregular endowment of research of commercialism, its little short-sighted snatches at profit by innovation and scientific economy, see how remarkable is the steady and rapid development of method and appliances in naval and military affairs! Nothing is more striking than to compare the progress of civil conveniences which has been left almost entirely to the trader, to the progress in military apparatus during the last few decades. The house-appliances of to-day for example, are little better than they were fifty years ago. A house of to-day is still almost as ill-ventilated, badly heated by wasteful fires, clumsily arranged and furnished as the house of 1858. Houses a couple of hundred years old are still satisfactory places of residence, so little have our standards risen. But the rifle or battleship of fifty years ago was beyond all comparison inferior to those we possess; in power, in speed, in convenience alike. No one has a use now for such superannuated things."

Wells adds that he thinks that the conceptions of order and discipline, the tradition of service and devotion, of physical fitness, unstinted exertion, and universal responsibility, which universal military duty is now teaching European nations, will remain a permanent acquisition, when the last ammunition has been used in the fireworks that celebrate the final peace. I believe as he does. It would be simply preposterous if the only force that could work ideals of honor and standards of efficiency into English or American natures should be the fear of being killed by the Germans or the Japanese. Great indeed is Fear; but it is not, as our military enthusiasts believe and try to make us believe, the only stimulus known for awakening the higher ranges of men's spiritual energy. The amount of alteration in public opinion which my utopia postulates is vastly less than the difference between the mentality of those black warriors who pursued Stanley's party on the Congo with their cannibal war-cry of "Meat! Meat!" and that of the "general-staff" of any civilized nation. History has seen the latter interval bridged over: the former one can be bridged over much more easily.

Suggested Readings

Clifford, John Gary. *The Citizen Soldiers: The Plattsburgh Training Camp Movement, 1913– 1920.* Lexington: University of Kentucky, 1972.

Cohen, Eliot A. *Citizens and Soldiers: The Dilemmas of Military Service.* Ithaca: Cornell University, 1985.

Karsten, Peter. *Soldiers and Society: The Effects of Military Service and War on American Life.* Westport: Greenwood, 1978.

Perry, Ralph Barton. *The Free Man and the Soldier: Essays on the Reconciliation of Liberty and Discipline.* New York: Scribner's, 1916.

Storr, Anthony. "Possible Substitutes for War." In *Aggression, Hostility and Violence,* eds. T. Maple and D. W. Matheson. New York: Holt, Rinehart & Winston, 1973, pp. 306–14.

Reading 35

CALCULATED DE-ESCALATION AS A STRATEGY

Charles E. Osgood

Notes from the Editor

In the late 1950s, social-psychologist Charles E. Osgood invented an approach to international conflict called Graduated Reciprocation in Tension-Reduction (GRIT). It is still one of the most celebrated proposals for reducing tensions in arms races or other diplomatic disputes. Indeed, there is some evidence to suggest that John F. Kennedy and his colleagues were aware of the general GRIT philosophy when they tried to move away from the brink of nuclear war during the Cuban Missile Crisis of 1962.

Osgood acknowledges the problems inherent in proposing unilateral initiatives. He is not a proponent, for example, of unilateral disarmament as are some pacifist groups. Rather, he lays out guidelines for small unilateral initiatives that might encourage the other side to do likewise while not risking military security to any great extent. As he points out, GRIT poses some level of risk for the initiator but he feels such a risk can be kept in the acceptable range while being significant enough to entice the opponent to take a comparable risk.

GRIT is not a blueprint for arms control. It makes no attempt to deal with the details of the very sensitive issue of verification, upon which many negotiations have foundered. Yet it is an excellent example of how academic specialists not directly involved in diplomacy, or even the study of international relations, can make contributions to global conflict resolution. The relatively new field of peace studies or peace science is full of behavioral scientists, scientists, and even humanists who are trying to contribute to the settlement of international disputes and a general reduction of international tension.

. . . For several years I have been trying to develop and justify an approach to international relations which I call *Graduated Reciprocation in Tension-Reduction*. The essence of the idea is that the tensions/arms-race spiral may provide the model for its own reversal. As a type of international behavior, *the arms race is a case of graduated and reciprocated unilateral action*. It is unilateral in that the nation developing a new weapon, increasing its stockpile, or setting up a new military base does not make its action contingent upon any prior agreement with the other side. It is reciprocal, however, because each increment in military power by one side provides the stimulus for the other to try to catch up and get ahead. It is necessarily graduated, first by the irregular and somewhat unpredictable occurrences of technological breakthrough and second by the oscillating nature of the threat stimulus itself.

But the arms race is obviously a *tension-increasing* system. One can readily conceive of a graduated and reciprocated, unilaterally initiated system that is *tension-reducing* in nature. The question is whether or not it is feasible under present conditions. I will try to demonstrate that given anything like the dedication and energy now being thrown into the arms race, it would be feasible, even though by no means magically simple.

This approach must be sharply distinguished from the kind of abject and complete unilateral disarmament sponsored by pacifist groups. To the contrary, what I am proposing is a flexible, self-regulating procedure in which the participants continually monitor their own actions on the basis of their evaluation of the reciprocating actions taken by the other side. It involves some risk, to be sure, but the risk is limited; merely going on doing what we are now doing involves infinitely greater risk! It is broader than disarmament, or even disengagement as usually conceived, since it would include programs of graduated unilateral actions of a tension-reducing nature in the areas of science and secrecy, social, economic, and cultural exchange, Communist China and the United Nations, controls and inspection, and so forth, as well as actual military and disarmament steps. It may be viewed as a kind of international (rather than interpersonal) communicating and learning situation, where the communication is more by deeds than by words and where what is learned is mutual understanding and trust.

However, being both unconventional and conciliatory in nature, this procedure is liable to suspicion abroad and resistance at home, particularly under conditions of the cold war mentality. Therefore it needs to be spelled out in detail, critically evaluated, and even tried out under both laboratory and field conditions. Specifically, it is necessary to indicate the characteristics that unilateral actions in such a program should have in order to maintain adequate felt security while nevertheless inducing reciprocation from an opponent; furthermore, we need to clarify the criteria for both determining the substance of unilateral initiatives and evaluating the bonafideness and significance of unilateral reciprocations. In other words, while admittedly idealistic in purpose, this rather novel approach must be shown to be realistic and feasible within the existing situation of competing sovereign states.

In the following analysis I will be speaking from the viewpoint of a nation which initiates such a policy of graduated reciprocation in tension-reduction. This is necessary to maintain a consistent orientation. But I want it understood that I have no particular nation in mind as the initiator—it could be either of the two polar nuclear powers, the United States or the USSR, or it could very well be some other nation or group of nations, present or future. Furthermore, just as with an arms race, once this kind of international behavior were underway, the distinction between initiation and reciprocation would become as meaningless as the distinction between stimulus and response within the central nervous system.

Maintaining Security

1. *Unilateral actions should not reduce a nation's capacity to inflict unacceptable nuclear retaliation on an opponent should it be attacked.* I would be the first to agree that nuclear deterrence does not provide any real security over the long haul, but on the other hand, highly invulnerable second-strike forces will exist in the near future, if not already, and under present levels of tension

they are not likely to be given up. Particularly if their retaliatory nature is made explicit, and moral prohibition against their first use is accepted by all sides, nuclear weapons can be viewed not only as a deterrent *but also as a security base from which limited risks can be taken.* I am assuming that since there is no necessary correlation between the tension-reducing impacts of actions and their military significance, a program of graduated reciprocation in tension-reduction could produce an atmosphere of mutual trust in which the nuclear deterrents themselves could ultimately be eliminated by negotiated agreement.

2. *Unilateral actions should be graduated in risk potential according to the degree of reciprocation obtained.* This is the essential self-regulating characteristic of the proposal. The magnitude of a unilateral step taken at a particular time would depend upon that nation's evaluation of the reciprocative behavior of the other. The process can be slowed down or speeded up, as conditions require, but it should be kept going.

3. *Unilateral actions should be diversified in nature so as not to weaken a nation progressively in any one sphere.* Diversity in areas of action both provides an essential flexibility of approach and prevents the unstabilizing effect of too large steps in a single sphere. The only common property of the actions envisaged in this proposal is their tension-reducing nature. This, as I pointed out earlier, can be cumulative over a highly diversified range of actions, e.g., student exchanges, sharing of scientific information, reducing trade barriers, diplomatic recognition, elimination of bases, and so on.

4. *Prior to announcement, unilateral actions should be unpredictable by an opponent as to their nature, locus, and time of execution.* This is to minimize the likelihood of encroachment. I submit that psychologically, an opponent is much less likely to encroach aggressively in an area after public announcement of intent by another than prior to it, and he is certainly less likely to gain world support if he does. However, if encroachments do occur they must be resisted just as firmly as if this policy were not in operation. Yet, this resistance should be pinpointed to the area of encroachment and the program of tension-reducing moves continued flexibly in other areas. This is clearly a different approach than the traditional, monolithic reaction of nations to tension-increasing events, but it is an approach that seems necessary in a nuclear age. Under conditions of nuclear deterrence, encroachments are likely to be tentative and probing in nature, and therefore can constitute a learning experience on all sides—learning that graduated reciprocation in reducing tensions is not synonymous with surrender.

Inducing Reciprocation

1. *Unilateral actions should be announced publicly at some reasonable interval prior to their execution and identified as part of a deliberate policy of reducing tensions.* Announcement prior to action is suggested as a means of augmenting pressure toward reciprocation, of avoiding the unstabilizing effect of unexpected moves, of providing time for preparing reciprocation, and, particularly, of influencing the interpretation of the action when it comes. Public an-

nouncement makes it possible to enlist pressures of world opinion toward reciprocation, and identification of each act as part of a deliberate policy is designed to make the pressures toward reciprocation cumulative.

2. *In their announcement, unilateral actions should include explicit invitation to reciprocation in some form.* Initiation and reciprocation need not be the same in kind nor even equal in quantity. There are some unilateral actions that could not be reciprocated in kind (e.g., if the United States were to denuclearize some Pacific base, the Chinese Communists could not reciprocate in kind) and the burden of the same rule may be quite different in two countries (e.g., absolute amounts of inspection permitted). On the other hand, the fact that reciprocation in some form is expected must be made explicit. The isolated unilateral gestures that have occasionally been made in the past have been largely abortive, in part because they did not call for reciprocation.

3. *Unilateral actions that have been announced must be executed on schedule regardless of prior commitment by the opponent to reciprocate.* This is the characteristic that distinguishes this policy from traditional bargaining and negotiating procedures; it is the characteristic that provides an increased degree of freedom on all sides for taking the initiative. Of course, if no reciprocation is forthcoming, or attempts are made to take advantage of the initiator, then the process slows down or stops. In this sense, reciprocation can be viewed as a kind of postcommitment that enables the policy to continue.

4. *Unilateral actions should be planned in graded series and continued over a considerable period regardless of immediate reciprocation or police action elsewhere.* Given the tense atmosphere in which such a strategy must begin, it is likely that initial actions would be greeted by cries of "cold war trick!"; but the bonafideness of the intent becomes more and more difficult to deny and rationalize as action follows announced action. Furthermore, the pressure toward reciprocation should cumulate over such a period of continued action. Here again we have a kind of international learning situation—in this case, unlearning the bogeyman image of the opponent, since the psychologic expectations and prophesies being made about him are being repeatedly denied.

5. *As far as possible, unilateral actions should be overt deeds rather than either positive or negative sanctions and should be as unambiguous and as susceptible to verification as possible.* Overt acts have the obvious advantage of bonafideness, particularly if the announced action includes invitation to observe and inspect. Sanctions, on the other hand, have no visible execution or test until their failure—the unilaterally imposed bans on nuclear testing are a case in point. This emphasizes another difference between this kind of policy and ordinary negotiations, a difference well expressed by the homely saying, "actions speak louder than words."

What about the problem of *evaluating reciprocations* (and, for that matter, the problem an opponent has in evaluating one's unilateral initiations)? There are two rather different questions here: One concerns the bonafideness of actions, which seems to come down to the adequacy of intelligence in the military sense; the other concerns the significance of actions, and this seems to be a matter for strategic analysis. To enhance *bonafideness,* both the initiator's unilateral acts and the reciprocations requested should be as unambiguous and susceptible to verification as possible; provisions for adequate inspection may be included in both initiations and requested reciprocations. As a matter of fact, it might be possible to get around the apparent deadlock on inspection by introducing it in small, manageable and perhaps palatable packages under such a program as this; if one side accepts an invitation to unilaterally inspect some specific action of the other, it becomes psychologically difficult to deny him the same privilege. As to the *significance* of reciprocations, two criteria would have to be kept in mind: first, that the risk potential in the unilateral actions by one party should be roughly balanced by the increased security gained through the reciprocations of the other party; second, that tension-decreasing steps in one area must be balanced against the total level of tension-increasing and tension-decreasing events in all areas. I realize that these estimations are not easy, but they involve the sort of strategic analysis that is going on all the time anyhow.

Finally, there are some additional criteria for selecting actions that should be mentioned. First, it is probably wisest to begin such a program with actions in areas other than the critical military and disarmament spheres, moving in toward these matters only when the general level of tension has been sufficiently reduced. Second, particularly in the early phases, unilateral initiatives should involve areas in which both parties in the conflict are known to be ready to move, in which restraints may already have been reciprocally self-imposed, and in which both are likely to see issues of human welfare rather than national security. Again, we have here a kind of learning situation on all sides, and it is important that the probabilities of reinforcement be high at first. And since we would wish the substance of our actions to be consistent with our long-term goals as well as our immediate needs to control tensions, they should be designed to gradually shape the world of tomorrow; therefore, unilateral initiatives and reciprocations should involve gradual transfer of sovereignty from national to international auspices, gradual lessening of the imbalance between "have" and "have not" countries, and gradual shifting of scientific research onto an international basis on the model of the IGY, particularly research having military implications where scientific breakthroughs have an unstabilizing impact.

Despite the unilateral initiative which characterizes this proposal, it should be apparent that the two parties in conflict are really dependent on each other for its success. This is because on each side there are competing factions spread over the spectrum of policy alternatives. If President Kennedy, exercising administrative initiative, were to announce and execute a carefully planned series of tension-reducing moves, opposition groups in the United States government, in its mass media, and in its public would become increasingly critical. The only way to quiet this opposition and keep the policy moving, in the long run, would be to receive reciprocation from the opponent. I am sure that much the same situation would hold in the case of Soviet initiation. Now it is true that the leadership of a nation would be risking its position by initiating such a policy and that an opponent might assist in the demise by withholding reciprocation—*but in doing so the opponent should be fully aware of the fact that he is strengthening forces more violently antagonistic to him and more likely to act inflexibly and irrationally in future relations.* Thus it would be to the advantage of both sides to be on the alert for tension-reducing probes from the other and to be prepared for reciprocations that will allow the process to continue.

Could the initiator of such a policy expect to obtain bonafide and significant reciprocation under present conditions? I cannot give an unqualified "yes" to this question. Here, obviously, lies the risk—but as I pointed out earlier, mere going on as we are involves even greater risk. And surely it would be cause for cosmic irony if two human groups in conflict were to bring their world down in destruction because of their threatening images of each other without ever testing the validity of these images. Despite the differences between us, there are many things we share; we share common modes of thinking and feeling, we share a common technology that is rapidly transforming us into one world whether we like it or not, and above all we share a common desire to get out of this dangerous situation and go on living. If my basic assumption about the contemporary motivation of international behavior is right—that it is based more on fear and insecurity than on any urge toward national aggrandizement—then I think reciprocation would be forthcoming, if not for reasons of good will then for reasons of good sense. And here another psychological principle applies: If two people are forced to keep on behaving *as if* they trusted each other, their beliefs and attitudes tend to fall in line with their behaviors. I think the same applies to nations.

Conclusion

The preservation of peace is the biggest problem of our time, and I have no illusions about my own capacity to comprehend it all. Although the problem has important psychological components, much more than psychology is involved—political science, economics, international law, communications, nuclear and space technology, diplomacy, and the military, to call only part of the roll. And no one as aware as I am of the strength of the contrary forces, of the deeply ingrained mechanisms of the cold war mentality, could be very sanguine about our chances of escaping from this situation unscathed.

On the other hand, I have convinced myself, at least, that such a policy of graduated reciprocation in tension control is feasible for our time. True, it would require extraordinary sensitivity, flexibility, and restraint from leadership on all sides, as well as high-level strategic planning and execution, but this could be viewed as a challenge rather than a flaw. If it were successfully initiated, such a policy could, over the short term, increase the stability of the military environment and perhaps create an atmosphere in which more significant steps toward disarmament could be taken; over the long term, it might offer a model for international relations that is more appropriate to this age of nuclear technology. I can do no better than close with a quotation from Albert Einstein that might have been written today: "The unleashed power of the atom has changed everything except our ways of thinking. Thus we are drifting toward a catastrophe beyond comparison. We shall require a substantially new manner of thinking if mankind is to survive."

Suggested Readings

Axelrod, Robert. *The Evolution of Cooperation*. New York: Basic Books, 1984.

de Callieres, Francois. *On the Manner of Negotiating with Princes*. Notre Dame: University of Notre Dame, 1963.

Deutsch, Morton. *The Resolution of Conflict: Constructive and Destructive Processes*. New Haven: Yale University, 1973.

Fisher, Roger, and William Ury. *Getting to Yes*. New York: Penguin, 1981.

Ikle, Fred Charles. *How Nations Negotiate*. New York: Praeger, 1964.

Lebow, Richard Ned. *Between Peace and War*. Baltimore: Johns Hopkins University, 1981.

Schelling, Thomas C. *The Strategy of Conflict*. New York: Oxford University Press, 1960.

Young, Oran, ed. *Bargaining: Formal Theories of Negotiation*. Urbana, University of Illinois, 1975.

Reading 36

AN OPEN LETTER TO U.N. CHIEFS

Richard Hudson

Notes from the Editors

Ever since the United Nations was founded in 1945, diplomats, scholars, and journalists have suggested ways to improve its peacekeeping and war prevention functions. They have tried to move the world body from a debating society to a genuine upholder of collective security, and possibly even to something of a world parliament. Richard Hudson, executive director of the Center for War/Peace Studies, offers his plan on the occasion of the fortieth anniversary of the United Nations.

The veto has been a particularly difficult problem for the Security Council, the UN agency that deals with collective security. Whenever the Council considers issues of vital importance to its five permanent members, a veto can be expected to quash any meaningful action. On the other hand, the General Assembly, which has no veto power, has only a limited role to play in collective security matters. Moreover, it is mistrusted by many major powers, especially the United States, because of the one-nation one-vote principle under which it operates. The weight of the vote of the smallest island nation in the Caribbean, for example, is equal to that of any major power. In the present international system, many of the small developing states in Asia, Africa, and Latin America are hostile to western and American policies.

Hudson's somewhat complicated proposals that call for the amending of two articles in the UN Charter are directed to solving these problems. While far from transforming the UN into a world government, they would increase the body's ability to deal with aggression and threats to peace. Hudson's Binding Triad and Magic 22 Formula seem equitable on the surface. However, many political and ideological issues confront anyone trying to implement them. Most important, they appear to call for a partial surrender of sovereignty to an international authority.

Dear Mr. President and Mr. Secretary-General:

With great respect for the organization you represent and high regard for both of you, I write to urge you as you prepare for the 40th anniversary of the adoption of the United Nations Charter to think in terms that may be considered radical in the glass house on the East River.

Mr. Secretary-General, at a press conference on July 5, 1984, in Geneva you said: "I personally hope and believe that the United Nations will make a great effort to become still more useful. It must always bear in mind that next year will mark the fortieth anniversary of the organization. I shall be rather like a person preparing for a celebration, who wants the outside of his house painted so as to present a better appearance."

Reprinted with permission of the author from *Global Report* 18, November/December 1984.

I would like earnestly to suggest that what the United Nations needs is not just a new paint job for its 40th birthday, but serious structural work on its foundation, a complete overhaul of its plumbing system, and the plugging of a good many leaks in its roof. In short, I argue that while the U.N. is not an international edifice beyond repair, it is much too rickety to be fixed up with cosmetics.

We are all familiar with the problems: the Security Council is time and again immobilized by the veto, and the General Assembly, with its one nation, one vote basis, passes great numbers of unbalanced, meaningless resolutions that in any event are only non-binding recommendations. I think that both of you, and the member states and the Secretariat staff, deserve praise for making the present hopelessly obsolete decision-making system work as well as you have. I know that both of you are painfully aware of the problems I mention.

Mr. President, in your statement to the General Assembly on being elected to your high post, you said: "Some member states are questioning the legitimacy of our organization. Some assert that the United Nations deliberative organs have ceased to honor the principle of objectivity, sobriety and fairness. It is even being suggested that these organs have served as instruments for the exacerbation of conflicts rather than for promoting understanding and reconciliation among states. Others bemoan the prevalence of double standards and absence of consistency in decisions."

And Mr. Secretary-General, in your report to the current 39th session of the General Assembly, you declared: "However, for all the accomplishments of the past decades, and they have been major, the fact of the matter is that the three main elements of a stable international order—an accepted system of maintaining international peace and security; disarmament and arms limitation; and the progressive development of a just and effective system of international relations—have yet to take hold as they should."

Two years ago, Mr. Secretary-General, in your first report to the General Assembly, you stated: "We are perilously near to a new international anarchy." That report inspired a series of Security Council "consultations" that are still continuing. I have talked with many of the participants in these consultations, and I have found that they have worked long and hard to try to find ways to make the Security Council function better. But the sad fact is that the Security Council is *not* working any better. In Lebanon alone, we have already witnessed two occasions this year on which the Council could have helped, but failed to do so. On the first, a French resolution to make U.N. peacekeeping forces available in Beirut could have aided in restoring stability there; it was vetoed by the Soviet Union. On the second, a resolution called upon the Israelis to open up roads between Israel-occupied areas in the south and the rest of Lebanon, and to treat civilians there better; it was vetoed by the United States.

I want to advance the argument to both of you, and to all other supporters of the United Nations who might read this open letter to you, that so long as efforts to improve the United Nations continue to operate on the assumption that the present U.N. Charter, without amendment, is adequate for making appropriate global decisions in our present interdependent and explosive world, these endeavors are doomed to failure. We are fortunate that the founders of the United Nations had the foresight to include Articles 108 and 109 in the Charter, which provide the means of amending the basic document of the world organization. In my view, it is tragic that the statesmen of the world have not seen fit to exercise these articles more often.

Let me set forth a proposal to amend two articles of the U.N. Charter, which I have been working on for more than 20 years. I believe that adoption of these two amendments would transform the United Nations into an organization that would provide a genuine peace system, replacing the present war system of international relations. The proposal is called the Binding Triad system of global decision-making.

The first amendment, to Article 18, would change the voting system in the U.N. General Assembly. Important decisions in the Assembly would still be adopted with a single vote, *but with three simultaneous majorities within that vote*. Approval of a resolution would require that the majority vote include two-thirds of the population of the members present and voting (as at present), nations representing two-thirds of those present and voting and nations representing two-thirds of the contributions to the regular U.N. budget of those present and voting. (Abstentions would not count.) Thus, in order for a resolution to be adopted it would have to be supported strongly by most of the countries of the world, most of the population of the world, and most of the political / economic / military strength of the world.

The second amendment, to Article 13, would increase the powers of the General Assembly, in most cases making its decisions binding instead of recommendations as at present. However, the Assembly would not be permitted "to intervene in matters which are essentially within the jurisdiction of any state," as the Charter already provides. If the jurisdiction were in doubt, the issue would be referred to the World Court, and if the court ruled that the question was essentially domestic, the Assembly could not act. Furthermore, the Assembly would be prohibited from employing military forces to carry out its resolutions; this would remain the prerogative of the Security Council, as at present. But the Assembly could provide peacekeeping forces to carry out a mandate. The Binding Triad system would be applicable not only to peace and security questions, but also to economic and social problems.

Roots Go Back to 1787

In a broad historical sense, the Binding Triad proposal traces its roots back to that long, hot summer in Philadelphia in 1787 when America's founding fathers drafted the U.S. Constitution. They convened under the Articles of Confederation, a document that bore striking similarities to the United Nations Charter. Its 13 members were sovereign, were not taxed but made voluntary contributions to joint efforts, provided forces as they wished (or did not wish) to the American army, and were engaged in a variety of unresolved boundary and trade disputes. Unfortunately, the Articles of Confederation provided a process of amendment even more difficult than that of the U.N. Charter—each of the 13 states had veto power over any amendment—so leaders of the American states struggled to write a new constitution that they hoped would meet the needs of the former colonies. They knew, above all, that they wanted to establish a representative government that would be strong enough to govern effectively, but not so strong that it could become authoritarian.

In the end, they produced the U.S. Constitution that we are now familiar with. One aspect of their handiwork is of particular interest now as the United Nations grapples with the problem of global decision-making. Small states such as Delaware and Rhode Island wanted the legislature to be based on equal voting strength for each of the sovereign states; larger states such as New York, Massachusetts and Virginia wanted a voting system that would reflect their greater power and populations. The upshot, as we know, was a bicameral system in which one house is based on the voting equality of states and the other is pro-rated on population.

In the years following World War II, as it was becoming evident that the United Nations was not living up to the hopes held for it in 1945, various proposals were made to improve the decision-making capacity of the United Nations. There was an urgency behind these efforts because of a feeling that the pre-Hiroshima U.N. Charter would not be an adequate instrument under which the world could disarm. The best known of these proposals was put forth by Grenville Clark and Louis B. Sohn in their book *World Peace Through World Law* (Harvard University Press, 1958). In the Clark-Sohn plan, which would have thoroughly revised the U.N. Charter, with the aim of making possible general disarmament and global development, the authors proposed that the General Assembly be given "final responsibility for the enforcement of the disarmament process and the maintenance of peace" and that voting power be based on seven categories of population. The way it worked out at that time (1957), four nations with populations of over 140 million (China, India, U.S.S.R., and U.S.A.) would have 30 votes, while eight nations with populations between 40 and 140 million (including two permanent members of the Security Council, France and the United Kingdom) would each have 16 votes. It seemed to me unrealistic to expect France or the U.K. to accept this scheme when it would mean their ending up with about half the voting strength of China or India, while at the same time—despite their greater political/economic/military strength than those two more populous countries—they would have had to give up their veto in the Security Council.

During the early 1960s, I was privileged to have a series of conversations with the sage Mr. Clark about the future of the U.N. and the best way to achieve world disarmament and development. We agreed on the extreme difficulty of achieving revision of the U.N. Charter. He settled on the alternative of trying to set up an International Disarmament Organization that for all practical purposes would have been outside the U.N., although technically it would still have been under the U.N. aegis. I could not accept this on the grounds that this would still not solve the critical problem of global decision-making. I am disturbed to see this idea being revived by some good friends of the U.N., and I feel as strongly now as I did then that this is the wrong road to take. I firmly believe that the U.N. Charter can be made to work, provided we wisely exercise Articles 108 and 109 which the framers so foresightedly gave us in San Francisco.

Mr. President, you said in your acceptance speech: "Twenty years ago, a distinguished son of Africa, symbolizing Africa's decade of independence and emancipation, was elected the nineteenth president of the United Nations General Assembly. It was a time of acute crisis for the organization and the shadow of imminent collapse hovered over the General Assembly. It was our good fortune that with exceptional skill and imagination, arrangements were found that ensured the survival of our organization."

I remember that 19th General Assembly of 1964 vividly. The problem you referred to is sometimes called "the Article 19 crisis," and the "distinguished son of Africa" was Alex Quaison-Sackey of Ghana. What happened, as we know, was that in 1960 the Soviet Union had voted approvingly in the Security Council for the U.N. operation in the Congo, which had become chaotic after winning its independence from Belgium. However, as the operation moved along the Soviet Union became increasingly disillusioned with it, charging that under Secretary-General Dag Hammarskjold the U.N. was tilting toward the pro-Western leader Mobutu and against the Soviets' friend Lumumba. (Mobutu is still there; Lumumba was assassinated.) As a result, the U.S.S.R. declined to pay its assessments for the Congo operation, and the United States determined to try to take away the vote of the Soviet Union in the Assembly under Article 19 of the Charter, which provides that a member two years in arrears in payments "shall have no vote." The Soviet Union made clear that if it were deprived of its vote, it would leave the Assembly, presumably for good, and maybe the U.N. itself. Some decisions were made informally with delegates filing by Quaison-Sackey in a U.N. basement office and whispering in his ear how they would vote if they could have voted. In the end, the U.S. had to back down since it faced the dilemma of either a humiliating loss in the vote or, if it won, of driving the Soviet Union out of the U.N. The Article 19 crisis reinforced my conclusion that the single most important need of the international community was for a system to make balanced, specific, creative decisions that could be effectively implemented.

Like the Article 19 crisis, the Binding Triad proposal for global decision-making I outlined earlier is also marking its 20th anniversary. In its initial version, called "A Proposal for a Peace-Keeping Majority in the United Nations" (published in *War/Peace Report*, February 1964), the idea was limited to peace and security questions and was based on a bicameral voting system requiring certain majorities in both the Security Council (but with no veto) and the General Assembly (with a population factor introduced). But by the time the next version was published (in *The Bulletin of the Atomic Scientists*, November 1976), I had concluded that it would be wise to make Charter changes only in regard to the General Assembly.

This brings to mind, Mr. Secretary General, a comment you made in answer to a question at your press conference of September 17, 1984: "Of course, any movement in the direction of a world government in this area will be most welcome by me, as a world citizen. But unfortunately, it is a difficult task because any revision needs the support of the five permanent members of the Security Council, and not even Article 43 has been fully implemented—which gives us an indication that unfortunately we are still far from a world government."

Leave the Security Council Alone

Here is my reasoning as to why the Binding Triad amendments should leave the Security Council untouched. First, Charter amendments on the veto would probably be the hardest of all kinds to get. Second, I do not believe they are necessary to get a decision-making system that will work effectively in the global interest. You mentioned, Mr. Secretary-General, Article 43, which calls upon members to make available "armed forces" to the Security Council "for the purpose of maintaining international peace and security." I believe the time is long since past when the U.N. should think in terms of the use of "armed forces" to implement its decisions. Peacekeeping forces, yes, have already demonstrated their utility many times, and under the Binding Triad system could be expected to be employed even more, and with better mandates. But Security Council action under Chapter VII of the Charter—and particularly Article 42 which provides that the Council "may take such action by air, sea, or land forces as may be necessary to maintain or restore international peace and security—is, *and should be,* a dead letter. The only scenario I can foresee in which Chapter VII should be invoked would be an attack on Earth from outer space, in which case I am sure you would see prompt and unanimous Security Council action employing armed forces.

The major thrust of the United Nations at this stage of history, in my view, should be to develop itself into an organization that can confront all our multifarious global problems and produce fair, imaginative, specific solutions to them. If the U.N. can succeed in doing this, it will not need "air, sea or land forces" to implement them—peacekeeping forces will be ample, and many decisions, probably most, will not need even those.

This is the purpose of the Binding Triad proposal for global decision-making. In order to test its viability and increase its credibility, in October of each of the three past years the Center for War/Peace Studies has invited a diverse group of diplomats, Secretariat members, academics, journalists, and non-governmental organization representatives to Lake Mohonk, New Paltz, N.Y., to carry out simulated tests on the Binding Triad system. The problems we have faced in our working groups have been arms control/disarmament, and Afghanistan (1981); the Middle East (the Israel-Palestinian conflict, in two working groups with the same mandate, to test the Binding Triad in a different way), and North-South talks (1982); and the militarization (or, hopefully the *de*-militarization) of space, Lebanon, and Antarctica (1983). Among the participants have been high level diplomats of all five permanent members of the Security Council and of many other countries. We have had present the computer and computer programmer enabling us to put the resolutions of these working groups to the test of the Binding Triad process. I think it is fair to say that the results ranged from slightly better to very much better than those the U.N. is producing on these same subjects. In fact, some of these resolutions have carried themselves into actual U.N. deliberations, and again I think it is fair to say that in this context the Mohonk resolutions have only gone downhill, becoming diluted and biased. For either of you, or anyone in the U.N. community, we will be pleased to provide reports of the Mohonk simulation tests. . . .

Mr. President and Mr. Secretary-General, I would like to raise with you a few of the key questions that have arisen in our discussions in the U.N. on the Binding Triad proposal.

The first reaction of the many small U.N. members to the Binding Triad usually is to object to the "Triad half" of the proposal. They view askance the prospect of losing their so-called automatic majority in the Assembly. However, they look with favor on the "Binding half." And as you might expect, the situation is precisely the reverse with the permanent members of the Security Council. Therefore, I argue, it will be necessary for both halves of the Binding Triad to be adopted together, with both sides trading off the half objectionable to them in order to gain the half they like. The bargain must be looked at not as a zero sum game in which one side will win and one will lose, but rather as a non zero sum game in which both sides can win—

or in which both sides can lose if they continue on the present perilous course. The great prize to be collectively won is a global order that can produce evenhanded, wise, specific solutions to our planet's problems—and most of all to create a peace system to replace the war system, making it possible for the world to proceed toward disarmament.

Many questions have arisen as to why this precise system of voting has been proposed for the Binding Triad. The rationale for the three legs of the Binding Triad goes like this:

One Nation, One Vote: The first leg of the Binding Triad is based on the sovereign equality of states. The primary reason for this, as was once said of Mt. Everest, is simply: "It's there." By itself, it is not working well, but is a logical place to start. Moveover, it is familiar to us all; if a photograph were taken of the General Assembly Hall after adoption of the Binding Triad, it would look exactly as it does today (except for the voting board, which would have spaces to display the results of the voting on the three legs). By beginning with a known quantity, it will be easier to project how the new system would work after the two Charter amendments are made, and thus diminish fears of governments of moving into a totally unknown area.

Population: The second leg of the Binding Triad, based on the population of states, might be called the democracy leg. It is often said in the U.N. that the one nation, one vote system is democratic, but this is spurious. A democracy is a government by the people, not nation states. The root *dem,* in both Greek and Latin, means *people; populace; population.* The extremely undemocratic nature of the one nation, one vote system can be demonstrated by comparing the most populous U.N. member, China (pop: 1,039,677,000), with the least populous member, Saint Christopher and Nevis (pop: 45,000). This means, since the two countries have an equal vote in the Assembly, that if you happen to be a citizen of Saint Christopher and Nevis you have, through your government, voting strength 23,104 times as great as that of a Chinese citizen.

Contributions to the Regular U.N. Budget: The third leg of the Binding Triad, based on assessments on members for contributions to the organization's regular budget, might be called the realpolitik leg. With assessments closely related to the members' gross national products, they represent in a rough manner the political/economic/military influence of nations in world affairs, ranging as they do from the maximum of 25 percent paid by the United States to the minimum of 0.01 percent paid by the majority of members. There have been suggestions of ways to bring in other factors on the third leg, such as giving increased voting weight to nations that raise their literacy rates or reduce military spending. On balance, however, it seemed wise to stick with the regular assessments basis both on the grounds of simplicity and because, again like Mt. Everest, "It's there." There will never be a perfect formula, and this one looks as if it could work fairly well.

The first two legs of the Binding Triad are rather cut and dried, as numbers of nations and their populations don't change very fast. But great care would have to be taken with the third leg to assure that an effective political balance was maintained. The regular U.N. budget is in global economic terms really very small—only about $750 million per year, or less than half the cost of one Trident submarine. Thus, unless careful limits were kept on contributions to the regular U.N. budget, a big power theoretically could "buy" the entire third leg. Of course, this would not be permitted. (However, there would be nothing to prevent rich countries from increasing contributions to voluntary U.N. programs, but those would not count in determining voting strength on the third leg of the Binding Triad.) The important point is, anomalous as it may at first seem, that under the Binding Triad many countries will want to *maximize* their contributions to the regular U.N. budget rather than to *minimize* them, as is the case now. Increasing one's contributions to the regular budget would be a very inexpensive way of acquiring new political influence.

The Magic 22 Formula: This situation in regard to the correlation of regular budget contributions and voting strength on the third leg of the triad gives rise to one particular difficulty: the Soviet bloc makes 16 percent of the regular budget contributions, compared to the United States' 25 percent. I can attest from conversations with many Soviet diplomats that this would not be an arrangement to their liking, and I think it is understandable. This has led me to propose what I call the "Magic 22 Formula," according to which the United States would be *required to reduce* its regular budget contribution from 25 to 22 percent, while the Soviet bloc would be *permitted to increase* its contributions from 16 to 22 percent. (This idea, on first presentation, usually gets a laugh from both U.S. and Soviet delegates.) By coincidence, the 22 percent figure represents two-thirds of a veto, and also by coincidence, China has 22 percent of the vote on the population leg. Thus, under the Magic 22 formula, the maximum voting strength that any nation or consistent voting bloc could have on any of the three legs would be the equivalent of two-thirds of a veto, with China having it on the second leg and the U.S. and the Soviet bloc on the third.

(Two-thirds of a veto, in practice, would be vastly different than the veto now operating in the Security Council. For example, the two resolutions on Lebanon cited earlier that were vetoed by the Soviet Union and the U.S. would almost surely have passed the Assembly under the Binding Triad system. In fact, they would probably have been of much higher quality—more comprehensive, more balanced, more specific, more creative, more implementable.)

Mr. President and Mr. Secretary-General, I don't know if I have been able to persuade you of the merit of the Binding Triad proposal. Even if I have, I know you will be quick to remind me of the enormous difficulty of winning its acceptance by two-thirds of the membership including the five permanent members of the Security Council. The Binding Triad proposal is asking no less than that the nations of the world transfer a limited portion of their sovereignty to a new United Nations in order to increase greatly the chances of avoiding World War III and moving toward a world organization under which members can afford to disarm. The way will be hard and long, but doing great things is never easy. And I would like to emphasize that while this initiative must necessarily start within the United Nations, I do not believe there is any chance that it can ever finally be accepted without mammoth pressure coming from outside the world organization.

Mr. Secretary-General, I cannot state the case more eloquently than you did in the closing words of your current annual report:

"In the United Nations we have now had nearly 40 years of experience, 40 years of change, and, for all the conflict of our time, 40 years without a global war. Let us look back at the road we have travelled, distill the experience and set out again refreshed and with a new determination. The purposes for which the United Nations was set up are essential for the future of our planet. The vision expressed in the Charter remains, and we should rally to it."

Let us prove that for the United Nations, with its immense unrealized potential so far, life truly does begin at 40!

With warm regards,

Sincerely,

Richard Hudson

Suggested Readings

Clark, Grenville, and Louis Sohn. *World Peace Through World Law*. Cambridge: Harvard University, 1966.

Cooper, Sandi E., ed. *Peace Projects of the Eighteenth Century*. New York: Garland, 1974.

Culbertson, Ely. *Total Peace*. Garden City, N.Y.: Doubleday, 1943.

Falk, Richard A., Samuel S. Kim, and Saul H. Mendlovitz, eds. *Studies on a Just World Order, I*. Boulder, Colo.: Westview, 1982.

Gould, Wesley, and Michael Barken, eds. *International Law and the Social Sciences*. Princeton: Princeton University, 1970.

Johansen, Robert C. *Toward an Alternative Security System*. New York: World Policy Institute, 1983.

Mazrui, Ali A. *A World Federation of Cultures: An African Perspective*. New York: Free Press, 1977.

CHAPTER 7

Nuclear War

Since the 1960s, fears of nuclear war have increased dramatically. The major powers have introduced new generations of weapons systems, while others still on their drawing boards have contributed to a frenzied renewal of the arms race with all of its inherent dangers. In addition, the likelihood of unrestrained nuclear proliferation, the prospect of nuclear-armed terrorists and even the rise of terrorist states have led many to worry about the very future of civilization. Despite the positive developments of the recent Reagan-Gorbachev peace initiatives, the specter of nuclear war continues to threaten civilization.

The end of life as we know it could come quickly and in many ways. In our first selection in this chapter, a group of Harvard scholars look into "The Shattered Crystal Ball: How Might a Nuclear War Begin?" All of their doomsday scenarios appear plausible in today's international system. Not all of them lead inexorably to global incineration, however. Some experts believe that a limited nuclear war would be the outcome of the scenarios since rational leaders would know when to stop.

The great concern is that once Pandora's box is opened, who will be able to close it? Moreover, irrespective of the numbers of missiles exchanged, even a "small" nuclear war might lead to unimaginable destruction to our ecosystem. Scientists now take seriously the prospect of nuclear winter following a *limited* nuclear war.

Although nuclear disarmament is almost everyone's long-term goal, strategists differ over proposals to defuse the current crisis. One controversial suggestion is the adoption of a pledge by atomic powers not to be the first to use their weapons. Admiral John Lee sets forth the case for a "No First Use" pledge from the United States in the second selection in this chapter. Needless to say, Lee's proposal is not accepted by those who maintain that deterrence has worked, in part because American adversaries have had to tread cautiously because they did not know at what point Washington would pull the nuclear trigger.

For his part, Paul H. Nitze comes to the defense of American arms control policy in his speech, "The Objectives of Arms Control." Nitze outlines American and Soviet arms control accomplishments up to 1985, how deterrence has succeeded and will continue to keep the peace, and the rationale for the Strategic Defense Initiative or "Star Wars."

Although the success of the INF treaty in 1988 and the move to reduce long-range missiles have encouraged those who would like to create and preserve a world without nuclear weapons, the total zero option appears unlikely at this juncture. More important, as Plinio Prioreschi contends "In Defense of Nuclear Deterrence," it is precisely the existence of nuclear weapons that has created the great power peace since the 1940s. Adopting an unsentimental approach, most likely one of which Nitze would approve, Prioreschi is relatively pleased with the prospects for great power peace and international stability in the short run.

Nevertheless, most defenders of MAD (Mutually Assured Destruction) acknowledge that the world is experiencing a period of increased instability as new weapons systems are made operational and both sides jockey for the best advantage, given the new strategic calculus. J. David Singer is unwilling to approach such a problem with a business-as-usual approach. In his "Nuclear Strategies and Peace," the final selection in this volume, he first analyzes the current situation and then presents a list of actions that diplomats, as well as citizens, should take to ensure that the nuclear genie is never released from the bottle.

If there is one cause for hope in our present precarious position it is in the fact that all major powers and their citizenry are on record in support of the overall goal of nuclear disarmament. All would like to achieve true security for themselves in a peaceful international environment. The debate then is not over the goal but how to achieve it. It is an important debate that merits all of our attention and, when possible, active participation. If some of the ideas presented in this anthology inspire readers to become more actively engaged in the vital search for peace and justice, then it will have served its purpose well.

Reading 37

THE SHATTERED CRYSTAL BALL: HOW MIGHT A NUCLEAR WAR BEGIN?

The Harvard Nuclear Study Group

Notes from the Editors

In 1983, a group of Harvard scholars published Living with Nuclear Weapons, *designed as a primer on the contemporary nuclear debate. Generally avoiding specific solutions to the major problems, the authors attempted merely to illuminate the major issues.*

Perhaps their most useful contribution is the chapter on how a nuclear war might begin. The several scenarios they offer seem plausible, and all are based upon real-life situations. The theme of how a third world war might start is a frighteningly common one. Much of the western world has been exposed to the Dr. Strangelove *scenario in which madmen and a system gone haywire contribute to produce a war neither side wanted.*

In none of the Harvard Group's scenarios do the leaders of the superpowers act irrationally. Although the launching of a total nuclear war would clearly be an "irrational" act, the authors imagine how even the most rational leaders could coolly decide to press their buttons in order to defend their conceptions of national interest.

The question is grisly, but nonetheless it must be asked. Nuclear war cannot be avoided simply by refusing to think about it. Indeed, the task of reducing the likelihood of nuclear war should begin with an effort to understand how it might start.

When strategists in Washington or Moscow study the possible origins of nuclear war, they discuss "scenarios," imagined sequences of future events that could trigger the use of nuclear weaponry. Scenarios are, of course, speculative exercises. They often leave out the political developments that might lead to the use of force in order to focus on military dangers. That nuclear war scenarios are even more speculative than most is something for which we can be thankful, for it reflects humanity's fortunate lack of experience with atomic warfare since 1945. But imaginary as they are, nuclear scenarios can help to identify problems not understood or dangers not yet prevented because they have not been foreseen.

Many commonly held beliefs about the likely origins of nuclear war are, however, misleading. Focusing on less likely ways that nuclear war might occur creates unnecessary worries and enhances the possibility that more probable dangers will be ignored. This chapter presents several scenarios—some more likely than others—each a con-

Reprinted by permission of the publishers from *Living With Nuclear Weapons* (pp. 45–68), Harvard Nuclear Study Group, Cambridge, Mass.: Harvard University Press, Copyright © 1983 by the Harvard Nuclear Study Group.

ceivable path to nuclear war. Although examining such horrible events can be frightening, creating fear is not the purpose of the exercise. Rather, constructing scenarios can underline actions already taken to reduce the likelihood of war and also point to actions that can minimize future hazards.

Nuclear war would most probably begin for reasons similar to those which began wars in the past. Governments might see opportunities for quick and easy gains and, misjudging enemy reactions, could take steps toward nuclear war without being fully aware of the risks involved. Governments might, under other circumstances, believe that beginning a war was the lesser of two evils, a plausible belief if the other evil is the enemy striking first. These and many other causes have led to war in the past.

Nuclear war is possible. It could occur through purposeful choice, through miscalculations, or through a variety of accidents. It could be started by a political leader, by a military commander, or by a group of terrorists. It could come as a sudden surprise in a time of peace or as the seemingly inevitable culmination of a prolonged conflict between nuclear armed nations. We chose the following kinds of scenarios (some of which are more plausible than others) to illustrate a gamut of possibilities as well as to explore popular and current concerns: (1) surprise attack by one superpower on all or part of the nuclear forces of the other; (2) pre-emptive attacks launched in desperation in time of crisis because one side believes (rightly or wrongly) that the other intends soon to strike first; (3) escalation of conventional wars to nuclear ones; (4) accidental uses of nuclear weapons resulting from malfunctions of machines or of minds; and (5) nuclear wars initiated by other nuclear armed nations or by terrorist organizations. These categories are not unique; additional scenarios involving elements from two or more categories could easily be constructed. Nor is the list of scenarios exhaustive; not all the possible paths to nuclear war can be foreseen. Murphy's law—which states that if something can go wrong, it will—applies here as in all other human activities: military plans go awry, controls fail, misjudgments occur, and one mistake often seems to lead to another, in peacetime and in war. This should not breed despair; it should serve as a constant reminder of the need to control events so that events do not control us.

Scenarios

The Bolt from the Blue.   Imagine the following conversation. The date is November 1, 1991; the location, inside the Kremlin.

> *General Secretary* —*: "Comrade General, you have heard the debate. Some members of the Politburo favor your proposal for a surprise attack upon the United States. Others are highly opposed. We await your opinion. Can we go to war and win?"*
>
> *General* —, *Chief of Staff, Soviet Rocket Forces: "Yes! If war is to come, it must come soon, or all is lost. The counter-revolution in Eastern Europe has put our back against the wall. The American military buildup continues to threaten our socialist nation.*
>
> *"But let me explain how we can triumph if we attack quickly, with all our power. The Americans suspect nothing. We have greatly improved our hunter-killer submarine force and now can closely follow all their submarines; our ballistic missile submarines can*

maintain adequate attack forces off the enemy's coast. In only seven minutes our submarine missiles could destroy American bombers on their runways, the American submarines in the ports, and, as importantly, American military and civilian command centers. Without orders from these command posts, the missiles in the United States will not be immediately launched and will be destroyed when our ICBMs arrive 23 minutes after the submarine missiles land on target.

"We have, of course, supreme confidence in our military strength. But if a small number of America's nuclear missiles and bombers escape destruction from our overwhelming attack, our ballistic missile defense system and our air defense system will shoot them down. We can end the capitalist threat forever. Let us decide now to end this intolerable situation, destroy them before they gain in strength and threaten us even more."

General Secretary —: "Thank you. Comrades, the day of destiny may be upon us. How do you vote?"

Is this scenario possible? Yes. Is it likely? No. This bolt from the blue, commonly the most feared prospect, is a most unlikely scenario for the start of a nuclear war *as long as* no Russian military leader could ever report to the Politburo that a Soviet victory in nuclear war was probable or that the damage from American nuclear retaliation could be reduced to acceptable levels.

What military, political, and economic conditions would have to exist before Soviet leaders would seriously listen to the imagined general's proposal? First, nearly *all* American retaliatory forces and the entire command system would have to be highly vulnerable to a Soviet first strike. Currently, most of the Minutemen ICBMs (intercontinental ballistic missiles), U.S. bombers on airfields and submarines in port, and the American command, control, and communications network are theoretically vulnerable. But the forces that would survive a Soviet attack would still be enormously destructive. Most importantly, the American submarine force routinely at sea, which carries more nuclear warheads than does the entire Minuteman force, cannot now or in the foreseeable future be located or quickly destroyed by the Soviet navy.

Second, both Soviet ballistic missile defenses and air defenses would have to be improved greatly, perhaps beyond what is possible, before they could be expected to reduce the damage of the American retaliatory missile and bomber attacks to an acceptable level. Third, technical difficulties would plague the prospects of success in such a surprise Soviet attack: not only would it be enormously difficult to coordinate the actions of Soviet missile-bearing submarines, ICBMs, and anti-submarine warfare forces, but success would hinge on complete surprise being maintained. If Soviet strategic forces were put on full alert status, the possibility that the American intelligence network would miss the warning is exceedingly remote. Strategic Air Command bombers would be alerted and dispersed, American political leaders and military commanders could be sent to safer locations, and some submarines in port could be sent to sea. These actions would reduce still further the probability that a massive Soviet nuclear attack would be answered with only token nuclear retaliation. Finally, the United States could choose to launch its ICBMs on warning of the attack (i.e., while the attacking missiles were in flight toward their targets) or after the first attacking warheads had arrived.

The bolt from the blue is thus not likely now or any time in the foreseeable future. This scenario is, indeed, so farfetched that it is useful to consider only in one sense: it points to a set of combined circumstances which, as a matter of long-range policy, the United States must seek to avoid. There is clearly no reason that such a dangerous combination of circumstances need ever develop. The bolt from the blue could become plausible only if there was a major deterioration of Soviet-American relations and if Soviet nuclear forces, defensive preparations, and anti-submarine capabilities were greatly enhanced, while American counter-measures were unilaterally restrained.

A Limited Attack on the Minuteman Missiles.   Some defense specialists believe that while American nuclear retaliatory capabilities might successfully deter surprise attacks on American cities, as well as bolt-from-the-blue attacks on all of the nuclear forces, limited attacks on portions of America's nuclear arsenal are substantially more likely. This is one of the concerns that has fueled the debate over the basing mode for the MX missile, a replacement for the vulnerable Minuteman system. The feared scenario often runs something like this:

The decision in Moscow: In a deep crisis over the status of Berlin, the Politburo decides not to launch an all-out pre-emptive attack against American forces and command centers, but only to attack the Minuteman silos. A hot-line message is sent as soon as the warheads land: first, the Soviet Union will spare American cities if the United States refrains from retaliation and, second, the United States is urged to give in to Soviet demands in Europe.

The decision in Washington: The president asks the Joint Chiefs of Staff what military options exist, now that 90% of the Minuteman force is destroyed. They say that fifteen million Americans have just died in the Soviet attack and that an American response will likely trigger a Soviet attack on population centers. Should the president launch a retaliatory strike? Or should he give in to Soviet demands?

This Minuteman-only scenario rests upon a very questionable premise: that the Soviets would believe that the president of the United States would choose not to launch the ICBMs on warning or retaliate after 2,000 Soviet nuclear warheads have exploded here. The American submarines, moreover, could attack many Soviet military targets. A Soviet leader probably would assume that retaliation of some sort would be launched after 15 million Americans were killed. In such circumstances, it would be likely that the Soviets would try to reduce the American retaliation to whatever extent they could.

Thus, if the Soviets were to attack the United States on a large-scale basis, they would have great incentives to attack not only the land-based missiles, but also other American strategic forces and the American command, control, and communications network. There is little Soviet advantage to be gained by attacking the U.S. ICBMs alone, for they contain less than one-fourth of America's strategic nuclear warheads. It is not surprising that Soviet military doctrine, as far as American intelligence sources can determine, stresses that if nuclear war occurs, their nuclear forces would be used on a massive scale.

This Minuteman-only scenario, like the full-blown bolt from the blue, is far less likely than many other possible paths to nuclear war. These surprise attack scenarios preoccupy all too many defense analysts whose talents would be far better applied to preventing more likely dangers. And the attention of the public would be better directed to more realistic scenarios and more probable perils.

A Pre-Emptive War.   Not all wars begin with coolly calculated decisions. Indeed, under certain circumstances, a nuclear war could originate from a series of hasty decisions made in the midst of uncertainty. In fact, a nuclear exchange could be precipitated by a mistaken action, originally intended to deter war, which could produce a counter-decision to launch a pre-emptive strike.

Consider the following scenario. It is the opening page of an imaginary historian's future best-seller, *The Missiles of August: The Origins of World War Three.*

What was the cause of the war? The Greek historian Thucydides, in his history of the conflict between Athens and Sparta, differentiated between the immediate causes and the underlying causes of war. The latter can be compared to the mass of combustible material; the former is the match that sets the material ablaze.

On August 2, 19—, none of the American leaders in Washington knew that they were lighting a match. A number of years earlier, Soviet Premier Brezhnev had warned the United States that if NATO deployed Pershing II and cruise missiles in Western Europe, the Soviet Union would "take retaliatory steps that would put the other side, including the United States itself, its own territory, in an analogous position." On the last day of July, American intelligence satellites spotted cruise missiles being unloaded onto Cuban soil from Soviet ships and on August 1 Premier Andropov announced that he would remove the missiles only if the United States withdrew the NATO deployments.

The sole surviving member of the National Security Council later reported that the president's decision to attack the Cuban dockyard and the Soviet ships was taken overnight. "We had no choice. In a few days, those missiles—we didn't know how many—would have been scattered all over Cuba. This was the only way to get rid of the missiles. We told the Soviets that there would be no attack on Russia itself. Our nuclear alert was only meant to signal our strength."

This was not the view from Moscow. Two Soviet staff officers who survived reported that the Politburo was informed that the Americans must be about to launch a nuclear attack. The head of the KGB told the Politburo that if the Americans launched first, the vast majority of Soviet ICBMs would be destroyed and eventually up to 100 million Soviet citizens might die. But if the Soviet arsenal was used immediately to destroy American nuclear forces and command centers, the casualties after retaliation would probably be "only" between 10 and 20 million. He even told the group that there was a small chance that a pre-emptive attack would "decapitate" the American giant and that no response would come.

He was wrong. The Russians thought war was unavoidable and launched first in desperation and fear. Thirty-five million Americans were killed instantly. The retaliation was perhaps smaller than the first strike the Soviets feared, but it still left 25 million Russians dead.

Perhaps, however, it is misleading to start this history with the immediate cause of the war. The deeper causes go back to 1945. At the close of the Second World War, Soviet and American relations deteriorated rapidly. . . .

How plausible is such a pre-emptive war scenario? Although no precise probabilities can be given, of course, it is at least a possibility that in a deep and apparently irresolvable crisis the Soviets (or the United States) might launch their nuclear weapons first with full knowledge that many of its citizens might die, but fearing far worse casualties if they allowed the other side to attack first. A desperate decision indeed, but a possible one.

What conditions would increase the likelihood of such a tragic decision being made by the leaders of a superpower? First, the leaders would have to believe that the other side intended to strike first, and soon. This would require that the adversary's forces be at or moving toward (or be perceived to be at) a high state of alert—a condition likely to be met only in times of crisis. Second, the leaders would have to believe that the other side could carry out a relatively successful disarming first strike—a judgment which would depend upon the capabilities of the adversary's forces and the vulnerabilities of their own. Lastly, the leaders must be convinced that by launching a pre-emptive attack against the other side's nuclear forces, they could substantially reduce the casualties and damage that would ultimately be suffered by their own nation.

The possibility that such a scenario might happen does not, by itself, mean that the United States should never put its forces on alert in a crisis or that we should always back down in dangerous circumstances. Nor does it mean that American nuclear forces should not be aimed at Soviet weaponry. But the possibility of such an occurrence should, at a minimum, promote great caution in times of crisis, highlight the importance of clear and unambiguous military orders, and stress the need for retaliatory forces that are invulnerable and are perceived as such by both sides. Moreover, it should serve as a constant reminder that the security of both sides is diminished by either side's fear of being struck first or by either side's temptation to strike first.

Escalation: Conventional Steps to Nuclear War.   It is difficult, though clearly not impossible, to outline a credible scenario in which, during peacetime, a Soviet or an American leader would decide to launch an all-out nuclear attack. It is less difficult to imagine a war occurring between the conventional forces of the two superpowers. And once American and Soviet troops met in combat, the likelihood of the use of nuclear weapons would be increased.

The process by which a war becomes incrementally more violent, either through the plans of the combatants or unintentionally, is called escalation. Escalation from conventional fighting to nuclear war has been a continuing concern of defense planners since the Soviets developed their nuclear arsenal. This fear has, thus far, produced prudence: each superpower has been reluctant to use even conventional forces against the other. Can this prudence continue indefinitely? What would happen if Soviet and American conventional forces did clash somewhere?

We do not know. And this inability to know whether conventional war would escalate to a nuclear exchange both enhances prudence and perpetuates fear. Consider two possible scenarios for nuclear conflict developing through escalation:

War in Europe.   *Step 1:* East German workers, organized by an underground labor union, go on strike, demanding political changes in the government of their country. Martial law is imposed and riots ensue throughout the country. Russian troops help in the "police action." East Germans flee across the border into West Germany.

Step 2: Fighting breaks out between West German military units, who are aiding the refugees, and East German security forces. Soon Soviet forces join in the fighting. Two days later Soviet divisions cross into West Germany and the Soviet premier publicly warns the United States to "refrain from self-defeating threats."

Step 3: Other NATO forces—American, British, and Dutch—become involved in the fighting as the Soviets advance further into West Germany. As the Allies are being pushed back by the superior numbers of Soviet divisions, NATO leaders gather to decide on further military action. They publicly warn the Soviets to withdraw immediately or "suffer the gravest consequences." Four airfields along the Polish-Soviet border are attacked with nuclear-tipped cruise missiles, a communique announces, "as a demonstration of NATO resolve."

Step 4: The Soviet Union immediately fires nuclear missiles to destroy nuclear weapons sites in West Germany.

Step 5: ?? Does the war escalate to a full nuclear exchange or is a settlement possible? What would the United States do? What would the Soviet Union do next?

War in the Persian Gulf.   *Step 1:* The Iranian Communist party overthrows the increasingly unpopular government of Ayatollah Khomeini. Civil war breaks out throughout Iran and the new government requests that Soviet troops enter the country "to help restore order." Despite American warnings against such action Soviet forces cross into Iran and move toward Teheran.

Step 2: American troops are immediately sent to southwestern Iran to protect the West's oil supply sources. Advance parties of the two armies meet and engage in combat.

Step 3: As Soviet reinforcements begin to move into Iran, the president orders aircraft from an American aircraft carrier in the Indian Ocean to "close the mountain passes" along the Soviet supply route. Told that nuclear bombs might be needed, he refuses to give weapons release authority to the local commander. "The United States will not be the first to go nuclear," the president's message concludes.

Step 4: The American military commander orders six conventional air strikes against mountain passes in Iran. The next morning, Soviet bombers fly south and attack the American carrier task force with nuclear-tipped missiles. The aircraft carrier and many of its supporting ships are destroyed instantly.

Step 5: ? Does the president escalate further? Does the Soviet Union stop fighting? What happens next? How does the war end?

These paths to nuclear conflict (or others like them) are more likely than the previous scenarios of initial homeland-to-homeland exchanges for an obvious reason: once war begins, the balance between political and military considerations shifts decidedly toward the military side. The leader of a government is far more likely to authorize use of a small number of nuclear weapons during a conventional war than to initiate a full-scale nuclear conflict. But unless the war is somehow terminated, there will be continued incentives for further escalation.

Once a conventional war began, there would be two other factors, in addition to possible decisions to take incremental escalatory steps, that could lead to nuclear war. First, there would be increased possibilities of miscalculation leading to nuclear war. It is possible that at some stage in a conventional conflict a field commander might be given "pre-delegation of authority," the president's option of allowing commanders to decide themselves when to use tactical nuclear weapons. Once this is done, the likelihood of use through miscalculation or mistake in the "fog of battle" would greatly increase. Second, the pressures for pre-emptive nuclear strikes would likely be enhanced after the line between superpower peace and superpower war was crossed. Once the fighting began, one or both governments might decide that full-scale use of nuclear weapons was inevitable or very nearly so; thus, despite the terrible risks involved, a pre-emptive attack might be chosen, on the basis that striking first is better than being stricken first, though both are worse than the unavailable option of no nuclear war at all.

The maintenance of a conventional-nuclear "firebreak"—an often used metaphor borrowed from forest fire-fighting techniques—is most strategists' goal here. If a conventional conflict between the superpowers does someday occur, every effort should be made to terminate the war without the use of nuclear weapons; escalation to full thermonuclear war should be avoided. Withdrawing tactical nuclear weapons from sites near borders, where they might be used quickly in a war, and keeping strict political control over weapons release authority widen the firebreak between conventional and nuclear war. It is not clear, however, exactly how wide such a firebreak should be because of what was earlier described as the "usability paradox": if nuclear weapons are too usable, they might be used when and in a manner not controllable by government leaders; yet if it is certain that weapons will not be used, might this not encourage conventional aggression?

Tragic Accidents.   Could nuclear war begin purely by accident? Mechanical failures do occur, after all, even with (and perhaps especially with) the most sophisticated machinery. Human frailties always exist as well. And such frailties can produce highly irrational behavior at times, even when (and perhaps especially when) the psychological pressures to behave cautiously are enormous.

It is a common assumption that nuclear weapons are likely to be used, not through decisions of rational government leaders, but through mechanical or human accidents. Jonathan Schell, for example, has written that "the machinery of destruction is complete, poised on a hair trigger, waiting for a 'button' to be 'pushed' by some misguided or deranged human being or for some faulty computer chip to send out the instruction to fire." Is this true? Are the following scenes possible?

The Faulty Computer Chip War.   Deep inside a multimillion-dollar computer, used to process the military intelligence coming from American satellites, a 35-cent computer chip malfunctions. Suddenly the radar screens begin to flash. A thousand Soviet missiles appear to be coming over the horizon. "Oh, my God," the radar screen operator says. "This is it."

In the White House, the president is informed of the warning, now ten minutes old. "In twenty minutes the missiles will destroy our retaliatory forces, sir," his military aide informs him. As the president leaves the White House for his specially equipped command post airplane, he orders that all land-based missiles be launched immediately.

"I am not going to let our missiles be destroyed on the ground," he says as he climbs aboard the helicopter. "We'll fight. But the Russians started this war. Let the history books record that fact."

The Strangelove Scenario.   Individuals under pressure cannot always withstand the strain. Sometimes men snap. Late one night, a Soviet submarine commander walks into the control room of his new *Typhoon*-class submarine and, before the astonished ensign can react, he pushes a button sending a single SLBM, with twelve nuclear warheads in the nose cone, on its way to the United States.

"What have you done?" the ensign cries as he tackles the commander, wrestling him to the floor.

The commander appears startled. Then he smiles, looks up, and says, "The missile is going to down a Nazi bomber. I'm teaching those fascists a lesson. Remember Stalingrad!"

Although such imaginative scenarios are often discussed, they are, fortunately, extremely unlikely if not impossible. This is not because the problem of accidental war is not a serious concern. Rather the opposite is the case: precisely because the possibility exists that nuclear weapons could be used accidentally, the United States government has devised numerous precautions to prevent such accidents. Indeed, contrary to a popular belief, the chances of an American weapon being used accidentally are probably much less today than they were in the 1950s. For along with more sophisticated and more numerous weapons, more sophisticated and more numerous precautionary policies have been developed.

Four kinds of measures intended to minimize the chances of unauthorized or accidental use are worth noting. First is the "two-man rule," which requires parallel actions by two or more individuals at several stages in the process of communicating and carrying out any order to use nuclear weapons. Second is the system of Permissive Action Links (PALs), including a highly secure coded signal which must be inserted in the weapons before they can be used. Third, devices internal to the weapon are designed to ensure that an attempt to bypass the PALs system will disarm the weapon. Finally, the nuclear warheads themselves are designed to preclude accidental detonation as a result of exposure to heat, blast, or radiation. The Soviets share our concern with unauthorized and accidental nuclear war, and there is reason to believe that they too have taken measures to prevent it.

In this light, how credible are the two scenarios outlined above? There have been, it is true, many false alarms in the American nuclear attack warning system. Some of them have been traced to such minuscule components as an inexpensive computer chip. But none of these false alerts has even come close to leading the nation into war because the government has built redundancies into the system, precisely so that no president will ever have to rely on a single computer or single radar screen to make such important decisions. For this kind of accident to lead to war, several warning systems of different kinds (e.g., infra-red sensors on satellites, and radars on land) would have to fail simultaneously. Even that by itself would be unlikely to cause the president to order an immediate launching of ICBMs. His incentives to do so might indeed be small if the missiles were relatively invulnerable and if he had other nuclear systems at sea, not under attack. It is even possible to maintain a policy of not launching missiles in a retaliatory strike until after the damage of the enemy's first strike is assessed.

Of course, it is possible that a military commander could go insane (although the stability of American officers with such responsibilities is carefully tested). An insane American officer could not, in peacetime by himself, arm and deliver the nuclear weapons under his command. In the submarine case, to give but one example, it would take the simultaneous insanity of a number of American submarine officers for an unauthorized American launch to be possible. Given the Soviets' strong propensity for tight political control of their nuclear weapons, there is no reason to believe that the chances of unauthorized Soviet use are any greater.

Thus it is a mistake to believe that a simple accident or an unstable commander could easily lead to a nuclear exchange. In reality, the probabilities of such an event are very low. This should not, however, breed complacency about the prospect of accidental war, for two reasons. First, it is only through continual concern that the likelihood of accidental use of weapons is kept to low. Second, mechanical accidents and human frailties could become increasingly dangerous in times of deep crisis or conventional war, during which time command centers could be threatened or destroyed.

There will continue to be an uneasy balance between the degree of control required to ensure that weapons are not used accidentally and the degree of "usability" required to ensure that the weapons can be used if needed. Preventing accidental use is an important goal, but it cannot be the only objective of a nuclear weapons policy. Nuclear weapons must be usable enough to provide credible deterrence, but not so usable as to invite unintended use.

Regional Nuclear War.   One important reason why the world has seen nuclear peace since 1945 is that there has been no conventional war between the United States and the Soviet Union. In the future, if nuclear proliferation continues, there will be an increased danger of nuclear war breaking out between two nuclear armed Third World countries. Such an event might be more likely than nuclear war between the superpowers because many of the conditions that have led to the maintenance of nuclear peace—such as invulnerable second-strike forces, strong leadership control of nuclear weapons, and stable governments in nuclear weapons states—may be absent. The following is an imaginary future newspaper report of a nuclear war which neither Washington nor Moscow would be in a position to stop.

India Uses the Bomb, Pakistan Sues for Peace.   *New Delhi, India.—* The Indian government this morning announced that four nuclear bombs were dropped on Pakistan late last night. At noon, a Defense Ministry spokesman in Islamabad read a declaration over the radio accepting "unconditional surrender" on behalf of the Revolutionary Islamic Council of Pakistan. Thus it appears that the week-long war between India and Pakistan has come to a sudden end.

Sources inside the Indian Ministry of Defense have revealed that India's entire nuclear arsenal was used in this morning's pre-emptive attack against Pakistan's three major military airfields and its nuclear weapons assembly facility. When the Pakistani forces crossed the Indian border last week, Radio Islamabad announced that any Indian use of nuclear weapons would be met in kind. After last year's Pakistani nuclear test, the government in New Delhi took the threat seriously, the Ministry of Defense officials reported, and only decided to attack pre-emptively when Indian intelligence warned that Pakistan's weapons were being readied for use. "We had no choice," an official said. "The enemy was preparing for an attack. Fortunately, we knew where the bombs were kept, and destroyed them and their bomber aircraft simultaneously."

Meanwhile, in New York, the UN Security Council met throughout the night and . . .

Somehow this scenario appears less farfetched than most of the previously outlined scenarios for superpower nuclear war. It also appears less apocalyptic (at least from a non-Pakistani perspective). Indeed, its less-than-apocalyptic nature may be precisely the characteristic that makes it less farfetched. The dangers of this kind of nuclear war may be comparatively small today, but they will increase in the future as more countries acquire nuclear weapons. . . .

It is tempting, but incorrect, to think that a nuclear conflict between any two countries would not affect other nations. There is the possibility that one government in war would be allied to the Soviet Union and the other government to the United States, thereby raising the specter of the superpowers becoming involved in the war. Moreover, there is a danger that a nuclear armed country could use a weapon, intentionally or not, against a superpower.

Catalytic War.   There is yet another way in which the superpowers could be dragged into nuclear war by the actions of a third party. Imagine the two scenarios described below:

The French Connection.   A conventional conflict between NATO and the Warsaw Pact erupts and, despite the imminent collapse of the NATO front, the United States does not use nuclear weapons. The French government, however, launches a small number of its nuclear-tipped submarine-launched ballistic missiles against military targets, hoping to bring a halt to the Soviet advance. The Soviets do not know who launched the missiles, and respond by launching a nuclear attack against NATO military targets throughout Europe. The American president orders that NATO   Pershing IIs be used against military targets in the USSR. . . .

Mistaken Identity.   A war in the Persian Gulf has broken out between the United States and the Soviet Union. After a week of conventional fighting, nuclear-tipped cruise missiles are launched against the American carrier task force. The planes are Soviet models and bear Soviet markings; they are not manned by Soviet pilots nor are they otherwise under Soviet control. Some other country has intentionally and successfully disguised its aircraft, and the Americans mistakenly conclude that it is the Soviets who have initiated use of nuclear weapons. Does the American president escalate further? What might the Soviets do in the midst of this confusion? What happens next?

Clearly, such scenarios are possible. Under a number of circumstances another nuclear power might trigger a strategic nuclear exchange between the superpowers, a war that they had thus far avoided. The possibilities of such an event are greatly increased if conventional war occurs. Few strategists place the danger of catalytic war as high as nuclear war through escalation or pre-emption, but it still is a serious concern. Indeed, during the SALT I negotiations, the Soviet Union mentioned its concern that the growing Chinese nuclear arsenal might someday be used with such results.

Nuclear Terrorism.   What if a terrorist organization gained possession of a nuclear bomb? Could nuclear war occur as a result? Consider the following scenario, which was invented in the best-selling novel *The Fifth Horseman:*

On a snowy December evening, the President of the United States is told by his National Security Adviser that a tape recording in Arabic has just been delivered to the White House. It appears to be a message from Muammar al-Qaddafi, President of Libya, and claims that a nuclear weapon has been placed somewhere on Manhattan. Unless the United States forces Israel to withdraw to its 1967 borders, the bomb will be detonated.

"I must further inform you that, should you make this communication public or begin in any way to evacuate New York City, I shall feel obliged to instantly explode my weapon," the message concludes.

"A man like Qaddafi has got to know we have the capability to utterly destroy him and his entire nation in retaliation. He'd be mad to do something like that," the President tells his adviser.

But what should the president do? Is nuclear terrorism possible? How could it come about?

Terrorists might gain possession of an atomic bomb in one of several ways, including theft, purchase, or manufacture. If they were to steal it, and if it were of American origin, then the Permissive Action Links should frustrate any attempt to detonate it. But it is not at all clear just how confident a president might be in the ability of the PALs to resist a concerted attempt to bypass them, especially in light of the high stakes involved. And suppose the stolen bomb was not an American one. Other current and future nuclear weapons states may not have equipped their warheads with safety systems comparable to those developed by the United States.

A terrorist organization might purchase an atomic bomb from (or be given one by) a government that shares the terrorist group's goals. Indeed, this possibility is reason enough to work to inhibit the spread of nuclear weapons to additional countries.

Finally, terrorists might fashion their own nuclear explosive device. The highly enriched uranium or plutonium essential to the project might be stolen or bought, and a crude but workable bomb assembled. The task would be difficult, but not impossible. In any event, how confident could a president be that the terrorists' bomb would not work? And against whom could he threaten retaliation?

Conclusion: Continuing Issues

How should one think about the various paths to war outlined in this chapter? Five points need to be stressed. First, the set of scenarios presented here is not exhaustive. Surely each reader can think of other ways in which a nuclear war might begin. How probable are such scenarios? What can be done to minimize the likelihood of their occurrence? Also, the dangers of these scenarios could be compounded. Suppose, to give but two examples, mechanical failures in warning systems developed during a deep superpower crisis, or human frailty produced unstable commanders during a conventional war. Thus, when thinking of the potential dangers to be avoided in the future, one must not assume that decisions will always be deliberate, or that accidents will always develop when they can do the least harm.

Second, this chapter suggests that it is usually misleading to concentrate one's attention on the number of nuclear weapons when analyzing the likelihood of war. It is widely assumed that changes in the numbers of weapons in the superpower arsenals— either upward or downward—are the major determinants of the risks of war. Sheer numbers, however, matter far less than factors such as the vulnerability of weapons, the credibility of commitments to allies, and imbalances in conventional forces. In the short run, to give but one example, making command and control systems less vulnerable can be as important, and probably more so, in reducing certain risks of war than would changes in the numbers of weapons: improved command and control could reduce an enemy's incentives for a "decapitating" attack, and could improve our ability to follow a policy of "no retaliation until specifically ordered." And the long-run risk of nuclear war is likely to depend more on our ability to stem proliferation than on any other single factor. The common fixation on numbers of weapons in the superpower arsenals misses such important issues.

Third, there is no reason to assume that an all-out nuclear exchange, certainly the most frightening scenario, is either the only kind of nuclear war possible or even the most likely type of nuclear war. Nuclear war occurring through the escalation of conventional conflict appears more probable. Avoiding conventional war is, therefore, one of the most important ways of avoiding nuclear war. And maintaining strong and credible conventional forces may thus be an important component of preventing nuclear war. One should never forget that, despite the incentives to keep a conventional war limited, once fighting begins it would be difficult to control escalation to the nuclear abyss. But escalation should not be considered inevitable, for that could prove to be a self-fulfilling prophecy.

Fourth, it is noted that in none of these scenarios do leaders of the United States or the Soviet Union act insanely. But departures from rationality are not inconceivable; they must be taken into account in the design of measures to prevent nuclear war.

Finally, this glimpse at the shattered crystal ball should breed neither complacency nor despair. A horrible nuclear future is not inevitable, but only because great efforts have been made in the past to decrease its likelihood. The good news for the present is, then, that nuclear war is not probable. The bad news is that nuclear war, is and will continue to be, possible. To make sure that the possible does not become the probable is the continuing task of nuclear policy.

Suggested Readings

Burns, Grant. *The Atomic Papers: A Citizen's Guide to Selected Books and Articles on the Bomb, the Arms Race, Nuclear Power, the Peace Movement and Related Issues*. Metuchen: Scarecrow, 1984.

Douglas, James A., and Amoretta M. Hoeber. *Soviet Strategy for Nuclear War*. Stanford: Hoover Institution, 1979.

Ehrlich, Paul, et al. *The Cold and the Dark, The World after Nuclear War*. New York: Norton, 1984.

Ford, Daniel. *The Button*. New York: Simon & Schuster, 1985.

Hackett, John, et al. *The Third World War: August 1985*. New York: Macmillan, 1979.

Lebow, Richard Ned. *Nuclear Crisis Management: A Dangerous Illusion*. Ithaca: Cornell University, 1987.

Powers, Thomas. *Thinking about the Next War*. New York: Knopf, 1982.

Spector, Leonard S. *Nuclear Proliferation Today*. New York: Vintage, 1984.

Reading 38

NO FIRST USE

Admiral John Lee

Notes from the Editors
Admiral John Lee is a career naval officer who achieved the rank of Vice Admiral. Since his retirement, he has been associated with the Center for Defense Information, an organization that is often critical of American national security policies. In 1982, the Union of Concerned Scientists, another organization critical of American policies, brought together a group of military experts to produce a report on the No First Use issue. Admiral Lee is primarily responsible for the section reprinted here.

As of this writing (1988), the United States government has refused to declare that it would not be the first to use nuclear weapons in a future global conflict. In general, this is part of the American doctrine of flexible response, which maintains that if the Soviets think that a nuclear response is one of the options available to Americans, they will be more reluctant to launch a conventional war. With a large lead in conventional weapons, they (and the Chinese) themselves adopted a No First Use pledge.

Admiral Lee examines the American government's position on No First Use from political and military perspectives, as well as how that pledge might relate to the future of arms control negotiations. Generally, he finds little merit in his nation's position and suggests that an American No First Use pledge would lead to an increase in international stability and American security. Although Lee feels strongly about his position, he does deal fairly with opposing arguments.

Nuclear warfare is not merely an extension of conventional warfare to a higher level of violence. It is an entirely different phenomenon. Modern conventional warfare can produce vast death, destruction, and suffering, but at its worst, conventional warfare leaves populations and structures for recuperation. General, all-out nuclear war would destroy the peoples, institutions, and cultures of the targeted nations, as well as damage the rest of the planet to an unpredictable but dangerous degree. The survival of the engaged nuclear powers, their allies, and many other nations depends upon preventing, permanently, the outbreak of general nuclear war.

Prevention of general nuclear war is, therefore, an objective of absolute priority, an objective which must be pursued for the indefinite future, in times of calm and in times of international crisis, even during actual hostilities. Prevention must be at the heart of U.S. and alliance policy and strategy. Dependence on the threat or the use of nuclear weapons to achieve national or allied purposes should be reduced to a minimum, since any such dependence creates the risk of initiation and escalation of

Reprinted by permission of Admiral John Lee from *No First Use*, Union of Concerned Scientists, 1983, pp. 3–15.

nuclear war. There is no present substitute for the threat of nuclear retaliation to deter the hostile use of nuclear weapons. But it is not similarly inescapable to rely on nuclear forces to deter or defeat conventional attack or to accomplish other military operational objectives. To depend on the threat or use of nuclear weapons for these tasks will with high probability, sooner or later, in one crisis or another, bring on disaster.

Such nuclear dependence is, however, the basic U.S. and NATO strategy and has been so for a generation. This strategy assumes a Soviet superiority in conventional forces that can be met, ultimately, only by U.S. nuclear weapons. In the case of NATO, the U.S. has repeatedly declared its determination, if conventional defense were to fail, to initiate the use of nuclear weapons. In a number of other actual or potential situations, from Dien Bien Phu to the Persian Gulf, where conventional forces appeared unable to deal with a situation, the U.S. has contemplated using nuclear weapons. The nuclear concept is built intimately into the U.S. and NATO assumptions, plans, organization, posture, doctrines, and programs. The bulk of U.S. strategic study in the postwar era has been devoted to refining ideas for nuclear posture and nuclear employment designed not only to strengthen deterrence but also to seek concepts for using nuclear weapons in action without necessarily escalating to general nuclear exchange. In the last analysis, our strategy is a nuclear strategy.

In the early days of the atomic era, when atomic weapons were few in number and largely in U.S. hands, such a nuclear-based strategy was at least plausible. During that period, the U.S. could have used nuclear weapons and survived the Soviet response, badly damaged but still functional. In the last twenty years, however, with enormous arsenals deliverable by both sides, the probability has become overwhelming that neither the U.S. nor the Soviet Union would survive. The logic of the nuclear-based strategy has evaporated.

Today, the nuclear weapon is not operationally usable. Its only rational function— and this function is essential—is nuclear deterrence: to prevent the use of nuclear weapons by others. To call on the nuclear weapon for any other role will be, in the long run, fatal. In the words of Field Marshal Lord Carver, present U.S. and NATO nuclear-dependent strategy is "either a bluff or a suicide pact."

This critical dilemma can be resolved and U.S. and alliance policy and strategy can be put on a rational footing by a declaration that the U.S. will not be the first to use nuclear weapons in any hostilities—the No-First-Use declaration. The No-First-Use declaration will signal a decisive shift in fundamental national and alliance policy of thirty years standing. It will demand thorough rethinking of strategic doctrine and extensive military and political analysis and debate in the U.S. and the allied nations, including public discussion and the development of public support. Further, it will require substantive change in military doctrines, plans, forces, and programs. This preparatory process will not be quick, easy, or lacking in strong opposition in the U.S. and among the allies. The discussions and debates will themselves be productive, however, in enhancing public understanding and, ultimately, national and alliance unity of purpose and concept.

The effect of a No-First-Use declaration will be profound. On the political side, alliances will ultimately be strengthened and relations with the Soviet Union, especially in times of tension, made less apocalyptic. On the military side, restricting the role of nuclear weapons to nuclear deterrence or retaliation will cause basic changes in the conventional as well as the nuclear forces, markedly lowering the risk of nuclear conflict.

Political Effect of No-First-Use

For a generation, our allies have based their security on U.S. readiness to use nuclear weapons in defense against conventional attack. A No-First-Use declaration may initially be viewed as undermining that deterrence. However, the allies are conscious of the irrationality of defense by the threat of suicide. They are aware that they cannot be "defended" by nuclear warfare, but would be destroyed by it. And while the allies depend on the power of nuclear deterrence, they recognize the danger of its failing catastrophically, sooner or later, in one crisis or another. The allies need, as we do, a rational strategy offering reasonable hope of long-term survival.

In allied nations, as in the U.S., a spectrum of views has emerged on the relative merits of No-First-Use and the nuclear deterrence of conventional attack. Arriving at a meeting of the minds, here and abroad, will depend on reaching several shared appreciations:

- The distinction between conventional and nuclear war is of overpowering significance. Some elements in allied countries, scarred by the tragic experiences of the two great wars of this century fought on their soil, virtually equate conventional and nuclear war.
- Under No-First-Use, conventional war would not surely escalate to nuclear war, as many now assume.
- A sound conventional defense which provides a powerful conventional deterrent and, if called upon, a good promise of operational success, is within reach at manageable political and economic cost.
- The present strategy of first-use will very probably lead to the catastrophe of nuclear war; it is intellectually and morally insupportable; it is internally divisive for the nations of the alliance.

Once such points are broadly agreed upon, a No-First-Use strategy will be seen as a major advance in security for all allies. Allies will readily appreciate the impact of No-First-Use on several existing problems. One perennial weakness of our alliances has been concern about American reliability in crises. Some Europeans, in particular, have long doubted that the U.S. would actually use its nuclear weapons against a Warsaw Pact conventional attack, when the consequence would be the near certainty of its own destruction. An even more corrosive variant of this fear is that the U.S. and the USSR will find some way to confine nuclear operations to the territory of their allies and cooperate to maintain their own countries as sanctuaries. There are also those who fear that the U.S., provoked by excessive hostility to the USSR, could trigger hostilities needlessly.

No-First-Use would alleviate these concerns. The allies could be confident that the U.S., substantially relieved of the prospect of its own immediate destruction, deeply conscious of the importance of its allies to U.S. security, and with its own large forces in the front line, would fully participate in a mutual conventional defense. Nor would U.S. nuclear support be eliminated. It would be in reserve as a powerful deterrent of hostile nuclear attack before and during hostilities; and if, tragically, the USSR were to break the nuclear barrier, it would be a ready retaliatory force.

Other cracks in the unity of purpose of the U.S. and allied nations would be ameliorated by No-First-Use. We would all be largely freed from the absurdity of defending ourselves by threat of suicide. We would be liberated, in great measure, from the inhuman prospect of inflicting millions of deaths, on our own initiative, on mostly innocent people. We would be functioning under a comprehensible policy and strategy that would justify the necessary military measures—a strategy that would give grounds for hope for the long future.

The transition of the alliances to a No-First-Use basis will be laborious, time consuming, and probably stormy. Advocates of No-First-Use, in the U.S. and in allied nations, face a major task. The U.S. clearly must be ready to share in strengthening the conventional defense. Once No-First-Use is in effect, however, the alliances will be on a rational and realistic military footing with a sensibly reduced risk of nuclear catastrophe. Our alliances will be stronger and more dependable.

Predicting Soviet actions and reactions cannot be done with accuracy and is not attempted here. There are, however, a number of considerations that would flow from a U.S. No-First-Use declaration that the USSR might weigh in its decision-making.

Given the profound Soviet mistrust of the U.S. and its allies, as well as the impossibility of predicting any nation's action under ultimate stress, the USSR may never place complete confidence in U.S. No-First-Use. Nevertheless, the Soviets will analyze the national and inter-allied discussion and debate on the subject, and will observe the associated military measures. This should lead them to a cautious belief that No-First-Use is at least accepted policy and strategy in the West. Such a belief would support the apparent Soviet interest in maintaining the non-nuclear barrier. With its powerful, numerically superior conventional forces, enormous geographical expanse, and central strategic position, the USSR is nearly invulnerable to conventional attack; the U.S. and its allies cannot seriously contemplate invading the Soviet Union. Thus, as long as any hostilities remain conventional, the Soviet homeland should seem basically secure. If the nuclear barrier were breached, however, the USSR and its allies would almost certainly be destroyed as functioning societies. Even under the stress of conventional warfare, and—the extreme case—even with that warfare going badly for the USSR, avoiding escalation to nuclear weapons would be profoundly in the Soviet interest. Furthermore, cutting their losses, pulling back from unsuccessful external adventures, and awaiting a better opportunity would be in keeping with enduring Communist dogma and Russian historical experience. In sum, a U.S. No-First-Use declaration, with its related measures, could give Soviet decision-makers additional grounds to avoid a dangerous hair-trigger nuclear posture, to refrain from nuclear preemption, and to adhere to their own recent No-First-Use declaration.

One important consequence of these factors is to invalidate the common assumption that any major hostilities involving the U.S. and the USSR would surely be, or quickly become, nuclear.

Military Effect of No-First-Use

The effect of No-First-Use on the allied military structure would also be funda-mental. A basic assumption now shared by the U.S. and its allies is that the nuclear weapon is available as the final arbiter in major hostility. If conventional operations go badly or major objectives cannot otherwise be achieved, nuclear forces can properly be called on. In brief, nuclear operations are legitimate operations of war, usable when needed. Under No-First-Use, that assumption would no longer hold. The ultimate reliance on nuclear weapons to shore up conventional operations would be eliminated; nuclear first-use would be outside the boundaries of legitimacy for U.S. forces. No American combat commander would expect or recommend nuclear support of his operations, just as today he would neither expect nor recommend the use of other prohibited weapons such as nerve gas or biological weapons.

The mission of the conventional forces would be to succeed conventionally. The mission of the nuclear forces would be definite and limited—to deter or, failing that, to retaliate against hostile use of nuclear weapons. Each side would, of course, find it essential to provide for the possibility of the other using nuclear weapons in violation of the No-First-Use declaration, or for nuclear operations being triggered by accident, mistake, insubordinate initiative, or third parties. A nuclear threat would still exist, and each side would need to be able to retaliate. But reliance on nuclear forces to shore up our own conventional operations would be eliminated.

The conventional forces would no longer be, in the final analysis, a trip-wire for nuclear war. They would have to fulfill their mission themselves, without a nuclear crutch. That would require conventional forces capable of deterring, or if necessary stopping, conventional attack against essential objectives. Nuclear weapons and nuclear concepts are now deeply intertwined with nearly every element of the forces; all aspects would need to be reexamined and modified. The composition, size, structure, and priority of various combat, support, and infrastructure elements would be altered to some degree. Adequate stocks of nonnuclear combat consumables would be given a higher priority. Organization, task assignments, reserve force concepts, training, doc-trines, manuals, operational plans, and tactical concepts would all feel the impact. Weapon research, development, and procurement programs would need some redirec-tion. Perhaps most important, the sense of mission of the conventional forces, at all levels, would be revolutionized; from top to bottom the conventional forces would know that the whole combat responsibility was theirs, that nuclear weapons were not available to cover inadequacy, incompetence, or failure. The basic dignity of the conventional combat forces would be restored. The effect on their outlook, tone, and determination—and consequently on their effectiveness—would be substantial.

The nuclear forces would also change. Nuclear weapons whose functions can be discharged conventionally, such as antiarmor (neutron bomb), antiair, and antisub-marine, would lose their *raison d'être*. The present dangerous and vulnerable accu-mulation of tactical weapons located in or near potential combat zones would surely be rethought. Presumably, tactical weapons could be thinned out and moved to less provocative locations, greatly reducing pressures to use these weapons before losing them and also clearing out the prime targets for hostile preemptive attacks. The longer-range nuclear forces, theater and strategic, would also be altered. With an exclusively retaliatory mission, first-strike characteristics would be given less weight; the very short flight time and high accuracy of the proposed Pershing II, for example, would presumably be recognized as provocative and destabilizing rather than a deterrent. Invulnerability, reliability, and endurance would gain priority in strategic force programming. The bottomless requirements for nuclear forces generated by nuclear "war-fighting" scenarios would have even less validity; a straightforward deterrence and retaliatory mission for the nuclear forces should restrict requirements. It might be possible, at long last, to answer for nuclear weapons the question "How much is enough?"

Under No-First-Use, it will be essential to make clear that any hostile first-use of nuclear weapons will be met by nuclear retaliation. This will require maintaining the means, the preparations, and the plans—including graduated plans—for making retaliation certain. No-First-Use neither eliminates nuclear requirements nor nuclear danger. However, if the Soviet Union and its people are convinced they will be safe from our nuclear weapons unless, and only unless, their weapons are used against us or our allies—the No-First-Use concept—the nuclear dangers will be markedly reduced and genuine security greatly enhanced.

A No-First-Use declaration would demand and would generate major, substantive, military changes—changes both in concepts and in forces. Some have argued that No-First-Use would be merely declaratory diplomacy, that the decision whether to use nuclear weapons will be made on the basis of perceived national interest at the moment of crisis. This argument fails to recognize the weight a No-First-Use declaration would have after it had been built into our thinking, our preparations, and our military structure. While it will be operationally possible to violate the No-First-Use declaration and use nuclear forces, the weight of legitimacy, expectation, preparation, planning, and operations will all be against such action.

In essence, the U.S. and its allies will have calmly evaluated their true individual and collective interest and decided that nuclear war is inevitably destructive to that interest. No-First-Use, then, will not leave the nuclear decision to a moment of nearly intolerable stress in the heat of crisis; the U.S. and its allies will have made that decision and built it in advance into their entire military posture.

The Nuclear Policy of France and the United Kingdom

France and the U.K. have nuclear forces comprising both tactical and long-range nuclear weapons. While their arsenals are small compared to those of the superpowers, they are enormously powerful by conventional standards. Not only can they be used against Warsaw Pact forces in the field, but they can strike the Soviet Union itself.

The geopolitical considerations that impelled France to create an independent nuclear deterrent are of a character that make it unlikely that she will renounce first-use to repel an invasion of her territory, whether or not the U.S. were to adopt a No-First-Use policy. The merits of a U.S. No-First-Use declaration are not, however, dependent on the possibility of nuclear initiation by France or other nuclear-armed nations friendly to the U.S.

Relation of No-First-Use to Other Proposals for Nuclear Arms Control

Governments have successfully negotiated a number of arms control measures designed to lessen the nuclear risk. A variety of new projects are now being advocated within and outside of governments and by the public. Some of these measures and projects would eliminate specific weapons (Antiballistic Missile Treaty, Seabed Treaty, antisatellite negotiations, the U.S. Theatre Nuclear Forces Proposal); some would limit technical developments (SALT I and SALT II, The Freeze, a Comprehensive Test Ban); some would reduce numbers of weapons (SALT II, START, the Kennan-Gayler 50 Percent Cut Proposal, Mutual and Balanced Force Reduction); and some would establish nuclear-free or nuclear-restricted zones (Palme Commission, Nordic and Balkan nuclear-free zones, Indian Ocean negotiations, European nuclear-free zone, Treaty of Tlatelolco). The goals of these proposals are worthy: to strengthen deterrence, enhance stability, limit technological advances, reduce the arsenals, and, perhaps most important, act as steps in the process of bringing the nuclear threat under control. There is no conflict between any of these proposals and No-First-Use; they are mutually supporting.

There is a significant element missing in all these measures, however. None of them directly challenges the use of nuclear weapons. None of them changes the nuclear strategy, the operational expectations, the plans. Even if that whole list of measures were negotiated, ratified, and implemented, the operational and conceptual approach to nuclear warfare would be as it is today. (And the remaining nuclear arsenals would be more than adequate to destroy both sides.) With No-First-Use, on the other hand, a large part—probably the largest—of possible deliberate nuclear employment would be eliminated from legitimate planning and expectation. No-First-Use would mark a fundamental change in political and military leaders' concepts of the use of nuclear weapons. No other proposed arms control measure deals directly with this central issue of how we, and particularly how our leaders, think.

Arguments against No-First-Use

Renunciation of the first-use of nuclear weapons would strike at the foundation on which the U.S. and its allies have built their military defense for a generation. Quite naturally, the proposal has produced a number of opposing arguments. Some of these arguments—in particular the impact on the cohesion of our alliances, considerations bearing on Soviet decision-making, and the argument that a No-First-Use declaration would be without operational significance—have been discussed above.

The following four opposing arguments are probably the most significant of the remaining issues:

1. It is not possible to provide a conventional counter to Soviet conventional strength within the limits of economic and political practicability.

2. It is essential to prevent major conventional war as well as nuclear war; let us take the steps needed to enhance conventional strength but not declare No-First-Use,

because No-First-Use would erode nuclear deterrence of conventional attack and make conventional war more likely.

3. Limited nuclear war can be controlled and may be needed in an ultimate crisis; let us not close out the option.

4. Soviet communism is a malignant force dedicated to global domination; it must be stopped regardless of cost.

Discussion of these points follows.

Conventional Defense.   *It is not possible to provide a conventional counter to Soviet conventional strength within the limits of economic and political practicability.*

Since the U.S. post World War II demobilization, it has been an article of faith, here and abroad, that the Soviet Union has overwhelming conventional superiority. It has been taken as a given that in Central Europe, the Warsaw Pact could rapidly overrun NATO conventional defenses and that in other potentially contested areas around the Soviet periphery the USSR could rapidly prevail. This presumption of unmatchable Soviet conventional dominance is challenged herein; the following sections of this report (Parts II and III) argue that:

In Central Europe:

- NATO enjoys the intrinsic advantage of the defender: that defense can be sustained with forces numerically smaller than those needed by the attacker. The existing numerical balance in men and weapons is within the generally accepted range for successful defense.

- The common assessment of Soviet conventional dominance, while it fully considers NATO limitations, gives inadequate weight to some of the problems facing the Warsaw Pact, notably the questionable reliability and effectiveness of Soviet satellites, and the limitations and vulnerabilities of Warsaw Pact communications.

- NATO has in existence powerful conventional forces and ongoing programs for the enhancement of these forces. There are a number of material, organizational, and operational improvements, at manageable cost, that can substantially strengthen the defense. Taken together, these factors bring within reach a conventional defense able to powerfully deter conventional aggression and, if necessary, able to contain or repel conventional attack with high confidence.

- NATO superiority in advanced micro-technology exists and promises to continue. It is in this technological area that decisive and economical advances in weapons and control systems are most probable. Critical fields in which NATO can exploit its technological superiority with powerful effect include search and surveillance, target acquisition and fire control, communications, navigation command and control, and electronic warfare.

Outside Europe:

- There are no targets for U.S. or allied attack where nuclear weapons would have a critical advantage over conventional weapons. Nuclear exchanges, however limited, would be greatly to the disadvantage of the U.S. and its allies in operations around the Soviet periphery or at sea. The risk of escalation would be acute. First-use of nuclear weapons by the U.S. or its allies would therefore be irrational.

Deterring Conventional War. *It is essential to prevent major conventional war as well as nuclear war; let us take the steps needed to enhance conventional strength but not declare No-First-Use, because No-First-Use would erode nuclear deterrence of conventional attack and make conventional war more likely.*

This argument against a No-First-Use declaration was made in an exaggerated form by General Haig while he was Secretary of State. No-First-Use, he said, is "tantamount to making Europe safe for conventional aggression." Without the threat of nuclear response to conventional attack (i.e., without "extended deterrence"), the risk of undertaking such an attack would be greatly reduced. Consequently, conventional war would be more likely to occur. Conventional war alone would be a major disaster and it would also be likely to trigger nuclear war. On the operational level, if the threat of tactical nuclear response to conventional attack is removed, the attacker could concentrate his forces and add power to the attack. In brief, advocates of this argument recommend improving the conventional forces to reduce dependence on nuclear weapons while retaining the threat of first-use to maintain extended deterrence.

There are serious problems with this attempt to maintain the deterrent value of nuclear first-use:

- The threat of nuclear response to conventional attack is indeed very powerful, but it is an unacceptable risk for NATO to rely on such extended deterrence to succeed invariably for the indefinite future. A single failure, whether in the first or the nth East-West crisis, would spell catastrophe. A solid conventional defense, on the other hand, is a strong deterrent to conventional attack, and if that deterrence were to fail, the outcome, though tragic, could be faced and survived.

- There is substantial doubt on both sides of the Atlantic and both sides of the Iron Curtain that NATO would, in fact, use nuclear weapons to stop a Warsaw Pact conventional advance in view of the probability of mutual destruction. (In particular, it is difficult to conceive of the Federal Republic of Germany concurring in tactical nuclear employment when most of the weapons of both sides would presumably be aimed initially at targets in West Germany.) NATO's confidence in its nuclear defense, under first-use, is therefore limited and uncertain—a source of weakness.

- Under a first-use policy there is a high probability that any major hostility will become nuclear; this danger will be a source of political weakness in crisis.

- Concentration of forces offers advantages not only to the attacker but also to the counter-attacking defender; in any case, modern conventional weapons increasingly threaten concentrated forces.

The overriding problem with nuclear deterrence of conventional attack, however, is that under that strategy the option to use nuclear weapons first will always exist, and will always be the dominating military consideration, in calm and in crisis. Without No-First-Use, the essential basic change in nuclear thinking will not occur among government leaders, the military, or the public. Basing security on a threat of suicide will increasingly disaffect the public. Military commanders, in plans and in actual operations, will be driven to calling for nuclear support whenever they face difficult tasks. National leaders, working under the appalling stress of crises, with partial, delayed, and dubious information, will be under enormous pressure to issue the nuclear command. On the Soviet side, the desired change in perception will not take place. The Soviets will have no reason to consider the nuclear threat reduced or to refrain from hair-trigger postures. The pressures on the Soviets to avoid crossing the nuclear barrier will not be powerfully reinforced.

Such extended nuclear deterrence, therefore, does not provide security. Instead, it weakens public morale, it undercuts the ultimate resolution of conventional forces, it overloads national leaders, and it makes catastrophic nuclear war more probable. Conventional attack can rationally be deterred or met only with conventional forces.

On the immediate, practical level, it is unrealistic to advocate a solid conventional defense and, simultaneously, a first-use option. The necessary steps on the conventional side will not be taken and sustained unless the conventional mission is seen as clear, possible to achieve, and critically necessary for national and allied security. There is simply not the incentive to do what needs to be done on the conventional side while the nuclear option exists. According to NATO Supreme Allied Commander of Europe, General Bernard Rogers, "We have mortgaged our defense (of Western Europe) to a nuclear response." (*New York Times*, 10-14-82)

Changing fundamental national and alliance policy, taking the extensive doctrinal and material steps to implement that change, and conveying the change convincingly to deeply mistrustful Soviet opponents cannot be done without broad public and official support throughout the alliance. These objectives cannot be attained and maintained without a clear-cut public position that is widely accepted as rational and feasible and that offers a realistic hope for genuine security and a substantial, even if incomplete, release from the nuclear trap. A No-First-Use declaration is indispensable.

Limited Nuclear War.   *Limited nuclear war can be controlled and may be needed in an ultimate crisis; let us not close out the option.*

The last twenty years have seen the development of concepts and plans, and the procurement of weapons and equipment for "controlled," "limited," and most recently "protracted" nuclear war-fighting strategies. These strategies aim to produce a broader deterrence and, if used, to limit the range of destruction. The military objective of these strategies is to gain some operational advantage without escalating to full-scale nuclear exchange. These operations would try to halt a conventional attack, for example, or give the firing side a recognizable lead in the remaining nuclear balance, or wreck the opponent's political and military control system. These strategies envision a nuclear war fought to a successful conclusion. Their supporters argue that nuclear "war-fighting" capabilities enhance deterrence of hostilities generally and deterrence of escalation during hostilities, that limited nuclear war may be a necessary last resort at a critical moment, and that it should therefore not be debarred by a No-First-Use declaration.

However, the various limited nuclear war concepts have several overriding defects. Planning for limited nuclear war produces virtually bottomless requirements for nuclear forces: weapons, delivery vehicles, and systems of command, control, communications, and intelligence. Such planning is the primary stimulus for very large increases in nuclear forces and contributes to a corresponding buildup by the other side which must, under war-fighting concepts, again be matched.

No one has been able to produce a scenario for limited nuclear operations, on whatever scale, that would clearly work to U.S. and allied advantage. Scenarios with "favorable" outcomes depend upon a whole series of dubious assumptions. None has a firm stopping point. In the real world, they would, on balance, work to our operational disadvantage, produce more or less localized chaos, and almost irresistibly escalate.

The concept of limited nuclear war lowers the nuclear threshold. If the first critical breach of the nuclear barrier is thought to offer some possibility of success without ultimate disaster, the fateful decision, at some moment of terrible stress, will be dangerously more probable.

The decisive argument against limited nuclear war, however, is the high probability of unlimited escalation. Limited nuclear operations are fundamentally not manageable. For limited nuclear war to remain limited—to be brought to a stop short of complete catastrophe—the two sides, during actual nuclear exchange, would have to first work out and observe mutually tolerable operational limits—mutually accepted restraints on the kinds and locations of the targets they fired at and the numbers, sizes, and kinds of weapons they used. In addition, and this is even less conceivable, both sides would have to arrive at an agreed outcome, a stopping point, while still in mid-exchange, and with each side still possessing more than ample nuclear forces to carry the exchange up further steps and finally to destroy the other. They would have to do this with different information, different weapons, different operational concepts and mechanisms, under appalling stresses of event and time, with the continued existence of both literally in the balance, while pursuing diametrically opposed objectives, in the midst of "limited" but substantial nuclear exchanges and the resulting death, destruction, and chaos. In such circumstances, the chances of successful limitations are remote indeed.

In short, limited nuclear war, or any firing of nuclear weapons in anger, however limited, has a prohibitively high probability of escalating to a full-scale exchange and catastrophe for both sides. We should not initiate such use nor, for reasons given in the previous section, should we use the threat of limited nuclear war for extended deterrence. Preserving limited nuclear war options should not be allowed to stand in the way of No-First-Use.

If Defense Fails.   *Soviet communism is a malignant force dedicated to global domination; it must be stopped regardless of cost.*

The remaining general argument against No-First-Use poses the ultimate nuclear dilemma. What should be done in case nonnuclear defense fails?

It is the argument of this paper that under a No-First-Use declaration, with the consequently improved conventional concepts and posture, the U.S. and its allies would maintain a powerful conventional deterrence, and were that deterrence to fail, they could defend conventionally with high probability of success.

High probability is, of course, not certainty. There has never been nor can there be a way to predict the outcome of such hostilities with complete assurance; there are too many unknowns, too many contingencies, too much blind chance. There is, and there always will be, some possibility of the defense failing to hold.

Some argue that the Soviet advance must then be stopped by nuclear weapons, at any cost, including the common destruction of the nuclear powers and their allies. This is a counsel of despair; national suicide is not a rational solution. The only sane approach in the nuclear age is to fight on, conventionally, as long as it may take and as costly as it may be. When the situation is finally restored, there will at least be peoples, cultures, and national structures to carry out the rebuilding and restoration.

Implementation of a No-First-Use Declaration

It is the basic recommendation of this report that a process leading to a No-First-Use declaration be set in motion forthwith.

The public debate and the alliance decisions required by a declaration of No-First-Use will need time to complete. The implementation of the military measures will stretch over a number of years. To await completion of this entire process before making a No-First-Use declaration, as some have argued, would be to postpone it indefinitely; it will always be possible to question the completeness of military preparations. On the other hand, an immediate No-First-Use declaration is neither politically nor diplomatically possible; there must first be broad agreement nationally and internationally, and steps needed to implement No-First-Use must be at least in progress.

To achieve No-First-Use in a reasonable time scale, therefore, discussions within and between U.S. and allied governments should be started at once, leading to general agreement on the desirability of a No-First-Use declaration and on the military measures that the declaration would require. As soon as broad agreement has been reached and the program of military measures adopted and adequately advanced, the U.S. should formally issue a No-First-Use declaration.

Suggested Readings

Bundy, McGeorge et al. "Nuclear Weapons and the Atlantic Alliance." *Foreign Affairs* 60 (Spring, 1982), pp. 753–768.

Ehrlich, Robert. *Waging Nuclear Peace: The Technology and Politics of Nuclear War.* Albany: SUNY, 1985.

Kaku, Michio and Daniel Axelrod. *To Win A Nuclear War: The Pentagon's Secret War Plans.* Boston: South End, 1987.

McNamara, Robert S. "The Military Role of Nuclear Weapons." *Foreign Affairs* 62 (Fall 1983), pp. 59–80.

Pringle, Peter and William Aiken. *S.I.O.P.: The Secret U.S. Plan for Nuclear War.* New York: Norton, 1983.

Reading 39

THE OBJECTIVES OF ARMS CONTROL

Paul H. Nitze

Notes from the Editors

Paul H. Nitze, a special advisor to President Reagan on arms control, and an advisor to other presidents and secretaries of state and defense, presented a defense and explanation of American arms control policy in March of 1985. His speech offers a useful philosophical and strategic background discussion, a brief survey of current official American views of the Strategic Arms Limitation Talks (SALT), and subsequent developments. It concludes with a consideration of the difficult issues in Soviet-American negotiations, including the Strategic Defense Initiative (Star Wars) and the new generation of missiles.

From the American perspective, the Soviet Union has been engaging in a destabilizing arms buildup since the mid-1970s. Only in recent years has the United States begun to close the alleged gap. Nitze sees his counterparts in Moscow as rational, intelligent leaders who will only agree to mutual and verifiable arms control when they realize that they cannot beat the United States into submission with their massive building program. Nitze adopts the position that if you want peace, prepare for war, even nuclear war. To some degree, his and the Reagan Administration's position has been supported by the signing of the INF Treaty in December 1987.

The American arms-control expert claims to believe in disarmament. He does not, however, believe that the world can get there through freezes or wishful thinking. It will be a monumental task. In the meantime, nuclear deterrence is the only hope for keeping the peace, including the continuing development of the latest in offensive and defensive technology, consistent with previous arms control agreements.

Needless to say, the Soviet perspective is dramatically different from Nitze's, especially in terms of who is offensive and who is defensive in the arms race. Critics in the United States and its NATO allies would also find much to disagree with in his exposition.

Arms Control Objectives

The primary security objective of the United States and, I believe, of the Western alliance in general is to reduce the risk of war while maintaining our right to live in freedom. Consistent with this objective, we have long based our security policy on deterrence—that is, prevention of conflict by convincing a potential opponent that the problems, risks, and costs of aggression would far outweigh any possible gains he might hope to achieve.

Published by the United States Department of State, Bureau of Public Affairs, Office of Public Communication, Editorial Division, Washington, D.C., April 1985. Editor: Cynthia Saboe.

In the context, arms control should be viewed as one element of our security policy. It complements the measures that we must take unilaterally, such as maintaining weapons and forces necessary for an adequate deterrent.

Arms control is not a substitute or replacement for adequate defenses. Indeed, experience indicates that while arms control hopefully can play an important role in enhancing our security and bringing about a more stable strategic relationship, what we are able and willing to do for ourselves is more important. It provides the necessary foundation on which effective deterrence and arms control must rest. I remember one Soviet negotiator during SALT I [strategic arms limitation talks] saying, "We will do whatever is necessary to deter you; whether you are able to deter us is up to you."

The objective of reducing the risk of war is intrinsically linked to deterrence. Whether or not we have arms control agreements, it is necessary that the United States and its allies have sufficient military forces, both conventional and nuclear, to deter an armed attack by the Soviet Union and its associates.

Likewise, the Soviet Union undoubtedly is determined to have what they assess to be fully adequate military capabilities, whether or not there are arms control agreements between us. It has been our belief, however, that a relationship of offsetting deterrent capabilities can be made more secure, stable, and reliable—and perhaps less costly—if we and the Soviets can agree on effective, equal, and verifiable arms control constraints.

There are two important corollaries to the objective of reducing the risk of war through effective deterrence. These are the objectives of assuring parity, or at least rough equivalence between the capabilities of the two sides, and of assuring crisis stability—that is, reducing the incentives that a side might have in a crisis to strike first or in peacetime to provoke a crisis that might lead to a military confrontation.

Some commentators tend to emphasize one of these goals or the other. To my mind they are interrelated; we cannot tolerate either significant inequality or substantial crisis instability.

The greatest strain on deterrence could arise in a crisis or a series of crises stemming from a complex of factors difficult to control. In such a period, our military forces as a whole must have the necessary characteristics of effectiveness, flexibility, survivability, and diversity to dissuade the Soviet Union from contemplating reckless action.

We cannot be confident that an array of U.S. and allied forces manifestly inferior to those of the Soviet Union would provide an adequate deterrent to reckless action in such a period. Similarly, forces of roughly equal capability could be inadequate if a significant portion of them were vulnerable to destruction in a surprise or preemptive attack.

Consistent with the objectives of promoting stability and rough equality, arms control should aim to achieve sharp reductions in the levels of armaments. Reductions per se may not always be good; for example, reductions in the number of launchers can be destabilizing if they increase the ratio of warheads to vulnerable launchers. But well-conceived proposals embodying reductions which bring about improvements in the proper indices can do much to enhance stability.

Finally, the panoply of arms control agreements should deal with the relationship between offensive and defensive systems. I will return later to this subject in some detail.

For arms control agreements to be effective, there are a number of additional requirements. The agreements should be reasonably precise and unambiguous in their terms. While no agreement can be made completely unambiguous, the less ambiguity, the better.

Moreover, we should have confidence in our ability to verify adherence to an agreement's provisions, and the panoply of arms control agreements should be sufficiently comprehensive so that their constraints cannot be readily circumvented. And finally, we must have confidence that the parties will abide by the agreements into which they have entered, a requirement that has become increasingly important in view of findings of Soviet noncompliance with existing arms control arrangements.

In addition to the foregoing objectives and requirements, our arms control policy must merit the sustained support of Western publics and of Western congressional and parliamentary bodies. In the absence of such support, the Soviets will seek to drive wedges and exploit divisions; indeed, tough Soviet bargaining stances have always been complemented by hard-nosed propaganda and active measures campaigns designed to bring about unilateral Western concessions. Such public and legislative support will also be essential to carrying out the unilateral defense programs that must necessarily proceed in parallel with arms control.

These, then—in my view—comprise the basic objectives and requirements of arms control policy.

History as It Illuminates the Issues Concerning Objectives

Let me review the issues and conflicting views as to the objectives of arms control as they have evolved over the years following the dawn of the nuclear age in 1945.

Immediately after the Japanese surrender, President Truman asked some of us who had been engaged in the Strategic Bombing Survey in Europe to undertake a comparable mission with respect to the war in the Pacific. He asked us not only to report on the effects of air power in the Pacific war but, in particular, to survey in detail the effects of the atomic weapons used at Hiroshima and Nagasaki. We were also asked to offer recommendations for U.S. weapons, especially nuclear weapons.

We recruited a distinguished team of physicists, engineers, and other scientists who measured in minute detail the effects of blast, radiation, heat, and fallout on people, buildings, and on the Japanese will and ability to continue the war. The general public reaction after Hiroshima and Nagasaki had been that the destructiveness of atomic weapons was absolute and immeasurable. We were, nevertheless, directed to measure precisely what those weapons had done and what they had not done.

We were all shocked by the devastation of the two cities. The casualties and damage were immense. The destruction at Hiroshima was tremendous; part of Nagasaki survived, as it was shielded by a hill. Even at Hiroshima, however, the destruction was not absolute; trains were running through Hiroshima within 48 hours after the attack. Our computations, based on the effects of those relatively primitive bombs, indicated that the advent of atomic weapons had increased the potential power of air attack against undefended cities by 100- to 200-fold.

The policy implications we drew were several. Nuclear weapons provided an increase in the power of offensive weapons by more than a hundredfold, and future technology could be expected to increase it by another order of magnitude. In war, the temptation for an aggressor possessing nuclear weapons to employ a preemptive strategy could be immense. The importance of being able to control the relevant air space, which had been of high importance in a war fought with conventional-weapons, would be far greater in a world with nuclear arms.

We were faced with a grim realization: even if we had very good offensive and defensive capabilities and a nuclear war were, nevertheless, to occur, we could not be sure that some weapons would not get through, and even a few could cause immense damage.

Therefore, our policy should be one of maintaining a deterrent posture adequate to assure that no war would occur. Since we could not guarantee the means fully to protect our society from nuclear attack, we should develop forces that would make clear to a potential opponent that he could not achieve military gains through launching an attack against us or our allies and that the consequences for him of launching his attack would be so horrible that the potential gains of such aggression would not be worthwhile.

One important issue remained. Some thought the terror of nuclear weapons was such that their very existence would in itself prevent war. This view was held by those who considered the destructiveness of nuclear weapons to be absolute. Bernard Brodie was the first and most eloquent proponent of this position. He also argued that there was an absolute dichotomy between the view that the purpose of military forces was to deter and the view that their purpose was to deny an aggressor the possibility of military success.

The alternative position was that deterrence would be greatly strengthened by the ability to face an enemy with military capabilities and a strategy that would deny him the ability or perception that he might successfully prosecute a war-winning strategy and emerge from a war in a predominant military position.

This issue of what is required to assure deterrence—the mere existence of nuclear weapons or a manifest military capability sufficient to deny the enemy any realistic prospect of achieving his objectives—remains with us to this day. I believed then, and I believe now, that the latter position is the sensible one.

The question remains, now as then, how to maintain a sure ability to retaliate with devastating nuclear destruction but concurrently to increase our ability to deny an aggressor the possibility of military success and, thus, reduce our dependence on the threat of mutually devastating nuclear destruction.

The Interest in Nuclear Disarmament

Shortly after nuclear weapons appeared, strong interest arose in negotiating the elimination of all such arms. Immediately after the war's end, the Acheson-Lilienthal report proposed a world government restricted in its authority to nuclear matters but including everything to do with those matters. The idea was roughly translated into the Baruch plan for the international control of atomic weapons and technology and offered to the Soviets. They would have no part of it.

Interest in nuclear disarmament continued, however. Some years later, before the UN Committee on Disarmament, the Soviets presented a program for what they called "general and complete disarmament." But it soon became clear that their position was purely for propaganda purposes; they offered no practical way to get to their stated end.

While "general and complete disarmament" did not then appear to be a realistic or achievable goal, the Soviets, nevertheless, were reaping significant benefits in the propaganda field. The United States, the United Kingdom, France, and Canada in response changed their position to advocate "phased total disarmament," which meant approximately the same thing as "general and complete disarmament" but offered a somewhat more practical approach.

From that point on, the propaganda battle was a standoff. But the talks on the subject had little to do with actual steps toward the goal of eliminating nuclear weapons or toward reducing the risks of war.

The Shift Toward Arms Control and Limited Measures

When the Kennedy Administration took office, the debate between the West and the Soviet Union concerning "general and complete disarmament" versus "phased total disarmament" was continuing.

Thought in the Administration began to turn to the possibility of negotiating agreements more limited in their scope, with the hope that success in these agreements would open the possibility of more comprehensive agreements later. In other words, our interest turned toward arms control rather than disarmament.

Instead of total disarmament—in which security would have been entrusted to something akin to a world government—we set our sights on a more realistic plane. We accepted the prospect of deterrence based on the threat of nuclear retaliation and sought to make the strategic balance safer, more stable, and perhaps less costly.

As a result, the Limited Test Ban Treaty, the Outer Space Treaty, the Non-Proliferation Treaty, and the Seabed Arms Control Treaty came into being. These agreements were important in their own right, but they were peripheral to the central issue of achieving an agreement which would serve materially to reduce the risk of war.

Up until 1963, thought on arms control had concentrated on multilateral arrangements; it was thought that a bilateral agreement between the United States and the Soviet Union would not be sufficiently comprehensive and could lead to possible circumvention and undercutting by other nations. But in the spring of 1963, some of us in the Administration came to the conclusion that we weren't apt to get an international agreement on the central issues unless and until we could work out the main issues bilaterally with the Soviets.

We prepared a paper on the issues involved in a bilateral agreement limiting strategic nuclear delivery vehicles between the United States and the Soviet Union. The analysis suggested that the total elimination of nuclear weapons was not the optimum solution. This was because nuclear technology had become too widely known; the risk of clandestine or third-country production of nuclear weapons was too great. It seemed that a level of perhaps 500 strategic nuclear weapons on each side would provide a more stable and predictable future than none at all.

Then Secretary of Defense [Robert] McNamara agreed with these conclusions and took them seriously. This helped set the stage for his proposal to [Soviet Premier] Kosygin at Glassboro in June 1967 that we begin bilateral nuclear arms control negotiations. By 1967, the Soviets had come to the conclusion that such negotiations "might not be impossible." The invasion of Czechoslovakia in 1968 temporarily made them impossible; the SALT I negotiations, as such, did not begin until the fall of 1969.

SALT I and SALT II

SALT represented what we hoped would be a mutual effort to achieve effective arms control constraints providing for a stable strategic relationship between the United States and the Soviet Union at lower levels of arms.

In the late 1960s, we were completing our intercontinental ballistic missile (ICBM) and submarine-launched ballistic missile (SLBM) deployment programs and were pursuing an active anti-ballistic missile (ABM) program. The Soviets also had vigorous— and growing—programs in both the offensive and defensive fields. With respect to ABM, however, we in the United States were coming to the conclusion that the state of the technology at the time was such that ABM systems were not very reliable and could be overcome by deploying additional offensive systems at substantially lesser cost.

Deployment of such ABM systems might thus, it was feared, encourage a proliferation of offensive arms. Were defenses limited, on the other hand, it might be possible to work out reductions and tight limitations on offensive nuclear weapons. We, therefore, were prepared stringently to limit ABM systems.

SALT I produced the ABM Treaty and the Interim Agreement on offensive arms. We believed that those measures would be helpful to the security of both sides. That belief was based on three principal assumptions:

First, that the constraints on ballistic missile defenses, particularly those on large phased-array radars, would prevent breakout or circumvention;

Second, that both sides would adhere to the letter and intent of the agreements; and

Third, that with defensive systems severely limited, it would be possible in the following few years to negotiate comprehensive limits on strategic offensive forces and to establish a reliable deterrent balance at reduced levels.

We believed that those assumptions were shared by both sides.

The ABM Treaty seemed to me to be a useful and equitable agreement. It constrained not only the interceptor launchers, which were relatively simple and cheap and could be easily stored and rapidly deployed. More significantly, the treaty limited large phased-array radars—which were expensive and took years to build; were one side to build such a radar in a manner not permitted by the treaty, the other side would have considerable warning time to challenge the action and, if necessary, take countermeasures. The ABM Treaty offered promise for enhancing stability by setting the stage for comprehensive limitations on offensive arms.

Unfortunately, a number of Soviet actions since 1972—such as the construction of an early warning radar at Krasnoyarsk in violation of constraints on such radars provided by the ABM Treaty—have undermined the first two assumptions. They call into serious question Soviet intentions with regard to possible breakout as well as Soviet willingness to comply with arms control arrangements when Soviet military priorities are not consonant with them.

We were also disappointed with regard to the third assumption; we could not get the Soviets to agree to tight limitations on offensive arms comparable to those applied to ABM systems of reductions in such arms. Indeed, limiting defenses did not appear to have any effect on the Soviet offensive buildup.

Part of the problem was that the Soviets were doing well with respect to offensive systems. We had ceased building new ICBMs, ballistic missile submarines, and heavy bombers some years earlier; we were improving them through qualitative changes. The Soviet Union was actively deploying large numbers and new types of ICBMs and SLBMs. Momentum thus tended to favor the Soviets; they saw no reason to sign a piece of paper which would cause them to forgo that advantage.

The 1972 SALT Interim Agreement purported to freeze the offensive balance at the then-existing level. In fact, it did no such thing. It froze the number of operational ballistic missile launchers and those the Soviets claimed were under construction; the levels were grossly unequal. Those inequalities continue to the present day and have become more significant as the Soviets, as some then anticipated, have caught up to us in accuracy, MIRVing [multiple independently-targetable reentry vehicle], and other pertinent aspects of technology.

Our inability to negotiate tight limits on offensive arms was also in part linked to the relationship between the verifiability of an agreement and its comprehensiveness. It was our view that it would be in the interest of each side to provide sufficient information to the other so that each could verify and have confidence in the other's adherence to the terms of an agreement.

Because the Soviets refused to agree to such a cooperative approach to verification, the limitations of an agreement had to be restricted to large visible items such as missile silos and submarine missile tubes. They could not apply to smaller systems or components. Nor could they apply to the more significant—but more difficult to monitor—qualitative characteristics of weapons systems.

The rationale for concluding such a modest and unequal accord as the 1972 Interim Agreement was based upon two expectations, both of which subsequently proved to be ill-founded.

First, we thought the two sides could negotiate a more comprehensive agreement within the next 2 or 3 years, surely within the 5-year duration of that agreement.

Second, we underestimated the extent to which, and how quickly, actual Soviet force developments—particularly MIRVing—would take advantage of the loose offensive constraints of SALT I.

Compounding these weaknesses, SALT II incorporated many of the drawbacks of its predecessor.

It is hard to make a case that the Interim Agreement or SALT II met any of the principal objectives for arms control. One would truly be hard pressed to demonstrate how they embodied rough equivalence, lowered armaments, enhanced crisis stability, or reduced the risk of war.

SALT II, as its predecessor, focused on the wrong indices of power—launchers—giving both sides incentives to increase the number of weapons on their missiles, with negative implications for stability. Likewise, it did not provide for rough equivalence, allowing the Soviet Union unilateral rights, such as the right to heavy ballistic missiles.

And by no means has SALT reduced armaments—the number of warheads on U.S. and Soviet ballistic missiles has increased since 1972; the number of warheads on Soviet ballistic missiles has increased by more than 50% since 1979. And taking advantage of their much superior throwweight, the Soviet capability to destroy hard targets has increased by an even greater amount. All of this has taken place within the limitations of SALT.

The shortcomings of SALT II, in particular the fact that it would not provide for significant warhead limitations, came to be widely recognized. In fact, its proponents largely fell back on the rationale that SALT II was "better than no agreement." For some of us who have worked to clarify thinking on the objectives of arms control agreements, this was a defeatist criterion; it suggested loss of confidence in our ability to maintain an adequate deterrent posture without arms control and implied that we must, therefore, accept more or less what the Soviets would agree to.

In the START [strategic arms reduction talks] and INF [intermediate-range nuclear forces] negotiations earlier in this decade, the United States sought to rectify some of the inadequacies of the SALT experience. For example, we made warheads rather than launchers the principal units of account and tabled positions embodying significant reductions rather than merely legitimizing existing launcher levels and permitting increased warhead levels. Unfortunately, our efforts were largely overshadowed by the Soviet campaign to split NATO over the issue of INF.

The Debate Since the Mid-1970s

From the mid-1970s on, the debate on the question of arms control objectives seems to me to have been confused and confusing.

An issue raised in the 1970s has been the idea that the principal objective of arms control should be to "stop the arms race." Yet from 1972, when the Soviets passed the United States in the number, size, and throwweight of offensive missile systems, they proceeded to develop and deploy one generation after another of more modern systems. Meanwhile, we had frozen the number of our weapon systems and restrained our modernization programs.

It was in the Soviet interest to keep things that way. Their propaganda approach was and is keyed to the phrase "stop the arms race." To the extent the Soviets can use such phrases to encourage unilateral Western restraint, they can avoid serious negotiations in which they might have to concede some of their advantage.

To many in the United States, however, it seemed that the Soviets had been merely reacting to what we had done first, that they were merely catching up; if we were to stop, they would stop, too. For some 10 years, this and the trauma and aftereffects of the Vietnam war combined to restrain the United States from responding to continuing Soviet force developments.

Over the years, however, it became increasingly clear that the Soviets were not merely reacting; they were executing a deliberate long-term program to improve their capabilities, regardless of what we did. As former Secretary of Defense [Harold] Brown put it, "When we build, they build; when we don't build, they build."

Today, both sides express agreement on "radical reductions" as being an important objective. But, as I noted earlier, those reductions should be such that they improve stability and result in rough equality and not the reverse. Reductions to low and equal levels of ballistic missile warheads and redressing the imbalance in destructive capability can undoubtedly enhance the strategic situation, particularly if such reductions are structured so as to encourage survivable basing for strategic systems and "de-MIRVing" of forces with a dangerous capability against hard targets. Such reductions would greatly reduce the value—and, therefore, the likelihood—of a first or preemptive strike.

Reduction in the number of launchers alone, however—without regard to the number and power of warheads—could be grossly destabilizing. It would increase, not decrease, the existing inequality between the capabilities of two sides and could increase the incentive to go first or preempt in a crisis.

Others began talking in the late 1970s and early 1980s of a verifiable and comprehensive nuclear freeze. If a freeze is not comprehensive, it makes the situation worse, not better, and today's situation is not good. If a freeze is comprehensive, it will both freeze the present unequal situation into the future and not be verifiable.

What has been the basic difficulty with the arms control situation? I believe it goes back to the days before SALT I. We were then ahead in most of the measures of strategic capability. But we came to the conclusion that enough was enough. It was our hope that when the Soviets pulled even, they also would conclude that enough is enough. The evidence indicates that we were wrong.

Since 1972, the nuclear arms control problem has been one of attempting to square the circle. The Soviet side has been quite frank in saying it would not enter into an agreement which would change the correlation of strategic forces in a manner they deemed adverse to their interests. Once the Soviets judged the military correlation of forces had become favorable, they were adamant in refusing to consider any agreement which would result in rough equality or which would improve crisis stability. But any agreement which would not lead to these results was flawed from the point of view of the West.

My view is that we should get back to fundamentals. The issues are complex, but not too complex. Four really is greater than two. The Soviet leaders are not mad; they look to their interests through eyes trained in the Marxist-Leninist approach. Many of them are excellent logicians, strategists, mathematicians, and physicists. Their approach is usually relatively understandable and predictable—more so, perhaps, than the approach of Western governments.

What we must do is give the Soviets grounds for concluding that we in the West are prepared to maintain sufficient political will and military capability to ensure deterrence of any possible aggression, conventional or nuclear. We must bring them to realize that their buildup cannot and will not be translated into an exploitable military or political advantage. If it turns out that we have to go for a few more years without a formal agreement limiting offensive nuclear weapons, that is undesirable, but let us not panic; we have been living with that situation for some years.

At the same time, we should hold out a better alternative, one that would produce a more stable and reliable relationship from the perspective of both sides. To this end, let me outline the strategic concept that underlies the U.S. approach to the negotiations that began earlier this month in Geneva.

The U.S. Strategic Concept

As I have explained elsewhere, that concept can be summarized in four sentences:

During the next 10 years, the U.S. objective is a radical reduction in the power of existing and planned offensive nuclear arms, as well as the stabilization of the relationship between offensive and defensive nuclear arms, whether on earth or in space. We are even now looking forward to a period of transition to a more stable world, with greatly reduced levels of nuclear arms and an enhanced ability to deter war based upon an increasing contribution of non-nuclear defenses against offensive non-nuclear arms. This period of transition could lead to the eventual elimination of all nuclear arms, both offensive and defensive. A world free of nuclear arms is an ultimate objective to which we, the Soviet Union, and all other nations can agree.

For the immediate future, we will continue to base deterrence on the ultimate threat of devastating nuclear retaliation. We have little choice; today's technology provides no alternative. For now and the foreseeable future, we and our allies must, therefore, continue to maintain a modern and effective nuclear deterrent.

We will continue to press for radical reductions in strategic and intermediate-range nuclear arms, with attention, of course, to the proper indices of limitation. Reductions can be structured so as to produce a more stable balance and reduce the risk of war. In the Geneva talks, we are prepared to consider various means of bridging differences between the U.S. and Soviet positions in an effort to achieve equitable accords that entail real reductions.

We also remain committed to the ABM Treaty and will seek to reverse the erosion that has occurred in that regime as a result of Soviet actions such as the construction of the Krasnoyarsk radar. In the longer run, however, we want to consider the possibilities of a more defense-reliant balance.

Fifteen years ago, we concluded that defenses could be overwhelmed—at relatively less cost—by additional offensive arms. Technology, however, has advanced considerably since then. We now see the possibility that new defensive systems might lead to a more stable and reliable strategic balance and, ultimately, might provide the means by which we could move with confidence toward the complete elimination of nuclear arms.

In March 1983, President Reagan questioned whether we should confine ourselves to a future in which deterrence rests solely on the threat of offensive nuclear retaliation. His Strategic Defense Initiative (SDI) research program was, therefore, given the task of determining the feasibility of effective defenses against nuclear ballistic missiles. This includes possible defenses based both on earth and in space. The President has directed that the program be carried out in full compliance with the ABM Treaty. Its object is to provide the basis for an informed decision, sometime in the next decade, as to the feasibility of providing for a defense of the United States and our allies against ballistic missile attack.

We expect the Soviets will continue their investigation of new defensive technologies. Indeed, the debate over SDI has often lost sight of the fact that the Soviets, besides having the only operational ABM system, have long had a major research effort devoted to advanced ballistic missile defense technologies, including high-energy lasers and particle-beam weapons.

Should new defensive technologies prove feasible and meet our criteria, we would want, at a future date, to begin a transition to a balance in which we would place greater reliance on defensive systems for our protection and that of our allies. Such defenses could enhance deterrence by creating excessive complications for an aggressor's planning for a possible first strike, thereby lessening the chance that he might seriously contemplate it.

Let me note that the criteria by which we will judge the feasibility of new technologies will be demanding. They must produce defensive systems that are reasonably survivable; if not, the defenses could themselves be tempting targets for a first strike. This would decrease rather than enhance stability.

New defensive systems must also be cost-effective at the margin—that is, it must be cheaper to add additional defensive capability than it is for the other side to add the offensive capability necessary to overcome the defense. If this criterion is not met, the defensive systems could encourage a proliferation of countermeasures and additional offensive weapons to overcome deployed defenses, instead of a redirection of effort from offense to defense.

As I have said, these criteria are demanding. But they are necessary if we are to move toward a more stable balance at lower levels of arms. While our SDI research program will seek technical answers to technical questions, we are simultaneously examining the broader strategic implications of moving toward a more defense-reliant balance.

If the new technologies cannot meet the standards we have set and, thus, not contribute to enhancing stability, we would not deploy them. In that event, we would have to continue to base deterrence largely on the ultimate threat of nuclear retaliation, though hopefully at lower levels of arms. However, we have high expectations that the scientific and technical communities can respond to the challenge.

Let me be clear that SDI is not an attempt to achieve superiority. Through any transition our goal would be to maintain balance. President Reagan has made it clear that any future decision to deploy new defenses against ballistic missiles would be a matter for negotiation.

This does not mean a Soviet veto over our defense programs; rather, our commitment to negotiation reflects a recognition that we should seek to move forward in a cooperative manner with the Soviets. We have, thus, offered to begin discussions even now in Geneva with the Soviets as to the implications of new defensive technologies, whether developed by them or by us, and how we might together manage a transition to a more stable and reliable strategic relationship based on an increasing contribution of defensive systems in the mix of offense and defense.

Of course, arms control would play an important role in such a transition. Properly structured cuts in offensive arms are not only worthwhile in their own right, they could also facilitate the shift to a more defense-reliant posture.

Before negotiating such a cooperative transition with the Soviet Union, and throughout the transition period, we would consult fully with our allies. Such a transition would continue for some time, perhaps for decades. As the U.S. and Soviet strategic and intermediate-range nuclear arsenals declined significantly, we would seek to negotiate reductions in other types of nuclear weapons and involve, in some manner, the other nuclear powers.

Given the right technical and political conditions, we would hope to be able to continue the reduction of all nuclear weapons down to zero. By necessity, this is a very long-term goal. Its realization would, of course, have far-reaching implications for the global military balance at all levels. For example, the deterrent effect of nuclear weapons has helped to prevent conventional as well as nuclear conflict. Were we to move to a situation in which nuclear weapons had been eliminated, the need for a stable conventional balance would become even more important than today.

We would have to devote particular attention and effort to how, together with our allies, we might counter and diminish the threat posed by conventional arms imbalances through both conventional arms improvements and arms control efforts. Clearly, were we able to move cooperatively with the Soviet Union toward a nuclear-free world, that would presuppose a more cooperative overall relationship than exists at present— one in which efforts to establish a conventional balance at lower levels should also be fruitful.

The global elimination of nuclear weapons, if this were ever to become possible, would need to be accompanied by widespread deployments of effective non-nuclear defenses. These defenses would provide assurance that, were some country to cheat— for example, by clandestinely building ICBMs or shorter range systems, such as SS-20s—it would not be able to achieve an exploitable military advantage. To overcome the deployed defenses, cheating would have to be conducted on a large scale— of too great a magnitude to pass unnoticed before appropriate countermeasures could be taken.

Were we to reach the ultimate phase, deterrence would be based on the ability of the defense to deny success to a potential aggressor's attack—whether nuclear or conventional. The strategic relationship could then be characterized as one of mutual assured security.

Conclusion

Having thus outlined our strategic concept for the future, let me offer some comments.

In the 1950s, total nuclear disarmament was the declared objective of both sides but it was wholly impractical. Among other reasons, in an uncertain world, neither side could have the confidence necessary seriously to consider abandoning its nuclear weapons; defenses against them seemed impossible. Emerging defensive technologies may provide the hedge that we need to move away from primary reliance on nuclear weapons. I frankly do not see any way in which we could consider eventually moving toward extremely deep cuts in offensive nuclear arms—and their ultimate elimination—without some means to protect against cheating and other contingencies.

Let me caution, however, that for the foreseeable future—that is, in the near term and even in the early and intermediate stages of any possible transition—offensive nuclear arms and the threat of massive destructive retaliation they embody will be the key element of deterrence. This situation unavoidably will obtain for many, many years.

Let me also emphasize that the concept I have outlined is wholly consistent with deterrence. Not only in the near term but in both the transition and ultimate phases as well, deterrence would continue to provide the basis for the U.S.-Soviet strategic relationship.

As I said at the beginning of my remarks, deterrence requires that a potential opponent be convinced that the problems, risks, and costs of aggression far outweigh the gains he might hope to achieve. A popular view of deterrence is that it is almost solely a matter of posing to an aggressor high potential costs through the ultimate threat of devastating nuclear retaliation.

But deterrence can also function effectively if one has the ability, through defense and other military means, to deny the attacker the gains he might otherwise have hoped to realize. Our hope and intent are to shift the deterrent balance from one which is based primarily on the punitive threat of devastating nuclear retaliation to one in which nuclear arms are greatly reduced on both sides and non-nuclear defenses play a greater and greater role. We believe this would provide a far sounder basis for a stable and reliable strategic relationship and for a real reduction in the risk of war.

The concept I have outlined embodies much that is old and some things that are new. It requires that we rethink some of our strategic policy, and we should not shy away from doing so. Reducing the risk of war is a goal of vital importance to both the West and East. We should examine all ways by which we can advance that goal with clear, objective, and open minds. This includes frank discussion between allies. This is the manner in which our coalition of democracies must work; I am confident that together we will make the right choices.

Suggested Readings

Bearden, Steven L. *The Evolution of American Strategic Doctrine: Paul H. Nitze and the Soviet Challenge*. SAIS Papers in International Affairs, No. 4. Boulder, Colo.: Westview, 1984.

Drell, Sidney et al. *The Reagan Strategic Defense Initiative*. Cambridge: Ballinger, 1985.

Guerrier, Stephen W. and Wayne C. Thompson, eds. *Perspectives on Strategic Defense*. Boulder, Colo.: Westview, 1987.

Jasani, Bhupendra, ed. *Space Weapons: The Arms Control Dilemma*. London: Taylor and Francis, 1984.

Mandlebaum, Michael. *The Nuclear Question: The U.S. and Nuclear Weapons, 1946–1976*. New York: Cambridge University, 1979.

Stein, Jonathan B. *From H Bomb to Star Wars: The Politics of Strategic Decision-Making*. New York: Heath, 1984.

Reading 40

IN DEFENSE OF NUCLEAR DETERRENCE

Plinio Prioreschi

Notes from the Editors

An increasing number of government officials, scholars, and citizens today, who are anxious about the nuclear arms race support arms control, and even eventual total disarmament. There are those, however, like Plinio Prioreschi, who see the large nuclear arsenals maintained by the major powers as contributing to international peace.

In this selection from Man and War, *Prioreschi, a professor at Creighton University's Medical School, argues against those who are trying to dismantle the nuclear deterrent forces. For one thing, he thinks that the prospect of that is unlikely; once having uncorked the nuclear genie from the bottle, there is no way for the world to return to the prenuclear age. Problems of verification and the impossibility of destroying technological capabilities make the goal of complete nuclear disarmament a chimera.*

Making the best of a bad situation, Prioreschi contends that it is precisely the existence of nuclear arms that have kept the major powers from going to war with one another since 1945. They may not have kept the peace between all nations, but they have made a Soviet-American war virtually impossible, even in the face of such incidents in the Third World as the Russian invasion of Afghanistan in 1979 and the United States invasion of Grenada in 1983. Such regional conflicts in the prenuclear era often resulted in war between the major powers.

Prioreschi is nervous about the proliferation of nuclear weapons among less rational and more immature minor powers. Further, although he sees the arms race as essentially a positive factor in great power relations, a substitute for war, he is also nervous about the prospect that one side may make a major technological breakthrough that could tempt it to launch a first strike. Nevertheless, he is optimistic about the survival of the international system even though members of that system continue to develop ever more frightening weapons of total and irrevocable destruction.

A few centuries before Christ, having conquered the Italian peninsula, Rome turned toward the Mediterranean and met Carthage. The two giants locked in a struggle that lasted more than one hundred years and ended with the destruction of the African power. Rome became the master of the world.

Why did they not pursue politics of peaceful coexistence? The immense destruction and suffering of the Punic Wars would have been avoided. The energy and wealth spent to fight each other could have been used to explore and spread civilization in Africa and in the immense unknown territories of Europe and Asia. Peaceful coexis-

Reprinted by permission from Plinio Prioreschi, *Man and War* (New York: Philosophical Library, 1987) pp. 280–88, 294–95, 305–6.

tence would have generated prosperity for all, whereas the results of the wars were the destruction of Carthage and, in Italy, ravages of such magnitude that their consequences were felt for centuries. True, by eliminating Carthage, Rome became *caput mundi*, but surely the world was large enough for two *capita mundi*. Carthage could have colonized Africa, and Rome Europe. It would have been the golden age for mankind.

Why did they choose to fight? Simply because it was the natural and normal thing to do. Since the beginning of history, whenever two groups become dominant, conflict follows. The Romans and the Carthaginians were not abnormal or insane; on the contrary, had they chosen to live in peace, they would have behaved in an abnormal and unusual way.

Two thousand years later, in our time, two giants watch each other across oceans that, because of modern technology, are smaller than the ancient Mediterranean. Under usual circumstances, conflict would be inevitable. Other conflicts would follow in an unending series. War would be eliminated only in the very distant future, after man has climbed another step in his evolutionary scale.

This is what would happen under usual circumstances. The circumstances are not usual, however: for the first time in history, the country contemplating starting an all-out atomic war has the absolute certitude that at the end it will be among the losers. There is no doubt that this is, by far, the most powerful restraint that has ever interfered with man's propensity to wage war. It is easy to imagine that Hannibal would have become the most ardent advocate of peaceful coexistence if, when crossing the Alps, he would have become absolutely certain that the war against Rome was going to result in his suicide and the final destruction of Carthage. There is no doubt that the certainty of losing would have made lambs of Hitler and Genghis Khan.

For centuries, wise men and religious leaders have repeated that war is an abomination that makes all men and all countries the losers in the long run, and that peace would give humanity marvelous opportunities for progress. Wise words forever admired and ignored. The inner drive toward war was too strong to resist. Now, however, the nuclear age insures instant and complete extinction. In fact, war, instead of a means to achieve survival, becomes a means to assure the death, not only of individuals and families (a price often paid before), not only of countries and civilizations (a price occasionally paid before), but also of humanity and of the whole planet, an intolerable price. Therefore war shall be eliminated.

As a means that has become unable to achieve its end, war loses its imperviousness to ethics and logical reasoning and to religious convictions. Although its elimination will be ascribed to such reasoning and convictions and to deeply felt ethical principles, in reality it is the result of fear. Fear of extinction. War is abolished because atomic weapons have changed the terms of the equation: the old one was WAR = SURVIVAL, the new is WAR = DEATH. Now the instinct of survival is against war, and peace is inevitable because it is dictated not by logic, a weak persuader, but by an instinct, an irresistible one. Finally the old dream has become reality: war will be no more.

The war abolished by the existence of nuclear weapons is, of course, all-out war among the superpowers, and the question could be asked whether this represents any advantage over the old ways. In the past, it is true, great powers used to fight each other, but at least the very existence of humanity was not in danger. Today, even if the hydrogen bomb imposes restraint, there is always the possibility of the terrible consequences of a miscalculation or a mistake.

Is it better or worse? The question is idle.

In the first place, nuclear weapons are here to stay and little is gained by speculating about whether it would be better if they were not. Second, we must get used to the idea that technological progress will put at the disposal of man more and more energy, which, if misused, will wipe out larger and larger portions of the universe. If we extrapolate into the future the ever-growing capacity of man to manipulate energy, it is not only conceivable but probable that one day he will be able, not just to sterilize the earth's surface, but to disintegrate the planet itself and to wipe out the rest of the solar system. Therefore, it would appear advisable to stop worrying, accept the fact that man has at his disposal tremendous energies—that he will have more in the future, and make sure that accidents and miscalculations do not occur. We cannot turn the clock back to the pre-nuclear age and we may as well accept this as a fact.

If this is the case, we must accept the principle that each superpower, for the foreseeable future, will have enough atomic weapons to obliterate the world. This, on the other hand, by keeping man in a continuous state of fear will make him avoid major wars. Fear is a great pacifier. This may seem demeaning to our dignity, but we must remember that, in the past, peace was always maintained through fear. The *Pax Romana* and the *Pax Britannica,* for example, were imposed by the swords of the legions and the guns of the Royal Navy. The *Pax Atomica* will be maintained by the hydrogen bomb.

> One cannot know what the Cold War would have been like if there had been no nuclear weapons, but it is hard to believe that such an intense contest between such powerful states, involving political stakes as important as Western Europe, would have been so readily contained beneath the threshold of general war had it not been for the prospect of nuclear devastation.
>
> The thesis that nuclear weapons have made war obsolete is presented most fully and explicitly by Walter Millis. It is implicit in the copious peace literature since World War II; for example, the writings of Bertrand Russell, Charles Osgood, Erich Fromm, and Seymor Melman. The idea, however, is not confined to the peace group. General Douglas MacArthur, for example, declared that the science of destruction in the nuclear age has transformed the abolition of war from a moral question to a political necessity. President Johnson affirmed what every post-World War II President and many other heads of state have said in similar words when he declared: "There is no real comparison between the attitudes of most of the world's governments today and twenty-five years ago on the role of warfare as an instrument of national policy. War is obsolete, obsolete because there can be no winner. . . . The question is not whether the world can eliminate war. The question is when—when all nations will have the courage and the good sense to do so." This kind of hyperbole differs from the view of the peace group because it assumes that, until war is eliminated by some unspecified means, the war system must go on the same as ever, except that states must be especially cautious to avoid wars with a high risk of becoming nuclear. But it shares the basic assumption that war is obsolete because it must entail cataclysmic costs that are grossly disproportionate to any conceivable gains.

It is evident that peace, even a peace imposed by fear, is better than war, and even if small conflicts continue, nightmares like the First and Second World Wars will be eliminated.

Even if nuclear weapons prevent the superpowers from making war on each other, that does not mean, of course, that wars among small countries or so-called "proxy wars" are not possible and that the superpowers will not make war on small countries. The existence of nuclear weapons, however, has also modified this aspect of the dynamics of international relations.

If a superpower attacks a small country, the probability of all-out nuclear war is remote. When Russia invaded Afghanistan, it would have been absurd for the U.S. to even consider the possibility of a nuclear threat on the issue. When the United States invaded Grenada, Russia likewise refrained from bellicose threats. One could think that this would lead to frequent attacks of the superpowers on small countries. Yet this is not the case because the effect that a country's actions have on world opinion is important. The final purpose of each superpower is to convince the rest of the world that its system is superior, so that the resulting "ideological infiltration" may help in undermining the strength and prestige of the other superpower. In addition, it is in the interest of each superpower to reassure the other (as much as possible) concerning bellicosity and aggressive intentions. This is for various reasons, one of the most important being the following: deterrence does not work in an all-or-nothing way; there are degrees of deterrence which are proportional to the power of the deterrent country. In other words, if both superpowers have enough nuclear weapons to destroy each other, but one has just enough and the other ten times more than enough, the two opposing forces do not have equal deterrence. This is so because possible errors, malfunctions, miscalculations, unexpected occurrences, new discoveries, etc., will influence less the destructive capability of the country with the larger nuclear arsenal. It is in fact to be expected that in a serious crisis, all other elements being equal, the country with the smaller stockpile would have to give in. This being the case, each superpower wants to reassure the government of the other so that the latter will be less stimulated to increase its stockpiles.

International trust for a given country depends on two factors: military power (in this case trust means international confidence in the capacity of the country to apply military power effectively when necessary) and restraint in using power (in this case trust means international confidence in the "benignity" of the country). In the case of superpower politics, invasion of a small country tends to decrease the amount of international trust, as shown by the Vietnam and Afghanistan wars; the intensity of this effect depends, of course, on circumstances and on the effectiveness of superpower propaganda. It must be underlined, however, that, as far as world opinion is concerned, effective application of military power is more important than other considerations and that, therefore, the biggest decrease in trust, in the two examples above, was caused not so much by the conflicts *per se* but, for the Americans, by the loss of the war and, for the Russians, by their failure, so far, to win.

Clearly, if nuclear weapons have eliminated all-out war, they have not eliminated its deep cause, namely the instinct for survival. This being the case, man will find effective substitutes for war. As discussed before, war (victorious war, of course) brings survival by making the group capable of imposing on others its language, its values, and its way of life. Because man's nature and needs have not changed, the same results will be sought by other means such as ideology, science and technology, and economic predominance.

If Chinese were to become the language of science and technology, for example, and if the Chinese brand of Communism were to become the most successful political system, this would represent an accomplishment equivalent to victory in many wars. Every educated person would speak Chinese—at least as a second language, China would become the standard to imitate, and the survival of the "Chinese way of life" would be assured for a long period.

Substitutes for war, like ideological infiltration, the technology race, and attempts at economic dominance, therefore, are, like war, based on a powerful subconscious drive. For this reason it is useless to oppose them with ethical arguments. For example, how often have we heard that with the amount of money spent for landing a man on the moon we could have bought so many millions of tons of milk for starving children and built so many hospitals for the poor and so many houses to shelter the needy, etc. Inane arguments. The groups that will be more successful in the exploration and colonization of space may hope to obtain the same result as those groups that were most successful in the exploration and colonization of earth: survival (in the sense already discussed). The same applies also to ideological and economic dominance and to any other means that our subconscious will perceive as a substitute for war in the pursuit of immortality. The arms race, in this context, will be discussed later.

Considering how effective nuclear weapons are in preventing war, the question could be raised as to whether it would be advisable to distribute atomic stockpiles to all countries.

Many groups are at a primitive technological level and the sudden acquisition of nuclear weapons would find them psychologically unprepared. There is no historical precedent to indicate what the reaction of a backward country would be to the sudden acquisition of military power several orders of magnitude above what it possessed before. Perhaps we may consider some of the Middle East nations which suddenly became rich with the sale of oil as examples of countries that have suddenly acquired enormous power (although economic in this case and not military). It would appear that, in some cases at least (e.g., Iran under the Shah), the sudden wealth may have been a destabilizing factor. We may assume, therefore, that the sudden acquisition of enormous military power would create an even more unstable, dangerous situation. On the other hand, if nuclear weapons are obtained as the result of long, slow technological progress, the government and the ruling class will have had more time to adjust to the responsiblity of power.

It is evident, therefore, that the spread of atomic weapons should be limited as much as possible among the countries that do not have nuclear capabilities, even if this means that those countries will continue to engage in war. After all, a conventional war between Libya and Albania, let's say, would be of less concern than their possession of atomic weapons. As for the countries with nuclear capability but no weapons, they are performing a tactical maneuver dictated by political circumstances. It is evident, for example, that Canada has not acquired nuclear weapons not because of ethical scruples but because it finds it cheaper, and politically advantageous, to rely on the U.S. nuclear deterrence.

While an all-out confrontation between the superpowers is kept in check by the Pax Atomica, wars between non-nuclear countries and conventional wars in which the superpowers are more or less directly involved will continue for a long time to come. The disappearance of "Great Wars" or "World Wars" however, is to be considered a tremendous step forward. The fear of nuclear annihilation is the price that we have to pay. There is no doubt that in the third century B.C., the possibility that humanity could perish was more remote than now. On the other hand, if Rome and Carthage had nuclear weapons, Carthage would still exist.

What about nuclear disarmament? Like ritualized dances, disarmament conferences have no value other than psychological. The thought that governments are involved in discussions to reduce the stocks of nuclear weapons, with the goal of eliminating them altogether, gives us reassurance. In reality, of course, the governments involved know very well that, under no circumstances, will nuclear weapons be eliminated and that eventual agreements will only be on marginal details with no great impact.

Besides insurmountable problems of verification, the abolition of nuclear weapons would create a very unstable situation: first, by throwing the world back to the pre-nuclear age when high risks were taken, in the political arena, because the worst that could happen was a conventional war for which the country taking the risk was prepared; second, by increasing the danger of nuclear war because, as mentioned before, even if nuclear weapons were eliminated, the capacity to produce them would not be, and a conventional war would cause the resumption of their production and their use; third, by increasing the possibility that any country, especially a third-rate one, could surreptitiously prepare a few nuclear weapons and use them in relative security from retaliation.

In addition, the existence of nuclear weapons generates the nuclear arms race, which, contrary to common belief, contributes to the maintenance of peace. While the arms races of the past were preparations for war, the nuclear arms race *replaces* war. The race consists, of course, not so much in accumulating more and more weapons but, more importantly, in a competition to achieve technological breakthroughs. When one is achieved by one side, everything else being the same, it becomes the equivalent of winning a battle or, in exceptional cases, even a war, because, depending on the importance of the breakthrough, the side with the new technological edge may gain an advantage so substantial that it may be able to impose its will on the other side. Which, of course, is the objective of war, in this case reached without violence. The drive toward war is, in this way, channeled toward technological competition instead of violent conflict. In addition, the capacity for winning the arms race is related to power and to all other elements that make a group more capable of competing with other groups. The arms race is, therefore, a valid substitute for war and, as such, replaces it. . . .

The centripetal force has acted throughout history on larger and larger groups, from the tribe to the city-state to modern nations. As modern technology has reduced the difficulty inherent in a process of identification encompassing large distances and peoples of different languages and customs, the centripetal force may start to act on an even larger group: the entire civilization. Until now we in the West, for example, have recognized that we belong to a single civilization, but this has not prevented us from slaughtering each other and from depicting each other as subhuman. Even if, in the past, our fury may have prevented us from realizing that most of our wars were in reality civil wars, the time has come for us to do so now. We may have already started. Nowadays the idea that there may be a war between the U.S. and England or between Spain and Italy strikes us as absurd. Military and economic reasons may be in part responsible for our reaction, but the feeling that we belong to the same culture, to the same civilization, undoubtedly plays a role. The Second World War was not only the last all-out war but also the last civil war of Western civilization. This does not mean that minor wars between some smaller countries (e.g., in South America) will not take place; what we will not see again, as a first step, are major wars among the more developed members of our civilization.

It would be even better, of course, if we were to realize that, as all civilizations are part of the Human Civilization, all wars are civil wars. Unfortunately, for the moment, this is only an intellectual understanding that does not reach our inner drives, and it is premature to hope that we will behave accordingly in the foreseeable future. We must therefore rely on something else (namely the fear of atomic annihilation) to prevent the recurrence of the "World Wars" of the past. . . .

As for nuclear deterrence, we have concluded that, at present, it is our best hope for the elimination of war. So far, prophecies of doom have been proven wrong. In 1960, the novelist and scientist C. P. Snow said:

> Within, at most, ten years, some of those [nuclear] bombs are going off. I am saying this as responsibly as I can. *That* is the certainty. On the one side [arms control], therefore, we have a finite risk. On the other side [arms race] we have a certainty of disaster. Between a risk and a certainty, a sane man does not hesitate.

It is evident that the mistake of Mr. Snow was to think in the old manner. He thought of atomic bombs not as entirely new weapons but as more powerful, old-fashioned bombs—and, of course, if it were so, he would have been right. On the other hand, Benjamin Franklin clearly perceived the advantages of an entirely new weapon:

> In November 1783, King George III and the court at Windsor were treated to an exhibition of a hydrogen balloon. . . . The potential value of the balloon in warfare, however, was recognized quickly. . . . Benjamin Franklin expressed the situation clearly in a letter dated soon afterward:
>
> "The invention of the balloon appears, as you observe, to be a discovery of great importance. Convincing sovereigns of the folly of wars may perhaps be one effect of it, since it will be impossible for the most potent of them to guard his dominions. Five thousand balloons, capable of raising two men each, could not cost more than five ships of the line, and where is there a prince who could afford to cover his country with troops for its defense as that ten thousand men descending from the clouds might not in many places do an infinite amount of damage before a force could be brought together to repel them?"

It is evident that the idea that man can be scared out of war is not new. Benjamin Franklin was wrong simply because balloons, as weapons, turned out to be not as dangerous as it was thought. Nuclear weapons, however, *are* as dangerous as we think; therefore all-out wars will be no more. One of the great dreams of mankind has become reality, and we may perhaps realistically start to hope that the day when all wars will be eliminated may not be too far away.

Suggested Readings

Calvocoressi, Peter. *A Time for Peace: Pacifism, Internationalism and Protest, Forces in the Reduction of War*. London: Hutchinson, 1987.

Gaddis, John. *The Long Peace*. New York: Oxford University Press, 1987.

Jervis, Robert. *The Illogic of American Nuclear Deterrence*. Ithaca: Cornell University, 1984.

Meyer, Stephen M. *The Dynamics of Nuclear Proliferation*. Chicago: University of Chicago, 1984.

Pipes, Richard. *Survival Is Not Enough*. New York: Simon & Schuster, 1984.

Reading 41

NUCLEAR STRATEGIES AND PEACE

J. David Singer

Notes from the Editors

Twenty-six years ago, J. David Singer wrote Deterrence, Arms Control and Disarmament *(1962), and when reissued in 1984, it seemed to need little revision. The problems of the arms race that confronted the United States and the Soviet Union in the early sixties are essentially the same today, despite the dramatic technological and systemic changes we have experienced.*

Singer's arguments were not—and still are not—accepted by everyone. In the first place, he suggests a basic symmetry in the strategies and goals of the two antagonists and does not consider the United States to be very much nobler than the Soviet Union. He assumes that neither side wants to launch or engage in a nuclear war and that we might do well to put ourselves in Russians' shoes in order to see how American "defensive" strategies are perceived in the Kremlin.

Some will take issue with Singer's critique of a first-strike strategy, his opposition to the MX and "Star Wars," as well as his notion that a rough arms parity exists between East and West. Nevertheless, this selection, an updated and abbreviated version of the Epilogue to the second edition of his book, does lay out most of the main issues in the current nuclear debate and reflects the language and concepts of that debate. He concludes with suggestions for initiatives that the United States might take to loosen the nuclear-arms-control logjam. They may seem utopian and unrealistic, but these are menacing times, and conventional half-measures are unlikely to suffice.

Nothing has occurred, politically or technologically, to impel any change in the original assumptions, but let me reiterate those that seem today the most crucial or the least understood. On the *weapons technology* side, it is even more clear today than at the dawn of the nuclear-missile era that: (a) there is no adequate defense against this lethal combination; while some fraction of an attacking force might be deflected or intercepted, enough will get through to cause untold devastation; (b) highly accurate delivery vehicles are as much of a threat to those possessing them as to those against whom they are targeted; despite any disclaimers, they just look too much like first-strike weapons and thus incite the development of similar silo-busting, hard-target capabilities on the other side; (c) weapon launchers that are relatively vulnerable—because of their location, lack of mobility, or easy detectability—are also a threat to their owners; inasmuch as they are of little value as a retaliatory force, the inevitable worst-case inference is that they *must* go first: either use them or lose them; and (d) numerical superiority, even by several orders of magnitude, is of no military value; even if heavily outnumbered, there will always be enough retaliatory weapons to ride out any conceivable opening salvo and to then deliver untold destruction upon the attacking nation. These elemental realities were perfectly visible in the 1960s, and even more apparent in the 1980s, and their implications for national security are as inescapable now as they were then.

Similarly, and despite a good many changes in the global system and the nations that comprise it, the basic *political assumptions* would still seem to hold: (a) the international system remains as anarchic and ungoverned now as then, with neither the institutions, the norms, nor the incentives and constraints strong enough to generate any important shifts away from the heavy reliance on military force as the major instrument of major power policy; (b) despite the rise and demise of the Khrushchev and Brezhnev regimes in the U.S.S.R., that society remains today a complex and relatively pluralistic one in which governance depends upon effectively reconciling the often incompatible interests of the military, heavy industry, agriculture, the consumer goods sector, and perhaps the final arbiter, the provincial party organizations; like his predecessors, Gorbachev cannot govern—and certainly cannot institute important reforms in internal or foreign policy—without a coalition that includes several (but not all) of these elements; this "classless society" has not only distinct classes and strata, but sectors, factions, and interest groups as well; (c) any effort by the U.S. or the U.S.S.R. to modify the national security policies of the other must recognize, and seek to exploit, the very different and deep-seated interests of the various sectors, strata, and elements that constitute these two societies; to the extent that each continues the basic lines of existing policy, each merely strengthens the stranglehold that the now-dominant forces enjoy in both societies; (d) in both the U.S. and the U.S.S.R., the political and economic elites continue to persuade—but less easily—the citizenry and its "representatives" that the other nation is hostile in intent, intractable in its expansionistic goals, and menacing in its military capabilities; in the U.S. those who challenge the dominant line merely remain peripheral, even when granted a periodic notoriety, but in the U.S.S.R., the costs are greater and the challenge is carefully muted; (e) the governments and political parties of the super powers' allies remain as unwilling and unable as ever to offer a serious challenge to the cold war doctrines that continue to paralyze the political centers of Washington and Moscow.

Given this terse reiteration of my technological and political assumptions, let me turn to the two basic dilemmas whose implications are profound, yet remain less than fully appreciated in all too many circles.

The Arms-Tension Dilemma

. . . Nations arm—and over-arm—for many reasons, of which self-defense is merely the most obvious and legitimate. They also arm for aggrandizement, to exercise clout in the world arena, to maintain or expand a sphere of influence, to inhibit other nations' efforts to encroach on their turf, to support their colonists, to help defend friendly regimes, and so forth. Then there are the essentially domestic incentives: to absorb the unemployed or other potential trouble-makers, to stimulate the economy, to aid certain industries, to develop a lucrative export activity, to maintain political order, and to perpetuate a given regime.

Most important, of course, is the fact that each incremental addition to a nation's military establishment or its arsenals will increase the political and economic power of those who favor such arming—and thus decrease the power of those opposed. Thus, as the Soviets and the Americans moved—for several of the reasons listed above—to bolster their military capabilities in the post-World War II period, they set in train a process that became increasingly self-amplifying. On the one hand, these early efforts to enhance preparedness created and strengthened *domestic* elements whose interests would naturally incline toward more of the same; the more we spend on arms, the greater the influence of those who want to spend more on arms. And on the other hand was the equally powerful *external* stimulus; the greater the preparedness levels in one of the rival powers, the more credible and potent the demand for more on the other side. Today, those who see the dangers and have to suffer the costs of excessive military outlay have considerably less political influence than they had when the arms race was in its infancy. Even in the U.S., where the opportunities for political expression and organization are relatively unhampered, militarization has gone so far, and so many vested interests have become so solidified, that hitherto influential groups seem incapable of slowing or halting the tide, if they have not themselves been co-opted.

While overstated for the sake of brevity, this line of reasoning has ominous implications for efforts to resolve the arms-tension dilemma. First of all, it illuminates the naivete of the traditional Western argument that nations arm primarily in response to political tension and competition, and will disarm when the sources of that tension are reduced or eliminated. It may come as a surprise to contemporary observers, but for a good many years even people as sophisticated as George Kennan and the late Hans Morgenthau took this position, and thus dismissed as impractical any moves toward arms reduction. Their stance was that weapons were merely the symptom, and would naturally disappear from the nation's arsenal once the political conflicts were resolved. While these two scholars ultimately turned away from such a position, they certainly helped to discredit the advocates of arms control and arms reduction, and the legacy of such foolishness remains to haunt us to this very day.

But the advocates of negotiated arms reduction have faced an equally intractable side of the arms-tension dilemma. We—and I was clearly in this camp—underestimated the political (and even the emotional) resistance to arms control, reduction, or elimination. The forces that favored maintenance or expansion of their nation's military capabilities found it an easy task—at least by the early 1960s—to discredit and sabotage any meaningful negotiations for arms reduction. Even when their arguments were specious, exaggerated, or downright dishonest, they could easily carry the day, not only in Moscow and Washington, but in the capitols of virtually every European nation, East or West. The cold war cheerleaders were well ensconced in the media, the political parties, the universities, the churches, and the professional associations, and it was a simple matter to challenge the patriotism and political virility of those who dared question strategies of "peace and strength. . . ."

The opponents of meaningful negotiation of arms reduction were sufficiently powerful on both sides by the middle 1950s that only the most optimistic could still hold out any hope for progress through this channel. Remember that it was in May of 1955 that the British, French, Soviets, and Americans had come very close (perilously close?) to agreement on strategic and conventional arms reduction after long and painful negotiations, only to have the Eisenhower-Dulles administration abruptly and unilaterally withdraw its support, bringing serious negotiations to a halt.

The history of major power negotiations in the three decades since was appallingly similar in result, if not in procedure. While we saw a negotiated ban on some nuclear weapons testing and on the deployment of large-scale ballistic missile defenses (BMD), and the SALT agreements set some upper limits on certain strategic weapon systems, and fragile constraints against biological and chemical weapons were established, there had been no progress at all in the efforts to reduce or limit conventional arms, and no negotiated reductions whatsoever in nuclear capabilities. But in 1987, we finally saw signs of progress. Largely as a result of a steady barrage of Soviet initiatives from the reform-minded (but hardly pacifistic) Gorbachev regime, negotiations on the elimination of intermediate range missiles and their warheads in Europe culminated in a formal agreement. At this writing, it looks as if the U.S. Senate will endorse the treaty, thus giving some impetus to the arms reduction-political settlement process. Both powers and their allies have agreed in principle to a follow-up reciprocal 50% reduction in existing ICBM forces, but this potentially dramatic move is threatened by U.S. reluctance to slow down research and development on a new and exotic generation of ballistic missile defense known as SDI or Star Wars. Given the probability of a very low interception capacity when and if deployed, this version of BMD could only be effective against a weak and disorganized attack on North America, that could come only from a non-super-power or from a superpower that had already been subjected to a "disarming" first strike. No wonder that the Soviets view it with alarm.

Given the arms-tension dilemma, and this brief deviation from its inhibiting effects, what is needed now is a sequence of moves by one of the adversaries (and we will use the U.S. here for illustrative purposes) that could achieve all of the following: (a) reduce the vulnerability of our strategic forces; (b) reduce the Soviet belief that the U.S. might, under certain conditions, be the first to use strategic nuclear weapons; (c) reduce our incentive to launch a nuclear strike on the basis of political perceptions, early warning signals, or anything other than unambiguous evidence that a major nuclear assault has begun; (d) reduce the magnitude of destruction if the Soviets were to strike against North America in either the preemptive or retaliatory mode; (e) reduce the political credibility and clout of the more hard-line and belligerent elements in the U.S.S.R.; (f) reduce the economic and political influence of the more hard-line and belligerent elements in the U.S.; (g) strengthen, albeit incrementally, the anti-militaristic forces in both super powers, and perhaps throughout East and West Europe as well; and (h) reduce the U.S. budget deficit and the other counter-productive effects of excessive military spending.

This is, admittedly, a tall order, but if I may be permitted a facetious aside, modest in comparison to all the good things that were/are supposed to follow from such "positive" moves as deploying tactical nuclear weapons in Europe, MIRVing our

ICBMs, enlarging our warhead stockpile, increasing the accuracy of our missiles, deploying the MX, threatening to deploy the neutron (enhanced radiation) weapon in Europe, and most recently, the renewed effort to develop an anti-ballistic missile on the dubious premise that it would be a purely defensive weapon. Each of these U.S. "initiatives" was sold on the grounds that in one way or another, it would make the Soviets more docile, our allies more confident, ourselves more secure, or our economy more vigorous.

Is there indeed a strategy that might have a chance, however slight, of advancing this eight-dimensional objective? In my view, there is, and I put it forward later in this chapter with reluctance, if not embarrassment, not because it does not strike the objective observer as a reasonable set of moves, but because it goes contrary to the unreasonable but widely-shared conventional wisdom of the post-World War II era. The attentive public, not to mention the political elites, counter-elites, media people, and reference figures have been so badly informed and so well manipulated that most of them in America, Soviet Russia, and West and East Europe believe all sorts of strange things about the East-West rivalry.

Among the strange assumptions that still seem to dominate the conventional wisdom of East and West these days are the following: (a) that the hardware of military capabilities is readily convertible into the currency of political influence; (b) that our strategic security is a direct function of our relative military superiority, and that one can never have too much in the way of weaponry; (c) that the other super power arms to intimidate, if not obliterate, us and our allies and to accelerate its drive toward global domination; (d) that our own political leadership, despite many lapses in performance, basically knows what it is doing in the national security field; (e) that a concession by the other side is a sign of their weakness, or an effort to lull us into a sense of complacency; (f) that until the other side's political leadership is changed, they cannot be trusted to honor arms reduction agreements, at least not without stringent inspection and verification arrangements; (g) any unilateral arms reductions on our part would either weaken our security position or encourage the adversary to think that we have lost our will to stand up to them; and (h) our side has no intention of initiating nuclear war and would certainly resort to it only in retaliation against the adversary's first use. While not everyone on both sides accepts every one of these premises, most seem to be accepted by many, and some of them are even believed by those holding top positions in the politico-military hierarchies. And as suggested, they help not at all to resolve the arms-tension dilemma, but to perpetuate its ominous auguries.

The Mutual Vulnerability Dilemma

There is—in addition to the arms-tension-political settlement dilemma—a second, equally vexing and equally unexamined dilemma. Simply put, it is the drive on the part of both ourselves and the Soviet Union since the early 1960s (perhaps even sooner in the U.S.) to achieve a pair of utterly incompatible objectives. On the one hand, we have sought to make our own strategic forces as *in*vulnerable to attack as we can, and on the other, to make the opponents' forces as *vulnerable* as we feasibly can.

This pair of objectives suffers from two fundamental flaws. First, it is dangerous—albeit tempting—to try to increase the vulnerability of the opponents' forces, via numbers, accuracy, and yield; the net effect of the enterprise is to heighten their sense of fear rather than their sense of security. This serves not to make them more prudent and cautious, but to make them more adventurous in the ways in which they deploy and exploit their own strategic forces. It strengthens the hand of those who want to match, counteract, or overcome our strategic advances, and weakens the hand of those who seek stability, restraint, and greater attention to the solution of their domestic problems. In sum, any effort to make the other side's forces more vulnerable will almost guarantee the continued success of their more hawkish elements and the failure of the more dovish ones.

Second, the objective is technologically unattainable. Even with the impending advances in the accuracy, as well as numbers and yield, of our submarine-based missiles (and theirs), a "credible first-strike" force must continue to have a strong land-based component. And whether one side's effort to degrade the survivability of the other's rests on one leg of the triad or another (even with stand-off cruise missiles, the manned aircraft remains essentially a second-strike weapon), the net effect is to drive that opponent to responses that contribute to overall instability. On the one hand, they can try to *overcome* that threat by hardening, concealment, and dispersal, which need not be overly destabilizing, and then renew their efforts—as we now see again—to build more active BMD defenses, which *is* highly destabilizing. On the other hand, they can, and usually will, seek to *counter,* rather than merely overcome, by increasing the accuracy, yield, and numbers of their forces, further accelerating the upward spiral in strategic arms acquisition.

In spite of these inexorable implications of the mutual vulnerability dilemma—and they were apparent as early as the middle 1950s—first the U.S. and then the U.S.S.R. began to pursue this dangerous chimera. While the conceptual and the weapons design search for the impossible began in the think tanks in the 1950's, it was not until the 1960 Presidential campaign that it received a meaningful political stimulus. It was then that the Democrats asserted the existence of a "missile gap," not because a Soviet edge—even *had* it existed—could threaten the finite or minimal deterrent resting on mutual assured destruction. Rather, it was a concern that the U.S. might be losing its earlier strategic preponderance, and thus the possibility, however remote, of posing a credible pre-emptive threat to the Soviets.

After a successful campaign and his inauguration, Kennedy and his Defense Secretary began to articulate, develop, and contract for a military posture quite different from the old "massive retaliation." Despite the warnings of those of us in the finite deterrence school, [Robert S.] McNamara and his colleagues shifted toward a "deterrence plus" strategy, requiring a nearly infinite number of more accurate missiles capable of threatening the entire Soviet land-based missile system. Although often couched in terms of making nuclear war less destructive and more civilized, the new and more explicit counter-force targeting doctrine (as distinct from counter-city or counter-value targeting) was intended to intimidate the Soviets, reassure our NATO allies, and make offensive war a legitimate option in the nuclear missile era.

Not surprisingly, Soviet military planners, fearing their own "window of vulnerability," not only accelerated the production and development of more ICBMs so as to preclude a disarming first strike by the West, but also began to toy with a number of first-strike options of their own, especially vis-à-vis European targets. Overcoming the threat of a disarming first strike was—as many of us noted—a simple matter of just adding to the number of launchers and warheads. Given the limitations of accuracy and reliability of the *offensive* weapons and the possibilities for dispersion and hardening of the retaliatory force, there is not and will not be for decades, if ever, any way to wipe out a large enough fraction of that force (not to mention the sea- and air-based components), and thus enjoy immunity from massive retaliation.

I dwell on this matter because it was the swing away from a basically finite and retaliatory strategy on both sides—and toward a mixed strategy known as deterrence plus, flexible response, damage limiting, war fighting, counter-force, escalation dominance, and so on—that gave new impetus to the strategic arms race beginning in the early 1960s. As noted above, mutual assured destruction is a simple objective, easily acquired and maintained, whereas trying to eliminate the adversary's ability to inflict that retaliatory destruction is virtually impossible. Despite this technological reality, both superpowers have sought to negate it by measures that are not merely astronomically expensive, but threatening, provocative, and destabilizing. To reiterate, until we give up the quixotic search for an effective first-strike capability, with numbers, mobility, and accuracy, coupled with ballistic missile defenses and crisis relocation programs as the inexorable accompaniment, there is little chance of breaking out of the strategic arms race.

Indicative of the mutual vulnerability dilemma and our inability to grasp its implications was the April 1983 report of the President's Commission on Strategic Forces, assigned the problem of finding an acceptable basing mode for the next generation of intercontinental ballistic missiles, labeled MX. Although its chairman, General Brent Scowcroft, emphasized that the group's mission would extend to the entire range of strategic doctrine, and could thus consider the "orphan option" and recommend against *any* home, ashore or afloat, for the new missile, so rational a recommendation was not forthcoming. Though the chairman was as independent an agent as one can find in Washington or Moscow, the group's composition was all too accurate a reflection of the dominant political and economic forces in America today, even including a vice-president of AFL-CIO. When the role of rational problem solving in government diminishes as far as it has in the modern industrial society, and government is by a coalition of parochial interest groups, each willing to tolerate the others' claims as long as *it* gets an acceptable piece of the action, there is no effective voice for the national interest or the general welfare. Thus, the commission's recommendations represented both a political compromise and an inability to withstand those strategic temptations, urging that the MX is necessary to the nation's very survival, while reducing the number to 100, and instead of a new basing mode, such as the race-track or dense pack, deployment would be in existing Minuteman silos.

The proposals proceed from three of the assumptions that we earlier labeled as strange. One of these was that the key to deterring Soviet military adventure is to demonstrate U.S. resolve; abandoning MX would allegedly convey a loss of such resolve. Equally strange, there was and is no awareness that Soviet deployment of new weapons systems has been and again might be largely a consequence of the American drive for a highly accurate, multiple warhead, and relatively vulnerable new generation of ICBMs based in Minuteman silos.

The third strange assumption was that today's technology really makes possible a Soviet first strike of disarming proportions, but not vice-versa. To quote: "The Soviets nevertheless now probably possess the necessary combination of ICBM numbers, reliability, accuracy, and warheads yield to destroy almost all of the 1,047 U.S. ICBM silos, using only a portion of their own ICBM force . . . the U.S. ICBM force now deployed cannot inflict similar damage, even using the entire force." This assertion was markedly at variance with the evidence, and inconsistent with the projections that are shared by many non-governmental analysts. While one would not quarrel with the general assumption of vulnerability, one assuredly *would* quarrel with the assertions that: (a) a portion of the Soviet land-based force could destroy almost all of the U.S. silos, rather than perhaps 80 or 90 percent; and (b) that the entire U.S. force cannot do likewise to the Soviets. If the Commission's was indeed an accurate assessment, then an intriguing question arises: why spend an estimated 15 billion dollars on a new and more accurate, higher yield, and more destabilizing missile, and then put it into these highly vulnerable Minuteman silos? When we try to salvage strategies that are basically bankrupt, logical consistency is clearly not a constraint.

Even more serious is the familiar worst case assessment: allusions to a Soviet breakthrough in anti-submarine forces, threatening the survivability of the U.S. sea-based deterrent. . . . Considering the infrequency with which the U.S.S.R. has made any breakthrough before the U.S., and our own lack of success in ASW technology, this seems a weak reed on which to build the case for a new — and far more vulnerable — land-based deterrent.

Again, even if the Scowcroft Commission's members *were* on solid empirical or logical ground regarding the desirability of going ahead with MX, their second major recommendation calls for considerable scrutiny. This was the call for a new land-based missile that would be smaller and more mobile and carry only a single warhead. The single warhead principle is, of course, a sound one, inasmuch as it offers a target that is not only less lucrative to the Soviets, but also — given a fixed number of missiles — is less threatening to their land-based systems. Another virtue is that monitoring an arms limitation agreement would be easier were all missiles armed with only one warhead; as many of us have noted, the number of *missiles* in an arsenal is no measure of its threat to the other's forces. The number of deliverable *warheads* is the appropriate indicator, and a limitation on these is what we should pursue. Further, by spreading one's warheads among many missiles, rather than putting all of them into a very few baskets, one increases their survivability.

The question remains, however, as to whether there are any compelling military reasons for continuing to add to one's land-based forces. Partly, of course, the explanation is found in the domestic political clout of the U.S. Air Force and its symbiotic relationship to the major aerospace firms, along with those Congressmen and other influentials who are, for a variety of reasons, closely associated with that particular coalition. The military justifications would seem to be two-fold, neither of them persuasive. First, there is the higher accuracy and yield that the land-based mode offers, enhancing our counter-force threat in pursuit of those dubious political and strategic objectives mentioned earlier. Second, there *is* the possibility of an ASW breakthrough that might jeopardize the survivability of our sea-launched ballistic missile force.

The trouble with the first justification is obvious: *All* land-based forces are quite vulnerable now, and modernization will make them even more provocative. And the trouble with the second is that it tacitly rejects the desirability and feasibility of winding down the strategic arms race. That is, it assumes that we have no choice but to continue the fruitless search for a nuclear "deterrent" that is relatively invulnerable and at the same time able to threaten the destruction of the opponent's silos and other military targets. As we have already noted, there is no way, now or in the relevant future, to achieve these incompatible objectives, and to pursue that chimera is to guarantee a perpetuation of the strategic arms race.

Some indication of a gradual movement away from the Scowcraft commission's assumptions is found not only in the INF agreement but also in the January 1988 report of the bi-partisan Commission on Integrated Long-Term Strategy, co-chaired by Deputy Defense Secretary Fred Ikle and Albert Wohlstetter, a Pentagon consultant and former Rand employee, and including Henry Kissinger and Zbigniew Brzezinski. These far-from-dovish analysts, in emphasizing the need to focus more on the dangers of regional Soviet aggression and less on the probability of a major assault on Europe or North America, noted "we cannot rely on threats expected to provoke our own annihilation if carried out." Thus, without explicitly backing away from the lethal mix of counter-force nuclear capabilities and strategic defense, they seem to suggest the desirability of some reallocation of military resources. While none of this directly points to a turning away from those strange notions identified above, it could be taken as a tacit recognition that strategic deterrence-plus strategies leave something to be desired.

On the other hand, as suggested earlier, there remains this resurgence of interest in the anti-ballistic missile (ABM) and other ballistic missile defense [Star Wars]. Both super powers have continued research in this area of weapons technology, and President Reagan's March 1983 call for an acceleration of such efforts is not only in itself a destabilizing move, but would, if heeded, almost certainly lead to an abrogation—formal or otherwise—of the very sensible 1972 treaty limiting the deployment of such weapons to agreed installations around either Moscow and Washington or a single ICBM site of their own choosing. Despite the attractiveness, at first blush, of shifting from offensive to defensive weapons, the argument against BMD systems is a simple and compelling one. The technological difficulty of designing and building any system, whether based on missiles, laser, or particle beams, is such that it can easily (now, and in the decades ahead) be saturated and overcome by merely increasing the number of incoming warheads. As noted on several occasions, each side has so large an arsenal that it could overwhelm any conceivable BMD system.

But suppose that instead of facing thousands of incoming warheads, such a system need only cope with a few hundred? In that case, projected BMD designs might conceivably have a chance of intercepting or deflecting all but perhaps a few dozen of them. Certainly, no strategic attack is going to be launched with only a few hundred warheads, but if the would-be attackers are themselves the *victims* of a prior attack, a very large fraction of their offensive land-based weapons would never get off the ground. Their retaliatory blow might be so crippled, weak, and disorganized that the BMD of the side that struck first might well be able to fend off the bulk of the few remaining weapons. If, in addition, the original attackers also had a fairly extensive "passive" defense system (population shelters, evacuation planning, and perhaps underground factories), one could imagine the resulting damage to be less than "unacceptable." In reality, such an outcome seems close to impossible, but strategists get paid to think about the impossible as well as the unthinkable. Thus, by making a few quick and dirty assumptions, one could conjure up the scenario whereby "we" might be able to get away with a nearly disarming first strike and then ride out the feeble retaliatory blow. Once it becomes thinkable that "we" could do so, it is a brief step to thinking that "they" could do it to us. If active and passive defenses are virtually useless against a first strike, but could conceivably be moderately effective against a second strike, no government committed to a retaliatory strategy only would be interested in acquiring them. But if a government was divided on the issue, and there were some incentives for leaving the adversary in doubt—and both seem to be true for both the U.S. and U.S.S.R. today—a case *could* be made for both active and passive defense systems. But, in my view, now and when this book first appeared, acquiring or maintaining any sort of defense against nuclear weapons is not merely a tragic waste of resources, but a highly provocative act in itself.

Similar considerations apply to anti-satellite weapons as well. Up to the present, orbiting satellites are used primarily for observation and communication purposes, and there are not yet any nuclear weapons in outer space. Assuming that the superpowers can resist the temptation that this burgeoning technology will offer, and not act stupidly enough to put weapons in orbit, the problem could be a manageable one. Observation satellites are generally considered desirable because they enhance each side's ability to know what the other's weapons testing, production, and deployment patterns are without on-site inspection, and despite an emerging propaganda program to the effect that some of the newer weapons will be able to avoid detection, satellites will continue to play a stabilizing role. The more we know about one another's capabilities, the harder it is for the worst-case analysis people on both sides to beat the drums for yet another qualitative or quantitative increase on the grounds that the opponent may already have such and such a capability. But the opposite side of that coin is that they also make it easier to pinpoint the other's missile sites and other land-based military targets. As a result, some would advocate a ban on such satellites, and others would join the advocates of the development of anti-satellite weapons. In my view, an anti-satellite system would be yet another expensive and destabilizing enterprise, and if . . . there *were* no land-based missiles, the only reasonable argument for trying to destroy the other's surveillance satellites would disappear.

These, then, are some of the implications of the mutual vulnerability dilemma, and we ignore them at our peril. The technology, despite any conceivable advances in the next few decades, leaves the offensive forces with an overwhelming advantage.

We can choose to recognize this reality and utilize it to the mutual advantage of all, or we can continue the fruitless search for ways to degrade the opponent's retaliatory capacity, thereby jeopardizing our own security as well as his.

Some Critical Initiatives

Having outlined some of the more questionable premises behind the conventional and general wisdom, and explored the arms-tension and mutual vulnerability dilemmas, let me now try to . . . expand upon some . . . initiatives . . . that might point to a possible exit from this road to nuclear war.

The first requirement, and the very linchpin of a strategy for slowing and reversing current trends, is for the U.S. government to decide that it will never, under any circumstances, fire any nuclear weapons unless the adversary has done so first, and to then join the other nuclear powers in a no-first-use declaration. Obviously, if all the powers made, and adhered to, such a commitment the likelihood of nuclear war would diminish nearly to zero. But it is equally obvious that the problem is not quite that simple; in today's world, such a statement, unilateral or with others, would not carry a great deal of credibility. After all, similarly pious statments have been made before (the League of Nations Covenant, the Kellogg-Briand agreement, and the UN Charter, for 20th century examples), yet the signatory governments all armed for, and participated in war, within ten or fifteen years after renouncing it as an instrument of national policy. What is proposed here is nothing so radical as a total renunciation of war, or even a renunciation of nuclear war; it is only the renunciation of the option to *initiate* nuclear war.

Why, one might ask, would such a decision and its announcement be of any real importance, given that it would be a mere paper statement, with neither historical precedent nor actual behavior to give it any credence? The answer lies, of course, in the political process that would have to precede so crucial and dramatic a shift in strategic doctrine. It is clearly not a shift that will come easily or painlessly. It will require not only an intellectual recognition of the propositions spelled out above, and a closer examination of the moral implications of our strategic options. It will also require the political courage to face the entrenched interests, both material and psychological, that have developed over the past thirty-five years, or longer, if we think of the deep historical and cultural roots that so influence national security considerations in the U.S. and almost every country of the world.

How might these processes get under way? The enterprise must begin—and already has begun—in the minds of a few specialists, who then make the effort and take the risks necessary to disseminate the idea. Thus, I join those others, in America and elsewhere, who seek to change the agenda of national security deliberations, not by reiterating how terrible nuclear war will be, or by castigating one or another nation, government, or political party, but by building from the preceding analyses and expanding upon an earlier set of proposals. If the reappearance of this study, with the addition of this Epilogue, helps to reinforce colleagues, known and unknown, who see the problem in similar terms, or to stimulate a few journalists, or energize a handful of politicians, it will have been worth the effort. The process must begin with a few people who can help to bring such views as these to public attention, after which there is some chance that they will be picked up, discussed, criticized, endorsed, modified, and even excoriated, but not ignored. Then, by the familiar process of diffusion, it might be adopted by some office-holders or office-seekers, and perhaps by a few brave souls in Congressional offices, federal agencies, allied or non-aligned governments, and so forth. But until the "no-first-use" issue becomes more salient and more visible, those who currently hold power in the U.S. need not—and surely will not—address it. That it has not yet become sufficiently salient is indicated by the brevity and disdain with which the administration noted the *Foreign Affairs* article by McNamara and his colleagues, plus the fact that neither the Scowcroft nor the Long-Term Strategy report even raised the issue.

But if the proposition *were* to get wider attention, and if the leadership of trade unions, professional societies, commercial firms, universities, religious groups, and so forth began to examine its implications seriously, then some important changes might begin to occur. As more and more people begin to recognize the foolishness of current national security policies in the West, and the political process begins to accelerate, labor would be less likely to vote for jobs that perpetuate the arms race, industry might be more insightful as to the roots of inflation, clergymen might re-examine the relevance of "proportionality," journalists might be a bit less credulous after a slick audio-visual "briefing," foreign service officers might be not quite so awed by Pentagon systems analysts, professors might subject the competence of government leaders to closer scrutiny, party workers might look beyond the next election, and plain citizens might wonder whether patriotic sloganeering and condemnation of "the enemy" is equivalent to statesmanship. It will take a lot of questioning, a good deal of courage, and a fair amount of homework, but we have risen to the demands of such an occasion before, and might just do so again.

Were such a process of discussion, debate, soul-searching, and political jousting to take hold, what sorts of scenarios, domestic and international, might have to be contemplated? On the international scene, the answer has already been suggested: (a) Western acceptance of strategic parity with the U.S.S.R.; (b) turn away from any effort to degrade the survivability of Soviet nuclear forces; (c) give up any delusions of blackmailing the adversaries into compliance via the threat of a preemptive strike; (d) work with our European allies to strengthen NATO's conventional forces; and (e) attend to the need for a stronger United Nations system.

On the domestic scene, the picture is not quite as obvious, but the general outlines are clear, with the costs perhaps even higher than in the global arena. Our country, like the Soviet Union, is today a highly militarized one; perhaps not quite the "garrison state" of which Lasswell and others have written, but nevertheless one in which two critical conditions obtain. One of these is the extraordinary breadth and depth of dependence on continuation of the strategic arms race; the "military-industrial complex" phrase barely captures that pervasiveness. More accurate would be "the military-industrial-trade union-journalist-legal-academic-research-religious-political party-government agency complex." In virtually every sector and strata of American society, we find a good many people and groups who benefit materially and psychically—at least in the short run—from a perpetuation of this dangerous and expensive arms accumulation. A good many of them will have to suffer some economic or social losses if they want to either lead or acquiesce in a turning away from the nuclear arms race. In the early stages of such a demilitarization sequence, it will still be socially deviant and thus costly to challenge the prevailing beliefs in many circles. Friendship, status, credibility, professional advancement, and occasionally jobs and marriages, will be jeopardized.

What we are discussing of course is radical socal change, albeit incremental in nature, but without the sort of powerful constituencies that aided such radical changes as the New Deal or the turn away from institutionalized racial discrimination. To ease and hasten that change, and to prevent its reversal, a fair amount of thinking and organizing and planning will be necessary. In the schools and colleges and churches and professional societies and labor unions and news rooms and barracks and officers clubs and board rooms and university cafeterias, we will need to anticipate and respond to the problems and dislocations. (There are people in some professions, such as agriculture and medicine, who are less implicated in the preparation for nuclear war, but even they may be implicated psychologically to the extent that they tend to be politically conservative and traditionally close to the ideological mainstream.) One obvious area in which considerable planning will be essential is that of the economy. It would not only be unfair to jeopardize the livelihood of those who have come to depend on the arms race for their paycheck, but naive to expect that they will come around to a more prudent and realistic position on national security policy until they see reasonable job alternatives. One implication of this is that those of us who are less vulnerable to the costs of a demilitarizing society, and who have easier access to the relevant information, should be in the forefront of the social and economic conversion effort. More specifically, the sooner that academics and media people, for example, begin to de-couple their professional lives from the militarization of America, the sooner others will find it feasible to do so. To illustrate, for political science, anthropology, or psychology professors to do contract research on how to threaten the U.S.S.R., or manipulate third world societies, or make combat crews more effective, or journalists to ride around on aircraft carriers, while preaching the need for a demilitarization of our country would indeed be morally scandalous, not to mention politically counter-productive.

Needless to say, we are looking here at a process that is not only two-tracked—weapons deployment and domestic politics—in the U.S., but also two-tracked in the U.S.S.R. That is, these American initiatives are supposed, in due course, to encourage some sort of response from the Soviet side. The premise is that there are some groups and factions in the U.S.S.R. who favor, for national security as well as domestic political reasons, a slowing down of the nuclear arms race. And if U.S. initiatives can be designed to strengthen the hand of those elements, and make their position more credible and influential, there could well be some reciprocal moves by the U.S.S.R. My reading of the Soviet scene, and the coalition of forces upon whom the Gorbachev regime depends, suggests that such reciprocal moves are indeed likely. But not soon; the militarization of the Soviet-American relationship and thus the militarization of the two societies has gone on too long. The forces of reason and humanity can still be found in the Soviet Union, but it will take creative and courageous initiatives from our side to amplify and then legitimate those forces, as well as a fair amount of time.

Thus, we need to go beyond the no-first-use decision, which is absolutely necessary to any success, but far from *sufficient*. The obvious requirement, once the basic decision has been taken, expressed, and explained, is to back it up with action: (a) publicly abandon plans for *any* new land-based missiles, whether in America or in Europe; and (b) begin a phased, publicized, dismantling of existing land-based systems. Part (a) refers, of course, to the still-controversial MX, the midgetman proposed by the Scowcroft Commission, and the emerging new family of counter-force-capable submarines. And part (b) applies to the 1,050-odd Minutemen in the U.S. To reiterate, we could phase out every one of these weapons without jeopardizing our security— or that of our NATO allies—in any way. Further, to the extent that these relatively accurate, high yield, multi-warhead—and vulnerable—systems actually encourage those on the Soviet side who are most paranoid about our strategic doctrine and/or most enamored of a first-strike posture for themselves, their elimination would actually enhance our own security. And, if the cumulative odds *do* culminate in a nuclear exchange, the fewer missile sites there are in America, the fewer targets there will be, and thus fewer attacking missiles and fewer casualties.

But the major reason for such a phasing-out program is not to make nuclear war less destructive but to make it less likely. And to achieve this, we must get maximum political mileage out of so dramatic an act as eschewing future land-based missiles and dismantling existing ones. Thus, the phase-out should be visible, explicit, and deliberate, neither so rapid as to muddle the message nor so slow as to make it less than credible. My sense is that the schedule could extend over a three or four year period, and probably should not be contingent upon a Soviet response; at the least, we ought to reduce down to about half of the force, regardless of what the Soviets do. And even if there is still no reciprocity, the program should continue on schedule.

What might we expect from the adversary? The obvious Soviet response is that of a reduction of their own land-based inter-continental missiles. But given their greater reliance on the ICBM, carrying as it does over 65% of their strategic warheads compared to 25% for ourselves, we need not be surprised that they respond not only slowly, but with an insistence on retaining a marginal land-based edge during such a phase-out. There would seem to be two possible initiatives on our part to reassure the adversary and to thus encourage the dismantling of an ever-increasing fraction of their ICBM force. One, already suggested, is to renounce explicitly the possibility of first use. The other is to curtail drastically research and development on strategic defenses, allocating fewer resources and restricting all research to the laboratory, with no field testing of the system or its components. Even if the former move is not taken, the second might well suffice in the short run and induce Soviet agreement to a major reduction of strategic offensive forces; this, indeed, is what the 50 percent START proposals are all about. In pursuit of this more stable arrangement, and at lower levels of destructiveness, we need to help the Soviets preserve a relatively invulnerable retaliatory capability, but given their failure to develop the sea- and air-launched legs of the strategic triad, the problem is more difficult. Thus, another option might be to move toward greater parity in the submarine and bomber forces if they begin to phase out their land-based systems, preferably via negotiated reduction in our B-52 and Poseidon and Trident forces.

Enough has been said here to make my basic position clear. If the U.S. can make the painful and unconventional transition to the no-first-use doctrine and to a purely retaliatory strategic force, and the postulated political changes begin to develop on both sides, the initiative will have achieved its purpose. Both powers will be markedly less vulnerable to (or tempted by) a preemptive attack, the re-distribution of political power within the two superpowers will have commenced, and the diplomatic climate will have improved considerably.

Under such conditions, formal negotiation might become a more viable option. But even then, there will be a good many "confidence-building measures" that can and should be taken unilaterally. Some of these can be *un*conditional: A cessation of the field testing—but not laboratory research—of nuclear devices in all environments, ballistic missile defenses, and anti-satellite weapons, and thinning out tactical nuclear installations in Europe, for example. Others could be contingent on eventual and incremental reciprocity: deploying SLBMs outside of range of the Soviet Union, deMIRVing these SLBM missiles, postponing deployment of the Trident II (D-5) system, and reducing or abandoning the projected deployment of whatever other hard-target systems are currently in the pipeline. But as and when we and the U.S.S.R. have made a real beginning toward the establishment of a relatively stable and non-provocative nuclear balance, formal negotiations for such purposes as a production freeze will become not only more feasible, but more necessary. One reason for a return to negotiated reductions is that, as strategic stockpiles are brought down to much lower levels, cheating could begin to make a significant difference. In today's strategic context, there is no advantage in a numerical superiority of even large proportions; no matter what, the victim of a first strike can inexorably inflict unacceptable damage upon the attacker's land, factories, cities, and people. But as the minimum deterrent thresholds are approached, numerical discrepancies could become more critical, making verification much more important.

When and if that desirable state of affairs is approximated, we will still face a good many problems of international security. We will, for example, remain in the grip of conventional arms rivalries all around the world, nuclear proliferation will still threaten us, disposing of the fissionable materials from dismantled weapons will probably remain a thorny matter, and a plethora of social, economic, and political issues will still abound. Further, there will remain the danger of a reversal of the arms reduction process, with the ominous threat of a return to the perilous circumstances of today. But if strategic arms reduction is understood to be part of a more pervasive restructuring of the global system, and if we go about the task in a workmanlike and imaginative fashion, these dangers need not be insuperable.

The creation of an arms reduction inspectorate, . . . the steady growth of a supranational constabulary, and the strengthening of the UN Secretariat could all make for crucial transformations, perhaps irreversible transformations, in the way that the global village is governed. It is, indeed, a tall order and the time is short, but a combination of imagination, courage, intelligence, farsightedness—and good luck—might well carry us out of this menacing epoch and into one in which the *real* issues of the human condition might be addressed in a civilized manner. . . .

Suggested Readings

Burton, John W. *Peace Theory: Preconditions of Disarmament*. New York: Knopf, 1962.

Dyson, Freeman J. *Weapons and Hope*. New York: Harper & Row, 1984.

Fisher, Dietrich. "Defense Without Threat: Switzerland's Security Policy," in Peter Wallensteen et al., eds., *Global Militarization*. Boulder: Westview, 1985, pp. 173–90.

Gayler, Admiral Noel. "The Way Out: A General Nuclear Settlement," in Guyn Prins, ed., *The Choice: Nuclear Weapons Versus Security*. London: Chatto and Windus, 1984, pp. 234–43.

Gorbachev, Mikhail. *Perestroika: New Thinking For Our Country*. New York: Harper & Row, 1987.

Herken, Gregg. *Counsels of War*. New York: Oxford University, 1987.

Jervis, Robert. "Deterrence Theory Revisited," *World Politics* 31 (January 1979), pp. 314–22.

Krepon, Michael. *Strategic Stalemate: Nuclear Weapons and Arms Control in American Politics*. London: Macmillan, 1985.

About the Editors

Melvin Small and *J. David Singer* began their collaboration in 1963 when Small was a graduate student in history and Singer a professor of political science at the University of Michigan. Singer had just launched the Correlates of War project, an ambitious study of the causes of war that relies heavily on the use of real historical data. Although Small was a specialist in American diplomatic history, his willingness to venture into the alien world of the quantitative social scientist made him a rare diplomatic historian of any sort.

Small is a professor and former chair of the History Department at Wayne State University. He also served as chair of the board of its Center for Peace and Conflict Studies. With Singer, he coauthored *The Wages of War, Resort to Arms,* and scores of articles on war, alliances, and diplomacy. In his other life as a more conventional historian, he has written *Was War Necessary, Johnson, Nixon, and the Doves,* and has edited *Public Opinion and Historians.*

Singer is coordinator of the University of Michigan World Politics program and founder and director of the Correlates of War (COW) project. Over twenty-five years old, the COW project has played an important role in the development of the modern field of international relations. A former president of the International Studies Association, Singer is author or editor of numerous books and articles, including *Deterrence, Arms Control, and Disarmament, Human Behavior in International Politics, Explaining War,* and *To Augur Well.*

A NOTE ON THE TYPE

The text of this book was set in 10/12 Times Roman, a film version of the face designed by Stanley Morison, which was first used by *The Times* (of London) in 1932. Part of Morison's special intent for Times Roman was to create a face that was editorially neutral. It is an especially compact, attractive, and legible typeface, which has come to be seen as the "most important type design of the twentieth century."

Composed by Graphic World, Inc.

Printed and bound by Malloy Lithographing, Inc.